WOMEN, THE FAMILY, AND FREEDOM

THE DEBATE IN DOCUMENTS

Volume One, 1750-1880

Women, the Family, and Freedom

THE DEBATE IN DOCUMENTS

EDITED BY

Susan Groag Bell & Karen M. Offen

VOLUME ONE, 1750-1880

STANFORD UNIVERSITY PRESS, STANFORD, CALIFORNIA

1983

Acknowledgments will be found on p. 553

STANFORD UNIVERSITY PRESS
Stanford, California
© 1983 by the Board of Trustees of the
Leland Stanford Junior University
Printed in the United States of America
Cloth ISBN 0-8047-1170-4
Paper ISBN 0-8047-1171-2
LC 82-61081

PREFACE

THIS BOOK explores the debate in Western nations over women, their relationship to the family, and their claims to freedom, from the Enlightenment to the mid-twentieth century. Statements of prevailing ideas, all published in their time, are juxtaposed with contemporary challenges to these ideas. The debate is presented in parts and chapters. Each part of the book is introduced by an essay that places the documents in their historical context. Within each thematic chapter, each set of documents is preceded by a headnote establishing context and background. When possible, we have provided selections that can be read in their entirety. When that was impossible, we have cut longer works in a manner that preserves the integrity of the author's argument.

In our presentation of the debate, we balance well-known male and female writers against others who are less well known. We shall introduce texts by a number of forgotten women authors as well as by better-known women, all of whom made significant contributions to this debate. Many of the texts included here have never before been available in English; others are only accessible with great difficulty.

As authors and editors we intend this collection to be a contribution to the study of the history of ideas and to the field of women's studies. It should also provide much-needed material for studies in the humanities, in sociology, in law and political theory, and in comparative literature. As historians, our original intent was to analyze and understand the historical development of this vigorous debate. As our book neared completion, however, we came to view "Women, the Family, and Freedom" as more than a documentary history. For, in fact, the "woman question" still lies embedded in the heart of the Western debate about individual liberty; its resolution is central to the full realization of such liberty within the framework of the democratic state.

This project would not have been possible without the help of many people and institutions. We wish to thank the libraries in which we worked during the last five years, and their staffs: the Bibliothèque Marguérite Durand, Paris (especially Madame Léautey); the Bibliothèque Nationale, Paris; the Bodleian Library, Oxford; the British Library,

London; the Perkins Library and the Medical Center Library, Duke University; the Fawcett Library, London (especially David Dougan); the Georgetown University Library, Washington, D.C.; the Hoover Institution of War, Revolution, and Peace, Stanford University (especially Helen Berman and Agnes Peterson); the Johns Hopkins University Library; the Lane Medical Library, Stanford University Medical Center; the Library of Congress (especially Sarah Pritchard and Kay Blair); the Library of the National Institute of Education, Washington, D.C.; the National Library of Medicine, Bethesda, Md.; the New York Public Library; the Newnham College Library, Cambridge University (especially Ann Phillips); the Stanford University libraries (especially Peter R. Frank, Joanne E. Hoffman, James M. Knox, Mary Jane Parrine, and Elfriede Wiesendanger); the Doe Library, University of California, Berkeley; the McKeldin Library, University of Maryland, College Park; the Louis Round Wilson Library, University of North Carolina, Chapel Hill; the Walter Clinton Jackson Library, University of North Carolina, Greensboro; and the Widener Library, Harvard University.

Those who aided us in procuring particular documents are acknowledged in the source notes. We are also, however, indebted and grateful to the following friends and colleagues, whose interest and assistance made the creation of this work such a pleasure: Renate Bridenthal, Anna Davin, Natalie Zemon Davis, Helene Eisenberg, Stephanie Fierz, Steven C. Hause and Anne R. Kenney, Sondra Herman, Leslie Parker Hume, Claudia Koonz, Carolyn C. Lougee, Claire Goldberg Moses, Winifred A. Myers, Richard K. P. Pankhurst, Agnes F. Peterson, Mollie Schwartz Rosenhan, Jane Slaughter, Bonnie G. Smith, Peter Stansky, Louise Tilly, Nicolas Walter, and Marilyn Yalom. Affiliated and visiting scholars and staff members at the Center for Research on Women, Stanford University, have provided a stimulating environment in which to work. Students in our undergraduate history colloquium on European women, the family, and social thought enriched our insights by their enthusiastic grappling with the documents in this book.

We acknowledge our appreciation to Norris Pope, Stanford University Press, who believed from the start in the potential of this book, and to Madeleine Gleason, who edited the text with uncommon grace and thoroughness. Helen L. Bryson provided enormous help in preparing the Index. Finally, we thank Ronald L. Bell and George R. Offen for their unfailing support.

S.G.B.
K.M.O.

Center for Research on Women,
Stanford University

CONTENTS

14. Women and the Civil Law   445
15. Women, Work, and the Professions   456
16. Women and the Vote   482

    Suggested Further Reading   521
    Bibliography   527
    Acknowledgments   553
    Index   555

DOCUMENTS

Chapter 6. "Woman's Sphere" and Women's Work

Chapter 7. Men, Women, and Political Rights Before 1848

PART III. Women, Revolution, and Reaction, 1848-1860

Chapter 8. Women's Political Consciousness in a Revolutionary Age

Chapter 13. New Controversies over Women's Education

Chapter 14. Women and the Civil Law

Chapter 15. Women, Work, and the Professions

Chapter 16. Women and the Vote

WOMEN, THE FAMILY, AND FREEDOM

THE DEBATE IN DOCUMENTS

Volume One, 1750-1880

GENERAL INTRODUCTION

"... History, real solemn history, I cannot be interested in. Can you?"

"Yes, I am fond of history."

"I wish I were too. I read it a little as a duty, but it tells me nothing that does not either vex or weary me. The quarrels of popes and kings, with wars or pestilences, in every page; the men all so good for nothing, and hardly any women at all—it is very tiresome. . . ."

Jane Austen, *Northanger Abbey* (1803), ch. 14.

THE OMISSION of women from the histories discussed by Jane Austen's characters is misleading. The debate about women was unmistakably present in the dialogues of popes and kings, and in the consideration of wars and natural disasters, even though the chroniclers did not refer to it. Indeed, the "woman question" may be the most central, yet overlooked, "quarrel" in the political and intellectual history of Western nations. It became an issue precisely because it challenged long-standing ideas of male dominance, which had remained implicit in Western political and social thought—published by men—until the seventeenth century.[1]

This book explores the debate in Western nations over women, their relationship to the family, and their claims to freedom, from the Enlightenment to the Atomic Age. Our focus is on the controversies over women's legal status, education, employment, and participation in political life. The authors of these texts came principally from Britain, France, and Germany, though there were significant participants also from Scandinavia, Russia, Italy, and the United States: the debate was truly international. Here, in contrast to the books read by Jane Austen and her contemporaries, women are on every page. They are subjects and participants in a controversy that began to boil shortly before Austen's birth. There is admittedly some peril in singling out an issue that has long been treated as peripheral—or as irritating in its refusal to be ignored—and redefining it as central. Therefore, in order to document our argument, we have incorporated (in the sound tradition of Renaissance humanists) the texts themselves. Only by returning to the words of the participants

[1] For insight into the "assumption of masculinity" in English political thought, see H. Smith 1981.

in the debate and considering their analyses of the woman question both textually and contextually can we achieve the deeper historical insight into women's plight that the poet Adrienne Rich doubtless had in mind when she wrote: "We need to know the writing of the past, and know it differently than we have ever known it; not to pass on a tradition but to break its hold over us."[2]

It is of course true that the analysis of women's position relative to men (by men) is as old as recorded history. Indeed, there are many who remind us that the woman question, as we are referring to it here,[3] will be posed as long as the physical burden of reproduction and the psychological and social burden of child-rearing continue to fall more heavily on one sex than on the other. Indeed, some would insist that the woman question will never be resolved as long as this reproductive imbalance, coupled with men's muscular superiority (and monopoly of force), continues to exist. Others argue that only if the structure of human societies can be radically altered, and the burden of child-rearing shared, can women's social disabilities be alleviated. It is an historical fact, however, that man's social power, once predicated solely on physical strength, has in recent times been diluted by other types of power, both intellectual and economic, which women—given the opportunity—can wield as advantageously as men.

Whatever the ultimate solution to this perplexing problem, the woman question itself has a history. Nowhere has the issue been examined with such persistence as in Western societies since the Renaissance and the Reformation.[4] With the closing of the nunneries in Protestant societies, women's only respected alternative to marriage and motherhood was abolished; all others remained devalued. During the next two hundred years, single, childless, deserted, and widowed women began to be char-

---

[2] Rich, "When the Dead Awaken . . ." (1971), in Rich 1979.

[3] We have here adopted the convenient term used by many nineteenth-century Continental writers, mainly French and German, and introduced prominently into English usage in 1884 by Theodore Stanton. Unless they are used by the historical authors themselves, we are deliberately avoiding the terms *feminist, antifeminist, feminism,* and *antifeminism* to characterize challenges and dissenting ideas put forward against entrenched and prevailing points of view on women's position. We aim to circumvent current misunderstandings about the evolution of historical demands made on women's behalf during the last three centuries; most of these misunderstandings arise from present-day efforts to eradicate notions of inherent sexual characteristics and the sexual division of labor and to celebrate the individual. Many of these notions remained unchallenged, however, by eighteenth- and nineteenth-century advocates of women's rights who described themselves, and were in turn described by their contemporaries, as *feminists*. Instead, we have tried to clarify the societal context of those dissenting ideas generally subsumed under the categories of "the emancipation of women," "the women's rights movement," etc., as required to pinpoint the specific character of the demands made by individual women for legal, educational, economic, moral, or political reform and the organized efforts they and their male supporters undertook to achieve them.

[4] The argument that follows draws on evidence gathered by many historians of medieval and early modern Europe, including K. Thomas 1971; Midelfort 1972; J. Douglas 1974; Davis 1975; Power 1975; Kelly-Gadol 1977; Monter 1976, 1977; and Wemple & McNamara 1977.

acterized as deviants. Indeed, the rampant persecutions of women for witchcraft in the sixteenth and seventeenth centuries may be viewed as an expression of a male-dominated society's intolerance of "uncontrolled" women. The emphasis by religious reformers and counterreformers alike on marriage and motherhood as women's ultimate and all-consuming destiny permitted no other options. The ancient Hebraic concept of the patriarchal family was now supported by a fragmented yet newly reinvigorated Christianity. This is indeed a legacy that has continued to plague women and to define their lives well into the twentieth century.

With the rise of capitalism in the late Middle Ages, the patriarchal family structure became based increasingly on absolute individual property rights. Paradoxically, however, this development fostered a demand for individual liberty and political rights within the state—for male heads of households. In less economically favored societies this demand, conceptualized by Western philosophers as an abstract ideal of human freedom, was conspicuously absent. The ideal of individual liberty stimulated educated women to evaluate their own opportunities for individual growth, only to discover, time and again, that these abstract ideals had never been intended to apply to them.

By the eighteenth century the contrast between women's subordination in organized society and their intrinsic moral equality with men in the state of nature (or the nature/culture dichotomy) first became, in the works of some philosophes, a topic of general interest in Western social thought. By this time the assumption of male superiority had, no doubt in response to repeated challenges, become an explicit assertion of male rights.[5] Women's claims to individual liberty were at first ridiculed, then denied on the grounds that their capacities (and indeed their very natures) were inferior to those of men. The argument also insisted that women's functional role must be located elsewhere than that of men—in the "private" sphere of the family, not in the "public" world of political and economic life. Hence, a profound tension arose for those women who sought freedom on what were, quite literally, men's terms. Against them the claims of the family were repeatedly pressed.

The pursuit of self-determination or autonomy is undoubtedly the

[5] For a provocative interpretation of seventeenth-century English political thought predicated on the assumption of "possessive individualism," see MacPherson 1962. See also Schochet 1975 on "patriarchalism and political thought," and Stone 1977, who has investigated the changes in family structures that underlay this ideological evolution in England. The implications of English liberal thought for women have been explored by Brennan & Pateman 1979; Shanley 1979; and Pateman 1980. As Keohane 1980a has pointed out, French political theory from the Renaissance to the Enlightenment also assumed masculinity; yet from the later seventeenth century on, when Poullain de la Barre challenged masculine prerogative on the grounds of reason, political theorists and social commentators from Montesquieu to Voltaire and Choderlos de Laclos felt obliged to remark that the subjection of women by men in organized society was a direct consequence of applied physical strength by men. See Weinstein & Platt 1969 on the "wish to be free" in French political thought; see also Alstad 1971; Hine 1973; and O'Reilly 1973. On French family structure in the *ancien régime*, see Flandrin 1979.

most compelling of the themes that, explicitly or implicitly, inform discourse about the woman question.[6] Since Christine de Pizan penned her *Citie of Ladies* in fifteenth-century France, women have become ever more articulate in resisting men's claims to govern them both in the family and in society at large. But in the eighteenth century the trickle of writings on this subject became a stream, and in the nineteenth century, a torrent. By 1854, when John Stuart Mill and Harriet Taylor Mill worked through the ideas that led to the classic essay *On Liberty*, in which they pondered the social limits of individual liberty, they had the woman question squarely in mind.[7]

Over the course of two centuries, from 1750 to 1950, during which challenges were mounted against the institution of monarchy in the name of individual liberty, two conflicting themes in the debate over women were paramount. The first was the realization by an ever growing number of women that men's struggle for personal and political liberty against the authority of state and church could be applied directly to their own subordinate situation in the patriarchal family. The second was the explicit concern of men in positions of political and intellectual authority to maintain a sexual division of labor and of social roles in the face of vehement challenges to their authority. Both these themes were central to Western preoccupations about the nature and limits of authority, hierarchy, and freedom.

The documents in this collection are organized to highlight the conflict between these two themes. They cover aspects of life such as marriage, sexuality, education and intellectual creativity, participation in the labor force, and legal or political rights. All of these challenges to male control were motivated and buttressed by arguments about women's need to exercise self-determination over the course of their lives. To this contention religious and secular authorities replied that, in the interests of the family, women must put aside their own conflicting needs. Women must raise and care for their children and serve the male heads of households. In female hands, they asserted, individualism amounted to egotism, and liberty only fostered license. Thus, Western women's claims to freedom have repeatedly provoked sharply stated counterclaims by defenders of the patriarchal family. Nevertheless, as this uneven dialogue developed, the double standard of individual freedom, in which men could test the limits of autonomy while denying the same possibility to women, was rendered visible, even conspicuous. It thus became susceptible to criticism and reform.

In the early nineteenth century, with the expansion of the market econ-

---

[6] We understand the term *autonomy* or personal liberty for women to mean having the possibility for individual self-determination, self-command, a choice of social functions or roles, and the exercise of societal rights contingent on the fulfillment of responsibilities common to both sexes, in the absence of direct and formal control by men. For a different use of the term, see Degler 1980, who speaks of autonomy *within* the male-headed family.

[7] Although *On Liberty* appeared solely under Mill's name, he made the extent of his wife's co-authorship abundantly clear in his dedication of the work. Both Hayek 1951 and C. Shields 1956 insist on Harriet Taylor Mill's joint authorship.

omy, the conditions for autonomous action by individuals changed. For women, these new conditions presented a problem that even the most sensitive male champions of the women's cause found difficult to resolve objectively. Even John Stuart Mill, writing in the mid-nineteenth century, took it for granted that a married woman, however desirous of autonomy, would be economically dependent upon her husband while she reared children. Mill's longtime companion and later wife, Harriet Taylor, insisted, however, that in nineteenth-century capitalist society not only single but also married women required economic independence in order to support that self-determination she and Mill sought for women and men alike. Indeed, ever since the heyday of the Saint-Simonian and Fourierist women in the 1830's, social critics have insisted on the centrality of women's need for economic parity with men, and have argued for institutionalized help with housework and childcare, and for open access to birth-control information.[8]

Neither capitalist nor socialist leaders have been able to resolve the problems women face in any known industrial society where competition and meritocracy prevail. Although many socialist political leaders, including the Bolsheviks of revolutionary Russia, have long shown concern for the situation of women, those who have acquired political power have never fully provided the kinds of institutions necessary for relieving women of the double burden of unpaid work at home and paid work in the labor force. Nor have they demanded that men participate equally in the raising of children or household maintenance. Male leaders of revolutionary movements—and most women revolutionaries too—preferred to postpone resolution of the woman question until after the defeat of capitalism, with the thought that any other approach might serve only to split the working class.[9] However, the egalitarian ideals of socialism remained as an inspiration for women within socialist movements. In the meantime, a long line of women social critics from Jeanne Deroin in early nineteenth-century France to Alva Myrdal in twentieth-century Sweden elaborated women's perspectives on these issues to produce an ideologically and politically significant platform for harnessing the aid of reformist governments in support of women's bid for autonomy.

This book, then, presents a study of the tension between the family and freedom that women experienced at three increasingly complex levels of interaction with others: in the couple, in the family, and in the state. To elaborate, the first level concerns the personal and sexual relationships between women and men as institutionalized in marriage. The second

[8]For the development of this economic argument, see Thibert 1926; Altman 1977; S. J. Moon 1977; and Moses 1982.

[9]The tensions between European women who espoused "socialist-feminist" theories and the men who headed revolutionary political movements have been systematically studied by Sowerwine 1975, 1976, 1977, 1978, 1979, and 1982; Boxer 1975, 1978; Quataert 1979; Boxer & Quataert 1978; and Slaughter & Kern 1981. See also Slaughter 1979. For evidence of continued present-day tensions, see Eisenstein 1980; Hartmann 1981; Sargent 1981; and MacKinnon 1982.

level, the family, constituted with the arrival of children, is understood in recorded Western history to be the fundamental unit of organized society. The family's historic structure has presupposed male authority over family members and property, and a sexual division of labor. The third level of interaction and complexity concerns the relationship between family members of both sexes and the state. During the last two or three hundred years, statesmen attempted to appropriate the traditional role of the church in dictating behavior. In the process, the authority of the male head of the family was at first reinforced but subsequently eroded, and thereby the justice of some of women's claims for greater self-determination was acknowledged. Democratic political movements played a significant role in determining how such rearrangements were to be carried out.

The volumes are divided into six parts, according to the periodization most often used by historians of modern Europe. Because the woman question *had* become a subject of public discussion in the period we are treating here, the debate waxed and waned in rhythm with the chronology of political and intellectual history, as it has traditionally been studied. Republican ideology and revolutionary events affected it profoundly, as did governmental countermeasures to repress the spread of "subversive" ideas. We have tried to incorporate the dispute between religious and secular authorities, as well as to examine the development of secular discourse by traditionalists, liberals, and socialist challengers. This approach establishes firmly the intrinsic and complex connection between the debate over female emancipation and the development of the political, economic, and social institutions of the Western nations.

The texts selected to illustrate the debate on the woman question represent only a small portion of those extant, but we believe that they illuminate vividly, better than any synthetic discussion could, how—despite many setbacks—received ideas about women have been repeatedly and persistently attacked and challenged. The documents come from a variety of published sources: periodicals, books, tracts, pamphlets, newspapers, laws and legal commentaries, and—not least—fiction. Indeed, in the period covered by our inquiry both the drama and the novel became increasingly important vehicles for discussing the woman question. The novel in particular, because of its focus on private life, proved suitable for exploring the tensions between women, the family, and freedom in ways that more conventional forms of public expression could not.[10] Moreover, women themselves constituted by far the greater part of the readership of the novel, which became the literary form *par excellence* during the period we are considering.

The international and cross-cultural character of the debate will quickly be apparent from the table of contents. Discussion on women's

[10] On the importance of the novel as a vehicle of social criticism, see D. O. Evans 1923, 1930; Van Tieghem 1927; Watt 1957; G. May 1963; and Clements 1973.

position, as on related sociopolitical issues such as freedom and slavery, never respected national boundaries. Social criticism originating in the urban centers of France or England crisscrossed the Channel, traveled north via the North and Baltic Seas to the capital and port cities of Scandinavia, Poland, and Russia, and to the seaports of the old Hanseatic League, and quickly sailed west to the Americas. Thus, ideas elaborated in London or Edinburgh rapidly reached a reading public not only in the Low Countries and in New England but in Stockholm, Hamburg, Königsberg, and St. Petersburg as well. Within months of publication the works of the Marquis de Condorcet, Mary Wollstonecraft, George Sand, and John Stuart Mill found translators (many of whom were women), reviewers, advocates, and detractors in other countries. In the nineteenth century intellectual networks soon assumed organizational forms through loose international alliances—a development that held true as much for partisans of the women's movements as for the better-known antislavery, socialist, and pacifist movements. Indeed, it would not be amiss to state that the international intellectual ferment surrounding the cause of women has, until recently, been one of Western civilization's best-kept secrets.

Though women's search for freedom is the overt theme running through this debate, there is a less explicit theme whose importance must not be underestimated. Surely men's opposition to liberty for women through the centuries has been motivated not solely by sheer pride, prejudice, or selfish convenience, though all these factors may have entered in. A persistent undercurrent in these texts suggests that, for many male participants in the debate, it was ultimately their fear of female sexuality—their vulnerability to women's attractiveness and consequent female power to distract them from their own quest for autonomy, that fueled their resistance.[11]

Beginning with Jean-Jacques Rousseau's surprisingly explicit statements on the matter, this male fear of "excessive" or "unleashed" female sexuality recurs in various guises throughout these two hundred years of social thought, culminating with Jean-Paul Sartre's image of woman's sex as "a mouth, and a voracious mouth, which devours the penis."[12] Indeed, it may well be that the long-standing dichotomy of male activity and female passivity postulated by male writers was nothing more than a rationalization of their deep-seated fears of female sexuality. Certainly, such notions provided the underpinnings for the oft-repeated contrast (rarely argued to women's benefit) between male intellectuality and female sensuality (reason versus instinct) that has so dominated Western thought on the subject of the sexes. This dichotomy, which found its

[11] This theme has been explored at the psychological level by Hays 1964; Masters & Lea 1964; Stern 1965; and Lederer 1968. More recently, its historical dimensions have been probed by Figes 1970 and Stearns 1979.

[12] Jean-Paul Sartre, *Being and Nothingness,* tr. Hazel E. Barnes (New York, 1956), p. 614.

clearest early statement in the works of Aristotle (active sperm, passive egg), was elaborated upon in our period by Rousseau, Wilhelm von Humboldt, John Ruskin, and Johann J. Bachofen.[13]

When dissenting women spoke initially, however, it was to argue that these notions of sexual polarity should work more to women's advantage. Mary Wollstonecraft wrote firmly and convincingly, "I do not want women to have power over men but over *themselves*." In the 1840's Louise Otto in Germany, Jeanne Deroin in France, and Marion Kirkland Reid in Great Britain all presented a vision of sexual complementarity that was not predicated on dominance/submission relationships. These women seemed unaware of men's "hydraulic theory" of sexual relationships, in which the rise of the "weaker" sex necessarily implied the diminution of the "stronger." Paradoxically, most women writers seemed not to recognize the conflicts created for men by women's sexual power over them, much less men's fear of losing authority they had established over women. Indeed, women appeared oblivious to the prospect that the liberation of women from male authority might provoke a crisis of virility among men in the view of men who equated virility with dominance. Nevertheless, a few women publicly countered men's arguments from sexual fear by standing them on their heads. "Sophia" criticized men for not controlling their own passions, and Hedwig Dohm chastised one German statesman for his conviction that the very presence of women delegates in a parliamentary assembly would so stir men's senses as to render them incapable of conducting their business; she suggested that men should be forced to curb their own sensual appetites just as women were asked to do.

These documents demonstrate that some aspects of the challenge to the assertion of male rights, though long articulated, are as current today as they were two hundred years ago. Yet present-mindedness is ever a potential hazard for the reader, as for the historian. We have attempted to combat this tendency whenever possible. For example, modern readers are often struck by inconsistencies and contradictions in the works of eighteenth- and nineteenth-century authors. These apparent discrepancies often resolve themselves, however, when the authors' ideas are interpreted with due regard for their own times and personal experiences. Our contextual approach offers readers a keener sense of the ways in which political and social ideas affecting women have developed historically than does a strictly thematic approach centered on the evolution of pro- or anti-women's rights rhetoric.

We believe that biography is central to the formulation of historically significant ideas about women and the family. The emotional intensity of the debate on the woman question underscores the vital importance of the personal and social circumstances of the participants. There is probably no other intellectual issue where the finer details of an author's expe-

[13]See in particular Stern 1965, ch. 4, and Merchant 1980. On the impact of Aristotelian ideas about women, see Horowitz 1976.

rience play such a vital part in framing his or her public statements. Not only is the author's sex itself important here, but also his or her age, relationship to parents, marital status, sexual orientation and experience, and relationship to children. It is astonishing, for example, to discover how many authoritative statements on marriage, the family, women's place, and even child-raising have been made by confirmed bachelors. These have long been treated as "objective" by virtue of the sex of the writer, whereas the statements of women such as Mary Wollstonecraft, Caroline Norton, or Juliette Lambert Adam, all of whom experienced the conflicts inherent in marriage and motherhood, are treated as "subjective." Events of the life-cycle render most "objectivity" subjective; one has only to examine the texts of Rousseau, Margaret Oliphant, Jules Michelet, Charlotte Perkins Gilman—or, for that matter, Sigmund Freud or Simone de Beauvoir—in light of their personal histories to appreciate the extent to which this is so. There is admittedly a fine line separating the use of biographical material as a sensitive interpretative tool from its use for *ad hominem* reductionism. We have naturally tried to avoid the latter. Yet, the evidence we have considered suggests the measure of truth in Lou Andreas-Salomé's observation, in a letter to Nietzsche, that all philosophical systems could be reduced "to personal dossiers on their authors." [14]

The primary source materials amassed in this collection highlight a number of considerations peculiar to the history of women. One of the most fascinating of these is how social convention has operated to attribute women's challenging ideas to men—even when the men themselves, such as William Thompson and John Stuart Mill, acknowledged a woman's contribution. But how did women's input remain unacknowledged? What of the unmentioned but obvious impact on the celebrated British theologian and educator Frederick Denison Maurice of the work and publications of his older sister Mary? Or the importance of the arguments of the Saint-Simonian women and Flora Tristan for the thought of Karl Marx and Friedrich Engels?

Another consideration arises from the cross-cultural nature of the debate and is emphasized by the comparative approach to its history: this concerns the uneven development of ideology and practice. We see, for example, that European arguments for women's emancipation—especially those generated by the French, the British, and later by Scandinavian writers—were developed with more intellectual rigor, more radically, and earlier than similar arguments in the United States. Yet it was in America that practical experiments in sexual equality, education, and legal reform, and the organized woman's movement itself, developed faster and more effectively than anywhere else. Similarly, experimental communities based on the ideas of Owen and Fourier, which incorpo-

---

[14] Quoted in Nietzsche's reply to Lou Andreas-Salomé, 16 Sept. 1882, by Binion 1968, n. 192. Nietzsche went on to develop her thought in *Beyond Good and Evil*: "Gradually I have come to realize what every philosophy has been to date—its author's confession and a sort of unintentional and unrecognized memoir."

rated attempts to reorganize housework for women, fascinated thinking persons on both sides of the Atlantic.[15] On the practical side, however, schools training women to become teachers originated in New England in the 1820's, whereas similar establishments only appeared in Britain in the 1840's and in Germany in the 1880's. Major reforms in marriage law, though first proposed in France during the Enlightenment and in England in the 1830's, were first forthcoming in American states during the 1840's; British women had to wait for similar reforms until the 1850's.

These differing developments are clearly attributable to the varied political and economic circumstances surrounding radical ideas and affecting their practical implementation. Within the United States, and within Imperial Germany after 1870, regional variations and local control must be taken into account. Social class and ethnic distinctions likewise influenced the development of women's own critique of their position, as well as their ability to act. When one contemplates the brutal post-1848 repression of women's activism (along with working-class activism) by the French and Prussian governments, and the continual constraints imposed even after freedom of the press and association were accorded—by having constantly to apply to the police to hold meetings or rallies, or to publish a political paper—one's appreciation of the difficulties facing the nineteenth-century European women's movement increases immensely. Similarly, the nervousness of many American women's rights advocates over the free-wheeling, anticlerical ideas of Elizabeth Cady Stanton, after her European visits, is highly significant. In both the range and extent of her critique, Stanton clearly showed the influence of European radical ideas; since her honeymoon visit to London in 1840, she was increasingly in touch with the women's rights radicals of England and France. Indeed, the relatively muted ideological character of the American women's rights movement was no doubt a product of its leadership's concerns for retaining respectability in order to succeed with their most pressing demand, the vote. This could be accomplished by avoiding thorny issues. For instance, the opinion that a loveless marriage was no marriage at all—a theme developed in French literature by George Sand and others in the early 1830's—was still considered scandalous when Victoria Woodhull dealt with it in print in New York in 1872.[16] Yet tact alone was not responsible for the American movement's successes; these were also attributable in part to the general level of prosperity in the New World, and, importantly, to the fact that there was far less class stratification and bitterness in America than in Europe. Moreover, America offered fewer legal obstacles to organized political and social action by ordinary citizens. European women were eminently aware of this. Some of them, along with their male allies, drew on the American experience to strengthen their own arguments for improving the position of their coun-

[15] See Hayden 1981 for a comparative survey of "feminist" architecture during this period.
[16] See Leach 1980.

trywomen. Hedwig Dohm in Germany, Fredrika Bremer in Sweden, and Léon Richer in France all appealed to national pride as a political tool, claiming that in one or more other countries things were improving for women more quickly than at home, and that something must be done immediately to redress the balance.

"Why bother," some ask, "with reconstructing or comprehending the history of the debate on the woman question. Surely, everything that is happening in this matter is happening now. Today women have the capacity, the tools, and—above all—the freedom to make their own choices. The patriarchy is defunct!" Such a view is unjustifiably sanguine. Those who initially believe it sooner or later encounter the persistence of the tension for women between the family and freedom, both in their own lives and in the lives of others. They are forced to reopen the debate, to rethink the issues, to reinvent the wheel.

We would suggest that reinventing the wheel is hardly necessary. It is more efficient to build on what is already in place. The woman question has recurred with cyclical regularity, though with new phases and emphases in each generation. Their development can be closely connected, as we have tried to show in this book, to war, peace, economic swings, advances and retreats in political liberty, and various currents in social and intellectual thought. Women have, in fact, a true intellectual heritage on which they can call when considering their situation. Its story is sobering, yet it suggests that prevailing ideas have been, and continue to be, successfully challenged. And the fact that this story has not been readily accessible to both men and women as part of their education should not be taken to mean that it never existed. Here a part of it is recovered, restored as it were to the annals of history, in order to redress the balance. For we believe, with the Vicomte de Ségur, that "the proper study of mankind includes the study of both sexes."[17]

[17] Alexandre-Joseph-Pierre, Vicomte de Ségur, Preface to *Women: Their Condition and Influence in Society*, 3 vols. (London, 1803), I, iii.

PART I

Women and the "Rights of Man" in the Age of Republican Revolutions, 1750-1830

AT THE OUTSET of the French Revolution on August 27, 1789, the National Assembly published a *Declaration of the Rights of Man and Citizen*. This statement of principle asserted that "Men are born and remain free and equal in rights"; that the rights of men and citizens were "liberty, property, security, and resistance to oppression"; that the law "must be the same for all," and that all citizens were "equally admissible to all public offices, positions, and employments, according to their capacity, and without other distinction than that of virtues and talents."[1]

The declaration owed its premises and much of its language to Enlightenment social criticism and, more immediately, to the Virginia "Declaration of Rights" adopted thirteen years earlier by the assembly in Williamsburg.[2] The men elected to represent the French people, however, excluded all women from the basic tenets of the Assembly's *Declaration of the Rights of Man*. Unacknowledged, indeed implicitly rejected, was the contribution of aristocratic and bourgeois French women over the previous two centuries to preparing the seedbed for Enlightenment philosophy by fostering discussion and social criticism in their salons; unacknowledged were women's published indictments of the inadequacy of their education and of their subordinate position in marriage.[3] In women's history, therefore, the Declaration of the Rights of Man was a landmark of a different sort than it has generally been considered for men; it symbolized the fact that the much-admired revolutions of reason were to be revolutions in the status of men—but not in the status of women.

The ideas so eloquently expressed in the French Declaration were dis-

---

[1] "Declaration of the Rights of Man and Citizen," in *A Documentary Survey of the French Revolution*, ed. John Hall Stewart (New York, 1951), p. 114.

[2] Pointed out by Palmer 1959, I, 487. The texts of both documents are reproduced in *ibid.*, pp. 518-21.

[3] Indeed, these very activities by women were ultimately repudiated by the men of the Revolution and their descendants. A classic nineteenth-century indictment is the Goncourt brothers' *Woman of the Eighteenth Century*, originally published in Paris in 1862.

tilled from a century of European and American published thought and private conversation that subjected once unquestioned beliefs, customs, and institutions of feudal Europe to the crucial test of reason. Critics drew on their philosophical ancestors in the Graeco-Roman tradition to furnish grist for their mills; classical Greek and Roman ideas and symbolism, on matters ranging from art to politics, became an important component of the vocabulary of eighteenth-century Enlightenment thinkers. The contributions of the "ancients" were supplemented by the more recent and much-discussed scientific materialism of Bacon, Descartes, and Newton, and the educational and political speculations of Locke and Montesquieu. Similarly, eighteenth-century European social critics found inspiration in the mechanical innovations then being applied to industrial production, and in the discoveries of medical physiologists about the human body itself. Drawing on these two sources they invoked concepts of "natural laws" and "natural rights" to question not only the extravagance and corruption of courtly life, but the legitimacy of royal authority and the truth of revealed religion as well.[4]

While monarchist and clerical intolerance and corruption had provoked republican and secular Enlightenment responses in France, political and social criticism in England was tempered by a less authoritarian and less arbitrary political and religious rule. The tolerated existence of a multitude of dissenting religious sects, to which most philosophical radicals such as Mary Wollstonecraft belonged, indicated that disagreement with the Anglican religious establishment did not necessarily imply revolt against revealed religion itself. This fact sharply differentiated English Enlightenment thought from that in France and in most other authoritarian nations where the alliance of State and Church allowed no room for disagreement. Only in France had the term *savant*, or intellectual, become synonymous with a "secular," anticlerical, or purely materialist approach. British intellectuals such as Dr. Samuel Johnson were more concerned to find reason in the Creator's methods than to reject those methods entirely. Thus "natural law" and the law of God could be interchangeable in England, while these concepts appeared as contradictory in secular French (Enlightenment) thought. Although republican idealism appealed to a number of "free thinkers" in Britain, greater freedom of religion meant that orthodox belief in a beneficent creator remained a more integral part of British intellectual thought throughout the eighteenth and the early nineteenth centuries. Eighteenth-century travellers such as the French philosophe Voltaire were intrigued by the greater liberty of individuals in England and by encounters with British intellectuals who upheld and defended Christian doctrine. Indeed, French writers frequently published their more controversial criticism disguised as spurious translations from the English in order to circumvent France's heavy-handed censorship.[5]

[4]For important interpretations of the continental Enlightenment, see Hazard 1963a, 1963b; Gay 1966, 1969, 1973; and Roger 1971. For the Enlightenment in America, see H. May 1976.

[5]For the English Enlightenment, see Stephen 1876, 1900; and Halévy 1928.

By mid-century some critics in France had begun to reexamine the organization of the family in light of natural law theories; they devised new secular definitions to replace older religious justifications of "woman's place." Until recently, however, modern scholars of eighteenth- and early-nineteenth-century thought devoted little attention either to the Enlightenment debate about women or to the family as a social issue. Their attention focused on those aspects of the critique directed toward those highly organized and highly visible institutions—church and state—from which women had always been excluded. Consequently, the efforts of Enlightenment and revolutionary thinkers to confront the institution of the patriarchal family, its social role, and women's position within it, and to redefine it in secular terms, were for all practical purposes ignored.[6]

In Part I we have assembled a number of these ignored documents; they offer a suggestive sampling of the way the woman question was debated between 1750 and 1830. The texts are organized in three sections, which address the three most important public issues concerning women during this period: male authority over women in marriage, female education, and women's position in the new revolutionary republics of France and the United States. They include reactions to these issues generated in other countries where their significance was understood. These three issues allow us to understand the conflict that articulate women increasingly perceived between the redefinition of the patriarchal family and their own quest for self-esteem and personal freedom. This conflict was first posed in the language of natural law during the eighteenth century, as women and their male defenders juxtaposed "liberty" with "servitude," and "equality" with "inferiority," in an attempt to define their position.

Historical accounts of the thought of this period have traditionally centered on a cluster of significant male writers whose works are landmarks in the history of critical thought.[7] But women's participation in this intellectual movement is likewise relevant. Even though women were not publishing works comparable to those of Newton, Locke, Montesquieu, or the Encyclopedists clustered around Diderot, a small but growing number of them published their opinions on a variety of related subjects, helping to spread the new ideas among their contemporaries, and—most significantly—applying Enlightened reason to their own situation. This collection includes a number of important statements by such women, and by their male champions as well.

The problem that women writers and their allies confronted was extremely sensitive. They were deliberately crossing a boundary of social organization that had previously been sacrosanct; they were extending

[6] The counter-movement was launched by Ariès 1962, whose focus was on changing attitudes toward male children. Of particular relevance to this study are Alstad 1971; Schochet 1975; Shorter 1975; Stone 1977; and Flandrin 1979.
[7] For discussion of their contributions, see Williams 1971; Clinton 1975; Fisher 1975; LeGates 1976; Kleinbaum 1977; the essays in Fritz & Morton 1976; and the essays in Jacobs et al. 1979. For a major new work on the woman question, also focused on the ideas of male writers, see Hoffman 1978.

the reasoned critique of received authority to a question that was at once personal and institutional: the absolutism of male physical strength in the social relationship of the sexes. The writers of the French Enlightenment, the so-called philosophes who hoped to change French political and clerical absolutism through reasoned reform, effectively goaded their audience into discussion of the woman question. With the publication in 1748 of the widely read treatise *L'Esprit des lois* by the jurist Montesquieu, which explored the structure of government and social institutions, including the subordination of women in families, a new wave of publications on the subject appeared. Many of the best-known male writers—Voltaire, Diderot, d'Alembert, and the controversial Rousseau—all addressed the woman question, with varying degrees of originality. Less well known, but highly significant for understanding the development of the debate, were the female voices that began to be heard: the pseudonymous Sophia (Doc. 1), whose work appeared both in England and in France, and Madame de Beaumer (Doc. 2), friend of the *Encyclopédistes* and self-assured challenger of male authority.

The connection to the *Encyclopédie* was particularly important. This vast reference work, coauthored and edited by Diderot and d'Alembert, with major assistance from the Chevalier de Jaucourt (Doc. 6), ambitiously stated that its goal was to enlighten all humankind by attempting to "set forth as well as possible the order and connection of the parts of human knowledge."[8] The Encyclopedists' concern with the dissemination of knowledge, obtained through critical reasoning and understanding of nature, effectively unified Enlightenment philosophy; in the process they challenged traditional thinking about the relationship of the sexes and underscored the role of education as the cornerstone for liberty and equality. The ideas of these French Enlightenment writers on women's position at mid-century stimulated an outburst of publications on the subject by educated persons in other countries.

The mounting critique of the position of women provoked considerable resistance as it evoked the realization that the structure of the family in European societies, and indeed the principle of male authority itself, was being called into question. Advocacy of divorce and of marriage for love instead of for money was viewed as thoroughly subversive. To counter such ideas, Enlightenment jurists developed new secular rationalizations for women's subordination in marriage, to replace the biblical and canonical justifications that had previously sufficed. The Prussian jurist Samuel von Cocceji (Doc. 4), working to codify German law under the authority of his king, Frederick the Great, incorporated many Enlightenment notions about nature's importance for regulating human af-

---

[8] Jean Le Rond d'Alembert, *Preliminary Discourse to the Encyclopedia of Diderot* (Indianapolis, Ind., 1977), p. 4. Originally published in Paris, 1751. On the perilous publishing history of the *Encyclopédie*, see Darnton 1977. For the relationships of Encyclopedists to women writers and their views on the woman question, see Pellison 1910; Williams 1971; Gardner 1979; Jacobs 1979; and Niklaus 1979. See also the works listed in the Suggested Further Reading for *L'Encyclopédie* (Louis, Chevalier de Jaucourt).

fairs and producing the best effect on individuals; woman's place, however, the Code stated, must be strictly circumscribed in order to realize nature's plan. The British jurist William Blackstone (Doc. 5) revealed a similar attitude in his commentaries on the laws of England. Several decades later, the American statesman Thomas Jefferson, who captured in enduring prose the Enlightenment concept that men were "endowed by their Creator with certain unalienable rights, that among these are Life, Liberty, and the pursuit of Happiness," admitted nevertheless to a firm conviction that women's happiness lay in the domestic sphere, under male protection.[9] Jefferson's contemporary, Judith Sargent Murray (Doc. 3) countered such views by arguing that self-reliance, not arbitrary male protection, was the key to women's happiness as well as to their liberty. In the Baltic city of Königsberg, the philosopher Immanuel Kant (Doc. 27) painstakingly worked out the new secular foundations for an ethical morality, yet he found it impossible to envision the status of women in the same terms as that of men. But in the very same East Prussian city Kant's friend Theodor von Hippel (Doc. 29), the president of the municipal Council, composed what was undoubtedly one of the most stunning theoretical arguments of the period for the complete emancipation of women. Wherever the controversy arose, opinions conflicted. Dissenting views provoked the recasting of earlier prevailing views in new terms.

Of unusual importance in the new phases of this debate was the contrast that both the critics of women's position and the defenders of the status quo saw between the Old World and the New. The increasing familiarity of Europeans with stories of settlers and their encounters with Indian aborigines in their colonies across the seas added a new dimension to the eighteenth century's already extensive fascination with nature; thus arose the mythology of the "noble savage" and the "state of nature." To the social critics of eighteenth-century France in particular, the simplicity and honesty of American life seemed to contrast admirably with the contrived artificiality of court life under Louis XV and XVI. Meanwhile, in the revolutionary new United States of America, the leaders of the Republic sought corroboration in the Roman definition of virtue as male.[10] Both critics and defenders of women's subordination could find ammunition in this mixture of classical precedent with the mythology of natural law. Champions of women appealed to the natural equality between men and women that must have preceded social institutions, while social critics such as Rousseau (Doc. 10) invoked the state of nature to reframe the biblical view that women's natural place in civilized society was not merely as helpmeet but as mother.[11] Indeed, the exercise of rethinking woman's role with reference to nature with which Rousseau used to censure aristocratic French women's ostensible frivolity on the

[9] Jefferson to Anne Willing Bingham, 7 February 1787, in *The Papers of Thomas Jefferson*, ed. Julian Parks Boyd, II (Princeton, N.J., 1955), 122-24.

[10] This point is underscored by Kerber 1980.

[11] See especially the recent analysis of Keohane 1980a.

one hand, and their intellectual pretensions on the other, effectively elaborated a new ideal of motherhood; in the short term it popularized the idea that upper-class women should breast-feed and care for their own infants. And in the long term women themselves expanded the exercise, especially in the aftermath of the American and French revolutions, to justify a special and important role for themselves in the new republics as molders of character—an idea that is clearly present in the writing of Mary Wollstonecraft and others.[12]

What is perhaps most fascinating—and, to women, most alarming—to discover in the debate is the firmness with which Enlightenment writers from Rousseau to Johann Wolfgang von Goethe (Doc. 28) reasserted that within a framework of separate spheres woman's role was to be natural comforter and domestic muse for the new public man. To twentieth-century readers this may raise suspicions that these men implicitly equated the term *human* solely with *male*; more probably, however, it underscores their explicit apprehension, as they realized that the logical conclusion of the Enlightenment slogan "free and equal," which they bandied about with such fervor, threatened—when applied to the patriarchal family—to destroy the basis of society as they knew it. Indeed, such men—and more than a few women such as the popular evangelical writer Hannah More (Doc. 20)—reacted with alarm to the notion that women might press these secular ideals of equality and liberty to such a logical conclusion.

Rejecting the teachings of authoritarian religion on such matters, therefore, they found it necessary to rejustify distinctive roles for the sexes in functional terms. Thus, they redefined male and female activities into separate spheres of equal weight: one public or civic, the other private, domestic, and maternal. The equivocal approach of Goethe is particularly suggestive: he paid tribute to women's intellect, their mental and physical strength, and insisted on their independence. Nevertheless, he demanded that they continue to nurture and promote the spirit of domestic harmony so that men might be free to accomplish heroic feats in the public sphere. Although, in retrospect, one might have expected such fierce critics of religious intolerance, absolutism, and slavery, to have supported complete equality of women and men, one finds instead constant equivocation. Indeed, such champions of women's rights as the Marquis de Condorcet (Docs. 19, 24), who argued for women's civic rights on the principle of "human rights," contended that women needed these rights and equal education to enhance their situation as mothers. Neither he nor any of his colleagues could view women solely as individuals, with the same potential for civic, economic, or professional contribution as men. Even Mary Wollstonecraft (Doc. 12) coupled her progressive views on independence for women with an explicit acknowledgment of their unique maternal role. Only Hippel (Doc. 29) dealt with the woman ques-

---

[12] For the United States, see Cott 1977; R. Bloch 1978a; Kerber 1980. For France, see Darrow 1979 and Pope 1980. For England, see Myers 1982.

tion solely on the level of theory, advocating full and equal civic rights for women as individuals.

Thus one finds that in the works of many Enlightenment social critics bio-social definitions of womanhood, centering on child-bearing and child-raising, became explicit in their restatements of woman's reason for existence. Rousseau, who insisted on the centrality of reproduction, remarked that a country woman with only five surviving children was considered "unfruitful" (Doc. 10). And indeed, the population explosion that began in Western Europe in the second half of the eighteenth century (as famines ceased and the death rate began to drop) was such that later social commentators, like the English clergyman Thomas Malthus, became deeply concerned about the prospect of mass starvation, should the population continue to increase at such a rate. Obviously, these demographic factors did nothing to undermine the persistent view that women, who bore children, should be supported and supervised by men; indeed, they could be cited by secular and religious detractors to rearticulate the legitimate concerns about women's vulnerability in terms of their inferiority, and—by logical extension—to rationalize the consignment of women to a legally subordinate position. Such a development is evident in both the Prussian Laws of 1794 and the French Civil Code of 1804 (Docs. 7, 8).

The questioning of women's subordinate status in marriage was, of course, closely connected to the problem of female education. Indeed, the long-standing debate on the education of women likewise entered a new phase in the mid-eighteenth century. In 1761 Jean-Jacques Rousseau (who had attracted a large female audience with his novel *La Nouvelle Héloïse*) asserted that women, created to please men, should be educated exclusively to be good wives and mothers; such mothers, in turn, would raise daughters entirely absorbed in pleasing men. Rousseau's youthful enthusiasm for natural, unrestricted self-realizing human development, for a social contract that would eliminate inequality, for a good yet simple life, has inspired the dreams—and nightmares—of successive generations of social reformers. Paradoxically, these egalitarian dreams seemed to require the backing of an unchanging and stable nurturing force. Fundamental to Rousseau's thought, therefore, lay the most conservative, the most time-honored assumptions about the social relations of the sexes. He reconsecrated for all women a role exclusively within the family on the grounds of biological determinism and gave new authority to deep-rooted attitudes concerning the "separate [male and female] spheres."[13]

Though a few women writers initially applauded Rousseau's overall assertions, a cluster of well-known female authors in France and England indignantly challenged his views on woman's nature and role. The most eloquent among them were Catharine Macaulay and Mary Wollstonecraft in England, and Germaine de Staël in France (Docs. 11-14). They protested against Rousseau's argument from differing points of view,

[13] Keohane 1980a.

raising issues as diverse as the importance of emotional independence for wives, economic independence for single women or widows, and that nefarious influence we now call sex-role conditioning. Against Rousseau's assertion that because all girls enjoyed playing at mothering dolls they were inherently competent "nurturers," the authors pointed out that girls were conditioned for this role by a society that allowed them to play with nothing but dolls. Catharine Macaulay further proposed that boys—as well as girls—should be taught the "graces," in order to blur the strong sexual dichotomy and dependence of weak women on strong men on which Rousseau insisted. Madame de Staël, a brilliant and creative writer, was personally outraged by Rousseau's denigrating aspersions against married women authors, whose writing (he implied) would cause them to neglect their wifely duties. Staël's works were translated into English and German, Wollstonecraft's into French and German, and Macaulay was read on the Continent and in the United States— Condorcet, von Hippel, and Judith Sargent Murray were all familiar with her books.

Rousseau's ideas on woman's nature and proper social role inspired protest not only among angry women. A generation later his arguments and those of his followers became a springboard for philosophical and literary discussion throughout Europe. In Germany, the linguist Wilhelm von Humboldt and the literary critic Friedrich von Schlegel held a debate in 1795 over the significance of contrasting gender characteristics (Docs. 15, 16). Based upon allusions to Plato, Aristotle, and Greek art, the debate stimulated thought and discussion in intellectual circles in Berlin. Schlegel's support for platonic androgyny was soon forgotten, however, while the views of Humboldt and of his contemporary, the poet Goethe (Doc. 28), prevailed throughout the German states and the Western world. Through Goethe's works in particular, these ideas carried new authority in English-speaking countries.

With the republican revolutions of the later eighteenth and early nineteenth centuries, Enlightenment social criticism provided ammunition for action against the established order. The question of women's relationship to the new republican states immediately came to the fore. Although the issues that precipitated the 1789 Paris revolt were economic —poor harvests, rising grain prices, and an expanding urban population unable to feed itself—the underlying discontent of the eighteenth century, both in Europe and in the American colonies, was expressed in political terms: men objected to autocratic and arbitrary government. Individual desire for the right to self-government, which followed naturally from Enlightenment emphasis on individual liberty, manifested itself in such practical demands as the right to vote—for men of property, that is—and the right to elect a representative government. The American colonists, cognizant of their heritage of governmental self-determination, adopted this method when agitation for revolution against British "tyranny" erupted; they were well versed in conducting their own affairs and continued to do so, in accord with a vision of government that excluded all women except queens. Yet the women, watching, did not always remain silent. "Remember the Ladies," Abigail Adams counseled her husband John, as he and his colleagues in the Continental Congress were drafting the American Constitution, and Adams himself queried, "Why exclude women?"[14] In America there were advocates of a private role for women with a public dimension; although they could not envision full citizenship, they emphasized the centrality of women's role as the wives and mothers of citizens. Judith Sargent Murray, Benjamin Rush, and others argued that, as mothers of future generations of men who would become the leaders of the new republic, women deserved and required a good education—an argument that was elaborated and expanded in the following century in the justification for founding schools for girls.[15]

In monarchical France, the course of the revolution was far more turbulent. In a highly volatile conflict, religious and anti-religious factions, agricultural and commercial interests, craft guilds, and paupers were all at loggerheads. Many believed that a completely new system of government would have to evolve from the tumult. A few voices urged that liberty and equality in law be granted to women as well as men, advocating their full participation in government and even in the military defense of the nation.[16]

Parisian women such as Etta Palm d'Aelders (Doc. 25) organized clubs whose primary aims were to influence the course of revolutionary politics; they were expressly concerned with women's emancipation and with establishing their right and capabilities to participate in the new government. The new Republican Assembly acknowledged addresses from a few men and women advocating equal legal and political rights for women. Indeed, during one session, a delegate from the provinces, Pierre Guyomar, rose to accuse his colleagues of being a "formal male aristocracy."[17] A few women addressed the National Assembly directly, and Olympe de Gouges remonstrated (Doc. 26) against the omission of women from the general dispensation of "rights and equality." The all-male National Convention elected in 1792 did make some important changes: in the interests of equalizing property rights, it revoked the laws on primogeniture, thereby permitting daughters to inherit family property equally with sons, and it took control of marriage away from the church, passing liberal laws governing marriage, divorce, and the legitimation of children.[18] The people's representatives balked, however, at the prospect of women's participation in governing the state. When the Jacobin radicals triumphed in late 1793, it became clear that the most

[14] Rossi 1973b, pp. 10, 14, quoting *The Adams Papers*, ser. 2, *Adams Family Correspondence*, ed. L. H. Butterfield (Cambridge, Mass., 1963).

[15] On women and the American Revolution, see Kerber 1974, 1976, 1980; J. Wilson 1976; and Norton 1980.

[16] On women and the French Revolution, see Abray 1975; Devance 1977; Graham 1977; and chs. 1, 5, and 9 in Berkin & Lovett 1980. See also the documents in Duhet 1971; and Levy, Applewhite & Johnson 1979.

[17] Cited in Abray 1975, p. 48.

[18] For a recent analysis of these laws, see Traer 1980.

persuasive advocates of women's rights were allied with the moderate—
and losing—factions. The execution of the king was followed by the
guillotining of outspoken monarchists, including Olympe de Gouges.
That she had dared to meddle in politics at all, let alone to promote
women's liberty and equal rights, was deemed a serious crime: "she
wanted to be a statesman, and it seems the law has punished this conspir-
ator for having forgotten the virtues that suited her sex," thundered *La
Feuille de Salut Public*, following her execution.[19]

After 1799 the authoritarian rule of France (1799-1814) by Napoleon
Bonaparte, inspired by legal and political ideas reminiscent of imperial
Rome—the sequel to the republican part of the classical tradition admired by Enlightenment thinkers—and culminating in his military conquest of large parts of Europe, ended all attempts to realize liberty and
equality for women, whether in the law or in the polity. His outspoken
belief that women were meant to be men's property and to produce children for them, embodied in the Civil Code of 1804 (Doc. 8), shaped not
only the new legal position of Frenchwomen, but also that of women in
many other parts of Europe where the French code was subsequently
adopted. "The wife," stated Article 213 dogmatically, "owes obedience
to her husband." Thus, the French wife had only fractionally more real
freedom in the law than the Englishwoman whose existence as a civil
personality was, as Blackstone had pointed out, "suspended during
marriage."[20]

The eighteenth-century French arguments for women's rights and
equality, demanding women's civic participation in the governmental
process either by voting or through legal and judicial involvement, were
not extinguished by the repression, even though their advocates were imprisoned or executed. Instead, these ideas were developed and spread in
other parts of the Western world. Among the most vocal advocates were
such British travellers to France as the young Mary Wollstonecraft, friend
of Thomas Paine and William Godwin, and foreign observers such as
Hippel, who from the eastern end of the Baltic Sea responded immediately in 1792 to women's omission from the French Declaration of
Rights (Doc. 29).

These ideas could not, however, be translated into action during the
post-revolutionary repression that affected all Europe. Even the circle
of British radicals like James Mill (Doc. 31) that surrounded the philosopher Jeremy Bentham hesitated before the Enlightenment emphasis
on "natural rights," developing instead a philosophy that sanctified individual property rights while yet seeking "the greatest happiness of the
greatest number." They were quite clear, however, that women's greatest
happiness did not lie in governing the state. In England, as agitation

[19] "Aux Républicaines," reprinted in the *Gazette Nationale, ou le Moniteur Universel*,
no. 59 Nonidi, 29 Brumaire, l'An 2ᵉ (19 November 1793), p. 450.

[20] In post-revolutionary America state courts slowly began to break away from the English common law on matters of women's property. See Rabkin 1974, 1980; and Salmon
1979, 1980.

mounted for suffrage reform, the ideas of the radical Irish aristocrat Anna Doyle Wheeler were published under the name of her friend William Thompson (Doc. 32). Another contributor to this agitation was Eliza Sharples (Doc. 33), an active orator in the circle of politically oriented artisans (including numerous women) that surrounded the reformer Richard Carlile. Sharples and Carlile resurrected the radical republican ideals of an earlier generation, and did not draw a line when it came to including women's participation in their discussion.[21]

Only toward 1830 did a more favorable political climate allow these ideas to be spread to a wider and more responsive public. New secular definitions of women's role and education bounded women's position but did not muzzle protest. In the meantime the Enlightenment focus on reason, social criticism, and the importance of knowledge contributed to the creation of a broader and more politically aware reading public, especially among women, which in the nineteenth century fostered an ever-growing block of support for women's rights.

[21] Royle 1974.

CHAPTER I

Male Authority in Marriage

Mid-Century Criticism of Male Authority in Marriage and Society

SOURCES

1. Sophia, A Person of Quality [pseud.], *Woman Not Inferior to Man or, A Short and Modest Vindication of the Natural Right of the Fair Sex to a Perfect Equality of Power, Dignity, and Esteem, with the Men* (London, 1739), pp. 1-3, 7-9, 56. The editors are grateful to Barbara Brandon Schnorrenberg, Birmingham, Alabama, for making her copy of this document available to them.

2. Madame de Beaumer, "Avant-Propos," *Journal des Dames* (March 1762), pp. 223-26. The editors are grateful to Professor Nina Gelbart, Occidental College, for bringing Madame de Beaumer's editorials to their attention. Tr. KMO.

3. Judith Sargent Murray, "Desultory Thoughts Upon the Utility of Encouraging a Degree of Self-Complacency, Especially in FEMALE BOSOMS," *Gentleman and Lady's Town and Country Magazine* (Boston), I, no. 6 (October 1784), 253.

The critique of male authority over women gained momentum throughout the eighteenth century. Appropriating the tools of Enlightenment criticism for their own ends, women rejected time-honored assumptions of male superiority and questioned the basis for male rights and authority over women's minds and bodies. Opinions that they might once have stated only privately found their way into print, reaching a wider audience among those women and men—privileged by birth, wealth, or acquired position—who formed the reading public of mid-eighteenth-century Western Europe and Colonial America. The three selections that follow illustrate the development of this critique in England, France, and post-revolutionary America. They reveal the increasingly assertive tone that characterized the women's critique between the 1740's and the 1780's.

The first selection is from an English tract entitled *Woman Not Inferior to Man* (1739) by the unidentified "Sophia, A Person of Quality." Sophia rejected all arguments concerning female inferiority based on anatomical difference. She insisted that women's faulty education over the centuries was to blame for any social inferiority that had subsequently become institutionalized. Moreover, Sophia argued, properly educated women would be suited to govern, to fill public offices, and to offer instruction in the sciences; she even devoted a special chapter to discussing women's capability to assume military functions. Although she may have derived many of these arguments from the seventeenth-century French author

Poullain de la Barre (whose treatise on women's natural equality with men she could have read either in French or in the English translation of 1677), she adapted them to the English scene by pointing to British heroines like Boadicea and Queen Elizabeth and to female scholars of her own day to emphasize her points.

Sophia's claims did not go unchallenged. Also in 1739 an anonymous "gentleman" answered her with a pamphlet entitled *Man Superior to Woman, or, A Vindication of Man's Natural Right of Sovereign Authority over the Woman.* In 1740 Sophia replied with an even longer treatise, in which she demolished these arguments and stated her own. Her treatises were reprinted and adapted under similar titles in England throughout the next forty years: in 1750 as *The Triumph of Beauty*; in French translation as *La Femme n'est pas inférieure à l'homme*, reprinted the following year as *Le Triomphe des dames*, by "Miladi P***." Scholars have attributed the French translation variously to Madeleine d'Arsant de Puisieux and to her estranged husband Philippe de Puisieux. The former attribution takes on added significance when it is noted that Madeleine de Puisieux had for years been deeply involved in a liaison with the brilliant young French social critic Denis Diderot, who was then preparing his plans for the great *Encyclopédie.*

The second selection, still more assertive in tone, is an editorial by Madame de Beaumer (d. 1766), the first of three women editors of the *Journal des Dames.* The *Journal* had been founded in Paris in 1759 with the idea of encouraging women to write seriously and to publish their literary efforts; late in 1761 Madame de Beaumer took over the editorship. Little is known about her life, save that she had lived for some time in Holland, had acquired a certain notoriety as a *bel esprit*, and claimed to be related to a distinguished French military leader, the Maréchal de Belle-Isle. During her two-year tenure as editor, Beaumer projected an image of considerable success, boasting that the *Journal des Dames* could be purchased in eighty-one European cities. She ardently defended the talents and prerogatives of her sex against all detractors. "Halt, Messieurs the critics," she wrote in her first editorial of October 1761; "You should know that it is a woman who addresses you, that she has been charged with the conduct of this Journal and that she cannot say enough good things in favor of her sex, whose sole right is the right to subdue you." Madame de Beaumer's connection with a major contributor to the *Encyclopédie* and one of the most radical male critics of women's subordination—the Chevalier de Jaucourt (Doc. 6)—is established by the fact that his address is given as an editorial and subscription address for the *Journal des Dames* during this period.

The third selection, from the United States, presents a critique of women's situation following the revolutionary war, by a Massachusetts woman. Her views are informed by the intense experience of American women during the struggle for liberty and human rights, and by her own personal situation. Judith Sargent (Stevens) Murray (1751-1820), a gifted essayist and poet, had shared her early education with a brother destined for the ministry and Harvard College. At the age of eighteen she had married her first husband John Stevens, a New England merchant and sea-captain who experienced financial problems during the Revolution and fled to the West Indies, where he died. Her earliest known publication, of 1784, here reprinted, contains the nucleus of her thought. Here, in deceptively respectful but firm language, she critiqued women's situation not only in terms of current discussion on political freedom, but also with reference to religious emphasis on the immolation of self. Writing at the age of thirty-three, after an unsuitable early marriage, she insisted that young girls must be taught self-worth and self-reliance as independent human beings. This would arm them against the fear of becoming "Old Maids," should they not marry the first flatterer to present himself, in order to arrive at the sole state acceptable for a woman in contemporary society—the married state. Following her second marriage to a clergyman, the Reverend Murray, and the birth of several children, she resumed her explorations of American women's education and status in the 1790's.

---

1. Sophia [pseud.] (1739)

If a celebrated Author had not already told us, that *there is nothing in nature so much to be wonder'd at as* THAT WE CAN WONDER AT ALL; it must appear to every one, who has but a degree of understanding above the idiot, a matter of the greatest surprize, to observe the universal prevalence of prejudice and custom in the minds of the *Men*. One might naturally expect to see those lordly creatures, as they modestly stile themselves, everywhere jealous of superiority, and watchful to maintain it. Instead of which, if we expect the tyrannical usurpation of authority they exert over us *Women*, we shall find them industrious in nothing but courting the meanest servitude. Was their ambition laudable and just, it would be consistent in itself, and this consistency would render them alike imperious in every circumstance, where authority is requisite and justifiable: And if their brutal strength of body entitled them to lord it over our nicer frame, the superiority of reason to passion, might suffice to make them blush to submit that reason to passion, prejudice, and groundless custom. If this haughty sex would have us believe they have a natural right of superiority over us, why do not they prove their charter from nature, by making use of reason to subdue themselves. We know we have reason, and are sensible that it is the only prerogative nature has bestow'd upon us, to lift us above the sphere of sensitive animals: And the same reason, which points us out our superiority over them, would light us to discern the superiority of *Men* over us, if we could discover in them the least degree of sense above what we ourselves possess. But it will be impossible for us, without forfeiting that reason, ever to acknowledge ourselves inferior to creatures, who make no other use of the sense they boast of, than basely to subject it to the passions they have in common with Brutes. Were we to see the *Men* every where, and at all times, masters of themselves, and their animal appetites in a perfect subordination to their rational faculties; we should have some colour to think that nature designed them for masters to us, who cannot perhaps always boast of so compleat a command over ourselves. But how is it possible for us to give into such a notion, while we see those very men, whose ambition of ascendency over us, nothing less than absolute dominion can satiate, court the most abject slavery, by prostituting reason to their groveling passions, suffering sense to be led away captive by prejudice, and sacrificing justice, truth, and honour, to inconsiderate custom? . . .

Hitherto the *difference* between the *sexes* has been but very slightly touch'd upon. Nevertheless, the *Men*, biass'd by custom, prejudice, and interest, have presumed boldly to pronounce sentence in their own favour, because possession empower'd them to make violence take place of justice. And the *Men* of our times, without trial or examination, have taken the same liberty from the report of other *Men*. Whereas to judge soundly, whether their sex has received from nature any real super-eminence beyond ours; they should entirely divest themselves of all *interest* and *partiality*, and suffer no bare reports to fill the place of argument, especially if the Reporter be a *party* immediately concern'd.

If a *Man* could thus divest the partiality attach'd to this self, and put on for a minute a state of neutrality, he would be able to see, and forced to acknowledge, that *prejudice* and *precipitance* are the chief causes of setting less value upon *Women* than *Men*, and giving so much greater excellence and nobility to the latter than to the former. In a word, were the *Men Philosophers* in the strict sense of the term, they would be able to see that nature invincibly proves a perfect *equality* in our sex with their own.

But as there are extremely *few* among them capable of such an ab-stracted way of thinking, they have no more right to act the judges in this matter than ourselves; and therefore, we must be obliged to appeal to a more *impartial judge*, one incapable of siding with any party, and conse-quently unsuspected on both sides. *This* I apprehend to be *rectified rea-son*, as it is a pure intellectual faculty elevated above the consideration of any sex, and equally concern'd in the welfare of the whole rational spe-cies in general, and in particular. *To this Judge* we leave our cause, by the decision of this we are prepar'd to stand or fall; and if, upon the evidence of *truth*, *reason* should declare us inferior to *Men*, we will chearfully ac-quiesce to the sentence. But what if we obtain a decree in our favour, upon impartial examination? Why then all the authority, which the *Men* have exerted over us hitherto, will appear an unjust usurpation on their side; for which nothing can make tolerable atonement, but their restor-ing to us the state of equality *nature* first placed us in. . . .

What I have hitherto said, has not been with an intention to stir up any of my own sex to revolt against the *Men*, or to invert the present order of things, with regard to *government* and *authority*. No, let them stand as they are: I only mean to shew my sex, that they are not so despicable as the *Men* wou'd have them believe themselves, and that we are capable of as much greatness of soul as the best of that haughty sex. And I am fully convinced, it wou'd be to the joint interest of both to think so.

2. Madame de Beaumer (1762)

The success of the *Journal des Dames* allows us to triumph over those frivolous persons who have regarded this periodical as a petty work con-taining only a few bagatelles suited to help them kill time. In truth, Gen-tlemen, you do us much honor to think that we could not provide things that unite the useful to the agreeable. To rid you of your error, we have made our Journal historical, with a view to putting before the eyes of youth striking images that will guide them toward virtue; it is for virtue that we are formed, and only by aspiring to virtue can we be esteemed. An historical *Journal des Dames*! these Gentlemen reasoners reply. How ridiculous! How out of character with the nature of this work, which calls only for little pieces to amuse [ladies] during their toilette. Well! It is precisely this that I wish to avoid. A female philosopher seeks to instruct; she makes too little of the toilette, in order to contribute to its pleasures. Please, Gentlemen *beaux esprits*, mind your own business and let us write in a manner worthy of our sex; I love this sex, I am jealous to uphold its honor and its rights. If we have not been raised up in the sciences as you have, it is you who are the guilty ones; for have you not always abused, if I may say so, the bodily strength that nature has given you? Have you not used it to annihilate our capacities, and to enshroud the special prerogatives that this same nature has bounteously granted to women, to compensate them for the material strength that you have—advantages that we surely would not dispute you—to truly appreciate vivacity of imagination, delicate feelings, and that amiable politeness, well worth the strength that you parade about so.

We would be well avenged, Gentlemen, if today, like our ancient Amazons, we could make you spin or make braids; especially you, the Frivolous Gentlemen, so enamoured of yourselves, just like Narcissus, you pass part of your time trying on the latest styles, artistically powdering and rouging yourselves, and placing beauty spots artistically; you chatter continually while you pick at your plates; yes, you are even more effeminate than the Coquettes you are seeking to please. Inasmuch as heaven has given you strength, do not debase it; use it in the service of the King and for the fatherland; become good Compatriots; Go to the battlefields, confront and confound our enemies; throw yourselves at the feet of the French Monarch, who is worthy to be king of the entire universe, and leave to us the task of cultivating *belles lettres*. We will prove to you that they are in good keeping in our hands. In this certitude, we will continue the new *Journal des Dames* and we will do everything in our power so to render it as to leave nothing to be desired in its execution.

3. Judith Sargent Murray (1784)

A young lady, growing up with the idea, that she possesses few, or no personal attractions, and that her mental abilities are of an inferior kind; imbibing at the same time, a most melancholy idea of a female, descending down the vale of life in an unprotected state; taught also to regard her character [as] ridiculously contemptible, will, too probably, throw herself away upon the first who approaches her with tenders of love, however indifferent may be her chance for happiness, least if she omits the present day of grace, she may never be so happy as to meet a second offer, and must then inevitably be stigmatised with that dreaded title, an Old Maid,

must rank with a class whom she has been accustomed to regard as bur-
thens upon society, and objects whom she might with impunity turn into
ridicule! Certainly love, friendship and esteem, ought to take place of
marriage, but, the woman thus circumstanced, will seldom regard these
previous requisites to felicity, if she can but insure the honors, which she,
in idea, associates with a matrimonial connection—to prevent which
great evil, I would early impress under proper regulations, a reverence of
self; I would endeavour to rear to worth, and a consciousness thereof; I
would be solicitous to inspire the glow of virtue, with that elevation of
soul, that dignity, which is ever attendant upon self-approbation, arising
from the genuine source of innate rectitude. I must be excused for thus
insisting upon my hypothesis, as I am, from observations, persuaded,
that many have suffered materially all their life long, from a depression of
soul, early inculcated, in compliance to a false maxim, which hath supposed pride would thereby be eradicated.

Woman as Wife in Eighteenth-Century Law

SOURCES

4. *The Frederician Code* (Edinburgh, 1761), part 1, book 1, Title VIII, pp. 37-
39. Originally published in German, Berlin, 1750.

5. Sir William Blackstone, *Commentaries on the Laws of England*, 11th ed.
(London, 1791), book 1, ch. 15, pp. 433, 442-45. Lectures presented at Oxford,
1756. Originally published in Oxford, 1765-69.

6. Louis, Chevalier de Jaucourt, "Femme (Droit Nat.)," in *L'Encyclopédie*, VI
(Paris, 1756), 471-72. Tr. KMO.

The critique of male authority over women highlighted in the previous section
provoked mid-century restatements or secular rationalizations to justify women's
subordination. Secular restatements draw not on theological tradition or sanctions but on the secular sanctions of natural law. Thus it was that the debate on
the "woman question" entered a new phase, which is highlighted here by the jux-
taposition of three important texts on the legal position of the wife, all published
in the 1750's: the first from the unified Prussian Frederician Code, the second
from Sir William Blackstone's *Commentaries on the Laws of England*, and the
third from the celebrated French *Encyclopédie*.

The Frederician Code, officially known as *Das allgemeines Landrecht*, was the
supreme achievement of Frederick the Great's chief minister of justice, Samuel
von Cocceji (1679-1755). Cocceji devoted his life to reforming the Prussian judicial system and administration. In his last years he drafted the first two sections of
a unified code, which included the major laws governing marriage and the family.
The remainder of the code was not completed and published until some forty
years after his death (Doc. 7).

Cocceji's code reflects his deep reliance upon the Roman law tradition, as well
as his "enlightened" belief in natural rights, which he equated with reason itself.
In formulating the code, he attempted to apply these two strains of thought to
German custom laws. The Edinburgh translation reprinted below, dating from

1761, expressly states on the title-page that the Code is "founded on Reason and the constitution of the Country," that is, on a blend of Enlightenment philosophy and traditional custom, and states at the outset that, "judging by the sole light of reason, the husband is master of his own household and head of his family." So intriguing was this codification of Germanic law to judicial experts in other parts of Europe that within a decade of its initial publication the Prussian code had been translated into French and English.

The English jurist William Blackstone (1723-1780) stated similar views on the wife's legal position in his *Commentaries on the Laws of England*, which he had first delivered as lectures at Oxford University in 1753. In his discussion on marriage, Blackstone makes it clear that in English law marriage is considered strictly as a civil contract, without regard to its possible religious significance. In several respects, however, Blackstone seems to epitomize the eighteenth-century Panglossian world-view, attacked by Voltaire, which assumes that "all is for the best in this best of all possible worlds." This is abundantly clear when he writes that the laws of England—even those that clearly restrict women—are made for the protection and benefit of the English wife.

Although Blackstone was long recognized as one of the foremost influences on British and American law, he is now viewed more as a rhetorician than a precise analyst of the law. He has been accused of blurring the distinction between *natural law* and *positive law* made by French political theorists such as Jaucourt (see below). Blackstone identified natural law (or God's law) with the man-made *common law* of England. His confusion of these terms nevertheless appealed greatly to English believers in natural laws and rights, thus helping to clothe in new language traditional views on woman's place. His famous dictum that "the very being or legal existence of the woman is suspended during marriage," thus took on a "natural" authority, as did the "reasoned" mastery of the husband in the Prussian legal code. Indeed, Blackstone's categorical pronouncement exerted a great influence on nineteenth-century women's lives in England and particularly in the eastern United States, where from the beginning of the Republic his *Commentaries* were used as the basic legal textbook for training lawyers.

While Blackstone in England and Cocceji in Prussia used the concepts of reason and natural law to consolidate their conservative appreciation of the status quo, the Encyclopedists in France used the same concepts to buttress their arguments on behalf of change. The *Encyclopédie*, published in twenty-one volumes between 1751 and 1772, was perhaps the greatest monument of French Enlightenment thought. The eighteenth-century preoccupation with knowledge and reason found its expression in a proliferation of dictionaries and encyclopedias of learning, published in French, English, and German. However, the *Encyclopédie* designed by Denis Diderot and his collaborators differed from both previous and contemporary works of the kind in that it consciously attacked prevailing thought and institutions from the standpoint of natural law. In fact, the public uproar after the publication of the first volume in 1751 was so tremendous that it nearly jeopardized completion of the work. However, with the help and patronage of various important people, including Madame de Pompadour, the king's mistress, Diderot was finally authorized to publish the remaining volumes.

Implicit in many articles of the *Encyclopédie* was the suggestion that its authors were unbelievers, attacking the Church, the law, despotic government, and even Christianity itself. This point of view is exemplified in one of the three articles on "Woman," which deals with the wife's position in the law. The author, Louis, Chevalier de Jaucourt (1704-1780), was a Huguenot nobleman and one of

Diderot's most faithful collaborators; he wrote approximately one-fourth of the articles in the *Encyclopédie*. Like the other philosophes, Jaucourt emphasized the distinction between natural law and positive law—that is, between God's law (or the law of natural reason) and man-made law, whether derived from custom or consolidated in a legal code. Jaucourt concluded that, by invariably subjecting the wife to her husband, positive law had erred. He even suggested that marriage contracts between husband and wife be based not only upon property but upon intellectual capabilities as well.

In fact, English common law had to some extent provided an equivalent to the contract system recommended by Jaucourt. English laws of equity, administered by special courts, provided remedies for wrongs overlooked by the common law. They made it possible for wealthy English or American fathers to ensure their daughters' ability to administer or retain property in marriage and widowhood, through the use of trusts, administered by equity law and equity courts. Marriage and property settlements could thus be arranged to give the propertied woman a reasonable amount of self-determination. Of course, both equity law in England and the contract arrangements suggested by the Chevalier de Jaucourt were available only to those who could pay substantial legal fees; this effectively restricted their utility to members of the wealthy aristocracy and upper-middle classes. The vast majority of English women under "cover" of their husbands had no more legal self-determination than the French women whose position Jaucourt wished to change, or the Prussian women subject to the Frederician Code.

---

4. The Frederician Code (1750)

Title VIII
Of the rights of the husband with regard to his wife; and those of the wife with regard to her husband, proceeding from the family-state

1.

As the domestic society, or family, is formed by the union of the husband and wife, we are to begin with enumerating the advantages and rights which result from this union.

2.

The husband is by nature the head of his family. To be convinced of this, it is sufficient to consider, that the wife leaves her family to join herself to that of her husband; that she enters into his household, and into the habitation of which he is the master, and grants him rights over her body, with intention to have children by him to perpetuate the family.

3.

Hence it follows, judging by the sole light of reason, that the husband is master of his own household, and head of his family. And as the wife enters into it of her own accord, she is in some measure subject to his power; whence flow several rights and privileges, which belong to the husband with regard to his wife.

For, (1) the husband has the liberty of prescribing laws and rules in his household, which the wife is to observe.

(2) If the wife be defective in her duty to her husband, and refuse to be subject, he is authorised to reduce her to her duty in a reasonable manner.

(3) The wife is bound, according to her quality, to assist her husband, to take upon her the care of the household affairs, according to his condition.

(4) The husband has the power over the wife's body, and she cannot refuse him the conjugal duty.

(5) As the husband and wife have promised not to leave each other during their lives, but to share the good and evil which may happen to them; the wife cannot, under pretext, for example, that her husband has lost his reason, leave him, without obtaining permission so to do from the judge.

(6) For the same reason, the wife is obliged to follow her husband, when he changes his habitation; unless, (a) it has been stipulated by the contract of marriage, or otherwise, that she shall not be bound to follow him if he should incline to settle elsewhere; or, (b) unless it were for a crime that the husband changed his habitation, as if he had been banished from his country.

4.

The wife likewise enjoys certain rights and privileges with respect to her husband. For,

(1) As it is in quality of an assistant that the wife enters into the family with her husband, she ought to enjoy all the rights of the family. Thus she carries her husband's name and arms, she partakes his rank, she is under the same jurisdiction as he, &c. These advantages are continued to her even after her husband's death, as long as she remains a widow.

(2) The husband is bound to defend his wife, as well before the judge as elsewhere; wherefore also he may appear in a judicature for her, without a letter of attorney, provided he give security, that she shall ratify what he does.

(3) The wife hath the power of her husband's body, who cannot refuse to pay her the conjugal duty, when he is not prevented by sickness or other accidents.

(4) By virtue of these engagements, the husband cannot, without committing adultery, have criminal correspondence with another woman.

(5) Neither can he separate from his wife, without very important reasons.

(6) The wife succeeds to an equal portion with her children in her husband's effects; unless, by contract of marriage, or other settlements, the succession be otherwise regulated. From this law are excepted the provinces, in which the statutes of the country settle on the conjunct survivor, a certain portion which is called *portionem statutariam*, and those in which the community of goods is introduced.

(7) The husband is obliged to maintain his wife according to his rank

and condition, whether he took her without dowry, or she lost her fortune after her marriage.

(8) In these cases he is also obliged to bury her at his own charge.

5. Sir William Blackstone (1756)

The second private relation of persons is that of marriage, which includes the reciprocal right and duties of husband and wife; or, as most of our elder law books call them, of *baron* and *feme*. . . .

Having thus shewn how marriages may be made, or dissolved, I come now, lastly, to speak of the legal consequences of such making, or dissolution.

By marriage, the husband and wife are one person in law: that is, the very being or legal existence of the woman is suspended during the marriage, or at least is incorporated and consolidated into that of the husband: under whose wing, protection, and *cover*, she performs every thing; and is therefore called in our law-french a *feme-covert, foemina virs co-operta*; is said to be *covert-baron*, or under the protection and influence of her husband, her *baron* or lord; and her condition during her marriage is called her *coverture*. Upon this principle, of an union of person in husband and wife, depend almost all the legal rights, duties, and disabilities, that either of them acquire by the marriage. I speak not at present of the rights of property, but of such as are merely *personal*. For this reason, a man cannot grant any thing to his wife, or enter into covenant with her: for the grant would be to suppose her separate existence; and to covenant with her, would be only to covenant with himself: and therefore it is also generally true, that all compacts made between husband and wife, when single, are voided by the intermarriage. A woman indeed may be attorney for her husband; for that implies no separation from, but is rather a representation of, her lord. And a husband may also bequeath any thing to his wife by will; for that cannot take effect till the coverture is determined by his death. The husband is bound to provide his wife with necessaries by law, as much as himself: and if she contracts debts for them, he is obliged to pay them; but for any thing besides necessaries, he is not chargeable. Also if a wife elopes, and lives with another man, the husband is not chargeable even for necessaries; at least if the person, who furnishes them, is sufficiently apprized of her elopement. If the wife be indebted before marriage, the husband is bound afterwards to pay the debt; for he has adopted her and her circumstances together. If the wife be injured in her person or her property, she can bring no action for redress without her husband's concurrence, and in his name, as well as her own: neither can she be sued, without making the husband a defendant. There is indeed one case where the wife shall sue and be sued as a feme sole, *viz.* where the husband has abjured the realm, or is banished: for then he is dead in law; and, the husband being thus disabled to sue for or defend the wife, it would be most unreasonable if she had no remedy, or could make no defence at all. In criminal prosecutions, it is true, the wife may be indicted and punished separately; for the union is only a civil union. But, in trials of any sort, they are not allowed to be evidence for, or against, each other: partly because it is impossible their testimony should be indifferent; but principally because of the union of person. . . .

In the civil law the husband and the wife are considered as two distinct persons; and may have separate estates, contracts, debts, and injuries: and therefore, in our ecclesiastical courts, a woman may sue and be sued without her husband.

But, though our law in general considers man and wife as one person, yet there are some instances in which she is separately considered; as inferior to him, and acting by his compulsion. And therefore all deeds executed, and acts done, by her, during her coverture, are void; except it be a fine, or the like matter of record, in which case she must be solely and secretly examined, to learn if her act be voluntary. She cannot by will devise lands to her husband, unless under special circumstances; for at the time of making it she is supposed to be under his coercion. And in some felonies, and other inferior crimes, committed by her, through constraint of her husband, the law excuses her: but this extends not to treason or murder.

The husband also (by the old law) might give his wife moderate correction. For, as he is to answer for her misbehaviour, the law thought it reasonable to intrust him with this power of restraining her, by domestic chastisement, in the same moderation that a man is allowed to correct his apprentices or children; for whom the master or parent is also liable in some cases to answer. But this power of correction was confined within reasonable bounds, and the husband was prohibited from using any violence to his wife, *aliter quam ad virum, ex causa regiminis et castigationis uxoris suae, licite et rationabiliter pertinet.* The civil law gave the husband the same, or a larger, authority over his wife: allowing him, for some misdemesnors [*sic*], *flagellis et fustibus acriter verberare uxorem*; for others, only *modicam castigationem adhibere.* But, with us, in the politer reign of Charles the second, this power of correction began to be doubted: and a wife may now have security of the peace against her husband; or, in return, a husband against his wife. Yet the lower rank of people, who were always fond of the old common law, still claim and exert their antient privilege: and the courts of law will still permit a husband to restrain a wife of her liberty, in case of any gross misbehaviour.

These are the chief legal effects of marriage during the coverture; upon which we may observe, that even the disabilities, which the wife lies under, are for the most part intended for her protection and benefit. So great a favourite is the female sex of the laws of England.

6. *L'Encyclopédie* [Louis de Jaucourt] (1756)

WIFE (Natural Law) Latin: *Uxor*, female of *man*, considered such when she is united to him by bonds of marriage. (See also *marriage* and *husband*).

The Supreme Being having considered that it would not be good for man to be alone, inspired him to wish to be joined in a close association with a companion, and this association is formed by voluntary agreement between the parties. Because this association has as its principal aim the procreation of, and the care of children which they will bear, it demands that the father and mother devote all their care to the nourishment and raising of these pledges of their love until they are at the stage of maintaining and managing themselves.

But while the husband and wife have basically the same interests in this association, it is nevertheless essential that the governing authority belongs to one or the other: therefore the positive law of civilized nations, the laws and customs of Europe unanimously and definitely give this authority to the male, as to one who, possessing a much greater force both of mind and of body, contributes more to the common good in both human and sacred things; thus the wife must necessarily be subordinate to her husband and obey his orders in all domestic affairs. This is the perception of all ancient and modern legal authorities and the formal decision of legislators.

Thus the Frederician Code, which was published in 1750, and which attempted to introduce a sure and universal law, declared that the husband is even by nature the master of the household, the head of the family; and so far as the wife enters into this of her free will, she is in some measure in the power of the husband, from whence proceed various prerogatives that concern him personally. Finally, the Holy Scriptures dictate to the wife to submit to him as to her master.

However, the reasons that can be alleged for marital power could be contested, humanly speaking; and the character of this work allows us to put them forward firmly.

It appears then, first, that it would be difficult to demonstrate that the husband's authority comes from nature, inasmuch as this principle is contrary to natural human equality; and it does not follow from the fact that one is fitted to command, that one actually has the right to do so. Second, a man does not invariably have more strength of body, of wisdom, of mind, or of conduct than a woman. Third, the precepts of Scripture [on subordination] being established as a punishment is sufficient indication that it is only positive law.* One may then argue that in the married association there is no subordination other than that of the civil law, and consequently nothing prevents individual agreements from changing the civil law, since natural law and religion determine nothing to the contrary.

We do not deny that in an association of two people it does not necessarily happen that the deliberative law of one or the other prevails; and since ordinarily men are more capable than women of governing their personal affairs well, it is judicious to establish as a general rule that the

---

* The author is here probably referring to Eve's punishment as described in the book of Genesis.—EDS.

voice of the man should prevail, so long as the parties have not come to some contrary agreement, because the general rule proceeds from human institutions and not from natural law. In this way a woman knowing the precept of the civil law, and who has contracted her marriage purely and simply has thus tacitly submitted herself to that civil law.

But if some woman, persuaded that she has better judgment and conduct, or knowing that she has a greater fortune or position than the man who presents himself as a suitor, stipulates contrary to the intent of the law and with the consent of the husband—according to natural law ought she not to have the same power as that given to the husband by the prince's law? The case of a queen who, as the sovereign of her domain, marries a prince below her rank or, if you will, one of her subjects, suffices to show that the authority of a wife over her husband even in matters concerning the government of the family is not incompatible with the nature of conjugal association.

Indeed in the most civilized nations there have been marriages in which the husband is subject to the empire of the wife; a princess, the heir of a kingdom, has been known to conserve her sovereign power in the state during her marriage. No one ignores the conventions of marriage that existed between Philip II and Queen Mary of England; or those of Mary Queen of Scots and those of Ferdinand and Isabella for jointly governing the kingdom of Castille. . . .

The example of England and Russia shows clearly that women can succeed equally both in moderate and in despotic government; and if it is not against reason and against nature that they rule over an empire, it seems that it should not be contradictory that they could also be the heads of a family.

When the Lacedaemonians were on the threshhold of marriage, the woman dressed as a man and this was the symbol of equal power that she would share with the husband. . . .

Nothing at all prevents (because we are not concerned here with establishing our case by citing unique examples that prove too much); nothing prevents, I maintain, a woman from having authority within marriage by virtue of agreement between persons of equal position, unless the legislator forbids all legal exceptions, the free consent of both parties notwithstanding.

Marriage is a contract by its very nature, and consequently in everything that is not forbidden by natural law, betrothal contracts between husband and wife determine their reciprocal rights.

Finally, why cannot the ancient maxim: The forethought of man gives rise to the precaution of law, be accepted in this instance so that it can be authorized with respect to dowries, the division of goods, and in a number of cases where the law applies only when the parties do not believe they can stipulate except as prescribed by law?

Woman as Wife in the Wake of the French Revolution

SOURCES

7. *Allgemeines Landrecht für die Preussischen Staaten,* ed. C. F. Koch (Berlin, 1862), Part II, Title I, pp. 1, 75, 77, 80, and Title II, p. 284. Originally published in 1792-94. Tr. SGB.

8. Henry Cachard, *The French Civil Code, With the Various Amendments Thereto, as in Force on March 15, 1895* (London, 1895), book 1, Title 5, ch. 6, pp. 59-61. Originally published in Paris, 1804.

9. Charles Fourier, *Théorie des quatre mouvements et des destinées générales,* 3d ed. (1841-48). Originally published in 1808, republished in his *Oeuvres complètes,* I (Paris, 1966), 131-33, 145-50. Tr. KMO.

The shocking speculations entertained by the *Encyclopédie* concerning the principle of male authority in marriage were not well received by more orthodox legal authorities. The *Allgemeines Landrecht,* developed by Prussian jurists since its inception in 1750 as the Frederician Code (Doc. 4), was finally completed in 1794 after Frederick II had died and the excesses of the French Revolution had shaken all Europe. Its new statutes made explicit the Prussian husband's and father's authority over such intimate personal matters as sexual intercourse and prescribed for wives the mandatory breast-feeding of infants. The editor of the third German edition of the Code (1862), Dr. C. F. Koch, appalled by some of the *Landrecht*'s stipulations, felt obliged to explain to his juridical audience that in the 1780's and 1790's, at the time of the laws' definition, marriage was considered a "police" or public order institution for the propagation of the human race. Thus it was illegal for either marriage partner to abstain continually from sexual intercourse (except for reasons of ill health or during lactation). In his commentary Dr. Koch exclaims: "What does this mean? How can one expect a moral woman to discuss this point [her sexual relations with her husband] before a group of totally unknown men [in a court of law]!" And again, when the law empowered the husband as legal head of the family to set the time limit for a wife's nursing of her children, Dr. Koch exclaims (sixty-eight years after the law was promulgated) that no civil laws of any other nation recognize such a legally binding force on breast-feeding, and that he doubts whether this article had in fact ever been invoked or brought before the court. Yet the French jurists were so impressed by the elegance of the Prussian *Landrecht* that it was officially translated in its entirety almost immediately after its German publication, at the time of Napoleon's coming of power.

In France jurists had long been trying to consolidate France's mixed heritage of written and custom law into a unified system. The Civil Code finally promulgated in 1804 by Napoleon was a synthesis of Enlightenment analysis and the emperor's own patriarchal convictions, the latter reinforced by his years of experience as a military officer. For Napoleon, women were quite simply destined to be men's property, to obey them, and to procreate on their behalf. Once, when Madame de Staël (Docs. 13, 14) asked him during a dinner party whom he considered the greatest woman, alive or dead, Napoleon responded, "The one who has made the most children."

The Civil Code, considered a triumph of the revolutionary state over the church, affirmed the French state's authority over the institution of marriage by making a civil ceremony obligatory for all couples. A supplementary religious ceremony could also be performed, but alone, it was no longer legally binding or sufficient. By law, the presiding official at the civil ceremony (usually the mayor) had to read aloud articles 212-26 of the Code, excerpted below, before pronouncing the contracting couple man and wife. Although the concept of marriage enshrined in the Code was indisputably authoritarian, it did not dispossess the wife to the same extent as the English common law. Even so, the Prussian *Landrecht* produced a situation more favorable to women, since they were given a higher level of control over their property than were French women. Wealthy French wives would exercise some degree of property rights, if they had contracted under a separate property or dowry agreement, rather than within the basic community property framework where the husband exercised complete control over familial assets. Marriage contracts were not uncommon; between 1856 and 1876, at least 40 percent of French marriages were preceded by a contract. As for divorce, this had been provided by the revolutionary legislators and was retained by the framers of the Civil Code, but in 1816 it was outlawed and was not reestablished until 1884.

Women's disadvantaged position in the Civil Code was not without its critics, however, even in the Napoleonic era. One of the most obscure, yet in the long run perhaps the most influential, of its critics was the self-educated salesman from Besançon Charles Fourier (1772-1837), who is often credited with inventing the word *féminisme*. The offspring of a prosperous merchant family whose fortune disappeared during the Revolution, Fourier liked to boast that he was "the only reformer who has rallied round human nature by accepting it as it is and devising the means of utilizing it with all the defects that are inseparable from man." Unique among the social critics of early nineteenth-century France, this bachelor visionary constructed elaborate schemes for societal reorganization. He considered himself the continuator of Newton's work on the laws of material attraction, extending its application to persons. Indeed he made the passionate attraction between men and women central to his visionary scheme. Only a few years after the promulgation of the Civil Code, Fourier published his major work, the *Théorie des quatre mouvements et des destinées générales* (1808), which contained many startling notions concerning women's situation in the societies of past, present, and future. Fourier's ideas on social reorganization subsequently influenced the formation of major experimental communities—in France, in Russia, and in the United States, where Robert Owen's settlement at New Harmony and Frances Wright's at Nashoba are among the best known. Moreover, Fourier's critique of the institution of marriage and the family in bourgeois society profoundly affected the course of European and American discussion on the position of women.

---

7. *Allgemeines Landrecht* (1794)

Part II, Title I.—Marriage.

Art. 1. The principal end of marriage is the procreation and upbringing of children.

Art. 2. A legal marriage may also be contracted solely for the purpose of reciprocal support.

Art. 173. Rights and duties of spouses commence immediately after the marriage ceremony.

Art. 178. A spouse may not continually refuse to perform the conjugal duty.

Art. 179. If the performance of this duty is detrimental to the health of one or the other of the spouses, it need not be demanded.

Art. 180. Nursing mothers are also legally authorized to refuse cohabitation.

Art. 184. The husband is the head of the conjugal society and his decision prevails in their joint affairs.

Art. 192. As a result of a publicly recognized marriage, a wife takes the name of her husband.

Art. 193. She shares in the rights of his status unless these are attached solely to his person.

Art. 194. She is obligated to administer the interior of the husband's household in a manner suiting his rank and status.

Art. 195. She may not exercise a specific trade for herself against her husband's will.

Part II, Title II.—Reciprocal rights and duties of parents and children

Art. 67. A healthy mother is required to breast-feed her child.

Art. 68. It is, however, the father's right to decide on the length of time she shall give her breast to the child.

8. The Napoleonic Code (1804)

Of the Respective Rights and Duties of Husband and Wife

212. Husband and wife owe each other fidelity, support, and assistance.

213. A husband owes protection to his wife; a wife obedience to her husband.

214. A wife is bound to live with her husband and to follow him wherever he deems proper to reside. The husband is bound to receive her, and to supply her with whatever is necessary for the wants of life, according to his means and condition.

215. A wife cannot sue in court without the consent of her husband, even if she is a public tradeswoman or if there is no community or she is separated as to property.

216. The husband's consent is not necessary when the wife is prosecuted criminally or in a police matter.

217. A wife, even when there is no community, or when she is separated as to property, cannot give, convey, mortgage, or acquire property, with or without consideration, without the husband joining in the instrument or giving his written consent.

218. If a husband refuses to allow his wife to sue in court, the Judge may grant the authorization.

219. If a husband refuses to allow his wife to execute an instrument, the wife can cause her husband to be summoned directly before the Tribunal of First Instance of the common domicil, and such Tribunal shall grant or refuse its consent in the Judges' room after the husband has been heard or has been duly summoned.

220. A wife may, if she is a public tradeswoman, bind herself without the husband's consent with respect to what relates to her trade, and in that case she also binds her husband if there is community of property between them.

She is not considered a public tradeswoman if she merely retails the goods of her husband's business, but only when she has a separate business.

221. When a sentence has been passed upon a husband which carries with it a degrading corporal punishment, even if it has been passed by default, a wife, even of full age, cannot, during the continuance of the punishment, sue in court nor bind herself, unless she has been authorized by the Judge, who may in such case grant the consent without the husband having been heard or summoned.

222. If a husband has been interdicted or is absent, the Judge may, with proper knowledge of the case, authorize the wife to sue in court or to bind herself.

223. Any general authorization, even given by a marriage contract, is only valid as to the management of the wife's property.

224. If the husband is a minor, the authorization of the Judge is necessary to the wife, either to sue in court or to bind herself.

225. A nullity based upon the want of authorization can only be set up by the wife, the husband, or the heirs.

226. A wife can make a will without her husband's consent.

9. Charles Fourier (1808)

Is there a shadow of justice to be seen in the fate that has befallen women? Is not a young woman a mere piece of merchandise displayed for sale to the highest bidder as exclusive property? Is not the consent she gives to the conjugal bond derisory and forced on her by the tyranny of the prejudices that obsess her from childhood on? People try to persuade her that her chains are woven only of flowers; but can she really have any doubt about her degradation, even in those regions that are bloated by philosophy such as England, where a man has the right to take his wife to market with a rope around her neck, and sell her like a beast of burden to anyone who will pay his asking price? Is our public opinion on this point much more advanced than in that crude era when the Council of Mâcon, a true council of vandals, debated whether or not women had a soul and decided in the affirmative by a margin of only three votes? English legislation, which the moralists praise so highly, grants men various rights that are no less degrading for the sex [women], such as the right of a husband to sue his wife's recognized lover for monetary indemnification. The

French forms are less gross, but at bottom the slavery is always the same. Here as everywhere you can see young women languishing, falling ill and dying for want of a union that is imperiously dictated by nature but forbidden by prejudice, under penalty of being branded, before they have been legally sold. Such incidents, though rare, are still frequent enough to attest to the slavery of the weaker sex, scorn for the urgings of nature, and the absence of all justice with respect to women.

Among the signs that promise the happy results to come from the extension of women's privileges, we must cite the experience of other countries. We have seen that the best nations are always those that accord women the greatest amount of liberty; this can be seen as much among the Barbarians and Savages as among the Civilized. The Japanese, who are the most industrious, the bravest, and the most honorable of the Barbarians, are also the least jealous and the most indulgent toward women; this is so true that the Magots of China travel to Japan to deliver themselves up to the love that is forbidden them by their own hypocritical customs.

Likewise the Tahitians were the best among the Savages; given their relative lack of natural resources, no other people have developed their industry to such an extent. Among the Civilized, the French, who are the least inclined to persecute women, are the best in that they are the most flexible nation, the one from which a skillful ruler can get the best results in any sort of task. Despite a few defects such as frivolity, individual presumptuousness, and uncleanliness, however, the French are the foremost civilized nation owing to this single fact of adaptability, the trait most alien to the barbarian character.

Likewise it can be seen that the most corrupt nations have always been those in which women were most completely subjugated. . . .

As a general thesis: *Social progress and historic changes occur by virtue of the progress of women toward liberty, and decadence of the social order occurs as the result of a decrease in the liberty of women.*

Other events influence these political changes, but there is no cause that produces social progress or decline as rapidly as change in the condition of women. I have already said that the mere adoption of closed harems would speedily turn us into Barbarians, and the mere opening of the harems would suffice to transport the Barbarians into Civilization. In summary, *the extension of women's privileges is the general principle for all social progress.*

CHAPTER 2

Woman's Nature and Education

Educating Women to Serve the Family and to Please Men

SOURCE

10. Jean-Jacques Rousseau, *Émile*, bk. 5, in *Oeuvres complètes*, ed. Michel Launay, 3 vols. (Paris, 1967-71), III, *Oeuvres philosophiques et politiques: de l'Émile aux derniers écrits politiques, 1762-1772*, 243-47. Originally published in The Hague, 1762. Tr. SGB and KMO.

Jean-Jacques Rousseau (1712-1778) was one of the most controversial and best known of the eighteenth-century thinkers engaged in the pursuit of earthly happiness. Born into a watchmaker's family in Calvinist Geneva, he lost his mother as an infant. Left by his father to shift for himself, Rousseau was untrained for a profession and lived by his wits, juggling changes in religion and friendships to further his ambitions. Although he did not marry until late in life, he had many affairs—mainly with motherly older women. In his early thirties he settled down in Paris with the illiterate Thérèse Le Vasseur, who bore him five children, all of whom he quickly dispatched to a foundling home. Such details about Rousseau's own life are important in view of his insistence in his writings on two tenets he derived from an attentive study of nature: first, that women, physically weaker and more passive than men, should necessarily be dependent on strong, active men; and second, that the primary function of woman is to breast-feed, care for, and educate her numerous children, sustained by and under the control of men.

Rousseau's first work, the prize-winning *Discours sur les arts et sciences* (1749), was published when he was thirty-seven, and heralded his literary genius. This was followed by the *Discours sur l'origine de l'inegalité* (1752) and the *Contrat social* (1762), both of which profoundly affected subsequent socio-political thought. His novel, *Julie, ou La Nouvelle Héloïse* (1760), about a passionate woman who was uplifted rather than destroyed by love, pioneered a new and well-received theme for fiction. His second novel, *Émile* (1761), was immediately translated into English both in London and in Edinburgh, and serves even today as a basis of discussion on educational method. Rousseau's Émile offered a new model for man, while his Sophie embodies his model woman.

These works brought Rousseau both money and fame in intellectual circles. Yet, the idea of the social contract displeased the monarchy; the passion depicted in his *Nouvelle Héloïse* was considered immoral; and *Émile* offended the defenders of organized religion by its sentimental deism. Rousseau was condemned by the Parlement of Paris and threatened with arrest. He sought refuge first in Neuchâtel (Switzerland), a Prussian dependency, and subsequently in Britain, where the distinguished writers David Hume and James Boswell took him under their protection. Eventually he was allowed to return to France, but for the rest of his life he feared persecution. His death, at the age of sixty-six, may have been self-inflicted.

The revolutionary premise behind all Rousseau's educational theories is his rejection of the centuries-old Christian belief that a child is born in original sin and is therefore an "evil spirit" who can be saved only by Christian belief and practice. In his rejection of both Calvinism and Catholicism, Rousseau substituted an unbounded optimism for the pessimistic Christian view of human nature. He insisted that a child is born innocent and good, and should be allowed to grow and develop without undue social constraint. Although he rejected the Christian notion of original sin in the new-born child, Rousseau nevertheless retained the view of women as rapacious temptresses. Thus, like the early and medieval Fathers of the Church, whose doctrines he professed to despise, he preached the controlling virtues of female modesty in order to protect men and prevent their sexual powers from being overtaxed.

Rousseau's power and influence lay in his limitations. His emotional intensity, which allowed him to ignore different sides of a question, swept up his readers, carrying them along in the wake of his enthusiasm; indeed, this may partly explain Rousseau's far-reaching influence as a force in Western thought. It was certainly this quality, coupled with his emphasis on the importance of a female education per se, that allowed many otherwise "shrewd-minded" women initially to accept his ideas with apparent sincerity. Even intellectuals such as Mary Wollstonecraft and Germaine de Staël (Docs. 12-14) only realized after years of reflection that Rousseau had in fact eliminated women from his schema for equality and, indeed, had excluded them from the social contract itself.

In this selection from *Émile*, Rousseau confronted the question of sexual differences. He argued that anatomical differences between the sexes profoundly condition their respective mental and emotional natures. After devoting the first part of his discussion to establishing "woman's nature," he then prescribes a suitable education for her.

---

10. Jean-Jacques Rousseau (1762)

Sophie should be as truly a woman as Émile is a man, that is, she must possess all those characteristics of her species and her sex required to allow her to play her part in the physical and moral order. Thus let us begin by examining the similarities and differences between her sex and our own.

Except for her sex woman is like a man: she has the same organs, the same needs, the same faculties. The machine is constructed the same way, the pieces are the same, they work the same way, the face is similar. In whatever way one looks at them, the difference is only one of degree.

Yet where sex is concerned woman and man are both complementary and different. The difficulty in comparing them lies in our inability to decide in either case what is due to sexual difference and what is not. From the standpoint of comparative anatomy and even upon cursory inspection one can see general differences between them which do not seem connected to sex. However, they are related, but by connections that elude our observations. How far such differences may extend we cannot tell; all we know for certain is that everything they have in common is from the species and that all their differences are due to sexual difference. Considered from these two standpoints, we find so many similarities and differences that it is perhaps one of the marvels of nature that two beings could be so alike and yet so different.

These similarities and differences must have an influence on morals; this effect is apparent and conforms with experience and shows the futility of the disputes over the superiority or the equality of the sexes—as if each sex, arriving at nature's ends by its own particular route, were not on that account more perfect than if it bore greater resemblance to the other. In their common qualities they are equal; in their differences they cannot be compared. A perfect woman and a perfect man should resemble one another neither in mind nor in face, and perfection admits of neither less nor more.

In the union of the sexes, each alike contributes to the common end, though in different ways. From this diversity springs the first difference that may be observed between man and woman in their moral relations. One should be strong and active, the other weak and passive; one must necessarily have both the power and the will—it is sufficient for the other to offer little resistance.

This principle being established, it follows that woman was specifically made to please man. If man ought to please her in turn, the necessity is less direct. His merit lies in his power; he pleases simply because he is strong. I grant you this is not the law of love; but it is the law of nature, which is older than love itself.

If woman is made to please and to be subjugated to man, she ought to make herself pleasing to him rather than to provoke him; her particular strength lies in her charms; by their means she should compel him to discover his own strength and put it to use. The surest art of arousing this strength is to render it necessary by resistance. Thus pride reinforces desire and each triumphs in the other's victory. From this originates attack and defense, the boldness of one sex and the timidity of the other and finally the modesty and shame with which nature has armed the weak for the conquest of the strong.

Who can possibly suppose that nature has indifferently prescribed the same advances to the one sex as to the other and that the first to feel desire should also be the first to display it. What a strange lack of judgment! Since the consequences of the sexual act are so different for the two sexes, is it natural that they should engage in it with equal boldness? How can one fail to see that when the share of each is so unequal, if reserve did not impose on one sex the moderation that nature imposes on the other, the result would be the destruction of both and the human race would perish through the very means ordained for its continuance. Women so easily stir men's senses and awaken in the bottom of their hearts the remains of an almost extinct desire that if there were some unhappy climate on this earth where philosophy had introduced this custom, especially in warm countries where more women than men are born, the men tyrannized over by the women would at last become their victims and would be dragged to their deaths without ever being able to defend themselves.

If female animals do not have the same sense of shame, what do we make of that? Are their desires as boundless as those of women, which are curbed by shame? The desires of animals are the result of need; and when the need is satisfied the desire ceases; they no longer pretend to repulse the male, they do so in earnest. . . . They take on no more passengers after the ship is loaded. Even when they are free their seasons of receptivity are short and soon over; instinct pushes them on and instinct stops them. What would supplement this negative instinct in women when you have taken away their modesty? When the time comes that women are no longer concerned with men's well-being, men will no longer be good for anything at all.

The Supreme Being has deigned to do honor to the human race: in giving man unlimited desires, at the same time he provided the law that regulates them so he could be free and self-controlled; and while delivering him to these immoderate passions he added reason in order to govern them. In endowing woman with unlimited desires he added modesty in order to restrain them; moreover he has also given a reward for the correct use of their faculties, to wit, the taste one acquires for right conduct when one makes it the law of one's behavior. To my mind this is certainly as good as the instinct of the beasts.

Whether the woman shares the man's desires or not, whether or not she is willing to satisfy them, she always repulses him and defends herself, though not always with the same vigor and not, therefore, always with the same success. For the attacker to be victorious, the besieged must permit or direct the attack. How adroitly she can force the aggressor to use his strength. The freest and most delightful of all the acts does not admit any real violence; both nature and reason oppose it; nature, in that she has given the weaker party strength enough to resist if she chooses; reason, in that real violence is not only the most brutal of all acts but defeats its own ends, not only because man thus declares war against his companion and gives her the right to defend her person and her liberty even at the expense of the aggressor's life, but also because the woman alone is the judge of the situation and a child would have no father if any man might usurp a father's rights.

Thus the different constitution of the sexes leads us to a third conclusion, namely, that the strongest seems to be the master, but depends in fact on the weakest; this is not based upon a foolish custom of gallantry, nor upon the magnanimity of the protector but upon an inexorable law of nature. For nature, having endowed woman with more power to stimulate man's desire than he is able to satisfy, thus makes him dependent on woman's good will and compels him in turn to please her so that she may consent to yield to his superior strength. Is it weakness that yields to force or is it voluntary self-surrender? This uncertainty constitutes the chief delight of the man's victory, and the woman is usually cunning enough to leave him in doubt. In this respect women's minds exactly resemble their bodies; far from being ashamed of their weakness they revel in it. Their soft muscles offer no resistance; they pretend that they cannot lift the lightest loads; they would be ashamed to be strong. And why? This is not merely to appear delicate, they are too clever for that; they are providing themselves beforehand with excuses and with the right to be weak if need be. . . .

There is no parity between man and woman as to the importance of sex. The male is only a male at certain moments; the female all her life, or at least throughout her youth, is incessantly reminded of her sex and in order to carry out its functions she needs a corresponding constitution. She needs to be careful during pregnancy; she needs rest after childbirth; she needs a quiet and sedentary life while she nurses her children; she needs patience and gentleness in order to raise them; a zeal and affection that nothing can discourage. She serves as liaison between the children and their father. She alone wins the father's love for the children and gives him the confidence to call them his own. How much tenderness and care is required to maintain the entire family in unity! Finally all this should not be a matter of virtue but of inclination, without which the human species would soon be extinct.

The relative duties of the two sexes are not and cannot be equally rigid. When woman complains about the unjust inequalities placed on her by man she is wrong; this inequality is by no means a human institution or at least it is not the work of prejudice but of reason. She to whom nature has entrusted the care of the children must hold herself accountable for them. No doubt every breach of faith is wrong and every unfaithful husband who deprives his wife of the sole reward for the austere duties of her sex is an unjust and barbarous man. But the unfaithful wife is worse. She dissolves the family and breaks all the bonds of nature; by giving her husband children who are not his own she betrays both him and them and adds perfidy to faithlessness. . . .

Thus it is not enough that a wife should be faithful, but that she should be so judged by her husband, by her neighbors and by the world. She must be modest, devoted, reserved and she should exhibit to the world as to her own conscience testimony to her virtue. Finally, for a father to love his children he must esteem their mother. For these reasons the appearance of correct behavior must be among women's duties; it repays them with honor and reputation that are no less indispensable than chastity itself. From these principles derives, along with the moral difference of the sexes, a new motive for duty and propriety that prescribes to women in particular the most scrupulous attention to their conduct, manners, and behavior. To advance vague arguments about the equality of the sexes and the similarity of their duties is to lose oneself in vain declamation and does not respond to my argument.

Is it not illogical to cite exceptions in response to general laws so firmly established? Women, you say, are not always bearing children. Agreed, yet it remains their particular mission. What! Just because there are a hundred large towns in the world where women live licentiously and have few children, would you maintain that it is their business to have few children? And what would become of your towns if the remote countryside, where women live more simply and more chastely, did not offset the sterility of the ladies. There are plenty of provincial areas where women with only four or five children are reckoned unfruitful. In conclusion, if a woman here or there has few children, what difference does it make? Is it any the less a woman's business to be a mother? Does it not accord with general laws that nature and morals both contribute to this state of things?

Even if we admit the possibility of such long intervals between pregnancies, can a woman change her manner of life so abruptly and without peril and without risk? Can she be a nursing mother today and a soldier tomorrow? Can she change her temperament and her tastes as a chameleon changes colors? Can she step suddenly from the shadow of the cloister and her domestic cares to the dangers of the elements, to the labors, fatigues, and perils of war? Can she be sometimes timid and sometimes brave, sometimes delicate and sometimes robust? If the young men raised in Paris can scarcely stand the soldier's profession, how can women who have never faced the sun directly and who scarcely know how to walk bear this after fifty years of idleness? Can they take up this arduous vocation at the age when men are leaving it? . . .

I am quite aware that Plato, in his *Republic*, assigns to women the same exercises as to men. Having excluded individual families from his government, and not knowing what to do with women, he finds himself forced to make them into men. This great genius has thought of everything: he even responded to an objection that perhaps no one would ever have made, but he has resolved the real objection poorly. I am not speaking of that alleged community of wives about which the oft-repeated reproach proves that those who make it have never read him. I am speaking of that civic promiscuity that mixes the two sexes in the same tasks, in the same work, and cannot help but engender the most intolerable abuse. I am speaking of that subversion of the sweetest sentiments of nature, sacrificed to an artificial sentiment that can only subsist because of them— as though it did not require a natural hold to form the bonds of convention! as though the love one has for one's dear ones were not the principle for that love one owes to the state! as if it were not by the small fatherland, the family, that the heart becomes attached to the larger fatherland, as if it were not the good son, the good husband, the good father who makes the good citizen!

Once it is demonstrated that man and woman are not, and should not be constituted the same, either in character or in temperament, it follows that they should not have the same education. In following the directions of nature they must act together but they should not do the same things;

their duties have a common end, but the duties themselves are different and consequently also the tastes that direct them. After having tried to form the natural man, let us also see, in order not to leave our work incomplete, how the woman is to be formed who suits this man.

If you would always be well guided, follow the indications of nature. All that characterizes sexual difference ought to be respected or established by nature. You are always saying that women have faults that we men do not have. Your pride deceives you; they would be faults in you but they are virtues in them; things would go less well if they did not have them. Prevent these so-called faults from degenerating, but beware of destroying them.

Women, for their part, are always complaining that we raise them only to be vain and coquettish, that we keep them amused with trifles so that we may more easily remain their masters; they blame us for the faults we attribute to them. What stupidity! And since when is it men who concern themselves with the education of girls? Who is preventing the mothers from raising them as they please? There are no schools for girls—what a tragedy! Would God, there were none for boys! They would be raised more sensibly and more straightforwardly. Is anyone forcing your daughters to waste their time on foolish trifles? Are they forced against their will to spend half their lives on their appearance, following your example? Are you prevented from instructing them, or having them instructed according to your wishes? Is it our fault if they please us when they are beautiful, if their airs and graces seduce us, if the art they learn from you attracts and flatters us, if we like to see them tastefully attired, if we let them display at leisure the weapons with which they subjugate us? Well then, decide to raise them like men; the men will gladly agree; the more women want to resemble them, the less women will govern them, and then men will truly be the masters.

All the faculties common to the two sexes are not equally divided; but taken as a whole, they offset one another. Woman is worth more as a woman and less as a man; wherever she makes her rights valued, she has the advantage; wherever she wishes to usurp ours, she remains inferior to us. One can only respond to this general truth by citing exceptions in the usual manner of the gallant partisans of the fair sex.

To cultivate in women the qualities of the men and to neglect those that are their own is, then, obviously to work to their detriment. Shrewd women see this too clearly to be duped by it. In trying to usurp our advantages they do not abandon their own, but from this it comes to pass that, not being able to manage both properly on account of their incompatibility, they fall short of their own possibilities without attaining to ours, and thus lose half their value. Believe me, judicious mother, do not make a good man of your daughter as though to give the lie to nature, but make of her a good woman, and be assured that she will be worth more to herself and to us.

Does it follow that she ought to be raised in complete ignorance and restricted solely to the duties of the household? Shall man make a servant of his companion? Shall he deprive himself of the greatest charm of society? The better to reduce her to servitude, shall he prevent her from feeling anything or knowing anything? Shall he make of her a real automaton? Certainly not! Nature, who has endowed women with such an agreeable and acute mind, has not so ordered. On the contrary, she would have them think, and judge, and love, and know, and cultivate their minds as they do their faces: these are the weapons she gives them to supplement the strength they lack and to direct our own. They ought to learn many things, but only those which it becomes them to know.

Whether I consider the particular destination of the female sex or observe woman's inclinations, or take account of her duties, everything concurs equally to convince me of the form her education should take. Woman and man are made for each other, but their mutual dependence is not equal: men are dependent on women because of their desires; women are dependent on men because of both their desires and their needs. We men could subsist more easily without women than they could without us. In order for women to have what they need to fulfill their purpose in life, we must give it to them, we must want to give it to them, we must believe them worthy; they are dependent on our feelings, on the price we place on their merit, and on the opinion we have of their charms and of their virtues. By the very law of nature, women are at the mercy of men's judgments as much for themselves as for their children. It is not sufficient that they be thought estimable; they must also be esteemed. It is not sufficient that they be beautiful; they must please. It is not sufficient they be well behaved; they must be recognized as such. Their honor lies not only in their conduct but in their reputation. It is impossible for a woman who permits herself to be morally compromised ever to be considered virtuous. A man has no one but himself to consider, and so long as he does right he may defy public opinion; but when a woman does right, her task is only half finished, and what people think of her matters as much as what she really is. Hence it follows that the system of woman's education should in this respect be the opposite of ours: among men, opinion is the tomb of virtue; among women it is the throne.

On the good constitution of mothers depends primarily that of the children; on the care of women depends the early education of men; and on women, again, depend their morals, their passions, their tastes, their pleasures, and even their happiness. Thus the whole education of women ought to be relative to men. To please them, to be useful to them, to make themselves loved and honored by them, to educate them when young, to care for them when grown, to counsel them, to console them, and to make life agreeable and sweet to them—these are the duties of women at all times, and should be taught them from their infancy. Unless we are guided by this principle we shall miss our aim, and all the precepts we give them will accomplish nothing either for their happiness or for our own.

Intellectual Women Reject Rousseau's View of Woman's Role

SOURCES

11. Catharine Macaulay-Graham, *Letters on Education* (London, 1787), pp. 46-50, 205-9.

12. Mary Wollstonecraft, *A Vindication of the Rights of Woman* (London, 1792), pp. 33-40 passim, 58, 75-76, 78, 80-81, 174, 175, 178, 179-82 passim, 183, 184, 207-8, 233-39 passim.

13. Germaine de Staël, *Corinne, or Italy*. Tr. Isabel Hill (New York, n.d.), pp. 215-17, 218-19. Originally published in Paris, 1807.

14. Germaine de Staël, "Lettres sur les écrits et le caractère de J. J. Rousseau, Seconde Préface, en 1814," *Oeuvres complètes de Mme la Baronne de Staël*, ed. Auguste-Louis, Baron de Staël-Holstein, 17 vols. (Paris, 1820), I, 5-10. Tr. SGB and KMO.

Two decades after Rousseau published *Émile*, his treatise on education, women on both sides of the Channel objected indignantly to his analysis of female characteristics and education.

The first of these arguments to appear was the *Letters on Education* (1787) written by the British historian Catharine Sawbridge Macaulay-Graham (1731-1791). She is best known for her *History of England*, the reputation of which endured through the nineteenth century. During the 1770's she became a leading spokeswoman for English republican radicalism, distinguishing herself as an opponent of the eloquent British statesman Edmund Burke. Catharine Macaulay's personal life was as unconventional as her published works. Once widowed, she married for the second time—at the age of forty-seven—a man of less than half her age. Secret extra-marital affairs with much younger men were fairly common among middle-aged women of her day (the romances of Lady Mary Wortley Montagu and Madame de Staël later became legendary), but Macaulay created a scandal by actually marrying her youthful lover.

In the *Letters on Education* Macaulay developed the long-standing argument that social convention, not nature, had caused woman's relative disabilities. She thought that girls as well as boys required a rigorous physical and mental training. Not only did she emphasize the values of co-education, as Condorcet was to do a few years later, but in advance of Condorcet she suggested that men should be taught "the graces" usually assigned only to females. Thus did Macaulay foreshadow twentieth-century ideas on the need to eliminate gender stereotyping.

In this respect, Macaulay was also in advance of Mary Wollstonecraft (1759-1797), who is undoubtedly the best known of the late eighteenth-century British women critics of woman's position in society. Wollstonecraft had read widely, taught as a governess, translated works from French and German, and published a variety of works of her own, including an essay on the education of daughters, several novels, and an answer to Burke's *Reflections on the French Revolution*, entitled *A Vindication of the Rights of Man* (1790). Her most enduring work, however, is the polemical and much-translated *Vindication of the Rights of Woman* (1792), from which the second selection is excerpted.

Wollstonecraft's unhappy childhood, her nonconformist religious convictions, and her need to support herself all contributed to her unconventional ideas on women's rights. Her stormy life included travel on the Continent, a few years living in revolutionary Paris, several intense love affairs, a daughter born out of wedlock, and two attempts at suicide. Many eighteenth-century women, both upper- and lower-class, bore their lovers' children, and society took this more or less in stride. Wollstonecraft's difficulty, however, was that she belonged to the middle class: unmarried and unprotected, she was forced to struggle with an entire range of complex personal problems within the obsessive middle-class framework of "respectability" that was less oppressive to women who were either richer or poorer than she.

Mary Wollstonecraft applied natural law and the rights of man to women's situation with a deeply felt passion arising from her own experience. She was encouraged to write and to publish by the group of British writers known as the Philosophical Radicals, who were active during the period of the French Revolution. This group, inspired by French and American Enlightenment and revolutionary thought, included Joseph Johnson, who published all her books, and William Godwin, whom she later married. Though her ideas inspired a number of less well-known women writers of her own day—as well as the poet Percy Bysshe Shelley, whom her daughter married—Wollstonecraft's real fame came half a century after her death, when a new generation of women's rights advocates in the United States, Britain, and France rediscovered her works.

Like Catharine Macaulay, whom she greatly admired, and Germaine de Staël, whom she criticized, Wollstonecraft took Rousseau to task for declaring that women's natural task in life was to please men. She rejected the notion that girls naturally wish to play with dolls. She advocated the same education for girls and boys and constantly reiterated the point that true equality and reciprocity of affection between the sexes can only be built on a base of intellectual—and economic—independence; indeed, she objected vehemently to the dependence of women upon men. Wollstonecraft's ideas on creating a financially independent, self-sufficient, free and equal woman of the future clearly represents her most important contribution to the debate on women's position. She was also, however, a woman of her time and experienced the ambivalence that has characterized many, if not most, female writers on the woman question. In the midst of *A Vindication*, Wollstonecraft acknowledged her admiration for what are now considered "traditional" ideas of married family life; woman's first duty, she argued, was to be a competent, knowledgeable mother. Even so, it should be noted, she envisioned an *independent* reciprocity between husband/father and wife/mother, based upon their respective functions as breadwinner and homemaker.

Wollstonecraft's work should be compared with that of Condorcet (Doc. 19), written in the same year, to see how she spoke to women from a woman's experience, while Condorcet clearly spoke to men from the experience of a man. Despite their differing perspectives, their recommendations for measures that would ensure human rights, equality, and a better understanding between the sexes are virtually identical. Indeed, it has even been suggested that Wollstonecraft helped Condorcet draft his program for educational reform. She had intended in a second volume to amplify her conviction that women should be represented in government and to develop her ideas on the legal position of women; she had planned, for example, to critique Blackstone's position that in marriage only the man is responsible, while his wife becomes (in Wollstonecraft's words) "a mere cypher." However, her untimely death of puerperal fever, following the birth of her second daughter, Mary Godwin, prevented her from completing this work.

The wealthy Geneva-born Anne-Louise-Germaine Necker, Baronne de Staël-Holstein (1766-1817), became one of the most prolific and internationally known

French authors and, by virtue of her forced exile from France because of her political activities against Napoleon, perhaps the best known woman of all Europe. In the same year that Catharine Macaulay published her own argument against Rousseau's *Émile* (1787), Staël wrote her *Lettres sur les écrits et le caractère de J. J. Rousseau.* At this time the twenty-two-year-old baroness found Rousseau's ideas enchanting and in her preface to these "letters" had almost nothing but praise for *Émile*; although she felt somewhat uneasy about his treatment of women and criticized him firmly for denying them any mental powers, she did not quite understand what was troubling her. She later wrote, "it was in vain, I agreed in every page with Rousseau; at the end of the book I told myself, it is certainly false." Despite her enthusiasm for Rousseau's emphasis on the "senses" (the eighteenth century's term for the nonrational aspects of human nature) she insisted that the senses must be tempered by intellect. She also believed that it would be preferable to develop in men those female virtues that they lacked rather than to dwell on woman's relative weakness and inferiority as Rousseau had done. Still in 1787 she approved of Rousseau's emphasis on sexual character differences and agreed with him that one of woman's most important roles was to contribute to the happiness of man.

Twenty-seven years, one husband, and seven lovers later, Staël published a "Seconde preface" to her *Lettres sur Rousseau.* By this time her opinion on the relationship between men and women had matured and crystallized. Objecting to Rousseau's "domestic slaves," whose purpose in life was to encourage and console men, Staël insisted that women must be taught to reason. The development of women's intellect would, she argued, as did Wollstonecraft, produce greater harmony in marriage and intensify the mutual understanding that creates greater happiness. Yet, going beyond this Staël wrote that for women in particular "the pleasures of the intellect are designed to calm the storms of the heart."

The selection from Staël's "Seconde preface" to the *Lettres sur Rousseau* is preceded by an excerpt from her novel *Corinne* (1807), in which she contrasted the educational and intellectual experiences of upper-class British women with those of the Continental women of her day.

---

11. Catharine Macaulay-Graham (1787)

[From Letter IV]

. . . The rules laid down by Rousseau, to pour instruction into the young mind, by using it to a close examination of sensible objects, and the methods which he prescribes to excite the attention of children, and to set their reasoning faculties in motion, is, I think, one of the most useful parts of this entertaining performance; but though I heartily concur with the ideas he has given on this subject, and would advise every tutor to read his Emilius with care; yet let him not be so charmed with the eloquence and plausibility of the author, as to adopt altogether the rules laid down in this work on the subject of instruction. We were not born to play all our lives; industry, both corporal and mental, is necessary to our happiness and advancement, both in this, and a future state; and when the organs of the brain have attained a sufficient firmness for the task of literature, young pupils ought to be exercised in the study of books, or such inveterate habits of idleness will be acquired as will be impossible afterwards to subdue.

The moderns in the education of their children, have too much followed the stiff and prudish manners of ancient days, in separating the male and female children of a family. This is well adapted to the absurd unsocial rigour of Grecian manners; but as it is not so agreeable to that mixture of the sexes in a more advanced age, which prevails in all European societies, it is not easy to be accounted for, but from the absurd notion, that the education of females should be of an opposite kind to that of males. How many nervous diseases have been contracted? How much feebleness of constitution has been acquired, by forming a false idea of female excellence, and endeavouring, by our art, to bring Nature to the ply of our imagination. Our sons are suffered to enjoy with freedom that time which is not devoted to study, and may follow, unmolested, those strong impulses which Nature has wisely given for the furtherance of her benevolent purposes; but if, before her natural vivacity is entirely subdued by habit, little Miss is inclined to show her locomotive tricks in a manner not entirely agreeable to the trammels of custom, she is reproved with a sharpness which gives her a consciousness of having highly transgressed the laws of decorum; and what with the vigilance of those who are appointed to superintend her conduct, and the false biass they have imposed on her mind, every vigorous exertion is suppressed, the mind and body yield to the tyranny of error, and Nature is charged with all those imperfections which we alone owe to the blunders of art.

I could say a great deal, Hortensia, on those personal advantages, which the strength of the mother gives to her offspring, and the ill effects which must accrue both to the male and female issue from her feebleness. I could expatiate on the mental advantages which accompany a firm constitution, and on that evenness and complacency of temper, which commonly attends the blessing of health. I could turn the other side of the argument, and show you, that most of the caprices, the teasing follies, and often the vices of women, proceed from weakness, or some other defect in their corporeal frame; but when I have sifted the subject to the bottom, and taken every necessary trouble to illustrate and enforce my opinion, I shall, perhaps, still continue singular in it. My arguments may serve only to strengthen my ideas, and my sex will continue to lisp with their tongues, to totter in their walk, and to counterfeit more weakness and sickness than they really have, in order to attract the notice of the male; for, says a very elegant author, perfection is not the proper object of love: we admire excellence; but we are more enclined to love those we despise. *

There is another prejudice, Hortensia, which affects yet more deeply female happiness, and female importance; a prejudice, which ought ever to have been confined to the regions of the east, because [of the] state of slavery to which female nature in that part of the world has been ever

---

* See Mr. Burke on the Sublime and Beautiful.

subjected, and can only suit with the notion of a positive inferiority in the intellectual powers of the female mind. You will soon perceive, that the prejudice which I mean, is that degrading difference in the culture of the understanding, which has prevailed for several centuries in all European societies. Our ancestors, on the first revival of letters, dispensed with an equal hand the advantages of a classical education to all their offspring; but as pedantry was the fault of that age, a female student might not at that time be a very agreeable character. True philosophy in those ages was rarely an attendant on learning, even in the male sex; but it must be obvious to all those who are not blinded by the mist of prejudice, that there is no cultivation which yields so promising a harvest as the cultivation of the understanding; and that a mind, irradiated by the clear light of wisdom, must be equal to every task which reason imposes on it. The social duties in the interesting characters of daughter, wife, and mother, will be but ill performed by ignorance and levity; and in the domestic converse of husband and wife, the alternative of an enlightened, or an unenlightened companion, cannot be indifferent to any man of taste and true knowledge. Be no longer niggards, then O ye parents, in bestowing on your offspring, every blessing which nature and fortune renders them capable of enjoying! Confine not the education of your daughters to what is regarded as the ornamental parts of it, nor deny the graces to your sons. Suffer no prejudices to prevail on you to weaken Nature, in order to render her more beautiful; take measures for the virtue and the harmony of your family, by uniting their young minds early in the soft bonds of friendship. Let your children be brought up together; let their sports and studies be the same; let them enjoy, in the constant presence of those who are set over them, all that freedom which innocence renders harmless, and in which Nature rejoices. By the uninterrupted intercourse which you will thus establish, both sexes will find, that friendship may be enjoyed between them without passion. The wisdom of your daughters will preserve them from the bane of coquetry, and even at the age of desire, objects of temptation will lose somewhat of their stimuli, by losing their novelty. Your sons will look for something more solid in women, than a mere outside; and be no longer the dupes to the meanest, the weakest, and the most profligate of the sex. They will become the constant benefactors of that part of their family who stand in need of their assistance; and in regard to all matters of domestic concern, the unjust distinction of primogeniture will be deprived of its sting.

[From Letter XXII]

Among the most strenuous asserters of a sexual difference in character, Rousseau is the most conspicuous, both on account of that warmth of sentiment which distinguishes all his writings, and the eloquence of his compositions: but never did enthusiasm and the love of paradox, those enemies to philosophical disquisition, appear in more strong opposition to plain sense than in Rousseau's definition of this difference. He sets out with a supposition, that Nature intended the subjection of the one sex to the other; that consequently there must be an inferiority of intellect in the subjected party; but as man is a very imperfect being, and apt to play the capricious tyrant, Nature, to bring things nearer to an equality, bestowed on the woman such attractive graces, and such an insinuating address, as to turn the balance on the other scale. Thus Nature, in a giddy mood, recedes from her purposes, and subjects prerogative to an influence which must produce confusion and disorder in the system of human affairs. Rousseau saw this objection; and in order to obviate it, he has made up a moral person of the union of the two sexes, which, for contradiction and absurdity, outdoes every metaphysical riddle that was ever formed in the schools. In short, it is not reason, it is not wit; it is pride and sensuality that speak in Rousseau, and, in this instance, has lowered the man of genius to the licentious pedant. . . .

The situation and education of women, Hortensia, is precisely that which must necessarily tend to corrupt and debilitate both the powers of mind and body. From a false notion of beauty and delicacy, their system of nerves is depraved before they come out of their nursery; and this kind of depravity has more influence over the mind, and consequently over morals, than is commonly apprehended. But it would be well if such causes only acted towards the debasement of the sex; their moral education is, if possible, more absurd than their physical. The principles and nature of virtue, which is never properly explained to boys, is kept quite a mystery to girls. They are told indeed, that they must abstain from those vices which are contrary to their personal happiness, or they will be regarded as criminals, both by God and man; but all the higher parts of rectitude, every thing that ennobles our being, and that renders us both innoxious and useful, is either not taught, or is taught in such a manner as to leave no proper impression on the mind. This is so obvious a truth, that the defects of female education have ever been a fruitful topic of declamation for the moralist; but not one of this class of writers have laid down any judicious rules for amendment. Whilst we still retain the absurd notion of a sexual excellence, it will militate against the perfecting a plan of education for either sex. The judicious Addison animadverts on the absurdity of bringing a young lady up with no higher idea of the end of education than to make her agreeable to a husband, and confining the necessary excellence for this happy acquisition to the mere graces of person.

Every parent and tutor may not express himself in the same manner as is marked out by Addison; yet certain it is, that the admiration of the other sex is held out to women as the highest honour they can attain; and whilst this is considered as their *summum bonum*, and the beauty of their persons the chief *desideratum* of men, Vanity, and its companion Envy, must taint, in their characters, every native and every acquired excellence. Nor can you, Hortensia, deny, that these qualities, when united to ignorance, are fully equal to the engendering and rivetting all those vices and foibles which are peculiar to the female sex; vices and foibles which have caused them to be considered, in ancient times, as beneath cultivation, and in modern days have subjected them to the censure and ridicule of writers of all descriptions, from the deep thinking philosopher to the man of ton* and gallantry, who, by the bye, sometimes distinguishes himself by qualities which are not greatly superior to those he despises in women.

12. Mary Wollstonecraft (1792)

. . . The most perfect education, in my opinion, is such an exercise of the understanding as is best calculated to strengthen the body and form the heart. Or, in other words, to enable the individual to attain such habits of virtue as will render it independent. In fact, it is a farce to call any being virtuous whose virtues do not result from the exercise of its own reason. This was Rousseau's opinion respecting men: I extend it to women, and confidently assert that they have been drawn out of their sphere by false refinement, and not by an endeavour to acquire masculine qualities. Still the regal homage which they receive is so intoxicating, that till the manners of the times are changed, and formed on more reasonable principles, it may be impossible to convince them that the illegitimate power, which they obtain, by degrading themselves, is a curse, and that they must return to nature and equality, if they wish to secure the placid satisfaction that unsophisticated affections impart. But for this epoch we must wait—wait, perhaps, till kings and nobles, enlightened by reason, and, preferring the real dignity of man to childish state, throw off their gaudy hereditary trappings: and if then women do not resign the arbitrary power of beauty—they will prove that they have *less* mind than man.

I may be accused of arrogance; still I must declare what I firmly believe, that all the writers who have written on the subject of female education and manners, from Rousseau to Dr. Gregory, have contributed to render women more artificial, weak characters, than they would otherwise have been; and consequently, more useless members of society. I might have expressed this conviction in a lower key; but I am afraid it would have been the whine of affectation, and not the faithful expression of my feelings, of the clear result which experience and reflection have led me to draw. . . .

Though, to reason on Rousseau's ground, if man did attain a degree of perfection of mind when his body arrived at maturity, it might be proper, in order to make a man and his wife *one*, that she should rely entirely on his understanding; and the graceful ivy, clasping the oak that supported it, would form a whole in which strength and beauty would be equally conspicuous. But, alas! husbands, as well as their helpmates, are often only overgrown children; nay, thanks to early debauchery, scarcely men in their outward form—and if the blind lead the blind, one need not come from heaven to tell us the consequence.

Many are the causes that, in the present corrupt state of society, con-

* *OED*: "The fashion, the vogue, the mode" (1769).—EDS.

tribute to enslave women by cramping their understandings and sharpening their senses. One, perhaps, that silently does more mischief than all the rest, is their disregard of order.

To do everything in an orderly manner, is a most important precept, which women, who, generally speaking, receive only a disorderly kind of education, seldom attend to with that degree of exactness that men, who from their infancy are broken into method, observe. . . .

This contempt of the understanding in early life has more baneful consequences than is commonly supposed; for the little knowledge which women of strong minds attain, is, from various circumstances, of a more desultory kind than the knowledge of men, and it is acquired more by sheer observations on real life, than from comparing what has been individually observed with the results of experience generalized by speculation. Led by their dependent situation and domestic employments more into society, what they learn is rather by snatches; and as learning is with them, in general, only a secondary thing, they do not pursue any one branch with that persevering ardour necessary to give vigour to the faculties, and clearness to the judgment. In the present state of society, a little learning is required to support the character of a gentleman; and boys are obliged to submit to a few years of discipline. But in the education of women, the cultivation of the understanding is always subordinate to the acquirement of some corporeal accomplishment; even while enervated by confinement and false notions of modesty, the body is prevented from attaining that grace and beauty which relaxed half-formed limbs never exhibit. Besides, in youth their faculties are not brought forward by emulation; and having no serious scientific study, if they have natural sagacity it is turned too soon on life and manners. They dwell on effects, and modifications, without tracing them back to causes; and complicated rules to adjust behaviour are a weak substitute for simple principles. . . .

. . . Riches and hereditary honours have made cyphers of women to give consequence to the numerical figure; and idleness has produced a mixture of gallantry and despotism into society, which leads the very men who are the slaves of their mistresses to tyrannize over their sisters, wives, and daughters. This is only keeping them in rank and file, it is true. Strengthen the female mind by enlarging it, and there will be an end to blind obedience; but, as blind obedience is ever sought for by power, tyrants and sensualists are in the right when they endeavour to keep women in the dark, because the former only want slaves, and the latter a plaything. The sensualist, indeed, has been the most dangerous of tyrants, and women have been duped by their lovers, as princes by their ministers, whilst dreaming that they reigned over them.

I now principally allude to Rousseau, for his character of Sophia is, undoubtedly, a captivating one, though it appears to me grossly unnatural; however it is not the superstructure, but the foundation of her character, the principles on which her education was built, that I mean to attack; nay, warmly as I admire the genius of that able writer, whose opinions I shall often have occasion to cite, indignation always takes place of admiration, and the rigid frown of insulted virtue effaces the smile of complacency, which his eloquent periods are wont to raise, when I read his voluptuous reveries. . . .

. . . Rousseau declares that a woman should never, for a moment, feel herself independent, that she should be governed by fear to exercise her *natural* cunning, and made a coquettish slave in order to render her a more alluring object of desire, a *sweeter* companion to man, whenever he chooses to relax himself. He carries the arguments, which he pretends to draw from the indications of nature, still further, and insinuates that truth and fortitude, the corner stones of all human virtue, should be cultivated with certain restrictions, because, with respect to the female character, obedience is the grand lesson which ought to be impressed with unrelenting rigour.

What nonsense! when will a great man arise with sufficient strength of mind to puff away the fumes which pride and sensuality have thus spread over the subject! If women are by nature inferior to men, their virtues must be the same in quality, if not in degree, or virtue is a relative idea; consequently, their conduct should be founded on the same principles, and have the same aim.

Connected with man as daughters, wives, and mothers, their moral character may be estimated by their manner of fulfilling those simple duties; but the end, the grand end of their exertions should be to unfold their own faculties and acquire the dignity of conscious virtue. They may try to render their road pleasant; but ought never to forget, in common with man, that life yields not the felicity which can satisfy an immortal soul. I do not mean to insinuate that either sex should be so lost in abstract reflections or distant views, as to forget the affections and duties that lie before them, and are, in truth, the means appointed to produce the fruit of life; on the contrary, I would warmly recommend them, even while I assert, that they afford most satisfaction when they are considered in their true, sober light. . . .

Let it not be concluded that I wish to invert the order of things. . . .

Youth is the season for love in both sexes; but in those days of thoughtless enjoyment provision should be made for the more important years of life, when reflection takes place of sensation. But Rousseau, and most of the male writers who have followed his steps, have warmly inculcated that the whole tendency of female education ought to be directed to one point:—to render them pleasing.

Let me reason with the supporters of this opinion who have any knowledge of human nature, do they imagine that marriage can eradicate the habitude of life? The woman who has only been taught to please will soon find that her charms are oblique sunbeams, and that they cannot have much effect on her husband's heart when they are seen every day, when the summer is passed and gone. Will she then have sufficient native energy to look into herself for comfort, and cultivate her dormant faculties? or, is it not more rational to expect that she will try to please other men; and, in the emotions raised by the expectation of new conquests, endeavour to forget the mortification her love or pride has received?

When the husband ceases to be a lover—and the time will inevitably come, her desire of pleasing will then grow languid, or become a spring of bitterness; and love, perhaps, the most evanescent of all passions, gives place to jealousy or vanity.

I now speak of women who are restrained by principle or prejudice; such women, though they would shrink from an intrigue with real abhorrence, yet, nevertheless, wish to be convinced by the homage of gallantry that they are cruelly neglected by their husbands; or, days and weeks are spent in dreaming of the happiness enjoyed by congenial souls till their health is undermined and their spirits broken by discontent. How then can the great art of pleasing be such a necessary study? it is only useful to a mistress; the chaste wife, and serious mother, should only consider her power to please as the polish of her virtues, and the affection of her husband as one of the comforts that render her task less difficult and her life happier. But, whether she be loved or neglected, her first wish should be to make herself respectable, and not to rely for all her happiness on a being subject to like infirmities with herself. . . .

I have, probably, had an opportunity of observing more girls in their infancy than J. J. Rousseau—I can recollect my own feelings, and I have looked steadily around me; yet, so far from coinciding with him in opinion respecting the first dawn of the female character, I will venture to affirm, that a girl, whose spirits have not been damped by inactivity, or innocence tainted by false shame, will always be a romp, and the doll will never excite attention unless confinement allows her no alternative. Girls and boys, in short, would play harmlessly together, if the distinction of sex was not inculcated long before nature makes any difference. I will go further, and affirm, as an indisputable fact, that most of the women, in the circle of my observation, who have acted like rational creatures, or shown any vigour of intellect, have accidentally been allowed to run wild—as some of the elegant formers of the fair sex would insinuate. . . .

I lament that women are systematically degraded by receiving the trivial attentions, which men think it manly to pay to the sex, when, in fact, they are insultingly supporting their own superiority. It is not condescension to bow to an inferior. So ludicrous, in fact, do these ceremonies appear to me, that I scarcely am able to govern my muscles, when I see a man start with eager and serious solicitude to lift a handkerchief, or shut a door, when the *lady* could have done it herself, had she only moved a pace or two. . . .

. . . Women, commonly called Ladies, are not to be contradicted in company, are not allowed to exert any manual strength; and from them the negative virtues only are expected, when any virtues are expected, patience, docility, good-humour, and flexibility; virtues incompatible with any vigorous exertion of intellect. Besides, by living more with each other, and being seldom absolutely alone, they are more under the influence of sentiments than passions. Solitude and reflection are necessary to give to wishes the force of passions, and to enable the imagination to enlarge the object, and make it the most desirable. . . .

In the middle rank of life, to continue the comparison, men, in their youth, are prepared for professions, and marriage is not considered as the grand feature in their lives, whilst women, on the contrary, have no other scheme to sharpen their faculties. It is not business, extensive plans, or any of the excursive flights of ambition, that engross their attention; no, their thoughts are not employed in rearing such noble structures. To rise in the world, and have the liberty of running from pleasure to pleasure, they must marry advantageously, and to this object their time is sacrificed, and their persons often legally prostituted. A man when he enters any profession has his eye steadily fixed on some future advantage (and the mind gains great strength by having all its efforts directed to one point), and, full of his business, pleasure is considered as mere relaxation; whilst women seek for pleasure as the main purpose of existence. In fact, from the education, which they receive from society, the love of pleasure may be said to govern them all; but does this prove that there is a sex in souls? . . .

It would be an endless task to trace the variety of meannesses, cares, and sorrows, into which women are plunged by the prevailing opinion, that they were created rather to feel than reason, and that all the power they obtain, must be obtained by their charms and weakness:

"Fine by defect, and amiably weak!"

I am fully persuaded that we should hear of none of these infantine airs, if girls were allowed to take sufficient exercise, and not confined in close rooms till their muscles are relaxed, and their powers of digestion destroyed. To carry the remark still further, if fear in girls, instead of being cherished, perhaps created, were treated in the same manner as cowardice in boys, we should quickly see women with more dignified aspects. It is true, they could not then with equal propriety be termed the sweet flowers that smile in the walk of man; but they would be more respectable members of society, and discharge the important duties of life by the light of their own reason. "Educate women like men," says Rousseau, "and the more they resemble our sex the less power will they have over us." This is the very point I aim at. I do not wish them to have power over men; but over themselves. . . .

It is vain to expect virtue from women till they are in some degree independent of men; nay, it is vain to expect that strength of natural affection which would make them good wives and mothers. Whilst they are absolutely dependent on their husbands they will be cunning, mean, and selfish, and the men who can be gratified by the fawning fondness of spaniel-like affection have not much delicacy, for love is not to be bought, in any sense of the words; its silken wings are instantly shrivelled up when anything beside a return in kind is sought. Yet whilst wealth enervates men, and women live, as it were, by their personal charms, how can we expect them to discharge those ennobling duties which equally require exertion and self-denial? . . .

Women are, in common with men, rendered weak and luxurious by the relaxing pleasures which wealth procures; but added to this they are made slaves to their persons, and must render them alluring that man may lend them his reason to guide their tottering steps aright. Or should they be ambitious, they must govern their tyrants by sinister tricks, for without rights there cannot be any incumbent duties. The laws respecting woman, which I mean to discuss in a future part, make an absurd unit of a man and his wife; and then, by the easy transition of only considering him as responsible, she is reduced to a mere cypher.

The being who discharges the duties of its station is independent; and, speaking of women at large, their first duty is to themselves as rational creatures, and the next in point of importance, as citizens, is that which includes so many, of a mother. The rank in life which dispenses with their fulfilling this duty necessarily degrades them by making them mere dolls. . . .

. . . The maternal solicitude of a reasonable affectionate woman is very interesting, and the chastened dignity with which a mother returns the caresses that she and her child receive from a father who has been fulfilling the serious duties of his station, is not only a respectable but a beautiful sight. So singular indeed are my feelings, and I have endeavoured not to catch factitious ones, that after having been fatigued with the sight of insipid grandeur and the slavish ceremonies that with cumbrous pomp supplied the place of domestic affections, I have turned to some other scene to relieve my eye by resting it on the refreshing green everywhere scattered by nature. I have then viewed with pleasure a woman nursing her children, and discharging the duties of her station with, perhaps, merely a servant maid to take off her hands the servile part of the household business. I have seen her prepare herself and her children, with only the luxury of cleanliness, to receive her husband, who returning weary home in the evening found smiling babes and a clean hearth. My heart has loitered in the midst of the group, and has even throbbed with sympathetic emotion, when the scraping of the well known foot has raised a pleasing tumult.

Whilst my benevolence has been gratified by contemplating this artless picture, I have thought that a couple of this description, equally necessary and independent of each other, because each fulfilled the respective duties of their station, possessed all that life could give.—Raised sufficiently above abject poverty not to be obliged to weigh the consequence of every farthing they spend, and having sufficient to prevent their attending to a frigid system of economy, which narrows both heart and mind. I declare, so vulgar are my conceptions, that I know not what is wanted to render this the happiest as well as the most respectable situation in the world, but a taste for literature, to throw a little variety and interest into social converse, and some superfluous money to give to the needy and to buy books. . . .

I know that, as a proof of the inferiority of the sex, Rousseau has exultingly exclaimed, How can they leave the nursery for the camp!

. . . Though I consider that women in the common walks of life are called to fulfil the duties of wives and mothers, by religion and reason, I cannot help lamenting that women of a superior cast have not a road open by which they can pursue more extensive plans of usefulness and independence. I may excite laughter by dropping a hint which I mean to pursue some future time, for I really think that women ought to have representatives, instead of being arbitrarily governed without having any direct share allowed them in the deliberations of government. . . .

But what have women to do in society? I may be asked, but to loiter with easy grace; surely you would not condemn them all to suckle fools and chronicle small beer! No. Women might certainly study the art of healing, and be physicians as well as nurses. And midwifery, decency seems to allot to them, though I am afraid the word midwife in our dictionaries will soon give place to *accoucheur*, and one proof of the former delicacy of the sex be effaced from the language.

They might also study politics. . . .

Business of various kinds they might likewise pursue, if they were educated in a more orderly manner, which might save many from common and legal prostitution. Women would not then marry for a support, as men accept of places under government, and neglect the implied duties; nor would an attempt to earn their own subsistence—a most laudable one!—sink them almost to the level of those poor abandoned creatures who live by prostitution. For are not milliners and mantua-makers reckoned the next class? The few employments open to women, so far from being liberal, are menial; and when a superior education enables them to take charge of the education of children as governesses, they are not treated like the tutors of sons. . . . [Thus] these situations are considered in the light of a degradation; and they know little of the human heart, who need to be told that nothing so painfully sharpens sensibility as such a fall in life.

Some of these women might be restrained from marrying by a proper spirit or delicacy, and others may not have had it in their power to escape in this pitiful way from servitude; is not that government then very defective, and very unmindful of the happiness of one half of its members, that does not provide for honest, independent women, by encouraging them to fill respectable stations? . . .

Another argument that has had great weight with me, must, I think, have some force with every considerate benevolent heart. Girls who have been thus weakly educated, are often cruelly left by their parents without any provision; and, of course, are dependent on, not only the reason, but the bounty of their brothers. These brothers are, to view the fairest side of the question, good sort of men, and give as a favour, what children of the same parents had an equal right to. In this equivocal humiliating situation, a docile female may remain some time, with a tolerable degree of comfort. But, when the brother marries, a probable circumstance, from being considered as the mistress of the family, she is viewed with averted looks as an intruder, an unnecessary burden on the benevolence of the master of the house, and his new partner.

Who can recount the misery, which many unfortunate beings, whose minds and bodies are equally weak, suffer in such situations—unable to work, and ashamed to beg? . . .

. . . I then would fain convince reasonable men of the importance of some of my remarks; and prevail on them to weight dispassionately the whole tenor of my observations. I appeal to their understandings; and, as a fellow-creature, claim, in the name of my sex, some interest in their hearts. I entreat them to assist to emancipate their companion, to make her a *help meet* for them!

Would men but generously snap our chains, and be content with rational fellowship instead of slavish obedience, they would find us more observant daughters, more affectionate sisters, more faithful wives, more reasonable mothers—in a word, better citizens. We should then love them with true affection, because we should learn to respect ourselves; and the peace of mind of a worthy man would not be interrupted by the idle vanity of his wife, nor the babes sent to nestle in a strange bosom, having never found a home in their mother's. . . .

After the age of nine, girls and boys, intended for domestic employments, or mechanical trades, ought to be removed to other schools, and receive instruction in some measure appropriated to the destination of each individual, the two sexes being still together in the morning; but in the afternoon the girls should attend a school where plain-work, mantua-making, millinery, &c., would be their employment.

The young people of superior abilities, or fortune, might now be taught, in another school, the dead and living languages, the elements of science, and continue the study of history and politics, on a more extensive scale, which would not exclude polite literature.

Girls and boys still together? I hear some readers ask: yes. And I should not fear any other consequence than that some early attachment might take place; which, whilst it had the best affect on the moral character of the young people, might not perfectly agree with the views of the parents, for it will be a long time, I fear, before the world will be so far enlightened that parents, only anxious to render their children virtuous, shall allow them to choose companions for life themselves.

Besides, this would be a sure way to promote early marriages, and from early marriages the most salutary physical and moral effects naturally flow. . . .

In this plan of education the constitution of boys would not be ruined by the early debaucheries which now make men so selfish, or girls rendered weak and vain by indolence and frivolous pursuits. But, I presuppose that such a degree of equality should be established between the sexes as would shut out gallantry and coquetry, yet allow friendship and love to temper the heart for the discharge of higher duties.

These would be schools of morality—and the happiness of man, allowed to flow from the pure springs of duty and affection, what advances might not the human mind make? Society can only be happy and free in proportion as it is virtuous; but the present distinctions, established in society, corrode all private and blast all public virtue.

As the rearing of children—that is, the laying a foundation of sound health both of body and mind in the rising generation—has justly been insisted on as the peculiar destination of woman, the ignorance that incapacitates them must be contrary to the order of things. And I contend that their minds can take in much more, and ought to do so, or they will never become sensible mothers. Many men attend to the breeding of horses, and overlook the management of the stable, who would—strange want of sense and feeling!—think themselves degraded by paying any attention to the nursery; yet, how many children are absolutely murdered by the ignorance of women! . . .

. . . Fulfilling the duties of a mother, a woman with a sound constitution may still keep her person scrupulously neat, and assist to maintain her family if necessary, or, by reading and conversations with both sexes indiscriminately, improve her mind. For nature has so wisely ordered things, that did women suckle their children they would preserve their own health, and there would be such an interval between the birth of each child that we should seldom see a houseful of babes. And did they pursue a plan of conduct, and not waste their time in following the fashionable vagaries of dress, the management of their household and children need not shut them out from literature, or prevent their attaching themselves to a science with that steady eye which strengthens the mind, or practising one of the fine arts that cultivate the taste. . . .

But, we shall not see women affectionate till more equality be established in society, till ranks are confounded and women freed; neither shall we see that dignified domestic happiness, the simple grandeur of which cannot be relished by ignorant or vitiated minds; nor will the important task of education ever be properly begun till the person of a woman is no longer preferred to her mind. For it would be as wise to expect corn from tares, or figs from thistles, as that a foolish ignorant woman should be a good mother. . . .

That women at present are by ignorance rendered foolish or vicious is, I think, not to be disputed; and that the most salutary effects tending to improve mankind might be expected from a REVOLUTION in female manners, appears, at least with a face of probability, to rise out of the observation. . . .

From the tyranny of man, I firmly believe, the greater number of female follies proceed; and the cunning, which I allow makes at present a part of their character, I likewise have repeatedly endeavoured to prove, is produced by oppression. . . .

Be just then, O ye men of understanding! and mark not more severely what women do amiss, than the vicious tricks of the horse or the ass for whom ye provide provender—and allow her the privileges of ignorance, to whom ye deny the rights of reason, or ye will be worse than Egyptian task-masters, expecting virtue where nature has not given understanding!

13. Germaine de Staël (1807)

Lord Edgarmond was my father. I was born in Italy; his first wife was a Roman; and Lucy, whom they intended for your bride, is my sister by an English lady—by my father's second marriage. Now hear me! I lost my mother ere I was ten years old, and as it was her dying wish that my education should be finished ere I went to England, I was confided to an aunt at Florence, with whom I lived till I was fifteen. My tastes and talents were formed ere her death induced Lord Edgarmond to have me with him. He lived at a small town in Northumberland, which cannot, I suppose, give any idea of England, yet was all I knew of it for six years. My mother from my infancy impressed on me the misery of not living in Italy; my aunt had often added that this fear of quitting her country had broken her heart. My good aunt herself was persuaded too that a Catholic would be condemned to perdition for settling in a Protestant country; and though I was not infected by this fear, the thought of going to England alarmed me much. I set forth with an inexplicable sense of sadness. . . .

Lady Edgarmond met me politely, but I soon perceived that my whole manner amazed her, and that she proposed to change it if she could. Not a word was said during dinner, though some neighbors had been invited. I was so tired of this silence that, in the midst of our meal, I strove to converse a little with an old gentleman who sat beside me. I spoke English tolerably, as my father had taught me in childhood; but happening to cite some Italian poetry, purely delicate, in which there was some mention of love, my step-mother, who knew the language slightly, started at me, blushed, and signed for the ladies, earlier than usual, to withdraw, prepare tea, and leave the men to themselves during the dessert. I know nothing of this custom, which 'would not be believed in Venice.' Society agreeable without women! For a moment I thought her ladyship so displeased that she could not remain in the same room with me; but I was reassured by her motioning me to follow and never reverting to my fault during the three hours we passed in the drawing-room, waiting for the gentlemen. At supper, however, she told me gently enough, that it was not usual in England for young ladies to talk; above all, they must never think of quoting poetry in which the name of love occurred. "Miss Edgarmond," she added, "you must endeavor to forget all that belongs to Italy; it is to be wished that you had never known such a country." I passed the night in tears, my heart was oppressed. In the morning I attempted to walk; there was so tremendous a fog that I could not see the sun, which at least would have reminded me of my own land; but I met my father, who said to me: "My dear child, it is not here as in Italy; our women have no occupations save their domestic duties. Your talents may beguile your solitude and you may win a husband who will pride in them; but in a country town like this all that attracts attention excites envy and you will never marry at all if it is thought that you have foreign manners. Here, every one must submit to the old prejudices of an obscure county." . . .

Toward the close of autumn the pleasures of the chase frequently kept my father from home till midnight. During his absence I remained mostly in my own room, endeavoring to improve myself; this displeased Lady Edgarmond. "What good will it do?" she said; "will you be any the happier for it?" The words struck me with despair. What then is happiness, I thought, if it consists not in the development of our faculties? Might we not as well kill ourselves physically as morally? If I must stifle my mind, my soul, why preserve the miserable remains of life that would but agitate me in vain? But I was careful not to speak thus before my stepmother. I had essayed it once or twice, and her reply was that women were made to manage their husbands' houses and watch over the health of their children; all other accomplishments were dangerous, and the best advice she could give me was to hide those I possessed.

14. Germaine de Staël (1814)

It has virtually never been denied that literary tastes and studies are of great advantage for men; but there is very little agreement on how these same studies might influence women's destiny. If it were a question of imposing domestic slavery upon them, one should beware of increasing their intelligence, for fear they might be tempted to revolt against such a fate; but since Christian society demands nothing unjust in family relationships, the more one's reason is enlightened the more it tends to submit to moral laws. Reflecting on these laws, it can be clearly seen that sooner or later they govern the world with no less infallibility than those of physics.

It is true that one's emotions can sweep one away but this occurs in spite of enlightenment, not because of it. It often happens that women of superior intellect are also persons of very passionate character; the dangers of this character are always diminished rather than increased by literary culture; the pleasures of the intellect are designed to calm the storms of the heart.

The organization of today's society threatens us far more with negative faults of coldness and egotism, than with exultation of any sort. The common man and the common woman can be possessed of very beautiful and fine qualities despite a lack of intellectual cultivation; but among the elegant and leisure class the habits one acquires wither the soul unless supplemented with revitalizing studies; if not combined with extensive literary instruction, worldly habits teach only the easy repetition of clichés, the expression of one's opinions in formulae and of one's character in well-mannered courtesies. If, then, you have not found in a distinguished education some compensation for all these sacrifices; if in the elevation of the mind you do not encounter what is natural, and in the knowledge of truth, candor; if, finally, you do not breathe the air of a larger realm, you are nothing but a well-bred doll, who always sings the same song, even when she changes the words. When it comes about (which is not at present the case) that only a woman thus disciplined submits more easily to marital authority, what then becomes of the communication between souls when the minds are not developed along similar lines? And what ought one to think of a husband of so little pride that he prefers blind obedience to enlightened sympathy from his wife? The most touching examples of married love have been shown by women worthy of understanding their husbands and of sharing their lot; marriage is not realized in its full beauty until it can be founded on reciprocal admiration.

Nevertheless, many men prefer women to be completely devoted to the care of their households, and to be entirely guaranteed of this they would not be upset if the women are incapable of understanding anything else. This is a matter of taste. However, since the number of distinguished people is very small, those who do not want a distinguished wife will have plenty of others to choose from. Some people say that they do not exclude the cultivation of intellect in women; but they do not want this intellect to inspire women with the desire to become authors and so distract them from their natural duties, and to enter into a rivalry with men, inasmuch as they are created solely to encourage and to console men. I must say that I would feel greater respect for a woman of great genius who does not strive after personal success, than for one who seeks it fervently; but one must scorn only what one can obtain. A Parisian always ducks when he passes under the Porte Saint-Denis, even though it is a hundred feet high; it is the same with women who pride themselves on fearing fame without ever having had the talent to achieve it. Doubtless these talents have their inconveniences as do all the most beautiful things in life; but even these seem preferable to the lassitude of a restricted intellect that sometimes scorns what it cannot achieve or affects what it does not know how to feel. Thus, from the standpoint of our self-esteem alone, a deeply intense life always produces increased happiness: melancholy, to be sure, enters more often into souls possessed of a certain energy; but all things considered there is no one who ought not to thank God for having been granted an extra talent.

German Idealists Debate Women's Intellectuality and Creativity

SOURCES

15. Wilhelm von Humboldt, "Über den Geschlechtsunterschied und dessen Einfluss auf die organische Natur," *Die Horen*, I, pt. 2 (Tübingen, 1795), 111, 117, 118, 119. Reprinted in Stuttgart, 1959. Tr. SGB. The editors are grateful to Professor Katharina Mommsen, Stanford University, for bringing the Humboldt-Schlegel debate to their attention, and to Professor Lilian Furst, University of Texas, for help with the translation.

16. Friedrich von Schlegel, "Über die Diotima," in *Friedrich Schlegel, seine*

prosaischen Jugendschriften, 2d ed., ed. J. Minor, 2 vols. (Vienna, 1906), I, 58-59. Originally published in *Berlinische Monatsschrift*, 1795. Tr. SGB.

The eminent linguist and statesman Wilhelm von Humboldt (1767-1835) earned a reputation in German literature through his close association with the poet Friedrich von Schiller. He left his mark on German society, however, as the architect of nineteenth-century German education. During his twenties Humboldt became closely associated with the young intellectual men and women of Berlin. In 1795 he published a series of essays on the sexes in Schiller's new journal *Die Horen*, from which these selections dealing with women are excerpted. Following a line of thought that harks back to Aristotle, Humboldt (who was steeped in Greek literature) considered man the active creator of life, while woman remained a passive recipient, who only responds creatively after male stimulation. It is significant that Humboldt, whose life interest was to clarify the complexities of language, should have produced a piece so opaque as the selection here reprinted while writing about creativity. Moreover, his own metaphor in developing his thoughts on *mental* creativity is completely physical. He described the male sex-drive and ignored both the female sexual initiative and the fact that the mental creativity of women might require the same total commitment of time and energy that he reserved for men. In these excerpts he posited a correlation between sexual power and creativity, reminiscent of the story of Samson and Delilah but anticipating Freud as well.

In answer to Humboldt the German literary critic Friedrich von Schlegel (1772-1829) extolled the beauty and wisdom of androgyny over Humboldt's exaggerated "pure" masculinity and femininity. Schlegel objected to both Humboldt's and Rousseau's views that women were incapable of intellectual and artistic creativity; he countered Humboldt's Aristotelianism by evoking the "Diotima" dialogue from Plato's *Symposium*. No doubt Schlegel was deeply influenced in his more liberal opinion of female talent by his recent friendship with the brilliant young widow Caroline Michaelis, who subsequently married Schlegel's brother August. This experience may also have disposed him to pursue in 1798, and to marry, the gifted and unhappy Dorothea Mendelssohn von Veit, who became a novelist in her own right and later translated Madame de Staël's *Corinne* (Doc. 13) into German. Schlegel subsequently incorporated many of his views on women into his famous and controversial novel, *Lucinde* (1799), which was read in secret by many young upper-class German women during the early nineteenth century.

---

15. Wilhelm von Humboldt (1795)

Here begins the difference between the sexes. Creative force is more attuned to aggressive movement while receiving force is more attuned to regressive movement. That which animates the former we call male; that which inspires the latter—female. All that is male shows more spontaneous activity; all that is female more passive receptivity. . . .

Thus, poetic force, as it evokes image after image in the heat of inspiration blocks the senses to external impressions; and the senses, in like fashion, as they embrace reality with pulsating passion, restrain it from bold ascent into the land of the imagination.

Masculine force, destined to create, gathers of its own accord, through its own momentum. It concentrates all its substance into an undivided whole. The richer and more manifold the substance is, the more exhausting the effort, but also the greater the effect. The substance must not be predisposed to union through its own nature. But from its own nature, as from a governing principle, it must receive its directive. Concentrated into itself in this way, it acts outward from its own core. Driven by a stirring desire for activity, it yearns for an object it can penetrate; totally self-absorbed in its own activity, it is at this moment insensitive to any receptivity. Such an effort is, however, soon followed by exhaustion, and it resembles a wind that brings intense animation but quickly subsides. With the sense of its ebbing strength its longing for receptiveness awakens and it welcomes rest where previously it had been exclusively creative. Thus it is as it is through its own nature and by its particular form. The man whose breast is filled with a bold urge to activity feels constrained within himself. With an observant mind he has gathered much experience on his journey through life with which to externalize the high ideals from within his inner being; manifold feelings stir him, at times the dignity of the new creation for which he yearns, at others a sympathetic empathy with the creatures he strives to ennoble. His breast is not large enough to contain all these lofty images, and a seething thirst for activity drives him on. He seeks a world that will correspond to his longing. Without thought of himself or his own pleasure, he impregnates it from the abundance of his strength. The new creation stands before him, and he relaxes joyously in contemplation of his children.

Female force, destined for recessive movement, centers on an external object and through external stimulation. Because the substance that is hers in ample abundance is consolidated by virtue of its particular nature, it functions more through its passive than through its self-activating capacity. With the degree of its diversity the beauty of its function increases proportionately, but not its effort. Rather, this is facilitated by the multiplicity of the points of contact, and its degree is determined only by the closeness of the union, which is dependent upon mutual harmony. The substance of female force stands in lesser need of the dominance of a unifying principle, but consolidates itself through its own homogeneity. In this unified entity she reacts to an aggressive movement with ever-mounting frenzy until finally her whole activity is in play. But since her particular nature gives her a greater tolerance for resistance and since she is devoid of the searing ardor that consumes masculine nature, she compensates for the slowness of her movement by sustaining it longer. So she owes to the qualities of her substance a part of her movement that is fostered and nurtured by it. A heart that is stirred by manifold emotions and inspired by noble aspirations, that feels rich within itself but lacks the boldness of spirit to set its own course, is tortured by restless longing. Uncomprehending of itself and needy in the midst of overabundance, it desires a being who will lovingly untangle the knots of its feelings. The more deeply the source of this confusion lies, the harder it is to meet its desires, but the more fervently also will it adhere to the object once it is found. The longer it remains by her side, the more points of contact it will discover, and it will not leave her until the seed has ripened into the mature fruit.

Thus it is not by degree, but by their intrinsic essence, that creative and receptive forces are distinct from one another. Mere "acceptance" is not "receiving," but stands as far beneath as "giving" stands beneath "creating." Both of them—"creating" and "receiving"—are higher and more potent energies, each a product of "giving" and "accepting." A fruitful input of its own must accompany what the one ejects just as it must comprise what the other receives. The real difference in the character of these two forces lies in the fact that more substance, more body is innate to the receiving and more soul to the creating, that is, insofar as soul designates every self-activating principle.

16. Friedrich von Schlegel (1795)

However short, there was nonetheless a time when it is fair to say that Laconian women possessed manly strength and independence and, conversely, Laconian youths possessed womanly humility, modesty and gentleness.

But did not these manly practices of Spartan girls, like the intellectual education of Pythagorean women, of necessity destroy womanliness? They seem to us as contrary to reason as Plato's assertions, and offend our whole sense of innate being. They may be justified as follows: . . . Once what is essential is separated from what is peripheral, the principle is irrefutable: womanhood, like manhood, should be elevated into a higher humanity. Despite its failure, the attempt still remains praiseworthy as an attempt to attain in the *mores* and in the state what the idealized art of Attic tragedy had in effect attained: subordinating gender to species, without, however, destroying it completely. What is uglier than that overwrought womanliness, what more disgusting than that exaggerated manliness that prevails in our customs, in our opinions, and extends also to our art? For indeed, this pernicious attitude extends its influence even over artistic representations, which should be idealized, as well as over endeavors to develop the concept of womanliness in utmost purity. The components of pure womanliness and of pure manliness are regarded as necessary characteristics that would destroy the freedom of the spirit. They are, however, no more than nature's enticements or palliatives. To control them without destroying them, to bow to necessity while still deferring to nature: that is the height of freedom. What is more, too many characteristics are subsumed under the concept of pure womanliness, which may well have only two components: intensity of feeling and tenderness, just as the concept of manliness consists of solidity and certitude. Some characteristics are deduced from experience, and are pertinent only to a distorted womanliness: tenacity and simplicity as desiderata of this sex. This denotes, however, nothing other than a total absence of character, a readiness to accept the prescription for her bearing from another being; this unity, imposed from without, is admittedly closer to perfection than the man's tenacity, which is the hard-won product of active inner struggle. Yet it is precisely the man's domineering vehemence and the woman's selfless devotion that are in themselves exaggerated and ugly. Only independent womanliness, only gentle manliness are good and beautiful. . . .

Educating Women for Citizenship in the New Nations

SOURCES

17. Nicolas Baudeau, "De l'Education nationale," *Ephémérides du Citoyen, ou Chronique de l'esprit national*, 4, no. 4 (12 May 1766), pp. 49-55, 57-58, 59-60, 61-64. Tr. KMO.

18. Benjamin Rush, *Thoughts upon Female Education, Accommodated to the Present State of Society, Manners, and Government in the United States of America* (Philadelphia and Boston, 1787). Reprinted in *Essays on Education in the Early Republic*, ed. Frederick Rudolph (Cambridge, Mass., 1965), pp. 27-28, 35-38, 38-40.

19. Marie-Jean-Nicolas Caritat, Marquis de Condorcet, "Sur l'Instruction publique: Première mémoire: Nature et objet de l'instruction publique," in *Oeuvres de Condorcet*, ed. A[rthur] Condorcet O'Connor and F. Arago, 12 vols. (Paris, 1847-49), IX, 215-24. Originally published in the *Bibliothèque de l'homme public, ou analyse raisonnée des principaux ouvrages françois et étrangers, etc.*, ed. M. Condorcet et al., seconde année, I (Paris, 1791), 64-77. Tr. KMO and SGB.

As we have seen, literary women in different parts of Europe objected strongly to the philosophical implications of Rousseau's prescription for female education, that is, for personal service to the individual man. However, another approach emerged from Rousseau's analysis that still viewed women functionally, but more politically: this was the view that women of all ranks must be well educated in order to raise good citizens for the nation-state. It was a view that in fact did offer women a meaningful role in the formation of the democratic state—and on which they themselves were not hesitant to capitalize, especially in the nineteenth century, in order to promote further educational reforms on their own behalf. Out of this grew yet a third view of women's education, based on equality of natural rights.

The first selection is from an essay on national education by the French physiocrat abbé Nicolas Baudeau (1730-1792?). In what has been called the most significant article written in the 1760's, Baudeau argued that the state should offer all French girls, of whatever social rank, a public education in order to fit them to be good citizens, good wives, and good mothers. Of particular interest is his carefully qualified use of the Spartan precedent, a use that clearly reveals him as a "modernist," as well as his objections to the training French girls were receiving at home (an attitude that he shared with his predecessor, Archbishop Fénelon).

Baudeau's arguments had a considerable impact not only in France but also throughout Europe, as the subsequent educational initiatives for girls undertaken by Frederick the Great of Prussia, Catherine the Great of Russia, and Joseph II of Austria all attest.

In the second selection, Benjamin Rush (1746-1813), a Philadelphia physician and professor of chemistry, and one of the signers of the Declaration of Independence, presented an American perspective on female education. Rush attended the College of New Jersey (now Princeton) and studied medicine at the University of Edinburgh, during which time he met David Hume and other luminaries of the Scottish Enlightenment and went on the "grand tour" of the Continent. During his stay in Paris he was particularly impressed with the upper-class women of France, and apparently he also became familiar with the educational writings of Fénelon, whose approach to female education seems to have significantly influenced his own. In this influential essay, which Rush presented as a speech at the newly founded Young Ladies' Academy in Philadelphia (of which he was a trustee), the doctor underscored the unique features that condition life for young American women in the new republic—especially early marriage. He recommended a program of solid practical studies in English composition and bookkeeping while discouraging the cultivation of showy accomplishments—including the acquisition of French. But his principal argument is that the survival of the new nation itself is at stake if women are unable to educate their sons to principles of liberty in government. This argument was later developed and strengthened to women's advantage by Judith Sargent Murray (Doc. 3) in the 1790's.

The selection by the Marquis de Condorcet (1743-1794), a French contemporary of Rush, offers a more radical proposal for female education. One of the great humanistic thinkers of the French Enlightenment and a distinguished mathematician and philosopher, Condorcet was equally well versed in political and educational theory. He was one of the few philosophes to play an active role in the early years of the French Revolution—and the only one to espouse the cause of women's rights, which he first took up in 1787 in his *Lettres d'un bourgeois de New Haven à un citoyen de Virginie.* This interest may have developed out of his long friendship with Madame de Suard and his marriage to the brilliant Sophie de Grouchy. In 1792 Condorcet presented a broad and comprehensive plan for state education to the newly elected Convention of the Republic. In this plan he advocated the same program of basic instruction for girls and boys, the coeducation of the sexes (which was deemed unacceptable by Baudeau), and higher education for women; he also espoused women's entry into suitable professions. Though he predicated his arguments on a traditional role division, Condorcet moved beyond this division to argue for equal education from the standpoint of natural rights. Public coeducation, he argued, would be democratic; it would improve morals and lessen the false attitudes caused by artificial segregation of the sexes. Indeed, in this "première mémoire" *Sur l'Instruction Publique,* Condorcet presented views strikingly close to those of Mary Wollstonecraft (Doc. 12), who was also in Paris during this period, and to Theodor von Hippel (Doc. 29), who was writing in Germany in the same year. "After all," wrote Condorcet, "women have the same [natural] rights as men. They ought then to have the same facilities to acquire the knowledge that alone can give them the means truly to exercise these rights with the same independence and to the same extent." This reference to independence, it should be noted, is the only one in which Condorcet demonstrated an explicit concern for the quality of women's lives. This is perhaps not surprising, for he addressed the memorandum to men; he was attempting to convince an all-male political constituency and was therefore presenting his suggestions for equal education in order to emphasize the benefits that would accrue to men from the equal education of both sexes. Condorcet included many of these ideas on women's education in his internationally known *Esquisse d'un tableau historique des progrès de l'esprit humain*, which he wrote in prison during the last year of his life. His views influenced the founders of the French Third Republic's system of secondary schools for girls, established in 1880.

---

17. Nicolas Baudeau (1766)

We think we have already demonstrated that all Citizens ought to receive public instruction in national schools, and that no one should be excepted, from the children born at Court to the most illustrious families of the Nation, who form the first class of pupils, down to the sons of the poorest villagers, who are in the fifth group in the order we have established. . . .

There remains but one single thing to discuss . . . but it should be regarded as one of the most interesting from the standpoint of morals, the perfection of the National Spirit, and public happiness. Up to this point we have considered only the children of our own sex. Now it is time to discuss the national education of French girls. We would compose a work about national education that was imperfect in every respect if we were to abandon half the State to prejudice, routine, and abuse. The half we will be here concerned with has perhaps more influence than the other half on the shaping of the French mind, on national character, and thereby on the public interest and the fate of [male] Citizens. Its effects are tangible and, in order to discover their first origin, we should probably go back to a time well before the origin of the French monarchy.

The legislators of ancient Greece regarded national education as their first object of concern and the instruction of girls as one of its most essential parts. The Romans, who never had any [educational] legislation to speak of, neglected the precious and sublime ideas of Lycurgus, Plato, and the other philosophers. Our own nation, which for several centuries has only imitated them [the Romans] all too much in the confusion of incomplete, obscure, and contradictory laws, still has no complete code on public schools; for a complete educational establishment we have only sparse sets of regulations and some schools here and there, of which only a few concern our French girls. Nevertheless, we can still find in them very useful views and excellent principles. These are analyzed with great precision in the latest work that appeared in 1764 on the education of *demoiselles*.

But the plan proposed in this treatise by Mademoiselle Despinassi [*sic*] involves only a private, domestic education, suitable for girls born in the two top classes of society. All the other [classes] also demand their own educational establishments, perhaps public establishments. This is precisely the question that presents itself for an answer at this time.

Let us therefore return to consider the first of our six problems: Which *Citoyennes* should receive a public education in national schools? We do not hesitate to give the same reply as before. Under the French Monarchy, all the Daughters of the Nation without exception, from the royal purple down to the shepherd's crook, should be given a common, public educational establishment. To justify this opinion, which will undoubtedly foster a great deal of opposition, especially from our female readers of the first rank [of society], we ought to explain our principles with greater clarity and apply them more forcefully.

We have declared ourselves to be the enemies of all private education for the Children of our own sex, in whatever rank the Heavens have allowed them to be born. We believe it should likewise be prohibited to all our young female citizens, and here are our reasons. It is only just to submit them to the most rigorous scrutiny.

Some of the ancients pushed their zeal for public education to the point of permitting the two sexes nothing but exercises in common; this was the usage of the Lacedaemonians [Laconians], who have been criticized so much, sometimes for very respectable reasons and motives and sometimes out of error or even out of prejudice. Our morals do not permit such an assemblage [of the sexes] and the Christian Religion repels still more the subsequent events, which Lycurgus seemed to desire and which we must fear. . . .

In defense of Lycurgus, whom we sincerely admire, we should say that his system of public instruction was in perfect harmony with all the rest of his legislation and, because of that, it merits praise. But we should add, arguing against the partisans of servile imitation, that it is in this very thing that he should not serve us as an example, for the very simple and essential reason that our Government, which is wholly different from the Spartan Constitution, requires an entirely different type of national education. . . .

While avoiding the extreme of offering a common public education to children of both sexes, however, it should be kept in mind that the educational establishments for each ought to have the same goal and to contribute to the welfare of the State according to the distinctive duties attached to the different classes of citizens. We must pose as a fundamental maxim that the Daughters of the Nation are destined each to become, within their class, *Citoyennes*, Wives, and Mothers. These three ideas should serve as a lodestone for the Speculators who would like to concern themselves with elaborating the system of studies and exercises that are appropriate.

In each status in civil life, women have duties to accomplish, talents and virtues they should acquire, to serve the public weal usefully and contribute to national prosperity. Thus for each of the five classes that compose the French nation, there should be a plan of education tailored as closely as possible to the duties that will be imposed on each, and to the services that can be expected from them. . . .

. . . Maternal tenderness ought to oversee [this plan], but ought not always to be in command of all the details. With the best will in the world, the Authors of our time lack enlightenment or, too often still, along with their knowledge they have not the straightforwardness of their intentions or the talents of soul necessary to direct the inclinations of young *Citoyennes* toward the public good.

Women teachers in household employ should be at least as suspect as men teachers, from the standpoint of true patriotism; their choice and their conduct require too much calculation for it to be possible to flatter oneself that a desirable success can be obtained from most of them.

Someone will no doubt object that the [existing] public schools for French girls are more poorly organized than those for the other sex; that legislative genius has never directed its torch toward this important object of national morals except for some weak sparks represented by the establishment of *Saint Cir* [sic] near Versailles, and that of *l'Enfant Jésus* at Paris, which are limited in their objective to the instruction of a few *demoiselles* descended from the impoverished nobility of our provinces. . . .

Ever confident in our ideas, we will insist, on behalf of the national schools for young French girls, on the same distinction that guided us in our earlier theories for other public studies: Fashion, which reigns supreme in France, permits princesses of the royal blood—even those closest to the throne—to receive in some sense a common educational establishment in some of our most celebrated monasteries for girls. This is one less prejudice for us to vanquish in order to establish our point of view.

We want all parents to follow such an example, just as many now do; but to obtain this much-desired uniformity, it would be helpful to found an establishment expressly for this purpose, near the Capital, corresponding to the first of the Colleges proposed for our own sex. It would have to have an educational plan suitable to the needs of women destined to live at Court or among the first dignitaries of the State. Their condition and their duties certainly demand virtues, talents, and particular knowledge. If you give them a small number of teachers, chosen with all the intelligence and uprightness imaginable, to shape their minds and hearts and communicate to them as much enlightenment as their sex and destination require, you would make of them excellent *Citoyennes*; a precious quality for women of the court, even though current abuses and prejudices would seem to exempt them from it. It would render them worthy wives for the Great Men of the Nation and would provide models who would be the more applauded since the contrary has been more common in our society. Finally, they would become mothers—to the public prosperity and the happiness of their children, whose educations they would then really merit supervising, a privilege so rare these days that one can advocate it without injustice.

Colleges would be established for the *Demoiselles* in each town; the State would thereby pay a most sacred debt to the impoverished nobility, which has exhausted itself in service to the State; by the same right the Bourgeoisie would have public schools for its daughters in all the good cities of the Realm; each parish in these cities would have schools for the daughters of artisans; and the project of giving each town its school-mistress, which we have already advocated so strongly in our "Writings on the Poor," would finally be realized.

This is to say, in sum, that all the *Citoyennes* born in the Realm, with-out exception, would be granted a public education in the national schools. We will explain at a later date what would be the objects of the lessons in each group and especially what teachers we would provide for them.

In each of the six questions we have announced, we will never fail to treat each successively with respect to both sexes, and to subdivide our reflections according to the distinction between the five states of the civil condition. We will view French women as *Citoyennes*, as Wives, and as Mothers, in search of the truths that ought to inform the theory of their educational establishments.

18. Benjamin Rush (1787)

The first remark that I shall make upon this subject is that female edu-cation should be accommodated to the state of society, manners, and government of the country in which it is conducted.

This remark leads me at once to add that the education of young ladies in this country should be conducted upon principles very different from what it is in Great Britain and in some respects different from what it was when we were a part of a monarchical empire.

There are several circumstances in the situation, employments, and du-ties of women in America which require a peculiar mode of education.

I. The early marriages of our women, by contracting the time allowed for education, renders it necessary to contract its plan and to confine it chiefly to the more useful branches of literature.

II. The state of property in America renders it necessary for the great-est part of our citizens to employ themselves in different occupations for the advancement of their fortunes. This cannot be done without the as-sistance of the female members of the community. They must be the stew-ards and guardians of their husbands' property. That education, there-fore, will be most proper for our women which teaches them to discharge the duties of those offices with the most success and reputation.

III. From the numerous avocations to which a professional life exposes gentlemen in America from their families, a principal share of the in-struction of children naturally devolves upon the women. It becomes us therefore to prepare them, by a suitable education, for the discharge of this most important duty of mothers.

IV. The equal share that every citizen has in the liberty and the possi-ble share he may have in the government of our country make it neces-sary that our ladies should be qualified to a certain degree, by a peculiar and suitable education, to concur in instructing their sons in the princi-ples of liberty and government.

V. In Great Britain the business of servants is a regular occupation, but in America this humble station is the usual retreat of unexpected indigence; hence the servants in this country possess less knowledge and subordination than are required from them; and hence our ladies are obliged to attend more to the private affairs of their families than ladies generally do of the same rank in Great Britain. "They are good servants," said an American lady of distinguished merit in a letter to a favorite daughter, "who will do well with good looking after." This circumstance should have great influence upon the nature and extent of female education in America. . . .

It should not surprise us that British customs with respect to female education have been transplanted into our American schools and families. We see marks of the same incongruity of time and place in many other things. We behold our houses accommodated to the climate of Great Britain by eastern and western directions. We behold our ladies panting in a heat of ninety degrees, under a hat and cushion which were calculated for the temperature of a British summer. We behold our citizens condemned and punished by a criminal law which was copied from a country where maturity in corruption renders public executions a part of the amusements of the nation. It is high time to awake from this servility—to study our own character—to examine the age of our country—and to adopt manners in everything that shall be accommodated to our state of society and to the forms of our government. In particular it is incumbent upon us to make ornamental accomplishments yield to principles and knowledge in the education of our women.

A philosopher once said, "let me make all the ballads of a country and I care not who makes its laws." He might with more propriety have said, let the ladies of a country be educated properly, and they will not only make and administer its laws, but form its manners and character. It would require a lively imagination to describe, or even to comprehend, the happiness of a country where knowledge and virtue were generally diffused among the female sex. Our young men would then be restrained from vice by the terror of being banished from their company. The loud laugh and the malignant smile, at the expense of innocence or of personal infirmities—the feats of successful mimicry and the low priced wit which is borrowed from a misapplication of scripture phrases—would no more be considered as recommendations to the society of the ladies. A *double-entendre* in their presence would then exclude a gentleman forever from the company of both sexes and probably oblige him to seek an asylum from contempt in a foreign country.

The influence of female education would be still more extensive and useful in domestic life. The obligations of gentlemen to qualify themselves by knowledge and industry to discharge the duties of benevolence would be increased by marriage; and the patriot—the hero—and the legislator would find the sweetest reward of their toils in the approbation and applause of their wives. Children would discover the marks of maternal prudence and wisdom in every station of life, for it has been remarked that there have been few great or good men who have not been blessed with wise and prudent mothers. Cyrus was taught to revere the gods by his mother Mandane; Samuel was devoted to his prophetic office before he was born by his mother Hannah; Constantine was rescued from paganism by his mother Constantia; and Edward the Sixth inherited those great and excellent qualities which made him the delight of the age in which he lived from his mother, Lady Jane Seymour. Many other instances might be mentioned, if necessary, from ancient and modern history, to establish the truth of this proposition.

I am not enthusiastic upon the subject of education. In the ordinary course of human affairs we shall probably too soon follow the footsteps of the nations of Europe in manners and vices. The first marks we shall perceive of our declension will appear among our women. Their idleness, ignorance, and profligacy will be the harbingers of our ruin. Then will the character and performance of a buffoon on the theater be the subject of more conversation and praise than the patriot or the minister of the gospel; then will our language and pronunciation be enfeebled and corrupted by a flood of French and Italian words; then will the history of romantic amours be preferred to the immortal writings of Addison, Hawkesworth, and Johnson; then will our churches be neglected and the name of the Supreme Being never be called upon but in profane exclamations; then will our Sundays be appropriated only to feasts and concerts; and then will begin all that train of domestic and political calamities.

But, I forbear. The prospect is so painful that I cannot help silently imploring the great Arbiter of human affairs to interpose his almighty goodness and to deliver us from these evils that, at least, one spot of the earth may be reserved as a monument of the effects of good education, in order to show in some degree what our species was before the fall and what it shall be after its restoration. . . .

I cannot dismiss the subject of female education without remarking that the city of Philadelphia first saw a number of gentlemen associated for the purpose of directing the education of young ladies. By means of this plan the power of teachers is regulated and restrained and the objects of education are extended. By the separation of the sexes in the unformed state of their manners, female delicacy is cherished and preserved. Here the young ladies may enjoy all the literary advantages of a boarding school and at the same time live under the protection of their parents. Here emulation may be excited without jealousy, ambition without envy, and competition without strife.

The attempt to establish this new mode of education for young ladies was an experiment, and the success of it hath answered our expectations. Too much praise cannot be given to our principal and his assistants, for the abilities and fidelity with which they have carried the plan into execution. The proficiency which the young ladies have discovered in reading, writing, spelling, arithmetic, grammar, geography, music, and their different catechisms since the last examination is a less equivocal mark of the merits of our teachers than anything I am able to express in their favor.

But the reputation of the academy must be suspended till the public are convinced by the future conduct and character of our pupils of the advantages of the institution. To you, therefore, YOUNG LADIES, an important problem is committed for solution; and that is, whether our present plan of education be a wise one and whether it be calculated to prepare you for the duties of social and domestic life. I know that the elevation of the female mind, by means of moral, physical, and religious truth, is considered by some men as unfriendly to the domestic character of a woman. But this is the prejudice of little minds and springs from the same spirit which opposes the general diffusion of knowledge among the citizens of our republics. If men believe that ignorance is favorable to the government of the female sex, they are certainly deceived, for a weak and ignorant woman will always be governed with the greatest difficulty.

I have sometimes been led to ascribe the invention of ridiculous and expensive fashions in female dress entirely to the gentlemen in order to divert the ladies from improving their minds and thereby to secure a more arbitrary and unlimited authority over them. It will be in your power, LADIES, to correct the mistakes and practice of our sex upon these subjects by demonstrating that the female temper can only be governed by reason and that the cultivation of reason in women is alike friendly to the order of nature and to private as well as public happiness.

19. Marquis de Condorcet (1791)

Instruction should be the same for women and men. We have proved that public education should be limited to instruction; we have shown that it is necessary to establish various degrees of such instruction. Thus nothing can prevent public instruction from being the same for women and for men. In fact, since all instruction is limited to revealing truth or developing its proof, it is hard to see why a sexual difference should demand a difference in the choice of truths or in the manner of their proving. If the complete system of public instruction, which aims to teach human individuals what they need for enjoyment of their rights and fulfillment of their duties, seems too extensive for women who are not called to any public functions, one can offer them only a survey of the primary levels of education, but without forbidding the higher levels to those who have greater capacity and whose families are willing to cultivate the same. If some profession is reserved exclusively for men, women will not be admitted to the instruction necessary for this particular profession; it would, however, be absurd to exclude them from that instruction intended for professions in which they can compete.

Women should not be excluded from that which relates to the sciences, because they can be useful to progress either by making scientific observations or in composing elementary texts. As for the sciences, why are they closed to women? Even if they were unable to contribute to scientific progress by making discoveries (which, moreover, can be true only of the highest order of discoveries, which require lengthy meditation and extraordinary mental powers), why should those women, whose life cannot be occupied by the exercise of a lucrative profession and who are not entirely taken up with domestic affairs, work usefully for the increase of enlightenment by engaging in observations demanding minute precision, extreme patience, and a sedentary and regular life? Perhaps they are even better suited than men to give method and clarity to elementary textbooks, since they are more disposed by amiable flexibility to commune with the minds of children whom they have watched in infancy and whose development they have followed with more tender interest. After all, an elementary book can be well composed only by those who have learned much of that which it encompasses; one is halted at every step by the limits of one's knowledge.

It is necessary for women to share instruction given to men: (1) *So that they may supervise the instruction of their children.* Public instruction, if it wishes to be dignified by that name, must be extended to the majority of citizens. It is impossible that children will profit from it if they are limited to the lessons they receive from a public-school master. They must also have a domestic tutor who can supervise their studies in the intervals of their public lessons. An instructor who can prepare them to absorb these lessons and facilitate the understanding of them, who can in fact supply that which can be lost through a moment of absence or distraction. Well, then, where can the children of poor citizens receive this help if not from their mothers, who, dedicated to the cares of the family or given to sedentary work, seem called to fulfill this duty. After all, the work of men, which almost invariably occupies them outside the home, would not permit men to devote themselves to it. It would seem impossible, then, to establish in public instruction that equality necessary to maintain the rights of men; without it one cannot even legitimately employ either the revenues of national properties or a part of the product of their contribution to politics, if women who have gone through at least the first levels of public instruction are not then put in charge of the instruction of their children. (2) *Because the lack of instruction of women introduces into the family an inequality detrimental to its happiness.* Moreover, one cannot establish instruction for men only, without introducing a marked inequality between husband and wife, between brother and sister, and even between the son and his mother. Nothing is more contrary to the purity and happiness of domestic morality. Equality is always, and especially in the family, the foremost element of felicity of peace, and of virtue. What authority can maternal tenderness achieve if mothers are ignorant and become objects of ridicule and contempt to their children? It may be said that I exaggerate this danger; that young people are acquiring knowledge that not only their mothers but also their fathers do not share, without which, however, the resulting disadvantages could be harmful. . . . (3) *Because this is a means of conserving for men the knowledge that they acquired in their youth.* I would add that men, who would profit from public instruction, would most easily conserve these advantages if they perceived an equal instruction in their wives; if they could read with them such books as would sustain their knowledge; if in the interval that separates childhood from their establishment as adults, the instruction that has prepared them for this period is not entirely foreign to those persons toward whom they are drawn by nature. (4) *Because women have the same right as men to public instruction.* After all, women have the same rights as men. They ought then to have the same facilities to acquire the knowledge that alone can give them the means truly to exercise those rights with the same independence and to the same extent.

Boys and Girls should be instructed together, and women ought not to be excluded from teaching. Since instruction should generally be the same, boys and girls ought to be taught together and entrusted to a master chosen freely from either sex.

In Italy women have sometimes taught with success. Several women have occupied professorial chairs in the most renowned Italian universities, and have gloriously fulfilled their professorial functions in the highest sciences without inconvenience or the least objection or even a joke in a country that one can hardly think of as free from prejudice and where society is neither simple nor pure in morals.*

The Necessity of combination to facilitate economy in instruction. The combination of children of both sexes in one school is almost essential for primary education. It would be difficult to establish two in each village and to find enough masters, at least at first, if they were limited to the choice from only one sex.

Far from being a danger, combination is useful for morality. Moreover, this combination, always in public and under the eye of the teachers, far from being a danger to morality would instead be a guard against those various types of corruption caused principally by the separation of the sexes toward the end of childhood and during the first years of adolescence. At that age the senses lead the imagination astray, and quite often they stray without return if a sweet hope does not fix them upon more legitimate objects. These degrading and dangerous habits are almost always the errors of youth mistaken in its desires, condemned to corruption by boredom and destroying in false pleasures a sensibility that torments their sad and solitary servitude.

One should not establish a separation that is real only in the wealthy classes. Under a free and equal constitution, creating a separation that, for most families, is purely illusory should not be permitted. After all, outside of the school it can never be real, neither in the country nor for the poorer citizens of the towns. Thus coeducation in the schools only diminishes the disadvantages that are unavoidable for those classes that are not exposed to the surveillance of witnesses of their own age or submitted to the vigilance of a teacher in ordinary daily life. Rousseau, who perhaps exaggerated the importance of moral purity, urged, in the interest of that very purity, that the two sexes should mingle during times of recreation. Would there be greater danger in uniting them for more serious pursuits?

Avarice and pride are the principal reasons for the separation of the sexes. Do not be misled; it is not the strictness of religious morality, this

---

* Laura Bassi was Professor of Anatomy and Françoise Agnesi Professor of Mathematics at Bologna.

ruse invented by sacerdotal politics to dominate the spirit—not to this severity alone must these ideas of rigorous separation be attributed. Pride and avarice have at least an equal part, and the hypocrisy of moralists has rendered self-interested homage to these vices. Most of these austere opinions are due, on the one hand, to the fear of unequal marriages, and on the other, to the refusal to sanction unions based upon personal affinity. It is necessary, then, far from favoring such opinions, to seek to fight them in the areas where one would like legislation to follow nature alone, to obey reason, and to conform to justice. In the institutions of a free nation, all should tend toward equality not only because this is a right of men but because the maintenance of order and peace urgently requires it. A constitution that established political equality will neither endure nor promote tranquility if it is mixed with institutions that maintain prejudices favorable to inequality.

It would be dangerous to conserve a spirit of inequality in women since that would prevent destroying it in men. The danger would be much greater if, while a communal education accustoms the children of one sex to think of themselves as equal, the impossibility of establishing a like education for those of the other abandoned them to a solitary and domestic education. The spirit of inequality thus conserved in one sex soon extends itself to both. This results in what we have witnessed up to now with the equality found in our colleges that disappears forever the moment the student believes he has become a man.

The education of boys and girls together in the same schools is favorable to competition and fosters a model based on sentiments of well-being rather than on self-serving sentiments like those fostered in colleges. Some may fear that instruction necessarily prolonged beyond childhood may be attended with too much distraction by individuals occupied with livelier and more stimulating interests, but this fear is not well founded. If these distractions are an evil, it is more than compensated by the emulation inspired by the desire either to merit the esteem of a loved one or to obtain that of the family. Such emulation is more generally useful than that based upon love of glory or, rather, pride, for the real love of glory is neither a child's passion nor likely to become a widespread human sentiment. To inspire the love of glory in mediocre men (and mediocre men can nevertheless achieve the highest prizes in their class) is to condemn them to envy. This last type of emulation excites hateful passions by inspiring children with the ridiculous sentiment of personal importance and produces more evil than good, in augmenting the activity of the mind.

Human life is not a battle where rivals fight for prizes; it is a journey made together by brothers, where each employs his strength for the good of all and is rewarded by the sweets of reciprocal benevolence, by the joy that comes from the feeling of having merited recognition or esteem. Emulation based upon the desire to be loved, or that of being considered for one's absolute qualities and not for one's superiority over others, can also be very powerful; it has the advantages of developing and strengthening those sentiments that usefully become a habit. On the other hand these laurels given by our *collèges*, which give our schoolboys the notion that they are already great men, only give rise to a puerile vanity from which a wise sort of instruction should seek to preserve us, if by misfortune the germ of it lies in nature and not in our maladroit institutions. The habit of wanting to be first is either ridiculous or a misfortune for the one who has contracted it, and a real calamity for those who are condemned to live with him. In contrast, the habit of meriting esteem leads to that internal peace which alone renders happiness possible and virtue easy.

Rethinking Female Education after the Revolutions

SOURCES
20. Hannah More, *Strictures on the Modern System of Female Education*, in *The Works; Including Several Pieces Never Before Published*, 4 vols. (Dublin, 1803), IV, 181-83, 187-89, 193-98. Originally published in London, 1799.
21. Vicomte de Bonald, "De l'éducation des femmes," from his *Législation primitive* (1802), in *Oeuvres complètes de M. de Bonald*, ed. l'abbé Migne, 3 vols. (Paris, 1859), I, 1398-1401. Tr. KMO.
22. "L. H.," "Über die Erziehung des Mädchens," *Jüdisch Deutsche Monatsschrift* (Prague), no. 3 (1802), pp. 72-87. Tr. SGB. The editors are grateful to Ruth Kestenberg-Gladstein, University of Haifa, for transmitting to them her German transcription of this document, the original of which is in the British Library, P.P. 4881.
23. Napoléon, "Notes sur l'établissement d'Écouen," addressed to the comte de Lacépède, grand chancellor of the Legion of Honor, 15 May 1807, as reprinted in Gabrielle Reval, *Madame Campan, assistante de Napoléon* (Paris, 1931), pp. 224-25, 225-27, 228-29. Tr. KMO.

After the French Revolution, discussion of female education took a distinctively conservative turn, as the following selections reveal. The secular political goals of a Condorcet were challenged by a resurgent moral conservatism that recast and reformulated female education in terms of traditional religious piety, chastity, and obedience, especially where women of the less privileged classes of society were concerned.

Against arguments for sexual equality in education and coeducation, the English Evangelical moralist Hannah More (1745-1833) argued forcefully for women's separatism, under the aegis of religion and the home. Daughter of a schoolmaster, precociously literate, she lived for most of her life in the west of England. As an adventurous young woman she visited London, where her witty verse plays captured the interest of the actor-playwright David Garrick. Through Garrick she became a valued member of the set of his friend the conservative Dr. Samuel Johnson. During another London visit, at the house of Elizabeth Montagu, known in her time as the "Queen of the Blues," Hannah More met Elizabeth Carter and Frances Boscawen, two members of the Blue-Stocking circle. She was quickly drawn into this group of intellectual women, who became her life-long friends and correspondents. Unlike the other Blue-Stockings, whose tastes were more purely literary, More earned a reputation for her and religious tracts and stories that lasted throughout the following century. Although in her own day her evangelical activism in some respects undermined the English religious establishment, her ideas found great favor with British counter-revolutionary thinkers. More disliked both the radicalism of Mary Wollstonecraft and the anti-religious, egalitarian sentiments voiced by French radical thinkers.

One of Hannah More's special interests was education, and she founded a number of small Christian schools near Bristol to teach miners, agricultural laborers, and their children to read—but not to write. True to her conservatism, More instructed her pupils to accept their place in the class structure. Her explicitly anti-democratic sentiments notwithstanding, her works were as popular in nineteenth-century America as they were in England. Some of her stories were also translated into French.

Hannah More wanted women, as well as the poor, to keep their place. She expressed her ideas on this subject in her book *Strictures on the Modern System of Female Education*, published in 1799. Indeed, she had been developing her analysis of women's education for some time. Only one year after the appearance of Wollstonecraft's *Vindication*, More wrote to a male friend: "I have been much pestered to read the 'Rights of Women,' but am invincibly resolved not to do it. Of all jargon I hate metaphysical jargon; besides there is something fantastic and absurd in the very title. How many ways there are of being ridiculous! I am sure I have as much liberty as I can make good use of, now I am an old maid [she was forty-eight], and when I was a young one, I had, I dare say, more than was good for me." More believed that the two sexes had different and contrasting characteristics—in her view, women were "soft and refined," and men were "judicious and firm." A righteous Christian, she claimed that she was speaking in women's true interest when she argued that women's struggle for power and equality in the secular world was pointless: "Christianity," she wrote, "brings that superinduced strength; it comes in aid of the conscious weakness, and offers the only true counterpoise to it." Yet even she conceded, in passing, that women's contemporary education was defective. Since, in her view, intellectual achievement was largely a product of mental concentration, women's poor intellectual showing might still be owing to lack of training rather than to an inherent difference in mentality.

Like Hannah More, the Vicomte de Bonald (1754-1840) advocated distinctively different education for young women, in the interest of maintaining rigorously separate spheres in a hierarchical society. An aristocrat and civil servant from southern France, Louis-Gabriel-Ambrose de Bonald was mayor of Millau before the outbreak of the French Revolution and subsequently served as chief administrator of the newly formed department of the Aveyron. As a faithful Catholic he was appalled by the revolution's secularization of the clergy in 1791; he resigned soon thereafter and left France, when it had become apparent that both his life and his property were in danger. After passing several years with his two sons in relative poverty in southern Germany and Switzerland, he returned home by foot only to find that his wife and one of his daughters had died. He went into hiding in Paris, where he wrote several treatises on political theory that became extremely influential in counter-revolutionary thought and action throughout nineteenth-century Europe. Well known as a political writer, he later held important appointments under the restored Bourbon monarchy (1815-30). Despite his disagreements with Enlightenment secularism, an emphasis on nature pervades his thought.

In this selection from his work on *Législation primitive*, published early in Napoleon's reign, Bonald stated his views on separate spheres and the type of education that should be given to upper-class girls, preferably by their mothers, or, failing that, by nuns in convent schools.

The third author excerpted below wrote anonymously under the initials "L. H.," in the significant, though short-lived Prague *Jüdisch Deutsche Monatsschrift*. Like Bonald and More, this writer firmly believed in separate spheres and separate education for girls. In this 1802 article on girls' education, the writer reflected the heavily religious and self-consciously Jewish tone of other articles in this journal, which appeared at the high point of the Jewish Enlightenment in Bohemia. The articles were all merely initialled, but it is believed that the publishers and authors were connected with the family of the famous Prague physician Jonas Jeitteles and his son, the rabbi and poet Baruch Benedict Jeitteles (1762-1813). Baruch Jeitteles had married a wealthy woman, Fradel Porges, whose dowry and inheritance supported his household and his library, and who was occasionally acknowledged by his students as their patroness.

The Jeitteles had explicitly disavowed the circle of learned Jewish women who dominated the salons of Enlightenment Berlin and instead had embraced a Rousseauistic argument concerning woman's domestic position, upon which this article elaborates. Indeed, the *leitmotif* of the entire journal was the specific and separate destinies (*Bestimmung*) according to which men and women should organize their lives. In order to emphasize the distinctive cultural characteristics of the Prague Jews, who were less assimilated than their Prussian counterparts, as well as to differentiate themselves from the leaders of the Prussian Jewish Enlightenment, the editors of the *Jüdisch Deutsche Monatsschrift* used the Hebrew alphabet, although in many articles (for example, the one excerpted below) the language was an almost grammatical transliterated German. Yet the publishers often resorted to the less distinguished women's German, or "Weiberdeutsch," so that no one could mistake their message of wishing to remain unassimilated.

The last selection is from a letter by the French Emperor Napoleon I (1769-1821) about the school he was founding at Écouen for daughters of meritorious army officers and career government employees. Here Napoleon specified the type of schooling he believed these young women should have, and gave his rationale. The school subsequently became a model of its kind, and its graduates were sought after as wives and as teachers for other young girls.

---

20. Hannah More (1799)

The practical use of female knowledge, with a sketch of the female character, and a comparative view of the sexes.

The chief end to be proposed in cultivating the understandings of women, is to qualify them for the practical purposes of life. Their knowledge is not often like the learning of men, to be reproduced in some literary composition, nor ever in any learned profession; but it is to come out in conduct. It is to be exhibited in life and manners. A lady studies, not that she may qualify herself to become an orator or a pleader; not that she may learn to debate, but to act. She is to read the best books, not so much to enable her to talk of them, as to bring the improvement which they furnish, to the rectification of her principles and the formation of her habits. The great uses of study to a woman are to enable her to regulate her own mind, and to be instrumental to the good of others.

To woman, therefore, whatever be her rank, I would recommend a predominance of those more sober studies, which, not having display for their object, may make her wise without vanity, happy without witnesses, and content without panegyrists; the exercise of which will not bring celebrity, but improve usefulness. She should pursue every kind of study which will teach her to elicit truth; which will lead her to be intent upon realities; will give precision to her ideas; will make an exact mind. She should cultivate every study which, instead of stimulating her sensibility, will chastise it; which will neither create an excessive or a false refinement; which will give her definite notions; will bring the imagination under dominion; will lead her to think, to compare, to combine, to methodise; which will confer such a power of discrimination, that her judgment shall learn to reject what is dazzling, if it be not solid; and to prefer, not what is striking, or bright, or new, but what is just. That kind of knowledge which is rather fitted for home consumption than foreign exportation, is peculiarly adapted to women.* . . .

For instance; ladies whose natural vanity has been aggravated by a false education, may look down on *œconomy* as a vulgar attainment, unworthy of the attention of an highly cultivated intellect; but this is the false estimate of a shallow mind. Œconomy, such as a woman of fortune is called on to practise, is not merely the petty detail of small daily expences, the shabby curtailments and stinted parsimony of a little mind, operating on little concerns; but it is the exercise of a sound judgment exerted in the comprehensive outline of order, of arrangement, of distribution; of regulations by which alone well-governed societies, great and small, subsist. She who has the best regulated mind will, other things being equal, have the best regulated family. . . .

A general capacity for knowledge, and the cultivation of the understanding at large, will always put a woman into the best state for directing her pursuits into those particular channels which her destination in life may afterwards require. But she should be carefully instructed that her talents are only a means to a still higher attainment, and that she is not to rest in them as an end; that merely to exercise them as instruments for the acquisition of fame and the promotion of pleasure, is subversive of her delicacy as a woman, and contrary to the spirit of a christian.

Study, therefore, is to be considered as the means of strengthening the mind, and of fitting it for higher duties, just as exercise is to be considered as an instrument for strengthening the body for the same purpose. . . .

As to men of sense, however, they need be the less hostile to the improvement of the other sex, as they themselves will be sure to be gainers by it; the enlargement of the female understanding being the most likely

---

* May I be allowed to strengthen my own opinion with the authority of Dr. Johnson, that a *woman cannot have too much arithmetic?* It is a solid, practical acquirement, in which there is much use and little display; it is a quiet sober kind of knowledge, which she acquires for herself and her family, and not for the world.

means to put an end to those petty and absurd contentions for equality which female smatterers so anxiously maintain. I say smatterers, for between the first class of both sexes the question is much more rarely and always more temperately agitated. Co-operation and not competition is indeed the clear principle we wish to see reciprocally adopted by those higher minds in each sex which really approximate the nearest to each other. The more a woman's understanding is improved, the more obviously she will discern that there can be no happiness in any society where there is a perpetual struggle for power; and the more her judgment is rectified, the more accurate views will she take of the station she was born to fill, and the more readily will she accommodate herself to it; . . .

But *they* little understand the true interests of woman who would lift her from the important duties of her allotted station, to fill with fantastic dignity a loftier but less appropriate niche. Nor do they understand her true happiness, who seek to annihilate distinctions from which she derives advantages, and to attempt innovations which would depreciate her real value. Each sex has its proper excellencies, which would be lost were they melted down into the common character by the fusion of the new philosophy. Why should we do away [with] distinctions which increase the mutual benefits and enhance the satisfactions of life? Whence, but by carefully preserving the original marks of difference stamped by the hand of the Creator, would be derived the superior advantage of mixed society? Is either sex so abounding in perfection as to be independent of the other for improvement? Have men no need to have their rough angles filed off, and their harshnesses and asperities smoothed and polished by assimilating with beings of more softness and refinement? Are the ideas of women naturally so *very* judicious, are their principles so *invincibly* firm, are their views so *perfectly* correct, are their judgments so *completely* exact, that there is occasion for no additional weight, no superadded strength, no increased clearness, none of that enlargement of mind, none of that additional invigoration which may be derived from the aids of the stronger sex? What identity could advantageously supersede such an enlivening opposition, such an interesting variety of character? Is it not then more wise as well as more honourable to move contentedly in the plain path which Providence has obviously marked out to the sex, and in which custom has for the most part rationally confirmed them, rather than to stray awkwardly, unbecomingly, and unsuccessfully, in a forbidden road? Is it not desireable to be the lawful possessors of a lesser domestic territory, rather than the turbulent usurpers of a wider foreign empire? to be good originals, than bad imitators? to be the best thing of one's own kind, rather than an inferior thing even if it were of an higher kind? to be excellent women rather than indifferent men?

Is the author then undervaluing her own sex?—No. It is her zeal for their true *interests* which leads her to oppose their imaginary *rights*. It is her regard for their happiness which makes her endeavour to cure them of a feverish thirst for a fame as unattainable as inappropriate; to guard them against an ambition as little becoming the delicacy of their female character as the meekness of their religious profession. A little Christian humility and sobermindedness are worth all the empty renown which was ever obtained by the misapplied energies of the sex; it is worth all the wild metaphysical discussion which has ever been obtruded under the name of reason and philosophy; which has unsettled the peace of vain women, and forfeited the respect of reasonable men. And the most elaborate definition of ideal rights, and the most hardy measures for attaining them, are of less value in the eyes of a truly amiable woman, than "that meek and quiet spirit, which is in the sight of God of great price."

Natural propensities best mark the designations of Providence as to their application. The fin was not more clearly bestowed on the fish that he should swim, nor the wing given to the bird that he should fly, than superior strength of body, and a firmer texture of mind was given to man that he might preside in the deep and daring scenes of action and of council; in the complicated arts of government, in the contention of arms, in the intricacies and depths of science, in the bustle of commerce, and in those professions which demand a higher reach, and a wider range of powers. The true value of woman is not diminished by the imputation of inferiority in those talents which do not belong to her, of those qualities in which her claim to excellence does not consist. . . .

In almost all that comes under the description of polite letters, in all that captivates by imagery, or warms by just and affecting sentiment, women are excellent. They possess in a high degree that delicacy and quickness of perception, and that nice discernment between the beautiful and defective which comes under the denomination of taste. Both in composition and action they excel in details; but they do not so much generalize their ideas as men, nor do their minds seize a great subject with so large a grasp. They are acute observers, and accurate judges of life and manners, as far as their own sphere of observation extends; but they describe a smaller circle. A woman sees the world, as it were, from a little elevation in her own garden, whence she makes an exact survey of home scenes, but takes not in that wider range of distant prospects which he who stands on a loftier eminence commands. Women have a certain *tact* which often enables them to feel what is just more instantaneously than they can define it. They have an intuitive penetration into character, bestowed on them by Providence, like the sensitive and tender organs of some timid animals, as a kind of natural guard to warn of the approach of danger, beings who are often called to act defensively.

In summing up the evidence, if I may so speak, of the different capacities of the sexes, one may venture, perhaps, to assert, that women have equal *parts*, but are inferior in *wholeness* of mind, in the integral understanding: that though a superior woman may possess single faculties in equal perfection, yet there is commonly a juster proportion in the mind of a superior man; that if women have in an equal degree the faculty of fancy which creates images, and the faculty of memory which collects and stores ideas, they seem not to possess in equal measure the faculty of comparing, combining, analysing, and separating these ideas; that deep and patient thinking which goes to the bottom of a subject; nor that power of arrangement which knows how to link a thousand connected ideas in one dependent train, without losing sight of the original idea out of which the rest grow, and on which they all hang. The female too, wanting steadiness in her intellectual pursuits, is perpetually turned aside by her characteristic tastes and feelings. Woman in the career of genius, is the Atalanta, who will risk losing the race by running out of her road to pick up the golden apple; while her male competitor, without, perhaps, possessing greater natural strength or swiftness, will more certainly attain his object, by direct pursuit, by being less exposed to the seductions of extraneous beauty, and will win the race, not by excelling in speed, but by despising the bait *.

Here it may be justly enough retorted, that, as it is allowed the education of women is so defective, the alleged inferiority of their minds may be accounted for on that ground more justly than by ascribing it to their natural make. And, indeed, there is so much truth in the remark, that till women shall be more reasonably educated, and till the native growth of their mind shall cease to be stinted and cramped, we have no juster ground for pronouncing that their understanding has already reached its highest attainable point, than the Chinese would have for affirming that their women have attained to the greatest possible perfection in walking, while the first care is, during their infancy, to cripple their feet. At least, till the female sex are more carefully instructed, this question will always remain as undecided as to the *degree* of difference between the masculine and feminine understanding, as the question between the understandings of blacks and whites; for until men and women, and until Africans and Europeans are put more nearly on a par in the cultivation of their minds, the shades of distinction, whatever they be, between their native abilities can never be fairly ascertained.

21. Vicomte de Bonald (1802)

Women belong to the family and not to political society, and nature created them for domestic cares and not for public functions. Thus their education should be domestic in its objective, and they ought to acquire it in the laps of their mothers, if our *moeurs* would always permit mothers to fulfill their obligation to raise their daughters, an obligation far more sacred than that of nursing their infants which modern philosophy has decreed. While awaiting this still-distant time, there is a need for educational houses where a [religious] order of unmarried women devotes itself to instructing this portion of the human species that is all the more important in society's eyes because it is charged almost exclusively with one day giving young children their basic education.

Orders of unmarried women are thus in the nature of society; they are

---

* What indisposes even reasonable women to concede in these points is, that the weakest man instantly lays hold on the concession; and, on the mere ground of sex, plumes himself on his own individual superiority; inferring that the silliest man is superior to the first-rate woman.

very necessary to the happiness of a large number of women. In a perfectly constituted society, every situation in life, every state of the soul ought to find the place that suits it; and when society puts up with these perilous vocations where a man sacrifices the care of his life to the necessity of retaining his livelihood, it ought to permit these professions where man disposes once and for all of his free will to better assure his liberty. There must be an asylum for misfortune, a rampart for weakness, a solitude for love, a shelter for misery, a means for exercising charity, a retreat for the repentent, a remedy for disgust with the world, for the infirmities of nature, for the wrongs of society. We do not understand well enough how few men there are who are capable of governing themselves, and how large is the number of those who are too happy to discover in the general rules of common reason, a rule of conduct that they cannot find in their own reason.

Religion founds monastic orders: the State makes them serve to comfort all the weaknesses of humanity, to educate children, to protect the weak sex, to comfort the handicapped, to instruct the people, to redeem captives, to civilize the savage, and religion marks these diverse tasks with this character of grandeur and divinity that it communicates to everything for which it serves as the [guiding] principle. Governments that are not deprived of this resource can find in the unlimited obedience of the religious, in the riches of the monasteries, and in the perpetuity of these large establishments, powerful means for administration that are sought elsewhere in vain and the loss of which is now regretted by the peoples who sacrificed them in the delirium of novelty.

The education of young girls should not be the same as that of young boys, because they have not received the same destiny from nature. Everything in their instruction should be directed toward domestic utility, just as everything in the education of young boys should be directed toward public utility. It is a false education that gives one's inclinations a direction that goes contrary to nature, that makes the sexes want to exchange occupations just as they would clothing, that women would voluntarily take a hand in the government of the State, and that men would find a bit too much pleasure in private life and in domestic enjoyments.

For a long time young men have been taught a great deal of botany, chemistry, natural history, etc., which are not very useful for the performance of public functions, and young women are taught foreign languages, sciences, and even certain arts, knowledge they should not acquire all the more because they require vanity to show it off, and which, if they cultivate successfully, takes away a good deal from their domestic duties, sometimes from their health, and nearly always from their natural charm.

Look upon nature, and admire how she distinguishes the sex she has called upon to exercise public functions from the one she has destined to the care of the family: from the earliest age, she endows the one with a taste for political and even religious *action*: the taste for horses, for weapons, for religious ceremonies. To the other she gives a taste for sedentary and domestic tasks, for household care, for *dolls*. These are the principles, and the best system of education should only result in their development. In this way nature inspires in the child a taste that will become a duty at a more advanced age, just as she introduces in a young people a custom that will become a law of their political society.

If the object of education is not the same for children of the two sexes, the means can be a bit different, and one must exercise extreme wisdom in the institutions, so that the communal education that suits men meant to live together in the courts, in the camps, on the ships, also suits women who are destined to live isolated in families. The powerful force of emulation, which works so well in the education of men because it awakens in them the most generous passions, must be employed with extreme caution in the education of women, in whom it might awaken vanity, the source of their misfortunes, their faults, their stupidities, and which, in women as in men, is born of the force of self-love and from the weakness of their talents.

Young men in their colleges duel with one another and love one another; young women caress each other and become jealous of each other. Thus it is especially useful in the education of women to establish the most rigorous uniformity in clothing, for it is remarkable how much they notice, even in the boarding schools, far more than young men, differences in the situation and fortunes of their parents.

In the education of young women one should speak to their hearts as much or even more than to their intelligence, lead them by a religion just as affectionate but perhaps even more enlightened and more grand than one finds in most convents; in a word, inspire them far more than teach them, because women have received their portion of intelligence in feeling. Because of this they know, without having learned, so many things that we learn badly without knowing them, which gives them a sense naturally more direct, although less reasoned, a surer though more hasty taste, a mind and manners that are less studied and by that very fact more loveable.*

22. *Jüdisch Deutsche Monatsschrift* (1802)

The splendor of women's intelligence should not be an intelligence of learning. Their model lies in natural simplicity. Their wisdom is to be found in sensibility, not in reasoning. One must strive to increase their moral sense, rather than their memory.

Traditionally girls have had the misfortune that little or no care has been bestowed upon their education and training; they are always at the mercy of good or bad coincidences, or the meeting of lucky or unlucky circumstances. Only rarely are we concerned with the development of

---

* In the convents physical education is too much neglected; exercise and food are generally not well enough attended to, and, out of fear of speaking to girls too much of marriage, they do not hear enough discussion of their duties.

their natural disposition as women, even more rarely with the development of the spirit and the moral ennoblement of their hearts as human beings; and almost never are we concerned with both of these! Let us praise benevolent providence, which is ushering in the dawn of an improved womanly culture. A dawn when men who are energetically working on the education of this noble half of humanity step forward, and to the joy of all friends of humanity we discover a most beautiful flowering of public and private education.

Only in our nation are there many who absolutely refuse to acknowledge the necessity of education for girls! Parents who recognize their duty to offer their son as much as possible, who do not object to giving up considerable sums in order to enhance his well-being, who sacrifice everything—at least after their fashion—to ensure his happiness; such parents do not consider it their duty to bestow equal concern upon their daughter. They do not think of her education and training, and believe they have done their part when they have given her nourishment, clothing, and a miserable dowry.

Is this peculiar behavior based in nature? Has the daughter been created out of worse stuff than the son? Is she perhaps an addition to creation who needs less improvement than the son? Have we not given life to them both? Should not the well-being and misery of both of them lie equally close to our hearts? Let us look about us! Let us listen to general experience! How frequently we find unhappy marriages. In one the husband is sighing about his undomesticated wife; in another a father is angry about a weak and too tender mother; here a frivolous and fluttery housewife can command neither respect nor the rights to which she is entitled and there she forfeits her unlucky husband's good name and credit. Does not the root of these sad happenings lie in education? Is not her neglected education the reason why the fault is to be found mostly on the side of the wife? Parents: Do you understand how much you are responsible for the welfare of your daughter and her own peace and comfort in old age. Do you see how experience strictly obliges you to *educate girls as well as boys.*

This is not the place in which to deal with general or particular rules for the education of girls. Nor do I want—at least at present—to offer a method for the teaching of our daughters. My most heartfelt desire is only that you should sincerely feel the great *destiny* of girls and that you should strive to make use of every sign that points to the realization of this destiny.

Girls have a dual destiny; as *human being* and as *wife.* Every sensitive and sensible being must strive for pure and enduring *happiness.* All knowledge bringing them closer to this goal is necessary and universal; this means it is indispensable for every person, regardless of sex or position. If then woman is to achieve her goal, her mental and physical qualities must be formed and developed as well as those of the man. The girl's intelligence must be enlightened, her powers of thought must be exercised, her heart must be ennobled, her will must be blessed, and her imagination must be led with gentleness. She must be made familiar with the varied positions and destinies of humanity, and also with passions, temperaments, and so forth. Only thus may right thinking be furthered, only thus may attitudes and judgments be protected from gross ignorance and damaging prejudice. Only thus can we unconsciously be led toward the recognition of human dignity, and he who is conscious of the inner dignity of a human being has crossed the halfway point on the road to virtue.

Morality and religion are closely allied with the cultivation of the intelligence. The vivacious spirit, the lively imagination and most delicate sensibility that differentiate women unmistakably from men—are often rocks upon which even the most solid virtue can be shattered. Armed with morality a girl will not be as easily led astray by the weaknesses of vanity and the glitter of coquetry; nor will she be as easily exposed to damaging errors and seductions. Moral and modest behavior will moreover support a girl in lively and constant cheerfulness and will make her receptive to the overwhelming joys of nature, and will prepare her for that bliss that nature has offered women in the loyalty of married love, in the joys of family ties, and in the tenderness of motherhood.

Whatever cultivation and morality may provide in peaceful and joyous times, religion can offer in times of unhappiness and suffering. Only religion is able to sustain the unhappy woman; only religion's healing powers are balm for the suffering woman. When her heart is filled with the idea of God and her childish faith in him, a woman can cope patiently with all the suffering that may be inflicted upon a family. Instead of defeating her, accidents can raise a woman's morale; instead of weakening her they can strengthen her courage; she will cheer her depressed husband; she will counsel him and bring him hope; she will double her motherly tenderness toward her children—and she will remain loyally virtuous even in suffering!

Culture, morality, and religion, then, are the most essential preparation—and cannot be instilled early enough if a girl is to achieve her goal —her destiny as a human being.

Since, when considering the education of an individual we must be guided by the particular position assigned to him in society, the education of woman must be guided by this same rule. In almost every cultivated country the narrow, unremarkable, but nevertheless important and extensive domestic sphere of activity is assigned to woman. Woman, to whom we thus entrust the rule of the home, is therefore obliged to be knowledgeable about all particulars of housewifery. Not only must she be adroit in all womanly dexterities and skills such as spinning, sewing, knitting, and so on, she must also understand the great art of transforming a man's home into a place of peace and joy by effective order and economy. She must know how to restrain and determine the family expenses and habits according to the husband's means and fortune; she must be as knowledgeable about the most useful domestic provisions as about the cost of various goods and their usefulness. She must never shop at the wrong time, but always with care; she must be sparing with her savings and always consider the future. As a mother on whom depends the education of her children, a woman must moreover have such knowledge as is essential for their education. From the moment of the child's birth, she must be able to develop and guide its mental and physical powers. Early on she must plant the seeds of virtue in their young souls, and aim to influence the tender heart of the child by her good example.

It is this destiny—parents!—that especially requires your activity and your concern. From her earliest infancy you must begin to familiarize a girl with womanly arts and skills as well as with the quiet virtues of domestic life such as order, simplicity, cleanliness, and so on. Even her universal destiny of human being may be furthered only insofar as it influences her particular destiny as wife, housewife, and mother. Mental and moral endowments must be developed so that her thoughts are corrected, her feelings ennobled, and her character strengthened. An important point that must never be forgotten in the education of girls is this: we must create a human woman and a womanly human being. The girl should become familiar with the entire range of domesticity as well as with the general knowledge of geography, history, natural history, and botany. But, to be sure, only with *general* knowledge! A girl does not require extensively learned studies in order to feel the dignity of humanity as a human being, and to arrange her activities with this understanding. How can learned treatises profit a wife, or how can absorption in the laws influence the life of a woman? On the contrary, such digressions surely cause more damage than usefulness in a girl, because the learned girl—instead of visiting the kitchen and cellar, which she might otherwise have done with delight—will soon prefer to flutter about in the realm of learning and live in an ideal rather than a real world.

If the girl is educated in this manner her education is one-sided and incompatible with the goal of happiness in society.

Therefore, parents, educate a girl to be a cultivated and skillful housewife. Think often of the sacredness and importance of her duty, and never lose sight of the goal you are striving to achieve!

What blessings you will enjoy in later days when the plant that you nurtured with such care has grown to maturity; when the silent virtue of your daughter affects her husband and children with such well-being; when the happiness of an entire family blossoms under the wise care of your daughter. Ah, then you will not remember the past with sorrow; but you will contemplate the future with delight. Because you will know that, when you must leave this stage, you will have created the foundation of your daughter's happiness.

23. Napoleon (1807)

The Écouen establishment must be handsome in its monumental aspect and simple in its educational aspect. Beware of following the example of the former establishment at St. Cyr, where considerable sums were spent and where the *demoiselles* were badly brought up.

The utilization and scheduling of time are the objects that will require your principal attention. What will be taught to the demoiselles who will be brought up at Écouen? We must begin with religion in all its rigor; in this matter do not admit any modification. In a public institution for demoiselles religion is a serious matter; whatever else may be said about it, it is the surest guarantee for mothers and for husbands. Make believers of them, not reasoners. The weakness of women's brains, the mobility of their ideas, their destination in the social order, the necessity for inspiring them with a constant and perpetual resignation and a mild and indulgent charity, all that cannot be obtained except by means of religion, a charitable and mild religion. . . . I am desirous that they may leave [Écouen] not as pleasing women but as virtuous women, that their pleasing qualities be those of morals and of the heart, not of the mind and of amusement. Therefore, there must be a director at Écouen, a man of spirit, of good moral character, and of a certain age; each day the pupils must participate in regular prayers, hear the mass, and receive lessons in the catechism. It is this part of education to which the most care should be given.

Next, the pupils should be taught to count and to write, and the principles of our language so that they know how to spell; they should be taught some geography and history, but should not be introduced either to Latin or to any other foreign language. The older ones might be taught a bit of botany, or offered an easy course in physics or natural history, though even that might have its drawbacks. In physics it should be limited to whatever might be necessary to prevent gross ignorance and stupid superstition, and should stick to the facts without going into arguments concerned either directly or indirectly with first causes. It can be decided later whether it would be useful to give those who come from a certain class a sum of money for their clothing. They could then accustom themselves to economizing, to calculating the values of things, and to reckoning for themselves. But, generally speaking, they should all be occupied for a good three-quarters of the day with manual work: they should make stockings, blouses, embroidery, indeed, every sort of woman's work. These girls should be considered as though they belonged to families who, in the provinces, have between fifteen to eighteen thousand *livres* annual income and who would bring to their husbands no more than twelve to fifteen thousand *livres*, and should be treated accordingly. In such situations it is evident that they should be no strangers to manual work in the household.

I do not know whether it is possible to show them a bit of medicine and pharmacy, at least the type of medicine that is the domain of a sick-nurse. It would also be good for them to know a little of that part of cooking that is called the pantry. It is my wish that a girl leaving Écouen to find herself at the helm of a small household know how to make her own dresses, mend her husband's clothing, make layettes for her children, procure comforts for her little family as befits the pantry of a provincial household, care for her husband and children when they are ill, and know in this respect, because it was inculcated in her early on, what sick-nurses have learned by practice. . . .

And should I be told that this establishment will not enjoy a great vogue, I will reply that such is my desire, because it is my opinion that of all possible educations, the best is that given by mothers. My intention is primarily to come to the aid of those girls who have lost their mothers or whose parents are poor, and if those members of the Legion of Honor who are rich do not deign to send their daughters, if those who are poor do wish to do so, and if these young people, once returned to their province, enjoy there the reputation of good women, I will have attained my objective completely. In such matters, one must proceed to the edge of ridicule: I am not raising vendors of style nor housemaids nor housekeepers, but wives for modest and poor households.

With the sole exception of the director, men should be excluded from the establishment: they should never enter the enclosure under any pretext. Even the garden work should be done by women. My intention in this respect is that the school at Écouen be under a rule quite as stringent as that of a convent of nuns. Even the directress ought not to be able to receive men except in the parlor, and if it is impossible to forbid letting parents enter in case of serious illness, it should be possible only with the express permission of the grand chancellor. I should not have to say that the employees of this establishment should be limited to older unmarried women or widows who have had no children, that their subordination to the directress must be absolute, and that they may neither receive men nor leave the establishment.

No doubt it would be equally superfluous to remark that there is no more ill-conceived idea, nothing more blameworthy than to have young girls participate in theatricals and to excite their emulation by means of class distinctions. This is good for men who may be called upon to speak in public and who, being obliged to learn many things, have the need to be sustained and stimulated by emulation; but in the case of girls, there must be no emulation among them, their passions must not be awakened nor their vanity, the most active passion of their sex, be called forth. Light punishments and the praise of the directress for those who conduct themselves well would seem to me to be sufficient. But classification by means of ribbons would seem to me to have no good effect if it has any goal other than to distinguish age-groups or if it establishes a sort of primacy.

CHAPTER 3

Revolutionary Republicanism, the Family, and Civic Rights for Women

The Case for Women's Rights as Citizens of the New French Republic

SOURCES

24. "Condorcet's Plea for the Citizenship of Women," tr. John Morley, *Fortnightly Review*, 13 (1 June 1870), 719-24; reprinted in Morley's *Critical Miscellanies* (London, 1871), pp. 367-72. As originally published: Marie-Jean-Antoine-Nicolas Caritat, marquis de Condorcet, "Sur l'Admission des femmes au droit de cité," *Journal de la Société de 1789*, 3 July 1790; reprinted in *Oeuvres de Condorcet*, ed. A[rthur] Condorcet O'Connor and F. Arago, 12 vols. (Paris, 1847-49), X, 121-30.

25. Etta Palm d'Aelders, "Adresse des citoyennes françoises à l'Assemblée Nationale" [July 1791] in her *Appel aux françoises sur la régénération des moeurs et necessité de l'influence des femmes dans un gouvernement libre* (Paris, 1791), pp. 37-40. Tr. KMO.

26. Olympe de Gouges, *Les Droits de la femme* (Paris, 1791). Tr. Nupur Chaudhuri, with SGB and KMO.

Women's political rights are conspicuous by their absence from official proclamations and from pronouncements by those who came to power during the French Revolution. Nevertheless, certain individuals were deeply concerned with this issue at the time, connecting it directly to the debate over slavery and natural rights. The selections reprinted here are from the three most incisive French contributors to this debate—the Marquis de Condorcet, Etta Palm d'Aelders, and Olympe de Gouges. The publications were the first to deal specifically with the issue of civic rights for women, and antedate the work both of the British Mary Wollstonecraft and of the German von Hippel (Docs. 12, 29) whose books on this topic appeared in 1792.

Elected to the Legislative Assembly in 1790, Condorcet (1743-1794; Doc. 19) published his essay "Sur l'Admission des femmes au droit de cité" in July of that year. This short and eloquent piece is devoted entirely to the discussion of women's rights. Basing his argument on the natural equality of all persons and on the natural rights possessed by all human beings, he concluded, first, that women must be granted the same civic rights as men; second, that women could be effective as actors in the political and legislative sphere; and, finally, that women should be allowed to vote. Condorcet's ideas on civic rights and equality were overruled by the revolutionary legislature, but his ideas on women resurfaced repeatedly in the nineteenth century. It is noteworthy that the British Liberal statesman and historian John Morley translated and republished "Condorcet's Plea for the Citizenship of Women" in the *Fortnightly Review* (June 1870) after the first round of the fifty-year-long British parliamentary debate on woman's suffrage.

The second selection is an appeal made in 1791 to the revolutionary legislators on behalf of women's rights by Etta Palm d'Aelders (1743-??), who headed a female delegation to the revolutionary assembly the following year. Born as Etta Lubina Derista Aelders in Groningen (Holland), she married Ferdinand Palm when she was nineteen. Following his disappearance in the Dutch Indies, Palm d'Aelders led a somewhat unsettled life and eventually made her home in Paris around 1774. She was connected with the circle of Madame de Condorcet and emerged as an orator on women's behalf in revolutionary club circles in November 1790. Throughout 1791 she championed the cause of women and advocated the organization of women to monitor revolutionary fervor in the provinces. Palm d'Aelders' interests ranged beyond the purely political. She wanted to provide sound apprenticeship programs for young girls, and had organized a society of women for this purpose. Her writing and speeches attest to her familiarity with classical culture; her rhetoric is sprinkled with frequent and pertinent references to the matrons of the Roman Republic. In 1792 the liberal statesman Lebrun sent her on a mission to lay the ground-work for a French revolutionary embassy to her native Low Countries. The selection here exudes the spirit of both Roman and French revolutionary republican ideals, exemplifying Palm D'Aelders' flair for assimilating and transforming her background knowledge into everyday terms. The proposed law she attacks—article XIII of the Police Code—accorded to *men only* the right to file a formal complaint against an unfaithful spouse. It further stipulated a two-year prison term for the wife, as well as giving husbands the opportunity to dispossess their wives of dowries or other property brought into the marriage.

Several months after Palm d'Aelders' appeal to the legislative assembly, Olympe de Gouges (1748-1793) proclaimed the "Rights of Woman." In her *Droits de la femme* she adapted the style and format of the famous *Declaration of the Rights of Man* (1789), invoking its principles on behalf of the female sex much as Elizabeth Cady Stanton and Lucretia Mott were to do with the Declaration of Independence sixty years later at Seneca Falls.

Born Marie Gouze, daughter of a butcher's family in Montauban, she educated herself and moved to Paris, where she wrote plays, novels, and political pamphlets under the name Olympe de Gouges. Her analysis of woman's position was far more radical than those of Wollstonecraft or Condorcet, yet she identified herself with the royal cause during the Revolution, addressing all her political writings—including those on women—to royal patrons. She was guillotined in 1793 by the Jacobins, who thereby made it unmistakably clear that the combination of her royalist politics with her "unwomanly" behavior and notions about women's position would not be tolerated in a radical republic.

Gouges addressed the *Droits de la femme* to Marie Antoinette. She called on the queen to turn away from counter-revolutionary intrigue with foreign powers and to champion instead the cause of women, in order to lead a long-overdue revolution in morals. "This revolution will occur," she wrote in the dedication, "only when all women are convinced of their deplorable fate and of the rights they have lost in society. Madame, support such a good cause, defend this unfortunate sex, and you will soon have one half the Kingdom on your side, along with at least one third of the other half."

The selection from Gouges' work includes the introductory exhortation, the preamble, all seventeen articles of the declaration, and the first section of the "Postamble." Of particular interest is her model of a marriage contract, which included a formula for legitimizing children "from whatever bed they might spring."

---

24. Marquis de Condorcet (1790)

It is in the power of habit to familiarise men with the violation of their natural rights to such a degree that, among those who have lost them, nobody ever thinks of reclaiming them, or supposes himself to have suffered any wrong. There are even some of these cases of violation, which have escaped philosophers and legislators, when they were devoting themselves with most zeal to the establishment of the common rights of the members of the human race, and to the foundation in these rights, and in them only, of political institutions.

For instance, have they not every one violated the principle of the equality of rights, in tranquilly depriving the half of the human race of that of assisting in the making of law; in excluding women from the right of citizenship? Is there a stronger proof of the power of habit, even over enlightened men, than the spectacle of equality of rights being invoked in favour of three or four hundred men that an absurd prejudice had deprived them of, and being forgotten in respect of twelve millions of women? For this exclusion not to be an act of tyranny, it would be necessary either to prove that the natural rights of women are not absolutely identical with those of men, or else to show that women are incapable of exercising them.

Now the rights of men result only from this, that men are beings with sensibility, capable of acquiring moral ideas, and of reasoning on these ideas. So women, having these same qualities, have necessarily equal rights. Either no individual of the human race has genuine rights, or else all have the same; and he who votes against the right of another, whatever the religion, colour, or sex of that other, has henceforth abjured his own.

With reference to the other horn of the dilemma, it would be hard to prove that women are incapable of exercising the rights of citizenship. Why should beings to whom pregnancy and passing indispositions are incident, not be able to exercise rights, of which nobody ever dreamt of depriving people who have the gout every winter, or who easily catch cold? Again, even if we admit in men a superiority of intelligence not the necessary result of difference of education—which is as far as possible from being proved, and which ought to be proved, to enable us to deprive women of a natural right without injustice—this superiority can only consist in two points. It is said that no woman has made an important discovery in science, nor given proofs of genius in art, literature, &c. But, we may presume, the franchise is not to be accorded only to men of genius. It is said, further, that no woman has the same range of knowledge, the same force of understanding, as certain men. But what follows from this, that, except a not very large class of highly enlightened men, there is entire equality between women and all the rest of men; that, this small class apart, inferiority and superiority are equally divided between the two sexes? Now, since it would be utterly absurd to confine to this superior class the rights of citizenship and the liability to public functions, why should we exclude women from them, any more than those among men who are inferior to a great number of women?

In short, will anybody contend that women have in intelligence or in heart any qualities that ought to exclude them from the enjoyment of their natural rights? Let us interrogate facts. Elizabeth of England, Maria Theresa, the two Catherines of Russia, proved that it was neither in strength of character nor courage of mind that women failed. Would not the rights of citizens have found a better champion at the States of 1614 in the adopted daughter of Montaigne, than in Councillor Courtin, who believed in sortilege and occult virtues? Was not the Princess des Ursins worth more than Chamillard? Would not the Marquise du Châtelet have composed a despatch as well as M. Rouillé? Would Madame de Lambert have made laws as absurd and as barbarous as those of D'Armenonville, against Protestants, thievish servants, smugglers, and negroes? As they cast an eye over the list of those who have been their rulers and law-makers, men have no right to be so lifted up.

Women are superior to men in the milder and domestic virtues; they know, as well as men, how to love liberty, though they do not share all its advantages; and in republics they have many a time sacrificed themselves for it. They have shown the virtues of citizens, as often as accident or civil troubles have brought them on a stage, from which among all nations the pride of men had repulsed them.

It has been said that women, notwithstanding much wit, judgment, and a faculty of reasoning carried as far as it has been by subtle dialecticians, have never been guided by what is called reason. This remark is untrue. They are not guided, it is true, by the reason of men, but they are guided by their own. Their interests not being the same by the defect of the laws, and the same things not having for them the same importance as for us, they may without failing in reason, make up their minds on other principles, and aim at a different end. It is not more unreasonable for a woman to take pains about her personal appearance, than it was for Demosthenes to take pains with his voice and his gesticulation.

It has been said that women, though better than men, more gentle, more sensitive, less subject to the harsher and more egoistic sort of vices, have not the sentiment of justice; that they obey feeling rather than conscience. This remark is more near being true, but it proves nothing. It is not nature, it is education, it is the manner of social life, which is the cause of this difference. Neither one nor the other has accustomed women to the idea of what is just, but only to the idea of what is amiable. Banished from affairs, from everything that is settled according to rigorous justice and positive laws, the matters with which they occupy themselves are precisely those which are ruled by natural amiability and by feeling. It is hardly fair, therefore, to allege as a ground for continuing to deny women the enjoyment of their natural rights, reasons which only possess a certain amount of substance because women do not enjoy these rights.

If we admitted such arguments against women, we must also deprive of the franchise the part of the people which, devoted to incessant labour, can neither acquire light nor exercise its reason, and soon we should come, step by step, to such a pass as only to permit citizenship in men who had gone through a course of public law. If we admit such principles, we must as a necessary consequence renounce the whole idea of a free constitution. The various aristocracies have only had similar pretexts for foundation or for excuse; the etymology of the word proves it.

You cannot bring forward the subjection of wives to their husbands, because, in the first place, it would be possible at the same time to destroy this tyranny of the civil law; and, in the second, one injustice can never be a reason for perpetrating another.

There only remain two objections to discuss. In truth, they only oppose to the admission of women to the right of citizenship motives of utility, which cannot outweigh a genuine right. The contrary maxim has too often been the excuse and pretext of tyrants; it is in the name of utility that commerce and industry groan in fetters, and that the African remains devoted to slavery; it was in the name of public utility that the Bastille was crowded with prisoners, that censors were appointed over books, that legal procedure was kept secret, that the torture was applied. Still, we may as well discuss these objections, so as to leave nothing unanswered.

We should have to dread, it is said, the influence of women over men.

We reply, to begin with, that this influence, like every other, is much more to be feared when used in private than in public discussion; that the influence which may be peculiar to women would lose all the more by this; as, if it extends over more than one individual, it cannot be durable after it is known. Again, as hitherto, women have never been admitted in any country to an absolute equality, as their empire has none the less for this existed everywhere, and the lower women have been placed by the laws, the more dangerous it has been, it does not seem as if we ought to have much confidence in this remedy. Is it not probable, on the contrary, that this empire would diminish, if women had less interest in maintaining it, if it ceased to be for them the only means of defending themselves, and of escaping from oppression? If politeness prevents most men from upholding their opinion against a woman in society, it is a politeness that has a good deal to do with pride; they yield a victory which has no consequences; defeat does not humiliate, because it is regarded as voluntary.

Does anybody seriously suppose that it would be the same in a public discussion on an important subject? Does politeness prevent people from pleading a cause in the courts against a woman?

But, we shall be told, this change would be contrary to general utility, because it would draw women away from the tasks that nature seems to have reserved for them.

This objection does not seem very well grounded. Whatever constitution is set up, it is certain that in the existing state of the civilisation of European nations, there will never be more than a very small number of citizens able to occupy themselves with public business. You would not be tearing women away from their housekeeping, any more than you tear the labourer from his plough or the artisan from his workshop. In the richer classes, we never see the women surrendering themselves to domestic cares in so continuous a manner, that we need be afraid of distracting their attention from them; and a serious occupation would certainly distract women from them much less than the futile tastes to which idleness and bad education condemn them.

The principal cause of this apprehension is the idea that every man admitted to enjoy the franchise thinks henceforth of nothing but governing; which may be true, to a certain extent, at the moment when a constitution is being established. But this stir and agitation could not be permanent. In the same way, we must not suppose that, because women might possibly be members of national assemblies, they would on the spot abandon their children, their households, their needle. They would be all the more fit to bring up their children and to form men. It is natural that the woman should suckle her children, and should attend to their first years. Kept to the house by these tasks, and being physically weaker than man, it is natural further that she should lead a more retired and domestic life. So women would be in the same class as the men, who are obliged by their position to attend to a business for a certain number of hours. This may be a good reason for not preferring them in the elections, but it cannot be the foundation of a legal exclusion. Gallantry would lose by this change, but domestic manners would gain by that, as by every other equality.

Hitherto all known nations have had barbarous or corrupt manners and customs. The only exception that I know of must be made in favour of the Americans of the United States, who are spread in a small number over a large territory. Hitherto, among all nations, legal inequality has existed between men and women; and it would not be hard to prove that in these two phenomena, equally general, the second is one of the principal causes of the first. For inequality necessarily introduces corruption, and is the most common, where it is not the only, cause of it.

It is singular enough that in many countries women should have been counted incapable of every public function, yet worthy of royalty; that in France a woman could have been regent, and that up to 1776 she could not be a *marchande de modes* at Paris; that, in fine, in the elective assemblies of our bailliages, that should have been accorded to a right of the fief which was denied to the right of nature. Several of our noble deputies owe to ladies the honour of sitting among the representatives of the nation. Why, instead of taking away this right from the owners of fiefs, not extend it to all those who have property, who are householders?

25. Etta Palm d'Aelders (1791)

The chains of Frenchmen have fallen with a clatter; the noise of their falling turned despots pale and shook their thrones. An astonished Europe is transfixed by the star that shines down on France and by the august Senate that represents a people who join the love of justice to the will to be free.

Yes, gentlemen, you have broken the scepter of bronze in order to replace it with the olive branch; you have sworn to protect the weak. It is your duty, it is your honor, it is in your interest to destroy to their very roots these gothic laws that abandon the weakest but most worthy half of humanity to a humiliating existence, an eternal slavery.

By recognizing man's rights you have restored his human dignity. Therefore, you will not leave women to suffer under an arbitrary authority. To do so would overthrow the fundamental principles on which rests the majestic edifice you are raising for the happiness of the French people through your unceasing labor. There is no time left for equivocation: philosophy has forced the truth out of the shadows. The hour has struck; justice, the sister of liberty, calls all individuals to equal rights without distinction of sex; the laws of a free people must be equal for all beings, like the air and the sunshine. Alas, too long have the imprescriptible rights of nature been misunderstood; too long have bizarre laws, the worthy product of centuries of ignorance, afflicted humanity; too long has the most odious tyranny been sanctioned by absurd laws.

But, gentlemen, Article XIII of the Police Code, which has been presented to you by the Committee on the Constitution, surpasses in its injustice anything that was accomplished during centuries of barbarism. It represents a refinement of despotism that renders the constitution odious to women. By degrading our existence in order to flatter your own conceit, [it will] lull you to sleep in the arms of a slave and thus blunt your energy, the better to enchain you.

August legislators, would you weigh down with chains the hands that helped you to raise the altar of the fatherland with so much ardor? Would you enslave those who contributed so zealously to make you free? Would you brand a Clelia, a Veturia, a Cornelia? No, no, conjugal authority should only be the result of a social pact. It is wisdom in legislation, it is in the general interest to establish a balance between despotism and license; but the powers of the husband and the wife should be equal and individual. The laws cannot establish any distinction between these two authorities; they must offer equal protection and must establish a lasting equilibrium between married persons. Would it not be unjust to sanction ease of access to vice for the husband, while the wife, whose fragile existence is subject to countless evils, would have for her part all the difficulties of virtue?

Fathers of the country, do not stain your immortal work by such a measure. No doubt a moral code is necessary—but morals are the work of time and education. They cannot be commanded. License is the natural result of the oppressive regime of indissoluble marriage and of the dull, enervating education of the cloisters, the haunts of ignorance and fanaticism that you in your wisdom have destroyed. You will crown your work by according girls a moral education equal to that of their brothers, for education is to the soul what dew is to plants. It fertilizes, makes blossom, strengthens, and carries the seed productive of virtues and talents to perfect maturity.

Representatives of the nation, vote down this unjust and unseemly code, in the name of honor, in the name of holy liberty. It would become the apple of discord in families and the tomb of liberty. Constraint withers the soul; the slave thinks only of breaking his chains, of avenging his servitude. No doubt the committee, in order to justify this odious article, consulted the theologians and not the philosophers. Well then, consult your own hearts! They will instruct you more fully than will the maxims of the jurists of past centuries—these men steeped in despotism, who consider the barrenness of their souls a result of virtue. Nature created us to be your equals, your companions and your friends; we are the mainstays of your childhood, the happiness of your mature years, and the consolation of your old age, all honorable titles that you must surely acknowledge.

26. Olympe de Gouges (1791)

Man, are you capable of being just? It is a woman who asks you this question; at least you will not deny her this right. Tell me! Who has given you the sovereign authority to oppress my sex? Your strength? Your talents? Observe the creator in his wisdom; regard nature in all her grandeur, with which you seem to want to compare yourself; and give me, if you dare, an example of this tyrannical empire.* Go back to the animals, consult the elements, study the plants, then glance over all the modifications of organized matter, and cede to the evidence when I offer you the means. Seek, search, and distinguish, if you can, the sexes in the administration of nature. Everywhere you will find them mingled, everywhere they cooperate in harmony with this immortal masterpiece.

Only man has fashioned himself a principle out of this exception. Bizarre, blind, bloated by science and degenerate, in this century of enlightenment and wisdom, he, in grossest ignorance, wishes to exercise the command of a despot over a sex that has received every intellectual faculty; he claims to rejoice in the Revolution and claims his rights to equality, at the very least.

* From Paris to Peru, from Rome to Japan, the most stupid animal, in my opinion, is man.

Declaration of the Rights of Woman and Citizen,

To be decreed by the National Assembly in its last meetings or in those of the next legislature.

PREAMBLE

The mothers, daughters, and sisters, representatives of the nation, demand to be constituted a national assembly. Considering that ignorance, disregard of or contempt for the rights of women are the only causes of public misfortune and of governmental corruption, they have resolved to set forth in a solemn declaration, the natural, inalienable and sacred rights of woman; to the end that this declaration, constantly held up to all members of society, may always remind them of their rights and duties; to the end that the acts based on women's power and those based on the power of men, being constantly measured against the goal of all political institutions, may be more respected; and so that the demands of female citizens, henceforth founded on simple and indisputable principles, may ever uphold the constitution and good morals, and may contribute to the happiness of all.

Consequently, the sex that is superior in beauty as well as in courage of maternal suffering, recognizes and declares, in the presence and under the auspices of the Supreme Being, the following rights of woman and citizen.

Article One. Woman is born free and remains equal in rights to man. Social distinctions can be founded only on general utility.

II. The goal of every political association is the preservation of the natural and irrevocable rights of Woman and Man. These rights are liberty, property, security, and especially resistance to oppression.

III. The principle of all sovereignty resides essentially in the Nation, which is none other than the union of Woman and Man; no group, no individual can exercise any authority that is not derived expressly from it.

IV. Liberty and Justice consist of rendering to persons those things that belong to them; thus, the exercise of woman's natural rights is limited only by the perpetual tyranny with which man opposes her; these limits must be changed according to the laws of nature and reason.

V. The laws of nature and of reason prohibit all acts harmful to society; whatever is not prohibited by these wise and divine laws cannot be prevented, and no one can be forced to do anything unspecified by the law.

VI. The law should be the expression of the general will: all female and male citizens must participate in its elaboration personally or through their representatives. It should be the same for all; all female and male citizens, being equal in the eyes of the law, should be equally admissible to all public offices, places, and employments, according to their capacities and with no distinctions other than those of their virtues and talents.

VII. No woman is immune; she can be accused, arrested, and detained in such cases as determined by law. Women, like men, must obey these rigorous laws.

VIII. Only punishments strictly and obviously necessary may be established by law. No one may be punished except under a law established and promulgated before the offense occurred, and which is legally applicable to women.

IX. If any woman is declared guilty, then the law must be enforced rigorously.

X. No one should be punished for their opinions. Woman has the right to mount the scaffold; she should likewise have the right to speak in public, provided that her demonstrations do not disrupt public order as established by law.

XI. Free communication of thoughts and opinions is one of the most precious rights of woman, since this liberty assures the legitimate paternity of fathers with regard to their children. Every female citizen can therefore freely say: "I am the mother of a child that belongs to you," without a barbaric prejudice forcing her to conceal the truth; she must also answer for the abuse of this liberty in cases determined by law.

XII. Guarantee of the rights of woman and female citizens requires the existence of public services. Such guarantee should be established for the advantage of everyone, not for the personal benefit of those to whom these services are entrusted.

XIII. For the maintenance of public forces and administrative expenses, the contributions of women and men shall be equal; the woman shares in all forced labor and all painful tasks, therefore she should have the same share in the distribution of positions, tasks, assignments, honors, and industry.

XIV. Female and male citizens have the right to determine the need for public taxes, either by themselves or through their representatives. Female citizens can agree to this only if they are admitted to an equal share not only in wealth but also in public administration, and by determining the proportion and extent of tax collection.

XV. The mass of women, allied for tax purposes to the mass of men, has the right to hold every public official accountable for his administration.

XVI. Any society in which the guarantee of rights is not assured, or the separation of powers determined, has no constitution. The constitution is invalid if the majority of individuals who compose the Nation have not cooperated in writing it.

XVII. The right of property is inviolable and sacred to both sexes, jointly or separately. No one can be deprived of it, since it is a true inheritance of nature except when public necessity, certified by law, clearly requires it, subject to just and prior compensation.

POSTAMBLE

Woman, wake up! The tocsin of reason is sounding throughout the Universe; know your rights. The powerful empire of nature is no longer surrounded by prejudices, fanaticism, superstition and lies. The torch of truth has dispelled all the clouds of stupidity and usurpation. Man en-slaved has multiplied his forces; he has had recourse to yours in order to break his own chains. Having become free, he has become unjust toward his mate. Oh Women! Women! when will you cease to be blind? What advantages have you gained in the Revolution? A more marked scorn, a more signal disdain. During centuries of corruption, you reigned only over the weakness of men. Your empire is destroyed; what then remains for you? The proof of man's injustice. The claim of your patrimony founded on the wise decrees of nature—what have you to fear from such a splendid enterprise? The good word of the legislator at the marriage of Canaan? Do you not fear that our French legislators, who are correcting this morality, which was for such a long time appended to the realm of politics but is no longer fashionable, will again say to you, "Women, what do we have in common with you?" You must answer, "Every-thing!" If, in their weakness, they are obstinate in drawing this conclu-sion contrary to their principles, you must courageously invoke the force of reason against their vain pretensions of superiority. Unite yourselves under the banner of philosophy; deploy all the energy of your character, and soon you will see these prideful ones, your adoring servants, no longer grovelling at your feet but proud to share with you the treasures of the Supreme Being. Whatever the obstacles that are put in your way, it is in your power to overturn them; you have only to will it. Let us turn now to the frightful picture of what you have been in society; and since there is currently a question of national education, let us see if our wise legisla-tors will think wisely about the education of women.

Women have done more evil than good. They have had their share in coercion and double-dealings. When forcibly abused, they have count-ered with stratagems; they have had recourse to all the resources of their charms, and the most blameless among them has not hesitated to use them. They have used poison and irons; they have commanded crime and virtue alike. For centuries, the government of France in particular has de-pended on the nocturnal administration of women; the cabinet had no secrets from their indiscretion: embassy, military command, ministry, presidency, pontificate, cardinalate—one might say everything profane and sacred subject to the foolishness of man has been subordinated to the greed and ambition of the female sex, which was formerly contempt-ible and respected but, since the revolution, is respectable and yet contemptible.

What could I not say about this paradox! I have only a moment for offering a few remarks, but this moment will attract the attention of the most remote posterity. Under the Old Regime, all were vicious, all were guilty; but could one not perceive the improvement of things, even in the substance of vice? A woman needed only to be beautiful or lovable; when she possessed these two advantages, she saw a hundred fortunes at her feet. If she did not profit from this situation, she had either a bizarre char-acter or a rare philosophy that led her to despise wealth; in such a case she was relegated to the status of a brainless person; the most indecent woman could make herself respected with enough gold; the buying and selling of women was a kind of industry taken for granted in the first rank of society, which, henceforth, will have no credit. If it did, the revolution would be lost, and under the new order we would remain ever corrupt. Still, can reason hide the fact that all other routes to fortune are closed to woman, whom man buys like a slave on the African coast? The difference is great, as we know. The slave commands the master; but if the master sets her free, without compensation, at an age when the slave has lost all her charms, what becomes of this unfortunate creature? A contemptible toy; even the doors of charity are closed to her; she is poor and old, they say; why didn't she know how to make her fortune? Other more touching examples suggest themselves to reason. A young person without experience, seduced by a man she loves, will abandon her parents to follow him; the ungrateful fellow will leave her after a few years, and the older she has grown with him, the more inhuman will his inconstancy be. If she has children, he will abandon her all the same. If he is rich, he will think himself exempt from sharing his fortune with his noble victims. If some commitment binds him to his duties, he will violate its power by using all legal loopholes. If he is married, other commitments lose their rights. What laws then remain to be made in order to destroy vice down to its very roots? One dealing with the sharing of fortunes between men and women, and another with public administration. It is clear that a woman born to a rich family gains a great deal from equal inheritance. But a woman born to a poor family of merit and virtue—what is her fate? Poverty and shame. If she does not excel in music or painting, she cannot be admitted to any public office, even though she might be quite capable. I wish only to give an overview of things. I will examine them more thoroughly in the new edition of my political works, with notes, which I propose to offer to the public in a few days.

I resume my text with regard to morals. Marriage is the tomb of confidence and love. A married woman can, with impunity, present bastards to her husband and the bastards with the fortune that does not belong to them. An unmarried woman has merely a slim right: ancient and inhuman laws have refused her the right to the name and property of the father of her children, and no new laws on this matter have been passed. If my attempt thus to give my sex an honorable and just stability is now considered a paradox on my part, an attempt at the impossible, I must leave to men yet to come the glory of discussing this matter; but meanwhile, one can pave the way through national education, the restoration of morals, and by conjugal contracts.

Model for a Social Contract Between a Man and a Woman

We, N & N, of our own free will, unite ourselves for the remainder of our lives and for the duration of our mutual inclinations, according to the following conditions: We intend and desire to pool our fortunes as community property, while nevertheless preserving the right to divide them on behalf of our own children and those we might have with someone else, mutually recognizing that our fortune belongs directly to our children, from whatever bed they might spring, and that all of them have the right to carry the name of the fathers and mothers who have acknowledged them, and we obligate ourselves to subscribe to the law that punishes the renunciation of one's own flesh and blood. We obligate ourselves equally, in case of separation, to divide our fortune, and to set apart the portion belonging to our children as indicated by the law; and in the case of perfect union, the first to die would assign half the property to their children; and if one of us should die without children, the survivor would inherit everything, unless the dying party had disposed of his half of the common wealth in favor of someone else he might deem appropriate.

Here is the general formula for the conjugal agreement I am proposing. Upon reading this unorthodox piece, I envision all the hypocrites, prudes, clergy, and their gang of diabolic followers rising up against me. But would this plan not offer to the wise a moral means of achieving the perfectibility of a happy government? I shall prove it in a few words. A rich and childless epicurean fervently thinks fit to go to his poor neighbor's house to augment his family. Once a law is passed that will authorize the rich man to adopt the poor woman's children, the bonds of society will be strengthened and its morals purified. This law would perhaps save the wealth of the community and check the disorder that leads so many victims into the refuges of shame, servility, and degeneration of human principles, where nature has so long bemoaned its oppression. May the critics of rational philosophy therefore cease to protest against primitive morals or else go bury themselves in the sources they cite.*

I should like a law that protects widows and maidens deceived by the false promises of a man to whom they have become attached; I would like this law to force a fickle-minded man to stand by his agreements or else provide an indemnity proportional to his fortune. Moreover, I would like this law to be rigorous against women, at least against those impudent enough to appeal to a law which they themselves have violated by their own misconduct, if this can be proved. At the same time, I would like prostitutes to be placed in designated quarters, as I discussed in 1788 in *Le Bonheur primitif de l'homme*. It is not the prostitutes who contribute most to the depravation of morals; it is the women of Society. By re-educating the latter, one can modify the former. At first this chain of fraternal union will prove disorderly, but eventually it will result in perfect harmony. I am offering an invincible means of elevating the soul of women; it is for them to join in all the activities of men. If man insists on finding this means impracticable, let him share his fortune with woman, not according to his whim, but according to the wisdom of the law. Prejudice will tumble down; customs and manners will be purified; and nature will recapture all its rights. Add to this the marriage of priests, the reaffirmation of the King on his throne, and the French government will never perish.

---

* Abraham had some very [*sic*] legitimate children with Agar, the servant of his wife.

German Responses to the Revolutionary Debate on Women's Role and Rights

SOURCES

27. Immanuel Kant, "The Character of the Sexes," in his *Anthropology from a Pragmatic Point of View*, tr. Victor Lyle Dowell; revised and ed. by Hans H. Rudnick (Carbondale, Ill., 1978), pp. 216-20. Originally published as *Anthropologie in pragmatischer Hinsicht abgefasst von Immanuel Kant* (Königsberg, 1798).

28. Johann Wolfgang von Goethe, *Wilhelm Meister's Lehrjahre*, in *Goethes Werke*, ed. Gustave von Loeper et al., sec. 1, vol. 23 (Weimar, 1901), p. 54. Originally published in 1795-96. Tr. SGB.

29. Theodor Gottlieb von Hippel, *Über die bürgerliche Verbesserung der Weiber*, in *Th. G. v. Hippel's sämtliche Werke*, etc., ed. Johann Georg Scheffner, VI (Berlin, 1828), 118-23, 193-96, 198, 201. Originally published in 1792. Tr. SGB.

From the German writers who contributed to the international Enlightenment debate on the woman question, three works of the 1790's demand our attention. To some extent these works were sparked by the Revolution. Two of them, the last philosophical treatise of Immanuel Kant and the novel *Wilhelm Meister* of Johann Wolfgang von Goethe, are considered integral works of prevailing Western thought. The third, a dissenting book by Theodor Gottlieb von Hippel, has been almost completely ignored.

The philosopher Immanuel Kant (1724-1804) epitomizes the internationalism of Enlightenment thought. His Scottish grandfather emigrated to East Prussia, and Kant spent his life in the city of Königsberg. He was deeply influenced both by the physical science of Newton and by the pragmatic philosophy of David Hume, and read, absorbed, and built on his own reinterpretation of Rousseau. For Kant, Rousseau was the "Newton of the moral world." In his own turn he profoundly influenced the thought of Goethe. He published the first part of his best known work, *Kritik der reiner Vernunft* (Critique of Pure Reason), in 1781.

The essence of Kant's thought is embodied in his 1784 essay, *Beantwortung der Frage, Was ist Aufklärung?* (Answer to the Question, What Is Enlightenment?). Here he stated that enlightened man is free from the guidance of others; he makes up his own mind; he "dares to know" and to have the "courage of his own understanding." Kant considered independence of mind the highest moral goal, one that separates man from beast. "In submissiveness," he wrote elsewhere, "there is not only something exceedingly dangerous, but also a certain ugliness. . . . An animal is not yet a complete being, because it is not conscious of itself. . . . the man who stands in dependence on another is no longer a man, he has lost his standing, he is nothing but the possession of another man." Moreover, according to Kant's "categorical imperative" man must act in such a way that his actions could always serve as the rule for action by others.

With respect to women, however, the loftiness of Kant's ideals and his analysis of the transcendent possibilities of man disappear before his acceptance of conventional views on the inferiority, submissiveness, and relative moral position of woman. Kant had, of course, read *Émile* (Doc. 10) and, in phrases clearly inspired by Rousseau, he considered woman's most necessary duty as the reproduction of the species. Her "natural talent [was] in mastering man's desire for her." In this selection from Kant's *Anthropologie*, his last work, written at the end of the century and acknowledged as the capstone of his philosophical system, woman is not to be concerned with the courage to know, or to think for herself; her primary role, similar to that of Rousseau's Sophie, is to advance the morality of man.

Johann Wolfgang von Goethe (1749-1832), often described as the greatest German poet, and certainly one of the most influential writers of his time, melded the classical and romantic streams of Enlightenment thought. His view of women has often been summed up in the much-cited phrase from *Faust*: "The eternal-womanly forever uplifts us" (*Das ewig Weibliche zieht uns hinan*). His views are in fact more complicated than this single phrase suggests. Goethe wrote a great deal about women and, in his fiction, created many convincing women ranging from erudite intellectuals to comfortable mother-figures. He loved many women during his long life, and his female companions and mistresses encompassed a wide spectrum of human character. It is perhaps significant, however, that the woman with whom he set up housekeeping and whom he finally married seventeen years after she had borne his child, was unable to be his intellectual companion and made no demands on his time, offering him primarily a comfortable and well-organized home.

The selection below is from the novel *Wilhelm Meisters Lehrjahre*, which Goethe wrote in the last decade of the eighteenth century. This concise statement of what later became known as the doctrine of the "separate spheres" differs from Rousseau's version, in which woman's function is solely to please man. Goethe's remarks on man's "unpleasing" political role in the immoral public sphere, which he contrasted to the loving and life-giving woman's domestic achievements, appealed not only to Europeans but also to English and American readers, who learned about his views from the widely reprinted 1824 translation by Thomas Carlyle. Mid-nineteenth-century American women read what was probably Carlyle's translation of our selection in the popular American women's magazine, *Godey's Lady's Book* (March 1850), a translation heavily slanted to emphasize the much-celebrated cult of domesticity. The translator added the word "holy" in describing the wife's position, and rendered the husband's role as that of the "happy prince," which illustrates not only Goethe's far-reaching influence, but also the liberties often taken by translators.

Theodor Gottlieb von Hippel (1741-1796), a Prussian legal and civic administrator, objected strongly to the exclusion of women from the "rights of man" philosophy. Like Rousseau, Hippel never married, but in 1774 he published anonymously a book entitled *Über die Ehe* (On Marriage), expounding his strong views on the subject. At that time his views were close to those of Rousseau and Kant: women belonged in a separate, distinct sphere as wives and mothers, and their entire lives should be a preparation for and execution of this role. Successive versions of the book published in 1775, 1792, and 1793, however, show a gradual change in his analysis of marriage and of woman's position. His legal practice had made him aware of the depth of prejudice and injustice against women, and by the time the third edition was published (1792) he had become convinced that women had been wronged and that they required equality with men both within marriage and in the public sphere.

In his *Über die bürgerliche Verbesserung der Weiber* (On Improving the Status of Women), 1792, Hippel calls for equality of political, educational, and professional rights for women. He wrote this work after realizing that women had not been awarded the rights of citizenship in the French revolutionary decrees. Hippel was acquainted with the history and literature of western civilization as well as that of his own day. Influenced by women's history as laid out by the contemporary French author Louise Keralio,* by the philosophic thought of the Scotsman David Hume, and by the principle of the categorical imperative, developed by his friend Immanuel Kant, Hippel argued that it was unethical to suppress women's freedom. He was thus more "Kantian" than Kant himself, in applying to the woman question the categorical imperative and Kant's concern with independence of mind and the dangers of submissiveness.

Although Hippel referred to Catherine Macaulay, he did not cite either Condorcet or de Gouges, with whom he had much in common. Hippel's book appeared in the same year as Wollstonecraft's *Vindication of the Rights of Woman*, but he went far beyond her ideas on women's rights to advocate equal opportunities for women in the professions, particularly in medicine, law, and the civil service.

Hippel stressed the full human complement of woman's personality. "Why should not women be persons," he asked: "why should not a woman pronounce the word I?" It is remarkable that while Goethe was suggesting in the 1790's that women should rule and administer the home, so that men could be free to administer the state, Hippel was arguing that women would make excellent administrators of the state, precisely because of their abilities in administering domestic economy. Thus, Hippel anticipated the "social feminism" argument of the French radical Jeanne Deroin (Docs. 70, 77) and the American Jane Addams by more than half a century. Moreover, like Plato and Condorcet, he argued that there are many first-rate women who could serve the state more effectively than the numerous second- and third-rate men who are so employed merely by virtue of being male. Since Hippel's career included experience as a lawyer, judge, civic counsellor, and president of the City of Königsberg, he was doubtless speaking from his own experience of professional and bureaucratic duties.

All of Hippel's work was published anonymously, because his king and benefactor, Frederick the Great of Prussia, objected to the pursuit of literary careers by civic administrators. The anonymity did not, however, prevent conventional reception of Hippel's changing viewpoints. The early editions of his anonymous book on marriage, which called for wives' subordinate dependence, were popular and sold well, while many copies of *Über die bürgerliche Verbesserung der Weiber* still remained on the publisher's shelves thirty-six years after publication.

---

27. Immanuel Kant (1798)

All machines, designed to accomplish with little power as much as those with great power, must be designed with art. Consequently, one can assume beforehand that Nature's foresight has put more art into the design of the female than the male, because Nature has equipped the male with greater strength than the female in order to bring both, who are also rational beings, together in intimate physical union for the most innate purpose, the preservation of the species. Moreover, for this capacity of theirs (as rational animals) Nature provided them with social inclinations so that their sexual partnership would persist in a domestic union.

* Louise Keralio Robert (1758-1821), French novelist, translator, revolutionary journalist, and author of *Histoire d'Elisabeth, reine d'Angleterre* (5 vols., 1786-89) and *Collection des meilleurs ouvrages françois composés par des femmes* (Paris, 1786-89).—EDS.

A harmonious and indissoluble union cannot be achieved through the random combination of two persons. One partner must subject himself to the other, and, alternately, one must be superior to the other in something, so that he can dominate or rule. If two people, who cannot do without each other, have identical ambitions, self-love will produce nothing but wrangling. In the interest of the progress of culture, one partner must be superior to the other in a heterogeneous way. The man must be superior to the woman in respect to his physical strength and courage, while the woman must be superior to the man in respect to her natural talent for mastering his desire for her. Under still uncivilized conditions, on the other hand, superiority is on the man's side only. Therefore in anthropology the nature of feminine characteristics, more than those of the masculine sex, is a subject for study by philosophers. Under adverse natural conditions one can no more recognize those characteristics than the characteristics of crab apples or wild pears, which disclose their potential only through grafting or innoculation. Civilization does not establish these feminine characteristics, it only causes them to develop and become recognizable under favorable circumstances.

Feminine traits are called weaknesses. People joke about them; fools ridicule them; but reasonable persons see very well that those traits are just the tools for the management of men, and for the use of men for female designs. The man is easy to fathom; but the woman does not reveal her secret, although she keeps another person's secret poorly (because of her loquacity). He loves domestic peace and gladly submits to her rule, so that he does not find himself hindered in his own affairs. She does not shy away from domestic strife which she carries on with her tongue, and for which Nature has provided her with loquacity and passionate eloquence which together disarm the man. He builds on the right of the stronger to give orders at home because he has the obligation to protect his home against outside enemies. She builds on the right of the weaker to be protected by her masculine partner against men, and she disarms him with her tears of exasperation by reproaching him with his lack of generosity.

In primitive cultures this is quite different. There the woman is a domestic animal. The man leads the way with weapon in his hand, and the woman follows him, laden with his household belongings. But even in a barbaric civilization with legal polygamy, the most favored woman in the prison-yard (called harem) knows how to win control over a man; and he has his hands full with bringing about a tolerable peace in the quarrel of many women about the one* (who is to dominate him).

*The old Russian story that wives suspect their husbands of keeping company with other women unless they are beaten now and then, is usually considered to be a fable. However, in Cook's travel book one finds that when an English sailor on Tahiti saw an Indian chastising his wife, the sailor, wanting to be gallant, began to threaten the husband. The woman immediately turned against the Englishman and asked him how it concerned him that her husband had to do this! Accordingly, one will also find that when the married woman practices obvious gallantry and her husband pays no attention to it, but rather compensates himself with drinking parties, card games, or with gallantry of his own, then not

In a civil society the woman does not submit herself without marriage to the desires of a man, and if she is married, then only in monogamy. Where civilization has not yet reached the level of feminine freedom in gallantry (that is, where the wife may openly admit to having lovers other than her husband), the man punishes the wife who threatens him with a rival. But when gallantry has become fashionable and jealousy ridiculous (as happens when a certain degree of luxury is reached), the feminine character reveals itself. By extending favors toward men, the feminine character lays claim to freedom and simultaneously to the conquest of the entire male species. Although this inclination is in ill repute, under the name of coquetry, it is not without a real justifiable basis. A young wife is always in danger of becoming a widow, and this leads her to distribute her charms to all men whose fortunes make them marriageable; so that, if this should occur, she would not be lacking in suitors.

Pope believes that one can characterize the feminine sex (the cultivated element of it, of course) under two headings, the inclination to dominate and the inclination to gratify. By the latter, however, must not be understood gratification at home, but gratification in public, which can work to her advantage and distinction. Then the inclination to gratify also dissolves into the inclination to dominate, and instead of giving in to her rivals' preoccupation with gratifying, she conquers all of them with her taste and her charm, wherever possible. However, even the inclination to dominate, like any inclination, cannot be used for characterizing the relationship of one class of people to another. The inclination to what is beneficial to them is common to all people; and the same also holds true for the inclination to dominate, as far as this is possible. Consequently, inclination does not characterize people. The fact that this female species is in a continual feud with its own kind, whereas it remains on rather good terms with the opposite sex, could be taken for a characteristic if it were not merely the natural consequence of rivalry among women for the favor and devotion of men. The inclination to dominate is the real goal, while public gratification, by which the field of their charm is extended, is only the means for providing the effect for that inclination.

We can only succeed in characterizing the feminine sex if we use the principle which served as Nature's end in the creation of femininity, and not what we have devised ourselves as its end. Since this end must still be wisdom according to Nature's design, despite the foolishness of men, these assumed ends will also be able to reveal their underlying principle which does not depend on our own choice, but on the higher design for the human race. These ends are (1) the preservation of the species, (2) the improvement of society and its refinement by women.

1. As Nature entrusted to the woman's womb her most precious

---

merely contempt but also hate overcomes the feminine partner, because the wife recognizes by this that he does not value her any longer, and that he leaves her indifferently to others, who also want to gnaw at the same bone. [On margin of MS: The woman wishes to be liked by all men, because if her husband should die, she will set her hopes on another man who likes her.—Ed. (Rudnick)] pledge, namely, the species, in the shape of the embryo by which the race was to propagate and perpetuate itself, Nature was concerned about the preservation of the embryo and implanted fear into the woman's character, a fear of physical injury and a timidity toward similar dangers. On the basis of this weakness, the woman legitimately asks for masculine protection.

2. Since Nature also wanted to instill the finer sensations, such as sociability and propriety, which belong to the culture, she made this sex the ruler of men through modesty and eloquence in speech and expression. Nature made women mature early and had them demand gentle and polite treatment from men, so that they would find themselves imperceptibly fettered by a child due to their own magnanimity; and they would find themselves brought, if not quite to morality itself, then at least to that which cloaks it, moral behavior, which is the preparation and introduction to morality.

28. Johann Wolfgang von Goethe (1795-96)

One evening, when the conversation turned to women, my satisfaction was unbounded. The subject arose quite naturally. A few ladies from the neighborhood had come to visit us and began the usual conversation about the education of women. They claimed injustice against our sex; that men wish to reserve all higher culture for themselves; that scholarship and science are denied to us; that we are expected to be nothing but playthings or housekeepers. Lothario said little to all of this, but when the group had become smaller he also spoke his mind on the subject.

It is strange, he concluded, that man should be criticized for wanting to put woman in the highest position that she is capable of occupying. After all, what position is higher than the government of the home? Man tortures himself with public affairs, he must acquire and safeguard property, he even takes part in the administration of the State—at every turn he is hampered by outside circumstances and, I might add, he governs nothing although he imagines himself to be governing. He must always be a politician, while he would prefer to be a man of good sense; he must be secretive, when he would prefer to be open; he must lie, when he would prefer to tell the truth. In order to work for an end he will never achieve, he must constantly relinquish that most splendid goal, his own inner harmony. Meanwhile, a sensible housewife truly governs her domain and facilitates every activity and every satisfaction for all members of her family. What, after all, is mankind's greatest happiness but the achievement of whatever we know to be just and good—and to know that we are truly the masters of the means to this end? And where but in our homes should or could our most immediate aims lie? Where, but in the place in which we rise in the morning and lie down to rest at night, do we expect and demand all those necessities that are constantly required and indispensable? Where but in this place, where food and wines and every kind of provision is always expected to be available for us and ours? What endless regular activity is required to produce a constant order of things in a lively, yet undisturbed continuum? How few men are able to exist and reappear regularly as a star and to preside over the day as well as the night. Can a man design his own tools, plant, harvest, preserve and distribute, glide through this round purposefully, calmly, and lovingly? A wife who has firmly grasped this authority thereby makes the husband whom she loves the true master. She concentrates her attention on every domestic art and craft and knows how to make the best use of them. Thus she is dependent on no one and creates for her husband that true inner and domestic independence which assures him that what he owns will be safe, and what he earns will be well used; therefore he is able to turn his mind toward great concerns. Then, if he is fortunate he may achieve for the state that which his wife achieves so well at home.

29. Theodor Gottlieb von Hippel (1792)

Men, would you not consider it barbaric and inhuman if out of fear you were denied all freedom merely because you might abuse it? What name, then, will you give to the fear that prevents you from returning the honor of freedom to the opposite sex? Times are no longer such that we can convince members of the other sex that guardianship still promotes their welfare as in the old days. Nor is it possible to convince them that such guardianship allows them to be more comfortable and carefree than emancipation, which would saddle them with responsibilities, cares, troubles, and a thousand discomforts of civic life, which at present they are fortunate to be hardly able to name. This is truly a shabby trick of inhuman despots wanting to ease the weight of the chains of their cowardly slaves. As though freedom, with all its discomforts, were not preferable to the most comfortable slavery! . . . And men, do you really believe that half the world exists merely for your pleasure, for your own desires, to satisfy your selfishness? Animals function; human beings act.—Why should a woman not be allowed to pronounce the word I? It is truly a gentle word for those who understand generous nature.— Whoever understands art is jealous and does not betray the master.—Is it not the greatest human privilege that we are able to know ourselves? Our worth is our own affair; our value is the concern of God and of the just. Did God overlook something while creating the other sex? Or is it men who sin against the other sex despite the will of the Creator? Why should women not be persons? Why can we not know: this is good for me and this is good, or this is advantageous and this is just? Many things, in fact most things that promote pleasure, do not by any means accomplish whatever is truly beneficial.—To be virtuous from genuine beneficence means, besides, to be truly virtuous.

Right now France, with its [ideas of] freedom, terrifies those powers that threaten to restrict the exaggerated decrees of the National Assembly. God! at the end of the eighteenth century—where no specter unless of considerable potency, perhaps a poltergeist, has any effect—it is possible to scare people with *freedom*! That it should come to this! Oh, even for him who has been raised in chains the name of freedom flashes like a divine spark, and because of this we are what we are. This spark diverts us so little from our path that it binds us even more firmly to the holiest of laws. The female sex lost its human rights through no fault of its own; merely through the development of human affairs in step with cultural progress. Neither by negotiation, nor by force has the female sex ever attempted to capture its civic rights, which unfortunately it lost very early with the growth of small family states. In fact, with complete self-denial, it awaits these civic rights today, out of our justice and generosity. Shall we let them wait in vain? Shall we rebuff with an honest and clear NO a petition submitted by nature on women's behalf, at a time when human rights are loudly proclaimed from the rooftops?

The new French constitution deserves a repetition of my reproaches, since it opted to forget one half of the nation. . . . All human beings have equal rights—all French men and women should be citizens and free. Those proposals for civic degradation, whereby in criminal cases deserving of such punishment men are proclaimed unworthy of the honor of French citizenship by means of a special ceremonial formula, are not extended to the other sex. In such cases women shall simply be berated with the curse: "Your fatherland has found you guilty of an infamous act." . . .

We are mistaken when we try to convince ourselves that women have no feeling for the matter of human honor involved in the struggles of freedom against tyranny. They have not only proved by their loud approbation that they know how to treasure the value of freedom and that the love of freedom can be highly volatile; but also they have worked hard to break the chains that bound the nation, and it was probably not their fault that they played only supporting roles in this spectacle.

Since the Revolution, Mademoiselle Keralio, the famous historian of Queen Elizabeth, has defended the rights of humanity with candor, truth, and firmness in her *Journal d'État et du Citoyen*. Women were aware of the setback, of the hollow silence, of their rejection from the service of the state on such a wondrous occasion. One of them dared to voice her indignation. In a letter directed to the National Assembly she noted that the constitution totally omitted women, although mothers ought to be citizens of the state. She begged for a decree by which mothers might be allowed to take a ceremonial oath in the presence of state officials. This honorable ceremony would have made it desirable to be a mother. History does not record what the representatives of the Nation resolved upon this address of a noble Frenchwoman. Today I commemorate her sadly. For today, on the 18th of March 1792 I read in the newspapers that, unmoved by her suggestions, the French have forced the other sex to appeal urgently for their rights. It would have been preferable to have offered the honors of citizenship to the other sex and avoided ridicule in such a serious matter. . . .

Still less should women be forbidden from taking part in the inner administration and economy of the state. After all, they are entrusted with the entire administration of their own homes, and the men themselves attest the laudable manner in which they carry out these duties. . . .

Whoever denies that the female sex is capable of perceiving matters in a large context, of organizing kingdoms and directing large-scale operations, of making wide-ranging plans, in short of elevating their understanding to take in universals, shows little knowledge of the world. He reaches conclusions concerning women's capabilities from the details that are at present mainly entrusted to them. . . . I would almost say the economy is a female matter, particularly when it concerns large-scale operations.—Since men have managed so masterfully, how shall I put it, to turn everything upside down. . . .

The idea that only equals should judge equals if justice is to become a live rather than a dead letter is gaining ever more credence. Would it not be a crying injustice, then, if women were to be excluded from the benches of judges and juries until this glowing spark bursts into flame? . . . [Hippel goes on to discuss the English jury system.]

In fact even in a monarchy everything could receive new impetus, and much that is now lame could become healed through a similar judicial administration. Both monarch and people would gain. But how would it be if the other sex were even to take part in legal practice, if quarrels and fights were to be settled not only by good men, but also by good women? Would judicial administration not be far more complete? Individuals who are merely following the letter of the law have no presence; they are in reality only useless slaves, who act as they are commanded, but produce nothing worthwhile thereby. Laws and human passions are often so closely connected that he who does not follow his intelligence and conscience (common sense) is, with the greatest legality, a rotten human being. Who but the other sex can discern this most clearly? Who should know better than women that the struggle through which others are gaining freedom is the test of true freedom? . . .

. . . What more should we desire than the highest human development? Should our laws not encompass everyone? Can an intelligent being be viewed merely as the means to [our] higher purposes? The common material principle that: those precepts according to which you live must be such that they can be used as general laws—is and remains a symbol of morality of all general laws and their highest principles. Am I reaching too far or can this philosophy become a manifesto of my suggestions? A good set of laws is surely the masterpiece of the human intellect. Whoever understands human nature knows that the morals of nations must attribute their cultures largely to the efficacy of their laws and will not be disturbed if I lead our jurists somewhat further back than they usually go themselves. Women already demonstrate in those areas where, in certain privileged cases, they act as judges, that they are mistresses of their art and put men, who usually spoil everything when they decide to become substitutes for their wives, to shame. . . .

The British Debate on Women's Role in the Family and the State

SOURCES

30. Charles James Fox, Speech in the debate on Mr. Grey's motion for a reform of Parliament (1797), in *The Parliamentary History of England*, XXXIII (London, 1818), 726-27.

31. James Mill, in *Encyclopedia Britannica*, supplement, 5th ed. (London, 1814), s.v. "Government." Reprinted as the *Article on Government*, 1825.

32. William Thompson [and Anna Doyle Wheeler], *Appeal of One Half the Human Race Against the Pretensions of the Other Half—Men—to Retain Them in Political and Thence in Civil and Domestic Slavery* (London, 1825), pp. v-xiv, 196-202, 209.

33. Eliza Sharples [Carlile], "The First Discourse of the Lady at the Rotunda," *The Isis, A London Weekly Publication*, 1, no. 1 (11 February 1832), 1-4.

Following the American and French Revolutions, British republican aspirations had to be dealt with by statesmen and authorities who feared an overthrow of the established order in the British Isles. They faced a variety of radical religious and political discontent, within the middle and working class, which was to bring about the passage of the Reform Act of 1832. This act extended voting rights beyond the wealthy aristocracy and middle class to some respectable—and financially stable—male artisan householders. Within the framework of discontent, the question of women's participation in politics was raised in Parliament, in philosophical radical literature, and in artisan discussion groups.

The first selection is from a speech made in Parliament May 26, 1791, by the liberal orator, Charles James Fox (1749-1806), who supported reform of the franchise as a necessity for quieting domestic unrest and improving the British position in the highly unpopular war against republican France. Fox, always a controversial figure, took pains to assure the House of Commons that unsuitable persons would not become enfranchised by the motion he proposed. He specifically used the example of woman's position to elucidate the necessary qualifications for the right to vote—legal and financial independence; both he and his listeners accepted the view that women "by law and by nature" cannot be independent (even when intellectually well qualified). Thus, it would clearly be "absurd" to enfranchise them.

Fox's rationale reappeared seventeen years later in an important article on "Government" by James Mill (1773-1836). Mill was the chief spokesman for Utilitarianism, the system supported by a group known as the British Philosophical Radicals, founded by Mill's friend Jeremy Bentham. The Utilitarian point of view is generally summed up by its principle of seeking to promote "the greatest possible happiness for the greatest possible number." Yet, even in new philosophical systems claiming to deal with humanity at large, women could be dismissed with ease. While Utilitarianism was concerned with the happiness and human rights of the individual, it is clear that in Mill's view political opinions are to be expressed and political rights exercised only by the male heads of families, whose opinions represent all members, including wives, adult daughters, and maiden aunts.

In 1814 Mill wrote several articles for the fifth edition of the *Encyclopedia Britannica*; the *Article on Government* was reprinted separately in 1825. Mill dismissed female voting rights in one cursory paragraph, reprinted below as the second selection. His analysis contributed directly to the passage of the British Parliament's landmark Reform Act of 1832, which extended voting privileges to a wider circle of property-holding males. It is not without importance that James Mill's son, John Stuart Mill (Docs. 105, 135) disagreed profoundly with his father's position and became the foremost advocate for woman suffrage among nineteenth-century male political thinkers.

In 1825, a radical Irish landowner William Thompson (1775-1833) published a reply to James Mill's article on government. His *Appeal of One Half the Human Race* was in fact the first British socialist analysis of the condition of women. Not the least of Thompson's many radical points is his explicit attribution of this work to Anna Doyle Wheeler (1785-1848). Although he had absorbed Wheeler's ideas to the point of making them his own, he had the honesty to acknowledge that he was merely their compiler and her scribe. Thompson's clear statement on this point—a first—raises the question whether many other publications by men on this and other topics may in fact have originated with women, only to be written up and published without acknowledgment under the names of men.

William Thompson and Anna Wheeler were both connected with Robert Owen's cooperative movement of the 1820's. Thompson, a political analyst, had already published an *Inquiry into the Principles of the Distribution of Wealth*, and had willed his estate to an Owenite community. Anna Wheeler was born into an enlightened Irish landed family and married off at fifteen. She spent the years of her unhappy early marriage bearing six children and reading the works of French and other revolutionary philosophers, including Mary Wollstonecraft. She finally deserted her ne'er-do-well alcoholic husband and spent several years on the Channel Island of Guernsey, where, as the governor's niece, she had the opportunity of meeting French radicals. Later she traveled to Paris and subsequently settled in London, where she provided a liaison between early French and British socialists. She encouraged the work of Charles Fourier (Doc. 35), supported the ideas of the radical Owenite Frances Wright, and shepherded Flora Tristan (Doc. 60) around London. Wheeler translated many articles by French socialist writers on women, contributed frequently to Robert Owen's journal *The Crisis*, and attracted considerable public attention through her lectures on women's issues.

In the *Appeal of One Half the Human Race* Thompson and Wheeler analyzed with careful logical irony James Mill's view that "women may be struck off from political rights without inconvenience." Their analysis cut far deeper than Wollstonecraft's; they not only addressed the public issues of legal and political equality, but also raised the issue of the sexual double standard, attacked the hypocrisy of marriage, and recommended the practice of birth control. Their critique owes something both to Fourier and to Owen, but it is their insight that the "accumulation of individual wealth will ever be whispering into man's ear preposterous notions of his relative importance over women" (p. 198) that makes the Thompson-Wheeler tract such a path-breaking contribution to the discussion of the woman question.

The *Appeal* was widely distributed in its time. Excerpts were translated into French before 1833, and Thompson's "Introductory Letter to Anna Wheeler" was included in a popular nineteenth-century American social anthology, *The Bible of Nature*, edited by George Henry Evans.

The final selection is from an 1832 speech by Eliza Sharples [Carlile] (1803/4-1861), republished in the radical weekly journal, *The Isis*, which she edited. Sharples, the daughter of a Lancashire textile manufacturer, had attended a boarding school until the age of twenty and was well read. A female cousin introduced her to the anti-clerical and anti-monarchical writings of the free-thought artisan leader Richard Carlile, which she found highly congenial. A repressive conservative government in Britain had repeatedly prosecuted and convicted Carlile during the 1820's for publishing cheap editions of seditious literature, among them reprints of Thomas Paine's works of the 1790's denouncing "kingcraft" and "priestcraft" and Carlile's own *Every Woman's Book* (1828), the first British work to describe methods of contraception. Carlile's book sold over 10,000 copies within five months of publication. After a short but intense correspondence with Carlile while he was in prison, Eliza Sharples arrived in London from Lancashire, in January 1832, to support his campaigns. When he was released, she lived with him until his death in 1843, and together they had four children. During his imprisonment, Sharples took over the organization and lectures at the "Rotunda," a radical meetingplace in the Blackfriars district of London. She edited and published *The Isis*, a title she also adopted as her pseudonym. She remained active in radical circles after Carlile's death, and later managed various other "free-thought" centers, including the Warner Street Temperance Hall. Here, her daughter wrote that Isis could "grace a rostrum but failed completely as a server of coffee." Nevertheless, in this center in the early 1850's she offered Charles Bradlaugh, who was to become one of the best known radical politicians of the nineteenth century, an opportunity to make his first public appearance.

Imbued with Enlightenment ideals, Sharples celebrated the power of the mind and reasserted the necessity of free thought and freedom of reason to combat entrenched superstition and prejudice.

---

30. Charles James Fox (1797)

My opinion is, that the best plan of representation is that which shall bring into activity the greatest number of independent voters, and that that is defective which would bring forth those whose situation and condition take from them the power of deliberation. I can have no conception of that being a good plan of election which should enable individuals to bring regiments to the poll. I hope gentlemen will not smile if I endeavour to illustrate my position by referring to the example of the other sex. In all the theories and projects of the most absurd speculation, it has never been suggested that it would be advisable to extend the elective suffrage to the female sex; and yet, justly respecting, as we must do, the mental powers, the acquirements, the discrimination, and the talents of the women of England, in the present improved state of society— knowing the opportunities which they have for acquiring knowledge— that they have interests as dear and as important as our own, it must be the genuine feeling of every gentleman who hears me, that all the superior classes of the female sex of England must be more capable of exercising the elective suffrage with deliberation and propriety, than the uninformed individuals of the lowest class of men to whom the advocates of universal suffrage would extend it. And yet, why has it never been imagined that the right of election should be extended to women? Why! but because by the law of nations, and perhaps also by the law of nature, that sex is dependent on ours; and because, therefore, their voices would be governed by the relation in which they stand in society. Therefore it is, Sir, that with the exception of companies, in which the right of voting merely affects property, it has never been in the contemplation of the most absurd theorists to extend the elective franchise to the other sex. The desideratum to be obtained, is independent voters, and that, I say, would be a defective system that should bring regiments of soldiers, of servants, and of persons whose low condition necessarily curbed the independence of their minds. That, then, I take to be the most perfect system which shall include the greatest number of independent electors, and exclude the greatest number of those who are necessarily by their condition dependent. I think that the plan of my hon. friend draws this line as discreetly as it can be drawn, and it by no means approaches to universal suffrage. It would neither admit, except in particular instances, soldiers nor servants. Universal suffrage would extend the right to three millions of men, . . .

31. James Mill (1814)

One thing is pretty clear, that all those individuals whose interests are indisputably included in those of other individuals may be struck off from political rights without inconvenience. In this light may be viewed all children up to a certain age, whose interests are involved in those of their parents. In this light also women may be regarded, the interest of almost all of whom is involved either in that of their fathers, or in that of their husbands.

32. William Thompson [and Anna Doyle Wheeler] (1825)

Introductory Letter to Mrs. Wheeler

Honored with your acquaintance, ambitious of your friendship, I have endeavoured to arrange the expression of those feelings, sentiments, and reasonings, which have emanated from your mind. In the following pages you will find discussed on paper, what you have so often discussed in conversation—a branch of that high and important subject of morals and legislation, the condition of women, of one half the human race, in what is called civilised society. Though not to me is that "diviner inspiration given," which can clothe with the grace and eloquence of your unpremeditated effusions the calm stream of argument; though, not having been in the situation you have been, to suffer from the inequalities of sexual laws, I cannot join with a sensibility equal to yours, in your lofty indignation and contempt of the puerilities and hypocrisy with which men seek to cover or to palliate their life-consuming and mind- and joy-eradicating oppressions, tempered always however with benevolence even to the foolish oppressors themselves; though I do not *feel* like you—thanks to the chance of having been born a man—looking lonely on the moral desolation around; though I am free from personal interest in the consideration of this question; yet can I not be inaccessible to the plain facts and reason of the case. Though long accustomed to reflect on this subject, to you am I indebted for those bolder and more comprehensive views which perhaps can only be elicited by concentration of the mind on one darling though terrific theme. To separate your thoughts from mine were now to me impossible, so amalgamated are they with my own: to the public this is indifferent; but to me how flattering, could I hope that any suggestions of mine had so amalgamated themselves in your mind!

The days of dedication and patronage are gone by. It is *not* with the view of obtaining the support of your name or your influence to the cause of truth and humanity that these lines are addressed to you. Truth must stand on its own foundation. . . .

I address you then simply to perform towards you a debt of justice; to show myself possessed of that sincerity which I profess to admire. I love not literary any more than any other species of piracy: I wish to give every thing to its right owner. Anxious that you should take up the cause of your proscribed sex, and state to the world in writing, in your own name, what you have so often and so well stated in conversation, and under feigned names in such of the periodical publications of the day as would tolerate such a theme, I long hesitated to arrange our common ideas, even upon a branch of the subject like the present. Anxious that the hand of a woman should have the honor of raising from the dust that neglected banner which a woman's hand nearly thirty years ago unfolded boldly, in face of the prejudices of thousands of years, and for which a woman's heart bled, and her life was all but the sacrifice—I hesitated to write. Were courage the quality wanting, you would have shown, what every day's experience proves, that women have more fortitude in endurance than men. Were comprehensiveness of mind, above the narrow views which too often marred Mary Wollstonecraft's pages and narrowed their usefulness, the quality wanting—above the timidity and impotence of conclusion accompanying the gentle eloquence of Mary Hays,* addressed, about the same time that Mary Wollstonecraft wrote, in the shape of an "*Appeal*" to the then closed ears of unreasoning men; yours was the eye which no prejudice obscured, open to the rays of truth from whatever quarter they might emanate. But leisure and resolution to undertake the drudgery of the task were wanting. A few only therefore of the following pages are the exclusive produce of your mind and pen, and written with your own hand. The remainder are our joint property, I being your interpreter and the scribe of your sentiments.

Too many years has remained uncontradicted the anathema of a school of modern philosophy against the claim to the equal use and enjoyment of their faculties of half the human race. In the ponderous though en-

---

* Mary Hays (1759-1843) was a novelist, an English women's rights advocate, and a friend of Mary Wollstonecraft.—EDS.

lightened volumes of the Supplement of the Encyclopædia Britannica, this dastardly anathema might have remained concealed from all eyes but those of the philosophers themselves, had not some patriotic men, over-looking perhaps the interests of women in their zeal for those of men, or not weighing the tendency of the paragraph, extracted the "Article on Government," with others, from the volume where its malignity towards half the human race slumbered, and re-printed it for gratuitous circula-tion; and had not the author of the "Article" expressly refused to omit or modify the offensive antisocial paragraph respecting women, though re-quested to do so by one whose lightest suggestion on such a subject ought to have been a command,* as his wisdom and benevolence surpass those of the disciples surrounding him, the faculties of many of whom seem calculated to gloat upon the least amiable features only of his philosophy.

Had such a paragraph as that in the title-page[†] been put forward by any of the vulgar hirelings or every-day bigots of existing institutions, it would have appeared to you and to me too worthless, from its palpable and audacious falsehood, to merit a reply. But put forward under the shield of philosophy, preached by the preachers of *Utility*—to what atrocities and absurdities might not the lustre and authority of such names give a pernicious colouring? Mr. Mill is not the only one of the new school of Utility who has misapplied the principle to the degradation of one half the human race. Another philosopher of the new school, Mr. Dumont of Geneva, another retrograde disciple of the great master of Legislation, though the collator and editor in French of Mr. Bentham's manuscripts, unites with the author of the "Article on Government" in his contemptuous exclusion of women. . . .

I therefore looked upon every day as lost till the rude gauntlet thrown down against half mankind was snatched up, and the inroad of barbar-ism, under the guise of philosophy, into the nineteenth century was ar-rested. Weary of waiting, the protest of at least one man and one woman is here put forward against doctrines which disgrace the principle of util-ity: the facts are denied, and the inferences controverted, even if the facts were true. Could any thing bring the principle of utility, or the search of the greatest amount of preponderant good, into disrepute, it would be the peculiarly inconsistent conduct in its abettors, of assuming the air of dogmatizing, and expecting that opinions should be believed, without proof, without reasons, on the faith of their wisdom. Of all reasoners, he that rests on the basis of utility is the least excused in advancing new opinions, or opinions on the truth of which great interests depend, with-out plainly stating the grounds of his opinions. Advocates as we are of the principle of Utility as the only test of morals, conduct so disgraceful to its admirers we will not follow.

You look forward, as I do, to a state of society very different from that which now exists, in which the effort of all is to out wit, supplant, and snatch from each other; where interest is systematically opposed to duty;

---

* Could this have been Jeremy Bentham himself?—EDS.
[†] Of Mill's article.—EDS.

where the so-called system of morals is little more than a mass of hypocrisy preached by knaves, unpractised by them, to keep their slaves, male as well as female, in blind uninquiring obedience; and where the whole motley fabric is kept together by fear and blood. You look forward to a better aspect of society, where the principle of benevolence shall supersede that of fear; where restless and anxious individual competition shall give place to mutual co-operation and joint possession; where individuals in large numbers, male and female, forming voluntary associations, shall become a mutual guarantee to each other for the supply of all useful wants, and form an unsalaried and uninsolvent insurance company against all insurable casualties; where perfect freedom of opinion and perfect equality will reign amongst the co-operators; and where the children of all will be equally educated and provided for by the whole, even these children longer the slaves of individual caprice.

In truth, under the present arrangements of society, the principle of individual competition remaining, as it is, the master-key and moving principle of the whole social organization, *individual* wealth the great object sought after by all, and the quantum of happiness of each individual (other things being equal) depending on the quantum of wealth, the means of happiness, possessed by each; it seems impossible—even were all unequal legal and unequal moral restraints removed, and were no secret current of force or influence exerted to baffle new regulations of equal justice—that women should attain to equal happiness with men. Two circumstances—permanent inferiority of strength, and occasional loss of time in gestation and rearing infants—must eternally render the average exertions of women in the race of the competition for wealth less successful than those of men. The pleasant compensation that men now affect to give for these two natural sources of inferior accumulation of wealth on the part of women (aggravated a thousand degrees by their exclusions from knowledge and almost all means of useful exertions, (the very lowest only excepted), is the existing system of marriage; under which, for the mere faculty of eating, breathing and living, in whatever degree of comfort husbands may think fit, women are reduced to domestic slavery, without will of their own, or power of locomotion, otherwise than as permitted by their respective masters.

While these two natural impediments in the way of the production or accumulation of wealth, and of course of the independence and equal enjoyments of women, exist—and exist they must—it should seem that the present arrangements of society, founded on individual competition, and of course allowing of no real compensation for these impediments, are absolutely irreconcilable with the equality, in point of the command of enjoyments, of women with men. Were all partial restraints, were unequal laws and unequal morals removed, were all the means and careers of all species of knowledge and exertion equally open to both sexes; still the barriers of physical organization must, under the system of individual competition, keep depressed the average station of women beneath that of men. Though in point of knowledge, talent, and virtue, they might become their equals; in point of independence *arising from wealth* they must, under the present principle of social arrangements, remain inferior.

No doubt, so much the more dastardly appears the baseness of man, that not satisfied with these indisputable advantages of organization in the pursuit of happiness on his own theatre of free competition, he paralyses to impotence even those means which Nature has given his feebler competitor, nor ceases his oppression till he has made her his slave. The more physical advantages Nature has given man, the *less* excusable is he in superadding factitious advantages, by the abuse of strength, to those which are natural and unavoidable. Were he generous, were he just, knew he how to promote his own happiness, he would be anxious to afford *compensations* for these physical inconveniences, instead of aggravating them; that he might raise woman to a perfect equality in all things with himself, and enjoy the highest pleasures of which his nature is susceptible—those of freedom, of voluntary association amongst perfect equals. Perhaps out of the system of "Association" or "Mutual Co-operation" such happiness is not to be expected.

But I hear you indignantly reject the boon of equality with such creatures as men now are. With you I would equally elevate both sexes. Really enlightened women, disdaining equally the submissive tricks of the slave and the caprices of the despot, breathing freely only in the air of the esteem of equals, and of mutual, *unbought, uncommanded*, affection, would find it difficult to meet with associates worthy of them in men as now formed, full of ignorance and vanity, priding themselves on a *sexual* superiority, entirely independent of any merit, any superior qualities, or pretensions to them, claiming respect from the strength of their arm and the lordly faculty of producing beards attached by nature to their chins! No: unworthy of, as incapable of appreciating, the delight of the society of such women, are the great majority of the existing race of men. The pleasures of mere animal appetite, the pleasures of commanding (the prettier and more helpless the slave, the greater these pleasures of the brute), are the only pleasures which the majority of men seek. . . .

. . . A mole cannot enjoy the "beauties and glories" (as a Professor terms them) of the visible world; nor can brute men enjoy the intellectual and sympathetic pleasures of equal intercourse with women, such as some are, such as all might be. Real and comprehensive knowledge, physical and moral, equally and impartially given by education and by all other means to both sexes, is the key to such higher enjoyments.

Even under the present arrangements of society, founded as they all are on the basis of individual competition, nothing could be more easy than to put the *rights* of women, political and civil, on a perfect equality with those of men. It is only to abolish all prohibitory and exclusive laws,—statute or what are called "common,"—the remnants of the barbarous customs of our ignorant ancestors; particularly the horrible and odious inequality and indissolubility of that disgrace of civilization, the present marriage code. Women then might exert in a free career with men their faculties of mind and body, to whatever degree developed, in pursuit of happiness by means of exertion, as men do. But this would not raise women to an equality of happiness with men: their rights might be equal, but not their happiness, because unequal powers under free competition must produce unequal effects.

In truth, the system of the most enlightened of the school of those reformers called political economists, is still founded on exclusions. Its basis is too narrow for human happiness. A more comprehensive system, founded on equal benevolence, on the true development of the principle of Utility, is wanting. Let the *competitive* political economists be satisfied with the praise of causing the removal of some of the rubbish of ignorant restrictions, under the name of laws, impeding the development of human exertion in the production of wealth. To build up a new fabric of social happiness, comprehending equally the interests of all existing human beings, has never been contemplated by them, and is altogether beyond the scope of their little theories; aiming at the utmost at increasing the number of what they style the happy middling orders, but leaving the great bulk of human beings to eternal ignorance and toil, requited by the mere means of prolonging from day to day an unhealthy and precarious existence. To a new science, the *social science*, or the science of promoting human happiness, that of political economy, or the mere science of producing wealth by individual competition, must give way. . . .

[From the Conclusion to the Appeal]

To obtain equal rights, the basis of equal happiness with men, you must be *respected* by them; not merely desired, like rare meats, to pamper their selfish appetites. To be respected by them, you must be respectable in your own eyes; you must exert more power, you must be more useful. You must regard yourselves as having equal capabilities of contributing to the general happiness with men, and as therefore equally entitled with them to every enjoyment. You must exercise these capabilities, nor cease to remonstrate till no more than equal duties are exacted from you, till no more than equal punishments are inflicted upon you, till equal enjoyments and equal means of seeking happiness are permitted to you as to men.

Still evils encompass you, inherent in the very system of labor by individual competition, even in its most free and perfect form. Men dread the competition of other men, of each other, in every line of industry. How much more will they dread your additional competition! How much will this dread of the competition of your industry and talents be aggravated by their previous contempt of your fabricated impotence! Hard enough, now, they will say, to earn subsistence and to acquire comforts: what will it be when an additional rivalship, equal to perhaps one third of actual human exertion, is thrown into the scale against them? How fearfully would such an influx of labor and talents into the market of competition bring down their remuneration!

An evil of no less magnitude, and immediately consequent on the preceding, opposes your happiness in the present state of social arrangements. Will man, laboring by individual competition, afford you any part of the fruits of his individual exertions as a compensation for the loss of time, pain, and expense incurred by women in bearing and rearing his and your common children? His present compensation of measured food, clothing, and idleness, with despotism over young children and inferior animals to compensate for his more lofty despotism over yourselves, coupled with personal insignificance, in what he calls his marriage contract, you know, or ought to know, how to appreciate. But not to say that this can only apply to that portion amongst you whom necessity compels to enter into so iniquitously partial a yoke; not to say that the duties and enjoyments of marriage might, if man ceased to be an ignorantly selfish creature, be rendered equal to both the contracting parties; the utmost compensation you could expect from this source would never afford you a permanent chance of happiness equal to that of men. You will always, under the system of individual competition and individual accumulations of wealth, be liable to the casualty of misery on the death of the active producer of the family, and occasional injustice from domestic abuse of superior strength and influence, against which no laws can entirely guard. Under the system of production by individual competition, it is impossible to expect that public opinion should be raised so high as to supply the defects of law, which can only repress—at the expense of the minor evils of punishment—the more flagrant and proveable acts of injustice, but can not take cognizance of those minute occurrences which so often form the groundwork of the happiness or misery of life. Superiority in the production or accumulation of individual wealth will ever be whispering into man's ear preposterous notions of his relative importance over woman, which notions must be ever prompting him to unsocial airs towards women, and particularly towards that woman who co-operates with him in the rearing of a family: for, individual wealth being under this system the one thing needful, all other qualities not tending to acquire it, though contributing ever so largely to increase the common stock of mutual happiness, are disregarded; and compensation for the exercise of such qualities or talents, for the endurance of pains and privations, would scarcely be dreamed of. If man, pursuing individual wealth, condescend to be equally instrumental with you in the production of children, the whole of the pleasure he takes care to enjoy and make the most of, as his by right of superior strength; but as to the pains and privations which his enjoyments may have entailed upon another, where is the bond that his labor should afford compensation for them?

Not so under the system of, Association, or of Labor by Mutual Co-operation.

This scheme of social arrangements is the only one which will complete and for ever insure the perfect equality and entire reciprocity of happiness between women and men. Those evils, which neither an equality of civil and criminal laws, nor of political laws, nor an equal system of morals upheld by an enlightened public opinion, can entirely obviate, this scheme of human exertion will remove or abundantly compensate. Even for the partial dispensations of nature it affords a remedy. Large numbers of men and women co-operating together for mutual happiness, all their possessions and means of enjoyment being the equal property of all— individual property and competition for ever excluded—women are not asked to *labor* as much in point of strength of muscle as men, but to contribute what they can, with as much cheerful benevolence, to the common happiness. All talents, all faculties, whether from nature or education, whether of min[d] or muscle, are here equally appreciated if they are spontaneously afforded and improved, and if they are necessary to keep up the common mass of happiness. Here no dread of being deserted by a husband with a helpless and pining family, could compel a woman to submit to the barbarities of an exclusive master. The whole Association educate and provide for the children of all: the children are independent of the exertions or the bounty of any individual parent: the whole wealth and beneficence of the community support woman against the enormous wrong of such casualties: they affect her not. She is bound by no motives to submit to injustice: it would not, therefore, be practised upon her. Here the evil of losing, by any accident, a beloved companion, is not aggravated to woman by the unanticipated pressure of overwhelming want. All her comforts, her respectability, depending on her personal qualities, remain unchanged: she co-operates as before to the common happiness, and her intelligent and sympathizing associates mitigate and gradually replace the bitterness of a last separation from the friend of her affections. Here, the daughter of the deserted mother could not, from want or vanity, sell the use of her person. She is as fully supplied with all comforts as any other member of the community, co-operating with them in whatever way her talents may permit to the common good. The vile trade of prostitution, consigning to untimely graves the youth and beauty of every civilized land, and gloated on by men pursuing individual wealth and upholding the sexual and partial system of morals, could not here exist. Man has, here, no individual wealth more than woman, with which to buy her person for the animal use of a few years. Man, like woman, if he wish to be beloved, must learn the art of pleasing, of benevolence, of deserving love. Here, the happiness of a young woman is not blasted for life by the scorn and persecutions of unrelenting hypocrisy, for that very indiscretion which weaves the gay chaplet of exulting gallantry round the forehead of unrestrained man. Morality is, here, just and equal in her awards. Why so? Because, man having no more wealth than woman, and no more influence over the general property, and his superior strength being brought down to its just level of utility, he can procure no sexual gratification but from the voluntary affection of woman: in proscribing her indiscretions, therefore, he must proscribe his own: and as far as the greatest degree of common happiness might require that such indiscretions should be equally repressed in the two sexes, so far and no farther would they be impartially discouraged in both. If women cease to be dependent on individual men for their daily support, if the children of all the pairs of the community are educated and maintained out of the common stock of wealth and talents, if every possible aid of medical skill and kindness is afforded impartially to all, to compensate for the bitterness of those hours when the organization of woman imposes on her superfluous sufferings; what motives, under such circumstances, could lead women to submit to unmerited reproach more than men, for those very acts in which men must from the very nature of things be equal participators? *No means of persecution being left to men*, all reproach not founded on reason and justice, all attempt at exclusive reproach, would be thrown back with laughter and contempt on the fools who harboured them. Woman's love must under such circumstances be earned, be merited, not, as now, *bought* or *commanded*: it would not be prostituted on heartless miscreants who could first steal the gem and then murder with their scorn its innocent confiding owner. Such men, in such an Association, might love themselves! a species of love, in which they would find no rivals to molest them! . . .

Arouse! awake! rescue your sex, your species, from the frightful circumstances that surround and degrade you:—demand your rights; or man, ungenerous man, intoxicated with his power, may become still more presumptuous and no longer measure or calculate the effect of his actions towards you, relying on your apathetic submission, while improvement in every other department of human exertion is on the advance.

33. Eliza Sharples [Carlile] (1832)

I purpose to speak, in my continued discourses, if this shall find favour with you, of superstition and of reason, of tyranny and of liberty, of morals and of politics.

Of politics! politics from a woman! some will exclaim. YES, I will set before my sex the example of asserting an equality for them with their present lords and masters, and strive to teach all, yes, *all*, that the undue submission, which constitutes slavery, is honourable to none; while the mutual submission, which leads to mutual good, is to all alike dignified and honourable. . . .

I have been full of superstition, but I trust, that I have ceased to be so; that I have gained some truth, and enough to become so pleased with it, as to proceed fearlessly in the pursuit of more. And thus it is that I stand here, a novelty among women, to call mankind from the ways and evils of error and of superstition to the paths and pleasures of truth. I can assure ye that there are no other thorns in this path, to molest the pursuit, than such as offended ignorance or dishonesty may strew there; and if your kind protection shall be the besom to sweep away those thorns from before my feet, I will follow with a basket and strew the path with flowers, with the aroma of Araby, and with the bloom of perpetual spring. . . .

Of tyranny I can only speak in denunciation: I am, in all its shapes, its enemy. Whether it come upon us in the name of heaven, garnished with holy cant and solemn drawling, in robed or mitred vaunting, or in his assumptions, in simple black and downcast looks, who calls himself the man of God; or whether it come in the name of the king, his ministers, the parliament, the law, or the administration of the law; whether it be from master to servant, from husband to wife, or from father to child; or whether it be in the customs of society, the manners of the people, or in long-established institutions, I am still its enemy. Here I challenge it to battle. On these boards, on other boards, through the medium of the Press, here and everywhere, that my voice can be heard or my pen can reach, I will struggle for more liberty;—not for myself, for I am free—for others who are not free. This bosom, sirs, has but one set of aspirations— they are for the increased liberty, virtue and happiness of the human race.

O Liberty! though abuses have been committed in thy name—though vice shelters itself under thy angel-wings, yet thou art virtue's God and I adore thee; I serve thee, and will strive to make thee known among men. Inspire my theme, and teach me how to be worthy of an administration in thy name. Here I bow to thee, and here I will teach others to bow themselves before no other God; for God is love and love is liberty.

. . . Give us free discussion. LET US HAVE NO PRIESTS. Let there be no impediment to our constant improvement, no prisons for honest talent, no tax on knowledge, no censorship on the press and the drama. Let us advance; and if Tyranny shall seek to arrest our march, let us unite to conquer it by the joint power of mind and matter moving in masses, and acting by and for and with the millions. The power of mind alone will do it. We have nothing to fear; let us unite and act. In our pursuit of knowledge, let us be as one mind. In our warfare with tyranny, let us be as one body. For mutual support, let us think of mutual good. For the soundness of our purpose, let us find a corresponding energy of action. Let us not be all things to all men; but one and the same character to all—and that a character working for the good of all.

Sirs, I shall seek to gather power around me in this establishment; and which of you will not accept me for your general, your leader, your guide? I will be worthy of the cause on which I ask you to embark. I have told you that I have left a happy home and comparative affluence, to launch the frail bark of my intellect, my soul, my genius, my spirit, on the ocean of politics; and I am fired with the daring to buffet its waves, and with the resolve to ride on the whirlwind, and to assist in the direction of the coming storm. I would that it should not be a storm; that all necessary should be accomplished with gentleness, with suasion, with kindness, with yielding, where yielding is required and proper, with resistance only where wrong is opposed; but, if human welfare require more than this, let more come on.

And to you, ladies, sisters, with your leave, I would say, I appeal, and ask in what way are you prepared to assist me? Will you gather round me, and give me that countenance in virtuous society which we all seek and need, and without which life to us is wretchedness. Will you not be offended at this step of mine, original to my understanding, but, I think, not unworthy of us, nor unbecoming in me? Are you prepared to advance, as you see I have already advanced? Breathes the spirit of liberty in you, or are you content to be slaves, because your lords may wish it? What say you, sisters? Will you advance, and seek that equality in human society which nature has qualified us for, but which tyranny, the tyranny of our lords and masters, hath suppressed? I have need of your assistance, as, I am sure, you have need of mine. I think we have souls, which no scripture has yet granted; that we are worthy of salvation, which no religion has yet promised us; that we are as men in mind and purpose; that we may make ourselves "helps meet for them," on the condition that they shall not seek our degradation, that they shall not be our tyrants, but that we shall be free to all the advantages, all the privileges, all the pleasures of human life.

Will you let your children gather round me, and learn from me a love of truth: not to learn to lisp the language of superstition with their first sweet prattlings, but that we may *teach the young idea how to shoot* in matters of reason, preserving the purity of the infant mind from those overwhelming corruptions which now pervade the general society.

Let your sons and your daughters come, and, as the Pagans of old personified and deified the virtues and the graces in their temples, and made a pursuit of them a matter of worship and religion, so here will I aspire to be, in example, an Isis Omnia. Here, in this temple, shall every virtue and every grace be taught; not in the sculptured marble or teinted painting alone, but in life and all its practices.

So, come, let us reason together; let us pursue that alone which will bear to be publicly reasoned upon; let us leave that of which we are publicly ashamed. Let us lead a new life, after being born again, to nobler purposes than those in which we have been educated. Let us be free! but let that freedom consist of wisdom, of honour, and of virtue.

And now, sirs, let me acquaint you with the particulars of my speculative undertaking. I take this building under my own care and management, very heavy as is the engagement; and moreover, I promise you to support, to the utmost, or in all the comforts that may be gathered in a prison, those two men, worthy of being called men, who, for their talent and honesty, exhibited in this place, have been led, not exactly like sheep to the slaughter, but nearly so: led to a prison, where one of them has had to endure all the horrors of confinement, which the magisterial barbarity of this age could inflict upon him. I do not shrink from them: I am proud of being associated with the names of Robert Taylor and Richard Carlile. But I stand not here to be the organ of their sentiments. I have formed a mind and found a soul of my own, and I stand here unpersuaded by any one, a free and independent woman.

PART II

Women and Their Sphere in the Romantic Era, 1830-1848

T HE CAREFUL new definitions of woman's sphere elaborated during the epoch of republican revolutions and counter-revolutions were, after 1830, subjected to renewed scrutiny. Both critics and defenders belonged to a new generation of writers, born after the eighteenth-century revolutions yet deeply affected by currents of Enlightenment ideas that had inspired them, and sensitive also to the events of their own time. To these critics, as to their predecessors, the woman question was an integral part of the social dissension born of the revolutions; it was intrinsically connected to the censure of both absolutist monarchy and aristocracy of birth and to the critique of the developing capitalist order, with its emerging aristocracy of wealth and "possessive individualism." [1]

These new thinkers and writers did not merely contemplate the social evils of their time; they took action. Some formed organizations of urban supporters dedicated to political and social reform; others founded counter-communities in isolated areas to see whether social change could be accomplished by restructuring human relationships, including male-female relationships, among a small group of willing individuals. In the meantime the defenders of organized religion and hierarchical social organization appropriated the very vocabulary and definitions of the secular Enlightenment to rephrase their own defense of social stability; this included the use of arguments from nature (drawing especially on the findings of physiologists) to bolster the traditional biblical case for female subordination. [2] All this ferment would seem to contradict the effectiveness of the system of ideological and political repression and censorship established in Europe as a response to the revolutions and

[1] We have borrowed the term from MacPherson 1962. For a sweeping overview of this period, see W. L. Langer, *Political and Social Upheaval, 1832-1852* (New York, 1969). See also Hobsbawm 1962 and Landes 1969.
[2] For the use of physiological arguments, especially by members of the medical profession, see Haller & Haller 1974; Smith-Rosenberg 1974; Knibiehler 1976a, 1976b; and Hellerstein 1980.

consolidated in Vienna in 1815 by the victors of the Napoleonic wars. The fears of Prince Metternich in Austria, Tsar Alexander I in Russia, and Lord Castlereagh in England about the unsettling influence of these radical ideas were not wholly unjustified.

In Part II we examine various aspects of this debate on the woman question, ranging over the development of challenges to women's situation in civil law and the inadequacy of their formal education, to explore the rearticulation of woman's sphere that accompanied the economic and political developments of the era. Politically speaking, the circumstances were somewhat special in each country, but there are general themes that run through all discussion. Concerning England, for instance, we have already alluded to the importance of republican agitation leading to the Reform Bill of 1832. Even at this time supporters of the extended franchise had made a convincing case for the vote for unmarried adult women, based on the same property considerations as those being prescribed for men. Then, in 1837, a young queen succeeded to the British throne. Although Victoria was personally uninterested in women's political emancipation, she did support efforts to promote women's education. Yet her very presence on the throne during her long reign (1837-1901) was to give constant impetus to those who argued for women's full participation in political life.

In France a new quasi-parliamentary monarchy under Louis-Philippe was established following the revolution of July 1830. The new regime was initially supportive of freedom of the press, of assembly, and of an extended franchise for men of property. The change of regime was accompanied by a rebirth of revolutionary rhetoric focusing on the position of women in the family. In this debate notions of "constitutionalism" and appeals to "freedom," both moral and material, for women were repeatedly advanced. Such terminology, spread by the so-called social novels and the theater as well as by essays and tracts, affected the debate throughout continental Europe, because of the continuing dominance of French as the language of intellectual as well as political discourse.[3]

Reconsideration of the problem of women's political and legal position in Great Britain and the United States consolidated itself in the movement to abolish slavery. The international slave trade had been outlawed by international treaty in 1815, and England had emancipated all her slaves in the British colonies in 1833. The institution of slavery, however, continued to flourish in the southern American states as well as in the island colonies of the French West Indies (until 1848), in Cuba, and in Portuguese Brazil. It was natural that women following the ancient Judæo-Christian tradition, emphasizing women's concern with charity and the welfare of the oppressed, should have become deeply involved in the anti-slavery movement. In England and the eastern United States they joined male abolition groups, but in the United States they also founded numer-

[3] On the importance of the French social novel and theater in spreading criticism during this period, see D.-O. Evans 1923, 1930, 1951; Siegel 1975; and P. Thompson 1977.

ous female anti-slavery societies. Prominent among their members in both English-speaking countries were Quaker women who, since the seventeenth century, had been the only Christian women permitted to participate in public religious meetings of their sect; over the years they had become accustomed to public oratory and public involvement. Yet when these women attempted to incorporate their Quaker practices into the anti-slavery movement, especially as public speakers, they elicited strong antipathy among both friends and foes.

Virtually all the American women who denounced female subordination during the 1830's and 1840's had become conscious of their own plight through male opposition to their active participation in the anti-slavery movement. The exclusion of America's women delegates from the 1840 World Anti-slavery Convention held in London radicalized a number of women who became activists in women's behalf, such as the Americans Lucretia Mott and Elizabeth Cady Stanton (Docs. 74, 76, 137) and the Scottish Marion Kirkland Reid (Docs. 54, 68). Perhaps as importantly, it established close personal and ideological ties of sisterhood between American and British women, friendships that ultimately led to the founding of international women's rights organizations.[4]

Slavery was at once a political, moral, and economic issue, and after 1830 the debate over woman's sphere likewise assumed an economic aspect. Here it joined the critique of capitalism, industrialization, and "wage slavery," spearheaded by the critics of capitalism who at this time became known as socialists.[5] Unlike those who felt optimistic and enthusiastic about the fruits of "progress" and those who vested great hope in the future of science and industry, these critics were appalled by the rampant growth of the market economy, the increasing power of capitalist entrepreneurs, the rising significance of industrial wage labor, and the developing sense of impotence among skilled artisans threatened with mechanization. They were particularly alarmed about women's employment and its impact on the separation of sexual spheres. At this point the emphasis on independence—of mind—for women expanded to a discussion of the independence of their material existence, which in turn raised a direct threat to the economic foundation of male authority in marriage. This issue is clearly addressed in the first set of selections, which juxtaposes the writings of the Saint-Simonian leader Prosper Enfantin, the social visionary Charles Fourier, and the Saint-Simonian women's advocate, "Jeanne-Victoire" (Docs. 34-36). For the first time, in the 1830's the restructuring of the household and the "right to work" for pay were posed as fundamental conditions of female emancipation in a society in

[4]On the radical background of Quaker women, see K. Thomas 1958. For their significance in nineteenth-century reform groups, see Lerner 1967, 1979 (ch. 8); and Melder 1977. For biographies of Lucretia Mott, see Cromwell 1958 and Bacon 1980. For the transatlantic links, see C. Taylor 1974.

[5]The term socialism was coined in 1834 by Pierre Leroux in his article "De l'individualisme et du socialisme," which appeared in the *Revue Encyclopédique*. See D.-O. Evans 1948, pp. 223-38, for a reprint of the original article.

which wealth, not rank, had become the single most important arbiter of power. Closely tied to this phenomenon was the new emphasis on harmony and on the association of individuals in groups organized to achieve social change. In this case these principles were invoked by women to unite members of their own sex across class lines. Class collaboration, not class conflict, was their goal, just as it was the men's goal.[6]

The prospect of material and moral independence for women provoked expressions of male consternation. Women's emancipation, men predicted, would be primarily a vehicle for promoting their freedom to indulge in sexual promiscuity—exposing blatantly, and for all to see, the fact that male control of women permitted men to impose a double standard of sexual behavior favorable to themselves. Advocates of women's emancipation were constantly challenged by their opponents to defend themselves and their cause against this charge and responded variously. Some women insisted on their own "respectability," while others argued for a single standard of restricted sexual freedom for both sexes. Still others insisted that sexual freedom was simply not on their agenda, despite the example of George Sand that was so often invoked against them.

The importance of the French contribution to international debate during this period on the amelioration of women's position within marriage cannot be overestimated. The arguments of the Saint-Simonians, of Charles Fourier and his followers, and the ideological novels of George Sand (Doc. 37) were read, discussed—and applied—throughout European intellectual circles during the next two generations. Saint-Simonism in particular was, according to historian Frank Manuel, "one of the most potent emotional and intellectual influences in nineteenth-century society."[7] Some examples of the dissemination of these ideas and their impact will illustrate the point. The manifestos of the Saint-Simonian women were translated by Anna Wheeler for Robert Owen's weekly, *The Crisis*, in London and from there transmitted to Owenite communities in America. In Russia the young social critic (and later revolutionary) Alexander Herzen went to prison in 1834 for the crime of possessing and promulgating the ideas of Prosper Enfantin; in Germany the leaders of "Young Germany" and, as a young woman, the German-born governess of Herzen's children, Malwida von Meysenbug, had also been swept up by Saint-Simonian ideas. George Sand's early novels were read not only by other Victorian novelists in England and the United States but also by aristocratic Russian girls in the elegant cloistered school of Smolny, by Polish women, and by German bourgeois girls like Louise Otto (Docs. 48, 78, 129).[8]

[6]See Thibert 1926, and the more recent contributions of S. J. Moon 1976a, 1976b, 1977, 1978a, 1978b; and Moses 1978, 1982.

[7]Manuel 1962, p. 135.

[8]For the Saint-Simonians' influence in Germany, see Butler 1926. For Herzen's experience, see Raoul Labry, *Alexandre Ivanovic Herzen, 1812-1870; essai sur la formation et le développement de ses idées* (Paris, 1928). For Meysenbug, see *Rebel in Bombazine: Memoirs of Malwida von Meysenbug*, ed. Mildred Adams (New York, 1936). On Sand's wide-ranging influence, see Malia 1961; P. Thompson 1977; and Stites 1978.

Sand's novels eloquently spread the eighteenth-century French argument that marriage for money, without love and without the possibility of divorce, amounted to socially sanctioned prostitution of women. This critique, effectively coupled with the insistence of the Fourierists on women's material independence from men, was developed in the pages of a Swedish novel, *Sara Videbeck* (Doc. 38). Yet a third, widely read French novelist, Honoré de Balzac, who like Sand addressed the problems of women in marriage, answered his colleague by portraying a woman who deployed a "rational" approach to property-based marriage by creating her own sort of independence within its confines. Balzac portrayed her strategy as taking control of her less-than-authoritarian husband and effectively negotiating her own terms for personal happiness.[9] As this literary examination of women's position unfolded, other critics, here represented by Madeleine Poutret de Mauchamps in France and Caroline Sheridan Norton in England (Docs. 40, 41), advocated legislative intervention to resolve specific grievances women had against their subordinate status in marriage.

By the 1830's the importance of appropriate education for women had been conceded; education for women was the keynote sounded by religious and secular moralists alike. But appropriate schools had to be established. As such schools were founded, the most striking characteristic is the way in which their founders, whose roots were often religious, repossessed the functionalist arguments once advanced by later eighteenth-century secular writers to educate women as mothers of citizens: they reemphasized the significance of women's familial role as mothers of good Christians. But what constituted an appropriate education for women in their separate sphere, beyond the rudimentary level of reading, arithmetic—and religious instruction—favored by Napoleon and Hannah More? Here opinions differed, and the rationalizations of the mother-educator were soon found among advocates not only of primary, but of secondary and even of vocational schooling for girls.[10]

The mother-educator rationale for girls' education was particularly evident in France, where arguments for improvements in women's formal schooling had acquired a thoroughly functionalist tone. This orientation permeates the selections from the Catholic spokesman Joseph de Maistre and the secular moralist Louis Aimé-Martin (Docs. 42, 43), whose works were widely read, in French and in translation, both in England and in the United States. Unlike Maistre, however, Aimé-Martin does acknowledge the importance of a more radical, individualistic counter-argument, which asserted that women should be educated for their own sakes. The formation of the moral woman, considered independently from moral man, needed no further justification. This argument was further elaborated with great exuberance by Auguste Comte (Doc. 63) as an underpinning for separate spheres and by Protestant Anglo-Saxon authors, here

[9] This seems to exemplify the strategy Carl Degler 1980 had in mind when he proposed the term "autonomy in marriage."

[10] For a comparative treatment of girls' education, see Stock 1978.

represented by the Scottish Marion Kirkland Reid (Doc. 44), but also by Margaret Fuller in the United States, to justify women's participation in the public sphere.

Reid's views challenged male authority in a way that few other Europeans or Americans could easily accept. Prevailing opinion acknowledged the far-reaching influence of women as mothers and wives and viewed control of this domestic influence as the key to maintaining formal authority in their societies. Consequently, both champions and secular opponents of organized Christianity confronted each other over control of formal education, which had long been the prerogative of the Church. One celebrated confrontation took place between two well-known writers, the Catholic diplomat Maistre and the anticlerical historian Jules Michelet (Docs. 45, 46); here, as in the arguments of Comte, women were clearly perceived as the prize in a male political struggle. By mid-century even the Virgin Mary would become a pawn in the Catholic Church's effort to maintain authority over women, as will be seen in Part III. However, the same attention to controlling women's influence can be seen to a lesser degree in Protestant countries wherever there was a state church opposed by dissenters, as in the various German states, in Scandinavia, and in England. Even in the United States, where church and state were separate, the educational enterprises of women like Catharine Beecher (Doc. 49) were formulated within an evangelical Protestant framework that insisted on the separation of spheres. Preachers paid heavy tribute to women's influence, while at the same time insisting on their subordination in marriage and opposing their active participation in the abolitionist movement.[11]

A related development in this period was the appearance of arguments, however tentative, for professional education of women—primarily as teachers. These arguments proceeded from the recognition not only of women's influence, but also of the existence of "surplus" middle-class women, especially in England, who were insufficiently wealthy to attract suitors of their own social class and who were untrained to do anything but marry well. The arguments are informed throughout by the acknowledgment that material independence for unmarried women is, in effect, vital to their survival when—as was more and more the case in England during this period of commercial boom and bust—male protection failed, fathers lost their business, brothers and would-be suitors departed for the empire. The eloquence of such hard facts made these arguments for more sustained training for women palatable even to those who believed that, in the best of all possible worlds, women ought to be protected by fathers or by husbands. Professional education for teaching or governessing, of course, offered cultivated unmarried women an opportunity for both self-support and training that could be put to use in a family setting, should the occasion arise; indeed, the trained teacher could easily be—and was—justified as a mere extension of the mother-

---

[11] In the contributions of Welter 1966, Sklar 1973, and A. Douglas 1977, the political implications of separate spheres are not emphasized to the extent we are doing here.

educator's role, as Mary Maurice (Doc. 47) suggested, or of the German-citizen-mother, as Louise Otto wrote at about the same time (Doc. 48).[12]

Dispossessed middle-class daughters were not the only women pressing out the carefully constructed boundaries of the separate spheres. Indeed, during this turbulent time the boundaries of woman's sphere were disputed as heatedly as any territorial limits in the westward expansion of the United States; some contests literally represented border skirmishes between opposing camps. Women could be found on both sides, as was the case in the well-known confrontation between Angelina Grimké and Catharine Beecher over women's participation in the American abolition movement (Docs. 49, 50). Here the conflict centered directly on the location of the line that separated the public from the private sphere and on whether "visible" action was an acceptable mode of political action for women. In the conflicting views of Sarah Stickney Ellis and Marion Kirkland Reid (Docs. 53, 54), the border skirmish erupted into open warfare. Both Beecher and Ellis left the unsettling impression that women should stay out of public affairs so that men might feel superior, and that woman's sphere itself was jeopardized when women intruded on male activities. In contrast, both Grimké and Reid suggested that the qualities of selflessness cultivated in the private sphere, especially those pertaining to motherhood and mothering, could be even more valuable to society if applied to the problems of public life. This was an argument destined for a long life in Western cultural intercourse, as the remainder of this book will demonstrate.

What seems clear enough is that separate spheres, so carefully re-defined in secular terms, were already under siege in the early nineteenth century; why else would so much ink have flowed in their defense? It is not necessary to insist on a "cult of true womanhood" unless the desired end is either unnatural—or in jeopardy. The cult of true womanhood was not assumed (as has previously been thought); it was asserted.[13]

In fact, two conflicting economic developments during this period affected the discussion of women's sphere. The first of these was an enhanced prosperity that lifted many women into the middle-upper classes for the first time; for these women, the possibility arose to elaborate the domestic sphere, to celebrate the "home" and fill it with meaning. As Barbara Welter has made clear, the "cult of domesticity" filled the pages of journals and publications of early nineteenth-century America; there women themselves celebrated the significance and increasing complexity of their work in the domestic sphere, a work from which they could and did derive both value and status.[14] At the same time, these women, and

[12] On the rationalization of mother-educator arguments to justify the training of women as teachers, see Sklar 1973 and Sugg 1978.

[13] For a schematic examination of the geography of separate spheres, see Hume & Offen, "The Adult Woman: Work," in Hellerstein, Hume & Offen 1981. See also Tilly & Scott 1978.

[14] On the elaboration of the cult of domesticity in England, see Branca 1975. For northern France, see B. G. Smith 1981. For the eastern United States, see Welter 1966; Ryan 1975; and, for the later period, Lasch 1977.

the men who joined them in celebrating domesticity, were horrified at a concurrent and conflicting development—the appearance of women in the newly visible industrial labor force, especially in the textile factories that mushroomed in England and were appearing in France, Germany, and the United States. Despite the fact that women had traditionally monopolized textile production when it had been a home industry, their high visibility as unskilled machine tenders seemed ominous. It was widely believed that the absence of these women from the home threatened the family by depriving children of care and supervision and husbands of their comforts; it was similarly believed that their presence outside the home removed them from the protection of male relatives and made them vulnerable, in the workplace and en route to it, to sexual harassment by other men. Finally, it was believed that these women, by tending machines, were displacing men, whose physical strength was rendered irrelevant by machines, from jobs they needed to support their families. These fears—and some characteristic remedies—emerge clearly from the selections in Documents 55-61.

Reluctantly, governments began to intervene to regulate female and child labor. In Europe, advocates of free-trade economics such as Sismondi were converted to state action in order to "protect" women and children. The British parliament took up the question in the early 1840's, prohibiting all underground work by women and children in mines and restricting the length of their workday in factories to ten hours. A similar proposal was brought before the French Chamber of Peers but had not been acted upon before the monarchy was overthrown in early 1848.[15] These were the first attempts by governments to establish differential protection for working women and children; they did so in the interest of maintaining the family and bolstering the economic role of male heads of households as well as protecting the health and welfare of other family members, and with the express purpose of reinforcing the separation of male and female spheres. But no Western government was interested in fostering women's economic independence at the expense of men. Women's arguments asking that the state limit male intrusion into *their* employments, such as selling ribbons in shops, were not acted upon.[16] Here too a double standard was imposed, with drastic repercussions for single, widowed, and deserted women.

[15] On pre-1848 factory legislation pertaining to English and French women, see Le Van Kim 1926 and Pinchbeck 1930. In 1840's Lyons, a proposal to extend the issue of regulatory *livrets* or worker passbooks to women workers outraged members of the city council, who insisted that the only women who should be registered with the police were the prostitutes; in contrast, the workingmen who published a workers' paper there approved. See Strumingher 1974. For English working-class men's opposition to women's employment, see B. Taylor 1979. For the elaboration of workingmen's attitudes toward the changing circumstances of their work, see E. P. Thompson 1963. For France, see Moss 1976 and Sewell 1980.

[16] For examples of these demands, see Constantin Pecqueur, *Economie sociale* (Paris, 1839); documents concerning the New York Ladies' Industrial Association, 1845, reprinted in *The Female Experience: An American Documentary*, ed. Gerda Lerner (Indianapolis, Ind., 1977), pp. 282-84; and Désirée Gay, editorials in *La Voix des femmes* (Paris), Apr.-June 1848.

The discussion of political participation in this period of expanding democracy was permeated by these contradictory attempts to restrict—and to extend—women's sphere of activity and to appeal to their special qualities in the process. The positions staked out by Beecher and Grimké in 1837-38 concerning women's political role were elaborated by the supporters and opponents of the Chartists in England in the 1830's, and by the working men of urban France, who mounted organized campaigns for further extensions of the franchise during the 1840's. Both working-class and middle-class women and men addressed the issue; advocates from both sectors developed solid arguments for women's participation in political life, while their opponents became increasingly entrenched in their categorical resistance. Some English Chartist women (Doc. 64) clearly directed their short-term efforts not toward furthering their own claims but to helping their husbands and fathers obtain the vote, all in the familial interest of the working poor; nevertheless they insisted firmly on their right as women to be interested in political matters. Further, they threatened to bring economic pressure, as women consumers, on the men of the newly enfranchised shopkeeping class, to make their wishes heard.[17] A stronger, more theoretical approach was developed by Chartist leader R. J. Richardson (Doc. 65) who, invoking Christian doctrine on the equality of souls before God, argued for women's full political participation. To strengthen his case he argued both on the basis of natural rights and on the basis of woman's important social role in the family and the special womanly qualities women will bring to politics, serving to temper the political work of men. Finally, Marion Kirkland Reid (Doc. 68), building on the arguments of the Philosophical Radicals (who had categorically denied women individual political rights), demonstrated why women need to elect their own representatives to legislatures to defend female interests. The stage was set for a far-reaching positive political involvement of women in the revolutions of 1848.

[17] On the Chartist women, see D. Thompson 1976.

The Dialogue Reopens on Marriage and Women's Legal Rights

Saint-Simonian and Fourierist Views on the Emancipation of Women

SOURCES

34. Prosper Enfantin, "Extrait de la parole du Père dans la réunion générale de la famille, le 19 Novembre 1831," *Oeuvres de Saint-Simon et d'Enfantin*, XLVII (Paris, 1878), 114-19. Tr. KMO.

35. Charles Fourier, "Les Saint-Simoniens," *Le Phalanstère*, 1st ser., 1, no. 8 (19 July 1832), 66. Tr. KMO.

36. *La Femme Libre* ["Jeanne-Victoire"], "Appel aux femmes," no. 1 (1832), pp. 1-3. English translation originally published in Robert Owen's *The Crisis* (15 June 1833), translated by A[nna] Wheeler. Revised translation by KMO.

A new wave of discussion about women's position burst forth in France in the 1830's, coincident with the resurgence of idealism, social criticism, and reform agitation that characterized the political and intellectual life of that period. The selections that follow exemplify the shift in emphasis from the abstract to the concrete, from women's moral emancipation to their material emancipation, and to a new insistence on group action.

Perhaps the most widely remarked critique of women's position in the first half of the nineteenth century was that of the Saint-Simonians in Paris. The Saint-Simonians had founded a secular religion devoted to realizing the ideas of the visionary social thinker Henri, comte de Saint-Simon. After his death in 1825, their principal spokesman was Barthélemy-Prosper Enfantin (1796-1864), a graduate of the École Polytechnique, who was known to his followers as "Father." The doctrines and activities of the Saint-Simonians were devoted to reordering the social organization of the materialistic, competitive society in which they lived. They hoped to realize an ambitious program for social progress by reconciling and harmonizing the opposing forces of industry and science, intellect and feeling, male and female attributes, leisured and working classes. But it was Enfantin's commitment to the much-misunderstood notion of "free love" (which was interpreted by his opponents as an explicit invitation to sexual promiscuity)—of rehabilitation of the flesh, in opposition to the Christian doctrine of mortification of the flesh—and to an androgynous leadership, which led to government prosecution of the followers in 1832 on charges of "public immorality" and to the sect's subsequent journey to the Near East on a fruitless search for a female Messiah. This selection from Père Enfantin's address to his followers in November 1831, which provoked a schism in the Saint-Simonian sect, sets forth his controversial revelations on the subject of female emancipation.

We have already encountered the startling social critique of Charles Fourier (1772-1837; Doc. 9) in response to Napoleon's treatment of marriage in the French Civil Code. In June 1832, when the Saint-Simonians were in great disarray, the sixty-year-old Fourier and his followers established a newspaper, *Le Phalanstère*, later renamed *La Réforme industrielle*. Here Fourier bitterly criticized the religious focus of the Saint-Simonians, and reminded the public of his own earlier contribution to resolving the woman question through reform of the household. He seems to have been the first thinker to write about the centrality of women's domestic responsibilities to their subordination in the family. He had developed this idea at length in designing his phalansteries—anticapitalist communal societies of the future—particularly in his work on the *Nouveau Monde industriel*, published in 1827 after he had moved to Paris from Lyons.

In response to Enfantin's call, the Saint-Simonian women (who had also been reading Fourier) did venture to speak out. In August 1832 a small group of working-class women, converted to Saint-Simonianism the previous year, founded a newspaper in Paris, *La Femme Libre*. Written by women for a female audience, this paper published thirty-one issues under various titles over the next two years. Like Enfantin, these women adhered to a complementary view of male and female attributes but, adopting the arguments of Fourier to their own ends, they insisted that women could fully exert their beneficent influence on society only when they had achieved economic independence from men. In addressing such questions they raised an issue that still remains current to this day. The selection by "Jeanne-Victoire" has been attributed to Jeanne Deroin (1805-1894; Docs. 70, 77, 84, 85, 87), a working-class woman who was active in the Saint-Simonian group and who later, during the Revolution of 1848, took an even more political role in demanding rights for French women.

---

34. Prosper Enfantin (1831)

Throughout our debates, one question has proved especially troublesome. It continues—and should continue—to occupy our attention: the question of the *emancipation of women*.

I have told you that I was the first to sense and to express the need for this emancipation; I must add that, in fact, I was the only one of the two of us (Bazard and myself) in a position to call women to a new life. This feeling impelled me to declare, at the moment we were going to embark upon founding a new MORAL ORDER, that any man who felt impelled to impose a LAW on woman was not a Saint-Simonian; and that the only position a Saint-Simonian could take with respect to woman was to declare himself incompetent to JUDGE her, inasmuch as she did not feel herself to be sufficiently emancipated to reveal freely everything she felt, everything she desired, everything she wanted for the future.

Thus, it was a matter of provoking the EMANCIPATION OF WOMAN.

The terms in which this challenge was made were broadcast among you in such a disorderly manner that it is essential for me to state them myself as I stand before you today.

THE MAN AND THE WOMAN, this is THE SOCIAL INDIVIDUAL, this is our deepest belief about the relationship of the two sexes; this is the basis for the MORALITY of the future. The *exploitation* of woman by man still exists, and this is why our apostolate is so necessary.

This exploitation, this subordination—contrary to nature as far as the future is concerned—has for its effects *lying* and fraud on the one hand, and *violence* and brutal passions on the other. These are the vices that must be ended.

The man who declares that it is his mission to EMANCIPATE WOMAN has to place himself in such a position that no woman, coming before him, will have to blush in confessing her life to him, in telling him who she really is, what she wants, and what she hopes for. This man must do this in such a way that nothing about his person suggests a symbol of Christian reprobation—and by Christian reprobation I understand the exclusion of woman from the temple, from politics, her subordination with respect to man. See in what condition I must place myself, and furthermore I must present myself to woman as one who rejects the anathema corresponding to the exclusion of woman in Christianity—the anathema against the *flesh*. This is what I have done; in declaring my personal convictions about the future of woman, I have had to express an opinion such that a man who would hear it would not adopt it; for if man had adopted it, if the *law* that I—a man—presented, had already been accepted by men, this *law* made without woman would have been imposed on women, who would thus forever remain in the subordination of slavery. But, just as I had predicted, my *law* finds itself rejected by men, and we await the woman who will, with the man, find the *definitive law* under which man and woman will be united and will live in a *holy equality.* . . .

You know that all our teachings about the past, and the principal means by which we classify historic facts can be reduced to this: humanity first developed *materially*, then *spiritually*. One day it must harmonize the development of the *mind* and of *matter*.

When humanity was under the sway of the law of the *flesh*, of the law of blood, the leaders were *violent men*, their inferiors *slaves*. When the *spirit* decided to resist the *flesh* and vanquish it through Christianity, it employed *lies*, miracles, and Jesuitism. Today the *violence* and the *lying* must cease; for Christian *ecstasy* and pagan *exaltation* have placed the *flesh* and the *spirit* in a state of hostility, and have consequently destined the *flesh* to *violence* and the *spirit* to *lying*. Thus, this war, this struggle, this hostile disposition must give way to *the law of love*, which will give satisfaction to both the flesh and the spirit, to industry and science, to cult and to dogma, to practice and to theory. The entire social problem of the future consists of comprehending how *sensual appetites* and *intellectual appetites* can be directed, ordered, combined, and separated in each epoch of human civilization, according to the progressive needs of humanity. The PRIEST ought then to offer himself to inspire and direct these two distinct natures, heretofore enemies, to direct them in a common love toward a common destiny, by attempting to shorten the distance that separates these two natures, and by opposing with all his might and with all his wisdom, with all his love, the development of a combat, of a *duel*, during their coming together.

Here is the policy, this is the government of the future. It consists of placing the theoretician and the practitioner, the men of the spirit and the men of the flesh, in such a relationship that the duel which has existed between them in the past no longer exists and that the successor to this duel is *harmony*.

You sense, in the terms I have just employed, that the problem is the same as that of the MAN and the WOMAN. Harmony must be reestablished between the man and woman; their relationship up till now has been either *violent* or *false*. The falseness and the violence must disappear.

35. Charles Fourier (1832)

[The Saint-Simonians] flatter women in order to profit from their influence in the intrigues of [their] religious schism. They promise a derisory freedom, for it is impossible to liberate one of the three sexes* in isolation; freedom must be simultaneously extended to men, women, and children. The first step toward freedom that the three sexes can take is to organize great households of seventeen to eighteen hundred persons, a scheme in which household work and child care will employ only a tenth of the women that are now required in our fragmented households. Once freed from this obligatory housework that is congenial only to a small number—certainly to no more than a tenth of the women—the other nine-tenths will be free to pursue lucrative jobs that appeal to them; the tenth occupied by the societal household will also be free, for they will have taken up this type of work because it *appealed* to them. Everyone will be delivered from an extremely tiring subjugation—that of asking periodically for money from a husband who is often in need of it himself. These are the principal servitudes that weigh upon women. They will find themselves free enough when they can earn plenty without having to ask their husbands for anything, or having to provide for children who will also earn money from the age of three or four on. Up to that age they will be raised at the expense of the phalange, by maids and teachers [*mentorines*] who love their work.

The Saint-Simonians have argued about women's emancipation in as thick-headed a manner as politicians concerning the sovereignty of the

---

*Fourier's "third sex" was envisioned (as he proposed originally in the *Théorie des quatre mouvements*) as an androgynous new sex, at once male and female and stronger than males. It would, as he put it, "confound the tyranny of men" by oppressing them and forcing them to protest against tyranny (as women were protesting against the tyranny of men) and to argue "that strength should not be the sole rule of right."—EDS.

people; before giving them the right to govern, they should be given the right to work and to eat well. Similarly, before women are dazzled with utopian visions of freedom, they should be freed from the chains of the [single] family household, chains so heavy that rich women have house-keepers and maids who are charged with such work; they are half-freed by virtue of this expenditure. But for every wealthy household, there are a hundred poor ones. It is misleading to preach liberty to women before they have discovered the *art of association* that would guarantee them first of all industrial independence and easy benefits. As for the other liberties, they can only be established by degrees, when fathers and husbands have voted unanimously for modifications that are recognized as compatible with the progress of wealth and sound morals and with the freedom of husbands themselves, who are certainly not free under "civilization."

36. *La Femme Libre* ["Jeanne-Victoire"] (1832)

At the moment when all peoples are aroused in the name of Liberty and the proletariat calls for its own emancipation, shall we women remain passive spectators of this great moment for social emancipation that is taking place before our eyes?

Is our own condition so happy that we ourselves have no demands to make? Until now woman has been exploited and tyrannized. This tyranny, this exploitation must cease. We are born free, like man, and half the human race cannot, without injustice, be in servitude to the other half.

Let us then understand our rights; let us understand our power. We have the power of attractiveness, the power of charms—an irresistible weapon. We must know how to employ it.

Let us refuse as husbands any man who is not sufficiently generous to consent to share his power; we want no more of this formula, *Woman, submit to your husband*!

We demand equality in marriage. We prefer celibacy to slavery!

We are free and equal to man; a powerful and just man [Enfantin] has so proclaimed, and he is understood by many who follow him.

Honor to these generous men! A halo of glory awaits them in the future. Let us lift our voices, let us claim our rights as citizens in the new temple, which recognizes rights for women equal to those for men.

Universal association is beginning; among nations there will no longer be relationships other than industrial, scientific, and moral; the future will be peaceful. No more war, no more national antipathy, love for all. The reign of harmony and peace will be established upon earth, and the moment has arrived when woman should have her place upon it.

Liberty, equality—that is to say, a free and equal chance to develop our faculties: this is the victory we must win, and we can succeed only if we unite in a single group. Let us no longer form two camps—that of the women of the people and that of privileged women. Let our common interest unite us. To this end, let all jealousy among us disappear. Let us honor merit, let us give precedence to talent, on whichever side it appears.

Women of the privileged class—you who are young, rich, and beautiful, you who think yourselves happy when, in your salons, you breathe the incense of flattery lavishly bestowed by those who surround you; you reign, but your reign is of short duration; it ends with the ball! When you return home you are slaves once again; you find there a master who makes you feel his power, and you forget all the pleasures you have tasted.

Women of every class, you can exercise a powerful action; you are called upon to spread the notion of order and harmony everywhere. Turn to the advantage of society-at-large the irresistible charm of your beauty, the sweetness of your convincing words, which can make man march toward the same objective.

Come inspire the common people with a holy enthusiasm for the immense task that lies at hand.

Come calm the warlike ardor of young men; the elements of grandeur and glory are in their hearts. But they see grandeur and glory only as helmets on their heads and lances in their hand. We will say to them that it is no longer a matter of destroying, but of building anew.

The ladies of Rome awarded wreaths to the warriors; we will weave wreaths of flowers to encircle the heads of the peaceable and moral men who will lead humanity toward a social goal and who will enrich the globe by means of science and industry.

European Novelists Critique Women's Subordination in Marriage

SOURCES

37. George Sand [Amantine-Lucile-Aurore Dupin, baroness Dudevant], *Indiana*, tr. George Burnham Ives (Philadelphia, 1900), pp. 204-8. Originally published in Paris, 1832.

38. Carl Jonas Love Almqvist, *Sara Videbeck*, tr. Adolph Burnett Benson (New York, 1919), pp. 108-9, 111-18. Originally published as *Det Går An* in Stockholm, 1839.

39. Honoré de Balzac, *The Two Young Brides*, with a critical introduction by Henry James (London, 1904), pp. 96-106. Originally published as *Mémoires de deux jeunes mariées* in Paris, 1842.

In the wake of the Saint-Simonian and Fourierist pronouncements, the critique of institutionalized marriage and family arrangements emerged as a significant theme in the works of European novelists, dramatists, and poets. Foremost among this new generation of literary figures who spearheaded the new social romanticism were George Sand and Victor Hugo, and Alfred, Lord Tennyson, in England.

These selections sample the range of concerns and demonstrate how novelists presented their social critique through female characters. The first excerpt is from

George Sand's first successful novel, *Indiana*, which she wrote in the same year that Enfantin was elaborating the Saint-Simonian critique of women's position. In that year George Sand, still the young and rebellious heiress Aurore Dupin, baroness Dudevant (1804-1876), nine years married and the mother of two young children, left her unsympathetic and domineering husband and moved to Paris with the intention of supporting herself as a writer. Her novel *Indiana* highlights the plight of a woman trapped in a loveless and indissoluble marriage; the confrontation scene exudes the emotion and rage of a woman's lived experience. The dialogue reproduced here follows the heroine's return home after a futile attempt to convince her lover to carry her off with him (so that she would not have to leave France with her husband, Colonel Delmare) and her close brush with suicide, from which she was rescued and returned to her husband by her protective cousin Sir Ralph.

The second selection comes from a Swedish novella by Carl Almqvist (1793-1866), a writer, educator, and clergyman. In *Sara Videbeck* he portrayed an independent-minded young woman in quiet revolt against the prevailing Swedish patriarchal social order. This radical novel, which anticipated Chernyshevsky's later treatment of a similar theme in *What is to be done?* (Doc. 100), offers a portrait of a young woman who demands from men not only economic and professional equality, but sexual independence as well. It scandalized Swedish conservatives and ultimately destroyed Almqvist's career in education and the ministry, forcing him to flee to America in 1851 to escape prosecution for debt. The scene reprinted here takes place during a decisive moment in the relationship between Sara, who is managing the family's small glazing business, and her new acquaintance and subsequent traveling companion, Albert, a sergeant in the Swedish army, who is clearly interested in establishing a more permanent relationship.

The third selection, from a novel in the form of letters between two close women friends, reveals the response of Honoré de Balzac (1799-1850) to his friend and colleague, George Sand, on the question of romantic love and woman's role in the social order. Upholding the monarchical principle of political and social authority, and positing the redemptive value of Catholic Christianity for social morality, order, and stability, Balzac supported the claims of the patriarchal family over and against those of its individual members. He envisioned no salvation for women except within this stabilizing framework. Yet, sensitive to women's gifts and complexities, and to their need for self-fulfillment (and in earlier times himself an outspoken critic of women's situation under the Civil Code), he portrayed through the character of Renée de Maucombe (later Madame de l'Estorade) the strategies of a young aristocratic woman intent upon making the most of an arranged marriage by manipulating her husband within the framework established by existing institutions. Balzac here suggested that women could achieve all they desired without seeking economic or legal independence.

---

37. George Sand (1832)

Madame Delmare, when she heard her husband's imprecations, felt stronger than she expected. She preferred this fierce wrath, which reconciled her with herself, to a generous forbearance which would have aroused her remorse. She wiped away the last trace of her tears and summoned what remained of her strength, which she was well content to expend in a day, so heavy a burden had life become to her. Her husband accosted her in a harsh and imperious tone, but suddenly changed his expression and his manner and seemed sorely embarrassed, overmatched by the superiority of her character. He tried to be as cool and dignified as she was; but he could not succeed.

"Will you condescend to inform me, madame," he said, "where you passed the morning and perhaps the night?"

That *perhaps* indicated to Madame Delmare that her absence had not been discovered until late. Her courage increased with that knowledge.

"No, monsieur," she replied, "I do not propose to tell you."

Delmare turned green with anger and amazement.

"Do you really hope to conceal the truth from me?" he said, in a trembling voice.

"I care very little about it," she replied in an icy tone. "I refuse to tell you solely for form's sake. I propose to convince you that you have no right to ask me that question."

"I have no right, ten thousand devils. Who is master here, pray tell, you or I? Which of us wears a petticoat and ought to be running a distaff? Do you propose to take the beard off my chin? It would look well on you, hussy!"

"I know that I am the slave and you the master. The laws of this country make you my master. You can bind my body, tie my hands, govern my acts. You have the right of the stronger, and society confirms you in it; but you cannot command my will, monsieur; God alone can bend it and subdue it. Try to find a law, a dungeon, an instrument of torture that gives you any hold on it! you might as well try to handle the air and grasp space."

"Hold your tongue, you foolish, impertinent creature; your high-flown novelist's phrases weary me."

"You can impose silence on me, but not prevent me from thinking."

"Silly pride! pride of a poor worm! you abuse the compassion I have had for you! But you will soon see that this mighty will can be subdued without too much difficulty."

"I don't advise you to try it; your repose would suffer, and you would gain nothing in dignity."

"Do you think so?" he said, crushing her hand between his thumb and forefinger.

"I do think so," she said, without wincing.

Ralph stepped forward, grasped the colonel's arm in his iron hand and bent it like a reed, saying in a pacific tone:

"I beg that you will not touch a hair of that woman's head."

Delmare longed to fly at him; but he felt that he was in the wrong and he dreaded nothing in the world so much as having to blush for himself. So he simply pushed him away, saying:

"Attend to your own business."

Then he returned to his wife.

"So, madame," he said, holding his arms tightly against his sides to resist the temptation to strike her, "you rebel against me, you refuse to go to Ile Bourbon with me, you desire a separation? Very well! *Mon dieu!* I too—"

"I desire it no longer," she replied. "I did desire it yesterday, it was my will; it is not so this morning. You resorted to violence and locked me in my room; I went out through the window to show you that there is a difference between exerting an absurd control over a woman's actions and reigning over her will. I passed several hours away from your domination; I breathed the air of liberty in order to show you that you are not morally my master, and that I look to no one on earth but myself for orders. As I walked along I reflected that I owed it to my duty and my conscience to return and place myself under your control once more. I did it of my own free will. My cousin *accompanied* me here, he did not *bring me back*. If I had not chosen to come with him, he could not have forced me to do it, as you can imagine. So, monsieur, do not waste your time fighting against my determination; you will never control it, you lost all right to change it as soon as you undertook to assert your right by force. Make your preparations for departure; I am ready to assist you and to accompany you, not because it is your will, but because it is my pleasure. You may condemn me, but I will never obey anyone but myself."

"I am sorry for the derangement of your mind," said the colonel, shrugging his shoulders.

And he went to his room to put his papers in order well satisfied in his heart with Madame Delmare's resolution and anticipating no further obstacles; for he respected her word as much as he despised her ideas.

38. Carl Almqvist (1839)

She raised her head from his breast, where it had rested for a time, meditated a little, and then said: "Since it is true that you are fond of me and I of you, we have that in common. That is a great deal, Albert. It is more than a good many have. But if we set about to have a mass of other, unnecessary things in common, then I will tell you what would happen. If you should take my little house, my means of sustenance, my property and money—insignificant enough in themselves, but of great value to me—why then I cannot deny that I might begin to be cross, because you might not know how to manage such affairs. I imagine that you hardly know yourself whether you do, since you have had no experience in looking after a house and trade. I am not certain; it is possible that my anxiety might be unjustified, and that you could manage all very well; still, the anxiety, Albert—. One thing at least I can tell you, that as soon as you noticed anything of the sort in me, you would become furious. Then I should go off alone by myself and nourish my secret thoughts. One moment I should think that I was doing you wrong; the next moment it might seem as if I were right, after all, in a few things at least. In these struggles and tortures of mind and soul we should waste time which could otherwise be spent profitably and usefully. . . . People should leave alone entanglements that may bring wretchedness; such are avoidable and should be shunned. They are not to be called trials, especially since they generally lead to hell, whither no kind Providence would want to drag those subject to it. But if you don't believe as I do, Albert, you are entirely at liberty, and—"

"At all events," interrupted the sergeant, "you are wrong, Sara, when you say that there is wickedness and unhappiness in all homes."

"In all?" she asked. "No, I have seen one or two where they lived happily, but that is not because they have been read together, which does not help matters in the other cases, but because they agree with all their soul or at least as much as is necessary, and that always helps."

"Read together? What do you mean?"

"Why, that some one has read a blessing over their heads. Dear Albert, sorceries are of no use. In this affair, as in all others, we must realize sometime that we must seek only what is really valuable and not build upon the worthless; for that breeds not only unhappiness but, what is worse, real vice. Because when love is gone it becomes a vice—"

"Sorceries? I like very much the beautiful prayer which is used, for instance, when two—"

Sara looked up with a wonderful expression. "God is my witness," she said in a scarcely audible but very clear voice; "God knows that I love prayers. I pray, Albert, and expect to pray, but I do not use prayers where they avail nothing, for that is sorcery and empty sound, if not something worse—blasphemy. Prayers? Oh, great God! Not the most beautiful of prayers can change black to white or white to black. If two stand beside each other and even then pretend a fondness they do not feel, does prayer convert the lie into truth? Or if they do not stand there and lie just then, but nevertheless promise what they may be utterly unable to keep afterwards, can that be prevented by any prayer read over their heads? . . ."

"Well, the reading does no harm, at least."

"Yes, indeed it does, for when we have once read the marriage ceremony over two persons who can only be a means of destruction and misery to each other, we still claim and insist that they must live together and crush each other henceforth, just on account of that reading, which took place needlessly once. It seems to me very harmful. Likewise, I dare say, it works mischief to use prayers in vain, and in most cases a terrible injury. Oh, my God—and how prayer, which is so holy and good, avails at the right time is something I know well."

"Dear girl, when did you pray last?"

"In Arboga—Albert." She whispered this very softly, and it sounded almost as though a *my* preceded the name Albert; yet the whole expression was too magical to be retained, although for a moment it was too deeply captivating ever to be forgotten. She was silent, but immediately afterward she added: "I repeat it, Albert, if you do not believe as I do you are free to do anything you wish with yourself and your property. Simply tell me, for in that case, I would just as soon have you go tonight or tomorrow morning and not come along to Lidköping, although God knows how much I should like to have your company on that sandy, disagreeable road."

"Merely on the road?"

Their warm glances met. . . .

"Let us then arrange things this way, Sara: each of us shall manage his or her own affairs. I will not let you direct mine, just as you shall not give me control over yours. We shall just have our love in common. But suppose that one of us should ever be in want, so that his own means were not enough to live on?"

"Wouldn't love be willing to help in such a case?" she demanded, continuing, "If you should get into trouble, Albert, wouldn't I give you of my resources as long as I had any and knew that you were no wretched squanderer? And if I should become very poor, it might happen that you—that you would be willing to give me something?"

"Good heavens, how you talk, Sara. When that feeling is mutual, have we not our resources in common already?"

"No, there is a vast difference. If I make you a present of money or anything else, you can do whatever you wish with it. No mischief will arise from that; it becomes yours just as what you had before. If you ask advice of me about the handling of it, I will answer you, and then afterward you may treat the advice as you think best. In that way, despite the gift, you remain free; neither will your affairs be disrupted nor your morals corrupted. Similarly, if you wish to make me a present of anything, you must make it on the same terms, as a pure and unselfish gift of love, for pleasure and service, which I may appropriate and use as I please and need. Such gifts and return gifts are an actual aid to man and not a mutual means of destruction such as the daily tangles that people are constantly getting into with one another."

"Can people never manage a household together, then?"

"Why, they may try. If the housekeeping goes well, they may continue with it, of course, just as you continue with anything else that goes well. On the other hand, if it goes wrong, it is wise to stop, just as you do with anything else that goes wrong. But love between two persons should, first of all, be protected from and undisturbed by dangers of that sort. However well it may turn out, love should never be made to suffer from or depend upon external domestic relations. My belief is that a man and a woman should never live together, because people who are in love provoke, irritate, and finally ruin each other more quickly than those who do not care so much about each other, and therefore regard many things with indifference. But if, after all, they insist upon the unnecessary pleasure of letting two heads rule over earthly affairs that are best managed and remain least involved when they are not joined together but handled by each one separately, according to the best of his ability—then, may they at least be prudent enough to stop before their love passes away, which may easily happen! For though no glass is more beautiful than the heart's fancy, no enamel is more brittle. That I can see."

"Why, it would be better, then, if we not only lived apart, but also refrained from seeing each other too often."

"Well, you expect to travel around a great deal, don't you, Albert?" she said with a glance that was far from pained.

"I must, I cannot avoid it."

"How gladly I shall think of you when you are away! You will have a hard time to keep yourself as handsome as the image of you in my soul when you are absent. But you can return and each time be doubly welcome!"

"But good heavens—"

"In that way love will last. You won't have to see me in all kinds of dull, stupid, and disagreeable—well, in moments when it is entirely unnecessary to see each other. If you, too, should have such moments, because you are a human being, Albert, I shall also be spared seeing you then."

"But great God, Sara, I don't understand—where will this end? May we not forget each other?"

"Those who are in daily contact and feel bored by it forget most quickly, Albert; or, if they do remember each other, it is with pain, just as one remembers a felon."

"Ugh!"

"Their bodies are intimate with their souls apart. As the Scriptures say: 'This people honoreth me with their lips; but their heart is far from me!'"

"You surely are a Dissenter!"

"If there must be a choice, then I prefer intimate souls with bodies apart."

39. Honoré de Balzac (1842)

From Mme de l'Estorade to Mlle de Chaulieu

La Crampade, *February.*

I was obliged to wait a little before writing to you, my dear Louise, but now I know, or I should rather say, I have learned, many things, and for the sake of your future happiness I must make them known to you. The difference between a young girl and a married woman is so great, that the girl is no more capable of conceiving it, than a married woman is capable of becoming a girl again. I preferred marrying Louis de l'Estorade to going back to the convent. That much is quite clear. After I had once guessed that if I did not marry Louis I should have to go back to my convent, I was obliged, in young girl's parlance, "to make up my mind to it." My mind once "made up," I set to work to consider my position, so as to turn it to the best possible account.

To begin with, the seriousness of the undertaking filled me with terror. Marriage is a matter of one's whole life; love is a matter of pleasure. But, then, marriage still endures after pleasure has passed away, and it gives birth to interests far dearer than those of the man and woman it binds together. It may be, then, that the only thing necessary to a happy marriage is that sort of friendship which, for the sake of the sweetness it brings, overlooks many a human imperfection. There was nothing to prevent my feeling affection for Louis de l'Estorade. Once I resolved never to seek in marriage those passionate delights on which we used to dwell so much and with such dangerous enthusiasm, I felt a sense of the sweetest calm within me. "If I cannot have love, why should I not seek for happiness?" said I to myself, "and besides, I am loved, and I will permit myself to be loved. There will be no servitude about my marriage, it will be a perpetual rule. What disadvantage can this state of things present to a woman who aspires to be absolute mistress of herself?"

This important point of being married, and yet not married, was settled in a conversation between Louis and myself, during which the excellence of his character and the goodness of his heart were both revealed to me. I greatly desired, my darling, to prolong that fair season of love and hope which, inasmuch as it involves no active enjoyment, leaves the virginity of the soul untouched. To grant nothing as a duty or in obedience to a law, to be a free agent, to preserve my own free-will—how sweet and noble that would be! A compact of this nature—one quite opposed to that of the law and even that of the sacrament—could only be arrived at between Louis and myself. This difficulty, the first on my horizon, was the only one that delayed the celebration of my marriage. Although from the very outset I had been determined to accept everything rather than go back to the convent, it is in our nature to ask for the greater advantage after we have obtained the least. And you and I, dear creature, are the sort of women who want everything. I kept watching my Louis out of the corner of my eye, saying to myself, Has misfortune made his heart good, or bad? By dint of study I discovered that his love for me amounted to a downright passion. Once I had obtained the status of an idol, when I saw him turn pale and tremble if I even glanced coldly at him, I realized that I might venture on anything. Of course I carried him off, far from the old people, to take long walks, during which I searched out his heart in the most prudent fashion. I made him talk; I made him tell me his ideas, his plans, his thoughts for our future. My questions revealed so much preconceived opinion, and made so direct an onslaught on the weak points of that hateful life *à deux*, that Louis, as he has since told me, was terrified at the thought that any maiden could know so much. As for me, I listened to his answers, the confusion of which proved him one of those people whom terror renders helpless. I ended by perceiving that chance had given me an adversary, whose inferiority was deepened by the fact that he had an inkling of what you so proudly denominate "the greatness of my mind." Broken down by suffering and misfortune, he looked upon himself as something not far from a wreck, and was torn by hideous fears. To begin with, he is thirty-seven and I am seventeen, and he could not survey the twenty years between us without alarm. Then, as you and I have agreed, I am very beautiful, and Louis, who shares our opinion on this subject, could not realize how sorely suffering had robbed him of his youth without a sensation of bitter regret. Finally, he felt that I, as a woman, was much superior to himself as a man. These three patent items of inferiority had undermined his confidence in himself. He feared he might not make me happy, and believed I had accepted him to avoid a worse fate. One evening he said shyly, that but for my dread of the convent I would not have married him.

"That is true," I answered gravely.

My dear friend, he made me feel the first throb of emotion with which a man can inspire us women. My very heart was wrung by the two great tears that rose to his eyes.

"Louis," I went on consolingly, "it rests with you to turn this marriage of convenience into a marriage to which I could give my full consent. What I am going to ask of you demands a much greater sacrifice on your part than the so-called 'servitude of love'—when that is sincere. Can you rise to the level of friendship, as I understand it? A man has only one real friend in his life, and I would be that friend to you. Friendship is the bond between twin souls, one in their strength, and yet independent of each other. Let us be friends and partners, to go through life together. Leave me my absolute independence. I do not forbid you to inspire me with the love you say you feel for me, but I do not desire to be your wife except of my own free-will. Make me desire to give over my free-will to you, and I will sacrifice it to you that instant. You see, I do not forbid you to import passion into our friendship, nor to disturb it with words of love, and I, on my part, will strive to make our affection perfect. Above all things spare me the discomfort the rather peculiar position in which we shall find ourselves might bring upon me in the outer world. I do not choose to appear either capricious or prudish, for I am neither, and I believe you to be so thorough a gentleman that I hereby offer to keep up the outward appearance of married life."

My dear, never did I see a man so delighted as Louis was with this proposal. His eyes began to shine—happiness had dried up all his tears.

"Consider," I said, as I closed the conversation, "that there is nothing so very extraordinary about what I am asking you to do. The condition I propose arises out of my intense desire to possess your esteem. Supposing you were to owe your possession of me merely to the marriage service, would it be a great satisfaction to you, in later days, to reflect that your longings had been crowned by legal or religious formalities, and not by my free-will? Supposing that while I did not love you, and owing simply to that passive obedience the duty of which my much-honoured mother has just impressed upon me, I should bear a child. Do you believe that I should love that child as dearly as one that was born of a mutual desire? Even if it be not indispensable that there should be love like the passion of a pair of lovers between a husband and wife, you will surely admit, sir, that it is indispensable there should be no dislike. Well, we shall soon be placed in a very perilous position. We are to make our home in the country. Should we not consider how unstable all passion is? May not wise folk arm themselves against the misfortunes arising from such changes?"

He was wonderfully taken aback to find me so reasonable and so full of sound reasoning, but he gave me his solemn promise, and thereupon I took his hand and squeezed it affectionately.

We were married at the end of that week. Once I was sure of my freedom, I applied myself with the greatest cheerfulness to the dull details of all the various ceremonies. I was able to be my own natural self, and I may, indeed, have been considered what would have been called in the language we used at Blois, "a very knowing little body." Onlookers took a young girl, delighted with the novel and promising position in which she had contrived to place herself, for a notable woman of the world. My dear soul, I had beheld, as in a vision, all the difficulties of my future life, and I was sincerely bent on making this man happy. Now, in the solitude in which we are to live, if the woman does not rule, the marriage state must soon become unendurable. The woman in such a case should possess all the charms of the mistress and all the good qualities of the wife. Does not the uncertainty which hangs about enjoyment prolong the illusion and perpetuate those flattering delights to which every human creature clings, and so rightly clings? Conjugal love, as I understand it, drapes the woman in a robe of hope, endues her with sovereign power, inspires her with exhaustless strength and with a vivifying warmth which causes everything about her to blossom. The more completely she is mistress of herself, the more certain she is to bring love and happiness into being. But I have specially insisted that all our private arrangements shall be veiled in the deepest mystery. The man who is subjugated by his wife is deservedly covered with ridicule. A woman's influence must be altogether secret. In our sex, charm and mystery are synonymous in all things. Though I set myself to raise up this crushed nature and bring back the lustre to the good qualities I have discovered in it, I intend it all to seem the spontaneous growth of Louis's character. This is the task, a not ignoble one, I have set before me. The glory of it may well suffice a woman. I am almost proud in my possession of a secret that fills my life, a plan which shall absorb all my efforts, which shall be hidden from every one, save yourself and God.

Now I am nearly happy, and perhaps I should not be altogether so, if I could not tell all I feel to one loving heart. For how can I say it to him? My happiness would wound him, I have been obliged to hide it from him. My dear, he is as delicate in feeling as any woman, like all men who have suffered acutely. For three months we lived just as we had lived before we married. As you will easily believe, I studied numberless little personal questions which have much more to do with love than any one would believe. In spite of my coldness, his heart unfolded as he grew bolder. I saw the expression of his face change and grow younger—the refinement I introduced into the household began to be reflected in his person. Gradually I grew accustomed to him, I made him my second self. By dint of looking at him, I discovered the agreement between his nature and his physiognomy. The "animal we call a husband," as you express it, disappeared from sight. One balmy evening I perceived a lover whose words touched my very heart, and on whose arm I leant with an unspeakable delight. And, last of all—to be as truthful with you as I would be with God, whom no man can deceive—curiosity, stirred, it may be, by the admirable faithfulness with which he kept his oath, rose up within my heart. Horribly ashamed, I fought against myself. Alas! when dignity is the only thing that holds one back, the intellect soon pitches on some compromise. All then was secret, as though we had been lovers, and secret it must remain between us two. When your own marriage comes, you will applaud my discretion. Yet nothing, be sure, was lacking that the most exquisite passion could desire, nor the unexpectedness, which is, in a manner, the glory of that special moment. The mysterious charm for which our imagination longs, the impulse which is our excuse, the half-extorted consent, the ideal delights over which we have dimly dreamt, and which overwhelmed our being before we yield to their reality, every one of these seductions, in all their most enchanting forms, was there.

I will confess to you that in spite of all these glories I have once more stipulated for my freedom, and I will not tell you all my reasons for so doing. You will certainly be the only creature upon whom even this half confidence shall be bestowed. The woman who gives herself to her husband, whether he adores her or not, would, I think, act very foolishly, were she not to conceal her feelings and her personal judgment concerning marriage. The sole delight I have known, and it has been a heavenly joy, comes from the certainty that I have restored life to that poor fellow, before I give life to his children. Louis has recovered his youth, his strength, and his spirits. He is a different man. Like some fairy, I have wiped out the very memory of his misfortunes. I have metamorphosed him; he has become a charming fellow. Now that he is sure I care for him, he displays his mental powers and constantly reveals fresh qualities. To be the constant spring of a man's happiness—when that man knows it, and mingles gratitude with his love—ah, my dear, this certainly develops a force within the soul far surpassing that of the most absorbing passion. This force, impetuous and lasting, uniform yet varied, evolves the family—that splendid work of womanhood which I can realize now in all its fruitful duty. The old father is not stingy any more. He gives everything I ask, unquestioningly. The servants are light-hearted; it seems as though Louis's happiness were reflected over the whole of this household which I rule by love. The old man has brought himself into harmony with all the improvements. He would not let himself be a blot upon my dainty arrangements. To please me, he has assumed the dress, and with the dress, the habits of the present day. We have English horses, we have a brougham, a barouche and a tilbury. Our servants are simply but carefully turned out, and we have the reputation of being spendthrifts. I apply my wits (joking apart) to keeping my house economically and giving the greatest possible amount of enjoyment for the smallest possible expenditure. I have already shown Louis how necessary it is for him to build roads, so as to gain a reputation of a man who takes an interest in the welfare of his neighborhood. I am making him fill up the gaps in his education. I hope soon, by the influence of my family and his mother's, to see him elected to the Conseil Général of his department. I have told him quite frankly that I am ambitious, and that I do not think it at all a bad thing that his father should continue to look after our property and save money, because I want him to apply his whole mind to politics; that if we have children I desire to see them all comfortable and well provided for under Government; that under pain of losing my regard and affection, he must become Deputy for his department at the next election; that my family will back up his candidature, and that we shall then have the pleasure of spending all our winters in Paris. Ah, my angel, the fervour of his obedience showed me how deeply I was loved!

Women Demand Legal Reforms in Marriage

SOURCES

40. M. Poutret de Mauchamps, "Petition au Roi, à Messieurs les Députés des départements, et à MM. les pairs du royaume de France. . ." *Gazette des Femmes*, 1, no. 2 (1 August 1836), 33-38. Tr. KMO.

41. Caroline Sheridan Norton, *The Separation of Mother and Child by the Law of "Custody of Infants," Considered* (London, 1838), pp. 1-3, 8-10, 24-25.

Demands for legal reform in the position of married women joined other demands for reform. In France, reformers addressed themselves to the inequitable situation of married women under the Civil Code and lobbied for the reinstitution of civil divorce, which had been suppressed by the legislature of the Restoration government under the impetus of the Catholic theorist Bonald (Doc. 21) and like-minded supporters. This petition to the king, demanding suppression of the infamous Article 213 of the Civil Code (Doc. 8), appeared in a women's newspaper published by a couple, Frédéric Herbinot and Marie-Madeleine Poutret de Mauchamps, under her name. Combining fashion news with what we would now call "consciousness-raising," the *Gazette des Femmes* persistently invoked the liberal charter of 1830 on behalf of equality for women.

A different sort of demand for change in the laws affecting married women in England came from Caroline Sheridan Norton (1808-1877). The granddaughter of the playwright and politician Richard Brinsley Sheridan, admired for her beauty and her wit, and herself an author, Norton learned about married women's nullity in English law not from Blackstone but from personal experience. Her husband, the son of a peer, beat her, took their three sons away from her while she was still breast-feeding the youngest (one son died without ever seeing her again), confiscated her property, and then—in order to embarrass her publicly—took the prime minister, Lord Melbourne, to court, falsely charging that he had committed adultery with her. To all of this Caroline Norton had no legal recourse whatsoever. All she had was her pen and some influential friends. The pamphlet from which the second selection is taken was circulated among persons of influence; it was soon followed by Norton's *Plain Letter to the Lord Chancellor*, which she published under a male pseudonym and sent to all members of Parliament. Caroline Norton's plea met with success, when in 1839 the Parliament passed an Infants' Custody Act to remedy the situation. The writer Ray Strachey has qualified this act as "a timid and hesitating measure, judged by modern standards, but nevertheless an immense and startling innovation."

---

40. Madeleine Poutret de Mauchamps (1836)

PETITION

To the King, to the Deputies from the Departments,
and to the Peers of the Realm of France,

To obtain the entire and complete suppression of Article 213 of the Civil Code . . . entitled *Of the respective rights and duties of spouses*, and thus conceived:—A husband owes protection to his wife, a wife obedience to her husband. . . .

Article 1 of the Charter of 1830 states: The French [*Les Français*] (which signifies French men and French women) are equal before the law, whatever their title and their rank.

Before demanding the frank and honest execution of this article of the charter, the spirit, letter, and the legal and social consequences of this article must be well understood.

For, what do these words, *before the law*, mean?

Do not the words *the law* mean *the laws*? Is it not a generic term signifying that French men and French women are equal before the laws, that is to say, that these laws must be binding not only on all French men and women, but further that the obligations, duties, advantages, and prohibitions as well as the authorizations contained in these laws ought to be applicable equally to French women and men, in such a way that both enjoy the same rewards and are held to the same duties. In other words, the laws, ordinances, and regulations that follow from Article 1 of the Charter should be equal, in this sense: that men cannot enjoy any right that women do not enjoy equally, and that women are not held accountable for any duty that men are not similarly obliged to honor.

Such is, such ought to be, in our view, *equality before the law*. . . .

Now I will offer several commentaries on the subject of the petition I have addressed to you.

Marriage is one of the ameliorations and conditions of the social and civilized state. In the wild or uncivilized state, woman and man are two animals whose bodily strength is unequal, from which it results that the man, being stronger than the woman, subjects her to his will just as he constrains horses and other animals. The intellectual level being nearly zero in the savage state, woman is nothing more than a domestic animal that man uses and abuses according to his whim, having not the right but the power of coercion over her, and even the power of life and death.

But in the social and civilized state, brute force has been reduced to its real value, and industry and mechanics work incessantly to replace the bodily strength of man by that of steam engines or others. Intelligence, the result of instruction, appears in all its splendor and utility; and as this intelligence, which comes from the intellectual faculties, is equal in woman and in man, the laws and institutions based on intelligence ought to accord to woman the same rights as are given to man. In fact, with respect to marriage, an institution unknown to savage peoples, but which in our civilized nation is one of the first requirements of society, marriage is positively considered as an association where the rights and duties are mutual. And for proof of this equality between spouses, suffice it to read Art. 212—of the Civil Code.—This article is thus conceived: "The spouses owe each other mutually fidelity, support, and assistance."

And note well, gentlemen, this article says everything. The word *mutually* is the truest expression of the equality of rights and duties of spouses. For if this mutuality no longer exists, if one or the other withdraws, then at that moment the association is flawed and the marriage is dissolved in fact. And just as in a commercial association: if one or the other of the associates, instead of depositing the society's receipts in the common account, keeps some of the money for his own profit to the detriment of his associate, the commercial society would be destroyed; the same would happen if *fidelity* is no longer mutual, if *support* and *assistance* are no longer mutual, at that point the marriage is broken. There is no longer a reciprocal obligation to fulfill duties, because the duties would all be supported by one or the other alone, whereas the law states that they be *mutual* for both.

Thus we believe the drafting of art. 212 is excellent, and this article summarizes and contains all by itself all the duties of the spouse; nothing more, nothing less.

But if, in fact, this article 212 is the most just and complete conjugal contract, how does one explain, how should one understand, article 213. . . ?

In the former it states: The spouses *owe each other mutually*. And in the latter it states: The wife *owes obedience*. . . .

Gentlemen, you must acknowledge that these two articles are incompatible, and article 213 is *antipathetic* to the Charter of 1830.

It is here that equality before the law should be applied with complete equity. The woman owes no more obedience to her husband than the husband owes to his wife. . . .

Inasmuch as the elimination of article 213 is a question of good faith, I do not think it useful to cite the authors, more or less famous, who have written on this difficult problem. Your natural insight and your good sense will certainly be more help to me than all the old science of legislators who were certainly respectable in the time they lived, but who have no point of contact, no sympathy with the ideas and needs of our culture, our social organization, our constitutional charter, and our present legislation.

In the hope that you will accord your affirmative vote to my just demands and that you will send my petition on to the ministers of justice and interior so they can take action by presenting you as promptly as possible with the reforms and improvements absolutely necessary to the Civil, Commercial, Penal, Procedural, and Criminal Instruction Codes,

I present you, gentlemen, with the expression of my most distinguished greetings. . . .

M. Poutret de Mauchamps

41. Caroline Norton (1838)

The law which regulates the Custody of Infant Children, being now under the consideration of the legislature, it is very desirable that the attention of the public and of Members of Parliament in particular, should be drawn towards a subject, upon which so much misconception and ignorance prevails.

It is a common error to suppose that every mother has a *right* to the custody of her child till it attain the age of seven years. By a curious anomaly in law, the mother of a *bastard child* HAS *this right*, while the mothers of legitimate children are excluded from it,—the law as regards children born in wedlock being as follows.

The custody of legitimate children, is held to be the right of the Father *from the hour of their birth:* to the utter exclusion of the Mother, whose separate claim has no legal existence, and is not recognised by the Courts. No circumstance can modify or alter this admitted right of the father: though he should be living in open adultery, and his wife be legally separated from him on that account. He is responsible to no one for his motives, should he desire entirely to exclude his wife from all access to her children; nor is he accountable for the disposal of the child; that is, the law supposing the *nominal* custody to be with him, does not oblige him to make it a *bona fide* custody by a residence of the child under his roof and protection, but holds 'the custody of the father' to mean, in an extended sense, the custody of whatever stranger the father may think fit to appoint in lieu of the mother; and those strangers can exert his delegated authority to exclude the mother from access to her children; without any legal remedy being possible on her part, by appeal to the Courts or otherwise; the construction of the law being, that they have *no power to interfere* with the exercise of the father's right.

Should it so happen that at the time of separation, or afterwards, the children being in the mother's possession, she should refuse to deliver them up, the father's right extends to forcibly seizing them; *even should they be infants at the breast.* Or he may obtain, on application, a writ of habeas corpus, ordering the mother to produce the child in Court, to be delivered over to him; and should this order be disobeyed, he can cause a writ of attachment to issue against her; or, in other words, cause her to be imprisoned for contempt of court. The fact of the wife being innocent and the husband guilty, or of the separation being an unwilling one on her part, does not alter his claim: the law has no power to order that a woman shall even have occasional access to her children, though she could prove that she was driven by violence from her husband's house, and that he had deserted her for a mistress. The Father's right is absolute and paramount, and can no more be affected by the mother's claim, than if she had no existence.

The result of this tacit admission by law, of an individual right so entirely despotic, (the assertion of which *can* only be called for in seasons of family disunion and bitterness of feeling), is exactly what might have been expected. Instances have arisen from time to time in which the power has been grossly and savagely abused. It has been made the means of persecution, and the instrument of vengeance: it has been exerted to compel a disposition of property in favour of the husband, where the wife has possessed an independent fortune; it has been put into force by an adulterous husband to terrify his wife from proceeding in the Ecclesiastical Courts against him: in short, there is scarcely any degree of cruelty which has not been practised under colour of its protection. . . .

On what principle of *natural* justice the law is founded, which in cases of separation between husband and wife, throws the whole power of limiting the access of a woman to her children into the hands of her husband, it is difficult to say. A man should hardly be allowed to be accuser and judge in his own case, and yet such is the anomalous position created by the law. Whatever be the *cause* of separation, whether incompatibility of temper, or imputation of graver offence, the feelings on both sides must be very bitter, bitter almost to desperation, before the parties can consent to publish their quarrel to the world, and break through ties voluntarily formed, and cemented by holy vows. The husband who contemplates such a separation, is certainly angry, probably mortified, and in nine cases out of ten, *eager to avenge* his real or fancied injuries. To this angry man, to this mortified man, the law awards that which can rarely be entrusted to any human being, even in the calmest hours of life, namely, DESPOTIC POWER! Surely it requires no eloquence to move, no argument to convince, in a case like this. There stands the one man in the world who is least likely to be *able* to judge his wife with the smallest particle of fairness or temperate feeling, and HE is the man to whom the *real* judges of the land yield their right of protection, their intelligence of decision,—their merciful consideration of individual wrong,—and their consistency in securing, under all circumstances, PUBLIC JUSTICE. To *him* it is permitted to make the power of their Courts a MOCKERY, and (in homely but expressive terms) to "*take the law into his own hands.*"

Doubtless the claim of a father is sacred and indisputable, but when the mother's claim clashes with it, surely *something* should be accorded to her. There are other laws besides those made by men—what says the holier law, the law of nature?

Does *nature* say that the woman, who endures for nearly a year a tedious suffering, ending in an agony which perils her life, has no claim to the children she bears? Does *nature* say that the woman, who after that year of suffering is over, provides from her own bosom the nourishment which preserves the very existence of her offspring, has no claim to the children she has nursed? Does *nature* say that the woman who has watched patiently through the very many feverish and anxious nights which occur even in the healthiest infancy, has no claim to the children she has tended? And that the whole and sole claim rests with him, who has slept while she watched; whose knowledge of her sufferings is confined to the intelligence that he is a father; and whose love is *at best* but a reflected shadow of that which fills her heart? No! the voice of nature cries out against the inhuman cruelty of such a separation. . . .

Surely in this country, where hatred of all oppression is made a national boast, where if a master were to strike his footboy, an action would lie for assault and damages—where even offensive and violent language subjects a man to a penalty; in this country, and at this time, when all liberal opinions are encouraged and fostered, it is a strange and crying shame, that the only despotic right an Englishman possesses is to wrong the mother of his children! That compelled as he is by the equal and glorious laws of his nation, to govern even the *words in which his anger is expressed* to his fellow men and subjects, he may act what cruelty he pleases by his own fire-side, and he who dares not in the open street lay a finger on the meanest man there, may stand on his own hearth and tear from the very breast of the nursing mother, the little unconscious infant whose lips were drawing from her bosom the nourishment of life!

Is this the vaunted justice—the vaunted mercy of the English code? Shall it be said that there is in England a legal protection for *every* right and *every* claim, natural and artificial, except ONE; and *that* ONE is the tie between mother and child! Over *that* there is no protection; in support of *that* the Courts "have no *power* to interfere"; in making laws for the human race, the mothers of the human race were forgotten! They were *forgotten*; that is the word. There is no positive enactment that for any crime she can commit against the law, a woman's infant children shall be torn from her; but there is a negative rule, that if they *are*, by the father, taken from her, the law cannot compel restitution; nor even allow access! . . .

CHAPTER 5

Perspectives on Education, Influence, and Control of Women

European Views on Girls' Education and Women's Influence

42. Joseph-Marie, comte de Maistre, *Les Soirées de Saint-Petersbourg; ou entretiens sur le gouvernement temporel de la providence* (Paris, 1960), pp. 93-94. Originally published in Paris, 1821. Tr. KMO.

43. Louis Aimé-Martin, *The Education of Mothers; or, The Civilization of Mankind by Women*, tr. Edwin Lee (Philadelphia, 1843), pp. 47, 67-69. Originally published as *De l'Éducation des mères de famille, ou de la civilisation du genre humain par les femmes*, Paris, 1834.

44. Marion Kirkland Reid (Mrs. Hugo Reid), *Woman: Her Education and Influence* (New York, 1857), pp. 156-57. Originally published as *A Plea for Woman*, Edinburgh, 1843.

That the education of women should be improved was a point conceded by nearly everyone during the early nineteenth century. But the rationales for female education differed markedly, depending on views of the social function of education. Should women be educated for others or for themselves? This was the key question in virtually every debate over the establishment of schools for nineteenth-century European girls.

In these selections two men and a woman speak to this issue from widely different perspectives. Joseph-Marie, comte de Maistre (1753-1821), best known as the voice of the Catholic counter-revolution, was a Savoyard diplomat who, like Bonald (Doc. 21), lived through the French Revolution. He spent many years in Russia as Savoy's ambassador to Tsar Alexander I. His perspective on female education was wholly traditional, in the sense that he did not encourage intellectual cultivation of girls, believing that women's minds were weaker than those of men. Yet he laid great emphasis on the moral force of the Christian woman and, as he makes clear in this passage, he thought that women should be encouraged to assume the role of mother-educators for their children, especially for their sons. Maistre's emphasis was transmuted into a secular, spiritualist vein by Louis Aimé-Martin (1786-1847), a professor of history at the École Polytechnique in Paris. Aimé-Martin's prescriptive work on the education of mothers was widely

read and commented upon, not only in France, where it went through nine editions in the next thirty years, but in England and the United States as well. His
treatise was the result of his reflections on the current state of affairs in France,
nourished by his own editing of the works of the Catholic educational writers
Fénelon, Bernardin de Saint-Pierre, and the playwright Racine. Aimé-Martin considered his own book as a supplement to the program laid out by Rousseau
(Doc. 10), whom he criticized for stopping short of considering the moral education of children. He defended a sharp sexual division of labor, underscoring the
differences between men and women and idealizing women as a sort of household
deity in a manner that foreshadows Michelet (Docs. 46, 97).

A sharp contrast to both Maistre and Aimé-Martin is offered by a young, spirited Scottish woman, Marion Kirkland Reid (dates unknown). The daughter of a
Glasgow merchant, Marion Kirkland married the prominent educator and writer
Hugo Reid in 1839. In 1840, with her husband, she attended the World Anti-
Slavery Convention in London where she met a number of American abolitionist
women. Sensitized to the woman question, she published her *Plea for Woman* in
1843; in the preface she stated boldly that "the immediately exciting cause of
setting to write was the scornful sneers . . . of those who write the popular books
about woman, when they condescend to notice such opinions as mine" (p. 32).
Reid's book was reprinted in Great Britain and the United States. In this selection,
she acknowledges the importance of the mother-educator's role but insists that
such a role should in no way provide the primary reason for offering women a
sound education.

---

42. Joseph de Maistre (1821)

[From a discussion between the Old Count, the young Cavalier, and the
Senator. The old Count is speaking.]

Before giving you my opinion, Monsieur le Chevalier, please permit me
to congratulate you on having read Louis Racine before Voltaire. His
muse, the heiress . . . of another more illustrious muse, should be dear to
all teachers; for she is a family muse, who has sung only of reason and
virtue. If the voice of this poet is not striking, it is at least sweet and always to the point. His *Sacred Poetry* is full of thoughts, feelings, and unc-
tion. Rousseau has precedence in society and in the academies: but in the
Church I would stand up for Racine. I congratulated you for having begun with him, and I congratulate you again for having learned his work
while sitting on the lap of your excellent mother, whom I deeply worshipped during her life, and whom today I am sometimes tempted to invoke. It doubtless belongs to our sex to form geometricians, tacticians,
chemists, etc.; but what one calls *man*, that is to say *moral* man, is
formed when he is perhaps ten years old, and if he has not been formed at
his mother's knee, it will always be a great misfortune. Nothing can replace that education. If the mother has made it her special duty to impress the divine mark on the forehead of her son, one can be almost certain that the hand of vice will never erase it. The young man may wander
from the right path, no doubt, but he will follow, if you will permit the

expression, a *courbe rentrante* [self-correcting curve] that will bring him back to the starting point.

43. Louis Aimé-Martin (1834)

... The influence of women is extended over the whole of our lives; a mistress, a wife, a mother—three magic words which comprise the sum of human felicity. It is the reign of beauty, of love, and of reason; it is always a reign. A man consults with his wife, he obeys his mother, he obeys her long after she has ceased to live, and the ideas which he has derived from her, become principles which are frequently more powerful than his passions.

On the maternal bosom the mind of nations reposes; their manners, prejudices, and virtues—in a word, the civilization of the human race all depend upon maternal influence.

The reality of the power is admitted, but the objection is stated, that it is only exercised in the family circle, as if the aggregate of families did not constitute a nation! Do we not perceive that the thoughts which occupy the woman at home, are carried into public assemblies by the man? It is there that he realizes by strength, that with which he was inspired by caresses, or which was insinuated by submission. You desire to restrict women to the mere management of their houses—you would only instruct them for that purpose; but you do not reflect that it is from the house of each citizen that the errors and the prejudices which prevail in the world emanate. . . .

MARRIAGE is accused of all the evils which I have sketched—an unjust accusation; marriage is good; it is our methods of education which are bad. Whatever, therefore, would amend these methods would render the state of marriage more happy. What is required? only a very simple thing, but which has not yet been tried; viz. to accustom us from our childhood to all the thoughts and sentiments which are to fill up our lives. I would wish above all to fix the attention of young girls on the choice of their husbands; educate them for this choice: impress deeply in their souls the characters of true love, in order that they may not be deceived by whatever has only its appearance.

Are they not made for loving? Should not this happiness extend itself throughout their whole life? Is it not at the same time their supremacy, their power, and their destiny? And yet the old conventual prejudices which abhor love still subsist in families. Mothers forget, in the presence of their children, the perils with which this narrow education surrounds them, the illusions to which their ignorance gives birth, and the weaknesses which follow these illusions. To open the soul of young girls to true love is to arm them against the corrupting passions which usurp its name; and here the advantage is twofold, for by exalting the loving faculties of the soul, you in some measure paralyse the tumultuous passions of the senses.

Examine the first choice of a young girl. Amongst all the qualities which please her in a lover, there is perhaps not one which would be suitable in a husband; and, in fact, she frequently sees little else of him she loves than the beauty of his form, or perhaps the elegance of his dress. Is not this, then, the most complete condemnation of our systems of education? From an apprehension of too strongly affecting the heart, we conceal from women all that is worthy of love; we allow the sense of the beautiful which exists in them to be lost among futilities; the outside pleases them; what is within is unknown. When, therefore, after having been united for six months, they look for the delightful young man whose presence charmed them, they are often very much surprised to find in his place only an impertinent fellow or a fool. Yet this is what is commonly termed in the world a marriage of inclination.

It is true, that in the present state of our manners, young girls are seldom called upon to make their choice; their imagination is occupied, not with the husband, but with marriage. Whence it results that most girls have marriage for their object, without thinking much about the husband. On their part, the parents seek to match the fortunes; their aim, they say, is to secure the futurity of their children, and, absorbed with this idea, they treat of marriage as of an affair of commerce—as of a thing which gives a position in the world—forgetting that it is likewise a thing which causes happiness or unhappiness. Thus our foolish wisdom has succeeded in detaching love from marriage: we have made a bargain by which girls purchase the power of regulating the expenses of their household, of going out alone, and of seeking in the circle around them that half of their soul, that ideal being which youth dreams of, and will possess.

For, how much soever our educations may succeed in suppressing our inclinations, they cannot destroy them; man and woman are the same being, whom nature unconquerably tends to unite by love.

The actual system is then but a deception; it removes the danger from the paternal roof, to transport it to that of the husband. Singular education! the chief aim of which is to throw upon another the heavy load of our want of foresight.

Thus, in the present state of matters, young girls are unable to make a proper choice for want of experience, and the choice of parents is almost always bad for want of the recollection of what is required in youth. We are placed between two evils, without any chance of good.

In order to extricate ourselves from such a deplorable position, there is but one means, which consists of giving at the same time to girls more freedom and more enlightenment. I would imprint in their souls an ideal model of all human perfections, and teach them to subject their inclinations to the guidance of this model. While destroying their state of half-slavery, I would accustom them to rely upon their own powers, which is of more importance as regards the stability of their virtues than is generally supposed; by developing in them the innate sense of moral beauty, I would accustom them to seek for it every where, and to prefer it before all. Love need then, no longer be feared; this flame, which consumes, would then be no more than the flame which enlightens and vivifies.

44. Marion Kirkland Reid (1843)

We now come to the last great disadvantage under which the women of this country manifestly labour—namely, the want of the means, or at least, the great difficulty of obtaining the means of a good substantial education; occasioned, in a great measure, by public neglect and indifference.

The incalculable greatness of the evil influence which ignorance in its women must bring to bear on any community, and the evident tendency of a race of truly enlightened women to produce in their turn, a more enlightened race of men, are certainly very good public reasons for the discontinuance of this system towards women. But far from being the only reasons—as is often assumed—neither of these is the best or truest argument for doing away with a system so partial or injurious. The intrinsic value of a human soul, and its infinite capability of improvement, are the true reasons for the culture of any human being—woman no less than man. The grand plea for woman sharing with man all the advantages of education, is, that every rational being is worthy of cultivation, for his or her own individual sake. The first object in the education of every mind ought to be its own development. Doubtless, the improvement of the influence exerted upon others, will be a necessary consequence; but it ought never to be spoken of as the first inducement to it. It is too much the custom, even of the most liberal in these matters, to urge the education and enlightenment of women, rather as a means of improving *man*, than as, in itself, an end of intrinsic excellence, which certainly seems to us the first and greatest consideration.

Who Will Control Woman's Influence?

SOURCES

45. Joseph de Maistre, "Liberté civile des hommes," in *Du Pape* (Geneva, 1966; reprint of 1821 ed.), pp. 234-36. Originally published in Paris, 1817. Tr. KMO.

46. Jules Michelet, *Le Prêtre, la femme, et la famille*, in *Oeuvres complètes de J. Michelet*, IX (Paris, 1895), 3-9, 11-12, 26-29, 32. Originally published in Paris, 1845. Tr. KMO.

No one in early nineteenth-century Europe would have hesitated to admit that women were wielding influence. Instead the question had become: what kind of influence would they wield, and how? Thus it was that in this period a struggle began between the male proponents of secular scientism and the post-revolutionary Church for control of women's influence. In the first selection, the widely read Catholic theoretician Joseph de Maistre (Doc. 42) addresses the question of women's influence in a chapter of his work, *Du Pape*, which discusses the civil liberty of mankind. Maistre was deeply pessimistic about the fate of humanity in a secular society. Here he developed the argument that only the Pope, as guardian of the moral authority of Christianity, can ultimately effect the achievement of true freedom by overcoming the naturally servile tendencies of mankind. Woman, Maistre argues, is the key to the Church's acquiring proper redemptive influence over men, and in a Christian context alone has she been able to realize her potential as a moralizing force. Throwing down the gauntlet to Maistre, the famous French historian and secular moralist Jules Michelet (1798-1874) argues in the second selection the case for liberating women and their influence from the control of the Church. A widower in his late forties, in 1845 Michelet published *Le Prêtre, la femme, et la famille*, the first of a series of works read widely throughout Europe, partly history and partly polemics, that dealt with the subject of women. Evoking the vital role of woman as mother (and openly acknowledging the immense symbolic importance of his own mother, who had died when he was very young), Michelet addressed himself to the spiritual divorce that seemed to him to exist in the households of his contemporaries. While condemning the celibacy of the priests and their intrusive presence in the family lives of others, Michelet exhorted "men of progress" to oust the priests by reasserting command over the women in their own households. He sought to establish a secular patriarchy by nurturing women intellectually and making companions of them, in order to recapture them from the "forces of darkness" he perceived in Catholicism. In subsequent years, his concern with the subject of women and the family, and his adoration of female qualities and physical functions became obsessive, as his recently published diaries reveal. Although Michelet addressed his remarks in *Le Prêtre* primarily to men, women also found his doctrines strangely attractive; indeed, it was his treatment of the subject in *Le Prêtre* that won him the admiration of Athénaïs Mialaret, a young French governess in Vienna, and impelled her to return to France to become his second wife, his muse, and his collaborator.

---

45. Joseph de Maistre (1821)

Wherever a religion other than our own prevails, slavery is the order of things, and wherever our religion becomes weak, the nation becomes proportionately less susceptible to general liberty.

We have just seen the social order shaken to its foundations because there was too much liberty in Europe and not enough religion. There will be still more commotions and sound order will not be firmly restored until either slavery or religion is reestablished. . . .

Wherever servitude prevails, there can be no true morality, because of the disorderly rule of man over woman. [Even when she is] mistress of her rights and actions, she is still too weak to oppose the temptations that everywhere surround her. What will it be like when even her willpower cannot defend her? The very idea of resistance will vanish; vice will become a duty, and man, gradually debased by the availability of pleasures, will no longer be able to raise himself above the level of Asian morals.

Mr. Buchanan . . . has very rightly pointed out that *in every country where Christianity does not prevail, one can observe a certain tendency toward the degradation of women.* *

Nothing is more self-evident: it is even possible to assign the reason for this degradation that can be combatted only by a supernatural principle. Wherever our own sex can commandeer vice, there can be neither true morality nor true moral dignity. Woman, who can accomplish anything by working through man's heart, will likewise reciprocate every perversity she receives, and nations will stagnate in this *vicious circle*, from which they cannot possibly extricate themselves by their own endeavors.

By an entirely opposite operation, one that is quite as natural, the most effective way to perfect man is to ennoble and to exalt woman. To this end Christianity alone works tirelessly with infallible success, that is hindered sometimes more, sometimes less, according to the type and number of obstacles that lie in its path. . . .

Woman, more than man, owes her being to Christianity. From it she derives all her dignity. The Christian woman is truly a *supernatural* being because she is raised up and maintained by [this religion] in a state that is not *natural* to her. But by what immense services she repays this type of ennoblement!

Thus the human race is, for the most part, *naturally* servile, and can only be raised from that state by *supernatural* means. With servitude, there is no real morality to speak of; without Christianity, no general liberty; and without the Pope, no true Christianity, that is to say no Christianity that is active, powerful, converting, regenerating, conquering, perfecting.

46. Jules Michelet (1845)

[From the *Avant-propos*, January 1845]

Our subject is the family;

Of the refuge where we would all like to be able to find repose, after so many useless efforts and lost illusions. We return home very weary—but do we find repose?

We must not dissimulate, we must frankly avow just how things are: in the family there is serious disagreement, indeed, the most serious of all.

We can speak to our mothers, our wives, our daughters of those subjects we discuss casually—business, news of the day—but never of things that touch the heart and moral life, eternal things—religion, the soul, God.

---

* *Christian Researches in Asia*, etc., by Claudius Buchanan, D.D., London, 1812, p. 56.

Consider the moment when you would like to gather round with your own family in shared thought, at the evening meal, at the family table; there, in your own home, your very own house, you dare to say a word of these things. Your mother shakes her head; your wife disagrees; your daughter, although not saying a word, clearly disapproves.—They are on one side of the table; you are on the other—and alone.

One might say that in their midst, facing you, sits an invisible man, contradicting everything you say.

How can we be so astonished at this state of the family? Our wives and our daughters are raised, governed *by our enemies.*

Enemies of the modern spirit, of liberty and of the future. It would serve no purpose to cite such and such a preacher, or such and such a sermon. One voice to speak of liberty, fifty thousand to speak against it.—Who do you think is fooled by this crude tactic?

Our enemies, I repeat, in a more direct sense, being naturally envious of marriage and family life. This fact, I recognize, is less their fault than their misfortune. An old dead system that functions mechanically can only produce dead things. However, life speaks in them; they sense all too cruelly that they are deprived of a family and can only console themselves by troubling ours. . . .

So many establishments; so much money; so many pulpits from which to speak out; so many confessionals from which to speak softly; the education of two hundred thousand boys, of six hundred thousand girls; the direction of several million women, this is a large machine. The unity it exhibits today can, it seems, alarm the State. Far from being alarmed, the State, in forbidding association to lay persons, has encouraged it among ecclesiastics. It has allowed them to take the most dangerous initiatives among the poorer classes; meetings of workers, headquarters for apprentices, associations of domestic servants who report to the priests, etc., etc. . . . Yet, strange to say, with all this the clergy is weak. . . .

The mark of the importance of this epoch, I dare say its holiness, is conscientious work, which advances without distraction the common task of humanity and, at its own expense, facilitates the work of the future. Our ancestors dreamed a great deal, argued a great deal. We ourselves are workers, and this is why our furrows have been blessed. The land that the Middle Ages left to us, still full of brambles, has produced, thanks to our efforts, such a bountiful harvest that it already envelops and will soon hide the old inert boundary-marker that thought it could stop the plow.

And it is because we are workers, because we arrive home worn out every evening that we, more than the others, have need of repose for our hearts. Thus it is necessary that this hearth be truly our own hearth, and this table our own table, and that we do not encounter, instead of domestic peace, the old quarrel that has ended both in science and in the world at large, that our wife or our child does not tell us on the pillow a lesson learned from the very words of another man.

Women voluntarily follow the strong. How does it happen then that in this case they have followed the weak? . . .

Modern man, the man of the future, will not surrender woman to the influence of a man of the past. The guidance of the latter . . . produces spiritual marriage, a more effective marriage than any other. He who controls the mind controls all.

Remember well, young man, to marry a woman whose soul is controlled by another is to marry divorce.

This must not continue. Marriage must return to being marriage; in the pursuit of his ideas and progress, the husband must associate himself with his wife more intimately than he has done up to now, and he must assist her if she is weary, he must help her to walk at the same pace. Man is not the innocent victim of what he suffers today; he must also blame himself. In this time of ardent competition and difficult research, and in his daily impatience to advance toward the future, he has left woman behind. He has plunged ahead, and she—she has fallen back. This should no longer happen. Look here, take her by the hand. Do you not hear that your child is crying? You would seek the past and the future by different routes, but the child is here; you will find both together at the cradle of this child!

[*Preface of 1845*]

This book has had an unexpected effect on our adversaries. It has caused them to lose all restraint, all respect for themselves; how should I put it?—all respect for the sanctuary, for what they should be teaching us. Thus, from the pulpit they preach out in church against a living man; they call him by name; they single out the book and its author to the hatred of those who don't know how to read, and who will never read this book.—To hurl these furious preachers against us thus, the leaders of the clergy must feel themselves directly attacked.

We have touched their sensitive spot—Woman! This is the spot where they feel vulnerable. The direction, the government of women, is the vital part of ecclesiastical power, which they will defend to the death. Strike elsewhere, if you will, but not here. Attack the dogma, and in good time you will feel their violence and their cold declamation. But should you decide to touch them in their weak spot, matters become serious, and they no longer are recognizable. . . .

Laymen, whatever your status—magistrates, politicians, writers, solitary thinkers—today we must—more than ever—take up the cause of women. . . .

The day your own family members sense in you the man of the future and of magnanimous will, the family will be won over. Woman will follow you everywhere if she can tell herself, "I am the wife of a strong man." . . .

Man must nourish woman. Both spiritually and materially, he must nourish her who in turn nourishes him with her love, with her milk, and with her blood.

Our adversaries nourish women poorly, and we give them no nourishment at all.

To women of the leisured classes, to those who seem to be so sweetly protected by the family, to the brilliant, to the happy, we give no spiritual nourishment whatsoever.

And to poor isolated women, the hard-working and the forlorn, who attempt to earn their daily bread, we do not help them find material nourishment.

These women, who are or will become mothers, we let them fast (both spiritually and physically) and we are punished, especially by the coming generation, for our negligence in giving them the necessities of life.

Good will is generally not lacking, or so I would like to believe. But time and attention are lacking. We live in a rush; we scarcely live; we follow doggedly the most insignificant objectives and neglect the most important. . . .

Philosophers, physiologists, economists, statesmen, we all know that the excellence of the race, the strength of a people, depends especially on the situation of the woman. She who carries the baby for nine months does a great deal more for him than the father. Strong mothers will produce strong children.

We are all, and will always be eternally indebted to women. They are the mothers—that suffices. One must be miserably and damnably born to make financial speculations on the work of those who are the joy of the present and the destiny of the future. What they do with their hands is very secondary; we are the ones who must work. What do they do? they shape us—this is a superior type of work. To be loved, to give birth, then to give moral birth, to raise man up (this barbarous time does not yet understand this), this is the business of woman.

Schooling and Social Function

SOURCES

47. Mary Atkinson Maurice, *Mothers and Governesses* (London, 1847), pp. 24-25, 145-46, 148-49, 151-53.
48. Louise Otto, "Die Theilnahme der Frauen an den Interessen des Staates," in *Vorwärts! Volks-Taschenbuch für das Jahr 1847* (published in Leipzig by Robert Blum), V, 51ff. Reprinted in *Die deutsche Frauenbewegung*, II, *Quellen: 1843-1889*, ed. Margrit Twellmann (Meisenheim am Glan, 1972), pp. 11-15. Tr. SGB.

Out of two very different traditions—the radical Christian turned conservative in Britain, and the romantic-revolutionary nationalist in Germany—came two uncompromising demands for improved education for middle-class girls. Both are marked by a pronounced emphasis on the importance of girls' education for the good of the national state, therein reflecting the discussion presented above in Part I. In both cases, also, these demands were formulated by women whose par-

ents' financial security had disintegrated and who could therefore understand—
perhaps better than those still in comfortable circumstances—women's need to
achieve economic independence.

The first selection is by Mary Atkinson Maurice (b. 1797), one of seven sisters
of the far better-known British theologian, Christian socialist, and founder of the
Workingmen's College, Frederick Denison Maurice. Raised in the west of England, the Maurice children had grown up in the Unitarian tradition of their minister father, but this was gradually exchanged for various more conservative
Christian commitments. Indeed, it has been argued that Mary Maurice's brother
"saw the hoary institutions of the family, the nation, and the Church as divine."

When their father lost most of his fortune through poor investments, Mary
Maurice and her sister Priscilla turned to schoolteaching, with the learning they
themselves had acquired from a governess and private tutors at home. Mary
opened a girls' school at home, after preparing herself to administer it by studying
at first hand the school of the most distinguished British follower of Pestalozzi,
Dr. Mayo at Cheam. In 1829 she published a book on education entitled *Aids to
Mental Development, or Hints to Parents*, which was pirated by "A Lady of Philadelphia" and republished there in 1834. In 1847 Mary Maurice published the
important *Mothers and Governesses*, excerpted below, in which she advocated an
institutional and truly professional training for young women as teachers and
governesses. This book directly inspired her brother and his colleagues at King's
College and University College, London, to offer to teach future governesses at
the recently founded Governesses' Benevolent Institution. Within a year these activities led to the establishment of the first rigorous private secondary school for
English girls—Queen's College. Sponsored by Queen Victoria herself, the college
was inaugurated in March 1848 by Frederick D. Maurice's address, in which he
echoed many of his elder sister's ideas. Mary Maurice's recommendations for a
rigorous curriculum—including "natural philosophy" or sciences, and organized
physical exercise—were carefully followed in the early years of the college; they
are still among the features proudly referred to by the institution's current staff as
having a long historical tradition.

The second selection is from Louise Otto (1819-1895), novelist, poet, journalist, publisher, and women's rights activist, who became one of the founders and
principal organizers of the German women's movement. The fourth daughter of a
prosperous lawyer's family in Meissen (Saxony), she received an excellent education from tutors in French and German literature and in Latin. But she lost both
parents and her eldest sister by the time she was sixteen. As a young woman of
independent means in the 1840's, Otto became deeply involved with the problems of the working class after a visit to a married sister, then living in a factory
town. In 1845 she had witnessed a confrontation between the army and the citizens of Leipzig that had ended in bloodshed, an incident that confirmed both her
revolutionary romanticism and her compassion for the innocent and under-
privileged. Otto's idealism was grounded in a Christian faith that had been
strengthened by hearing the German Catholic orator, Johannes Ronge (Doc. 80)
preach before thousands in Dresden. She became a close friend of the political
reformer Robert Blum, who published this selection and who subsequently became a leading member of the Frankfurt Parliament during the Revolution of
1848. In this selection, "Women's Participation in the Interests of the State,"
Otto, like Mary Maurice who wrote in England in the same year, pleads for rigorous secondary education for girls of the middle classes.

47. Mary Atkinson Maurice (1847)

. . . Every young person ought to study, with the idea that she will in all probability have to teach what she is now acquiring. The only way to test our real knowledge of any subject, is to ask, Can I impart it to another? Have I so thoroughly made it my own, that I can reproduce it, not in the words in which I have learned it, but remodelled from my own mind? If not, let me go again over the lesson, till I can do so. It is true that numbers of young ladies may say, "But we are not to be governesses: why should we be obliged to learn, as if we were hereafter to support ourselves?" For this reason: that every woman is, or ought to be, a teacher, or at least she should be able to teach. If the casualties of life never force her from her home,—yet has she no sisters, or servants,—or is she not surrounded by the poor, and ignorant? Have these no claims upon her sympathies and care? May she not become a mother? Will she at once resign the charge of her children to other hands,—will she thus give up her best hold on their affections, and never make a part of their instruction her daily occupation? But if she denies herself this privilege, at least she should be able to judge, how far those whom she appoints her substitutes, are capable of fulfilling their office. We may therefore safely assert, that no woman is really able to perform the duties which devolve upon her, be her station what it may, unless she has herself been well educated. . . .

Now, is it not, because there is no regular authorized plan for the education of teachers that so many who are unqualified, presume to enter on the office? Girls generally have no opportunity of obtaining really sound instruction, though some by the exertion of their own energies, and from a real desire of improvement, make the most of their advantages, and determine to master whatever they undertake; but in many of these cases the health has been sacrificed, to the high principle and zeal, which enabled them to form the resolution. How then can these evils be remedied, for this is a question of great moment? The only efficient method seems to be, that of establishing regular training schools, under ecclesiastical superintendence, for the middling classes of society. They should be formed on a religious foundation, and scriptural teaching [should] be the basis of all other instruction. Masters of the first eminence should be engaged, for languages and accomplishments, and every facility should be afforded, for the acquisition of knowledge. Lectures should be given, in which the various branches of natural philosophy, should be illustrated by experiments. The terms of admission to these schools should be so moderate, as to enable those for whose advantage they are designed, to benefit by them, but at the same time so strict an examination as to competency should be made, before the admission of any pupil, and such high testimonials of character required, as would preclude their abuse, or the entrance of any who might not afterwards become valuable governesses. . . .

A clergyman and his wife should, preside over the whole, and on the latter, should devolve the important office, of forming the habits, and manners, of the young students. A spirit of social union and harmony, should be cultivated amongst the inmates; class singing should be universally taught and practised, and carried into the daily worship of the chapels, annexed to these schools. Great attention should be paid to exercise, and every thing connected with the bodily health, and vigour, of the residents.

Education should always be represented to them, as an honourable and dignified calling, next only to the sacred ministry of the Gospel. When such a system is thoroughly carried out, the condition of governesses will be altered—they cannot then any longer be looked down upon, for their education will place them in an advantageous position, and their help will be eagerly sought for. That this is the fact, is already shown, by the working of a school in the Regent's Park, which admits only a small number of the orphaned daughters, of clergymen, and officers. None but governess pupils are allowed to enter, and that after strict examination; every advantage is given by the attendance of the best instructors; and when they leave the establishment, situations are found for them, on good salaries, none being allowed to take less than a stipulated sum. We cannot give a higher proof of the estimate in which this school is held, than by alluding to the fact, that her Majesty has just selected a governess for the royal children, from amongst its inmates.

Great difficulties will no doubt arise, in the prosecution of the proposed plan, and especially on the ground of the risk, involved in its commencement. But this is never considered a sufficient barrier, to any public undertaking which holds out a fair chance of success, and therefore should not be so to one, which would prove so great a national blessing. It might even be commenced in such a manner, as to require very little expenditure. . . .

Is there not a strange inconsistency in our estimate of things, when we see the sedulous care that is taken to limit the exercise of professional duties, to those thoroughly qualified to practise them, and the carelessness that is felt about the education of ladies, to whom is to be committed the instruction and guidance, of the female part of our population, in the upper ranks of society? What would be thought of a neighbourhood, in which there was no medical attendant, who had walked the hospitals, or who had passed through the studies and examinations necessary to qualify a man for prescribing in sickness, or operating in cases of accident or injury? There are distinct professors to attend to the eye, and to the ear of the body, but the eye and the ear of the mind, may be entrusted to any one, who sets up for a teacher, and who needs but slender credentials to entitle her to practise her art.

The Governess Society has suggested the idea of a college in connexion with it. The plan has already been successfully adopted both in Scotland and America, though without restrictions as to the class admitted—and from the former, at least information could be gained as to the best mode of regulating such institutions in England.

These might be the means of raising the tone of education generally, and of leading to the formation of schools for girls, similar to the proprietary schools for boys, which are now become so universal. Let us then, not be daunted, but rather stimulated by the apparent obstacles, which present themselves, to carrying out that which would be really a national benefit. What good work at the onset did not meet with opposition and ridicule? it would be strange indeed, were it otherwise. But let us be convinced that it ought to be done, that there are means for doing it, and that it wants only energy and determination, to set heartily to the work, and we shall soon see female education in England, become the model for that of all other nations.

48. Louise Otto (1847)

In larger cities a number of institutions intended for girls of 13 to 18 years exist for the daughters of those in easy circumstances. But how badly they are organized! The girls learn nothing but French and English, dancing, music-making, drawing and embroidery. These subjects may well belong to female education, but they are of minor importance. Yet in our present mode of education what is minor has become of major importance.

These institutions ought to be in the hands of patriotically oriented women. There is no reason why English or Frenchwomen should not be employed, but they ought not to become constant companions of our young girls. For this we should seek true German women who find their highest calling in educating German maidens. Then we should choose men who are conversant with present-day conditions as teachers, especially for world history and natural sciences. Above all, the minor subjects previously enumerated should also include gymnastics.

The school should become a truly national institution befitting the temper of the time, and one in which German sensibility, sisterly equality and a noble simple manner are paramount.

It would perhaps be advisable—if it were feasible—to open such schools for girls in small towns and in the country, rather than in large expensive cities that offer too many distractions. Young girls will soon enough discover life in the great world, with its intoxication and its immorality. They should be kept from it as long as possible—but should be equipped with firm moral strength, with a sense of piety, with innermost German sensibilities. . . .

It is also essential, desperately essential, to offer women the opportunity to be able to earn their own livelihood if necessary.

Even in the lowest classes the earnings of women who are day laborers or in domestic service contrast markedly and poorly with those of men. . . . In the upper classes women are almost completely barred from helping themselves independently through life.

An embroideress or seamstress can barely earn five *Groschen* a day at present! Girls can seldom learn anything else, since in order to be able to teach foreign languages great skill, seldom achieved, is necessary. Nevertheless the only means by which women can support themselves is instructing in the French language, either by giving private lessons or as a governess, and a large number of them have adopted this course.

How shameful that a young German maiden must go abroad in order to acquire an earning capacity that will serve her in the Fatherland, only to find that genuine foreign women are preferred to herself [as language teachers—EDS.].

How shameful for young German maidens—but even more so for Germany itself which says to its daughters: Make sure that you sell yourselves soon to a husband who can support you decently and for whom in return you will keep house—whatever your heart may counsel. You must comply in order to follow your appointed womanly destiny, not in order to follow your womanly sensibilities.

But enough on this topic!

I blush over this debasement of marriage, over this mockery of all maidenly feeling and of all chaste morality. But whom shall I accuse? Mothers—who teach these attitudes? Daughters—who obediently follow them? No, I accuse Society, which forces both mothers and daughters into this situation.

If girls had an opportunity to gain some qualifications in order to achieve an independent position in life, things would be different. If women were capable of supervising female education (as indicated above) as teachers; or of occupying themselves with commerce—for which women are as suitable as men—it might be possible for German marriage to reestablish itself as a natural right and not to be degraded, as it now is in thousands of instances to a support-institution for the female sex.

German women must become independent; only then will they be capable of doing their duty on behalf of the State in a proper manner. This independence can be promoted only through individual development, because only an independent heart leads to independent action.

Most women remain children throughout their entire lives. First they reside under constant, even hourly, supervision in their parents' house and dare not consider any point of view other than that which prevails in the family. Then they become wives. If they love their husbands, their reorientation from prior attitudes to those of their husbands is easily achieved—whether or not it is a complete reversal; first they judge in the spirit of their parents, now they judge in the spirit of their husbands. First they aped one, now the other. Given such characterlessness, the existence of a woman's political opinion is of no account. Woman must be capable of independent judgment or she does injury to human dignity and to her own womanliness.

Independent action is as difficult for women as independent judgment— since one is a necessary consequence of the other. And yet every woman has the capacity to regulate her thoughts and activities without outside influence in her own noble and freely developed womanliness. In this womanliness she has a sacred defense against everything that could injure true morality and to which she could be vulnerable in a free and independent position.

In fact she will be able to develop her true womanliness more easily and much better when she is not endlessly led about on leading strings*; when she can hear and follow her own voice. . . .

You—German brothers: whose hearts glow warmest for our people, who have recognized that freedom is the supreme blessing, that it cannot infiltrate one place when it is absent in others. I beg you: Fight for the rights of German women, and since you no longer wish to tolerate the unemancipated among yourselves—help women to become spiritually emancipated.

And—you—German sisters, who have awakened to the clear day of the present, in which our people are fighting for their sacred rights, do not forget that the Fatherland has sacred claims on you. Awaken those sisters who are still asleep and educate your girls to become worthy companions of a happy people.

* Leading strings were a device used by adults to teach toddlers to walk.—EDS.

CHAPTER 6

"Woman's Sphere" and Women's Work

American Women Debate Women's Public Rights and Duties

SOURCES

49. Catharine Beecher, *Essay on Slavery and Abolitionism with Reference to the Duty of American Females* (Philadelphia, 1837), pp. 97-105.

50. Angelina Grimké, *Letters to Catharine E. Beecher, in Reply to an Essay on Slavery and Abolitionism, Addressed to A. E. Grimké* (Boston, 1838), letter 12 (2 October 1837), pp. 114-21.

When the young French aristocrat, Alexis de Tocqueville, visited the United States in 1831-32, to learn about democracy in action, he carried home a vivid picture of the social relationship of the sexes. "In no country," he remarked, "has such constant care been taken as in America to trace two clearly distinct lines of action for the two sexes and to make them keep pace one with the other, but in two pathways that are always different." Within only a few years, the apparent equanimity with which Tocqueville thought American women "made it their boast to bend themselves to the yoke" of marriage and retire into the sanctuary of domestic life was threatened by a new political development: the rise of organized opposition to the system of black slavery that made such a mockery of democracy in the Southern states. As women attempted to participate in this campaign, they quickly rediscovered the analogies that could be drawn between the legal status of the slave and that of the married woman, just as Condorcet (Doc. 24) had done in the 1780's.

One of the most articulate abolitionists was Angelina Grimké (1805-1876), the angry daughter of a wealthy South Carolina slave-holding planter and his wife. Following her older sister Sarah, Grimké had left her family as a young woman to join the Quakers in Philadelphia and later to campaign in the North as a public speaker against the iniquities of slavery—an act that earned her an overt condemnation from the consolidated forces of the Congregational clergy. In her 1837 *Appeal to the Christian Women of the Southern States*, she called on women to organize themselves against slavery and to mount petition campaigns to present women's views to state legislatures, a tactic that was already being actively employed in the North.

These selections highlight the subsequent debate between Angelina Grimké and the well-known New England educator Catharine Beecher (1800-1878).

Beecher presents a spirited assault on Grimké's proposal for female political action. In terms reminiscent of Bonald (Doc. 21) she defended the necessity of an explicitly hierarchical organization of political society, where husbands serve as the public representatives of families, and wives place themselves—willingly and dutifully—under male authority. Yet, imbued with a view of the unique nature that gives woman special prerogatives, Beecher urged women to cultivate those particular traits that will enable them to rule supreme in the domestic sphere, and thereby to affect political decisions indirectly. Overt political activity by women such as Angelina Grimké was, in Beecher's estimation, neither appropriate nor desirable. Instead, women should turn their energies toward teaching, a cause dear to Beecher's own heart. In reply, Grimké marshalled her counter-arguments under the banner of New Testament gospel, arguing that the moral equality of the sexes demands the political participation of both sexes in righting the wrongs of society.

---

49. Catharine Beecher (1837)

It has of late become quite fashionable in all benevolent efforts, to shower upon our sex an abundance of compliments, not only for what they have done, but also for what they can do; and so injudicious and so frequent, are these oblations, that while I feel an increasing respect for my countrywomen, that their good sense has not been decoyed by these appeals to their vanity and ambition, I cannot but apprehend that there is some need of inquiry as to the just bounds of female influence, and the times, places, and manner in which it can be appropriately exerted.

It is the grand feature of the Divine economy, that there should be different stations of superiority and subordination, and it is impossible to annihilate this beneficent and immutable law. On its first entrance into life, the child is a dependent on parental love, and of necessity takes a place of subordination and obedience. As he advances in life these new relations of superiority and subordination multiply. The teacher must be the superior in station, the pupil a subordinate. The master of a family the superior, the domestic a subordinate—the ruler a superior, the subject a subordinate. Nor do these relations at all depend upon superiority either in intellectual or moral worth. . . . In this arrangement of the duties of life, Heaven has appointed to one sex the superior, and to the other the subordinate station, and this without any reference to the character or conduct of either. It is therefore as much for the dignity as it is for the interest of females, in all respects to conform to the duties of this relation. And it is as much a duty as it is for the child to fulfil similar relations to parents, or subjects to rulers. But while woman holds a subordinate relation in society to the other sex, it is not because it was designed that her duties or her influence should be any the less important, or all-pervading. But it was designed that the mode of gaining influence and of exercising power should be altogether different and peculiar.

It is Christianity that has given to woman her true place in society. And it is the peculiar trait of Christianity alone that can sustain her therein.

"Peace on earth and good will to men" is the character of all the rights and privileges, the influence, and the power of woman. A man may act on society by the collision of intellect, in public debate; he may urge his measures by a sense of shame, by fear and by personal interest; he may coerce by the combination of public sentiment; he may drive by physical force, and he does not outstep the boundaries of his sphere. But all the power, and all the conquests that are lawful to woman, are those only which appeal to the kindly, generous, peaceful and benevolent principles.

Woman is to win everything by peace and love; by making herself so much respected, esteemed and loved, that to yield to her opinions and to gratify her wishes, will be the free-will offering of the heart. But this is to be all accomplished in the domestic and social circle. There let every woman become so cultivated and refined in intellect, that her taste and judgment will be respected; so benevolent in feeling and action; that her motives will be reverenced;—so unassuming and unambitious, that collision and competition will be banished;—so "gentle and easy to be entreated," as that every heart will repose in her presence; then, the fathers, the husbands, and the sons, will find an influence thrown around them, to which they will yield not only willingly but proudly. A man is never ashamed to own such influences, but feels dignified and ennobled in acknowledging them. But the moment woman begins to feel the promptings of ambition, or the thirst for power, her ægis of defence is gone. All the sacred protection of religion, all the generous promptings of chivalry, all the poetry of romantic gallantry, depend upon woman's retaining her place as dependent and defenceless, and making no claims, and maintaining no right but what are the gifts of honour, rectitude and love.

A woman may seek the aid of co-operation and combination among her own sex, to assist her in her appropriate offices of piety, charity, maternal and domestic duty; but whatever, in any measure, throws a woman into the attitude of a combatant, either for herself or others—whatever binds her in a party conflict—whatever obliges her in any way to exert coercive influences, throws her out of her appropriate sphere. If these general principles are correct, they are entirely opposed to the plan of arraying females in any Abolition movement; because it enlists them in an effort to coerce the South by the public sentiment of the North; because it brings them forward as partisans in a conflict that has been begun and carried forward by measures that are any thing rather than peaceful in their tendencies; because it draws them forth from their appropriate retirement, to expose themselves to the ungoverned violence of mobs, and to sneers and ridicule in public places; because it leads them into the arena of political collision, not as peaceful mediators to hush the opposing elements, but as combatants to cheer up and carry forward the measures of strife.

If it is asked, "May not woman appropriately come forward as a suppliant for a portion of her sex who are bound in cruel bondage?" It is replied, that, the rectitude and propriety of any such measure, depend entirely on its probable results. If petitions from females will operate to exasperate; if they will be deemed obtrusive, indecorous, and unwise, by those to whom they are addressed; if they will increase, rather than diminish the evil which it is wished to remove; if they will be the opening wedge, that will tend eventually to bring females as petitioners and partisans into every political measure that may tend to injure and oppress their sex, in various parts of the nation, and under the various public measures that may hereafter be enforced, then it is neither appropriate nor wise, nor right, for a woman to petition for the relief of oppressed females.

The case of Queen Esther is one often appealed to as a precedent. When a woman is placed in similar circumstances, where death to herself and all her nation is one alternative, and there is nothing worse to fear, but something to hope as the other alternative, then she may safely follow such an example. But when a woman is asked to join an Abolition Society, or to put her name to a petition to congress, for the purpose of contributing her measure of influence to keep up agitation in congress, to promote the excitement of the North against the iniquities of the South, to coerce the South by fear, shame, anger, and a sense of odium to do what she has determined not to do, the case of Queen Esther is not at all to be regarded as a suitable example for imitation.

In this country, petitions to congress, in reference to the official duties of legislators, seem, IN ALL CASES, to fall entirely without the sphere of female duty. Men are the proper persons to make appeals to the rulers whom they appoint, and if their female friends, by arguments and persuasions, can induce them to petition, all the good that can be done by such measures will be secured. But if females cannot influence their nearest friends, to urge forward a public measure in this way, they surely are out of their place, in attempting to do it themselves.

50. Angelina Grimké (1838)

Dear Friend: In my last, I made a sort of running commentary upon thy views of the appropriate sphere of woman, with something like a promise, that in my next, I would give thee my own.

The investigation of the rights of the slave has led me to a better understanding of my own. I have found the Anti-Slavery cause to be the high school of morals in our land—the school in which *human rights* are more fully investigated, and better understood and taught, than in any other. Here a great fundamental principle is uplifted and illuminated, and from this central light, rays innumerable stream all around. Human beings have *rights*, because they are *moral* beings: the rights of *all* men grow out of their moral nature; and as all men have the same moral nature, they have essentially the same rights. These rights may be wrested from the slave, but they cannot be alienated: his title to himself is as perfect *now*, as is that of Lyman Beecher: it is stamped on his moral being, and is, like it, imperishable. Now if rights are founded in the nature of our moral being, then the *mere circumstance of sex* does not give to man higher rights and responsibilities, than to woman. To suppose that it does, would be to deny the self-evident truth, that the 'physical constitution is the mere instrument of the moral nature.' To suppose that it does, would be to break up utterly the relations, of the two natures, and to reverse their functions, exalting the animal nature into a monarch, and humbling the moral into a slave; making the former a proprietor, and the latter its property. When human beings are regarded as *moral* beings, *sex*, instead of being enthroned upon the summit, administering upon rights and responsibilities, sinks into insignificance and nothingness. My doctrine then is, that whatever it is morally right for man to do, it is morally right for woman to do. Our duties originate, not from difference of sex, but from the diversity of our relations in life, the various gifts and talents committed to our care, and the different eras in which we live.

This regulation of duty by the mere circumstance of sex, rather than by the fundamental principle of moral being, has led to all that multifarious train of evils flowing out of the anti-christian doctrine of masculine and feminine virtues. By this doctrine, man has been converted into the warrior, and clothed with sternness, and those other kindred qualities, which in common estimation belong to his character as a *man*; whilst woman has been taught to lean upon an arm of flesh, to sit as a doll arrayed in 'gold, and pearls, and costly array,' to be admired for her personal charms, and caressed and humored like a spoiled child, or converted into a mere drudge to suit the convenience of her lord and master. Thus have all the diversified relations of life been filled with 'confusion and every evil work.' This principle has given to man a charter for the exercise of tyranny and selfishness, pride and arrogance, lust and brutal violence. It has robbed woman of essential rights, the right to think and speak and act on all great moral questions, just as men think and speak and act; the right to share their responsibilities, perils and toils; the right to fulfil the great end of her being, as a moral, intellectual and immortal creature, and of glorifying God in her body and her spirit which are His. Hitherto, instead of being a help meet to man, in the highest, noblest sense of the term, as a companion, a co-worker, an equal; she has been a mere appendage of his being, an instrument of his convenience and pleasure, the pretty toy with which he wiled away his leisure moments, or the pet animal whom he humored into playfulness and submission. Woman, instead of being regarded as the equal of man, has uniformly been looked down upon as his inferior, a mere gift to fill up the measure of his happiness. In 'the poetry of romantic gallantry,' it is true, she has been called 'the last *best* gift of God to man;' but I believe I speak forth the words of truth and soberness when I affirm, that woman never was given to man. She was created, like him, in the image of God, and crowned with glory and honor; created only a little lower than the angels,—not, as is almost universally assumed, a little lower than man; on her brow, as well as on his, was placed the 'diadem of beauty,' and in her hand the sceptre of universal dominion. Gen: i. 27, 28. 'The last *best gift* of God to man!' Where is the scripture warrant for this 'rhetorical flourish, this splendid absurdity?' Let us examine the account of her creation. 'And the rib which the Lord God had taken from man, made he a woman, and brought her unto the man.' Not as a gift—for Adam immediately recognized her *as a part of himself*—('this is now bone of my bone, and flesh of my flesh')—a companion and equal, not one hair's breadth beneath him in the majesty and glory of her moral being; not placed under his authority as a *subject*, but by his side, on the same platform of human rights, under the government of God only. This idea of woman's being 'the last best gift of God to man,' however pretty it may sound to the ears of those who love to discourse upon 'the poetry of romantic gallantry, and the generous promptings of chivalry,' has nevertheless been the means of sinking her from an *end* into a mere *means*—of turning her into an *appendage* to man, instead of recognizing her as *a part of man*—of destroying her individuality, and rights, and responsibilities, and merging her moral being in that of man. Instead of *Jehovah* being *her* king, *her* lawgiver, and *her* judge, she has been taken out of the exalted scale of existence in which He placed her, and subjected to the despotic control of man.

I have often been amused at the vain efforts made to define the rights and responsibilities of immortal beings as *men* and *women*. No one has yet found out just *where* the line of separation between them should be drawn, and for this simple reason, that no one knows just how far below man woman is, whether she be a head shorter in her moral responsibilities, or head and shoulders, or the full length of his noble stature, below him, i.e. under his feet. Confusion, uncertainty, and great inconsistencies, must exist on this point, so long as woman is regarded in the least degree inferior to man; but place her where her Maker placed her, on the same high level of human rights with man, side by side with him, and difficulties vanish, the mountains of perplexity flow down at the presence of this grand equalizing principle. Measure her rights and duties by the unerring standard of *moral being*, not by the false weights and measures of a mere circumstance of her human existence, and then the truth will be self-evident, that whatever it is *morally* right for a man to do, it is *morally* right for a woman to do. I recognize no rights but *human* rights—I know nothing of men's rights and women's rights; for in Christ Jesus, there is neither male nor female. It is my solemn conviction, that, until this principle of equality is recognised and embodied in practice, the church can do nothing effectual for the permanent reformation of the world. Woman was the first transgressor, and the first victim of power. In all heathen nations, she has been the slave of man, and Christian nations have never acknowledged her rights. Nay more, no Christian denomination or Society has ever acknowledged them on the broad basis of humanity. I know that in some denominations, she is permitted to preach the gospel; not from a conviction of her rights, nor upon the ground of her equality as a *human being*, but of her equality in spiritual gifts—for we find that woman, even in these Societies, is allowed no voice in framing the Discipline by which she is to be governed. Now, I believe it is woman's right to have a voice in all the laws and regulations by which she is to be *gov-*

erned, whether in Church or State; and that the present arrangements of society, on these points, are *a violation of human rights, a rank usurpation of power*, a violent seizure and confiscation of what is sacredly and inalienably hers—thus inflicting upon woman outrageous wrongs, working mischief incalculable in the social circle, and in its influence on the world producing only evil, and that continually. *If* Ecclesiastical and Civil governments are ordained of God, *then* I contend that woman has just as much right to sit in solemn counsel in Conventions, Conferences, Associations and General Assemblies, as man—just as much right to sit upon the throne of England, or in the Presidential chair of the United States.

French Social Theorists Insist on Woman's Private Sphere

SOURCES

51. Étienne Cabet, "La Femme dans la société actuelle et dans la communauté," *Douze Lettres d'un communiste à un reformiste sur la communauté* (Paris, 1841), pp. 55-59. Tr. KMO. The editors are grateful to Professor Ralph Giesey, University of Iowa, for transmitting a copy of this document.

52. Pierre-Joseph Proudhon, *Système des contradictions économiques, ou Philosophie de la misère* (1846), in *Oeuvres complètes de P.-J. Proudhon*, new ed., ed. C. Bouglé and H. Moysset, II (Paris, 1923), 196-99. Tr. KMO.

In contrast to Beecher and Grimké (Docs. 49, 50), whose dissent over woman's sphere was rooted in the existing socio-political structure of 1830's America, two French social theorists speculated on what that sphere might be in radically restructured societies in the future. Both were writing in an intellectual climate where Saint-Simonian and Fourierist ideas (Docs. 9, 34-36) were well known and controversial.

Étienne Cabet (1788-1856) was the best-known European advocate of communism during the 1840's, before he and a group of followers left France to found a communal society in Texas. The son of a Dijon cooper, Cabet first became a teacher, then entered the practice of law. In 1820 he migrated to Paris, where he became deeply involved in the secret political societies of the Restoration and took an active part in the revolution of 1830. In 1834 he fled to England, where he supplemented his own radical vision with the ideas of Robert Owen and More's *Utopia*. In 1840, following his return to France, he published a utopian novel, *Voyage en Icarie*. Cabet's vision of society, though secular, is permeated with Judæo-Christian values and is expressed in highly idealized terms; he also appealed to nature and reason to vindicate his vision of social harmony. Though Cabet proposed the collectivization of wealth, he did not postulate any fundamental restructuring of woman's sphere, presenting instead what was merely a more liberalized version of the patriarchal family as the essential social unit, centered on romantic womanhood. In this selection from his widely read *Lettres d'un communiste à un reformiste sur la communauté*, which he addressed to an unnamed female friend, the fifty-year-old Cabet presents his vision of woman, the family, and freedom in the society of the future.

In response to Cabet and other social visionaries of the 1830's and 1840's, Pierre-Joseph Proudhon (1809-1865) drafted a discussion of the connections between property, family, and the situation of women. Proudhon, a self-educated man, was a printer by profession. He had migrated from his home town of Besançon, via Lyons, to Paris, where he quickly entered working-class politics and socialist intellectual discussion. In contrast to Cabet, however, Proudhon never abandoned the peasant/artisan values of his youth. Opposed as he was to the communal holding of property, he argued instead for its broader distribution among the populace and advocated a type of populist capitalism based on owner-producer mutual societies. His writings on women reflect a deep-seated distrust of the female, bordering on misogyny, which recurs throughout his works and which the reader will encounter again in Part IV. When Proudhon published the *Philosophie de la misère*, from which this selection is taken, he was a bachelor in his mid-thirties.

---

51. Étienne Cabet (1841)

Inasmuch as aristocracy, or privilege, or inequality of wealth, or the simultaneous existence of opulence and misery is the *cause* of all of women's misfortunes, the true *remedy* is the destruction of this cause and the establishment of equality or democracy. And this is why I demand so ardently the destruction of the *bastilles*,* whose goal is to prevent every reform, every amelioration, every egalitarian and democratic system.

But democracy and equality can never be realized without the Community.—Thus one must establish the Community in order to assure and guarantee the happiness of women. Let us then examine their situation in the Community!

You know that the Community is the Association or Society organized on the basis of *equality* and *fraternity*, and UNITY in everything, in property, in industry, in education.

You know that the Nation forms but a single Society of citizens, all brothers and all equal in their rights; that the territory forms but a single domain, a single property, exploited in the common interest; that all the industries form but a single industry, directed and exercised in the common interest; that all the citizens are workers; that all receive the same elementary education, and the most perfect education; that machines, in infinite quantities, will render work moderate, of short duration, tolerable, free of danger, fatigue, and disgust; that production will be augmented enough to produce ease for all and to make poverty disappear completely; that every product of earth and industry will be gathered in common and distributed in equal portions to all in such manner that everyone will be equally well nourished, clothed, housed, and so that everyone will be able to marry and raise a family without ever having cares or

---

* An allusion to *La Bastille*, the legendary prison in Paris, which was considered a symbol of oppression and was torn down by the Paris crowd during the early days of the French Revolution.—EDS.

torments, and while enjoying all the fine arts and pleasures that do not trouble others.

The Community will give this happiness to women just as to men, because its fundamental principle is equality of rights and fraternity between man and woman. Moreover, all the favors of the Community will be directed toward women. . . .

One of the first articles of the Constitution of the Community proclaims that the *mass of men* owes gratitude, respect, affection, devotion, protection, care, and homage to the *mass of women*; that everywhere and always the first place and the first share should be for the women; and that, in all their meetings, the representatives of the People should concern themselves before all else with laws and measures that concern women.

Another article proclaims that every man owes gratitude, love, and veneration to his father and mother, and especially to his mother, friendship to his brothers and sisters, and especially to his sisters, love and devotion to his wife; love and protection to his children, and especially to his daughters.

Another proclaims that everyone should conduct himself toward his fellow citizens or his brothers as he would like them to conduct themselves toward him, that everyman owes to women, whether old or young, the same feelings and consideration that he would like to see other men show for his own mother and sister, wife and daughter. *Old women* should be, for everyone, the objects of a kind of *cult*.

All legislation, all acts of the magistrates will state, apply, and enact all these sentiments toward women.

Education will explain them and engrave them in the minds and hearts of young men; *mores* and *customs* will ensure their constant application.

In a word, man in the Community, taking Nature and Reason as his guides, will vest his happiness in woman, will almost make her his idol, and will devote himself unceasingly to enhancing her beauty, perfecting her, and making her happy. You will guess the consequences!

You can imagine all the care one will take of woman, from her birth, during her childhood and adolescence, to develop her health, her grace, and her beauty; to cultivate her intelligence; to enrich her mind; to perfect her heart; to make of her a companion worthy of man and capable of ensuring his happiness.

Her first fifteen or sixteen years will be consecrated to her physical, intellectual, and moral education. Just like man, she will be instructed in the elements of all the sciences and arts, by taking every means of making study as agreeable to her as it is easy. Special care will be taken to make of her a good girl, a good sister, a good wife, a good mother, a good housekeeper, a good *citoyenne*.

All women will work in the workshop and follow the vocation of their choice; but their work will be short and moderate, and everything will be done to render their work, like their studies, agreeable and easy; for them especially every machine will be invented that can lighten their burden.

It is unnecessary to add that the entire Community will spare no effort or consideration when it is a question of women who are pregnant or carrying a babe in arms.

Nor do I need to tell you that the Community allows *Marriage* and *Family*; and I will not even take the time to refute the opinion of certain individuals who, all too obsessed with the inconveniences that are present in the *Marriage* and *Family* of today, see no remedy except in suppressing *Marriage* and *Family*. This opinion, held by a very few, seems to me so erroneous, so false, so imprudent, so contrary to universal feeling, that it is simply crazy, if not perfidiously hostile to the Community.

Marriage and *Family* are not, in themselves, the evil, but their faulty organization, the bad education of the husband and wife, the dowry, the inequality of wealth, etc. etc. To remedy them, it is no more necessary to suppress *Marriage* and the *Family* than to suppress *Society* itself: it suffices to organize them better, by giving the future spouses a better education, by suppressing inequality of wealth and the dowry, by reestablishing divorce, by assuring the welfare of the two spouses and their children, by abolishing celibacy, by instituting equality and fraternity everywhere. When *Society, Marriage*, and the *Family* are well organized, it is evident that *Marriage* and the *Family* will no longer be inconvenient for Society and will offer nothing but advantages for man and woman alike. If some woman today, oppressed, tyrannized by her husband, dreams in her slavery and despair about absolute and perpetual independence of woman by the abolition of *Marriage* and *Family*, the mass of women undoubtedly prefer, like yourself, an institution that gives them a husband, a friend, a protector for their old age as well as for stormy times, and children who will prolong their happiness until they draw their last breaths.

Yes, *Marriage* and *Family* are, for woman, the source of a thousand moral pleasures far superior to other pleasures. Yes, *Marriage* and the *Family* conform more to the dignity, ease, and happiness of woman, than do isolation and independence. Yes, it is woman in particular who should desire the preservation of *Marriage* and *Family*, purged of all their vices.

Thus, in the Community everything combines to perfect *Marriage* and *Family*. Education disposes the young man to become a good spouse and a good father, along with becoming a good citizen, and inspires the girl to fulfill all her duties as a spouse and mother, as well as a good *citoyenne*. Everyone, men and women, will be able to get married, because the Community will assure their subsistence and that of their family, on the sole condition of moderate work. Everyone will perform it in the interest of order and Society; everyone will do it with enthusiasm, because it is the first order of Nature.

No more dowries; in consequence, no more reasons to be concerned, in choosing a husband or wife, with anything other than personal wishes, the qualities of the person, of mind and heart. Moreover, freedom to see each other a good deal before Marriage in order to get acquainted, and perfect freedom on the parents' part. Still again, no more poverty, no more worries; in consequence, all the conditions and guarantees for the happiness of the couple and the children. And if, by chance, their common life does not measure up to the hopes of early days, easy *divorce*. But you can guess that divorce will hardly ever be necessary.

You will also guess, no more disorders, no more troubles in households, no more infidelity, no more adultery, no more scandalous trials, no more poisonings.

No more young women seduced, betrayed, and abandoned. No more debauchery, no more prostitution, no more infanticide. No more intrigues, jealousy, envy. No more reprehensible coquetry, or false gallantry.

Everywhere purity, innocence, candor, sincerity. Ah! I would be so content if I could enumerate all the consequences for the happiness of women and the felicity of men!

Add to this all the enjoyments that Nature and the fine arts can give; for nothing can equal the productive power of the Community—and this Community will work unremittingly for the happiness of women!

Yes, the Community will be the *paradise* of women, whereas today it is hardly that for those women who live in the hell of our present Society.

And think also about the improvement in the human race after several generations! Imagine how much women will be able to be perfected both in their charms and in their beauty!

52. Pierre-Joseph Proudhon (1846)

. . . It is especially in the family that one discovers the profound meaning of property. The family and property march side by side, supporting each other, neither having either meaning or value except through the relationship that binds them.

With property the role of woman begins. The household, that totally ideal thing that some try in vain to render ridiculous, the household is the realm of woman, the monument of the family. Take away the household, take away this hearthstone, the center of attraction for the spouses, and only couples remain; there are families no longer. See the working classes in the large cities falling bit by bit into concubinage and debauchery; this can be attributed to the instability of their domicile, the inanity of the household, and the lack of property! Persons who possess nothing, who hold nothing dear and live from one day to the next, who can be sure of nothing, have no reason to marry; better not to obligate oneself than to obligate oneself for no reason. Thus the working class is dedicated to infamy; in the Middle Ages this was expressed through the *droit de seigneur*, and among the Romans through the prohibition of marriage among the proletariat.

For what is the household with regard to a changing society, if not simultaneously the foundation and the fortress of property? The household is every girl's first dream: those who talk so much of "attraction" and who want to abolish the household* will have to explain this de-

---

* Proudhon is here alluding to Fourier and his followers; see Docs. 9 and 35.—EDS.

pravity of women's sexual instinct. As for me, the more I think about it, the less I can justify the destiny of woman outside the family and the household. Between harlot or housewife (housewife I say, and not servant) I see no halfway point: what is so humiliating about this alternative? In what respect is the woman's role, charged with the conduct of the household and everything that pertains to consumption and to savings, inferior to the man's role, whose own function is to direct the workshop, that is to say, the government of production and exchange.

Man and woman are necessary to one another as the two constituent principles of work; in its indissoluble duality, marriage is the incarnation of economic dualism which, as we know, expresses itself in the general terms of consumption and production. It is in this view that the aptitudes of the sexes have been regulated, work for one, spending for the other; and woe to any union in which one of the parties does not live up to its obligation. The happiness that is promised to spouses will be changed into sorrow and bitterness; may they blame each other!

If only women existed, they would live together like a flock of turtledoves; if there were only men, they would have no reason to rise above monopoly or to renounce speculation; masters and valets alike would be seen sitting at the gambling table or bent under the yoke. But man was created male and female: whence the necessity for household and property. The two sexes must be united: from this mystical union, the most astonishing of all human institutions is born—an incomprehensible miracle—property, the division of the common patrimony into individual sovereignties.

See therefore that for every woman in the economic order, the household is the most desirable of possessions; property, workshop, work for its own sake; see what, with woman, every man desires the most. Love and marriage, work and household, property and *domesticity*—let the reader deign to supplement these—all these terms are equivalent, all these ideas are synonyms for, and create for future founders of the family, a long perspective of happiness, as to the philosopher they reveal an entire system.

On all this the human race is unanimous, except for socialism, which alone, in the wake of its ideas, protests against the unanimity of the human race. Socialism wants to abolish the household because it is too expensive; the family, because it inconveniences the fatherland; property, because it is prejudicial to the State. Socialism wants to change woman's role; from queen, as society has established her, socialism wants to turn her into a priestess of Cotytto*. . . . On the subject of marriage as on the subject of association, socialism has no ideas; and all its criticism boils down to an explicit vow of ignorance, a genre of argumentation that lacks authority or weight.

Is it not evident, in fact, that if the socialists thought it possible, with the aid of any known means, to offer abundance and even luxury to each

---

* One of a number of exotic goddesses worshipped by the populace in mysterious rites in third-century Athens.—EDS.

household, they would not argue against it so? that if they could reconcile civic sentiments with domestic affections, they would not condemn the family? that if they had the secret of rendering wealth not only common—which is nothing—but universal, which is something else altogether, they would allow citizens to live in small clusters as well as in common, and not trouble the public with their internal disputes? According to the socialists, marriage, the family, and property are things that contribute abundantly to happiness; the only criticism they have to make is that THEY DO NOT KNOW how to reconcile these things with the general welfare. Is this, I ask, a serious argument? As if they could judge from their own ignorance the subsequent development of human institutions! as if the legislator's goal was not to realize for everyone—not to abolish—marriage, family, and property!

British Women Disagree on the Boundaries of Woman's Sphere

SOURCES

53. Sarah Stickney Ellis, *The Wives of England* (London, 1843), pp. 70, 72, 76-77, 78-79, 101-2, 102-5.

54. Marion Kirkland Reid [Mrs. Hugo Reid], *Woman: Her Education and Influence* (New York, 1857), pp. 47-49, 54-59. Originally published as *A Plea for Woman*, Edinburgh, 1843.

In the debate about "woman's sphere," women, like men, offered widely differing opinions. An expedient argument for conscious female subordination was developed by Sarah Stickney Ellis (c. 1800-1872), a prolific English moralist and novelist whose works were widely read on both sides of the Atlantic. Ellis, who had been educated by the Quakers and later married the widely traveled preacher and missionary, William Ellis, in 1837, burst into print in 1838 with her advice book, *Women of England*, which was followed during the next five years by *Daughters of England*, *Wives of England* (excerpted here), and *Mothers of England*. In terms reminiscent of Rousseau (Doc. 10) and, more recently, *Total Woman*, Ellis not only counsels middle-class English wives to learn to manage their households well but, like Catharine Beecher (Doc. 49), urges them to cultivate a position subordinate to that of their imperfect—indeed selfish—husbands, the breadwinners. Going beyond Beecher, however, Ellis advises women to humor husbands by indulging them, especially when they return home tired from a hard day's work, to fortify male egos so that husbands truly feel like kings in their own households and thereby become aware of just how much they *need* their devoted wives. In a period when divorce was possible in England only for the very wealthy or the very influential, such advice may have had its practical utility.

In contrast, the Scottish writer Marion Kirkland Reid (Doc. 44), who was well versed in the writings of the liberal Unitarians, rejected the position of authors like Ellis. Reid argued that the boundaries of "woman's sphere" were not at all clear. She further asserted that the possession of civil rights and extensive education by women should enhance the performance of their traditionally assigned domestic duties without causing any deleterious side-effects.

---

53. Sarah Stickney Ellis (1843)

. . . It may be said to be a necessary part of man's nature, and conducive to his support in the position he has to maintain, that he should, in a greater degree than woman, be sufficient unto himself. The nature of his occupations, and the character of his peculiar duties, require this. The contending interests of the community at large, the strife of public affairs, and the competition of business, with the paramount importance of establishing himself as the master of a family, and the head of a household, all require a degree of concentrated effort in favour of self, and a powerful repulsion against others, which woman, happily for her, is seldom or never called upon to maintain. . . .

Those who argue for the perfect equality—the oneness of women in their intellectual nature with men, appear to know little of that higher philosophy, by which both, from the very distinctness of their characters, have been made subservient to the purposes of wisdom and of goodness; and after having observed with deep thought, and profound reverence, the operation of mind on mind, the powerful and instinctive sympathies which rule our very being, and the associated influence of different natures, all working together, yet too separate and distinct to create confusion; to those who have thus regarded the perfect adjustment of the plans of an all-wise Providence, I own it does appear an ignorant and vulgar contest, to strive to establish the equality of that, which would lose not only its utility, but its perfection, by being assimilated with a different nature. . . .

The love of woman appears to have been created solely to minister; that of man, to be ministered unto. It is true, his avocations lead him daily to some labour, or some effort for the maintenance of his family; and he often conscientiously believes that this labour is for his wife. But the probability is, that he would be just as attentive to his business, and as eager about making money, had he no wife at all—witness the number of single men who provide with as great care, and as plentifully, according to their wants, for the maintenance of a house without either wife or child.

As it is the natural characteristic of woman's love in its most refined, as well as its most practical development, to be perpetually doing something for the good or the happiness of the object of her affection, it is but reasonable that man's personal comfort should be studiously attended to; and in this, the complacence and satisfaction which most men evince on finding themselves placed at table before a favourite dish, situated beside a clean hearth, or accommodated with an empty sofa, is of itself a sufficient reward for any sacrifice such indulgence may have cost. In proofs of affection like these, there is something tangible which speaks home to the senses—something which man can understand without an effort; and he will sit down to eat, or compose himself to rest, with more hearty good-will towards the wife who has been thoughtful about these things, than if she had been all day busily employed in writing a treatise on morals for his especial benefit. . . .

It is unquestionably the inalienable right of all men, whether ill or well, rich or poor, wise or foolish, to be treated with deference, and made much of in their own houses. It is true that in the last mentioned case, this duty may be attended with some difficulty in the performance; but as no man becomes a fool, or loses his senses by marriage, the woman who has selected such a companion must abide by the consequences; and even he, whatever may be his degree of folly, is entitled to respect from her, because she has voluntarily placed herself in such a position that she must necessarily be his inferior. . . .

The first thing to be done in the attainment of this high object [i.e., to give men's minds a bias in favor of nobler things] is to use what influence you have so as not to lower or degrade the habitual train of your husband's thoughts; and the next is, to watch every eligible opportunity, and to use every suitable means, of leading him to view his favourite subjects in their broadest and most expansive light; while, at the same time, it is within the region of woman's capabilities, to connect them, by some delicate mode of association, with the general bearing of man's interests in this world upon his interests in eternity.

. . . Indeed that mode of conversation which I have been accustomed to describe as *talking on a large scale*, is, except on very important occasions, most inimical to the natural softness and attractiveness of woman. It is not, in fact, her forte; but belongs to a region of display in which she cannot, or at least ought not, to shine. The excellence of woman as regards her conversation, consists rather of quick, and delicate, and sometimes playful turns of thought, with a lively and subtle apprehension of the bearings, tendencies, and associations of ideas; so that the whole machinery of conversation, if I may be allowed to use such an expression, may be made, by her good management, to turn off from one subject, and play upon another, as if by the direction of some magic influence, which will ever be preserved from detection by the tact of an unobtrusive and sensitive nature.

It is in this manner, and this alone, that women should evince their interest in those great political questions which arise out of the state of the times in which they live. Not that they may be able to attach themselves to a party, still less that they may *make speeches* either in public or in private; but that they may think and converse like rational beings on subjects which occupy the attention of the majority of mankind; and it is, perhaps, on these subjects that we see most strikingly the wide difference betwixt the low views so generally taken, and those which I would so earnestly recommend. If, for instance, a wife would converse with her husband about a candidate for the representation of the place in which they live, she may, if she choose, discuss the merits of the colour which his party wears, and wish it were some other, as being more becoming; she may tell with delight how he bowed especially to her; and she may wish from her heart that the number of votes may be in his favour, because he kissed her child, and called it the prettiest he had ever seen. It is this kind of prattle which may properly be described as *small talk*, and which it is to be feared denotes a littleness of soul. Yet this style of talk may be, and sometimes is, applied by women to all sorts of subjects, not excepting politics, philosophy, and even religion. But, on the other hand, there is an opposite style of conversation which may be used with equal scope of application, on almost all subjects, whether high or low: and it is a truth which the peculiar nature of woman's mind renders her admirably qualified to carry out through ordinary life, that so intimately connected are our thoughts, and feelings, habits, and pursuits, not only with those of other beings of a similar nature, but with a state of existence in which that common nature will be more fully developed, that there is scarcely a fact presented to our knowledge, which has not a connection, either immediate or remote, with some great moral truth; and scarcely a subject brought under our consideration, which may not be ennobled by conducing, in some way or other, to the improvement of our moral being.

It will readily be perceived, however, that this exercise of the powers of conversation, would be utterly unattainable to a woman of ignorant or vulgar mind—that she would alike be incapable of comprehending the desirableness of the object, and the best mode of its accomplishment. And here I would again advert to an expression not unfrequently heard amongst young ladies, that they do not wish to be clever; by which we are left to suppose, by their neglect of their own minds, that they mean either well-informed, or capable of judging rightly. Yet without having paid considerable attention to the improvement and cultivation of their intellectual powers, how will it be possible for them to raise the general tone of thought and conversation at their own fireside?

54. Marion Kirkland Reid (1843)

Woman's sphere is a phrase which has been generally used to denote the various household duties usually performed by her; but this is employing the phrase in a very limited sense, and one that requires explanation. Strictly speaking, a person's sphere comprises the whole range of his duties; but taken in this limited sense, woman's sphere does not do this: for she has very many duties in common with man, besides those household requirements peculiar to her as a woman. The meaning usually attached to the phrase "duties of woman's sphere," would be much better expressed, were we to say, duties *peculiar* to woman's sphere. However, the phrase being an established one, we shall use it in its usual limited sense, having thus explained.

There is at present, we believe, almost every variety of sentiment on

this subject, from the narrowest and most bigoted to the most extended
and liberal; but we think that the three following classes of opinions will
be found, without much straining, to comprehend them all.

1st. Those who think that woman's sphere really and truly comprises
only her domestic duties, and that her mind ought never to stir beyond these.

2nd. Those who think her mind ought to be enlarged, and her condition improved in some respects; but that she ought not to be equally privileged with man.

3d. Those who think she has a just claim to equal rights with man.

We do not speak to those who hold the first class of opinions, their
prejudices being usually too obstinate and deep-seated for eradication;
they in general maintain, that intellectual culture would take woman out
of her proper sphere, that is, take her away from her domestic employments by raising her above them. Those who hold the second class maintain that woman may profitably cultivate her mind in literature, science,
or even politics; they declare that a more substantial education, far from
raising woman above her domestic duties, will both show her how important those duties are, and enable her to perform them much better. This
class maintain, of the possession of equal civil rights, what the first do of
a more enlightened education, that it would take woman out of her
sphere. We ourselves hold, we hope with many more, that woman has a
right to social equality; and we also maintain, that the possession of this
just right would not interfere in the slightest with her domestic duties, or
"woman's sphere," as it is called. Nay, we go still farther, and assert, that
the energy, self-reliance, and intelligence which the possession of this
right has such a tendency to foster and call into action, would be highly
favourable to a more enlarged view of those duties and a more active discharge of them.

There is a class of writers, mostly feminine, who use this phrase very
frequently; they are in general of the number of those who have escaped
in a great measure from the thraldom of old prejudices with regard to
women. They have all of them outgrown in some degree, many of them
altogether, the opinion, that with regard to woman it is best to "rear of
ignorance the safe high-wall"; but they seem to have almost a nervous
apprehension of being thought to step out of woman's proper place
themselves, or of trying to induce others to do so, when they advocate
such comparatively new opinions as the following: that woman's nature
is capable of, and would repay, as much cultivation as that of man; that it
is quite allowable, and even highly proper, that she should take an interest in politics, and try to influence all her friends towards her own side of
the question. The consequence of this apprehension is, that these writers
take every opportunity of deprecating the idea that their opinions have
any tendency to take woman out of what they call her sphere. . . .

. . . We think that the old prejudices regarding women convert the noble duty of self-renunciation into a most criminal self-extinction. These
old prejudices extinguish her individuality, oblige her to renounce the

good even more than the evil of her nature, and convert the inflexible rule of duty into a very flexible principle of submission to, and connivance at, all the weaknesses and wickednesses of man. No one will doubt this who has studied the *beau-ideal* of a wife in Chaucer's tale of Griselda, and which is, with some modification, too much the original character from which the good wife—having a bad husband—of modern story, is taken. A woman is thought perfect if she is represented as continuing to love, with the most ardent and constant affection, a monster who first gained her love by guile, and then treated her in so brutal a manner as to merit the contempt of the whole world. The love which is felt for such a being, if real, is a blind passion which ought to be reprobated rather than admired; but if a conviction of duty induces it, it is a pity to see so noble a principle so ill directed.

True self-renunciation strengthens and invigorates the mind; but such self-extinction as old custom prescribes to women enfeebles and debases it. No pure and noble-minded woman can long love affectionately, and submit passively to, a vicious and dissipated—or even to a good and virtuous tyrant—without having her own mind greatly deteriorated.

We believe that a great many of the loose and erroneous notions which people pick up, rather than acquire, regarding the nature of woman's duties, have their origin in the partial nature of the institutions of society with regard to her. Those institutions had their foundation, and were very valuable in times of strife and danger, when might almost constituted right; but when a more peaceful state of society has succeeded—when we hope right will be found to constitute might—is it not proper to examine the legacy which these stormy days have left us, and see whether, in our present condition, it is worth retaining or not?

Our own opinion of the true and extensive nature of woman's sphere will be seen more clearly in the course of the following pages; we only wish in this place to show some of the most obviously groundless conclusions which have been arrived at on the subject, and that the phrase has as yet no definite, precise, and unmistakable meaning. Those who wish woman to stand still, accuse those who wish her to advance of the high misdemeanor of taking her out of her sphere: these deny the charge, but throw the same imputation on those again who wish to see woman more free and independent. These last also deny the obnoxious charge, being unable to see an incompatibility, which the others do not attempt to prove but take for granted, between the possession of civil rights, and the performance of business duties.

For our own part, we should be as sorry as any one to see the domestic virtues of woman impaired; but we see no shadow of fear that such a consequence must necessarily follow the success of the opinions which we advocate. The fireside virtues are not properly cultivated by a mere housewife.

"Well ordered home man's chief delight to make,"

is a task which the accomplished woman can alone efficiently perform; she alone can make her fireside a scene of happiness and improvement to all who approach it; she alone can clearly show her children that the paths of wisdom and virtue are also those of pleasantness and peace; she alone will be as able and as solicitous to aid their mental development as to care for their physical comfort. All that unshackled self-dependence, all that freedom and elasticity of mind which social independence and equality, as we hope to convince the readers of the following pages, alone can thoroughly bestow, are not only favourable, but almost necessary to the right performance of those duties. Taking the phrase in its proper sense, we believe that the best and noblest of women will always find their greatest delight in the cultivation of the domestic virtues.

But although we are convinced that no elevation of the position of woman can ever withdraw domestic occupations and pleasures from forming a part, and perhaps even the chief part of her sphere, yet we are quite unable to see either the right or the reason which confines her to those occupations and pleasures. Nay! can any right be produced save that which is conferred by the strong right hand? Or any better reason than that it has been done from time immemorial?

There is yet another consideration connected with this subject, worthy of our attention. If all woman's duties are to be considered as so strictly domestic, and if God and nature have really so circumscribed her sphere of action—what are we to think of the dreadful depravity of thousands upon thousands of unprotected females, who actually prefer leaving their only proper sphere, and working for their own subsistence—to starvation? Is it not shocking to see their consciences so seared, that they are quite unaware of the dreadful nature of the course they are following? Ought not such wicked creatures to be exterminated? Or if we charitably allow them to cover their sins under the strong plea of necessity, what are we to think of that state of society which absolutely forces thousands of unfortunates to contradict their own nature—not by enlightening or enlarging their sphere—but by thrusting them entirely out of it? We say thrusting them entirely out, because we consider that domestic duties, though not occupying the whole of woman's sphere, ought always to form an integral part of it; and because few women are induced to work for themselves, except under the influence of such a pressure from without as obliges them to devote their whole time to any occupation they may choose, for obtaining subsistence, to the exclusion of course of all the peculiar duties of their sphere.

It may be said that this is merely an incidental evil; that it is a pity, but cannot be entirely avoided. Well! allowing that it is merely an incidental evil, still it is one which affects immense numbers of women; and if it is allowed to be in a great measure unavoidable, we would ask, is it fair to continue institutions which in their turn perpetuate those absurd prejudices which make it next to a certain loss of caste for any woman to attempt earning an honest and independent livelihood for herself? These prejudices have also had the very bad effect of limiting woman's choice of occupations to a few, and those the most tiresome and unhealthy of all the avocations which exist in the world.

We do not say, take away all occasion for woman being obliged to enter into an honourable and useful occupation; (for we think independence as necessary to the moral dignity of woman, as it confessedly is to that of man;) but we do say, either this must be done, or there is no excuse for not giving them as complete equality as law can give them. Even with perfectly fair play, they will still have plenty of difficulties to struggle with.

Putting, however, those cases out of the question, as exceptions to the general rule, where woman is forced to make what may be called unnatural exertions, and taking her in what is most certainly her natural, and we hope, also, her most frequent condition, that of a happy wife and mother, who requires to exert herself only to use judiciously the means supplied by her husband for their domestic comfort; still we say that this person's usefulness, even in the peculiar duties of her sphere, would not be at all impaired by her taking a more or less active interest, as her time might permit, in the welfare of her country.

Again we would repeat, that though no scheme would be of a healthy complexion, the object or the consequence of which was to take woman away from domestic occupations, (or in other words, make woman change places with man, for one of them must attend to these matters,) so neither is there justice, to either sex, in the social system which tries to confine them to those occupations. We say tries, for it only succeeds in throwing obstacles in the way of woman's sphere being enlarged judiciously, and in a right direction.

The Problem of Women in the Work Force

SOURCES

55. Jane Dubuisson, "Des femmes de la classe ouvrière à Lyon," *Le Conseiller des Femmes* (Lyons), 15 March 1834. Tr. KMO. The editors are grateful to Laura S. Strumingher, University of Cincinnati, for transmitting a copy of this article.

56. "Report of the Committee on Female Labor," *National Laborer*, 12 November 1836; reprinted from the *Documentary History of American Industrial Society*, 10 vols. (Cleveland, 1910-11), VI, *Labor Movement, 1820-1840*, pt. 2, ed. John R. Commons and Helen L. Sumner, 281-84.

57. *L'Atelier*, "Enquête—De la Condition des femmes," 3, no. 4 (30 December 1842), 31-32. The editors wish to thank Professor Edgar Newman, New Mexico State University, for a copy of this article.

58. Elizabeth Gaskell, *Mary Barton* (London, 1848), pp. 113-14.

The massive influx of women into mechanized textile manufacturing during the 1830's and 1840's set off a wave of debate throughout Europe and America concerning the suitability of paid labor for women. Although the vast majority of the women so employed were single, teen-age girls, concern about the propriety of such work for their futures as wives and mothers was widespread. The following selections, from France, England, and the United States, offer the perspectives of both middle-class and working-class observers.

The first selection comes from a pioneer women's publication in the silk manufacturing center of Lyons, France. During 1833-34 labor unrest was growing among the male artisans in the silk industry as increasingly large numbers of young women and children were hired to tend the steam-powered machinery being introduced in an old industry that had traditionally employed many women. With mechanization and increasing regimentation, however, many of them were working in excess of sixteen hours per day in poorly lighted, unsanitary, unventilated quarters, where advancement and better pay were all too often contingent on providing sexual favors for unscrupulous foremen or clerks, rather than on skill or hard work. *Le Conseiller des Femmes*, founded by Eugénie Niboyet (1800-1883), an energetic Protestant bourgeoise from Lyons who had participated in the Saint-Simonian circles of Paris, made an explicit effort to transcend mounting class conflict in France's second largest city. It called on women from both the bourgeois and the working-class worlds to rally under the banner of female solidarity to accomplish reforms on behalf of all women. However well-intentioned, the paper lasted only eleven months, foundering in the repressive wake of the 1834 silkworkers' riots. This article was written by Jane Dubuisson (dates unknown), one of Niboyet's associates in Lyons.

The second selection comes from a report presented at the 1836 convention of the National Trades' Union in Philadelphia. This group was the first national labor organization to be formed in the United States (in 1834); its delegates included shoemakers, hand-loom weavers, carpenters, mechanics, tailors, bookbinders, and other artisans from various East Coast cities. The subject of women's situation in cotton- and woolen-manufacturing establishments had first been brought to the attention of the association by a Boston delegate, Dr. Charles Douglass. The factory system that employed these women was viewed with great suspicion and mistrust, as a threat to the independence and intelligence of the common people. The 1835 convention had appointed a committee to investigate the situation of the women and to prepare a report, excerpted here, which was presented in 1836. Women's wage labor is viewed as part of a plot by capitalists to undermine the independence of working men.

The third selection, an unsigned article from *L'Atelier* (The Workshop), a Parisian workingmen's monthly newspaper, should be compared with the Americans' report. In 1841 the French Chamber of Deputies debated a bill proposing the regulation of child labor in manufacturing; in June *L'Atelier* launched an inquiry among its own working-class constituency about women's work and woman's role. Their report appeared in December 1842, following the shocking reports of English women working at heavy labor in the coal mines (alluded to here) that had created a sensation throughout Europe and led to parliamentary action prohibiting all such work for women. The reader should be alert to the inconsistencies in the French workers' analysis when, on the one hand, they advocate improvements in the condition of women workers and, on the other, argue for their removal from the labor force altogether.

The fourth selection is from the novel *Mary Barton* by the English novelist and reformer, Elizabeth Cleghorn Gaskell (1810-1865). Gaskell, born Elizabeth Stephenson, was nurtured by the British radical tradition associated with Unitarianism. As the wife of a Unitarian minister who brought her into the poverty-stricken homes of the Manchester working class, Gaskell constructed many of her novels on personal observations. She was further sensitized to the problems of women through her own experiences as the mother of four daughters. In this excerpt from her very successful first novel, set in Manchester in the late 1830's, the middle-aged Mrs. Wilson, who is the mother of Mary Barton's sweetheart Jem, tells Mary of her own experiences as a young working-class wife. As Gaskell develops the dialogue, she develops the point, through Mrs. Wilson's remarks, that by working in factories young unmarried women are forfeiting their domestic apprenticeship. Thus Gaskell makes explicit the primary concern underlying the complaints of reformers and workingmen alike in the 1840's—namely, that as increasing numbers of married or single women worked for pay away from their homes, domestic comforts would simply cease to exist.

---

55. Jane Dubuisson (1834)

For a long time eloquent pens and generous hearts have pleaded the cause of the unfortunate workers in our city but, with the exception of M. Jules Favre,* no one has considered the deplorable situation of the women and daughters of the working class. And by *working class* I mean not only those who work at the loom but also those directly or indirectly attached to the fabrication of silk; included in this group are the winders, fringers, stitchers, shawl cutters, etc. etc., in this unfortunate and useful portion of the population of our opulent city. Misery and its horrors do not even spare children. From the age of six an unfortunate little girl is harnessed to a mechanical wheel eighteen hours a day. She earns eight *sols*, spends two or at the most three of them to add an insufficient portion of coarse prepared food to her even coarser bread. Wilted by a type of work that exceeds her strength, brutalized by an existence that is entirely contrary to nature and that proceeds in hideously unclean, unhealthy workshops, this child vegetates in the most deplorable ignorance. If her sickly childhood withstands all these evils, she will arrive at an even more unfortunate adolescence. Restricted to the fabrication of *étoffes unis* (the most poorly paid), a woman works fifteen or eighteen hours, often Sundays and holidays, in order to earn a salary that just about suffices for half of her most urgent needs. Should she become weary of this situation that is killing her, and if the continuance of work permits her to do so—if, I say—a woman worker wishes to seek an occupation from which she can live, her native intelligence, suppressed since childhood, prevents her from entering any of those occupations that demand a bit of study. Does she wish to mill the silk? In order to get work, it is not sufficient to be able to do it well and to be scrupulously honest; she must first be recommended, by whatever possible means, to the clerk *who makes the decisions.*

This person, though of secondary importance himself, pays little attention to the orders of the boss [*chef*], or, if he cannot evade an order to give work to some woman worker who has not sought out his protection, she then becomes subject to a series of vexations that would reduce the most patient person to despair. Disgusted by a situation in which it is impossible to work except under a revolting patronage, the woman worker goes on to sacrifice a long and irretrievable period in a shawl-making

* Favre was an aspiring, reform-minded lawyer in Lyons who later became prominent in republican politics.—EDS.

workshop in order to learn a more lucrative trade. There she will first discover that the mistress of the workshop is a relative either of the head man or of his principal clerk, or belongs to them in some other fashion, the only conditions for obtaining a monopoly on the work of a shop. Thus the woman worker must either seek employment in workshops in which the mistress, following the example of the manufacturers, will make enormous profits by paying her only the most minimal wages (without overlooking any of the illicit and vexatious acts that it will be in her power to inflict) or the woman worker herself must accept ignoble and revolting conditions. And do not think that all those women who are exposed to so many horrible seductions give in, oh no! I have seen upright women, however miserable, who, given a choice between vice and hunger, refuse such shameful transactions and, thanks to this refusal, have their work taken away from them. Their work! Their daily bread! . . .

Thus the woman worker who has not been corrupted by misery and bad example must work all her life, sustain the most extreme deprivation, and, in the midst of this struggle between misfortune and infamy, must witness the early arrival of infirmities, an anticipation of old age. What she is not given, or more clearly, *what is stolen from her*, makes the fortune of those who do not blush to become rich off the sweat of the poor.

Perhaps someone will try to counter this tableau by pointing to the immense amount of charity that is distributed every year. But it is not charity that withers [these women]. What do these poor victims of greed desire? They ask for work, difficult, continuous work—work that will nourish them and that will not leave them with only starvation and the hospital* to look forward to!

When such abuses display themselves—bleeding, palpitating, hideous —should one not scorn this philanthropy that does not cure, because it does not recognize, the real wounds of humanity, the real evils that society endures? Oh! if you had seen, as we have, the bitter tears that flow from these eyes, reddened by working half the night, if you had heard the sorrowful cries of these ulcerated hearts, you would curse as we do these murderers who strike down a generation at its roots, who gnaw away at it slowly until, as a result of the evils with which they flood it, it is entirely extinguished.

56. National Trades' Union Committee on Female Labor (1836)

The Committee appointed to report on the evils of Female Labor, respectfully offer the following as the result of their opinions and conference on that subject, having in the discharge of their duty considered the subject in a moral, social, and pecuniary point of view.

First—Proceeding to explain and exhibit the errors of the system, and after to point out the only means of curtailing or arresting the evil.

---

* The hospitals of the nineteenth century served almost exclusively as a last resort for the sick and dying poor.—EDS.

The system of Female Labor, as practiced in our cities and manufacturing towns, is surely the most disgraceful escutcheon on the character of American freemen, and one [that], if not checked by some superior cause, will entail ignorance, misery and degradation on our children, to the end of time. "The physical organization, the natural responsibilities, and the moral sensibility of women, prove conclusively that her labors should be only of a domestic nature." But if the character and attributes of any of God's creatures have been subverted, it has been woman, when forced by adventitious circumstances to become the abused hireling and drudge of the speculator and monopolist. Let the Workingmen of the United States but consider what would become of the rising generation if the almost universal system of Female Labor should not be arrested. By reflecting one moment, every one can see the consequences, and although it may promise and offer temporary gain to some, it should be passed and heeded as "the song of the syren"—every thing at present or in future, is destroyed by the illusion. The health of the young female, in the majority of cases, is injured by unnatural restraint and confinement, and deprived of the qualities essentially necessary in the culture and bearing of healthy children. Their morals frequently depart before their health, in consequence of being often crowded in such large numbers, with all characters and all sexes; and what evil example this fails to do, necessity too often urges and palliates; and this one point of the subject, above all others, should arouse the jealous sensibilities of every moral man, and more particularly of every parent. These evils themselves are great, and call loudly for a speedy cure; but still another objection to the system arises, which, if possible, is productive of the other evils, namely, the ruinous competition brought in active opposition to male labor, actually producing a reversion of the very good intended to do the guardian or parent, causing the destruction of the end which it aims to benefit; because, when the employer finds, as he surely will, that female assistance will compress his ends, of course the workman is discharged, or reduced to a corresponding rate of wages with the female operative. By these means the parent, the husband, or the brother, is deprived of a sufficient subsistence to support himself and family, when without the auxiliary aid of the female, by his own labor alone he might have supported himself and family in decency, and kept his wife or relative at home, to perform the duties of the household. Nor is the evil lessened in the case of females who work singly, or in reduced numbers. If possible, their competition is still more ruinous; because, in the first instance, when congregated in large numbers, they are generally the assistants of machinery, which destroys the necessity of manual labor. But in the latter case, all being done by the hand, the female in a short time becomes so expert as entirely to supercede the necessity of the male; and this fact is apparent to every one, that, when the females are found capable of performing duty generally performed by the men, as a natural consequence, from the cheapness of their habits and dependent situation, they acquire complete control of that particular branch of labor. And if the evil stopped here, it might more readily be arrested; but the desire of gain is such that there is no limits that could confine it; and so long as employers are allowed to experiment on the labor of the sex, each trade, except it be of the most laborious character, is in danger of the innovation. The Committee will not attempt to conceal the fact, that a serious question meets us in our opposition to the system. "If the mechanical labor, or the opposition labor of females are destroyed, can they employ their time usefully and profitably?" and the Committee will answer, not without a corresponding change in society, which must be produced by the extension of knowledge and education. In the early ages, we find that the women were usefully, healthily, and industriously employed, although differently engaged from their present occupations; and if in those early days a sufficiency of labor was found, as a matter of course, at the present day, with the increased demand, a sufficiency can be had in the family of every one. The evil, however, has been saddled upon us, and it is our duty, as well as interest, to propose such remedies as the case may require. Females themselves are very blind as to their real interest, and imagine that each effort made to destroy the operation of the system, is destructive to their interest, whereas it is virtually calculated to remove and destroy the very evils they now labor under, and it would be folly to urge a different course, until they see the evil in all its colours. One thing, however, must be apparent to every reflecting female, that all her exertions are scarce sufficient to keep her alive; that the price of her labor each year is reduced; and that she in a measure stands in the way of the male when attempting to raise his prices or equalize his labor; and that there her efforts to sustain herself and family, are actually the same as tying a stone around the neck of her natural protector, Man, and destroying him with the weight she has brought to his assistance. This is the true and natural consequence of female labor, when carried beyond the necessities of the family. It is thus that the speculator can riot through his mines of gold, heedless of the tears and the degradation of his innocent victims. It is not enough that freemen have sunk below the level of humanity at the shrine of Mammon, but their wives and daughters must be offered at the pyre. Is not Avarice satisfied with a nation of Fathers and Sons, but our Wives and Daughters, the loved ones of our hearts and affections, shall be thrown into the spoilers' arms?

57. *L'Atelier* (1842)

We want to combat every aspect of the industrial disorder that dominates us, for every abuse that exists reinforces the others, to the point where one cannot deal with any one of them without the entire structure collapsing.

Without wishing to design a new system here, we think it is useful to present a few ideas on the unfortunate situation of working women. No doubt, many others have spoken of this before and better than we can, and others will speak of it again. But no one can do so with more first-hand knowledge than we have, and we would consider ourselves negligent in our duty if we did not attempt to expose the vices and disorders that we see about us and that have such a great influence on our existence and on our future.

One of the major causes of demoralization in our society is the position of women, especially working women. Although we do not share the ideas elaborated by some innovators, we think that there should be great concern about women in our society, in which they play such an important role. In no other country do they have as much influence in private life, or—we would declare—even in public life.

For every moral reform that is possible and realizable, we are convinced that the first step must be education. Certainly, that of women is so far neglected, so insignificant, that it must be given first priority.

One of the most important causes of demoralization for working women is the meagerness of salaries and the rapacity of the employers who, speculating on their misery and the ease with which workers can be gotten, make the women work at any price, because they—being isolated and informed only by the extreme need that impels them—always consent to the reductions imposed on their salaries.

Although women's work is less productive for society than that of men, it does, nevertheless, have a certain value, and, moreover, there are professions that only women can practice. For these, women are indispensable, as in every type of needlework, where there are so many specialties, and in many others that need not be enumerated. Well then, what do you think: It is these very workers in all these necessary trades who earn the least and who are subject to the longest layoffs. Since for so much work they earn only barely enough to live from day to day, it happens that during times of unemployment they sink into abject poverty, and far worse than that when they have children—a situation we see far too often.

One should not think that it is only in Paris where the misery of women workers is severe. In every large manufacturing center their position is the same: a great deal of work, little recompense; and from the standpoint of morality it is worse in the large factories, where men and women work in the same workshops and leave at the same hours, which means that morals are more dissolute than elsewhere. And this is so true, that in these places the degeneration has become so considerable that one can scarcely find men capable of serving as soldiers.

Who has not heard of the women silkworkers at Lyons and throughout the Midi—dirty, unhealthy, and badly paid work; of the women in the spinning and weaving factories of eastern and northern France, working fourteen to sixteen hours (except for one hour for both meals); always standing, without a single minute for repose, putting forth an enormous amount of effort. And many of them have to walk a league or more, morning and evening, to get home, which is often a cause for moral disorder. Nor should we neglect to mention the danger that exists merely from working in these large factories, surrounded by wheels, gears, enormous leather belts that always threaten to seize you and pound you to pieces. There is no factory in which some kind of accident has not happened—some woman worker caught by the hair or her clothing, and thereby pulverized; some mutilation of the fingers or the hands. What happens then? The employer pays the doctor; they take up a subscription in the workshop, and it ends there; nobody worries further about the unfortunate soul who has often lost her entire means of subsistence.

Is it not also deplorable to see pregnant women obliged to perform work that far exceeds their strength—to carry loads, pull carts, etc., thus exposing them to the possibility of hurting themselves seriously or contracting some incurable disease?

Do not accuse us of exaggerating for, on the contrary, we are understating the reality. When we spell out and call with all our might for social and industrial reforms, we know that we are on the path of justice; we know that the publicists and scholars are in front of us, and that behind us there is a mass of workers calling out for reform.

Among the causes of women workers' misery that we must consider is the competition that comes from work in the prisons. It could be said of this work that it is designed expressly to ruin the situation of free, upright women so that they too will take their turn in prison. The result of this competition is the lowering of the price of labor to such a degree that it becomes impossible for a worker to support herself by her labor. She then falls into prostitution; she becomes prison fodder and in her turn enters competition with the workers outside, who are scarcely free to choose between the most utter misery, the greatest privations, or prostitution. . . .

The existence of women who work as day laborers and are obliged to abandon their households and the care of their children to indifferent neighbors is no better; on the contrary, from the perspective of morality it is worse. This continual abandonment for the entire day accounts for the fact that some working-class children were picked up by the police, having contracted a taste for vagabondage and laziness. Certainly there are *salles d'asile* [day-care centers], but parents who go to work at five or six in the morning cannot take their children there at that time.

If the salary of the male worker were generally sufficient for the keep of his family—as it should be—his wife would not be obliged to frequent the workshops. She would be able, while doing a bit of work in her home, to raise her children, send them to school, care for them, and thereby avoid turning out bad subjects later on. And then the mother of the family would regain dignity in her own eyes; she would understand her dignity and her duties; and she would raise her daughters with the same feelings, so that they could someday also be good mothers.

But, unfortunately, things do not ever happen this way; moreover, how can one require habits of order and morality, of virtue and courage to resist misery from a goodly number of working women when, due to the weakness of their organs, the absence of all moral education, of any idea of duty, of self-respect, they find themselves thrown into the workshops from the most tender age, in contact with persons of every age, exposed to bad company, to overhearing conversations that would make men blush? The good tendencies they might have are suffocated by the scoffing and mocking of other women, especially certain old working women who, instead of preaching and setting a good example, get their revenge for not themselves being able to misbehave by encouraging girls to debauchery.

Young girls surrounded by such persons cannot help being corrupted in heart and mind, because the nullity of their education cannot put them on guard against all the grossness and immorality they hear about, and which, simply because it is spoken of around them, seems to them to represent the ordinary and routine life one must lead in order to be happy. . . .

In summary, we want the education of our daughters to be better directed, and salaries to be raised in a way that does not hurt anyone, which could very well be arranged with the organization of a conciliation board, as we have demanded, so that the wage scale could thus assure woman workers enough to live on.

Marriage must be made easier for women. They must be made into mothers who will raise their children to love their country and to respect their parents, and not—by necessity—make of them beggarwomen dragging their children behind them in order to arouse public pity; this vice, however uncommon, should not exist at all. One should be able to work in order to live, not to beg.

The situation of women workers could be improved by encouraging them, with some modifications, toward the system of association in work that we have explained many times and that we defend every day. We are persuaded that it would give good results. However, we believe that the condition of women will never really improve until workingmen can earn enough to support their families, which is only fair. Woman is so closely linked to man that the position of the one cannot be improved without reference to the position of the other; thus, the male worker must conquer his place; he must make his true rights in society understood, and women can still aid him in achieving this end. We are convinced that this mutual improvement cannot be achieved without association.

The improvement of the physical condition of the working women would have a great moral influence, for everyone knows that an excess of misery leads to degradation! How can it be that our economists, our leading philanthropists, have not sought to apply some remedy to the evil, since they know so well how to talk about it? But these gentlemen are more interested in their own glory than in the well-being of the masses and the solution to these questions. Instead of looking for ways to save money on hospitals, shelters, abandoned children, etc., they ought to be able to understand that if the condition of women workers could be improved, stabilized, better assured, the number of abandoned children would decrease greatly, the hospitals for old people would be less overcrowded, and thereby the Treasury would save a lot of money.

But we know that we can expect nothing from these types. It is up to the people to ponder these things and to instruct themselves, to propagandize, and to unite in order to seek guarantees against exploitation.

58. Elizabeth Gaskell (1848)

"If you'll believe me, Mary, there never was such a born goose at house-keeping as I were; and yet he married me! I had been in a factory sin' five years old a'most, and I knew nought about cleaning, or cooking, let alone washing and such like work. The day after we were married, he went to his work after breakfast, and says he, 'Jenny, we'll ha' th' cold beef, and potatoes, and that's a dinner for a prince.' I were anxious to make him comfortable, God knows how anxious. And yet I'd no notion how to cook a potato. I know'd they were boiled, and knowed their skins were taken off, and that were all. So I tidied my house in a rough kind o'way, then I looked at that very clock up yonder," pointing at one that hung against the wall, "and I seed it were nine o'clock, so, thinks I, th' potatoes shall be well boiled at any rate, and I gets 'em on th' fire in a jiffy (that's to say, as soon as I could peel 'em, which were a tough job at first), and then I fell to unpacking my boxes! and at twenty minutes past twelve, he comes home, and I had the beef ready on th' table, and I went to take the potatoes out o' th' pot; but oh! Mary, th' water had boiled away, and they were all a nasty brown mess, as smelt through all the house. He said nought, and were very gentle; but, oh, Mary, I cried so that afternoon. I shall ne'er forget it; no, never. I made many a blunder at after, but none that fretted me like that."

"Father does not like girls to work in factories," said Mary.

"No, I know he does not; and reason good. They oughtn't to go at after they're married, that I'm very clear about. I could reckon up" (counting with her finger), "ay, nine men, I know, as has been driven to th' public-house by having wives as worked in factories; good folk too, as thought there was no harm in putting their little ones out at nurse, and letting their house go all dirty, and their fires all out; and that was a place as was tempting for a husband to stay in, was it? He soon finds out gin-shops, where all is clean and bright, and where th' fire blazes cheerily, and gives a man a welcome as it were."

Alice, who was standing near for the convenience of hearing, had caught much of this speech, and it was evident the subject had previously been discussed by the women, for she chimed in,

"I wish our Jem could speak a word to th' Queen, about factory work for married women. Eh! but he comes it strong when once yo get him to speak about it. Wife o' his'n will never work away fra' home."

"I say it's Prince Albert as ought to be asked how he'd like his missis to be from home when he comes in, tired and worn, and wanting some one to cheer him; and maybe, her to come in by-and-by, just as tired and down in th' mouth; and how he'd like for her never to be at home to see to th' cleaning of his house, or to keep a bright fire in his grate. Let alone his meals being all hugger-mugger and comfortless. I'd be bound, prince as he is, if his missis served him so, he'd be off to a gin-palace, or summut o' that kind. So why can't he make a law again poor folks' wives working in factories?"

Mary ventured to say that she thought the Queen and Prince Albert could not make laws, but the answer was,

"Pooh! don't tell me it's not the Queen as makes laws; and isn't she bound to obey Prince Albert? And if he said they mustn't, why she'd say they mustn't, and then all folk would say, oh, no, we never shall do any such thing no more."

Solutions to the Problem of Women in the Work Force

SOURCES

59. "Report of the Committee on Female Labor," *National Laborer*, 12 November 1836; reprinted in the *Documentary History of American Industrial Society*, 10 vols. (Cleveland, Ohio, 1910-11), VI, *Labor Movement, 1820-1840*, pt. 2, ed. John R. Commons and Helen L. Sumner, 287-90.

60. Flora Tristan (Flore-Célestine-Thérèse-Henriette Tristan y Moscozo), *L'Union ouvrière*, 3rd ed. (Paris and Lyons, 1844), pp. 60-65, 67-69. Originally published in 1843. The editors wish to thank Professor S. Joan Moon, Sacramento State University, for sending them this document, and are indebted to Giselle Pincetl, San Diego State University, for permission to use her translation of this excerpt, which originally appeared in *Harvest Quarterly*, 7 (Fall 1977), 12-14.

61. Friedrich Engels, *The Condition of the Working Class in England* (Stanford, 1968), pp. 160, 161-65. Tr. W. O. Henderson and W. H. Chaloner. Originally published as *Die Lage der arbeitenden Klasse in England* (Leipzig, 1845).

The solutions proposed to the problem of female labor during the 1830's and 1840's differed in numerous respects. The solution envisioned by the artisans of the National Trades' Union (Doc. 56) in the United States lay in opposing factory labor as unhealthy for either sex; meanwhile they encouraged women workers to associate themselves in self-help societies and to affiliate with male workers. In France, where such pragmatic solutions were less easy to realize, Flora Tristan (1803-1844) proposed a more comprehensive solution to skeptical French workers, calling for better female education and for women's rights. Tristan, the illegitimate child of a wealthy Peruvian nobleman and a French woman, grew up in poverty. Following a series of dramatic events in her personal life, which brought her both fame and notoriety in France, Tristan embarked on a journey through the provinces with the mission of enlightening and emancipating working men and women everywhere, and advocating formation of a Workers' Union along Fourierist lines. Though Tristan fell ill and died while on this tour, her earlier published writings subsequently influenced other social critics and theorists, among them Karl Marx, who had arrived in France shortly before her death.

A third proposal was offered by Friedrich Engels (1820-1895). Engels was the rebellious son of a Rhineland textile manufacturer who was also part owner of a mill in Manchester. As a young man Engels was sent to England by his father to familiarize himself with the Manchester textile industry; during the twenty-two months of his stay, he poured over the reports of parliamentary reformers and other publications, combining the knowledge obtained from them with the more immediate insights gained from his friendship with a young Irish mill girl who introduced him at first hand to the harsh realities of working-class life. He concluded that there would inevitably be a confrontation between the working classes and the over-rich ruling class. In this selection Engels denounced the reversal of universally accepted male and female roles that accompanied economic depression in the industrial cities of England. He concluded, however, that the only way to eliminate sex roles was to eliminate the power relationship based on economics. Such an assertion, of course, does not address—much less resolve—the problem of who will do the housework, the problem confronted earlier by Fourier (Docs. 9, 35).

---

59. National Trades' Union Committee on Female Labor (1836)

We would not be understood by these suggestions to deprive the female portion of the community from earning by honest industry a livelihood, but to direct their attention to the other branches of female industry, better calculated to promote health of body, and the still more noble attainments, the cultivation of the mind, believing that there are sufficient openings for female industry and invention, much more profitable, and not requiring that labor of body, and constant incarceration required in factories.

That it must be destroyed by gradual means none can deny; a departure from which, if it were practicable, would reduce thousands to beggary, starvation, and crime.

That females themselves should arouse in this noble cause is again pressed by the committee, believing if the good and pure in all classes would but come out, much might be done to meliorate their condition. For instance, it is presumed there are twenty beneficial societies for females in the city of Philadelphia, composing in the aggregate 4,000 members. Now, if the humane in these societies could effect a reorganization in order to grant assistance to those imposed upon by employers, the good effects, no doubt, would be speedily felt. In addition to their beneficial dues, let them assess each member 6¼ cents monthly, making the sum in addition 75 cents yearly, which could be felt by none, but which by the increased number of females who would subscribe from motives of charity, might be raised to an amount calculated to defeat the oppression of the heartless employer; because if the employer can but manage without their assistance two weeks, he is sure of defeating them. And on the other hand, if they could stand for three weeks, the pressing demand for their labor and the impracticability of foreign assistance, would compel him to come to terms. This simple plan itself would give confidence to the female, throws her in the company of those who were her friends, and by their united energies would do more to raise each other than all the Dorcas Societies in the world, who subscribe themselves "charitable ladies," for giving a woman 12½ cents for making a shirt, equalled as they are in "charity" only by the United States' Clothing Department in the city of Philadelphia, which has ground the seamstress down to the above sum, 12½ for the same article.

In the city of Philadelphia a Society of Female Operatives exists, numbering near four hundred, governed on the same principles as the other Trade Societies, which, in time, no doubt, will effectuate much good; and two or three other societies are composed in part by females who have received a proportionate benefit with the males. Many means, no doubt, might be adopted to bring females in society, but until it is done, they have little hope of redress.

Another method might be resorted to. All those trades affected by female labor could regulate their laws in such way as to admit those females in their society, so that in case of difficulty they would be governed by their laws and receive their support—or raise the Society of females, and make one auxiliary to the other. Any of these measures might be tried without danger or loss, and there is no doubt one or the other with perseverance would succeed, but the committee would recommend the amalgamation of trade and beneficial Societies. While on this point of the subject, the committee cannot pass without a remark on the inconsistency of a certain class of females, and likewise to offer one more suggestion. The fact must be apparent to any one that Sunday School Societies and Temperance Societies have been mainly supported by females, as well also as Foreign and Domestic Missions. Now, is it not a singular fact, that females who would sacrifice their time and health to distribute tracts and collect moneys for the heathen, could not devote a mite for their own oppressed countrywomen without the sacrifice of time or health. We do not object to these objects by any means; but while they are discharging the duties of humanity they should not overlook their own sex and kin. Let them endeavour to take away the provocation to crime by giving the poor female a sufficiency for her labor to support herself and orphans, and that act will be as acceptable in the eye of Heaven as any ever discharged by mortal. Besides, their efforts to distinguish themselves, if their motives be pure, which we do not question, are not always crowned with success, agents and impostors frequently reaping the fruit of their labors; whereas, did they but collect but half the sum to give to destitute females forced to abandon their labor, they themselves could divide the tribute without the least danger of imposition. Of what avail has been all the sympathy expressed by some of the great men of this city? Have they ever proposed a single plan to benefit the female laborer? Much have they talked, but little have they done. We see among the fashionable ladies, monthly contributions started, extending, as they do, through all classes of females, for one thing or the other thing, but we do not see them propose a penny or twopenny tax on the female portion of the community for their unfortunate sisters in adversity. This would be a noble thing; and the committee will propose to the charitable in those districts where females are oppressed, to form themselves in general societies for the benefit of female laborers; and if the donation be but two cents monthly, that sum will answer every purpose, provided it is subscribed to generally. The question will then soon be settled, whether those who have done so much have done so from the dictates of conscience or for the applause of the world. The females employed in the Lowell Mills, by the adoption of such a suggestion, no doubt would have been able to starve their proprietors out, instead of being defeated, as they probably will be. But to prevent a similar recurrence, they should immediately adopt energetic measures, in the construction of Societies to support each other in trouble; and by their failure, composed as they are of 7,000 in all, let others be cautioned. This is the only effectual remedy to be applied at this time. We must first curb the excess before we destroy the evil.

In relation to the right or propriety of legislatures interfering with the domestic arrangements of manufacturers or speculators, workingmen should not say one word. "The evil has arisen from partial legislation," and let legislation correct the evil. Take away from the wealthy the temptation held out by poverty, and we will be more virtuous and more happy.

In concluding their report, the committee will observe the suggestions thrown out are gratuitous, believing that nothing can be done without the co-operation of the females; they however have proposed the above remedies, hoping that the day is not far distant, when some of them may be adopted to relieve this oppressed part of the community; they shall therefore close by offering the following:

RESOLVED, that in the opinion of this convention, the present system of Female Labour is highly injurious to the best interests of the working classes, to the great object of mental improvement, and consequent corruption of good morals.

RESOLVED, that this convention, from feelings of humanity, recommend to the different Unions the propriety of assisting with their advice and influence, the female operatives through out the U. States, in ameliorating their present unhappy situation, under the female system of labour.

60. Flora Tristan (1843)

. . . Woman is everything in the life of the worker: as mother she has an influence over him during his childhood, it is from her and her alone that he learns the first notions of the science of life, so important to master because it teaches us to live decently for ourselves and for others in whatever walk of life fate has placed us. As lover she has an influence over him during his youth, and what powerful influence has a beautiful girl who is loved! As wife she has an influence on three-quarters of his life; and finally, as daughter she has an influence on his old age.

You will observe that the workers' position is quite different from that of the rich. If a rich child's mother is incapable of raising him, he is sent to a boarding school or given a governess. If a rich young man has no mistress, he can study art or science to keep his heart and imagination occupied. If a rich man has no wife, he will easily find pleasures in society. If a rich old man has no daughter, he can find some old friends or young nephews who will gladly come and play cards with him. Whereas the worker, to whom all these advantages are denied, has only the company of the women of his family—his fellow sufferers—for his sole joy and comfort.

As a result it is imperative, in order to improve the intellectual, moral, and material condition of the working class, that women of the lower classes be given a rational and solid education, conducive to the development of their good inclinations, so that they may become skillful workers, good mothers capable of raising and guiding their children, and of tutoring them in their school work, and so that they may also act as moralizing agents in the life of the men on whom they exert an influence from the cradle to the grave.

Do you begin to understand, you, men, who cry shame before even looking into the question, why I demand rights for woman? Why I should like her to be placed on a footing of absolute equality with man in society, and that she should be so by virtue of the legal right every human being brings at birth?

I demand rights for women because I am convinced that all the misfortunes in the world result from the neglect and contempt in which woman's natural and inalienable rights have so far been held. I demand rights for woman because it is the only way she will get an education, and because the education of man in general and man of the lower classes in particular depends on the education of woman. I demand rights for woman because it is the only way to obtain her rehabilitation in the Church, the law, and society, and because this preliminary rehabilitation is necessary to achieve the rehabilitation of the workers themselves. All the woes of the working class can be summed up in these two words: poverty and ignorance, ignorance and poverty. Now, I see only one way out of this labyrinth: begin by educating women, because women have the responsibility for educating male and female children.

Workers, the way things stand now, you know what is going on in your homes. You, man—the master—with rights over your wife, do you like living with her? Tell me: are you happy? No, no, it is easy to see that despite your rights you are neither content nor happy. Between master and slave there can be nothing but the weariness caused by the weight of the chain that binds them together. Whenever freedom is lacking there can be no happiness.

Men keep on complaining about the surliness, the sly and underhandedly mean character that woman reveals in nearly all her relationships. Oh, I would indeed have a very poor opinion of the female race if, in the state of abjection in which the law and customs have maintained them, women submitted to the yoke that weighs upon them without uttering a word. Thank heavens, it is not so; their protest has been continuous since the beginning of time. But since the *Declaration of the Rights of Man*—a solemn act that proclaimed the neglect and contempt of the new men for them—their protest has become vigorous and vehement, which proves that the exasperation of the slave has reached its peak.

Workers, you have good sense and one can reason with you because your minds are not stuffed with a bunch of systems, as Fourier says, would you imagine for a moment that woman is by right the equal of man? Well, what would happen?

As soon as the dangerous consequences of the development of the moral and physical faculties of women—dangerous because of women's current slave status—are no longer feared, woman can be taught with great care so as to make the best possible use of her intelligence and work. Then, you, men of the lower classes, will have as mothers skillful workers who earn a decent salary, are educated, well brought up, and quite capable of raising you, of educating you, the workers, as is proper for free men. You will have well brought up and well educated sisters, lovers, wives, friends, with whom daily contacts will be most pleasant for you. Nothing is sweeter or more agreeable to a man's heart than the sensible and gracious conversation of good and well educated women.

We have given a brief outline of what takes place currently in workers' households. Let us now see what will take place in these same households when woman is equal to man.

The husband who knows that his wife's rights are equal to his does not treat her with the disdain and scorn that are shown to inferiors; on the contrary, he treats her with the respect and regard due to one's equal. Then, the woman has no more cause for irritation, and once the cause of irritation is removed the woman is no longer brutal, sly, surly, angry, exasperated, or mean. She is no longer considered as the husband's servant in the house, but rather as the man's partner, his friend and companion. She naturally takes an interest in their association and does her best to make the household prosper. Thanks to her practical experience and theoretical knowledge, she runs her house intelligently, economically, and methodically. Because she is well educated and aware of the usefulness of education, her highest ambition is to raise her children well, she lovingly instructs them herself, supervises their school work, and apprentices them to good employers. Finally she guides them in all manner of things with solicitude, affection, and good judgment.

The man, the worker, the husband who has such a wife, enjoys great peace of mind, satisfaction, and happiness. Aware of his wife's intelligence, good sense, and high-mindedness, he is able to discuss important matters with her, communicate his plans, work with her on ways to improve their position. Flattered by his trust, she helps him in his undertakings and business either with good advice or by her activity. The worker, who is himself well educated and well brought up, finds great joy in educating and developing the minds of his children. Workers, in general, are quite warm-hearted and love children. . . .

Workers, I have barely sketched a picture of the life the proletarian class would enjoy if woman were recognized as the equal of man. This should make you think about the existing evil and about the well-being that could exist. It should make you greatly determined.

Workers, you have no power to repeal old laws and make new ones; no, indeed; but you have the power to protest against the inequity and absurdity of laws that hinder the progress of humanity and make you suffer, you in particular. Thus you can—it is even your sacred duty—you can protest strongly with your ideas, your words, and your writings against all the laws that oppress you. Now, be sure you understand this well: the law that enslaves woman and deprives her of an education also oppresses you, proletarian men.

To raise him, educate him, and teach him the science of the world, the son of the rich has learned governesses and teachers, clever headmistresses, and finally, beautiful marquises, witty and elegant women, whose function consists in educating the youths of the upper class when they leave college. It is a most useful function for the well-being of those gentlemen of the high nobility. The ladies teach them politeness, tact, subtlety, open-mindedness, and good manners; in a word, they make of them men who know how to live, men of good breeding. If a young man shows any ability, if he has the good fortune to be under the protection of one of those lovely ladies, his success is assured. At thirty-five, he is certain to be an ambassador or a minister. Meanwhile, you, poor workers, to raise you, to educate you, you have only your mothers; to make of you men who know how to live, you have only the women of your class, your companions in ignorance and poverty.

Therefore it is not in the name of the superiority of woman (of which I shall no doubt be accused) that I tell you to demand rights for woman; no, indeed. To begin with, woman must be recognized as a full member of society before we can discuss her superiority. I rely on more solid arguments than that. It is in the name of your own interest, men, of your own improvement, men, and lastly, it is in the name of the universal well-being of all men and women that I urge you to demand rights for women and, in the meantime, to acknowledge them yourselves, at least in principle.

Thus, it is up to you, workers, victims of de facto inequality and injustice, finally to establish on earth the reign of justice and absolute equality between woman and man. Give a great example to the world, an example that will show your oppressors that you wish to triumph by right and not by brute force; you, the 7, 10, 15 millions of proletarians who could use that brute force.

While demanding justice for yourselves, show that you are just and fair; proclaim—you, the strong men, the men with bare arms—that you recognize woman as your equal, and that, as such, you recognize for her an equal right to the benefits of the UNIVERSAL UNION OF WORKING MEN AND WOMEN.

61. Friedrich Engels (1844)

. . . It is inevitable that if a married woman works in a factory family life is inevitably destroyed and in the present state of society, which is based upon family life, its dissolution has the most demoralising consequences both for parents and children. A married woman cannot really be regarded as a mother if she is unable to spare the time to look after her child; if she hardly sees the infant at all; and if she cannot satisfy her baby's elementary need for loving care. Such a mother is inevitably indifferent to the welfare of the child, which she treats without love and without proper care as if it were a stranger. Children who grow up under such conditions have no idea of what a proper family life should be. When they grow up and have families of their own they feel out of place because their own early experience has been that of a lonely life. Such parents foster the universal decadence of family life among the workers. Similar evil consequences for the family follow from child labour. When children earn more than the cost of their keep they begin to make a contribution to the family budget and to keep the rest as pocket money. This often occurs when they are no more than fourteen or fifteen. In brief, the children become emancipated and regard their parents' house merely as lodgings, and quite often, if they feel like it, they leave home and take lodgings elsewhere.

Very often the fact that a married woman is working does not lead to the complete disruption of the home but to a reversal of the normal division of labour within the family. The wife is the breadwinner while her husband stays at home to look after the children and to do the cleaning and cooking. This happens very frequently indeed. In Manchester alone there are many hundreds of men who are condemned to perform household duties. One may well imagine the righteous indignation of the workers at being virtually turned into eunuchs. Family relationships are reversed, although other social conditions remain unchanged. I have before me a letter written to Oastler by an English working man named Robert Pounder. . . . Pounder relates how a working class acquaintance of his, being on tramp in search of work, passed through St. Helens in Lancashire, and met an old friend: [Pounder wrote to Oastler]: *

. . . Well Sir he found him out—and when he got to is Cot what was it think you, Why a Low Damp Seller the Discriptun he gave of the funitoure was has follows, 2 old Chares, a round 3 legd table, a Box, no Bed Stocks, but a quantety of old Strow in one Corner with some Durty Bed Linen thrown opon it, and too peseses of wood was placed by the Fire Place, and when my poor friend Entered the Doar—poar Jack (for that is is name) was sat by th Fire Jarm on one of the Cloggs of wood and what wor he Dowing think you? Why he was sat mending is wife Stocking Eeels, with the Darning Neadle, but as soon has he sow is old Matey at the Door post, he endeverd to hide them—but Joe (for that is my poar friend's name) was to sharp for him and he sead 'Jack what Ever is thow Dowing? whear is the wife? what, that is not thy job, Im shour?' poar Jack was ashamed, and sead 'No I know that this is not my job, but t' poar wife is at the Mill, she has

* In order to enable his German readers to realise that the letter was written in dialect, Engels turned it into the sort of German that an uneducated worker would use and introduced deliberate mis-spellings. The translators have reproduced the relevant portions of the original letter of August 5th, 1844, from Oastler's periodical, *The Fleet Papers*, vol. 4, no. 35, August 31st, 1844, pp. 486-88.—TRANSLATORS.

to go at ½ past 5 oClock and work untill 8, and she is so poley that she is not able to to do Eneything when she comes home so I do all that I can for her, for I have no wark nore have Ed Eney for more then 3 years, and I think that I never shall heave Eney, Eney more.' And then Sir, he weept the big Tear,—'No, Joe, there is plenty of Wark for Wemen and Barns in this quarter but very Little for men—thou may as well go try to finde a hondred pounds, as go to find wark aboats heare—but I hed not ment neather thee nor eney one Els to have seen me mending t'wifes stockings, for its a poar job, but she is almost nockt of her feet—I ham sadly afrad that she will be thrown up altogather, and then, if she is, I do not now what is to become of us, for she as been t'man now for a Long time, and me t'woman— it is hard wark Joe';—and then poor Jack crayed bittly and sead 'It did not use to be so'—'No,' sead Joe, 'it did not Lad—and if thou has being out of wark so Long as that how Ever has ta Gotten on all t'time?' Well, Joe, I wall tell thee, as well as I can, I have gotten on in a very misserable way all the time—thow knows that when I Gat Wead—I had plenty of wark and something for warking, and thou nows that I was not Idle'—'No Jack thou wasn't'—'and we gat on very well—we gat a good firnished House' ('Ye Did Lad—has Ever Eney poar man need put a foot into')—'thire was no nead for—Mary to go to wark then—I could wark for us boath'—('yes that thou could') 'but now t'world is turned up side down, Mary has to turn out to wark and I have to stop at home to mind Barns—and to Wash and Clean—Bake and mend, for, poar Lass—when she comes home at night, she is down up—thou nows Joe this is ard wark for one that wants to Dow Different'.—Joe sead, 'I Lad it is ard Wark'—then poor Jack weept agane and sead that he wisht that he had never being Wead and that he never had being Born—but he did not think when Marred Mary that things would have comed to this, 'I have meney a cry about it', sead poor Jack.

Well Sir—when Joe heard poar Jacks tale, he towld me that he Could not help—Curseing both the factarys and the factary masters and the Government also for premetting it with all the Curseses that a mind Edecated in a factary is Capperble of.*

Can one imagine a more senseless and foolish state of affairs than that described in this letter? It deprives the husband of his manhood and the wife of all womanly qualities. Yet it cannot thereby turn a man into a

---

* Owing to Engels's misleading abridgement of the beginning of this letter it has previously been assumed that this incident took place in a house in St. Helens, but the relevant passage in the original letter, now reprinted for the first time, leaves the location vague:
'a shot time since a friend of mine that was out of work and who ust to work with me, at a former pearead, but who had being out of Wark for a Long time wor Compeld to go, on what we Labouring men Call, the tramp and having got to a place Calld Sant Hellins (I think it is in Lonckshire) and meeting with no sucsess, he thought that he would bend is way towards Monchester, and just as he was Leaving the place, he herd of one of his old mateys Leaving Close on the way—so he resolved that he would make him out if poseble—for he wishd to see him, thinking that he might perhaps help him to a job, and if not, he might give him a mouthfull of something to Eat, and a nights Lodgings, has he said he was very heardup' (*The Fleet Paper*, Vol. IV, no. 35, August 31, 1844, p. 487).

It would, of course, be a mistake to assume that the state of affairs reported by Pounder was in any way typical of St. Helens in the early 1840s, which was a town of heavy industry rather than a textile centre. T. C. Barker and J. R. Harris comment as follows: ' . . . it seems probable that the celebrated story recounted by Engels, of the poor, helpless wretch, found in a miserable, damp cellar at St. Helens mending the stockings of his wife who was out working, was a product of this period' of depression in 1841-3: *A Merseyside Town in the Industrial Revolution: St. Helens, 1750-1900* (1954), p. 321.—TRANSLATORS.

woman or a woman into a man. It is a state of affairs shameful and degrading to the human attributes of the sexes.* It is the culminating point of our highly-praised civilization. It is the final result of all the efforts of hundreds of generations to improve the lot of humanity both now and in the future. If all that can be achieved by our work and effort is this sort of mockery, then we must truly despair of humanity and its aspirations. If not, then we must admit that human society has followed the wrong road in its search for happiness. We shall have to accept the fact that so complete a reversal of the role of the two sexes can be due only to some radical error in the original relationship between men and women. If the rule of the wife over her husband—a natural consequence of the factory system—is unnatural, then the former rule of the husband over the wife must also have been unnatural. To-day, the wife—as in former times the husband—justifies her sway because she is the major or even the sole breadwinner of the family. In either case one partner is able to boast that he or she makes the greatest contribution to the upkeep of the family. Such a state of affairs shows clearly that there is no rational or sensible principle at the root of our ideas concerning family income and property. If the family as it exists in our present-day society comes to an end then its disappearance will prove that the real bond holding the family together was not affection but merely self-interest engendered by the false concept of family property.[†]

Enshrining Woman on the Patriarchal Pedestal

SOURCES

62. Auguste Comte, "Social Statics; or, Theory of the Spontaneous Order of Human Society," in *The Positive Philosophy of Auguste Comte*, tr. Harriet Martineau. 3 vols. (London, 1896), II, 280-81, 283, 284-86. Originally published as "Leçon 50" in Comte's *Cours de philosophie positive*, IV (Paris, 1839).

* Engels's 'Victorian' belief that women's place was in the home was shared by Peter Gaskell. See P. Gaskell, *The Manufacturing Population of England* (1833), pp. 166-7: "Nothing would tend more to elevate the moral condition of the manufacturing population, than the restoration of woman to her proper social rank: nothing would exercise greater influence upon the form and growth of her offspring, than her devotion to those womanly occupations which would render her a denizen of home. No great step can be made till she is snatched from unremitting toil, and made what Nature meant she should be—the centre of a system of social delights. Domestic avocations are those which are her peculiar lot. The poor man who suffers his wife to work, separated from him and from home, is a bad calculator."—TRANSLATORS.

†The great number of married women working in factories is shown by the following statistics issued by the factory owners themselves. In 412 factories in Lancashire 10,721 married women were employed. Only 5,314 of their husbands were also at work in factories; 3,927 of the husbands were engaged in other trades, while 821 were out of work and no information was available concerning 659 others. This shows that on the average in every factory two or even three husbands were being supported by their wives. [These statistics are to be found in the *Statement of Facts . . . submitted by the Deputation of the Master Manufacturers and Millowners in the County of Lancaster.* (See *Manchester Guardian*, May 1st, 1844, p. 5, cols. 4-5.)—TRANSLATORS.]

63. Auguste Comte, "The Influence of Positivism upon Women," in his "*General View of Positivism*," tr. J. H. Bridges (London, 1875; reprint ed., Stanford, Calif., n.d.), pp. 228-30, 231-32, 239-40, 275-77, 283, 286-88. Originally published in the first volume of his *Système de politique positive* (Paris, 1848).

The French philosopher Auguste Comte (1798-1857), one-time secretary and disciple of the comte de Saint-Simon, devoted his life to the formulation of a rigorously secular "science" of society, incorporating the concepts of statics and dynamics. Prior to 1842 Comte earned his living as a tutor and talent scout for the prestigious Parisian engineering school, the École Polytechnique. That year, when the final volume of his massive *Cours de philosophie positive* was published, this "father of modern sociology" lost his job and separated from his wife. In the first selection from the *Philosophie positive* (1839), Comte restated in the clinical language of nineteenth-century science long-standing European notions of female inferiority, thereby justifying old prejudices by clothing them in the more modern idiom of "objectivity." Like Michelet and Balzac, Comte was fascinated by recent developments in medical research, especially in comparative anatomy and physiology of the brain, which he incorporated into his theory of society by employing a highly charged biological vocabulary.

Within the next decade, however, Comte further developed and expanded his ideas about women and their social role within the constraints imposed by his convictions about male governance and the sexual division of labor. He had in the meantime rediscovered the importance of feeling through a passionate friendship with a much younger woman, Clotilde de Vaux, who had been deserted by her husband and was trying to make her own way as a writer. As a consequence of his infatuation, his concern for her welfare, and his idealization of her following her sudden and untimely death in 1846, Comte softened the edges of his earlier harsh postulates on female subordination. In its place he elaborated a romanticized and highly political restatement of the theory of woman's "moderating function" under man's protection. In 1847 Comte installed the worship of woman as the central tenet of his new "religion of humanity," which he had elaborated to cap his philosophical system. In the second selection, from his *Système de politique positive*, published in 1848, Comte lauded woman as the vehicle of feeling over reason and of morality over politics. Like Michelet (Doc. 46) he sought to enlist women on behalf of the forces of progress and to entice them away from Catholicism. He elaborated this campaign even further in the *Catechisme positiviste* (1851), in which his priest of the positive religion of humanity sought to instruct women to realize their exalted new potential as redeemers of Western society.

---

62. Auguste Comte (1839)

. . . As every system must be composed of elements of the same nature with itself, the scientific spirit forbids us to regard society as composed of individuals. The true social unit is certainly the family—reduced, if necessary, to the elementary couple which forms its basis. This consideration implies more than the physiological truth that families become tribes, and tribes become nations: so that the whole human race might be conceived of as the gradual development of a single family, if local diversities did not forbid such a supposition. There is a political point of view from which also we must consider this elementary idea, inasmuch as the family presents the true germ of the various characteristics of the social organism. . . .

We cannot too reverently admire that universal natural disposition, on which all association is grounded, by which, in the state of marriage, however imperfect, the strongest instinct of our animal nature, at once satisfied and disciplined, occasions harmony instead of the disorder which would arise from its license. It was not to be expected that, when the revolutionary spirit was attacking everything else, it should allow marriage to escape—connected as it has hitherto been with the theological philosophy. When the positive philosophy shall have established the subordination of the sexes, and in that, the principle of marriage and of the family, it will take its stand on an exact knowledge of human nature, followed by an appreciation of social development as a whole, and of the general phase which it now presents; and in doing this it will extinguish the fancies by which the institution is at present discredited and betrayed. . . .

What the ultimate conditions of marriage will be, we cannot know as yet; and if we could, this is not the place to treat of them. It is enough for our purpose to be assured that they will be consonant with the fundamental principle of the institution—the natural subordination of the woman, which has reappeared under all forms of marriage, in all ages, and which the new philosophy will place on its right basis—a knowledge of the individual organism first, and then of the social organism. Biological philosophy teaches us that, through the whole animal scale, and while the specific type is preserved, radical differences, physical and moral, distinguish the sexes. Comparing sex with age, biological analysis presents the female sex, in the human species especially, as constitutionally in a state of perpetual infancy, in comparison with the other; and therefore more remote, in all important respects, from the ideal type of the race. Sociology will prove that the equality of the sexes, of which so much is said, is incompatible with all social existence, by showing that each sex has special and permanent functions which it must fulfil in the natural economy of the human family, and which concur in a common end by different ways, the welfare which results being in no degree injured by the necessary subordination, since the happiness of every being depends on the wise development of its proper nature.

We have seen that the preponderance of the affective faculties is less marked in Man than in the lower animals, and that a certain degree of spontaneous speculative activity is the chief cerebral attribute of humanity, as well as the prime source of the marked character of our social organism. Now, the relative inferiority of Woman in this view is incontestable, unfit as she is, in comparison, for the requisite continuousness and intensity of mental labour, either from the intrinsic weakness of her reason or from her more lively moral and physical sensibility, which are hostile to scientific abstraction and concentration. This indubitable organic inferiority of feminine genius has been confirmed by decisive experiment, even in the fine arts, and amidst the concurrence of the most favourable circumstances. As for any functions of government, the radical inaptitude of the female sex is there yet more marked, even in regard to the most elementary state, and limited to the guidance of the mere family, the nature of the task requiring, above everything, an indefatigable attention to an aggregate of complex relations, none of which must be neglected, while the mind must be independent of the passions; in short, reasonable. Thus, the economy of the human family could never be inverted without an entire change in our cerebral organism, and the only possible result of a resistance to natural laws would be to deprive Woman of the enjoyment of her proper welfare by disturbing the family and society. Again, we have seen that, in the affective life of Man, the personal instincts overrule the sympathetic or social, which last can, and do, only modify the direction decided by the first, without becoming the habitual moving powers of practical existence. Here again, by a comparative examination, we can estimate the happy social position appropriated to the female sex. It is indisputable that women are, in general, as superior to men in a spontaneous expansion of sympathy and sociality, as they are inferior to men in understanding and reason. Their function in the economy of the family, and consequently of society, must therefore be to modify by the excitement of the social instinct the general direction necessarily originated by the cold and rough reason which is distinctive of Man. Apart from all consideration of material differences, and contemplating exclusively the noblest properties of our cerebral nature, we see that, of the two attributes which separate the human race from the brutes, the primary one indicates the necessary and invariable preponderance of the male sex, while the other points out the moderating function which is appropriate to Woman, even independently of maternal cares, which evidently constitute her most important special destination, but which are usually too exclusively insisted on, so as to disguise the direct social and personal vocation of the female sex.

63. Auguste Comte (1848)

. . . In the alliance which has been here proposed as necessary for social reorganization, Feeling, the most influential part of human nature, has not been adequately represented. An element is wanting which shall have the same relation to the moral side of our constitution, as the philosophic body has with Intellect, and the people with Activity. On this, as well as on other grounds, it is indispensable that Women be associated in the work of regeneration as soon as its tendencies and conditions can be explained to them. With the addition of this third element, the constructive movement at last assumes its true character. We may then feel confident that our intellectual and practical faculties will be kept in due subordination to universal Love. The digressions of intellect, and the subversive tendencies of our active powers will be as far as possible prevented.

Indispensable to Positivism as the co-operation of women is, it involves one essential condition. Modern progress must rise above its present imperfect character, before women can thoroughly sympathize with it.

At present the general feeling amongst them is antipathy to the Revolution. They dislike the destructive character which the Revolution necessarily exhibited in its first phase. All their social sympathies are given to the Middle Ages. And this is not merely due, as is supposed, to the regret which they very naturally feel for the decline of chivalry, although they cannot but feel that the Middle Ages are the only period in which the feeling of reverence for women has been properly cultivated. But the real ground of their predilection is deeper and less interested. It is that, being morally the purest portion of Humanity, they venerate Catholicism, as the only system which has upheld the principle of subordinating Politics to Morals. This, I cannot doubt, is the secret cause of most of the regret with which women still regard the irrevocable decay of mediaeval society.

They do not disregard the progress which modern times have made in various special directions. But our erroneous tendencies towards bringing back the old supremacy of Politics over Morality, are, in their eyes, a retrograde movement so comprehensive in its character that no partial improvements can compensate for it. True, we are able to justify this deviation provisionally, since the decay of Catholicism renders political dictatorship necessary. But women, having comparatively little to do with the practical business of life, can hardly appreciate this necessity without a more satisfactory theory of history than they at present possess. It is a complete mistake to charge women with being retrograde on account of these feelings of regret which are most honourable to them. They might retort the charge with far better reason on the revolutionists, for their blind admiration of Greek and Roman society, which they still persist in asserting to be superior to Catholic Feudalism; a delusion, the continuance of which is principally due to our absurd system of classical education, from which women are fortunately preserved.

However this may be, the feelings of women upon these subjects are a very plain and simple demonstration of the first condition of social regeneration, which is, that Politics must again be subordinated to Morality; and this upon a more intelligible, more comprehensive, and more permanent basis than Catholicism could supply. A system which supplied such a basis would naturally involve reverence for women as one of its characteristic results. . . .

Women will gladly associate themselves with the Revolution as soon as its work of reconstruction is fairly begun. Its negative phase must not be prolonged too far. It is difficult enough for them to understand how such a phase could ever be necessary; therefore they cannot be expected to excuse its aberrations. The true connexion of the Revolution with the Middle Ages must be fairly stated. History, when rightly interpreted, will show them that its real object is, while laying down a surer basis for Morality, to restore it to the old position of superiority over Politics in which the mediaeval system first placed it. Women will feel enthusiasm for the second phase of the Revolution, when they see republicanism in the light in which Positivism presents it, modified by the spirit of ancient chivalry.

Then, and not till then, will the movement of social regeneration be fairly begun. The movement can have no great force until women give cordial support to it; for it is they who are the best representatives of the fundamental principle on which Positivism rests, the victory of social over selfish affections. . . .

Spiritual power, as interpreted by Positivism, begins with the influence of women in the family; it is afterwards moulded into a system by thinkers, while the people are the guarantees for its political efficiency. Although it is the intellectual class that institutes the union, yet its own part in it, as it should never forget, is less direct than that of women, less practical than that of the people. The thinker is socially powerless except so far as he is supported by feminine sympathy and popular energy.

Thus the necessity of associating women in the movement of social regeneration creates no obstacle whatever to the philosophy by which that movement is to be directed. On the contrary, it aids its progress, by showing the true character of the moral force which is destined to control all the other forces of man. It involves as perfect an inauguration of the normal state as our times of transition admit. For the chief characteristic of that state will be a more complete and more harmonious union of the same three classes to whom we are now looking for the first impulse of reform. Already we can see how perfectly adapted to the constitution of man this final condition of Humanity will be. Feeling, Reason, Activity, whether viewed separately or in combination, correspond exactly to the three elements of the regenerative movement, Women, Philosophers, and People. . . .

Equality in the position of the two sexes is contrary to their nature, and no tendency to it has at any time been exhibited. All history assures us that with the growth of society the peculiar features of each sex have become not less but more distinct. By Catholic Feudalism the social condition of women in Western Europe was raised to a far higher level. But it took away from them the priestly functions which they had held under Polytheism; a religion in which the priesthood was more occupied with Art than with Science. So too with the gradual decline of the principle of Caste, women have been excluded more and more rigidly from royalty and from every other kind of political authority. Again, there is a visible tendency towards the removal of women from all industrial occupations, even from those which might seem best suited to them. And thus female life, instead of becoming independent of the Family, is being more and more concentrated in it; while at the same time their proper sphere of moral influence is constantly extending. The two tendencies so far from being opposed, are inseparably connected.

Without discussing the absurd and retrograde schemes which have been recently put forward on the subject, there is one remark which may serve to illustrate the value of the order which now exists. If women were to obtain that equality in the affairs of life which their so-called champions are claiming for them without their wish, not only would they suffer morally, but their social position would be endangered. They would be subject in almost every occupation to a degree of competition which they would not be able to sustain. Moreover, by rivalry in the pursuits of life, mutual affection between the sexes would be corrupted at its source.

Leaving these subversive dreams, we find a natural principle which, by determining the practical obligations of the Active to the Sympathetic sex, averts this danger. It is a principle which no philosophy but Positivism has been sufficiently real and practical to bring forward systematically for general acceptance. It is no new invention, however, but a universal tendency, confirmed by careful study of the whole past history of Man. The principle is, that Man should provide for Woman. It is a natural law of the human race; a law connected with the essentially domestic character of female life. We find it in the rudest forms of social life; and with every step in the progress of society its adoption becomes more extensive and complete. A still larger application of this fundamental principle will meet all the material difficulties under which women are now labouring. All social relations, and especially the question of wages, will be affected by it. The tendency to it is spontaneous; but it also follows from the high position which Positivism has assigned to Woman as the sympathetic element in the spiritual power. The intellectual class, in the same way, has to be supported by the practical class, in order to have its whole time available for the special duties imposed upon it. But in the case of women, the obligation of the other sex is still more sacred, because the sphere of duty in which protection for them is required, is the home. The obligation to provide for the intellectual class, affects society as a whole; but the maintenance of women is, with few exceptions, a personal obligation. Each individual should consider himself bound to maintain the woman he has chosen to be his partner in life. There are cases, however, in which men should be considered collectively responsible for the support of the other sex. Women who are without husband or parents should have their maintenance guaranteed by society; and this not merely from compassion for their dependent position, but with the view of enabling them to render public service of the greatest moral value.

The direction, then, of progress in the social condition of woman is this: to render her life more and more domestic; to diminish as far as possible the burden of out-door labour; and so to fit her more completely for her special office of educating our moral nature. . . .

But besides the pleasure inherent in their vocation, Positivism offers a recompense for their services, which Catholic Feudalism foreshadowed but could not realize. As men become more and more grateful for the blessing of their moral influence, they will give expression to this feeling in a systematic form. In a word the new doctrine will institute the Wor-

ship of Woman, publicly and privately, in a far more perfect way than has
ever before been possible. It is the first permanent step towards the worship of Humanity; which, as the concluding chapter of this introductory
work will show, is the central principle of Positivism, viewed either as a
Philosophy or as a Polity. . . .

Feudalism introduced for the first time the worship of Woman. But in
this it met with little support from Catholicism, and was in many respects
thwarted by it. The habits of Christianity were in themselves adverse to
real tenderness of heart; they only strengthened it indirectly, by promoting one of the indispensable conditions of true affection, purity of life. In
all other respects Chivalry was constantly opposed by the Catholic system; which was so austere and anti-social, that it could not sanction marriage except as an infirmity which it was necessary to tolerate, but which
was hazardous to personal salvation. Even its rules of purity, valuable as
they were, were often weakened by interested motives which seriously
impaired their value. Consequently, notwithstanding all the noble and
long-continued efforts of our mediaeval ancestors, the institution of the
worship of Woman was very imperfectly effected, especially in its relation
to public life. Whatever Catholic apologists may say, there is every reason
to believe that if Feudalism could have arisen before the decline of Polytheism, the influence of Chivalry would have been greater.

It was reserved for the more comprehensive system of Positivism, in
which sound practice is always supported by sound theory, to give full
expression to the feeling of veneration for women. In the new religion,
tenderness of heart is looked upon as the first of Woman's attributes. But
purity is not neglected. On the contrary its true source and its essential
value, as the first condition of happiness and of moral growth, are
pointed out more distinctly than before. . . . Positivism . . . teaches that
while the primary reason for insisting on purity is that it is essential to
depth of affection, it has as close a connexion with the physical and intellectual improvement of the individual and the race as with our moral
progress.

Positivism then, as the whole tendency of this chapter indicates, encourages, on intellectual as well as on moral grounds, full and systematic
expression of the feeling of veneration for Women, in public as well as in
private life, collectively as well as individually. Born to love and to be
loved, relieved from the burdens of practical life, free in the sacred retirement of their homes, the women of the West will receive from Positivists
the tribute of deep and sincere admiration which their life inspires. They
will feel no scruple in accepting their position as spontaneous priestesses
of Humanity; they will fear no longer the rivalry of a vindictive Deity.
From childhood each of us will be taught to regard their sex as the principal source of human happiness and improvement, whether in public life
or in private.

The treasures of affection which our ancestors wasted upon mystical
objects, and which these revolutionary times ignore, will then be care-

fully preserved and directed to their proper purpose. The enervating influence of chimerical beliefs will have passed away; and men in all the vigour of their energies, feeling themselves the masters of the known world, will feel it their highest happiness to submit with gratitude to the beneficent power of womanly sympathy. In a word, Man will in those days kneel to Woman, and to Woman alone.

CHAPTER 7

Men, Women, and Political Rights Before 1848

The Working-Class Discussion of Woman Suffrage

SOURCES

64. "Address of the Female Political Union of Newcastle-upon-Tyne to Their Fellow Countrywomen," in *The Early Chartists*, ed. Dorothy Thompson (Columbia, S.C., 1971), pp. 128-30. Originally published in the *Northern Star* (Newcastle upon Tyne), 2 February 1839.

65. R. J. Richardson, "The Rights of Woman," in *The Early Chartists*, ed. Dorothy Thompson, pp. 115, 124-25. Originally published as "The Rights of Woman; Exhibiting Her Natural, Civil, and Political Claims to Share in the Legislative and Executive Power of the State" (Edinburgh, 1840).

66. *L'Atelier*, "De la souveraineté," 4, no. 5 (February 1844), 67. Tr. KMO.

After fifty years of political agitation and the disappointment of the limited concessions made by Parliament in the 1832 Reform Act, English working-class radicals began the campaign for universal adult male suffrage known as "Chartism." Particularly in the North of England, the Chartists were remarked for their unusual literacy and their political eloquence; a number of the leading men in the movement attributed these traits to the fact that they had been carefully educated—and politicized—by the women who reared them. The "Address of the Female Political Union of Newcastle-upon-Tyne to Their Fellow Countrywomen," from the Chartist newspaper *Northern Star*, presents the prevailing Chartist view. It shows that these women were deeply concerned about—and understood—the impact of political events upon their lives, but that they expected to be politically active through their husbands and their sons. Moreover, they were hoping to exert their labor within their own households, rather than in the factory or in the marketplace.

A dissenting view is presented in the second selection, which is excerpted from a pamphlet on the political rights of women written by the Salford joiner and bookseller R. J. Richardson (dates not known) while he was in prison in 1840. Richardson disagreed with the Chartist majority view, arguing that women should be politically active in their own right. He insisted that women, as human beings, neglect their God-given duty if they do not participate in forging the laws of their own society.

The third selection comes from France, where, as in England, universal manhood suffrage without property qualification was strongly advocated during the

1830's and 1840's. This concise statement, which appeared in the French working-men's newspaper, *L'Atelier* (Doc. 57), bluntly presents the view predominant among Parisian skilled workers concerning women's position with respect to the vote.

---

64. The Female Political Union of Newcastle upon Tyne (1839)

Fellow-countrywomen,—We call upon you to join us and help our fathers, husbands, and brothers, to free themselves and us from political, physical, and mental bondage, and urge the following reasons as an answer to our enemies and an inducement to our friends.

We have been told that the province of woman is her home, and that the field of politics should be left to men; this we deny; the nature of things renders it impossible, and the conduct of those who give the advice is at variance with the principles they assert. Is it not true that the interests of our fathers, husbands, and brothers, ought to be ours? If they are oppressed and impoverished, do we not share those evils with them? If so, ought we not to resent the infliction of those wrongs upon them? We have read the records of the past, and our hearts have responded to the historian's praise of those women, who struggled against tyranny and urged their countrymen to be free or die.

Acting from those feelings when told of the oppression exercised upon the enslaved negroes in our colonies, we raised our voices in denunciation of their tyrants, and never rested until the dealers in human blood were compelled to abandon their hell-born traffic; but we have learned by bitter experience that slavery is not confined to colour or clime, and that even in England cruel oppression reigns—and we are compelled by our love of God and hatred of wrong to join our countrywomen in their demand for liberty and justice.

We have seen that because the husband's earnings could not support his family, the wife has been compelled to leave her home neglected and, with her infant children, work at a soul and body degrading toil. We have seen the father dragged from his home by a ruffian press-gang, compelled to fight against those that never injured him, paid only 34/- per month, while he ought to have had £6; his wife and children left to starve or subsist on the scanty fare doled out by hired charity. We have seen the poor robbed of their inheritance and a law enacted to treat poverty as a crime, to deny misery consolation, to take from the unfortunate their freedom, to drive the poor from their homes and their fatherland, to separate those whom God has joined together, and tear the children from their parents care,—this law was passed by men and supported by men, who avow the doctrine that the poor have no right to live, and that an all wise and beneficent Creator has left the wants of his children unprovided for. . . .

We have searched and found that the cause of these evils is the Government of the country being in the hands of a few of the upper and middle classes, while the working men who form the millions, the strength and wealth of the country, are left without the pale of the Constitution, their

wishes never consulted, and their interests sacrificed by the ruling factions, who have created useless officers and enormous salaries for their
own aggrandisement—burthened the country with a debt of eighteen
hundred millions sterling, and an enourmous taxation of fifty-four millions sterling annually, which ought not to be more than eight millions;
for these evils there is no remedy but the just measure of allowing every
citizen of the United Kingdom, the right of voting in the election of the
members of Parliaments, who have to make the laws that he has to be
governed by, and grant the taxes he has to pay; or, in other words, to pass
the people's Charter into a law and emancipate the white slaves of England. This is what the working men of England, Ireland, and Scotland,
are struggling for, and we have banded ourselves together in union to assist them; and we call on all our fellow country-women to join us.

We tell the wealthy, the high and mighty ones of the land, our kindred
shall be free. We tell their lordly dames we love our husbands as well as
they love theirs, that our homes shall be no longer destitute of comfort,
that in sickness, want, and old age, we will not be separated from them,
that our children are near and dear to us and shall not be torn from us.

We harbour no evil wishes against any one, and ask for nought but
justice; therefore, we call on all persons to assist us in this good work, but
especially those shopkeepers which the Reform Bill enfranchised. We call
on them to remember it was the unrepresented working men that procured them their rights, and that they ought now to fulfil the pledge they
gave to assist them to get theirs—they ought to remember that our pen-
nies make their pounds, and that we cannot in justice spend the hard
earnings of our husbands with those that are opposed to their rights and
interests.

Fellow-Countrywomen, in conclusion, we entreat you to join us to help
the cause of freedom, justice, honesty, and truth, to drive poverty and
ignorance from our land, and establish happy homes, true religion, righteous government, and good laws.

65. R. J. Richardson (1840)

. . . Having occupied some time in shewing you the natural degree of
woman, also her scriptural qualifications and her physical inequality, I
shall now proceed to the main feature of the question, or rather to the
question itself—'Ought Women to interfere in the political affairs of the
country?' As I have before prepared you, by an abstract dissertation upon
the natural rights of woman, I do most distinctly and unequivocally
say—YES! And for the following reasons:

First, Because she has a natural right.

Second, Because she has a civil right.

Third, Because she has a political right.

Fourth, Because it is a duty imperative upon her.

Fifth, Because it is derogatory to the divine will to neglect so imperative a duty. . . .

. . . I think, nay I believe, that God ordained woman 'to temper man.' I believe, from this reason, that she ought to partake of his councils, public and private, that she ought to share in the making of laws for the government of the commonwealth, in the same manner as she would join with her husband in the councils of his household. It is a duty she owes to herself, to her husband, to her children, to posterity, and to her common country. When we consider that it is to woman we owe our existence, that we receive from her our earliest thoughts and the bias of our minds—that we are indebted to her for all that makes life a blessing—would it not be unwise, ungrateful, and inhuman in man to deny them every advantage they can possess in society; and would it not be wrong and criminal, in the highest degree, in woman herself to neglect the most important part of her duty, namely, the making of good laws for the guidance of those whom she is instrumental in bringing into the world, and for the good government of the society of which she is an ornament and a member? Every bad law injures society in some way or other; an accumulation of bad laws weakens the bond of peace; and the continuance of bad laws destroys the freedom and happiness of mankind. If woman be silent in the passing of bad laws, she neglects her duty; if she is unconcerned about the accumulation of bad laws, she is criminally apathetic; and if she remains unmoved at the continuance of bad laws, she connives at her own ruin; is a party to her own disgrace; links the fetters to her own limbs; rivets the yoke of slavery to her children's necks, and deserves to be ruled over with a rod of iron. My last principal reason, viz. that it is derogatory to the Divine will to neglect so important a duty. I hope I have given sufficient proof in the foregoing pages of the rights and duties of women. I consider that she who neglects her country's good neglects her God. The Creator gave man the earth for his heritage, and bade him go forth, multiply, and replenish, and subdue it—not literally man, but mankind. How, then, can the earth be subdued but by government? and who are the governors and the governed?—Mankind; they are endowed with reason for that purpose, and by the force of such endowment, laws are made congenial with man's nature, for man's government, which constitutes society. There is no distinction made betwixt man and woman, therefore it is a duty imperative upon her to deliberate with man in all affairs of government, for with man she has a concurrent jurisdiction over the things of the earth. If she neglects her duty in the affairs of government, she does that which is derogatory to the Divine will; and, according to the true doctrine of rewards and punishments, brings the penalty of such derogation upon herself. If she fails to exercise a concurrent jurisdiction over the things of the earth, then does she again bring pains and penalties upon her own head, and her punishment is manifested in the passive obedience and slavish subjugation of which we have so many harrowing proofs.

66. *L'Atelier* (1844)

It is quite pointless to elaborate at length on the question of women's political incapacity. Everyone understands that her place is elsewhere than in the political arena; her place is at the domestic hearth. Public functions belong to man; private functions belong to woman—the latter are no less honorable, no less difficult than those functions belonging to man's nature. To refuse woman electoral rights does not make her inferior in any way—it simply submits her to a social necessity that requires a division of functions. If you remove woman from the function for which she is destined, lead her to the political theater and give her the right to speak there, you will have all the inconveniences of the babbling of infants and the influence of sensuality.

The Middle-Class Discussion of Woman Suffrage

SOURCES

67. *Woman's Rights and Duties Considered with Relation to Their Influence on Society and on Her Own Condition*, 2 vols. (London, 1840), I, 211-12, 213-15.

68. Marion Kirkland Reid (Mrs. Hugo Reid), *Woman: Her Education and Influence* (New York, 1857), pp. 70-76, 87, 89-91, 92-93. Originally published as *A Plea for Woman* (Edinburgh, 1843).

It was perhaps no coincidence that the anonymous female author of *Woman's Rights and Duties* published her tract in the same year that the World Anti-Slavery Convention was held in London. As in the case of Catharine Beecher and Mrs. Ellis (Docs. 49, 53), but going further than either, this author argued from a hierarchical view of society that placed men in control not only of the "public sphere" of political life but of the domestic sphere as well. She invoked "nature" to support a clearly counter-revolutionary point of view on the notion of women's participation in political life.

In contrast, Marion Kirkland Reid (dates not known; Docs. 44, 54) based her views on women's political rights on the utilitarian philosophy of Jeremy Bentham and James Mill (Doc. 31). Echoing William Thompson and Anna Doyle Wheeler (Doc. 32) she insisted that "all the arguments of those that may be called Benthamites apply equally to men and women," while dismissing the Utilitarians' statements that women did not need the vote. She went on to demolish the oft-cited assertions that women's domestic concerns would not allow them time for politics, or that politics might distract them from domestic duties. Finally she confronted the assertion that women's exposure to the coarser issues in political life might damage or destroy their gentle nature, arguing instead that there was no issue—especially one concerning women's fates and futures—that women should be barred from addressing. Arguments like Marion Reid's paved the way for the "social housekeeping" arguments that appeared with increasing frequency as the campaign for woman suffrage got underway.

---

67. *Woman's Rights and Duties* (1840)

Nature, then, having placed the stronger mind where she gave the stronger body, and accompanied it with a more enterprising ambitious spirit, the custom that consigns to the male sex the chief command in society, and all the offices which require the greatest strength and ability, has a better foundation than force, or the prejudices that result from it. The hard, laborious, stern, and coarse duties of the warrior, lawyer, legislator, or physician, require all tender emotions to be frequently repressed. The firmest texture of nerve is required to stand the severity of mental labour, and the greatest abilities are wanted where the duties of society are most difficult. It would be as little in agreement with the nature of things to see the exclusive possession of these taken from the abler sex, to be divided with the weaker, as it is, in the savage condition, to behold severe bodily toil inflicted on the feeble frame of the woman, and the softness of feeling, which nature has provided her with for the tenderest of her offices, that of nurturing the young, outraged by contempt, menaces, and blows.

It is therefore an impartial decree, which consigns all the offices that require the greatest ability to men. For, is it less the interest of woman than of man, that property, life, and liberty, should be secured—that aggression should be quickly and easily repressed—that contentment and order should prevail instead of tumult? that industry should be well paid—provisions cheap and plentiful—that trade should cover their tables and their persons with the comforts, conveniences, and luxuries which habit has rendered necessary, or an innocent sensibility pleasurable? Is it less momentous to them that religious opinions should be free from persecution—that a wise foreign policy should maintain those blessings in peace, and preserve us from the tribulation of foreign dominion? In objects of less selfish interest, are women less anxious than men, or more so, to see the practice of slavery expelled from the face of the earth? or our colonial government redeemed in every remaining instance, from the stain that has too often attended it, of being numbered with the most oppressive of European? . . .

Ills enough, Heaven knows! ensue from the weaknesses and incapacity of men, but to confer the offices, which demand all the skill and energy that can be had, on those who are weaker still, would be injurious alike to both. The commanding and influential stations in society belong, therefore, naturally and properly to the male sex: this of necessity entails the chief rule in private life also. But it is here that the rights of women come in, and that the danger of unjust encroachment upon them commences.

Everything that tends to lessen the comparative purity and refinement of women, is most pointedly adverse to their real interests; these are the qualities that enable them to be the guardians and sustainers of national morals: and their rights must be founded on their natural attributes and their moral dignity. To these respect and consideration cannot be denied, and every step mankind advances in civilisation gives strength to those sentiments. Women have neither the physical strength nor the mental power, to compete with men in the departments which depend on those qualifications; and however little we were to suppose their inferiority, in the long run they would always be defeated and discredited, in their competition for employment with the abler sex. Were so unnatural a state of society to arise, as that they should become the competitors instead of the assistants of man, they would lose their hold on his protection and tenderness, without being able to shield themselves from his harshness. The business of life would be far worse conducted, when the division of labour so clearly pointed out by nature was done away: and the just influence which women ought to have, would be destroyed by breaking down the barrier of opinion, which consigns them to the duties of a domestic and private station, and preserves them from the contamination of gross and contentious scenes.

But the same arguments that establish the right of the male sex to the sole possession of public authority, must leave the *chief* control of domestic life in their hands also. All the most laborious, the greater and more lucrative social offices, being filled by them, it follows, that generally speaking it is they who produce the wealth and property of society, and the property they create they have assuredly the best right to control; within the rules of virtue and law they may spend it as they will. The children whom the husband supports, the wife who accepts him, engaging to follow his fortunes, must be content to live as he pleases, or as his business requires. This is the law of nature and of reason. If his tastes or his profession be unpleasant to her, she must see to it beforehand; for ever after their interests must be one. In every important decision that is taken, one counsel must prevail: if it cannot be mutual, it must be assigned as a legal right to the owner of the property and the abler sex. Hence he is the head of the family; he must be responsible to law and opinion for the decorum of his house, and must have the power of restraining what he holds to be discreditable or wrong. Happy if he could be made equally responsible, even to his own conscience, for unjustly encroaching on rights which should never be taken from a woman, except for positive vice or incapacity! Her right to all the self-government that can be left to her, without deranging *his* purposes or *his* enjoyment, is as real as his own; and his purposes and enjoyments are not to be measured by mere pride or fancy, but by reason and justice; even then he remains judge in his own cause. As the right of man to the chief power, public and domestic, has been deduced from his greater ability, so the aptitude of the female mind and character for the details of domestic life, and the improvement of society in manners and morals, establish her rights also to a share of control; otherwise her utility must be greatly impaired, and her enjoyment cruelly and needlessly sacrificed.

68. Marion Kirkland Reid (1843)

The ground on which equality is claimed for all men is of equal force for all women; for women share the common nature of humanity, and are possessed of all those noble faculties which constitute man a responsible being, and give him a claim to be his own ruler, so far as is consistent with order, and the possession of the like degree of sovereignty over himself by every other human being. It is the possession of the noble faculties of reason and conscience which elevates man above the brutes, and invests him with this right of exercising supreme authority over himself. It is more especially the possession of an inward rule of rectitude, a law written on the heart in indelible characters, which raises him to this high dignity, and renders him an accountable being, by impressing him with the conviction that there are certain duties which he owes to his fellow-creatures. Whoever possesses this consciousness, has also the belief that the same convictions of duty are implanted in the breast of each member of the human family. He feels that he has a *right* to have all those duties exercised by others towards him, which his conscience tells him he ought to exercise towards others; hence the natural and equal rights of men.

We do not mean to enter into the question of the claim of all men to equal rights, but simply to state the foundation on which that claim rests, and to show that the first principles on which it does rest, apply to all mankind, without distinction of sex. The question of the equal right of all men to be represented in the legislature, would be the more out of place here, as it has already been ably discussed, and answered in the affirmative, by many of the greatest men of modern times; of these, Jeremy Bentham may be mentioned as the chief. Now, as all the arguments of those who may be called Benthamites apply equally to men and women, (with the exception of some counter objections in the case of woman, which we shall examine and show to be but trifling,) being built upon the grand characteristics of human nature, which are the same in both sexes, it is certainly inconsistent to allow those arguments weight in the case of one sex, and refuse it in that of the other. Perhaps those who refuse their assent to these doctrines—who cling to expediency, and put *right* altogether out of the question, are, to a certain length, excusable for denying equal civil rights to woman; but even these would find it difficult to assign any reason in favour of the expediency which they assert exists for the exclusion of *all* women from this right.

Our readers will, doubtless, soon observe, that throughout all the arguments we have used in these pages runs the idea of the equal right of all men to be represented—actually and really represented—in Parliament. Now this has been merely because we were not exactly aware of the grounds on which this privilege has been confined to persons having a house of ten-pounds' rent and upwards. Of course, we do not mean that all women should possess a privilege which has, as yet, only been conferred on particular classes of men; we only mean to insist that the right is the same in both sexes. If there be any particular reason for the exclusion from this privilege of a certain class among men, we would allow it to have weight for excluding the corresponding class of women, but for these alone. We would insist that, with whatever speciousness certain classes among men have been excluded from this right, it does not follow as a matter of course—as often assumed—that *all* women ought to be excluded. The class of women corresponding to the privileged class among men have still a claim; and the *onus probandi* against them lies with those who advocate the continuance of the system of exclusion.

The exercise of those rights would be useful in two ways: it would tend to ennoble and elevate the mind; and it would secure the temporal interest of those who exercise it.

No doubt can be entertained of the debasing nature of slavery. Its tendency to crush and extinguish the moral and spiritual, and to elevate the animal in human nature, is now generally acknowledged; but it does not seem to be so clearly perceived, that every degree of constraint partakes of the same tendency. Perfect liberty, we should say, is that which allows as much freedom to each individual human being, as is consistent with the same degree of freedom in every other human being. Everything short of this liberty, however far it may be from absolute slavery, yet partakes of its nature, and of its power of crushing, cramping, and debasing the human mind; of implanting a slavish spirit, and of substituting cunning for true wisdom. It prevents the human being from developing its powers; forbids independence of thought and action, without which there can be no virtue: and exercises in a thousand baneful ways, the most pernicious influence on the formation of individual character. What a cramping and keeping-down effect on the mind of women must this remark have, "What have women to do with that?"—the matter in question being one of interest to the whole human family—"let them mind their knitting, or their house affairs!" Now, this remark is, perhaps, only occasionally expressed in words, yet the spirit of it runs through all society: if not often *spoken* in conversation, it is constantly acted upon by our institutions.

Not only does civil liberty remove those evil influences, but it also substitutes ennobling influences in their place. The consciousness of a responsibility which the possession of a vote would bestow, the dignity of being trusted, the resolution to justify the faith placed in her truth and judgment, would call forth, in woman, noble powers, which, hitherto, have been too much suffered to lie dormant; powers which, when they have occasionally peeped forth in an individual, have but too often been greeted with laughter and ridicule, sometimes even with more serious obloquy. Thus, some of the gifted among women have been induced to hide their light beneath an exterior of levity and frivolity, while others have gained the pardon of the lord of the creation for encroaching on what he claims as his peculiar domain—the intellectual—by falling down and worshipping him, and then devoting their talents to instructing their sex in all the duties of this idolatry. The possession of the franchise would tend to raise woman above the bonds of this intolerable restraint; would give free play to her faculties, energy and individuality to all her powers. It would remove that inert and subdued state of mind which must be the result of a belief, that one is not fit for this or that thing of common sense and every-day life.

But besides all this, equal privileges are necessary for the mere tem-

poral interests of all; for no one can be supposed to know so well as the
individual himself, what is for his own peculiar advantage. Accordingly,
it is found, that when one class legislates for any other class, it attends
first to the bearing of that legislation on its own class interests; not perhaps, so much from selfishness (although that will help to blind the legislator) as because it *knows* what is for its own interest better than it possibly can know the interest of another class with whose mode of life, and
consequent wants and wishes, it never can be so familiar as with its own.
Each class, then, knowing what is best for its own peculiar benefit, will
have its interests best attended to by its own representative; and when all
are represented, those measures will be resolved on which favour the
happiness of the greatest number.

We are aware that it is said, that woman is virtually represented in Parliament, her interests being the same as those of man; but the many laws
which have been obliged to be passed to protect them from their nearest
male relatives, are a sufficient answer. The simple fact of such laws being
necessary, would be a strong presumption that woman requires to have
her interests really represented in the Legislature; but the manifestly unjust nature of the laws which this necessity has produced, convert presumption into proof, by showing most distinctly, that no sentiment, either of justice or gallantry, has been sufficient to ensure anything like
impartiality in the laws between the sexes. Those laws, then, are in themselves a convincing proof, first, that woman requires representation, and
second, that she is not represented. So utterly unjust are they—as we
shall show when treating more particularly on that subject—that no real
representative of woman could have any share in the making of them.
They are evidently the production of men legislating for their own most
obvious interests (I say obvious, because their own true and deep interest
was to do justice) without the slightest reference to the injustice they
were committing against women.

Members of Parliament are so deeply engaged with the party spirit of
politics, that the more special interests of woman, even though most intimately bound up with the general prosperity and well-being of the race,
are in great danger of being entirely lost sight of. Unless she be actually
represented, there is very little chance of woman's obtaining justice, even
in those matters where the laws are acknowledged to be partial—the evident results of class legislation. The justice of her complaints may be allowed; but if she has no one whose business it is to advocate her cause, its
justice will hardly prevent it from being laid on the shelf. It is a proverbial
saying, that "everybody's business is nobody's business"; and this is very
well exemplified in the manner in which woman is pretended to be represented now.

Denying that women are represented, infers another great wrong done
them. No taxation without representation, is the great motto of the
British constitution. Does the tax-gatherer pass the door of the self-
dependent and solitary female? Do the various commodities she consumes, come to her charged only with the price of their production and

carriage to her? Or is a fourth, or even a third, added to that price, which goes into the public treasury? If she must pay, why cannot she also vote? . . .

In proceeding to consider some of the most common objections against this change, it must be borne in mind that there is no reform against which it is not very easy to produce objections. But in arguing against any reform, it is not enough to show that there are objections to it—it must be shown that the objections against it are greater than the advantages which would arise from granting it.

The first objection I shall notice is, want of sufficient leisure: it may be said that woman has not time to spare from her domestic duties. . . .

The next objection we shall notice, is the fear that mixing in any degree in those weighty affairs may quite take away the relish for more domestic matters. But these so-much-despised domestic matters are really as important to the happiness of the human race as the duties attached to civil rights; and they lie too near the heart of woman ever to be neglected, in any great degree, even were they the most insignificant affairs conceivable. It sometimes happens that a merchant, manufacturer, or shopkeeper, runs mad with politics, and leaves his own business neglected, that he may have leisure to attend to that of the nation; yet, to prevent more mishaps of that kind, nobody proposes to take away the civil rights of merchants, manufacturers, or shopkeepers. Now, the domestic duties of woman being so much more closely, or at least more immediately, bound up in the affections than the business duties of man, there is much less risk of her ever falling into such an error. Is it to be so much as imagined, that any political excitement will be so apt to make a woman forget her children as to make a man forget his counting-house, counter, or spinning-jennies? Every heart, worthy the name, answers distinctly, and at once, No.

It may be objected, that such an introduction into the bustle of public life would injure the most charming characteristics of woman—her gentleness and modesty. What a satire is this upon the conduct of men in their intercourse with each other! Does it appear that their business habits are so rough that they are afraid to allow of women mingling with them, lest they should lose their natural gentleness, and become as uncouth and as uncultivated as themselves? Why! let them mend their manners, and the difficulty at once disappears. However, even although this mode of getting rid of the obstacle should not be approved of by those who alone can put it in practice, we have no doubt that gentleness and modesty are too deeply rooted in the very constitution of woman to be so early lost. We incline rather to hope that both parties may soon be improved by some amalgamation of manners—that women shall soon cease to be so soft and helpless, and men so rough and bearish. Having no fear that they can ever lose their distinctive marks, we confess we should like to see them approach each other a little nearer in character.

An objection something similar to the last is, that delicacy and decorum would suffer materially by the success of the opinions we advocate. . . .

We suppose that [this objection] alludes to those terrible disorders and desperate vices of society, a fearful and shuddering glimpse of which is all that her own ideas of propriety allow to a modest woman; and, if such be the case, we cannot help thinking that a better acquaintance with those dreadful evils, and even great efforts to amend them, are perfectly consistent with female delicacy: to the pure all things are pure. The possession of a truer and more complete knowledge on this painful subject, by women in general, would do more to lessen the numbers of the most unfortunate outcasts of society—many of them more sinned against than sinning—than all the secret discussions of the House of Commons. However pleasant it may be for women themselves to intrench themselves in decorum and refinement from so painful a knowledge, and however consonant such behavior may be to the prejudices of society—yet such is not the manner in which those terrible disorders can be remedied. It certainly seems to us that there are no vices so desperate that they ought not to be unfolded to female eyes, of which females are themselves the partakers and the most miserable victims. However painful the discussion of such subjects may be—and painful they must ever be to every refined and delicate mind whether male or female— yet, since the discussion is necessary, it ought not to be shrunk from. Since females are also even more interested than males in the suppression of those evils, we can see no propriety whatever in endeavouring to keep them in ignorance of their existence.

PART III

Women, Revolution, and Reaction, 1848-1860

The year 1848 marks a watershed in the history of the debate over women, the family, and freedom. For two decades after 1830, when the debate reopened in France, the "woman question" became a pivotal issue in the recasting of social ideology by Protestant Evangelical and Catholic Christians as well as for their secular rivals, the Liberals, Radicals, and Socialists, all of whom expressed themselves in the romantic idiom of the time. Then, in 1848, as revolutionaries challenged the monarchies and attempted to reformulate the authoritarian structure of governments in France, the Germanies, and Italy, women confronted them with a question central to the understanding of republican and democratic ideals— that of women's right to active participation in political affairs.

The sequence of revolutions began in February 1848 when the French monarchy was overthrown and a republic was proclaimed. Shortly thereafter the Austrian Empire also experienced political upheaval, followed by similar outbreaks in other major European capitals.[1] Within the first month of the new French republic a group of French women who had been active in Saint-Simonian and Fourierist circles organized to present their claims. Writing in their own daily paper, *La Voix des Femmes*, published in Paris from March to June 1848, these women presented a program that demanded political rights equal to those being considered for men, the representation of women by women in the Constituent Assembly, the consecration of women as "priestesses" of the new order, government action to guarantee women's independence through work (including employment by the state in national workshops for the unemployed and the protection of women's trades against invasion by men), and the founding of day-care centers for working-class families; also, the construction of apartment houses with central kitchens, central heat, central gardens, and reading rooms, mutually funded medical care and mid-

[1] For specific treatments of the 1848 revolutions, see Robertson 1952; Duveau 1969; Langer 1969; R. Lougee 1972; Price 1972; and Stearns 1974.

wifery expenses for women, and a vocational school for the daughters of residents.

It was an extraordinarily comprehensive program. And, indeed, the emphatic self-confidence displayed by these dissenting women of 1848 is impressive. These articles and tracts are tightly argued and assertive, as we see in Jeanne Deroin's manifesto and in her series of articles on "woman's mission" (Docs. 70, 77) and in Louise Otto's articles (Docs. 78, 89).

Women's political assertiveness was particularly apparent in the newspapers they founded to defend their interests in 1848: *La Voix des Femmes*, *Le Politique des Femmes*, and *L'Opinion des Femmes*, in Paris; the *Frauen-Zeitung* of Louise Otto in Leipzig, and the paper of the same name begun by Mathilda Franziska Anneke in Cologne. In these city settings women had found a public voice; the press gave them a means to spread their message, both as individuals and through group efforts.[2] In early May 1848 they opened a political club in Paris for women that met weekly to discuss women's issues. It soon attracted considerable notice and a good deal of ridicule; it even became a tourist attraction for visiting foreigners. And in early June it became the target for harassment by visiting men. After the widely reported uproar of one meeting chaired by Eugénie Niboyet in early June, she angrily criticized the "unrepublican" interlopers for their behavior. "If anything justifies and encourages us, Messieurs," she wrote, "it is your conduct at our meeting. You do not want to listen to us because you are beginning to fear us, and to you it seems easier to stifle us than to accord us justice. Behind your jeering, despotism reveals itself; behind your interruptions lurks malevolence. You well know that we do not wish to diminish you, yet you are afraid to see us rise."[3]

Niboyet's charges hit the mark. When the forces of counter-revolution reestablished their grip, they not only set limits on the access other men had to freedom of speech and association, but they also applied a double standard by barring women completely from such access, as the French decree on the clubs and the later Prussian law on association attest (Docs. 71, 86). The French decree was accompanied, only a few years later, by Napoleon III's formal exclusion of women from the right to publish newspapers discussing political subjects; similar laws and decrees were enacted throughout central Europe. Even women's right to petition the government for redress of grievances was threatened. Thus, by 1851 the women who had claimed the right to common participation in governmental affairs had been beaten back. Allied as they often were with male advocates of radical democratic reform, their defeat is perhaps not entirely surprising; what still astonishes, however, is the ruthlessness with which women's political activism was repressed on the Continent. Only in England and the United States (as evidenced by the Seneca Falls and later conventions, Docs. 74-76) were women legally free after 1848

[2]On the significance of the women's press in 1848, see Sullerot 1966a; Adler 1979; and Gerhard, Hannover-Drück & Schmitter 1980.
[3]In *La Voix des Femmes*, 8-10 June 1848.

to organize in unrestricted pursuit of political and economic freedom, though they were still subjected to misrepresentation and ridicule. Elsewhere the power of the state was turned against them, legally defining them out of political life, and silencing and dispersing the most articulate and committed leaders of this generation of innovating women.

Politically conscious women throughout the Western world quickly learned, however, through their own press and through their friends, of this repression; they understood its symbolic and practical significance. These events undoubtedly played a critical role in determining women in other countries, especially in the United States, to demand the vote on the same basis that it had been granted to men—whether wholly democratic, as it was (at least for white males) in the United States and as it had been in France from 1848 to 1851, or based on property qualifications, as it remained in England until 1918. The demand for woman suffrage and candidacy (eligibility for office) was a radical demand, a political demand, formulated in the language that the men who controlled (or who aspired to control) the state understood—and feared, as can be seen from the controversy over Jeanne Deroin's candidacy (Docs. 84, 85).[4]

In the meantime, women in countries less immediately affected by the continental revolutions had other incentives for initiating reforms in the legal and economic status of their countrywomen. Their campaigns were informational and propagandistic. In England, Harriet Taylor Mill, inspired by the conventions of American women in New York and Massachusetts, put the finishing touches to her thoughtful and firm essay, "The Enfranchisement of Women" (Doc. 88), published in 1851. Numerous English and Russian women played a highly visible role under excruciatingly difficult conditions by traveling far from home and nursing wounded soldiers during the Crimean War (1854-57). Because of her personality and high-level connections, Florence Nightingale was much discussed in the British press, thus alerting the civilian population to middle-class women's stamina and organizational capacities. Further, the women concerned with the founding of the well-respected institutions for aiding and educating teachers and governesses—such as Queen's College (Doc. 47), Bedford College, and the North London Collegiate School (1847-50)—also established, in 1857, the *English Woman's Journal*. It was staffed almost entirely by women, working at their own Victoria Press, who were dedicated to promoting women's educational and legal reforms. In 1854 one of its founder-members, Barbara Leigh-Smith Bodichon, had produced a lucid catalogue of facts concerning women's legal condition that sparked furious controversy. The selections printed here illustrate some of the ways in which articulate women could disagree about the very principle of women's legal subjection in marriage (Docs. 90-92). In the long run, however, this debate led to major reforms in women's status within the law. In the same period, between 1854 and 1856, the Scandinavian novelists Camilla Collett and Fredrika Bremer

---

[4]For rehabilitation of the argument that suffrage was a radical demand in the United States, see DuBois 1975.

contributed to mobilizing public opinion behind legal reforms for women in Norway and Sweden (Docs. 93, 94).[5]

In their writings, the women of this era invoked, once again, the potential contribution to public life of their intrinsic qualities as women and their practical experience as mothers—natural qualities and functional experience different from that of men. They demanded equality—but equality in difference. Such arguments, already developed by writers of both sexes in the 1830's and 1840's, permeated the arguments of women revolutionaries like Jeanne Deroin and Louise Otto. Moreover, all these women argued for the "domestication of the public sphere," to cite the felicitous phrase of historian Joan Moon.[6] Similar arguments would be heard again two or three generations later in the United States, in the reform efforts of Frances E. Willard, Charlotte Perkins Gilman, and Jane Addams (who are often erroneously credited with inventing this approach). The glorification of women's "otherness" as a tool for reform, however, viewed by many twentieth-century objectors as anathema, represented the cutting edge of change in the mid-nineteenth century; women had turned an ostensibly conservative male doctrine on its head and forged it into a revolutionary political tool.

There was yet another important development since 1830 that emerged in the rhetoric and ideology of the women of 1848: their reincorporation of liberal Christian humanist arguments. Anglo-Saxon women reformers such as Mott and the Grimké sisters in the United States and Anne Knight in Britain drew on a Quaker heritage (Docs. 50, 74, 73, respectively). Anglican women like Mary Maurice (Doc. 47) were able to proceed with educational reforms within the Established Church, which in England at least was able to incorporate reforms that did not challenge basic Christian doctrine. No longer (as in the eighteenth century) do we see the case for women's emancipation stated in purely secular terms. Even as traditionalist Christian defenders of the patriarchal order drew on secular Enlightenment arguments to bolster their case for preserving the status quo (see Introduction to Part II), women and men dedicated to improving the position of women drew on the arguments from equality of the sexes in natural law, and joined to them the doctrine of the equality of Christians, male and female—and Christians and Jews—before God.[7] Indeed, the arguments of women revolutionaries and their supporters throughout continental Europe were infused with appeals both to God and to natural law. Thus, the contest to control women's influence erupted in the wake of 1848 in a series of fascinating, yet relatively little-known developments whose true significance has been overlooked.

The campaign for celebration of womanhood common to the Saint-

[5] For further insight into the British campaigns, see Strachey 1928; F. Basch 1974; and Fredeman 1974. On the Scandinavian reform campaign, see Qvist 1960, 1969; and Wieselgren 1978.

[6] S. J. Moon 1976b.

[7] The argument that Christians and Jews were equal before God was elaborated by liberals in the German states, where Jews were emancipated from legal restrictions during the revolutions of 1848.

Simonians, to liberal Protestants, and secular Positivists was taken up by Roman Catholics. In the same year that Jeanne Deroin and Louise Otto asserted that women, because of their special role, had a unique mission to fill in a revolutionary world, Pope Pius IX launched the Catholic campaign for the "rehabilitation" of the Virgin through proclaiming the dogma of the Immaculate Conception of Mary (Doc. 79).[8] As in the Counter-Reformation of the sixteenth century the new pope was responding to Protestant *and* secular arguments. The papal campaign was variously appreciated. Dissident German Catholic leader Johannes Ronge (Doc. 80) objected to the supernatural elements of Mariolatry but applauded its redeeming contribution to the dignity of womanhood and of womanly love; on this basis he beseeched women to embark on a course of social action. And the former "father" of the Saint-Simonians, the railroad entrepreneur Prosper Enfantin, was reported to have remarked concerning the proclamation of the Immaculate Conception: "At last male paradise has come to an end. For look, woman is being introduced at God's side; on his very throne the Goddess is being seated. It is a guarantee for the future." And he added, "Out of religious law, this idea will sooner or later slip into civil law, and woman will become Man's equal. The Church has been allowed to take the lead in a matter that should have been resolved long ago."[9]

From this point on, without much further cross-fertilization, the woman question became central in controversies that developed internally within the various organized religious groups and among their secular opponents. In the face of the religious aspect of the campaign to rehabilitate women, the arguments of secular and anticlerical writers like Jules Michelet and P.-J. Proudhon (Docs. 97, 95) can be better appreciated. Proudhon challenged the very notion of female rehabilitation in his highly controversial work, *De la Justice*, while Michelet, arguing in the opposite sense in his *Love* and *Woman*, like Comte (Doc. 63) sought to extend the notion of woman as priestess, while confining her mission to the patriarchal hearth. The woman question is basic to the cosmology of both writers, and was recognized as such by their readers. The danger of these men's ideas for women's cause was also recognized by two articulate women—Juliette Lambert Lamessine [Adam] and Jenny P. d'Héricourt (Docs. 96, 98)—who wrote solid books of international significance refuting the new *summae* of Michelet and Proudhon. Even though the political press was unavailable to these women, the expression of their ideas in book form was still possible. Significantly, they both had personal contacts among the old Saint-Simonians, Fourierists, and Cabetistes, and neither woman was reticent about publishing her provocative opinions. With Juliette Adam, we find a woman restating and elaborating the argu-

---

[8] The dogma proclaimed, in effect, that the Virgin Mary was herself conceived free of original sin (i.e., asexually) by her own mother Elizabeth. For particulars, see Digby 1845-47; Doheny & Kelly 1954; O'Connor 1958; and Gruber 1967.

[9] Enfantin's remarks were reported by Maxime du Camp in his *Souvenirs littéraires*, II (Paris, 1892), 89.

ments presented since the early 1830's by the Saint-Simonian women, to the effect that women have a right to work, to self-support, as a guarantee of their personal dignity. This argument was quietly transported to Russia and elaborated by the Russian radicals Mikhailov and Chernyshevsky (Docs. 99, 100).[10]

By 1860, then, firm commitments to women's public involvement had been made by women themselves in the public sphere through political intervention, through founding their own presses, newspapers, and journals; and, in England and the United States, through creating establishments of secondary higher education for women.[11] The revolutions and the Crimean War had given women an opportunity to demonstrate to the world that they were quite capable of boldly confronting and criticizing the results of male violence. At the same time, economic development produced an ever-growing number of women who had to depend for survival on their own efforts. Moreover, the international connections fostered by war, revolution, and commerce reinforced the internationalism of the debate over women. These bold challenges appear to have forced defenders of the status quo to become yet more firmly entrenched in their assertions that, in order to uphold patriarchy, women's humanizing influence must be contained within the private/domestic sphere.

[10] On the transfer of this debate to Russia, see Stites 1969, 1978.

[11] The founding of girls' academies and teacher training establishments in the United States in the 1820's and 1830's has been well studied. See, in particular, Woody 1929; Flexner 1959; Newcomer 1959; Sklar 1973; Melder 1977; Scott 1978; and Green 1979. For the beginnings of such schools in England, see Tuke 1939; Grylls 1948; Scrimgeour 1950; Kamm 1965; and Kaye 1972.

CHAPTER 8

Women's Political Consciousness in a Revolutionary Age

Revolutionary Visions in Continental Europe

SOURCES

69. Karl Marx and Friedrich Engels, "Manifesto of the German Communist Party," *The Red Republican* (London), I, no. 23 (23 November 1850), 182. Translated by Helen Macfarlane. Originally published in German, London, 1848.

70. Jeanne Deroin, "Aux Citoyens Français!," *La Voix des Femmes*, no. 7 (27 March 1848); reprinted in Adrien Ranvier, "Une Féministe de 1848, Jeanne Deroin," *La Révolution de 1848*, 4, no. 24 (Jan.-Feb. 1908), 322-23. Tr. KMO.

Perhaps the most radical statement concerning the future of women and the family was that of Karl Marx (1818-1883) and Friedrich Engels (1820-1895; Doc. 61), who were convinced that only through class struggle and abolition of the links between private property and the family could women—and men—become truly free. The brilliant and belligerent Marx came from a prosperous, converted Jewish family in the Prussian Rhineland. In 1843 he arrived in Paris, armed with a doctorate in philosophy from the University of Jena and some experience as a journalist writing for a radical newspaper in Cologne; he was accompanied by his new wife, Jenny, daughter of the aristocratic family next door. In Paris he quickly immersed himself in the social reform discussions of the French theorists, especially Proudhon (Doc. 52), with whom Marx quarreled bitterly before he was expelled from the country at the request of the Prussian government in 1845. In 1847, the twenty-nine-year-old Marx, then living in Brussels, and his collaborator Friedrich Engels, the son of a wealthy German textile manufacturer who, like Marx, had become a political radical, composed this manifesto for the London branch of a small German revolutionary group in exile known as the Communist League. Though the document did not attract much notice at the time, it has since become a "classic" of the revolutionary literature of 1848. This excerpt presents in its entirety the *Manifesto*'s discussion of women and the family. The role of women here is curiously abstract; some notion of Marx's own views can, however, be extrapolated from a later manuscript by his daughter, who had asked him to name his favorite virtue in man and in woman. Marx's replies were, respectively, "strength" and "weakness."

A more characteristic statement of the French reform tradition was presented by Jeanne Deroin (1805-1894; Docs. 36, 77, 84, 85, 87), a self-educated working-class woman—married and a mother—who had first become committed to improving the condition of women through her involvement with the Saint-Simonians (Part II above). In contrast to Marx, Deroin was firmly committed to the advancement of class harmony, not class struggle, and to the non-combative cooperation of the sexes as well. She was more interested in reallocating private property and political power than in abolishing it. Within the first month of the new republic's existence and the provisional government's proclamation of universal manhood suffrage, Deroin confronted the republicans with the logical conclusion of their democratic doctrines—women's full participation in charting the course of the new regime. Writing in the daily women's paper founded by Eugénie Niboyet just the week before, Deroin had called on the republicans to nominate distinguished women as candidates to the Constituent Assembly that was to be elected in late April. Shortly thereafter she called for woman suffrage as well. The romantic rhetoric in which Deroin couched her demands in this article could not conceal from her contemporaries their radical nature; it appeared the very week that a delegation of women presented the provisional government of the new republic with a petition for women's political rights.

---

69. Karl Marx and Friedrich Engels (1848)

But do not dispute with us, while you measure the proposed abolition of Middle-class property, by your Middle-class ideas of freedom, civilization, jurisprudence, and the like. Your ideas are the necessary consequences of the Middle-class conditions of property and production, as your jurisprudence is the Will of your class raised to the dignity of law, a will whose subject is given in the economical conditions of your class. The selfish mode of viewing the question, whereby you confound your transitory conditions of production and property with the eternal laws of Reason and Nature, is common to all ruling classes. What you understand with regard to Antique and Feudal property, you cannot understand with regard to modern Middle-class property.—The destruction of domestic ties! Even the greatest Radicals are shocked at this scandalous intention of the Communists. Upon what rests the present system, the Bourgeois system, of family relationships? Upon Capital, upon private gains, on profit-mongering. In its most perfect form it exists only for the Bourgeoisie, and it finds a befitting complement in the compulsory celibacy of the Proletarians, and in public prostitution. The Bourgeois family system naturally disappears with the disappearance of its complement, and the destruction of both is involved in the destruction of Capital. Do you reproach us that we intend abolishing the using up of children by their parents? We acknowledge this crime. Or that we will abolish the most endearing relationships, by substituting a public and social system of education for the existing private one? And is not your system of education also determined by society? by the social conditions, within the limits of which you educate? by the more or less direct influence of society, through the medium of your schools, and so forth?

The Communists do not invent the influence of society upon education; they only seek to change its character, to rescue education from the influence of a ruling class. Middle-class talk about domestic ties and education, about the endearing connection of parent and child, becomes more and more disgusting in proportion as the family ties of the Proletarians are torn asunder, and their children changed into machines, into articles of commerce, by the extension of the modern industrial system. But you intend introducing a community of women, shrieks the whole Middle-class like a tragic chorus. The Bourgeois looks upon his wife as a mere instrument of production; he is told that the instruments of production are to be used up in common, and thus he naturally supposes that women will share the common fate of other machines. He does not even dream that it is intended, on the contrary, to abolish the position of woman as a mere instrument of production. For the rest, nothing can be more ludicrous than the highly moral and religious horror entertained by the Bourgeoisie towards the pretended official community of women among the Communists. We do not require to introduce [a] community of women; it has always existed. Your Middle-class gentry are not satisfied with having the wives and daughters of their Wages-slaves at their disposal—not to mention the innumerable public prostitutes—but they take a particular pleasure in seducing each other's wives. Middle-class marriage is in reality a community of wives. At the most, then, we could only be reproached for wishing to substitute an open, above-board community of women, for the present mean, hypocritical, sneaking kind of community. But it is evident enough that with the disappearance of the present conditions of production, the community of women occasioned by them—namely, official and non-official prostitution—will also disappear.

70. Jeanne Deroin (1848)

The reign of brute force has ended; that of morality and intelligence has just begun. The motives that led our fathers to exclude women from all participation in the governance of the State are no longer valid. When every question was decided by the sword, it was natural to believe that women—who could not take part in combat—should not be seated in the assembly of warriors. In those days it was a question of destroying and conquering by the sword; today it is a question of building and of organizing. Women should be called on to take part in the great task of social regeneration that is under way. Why should our country be deprived of the services of its daughters?

Liberty, equality, and fraternity have been proclaimed for all. Why should women be left only with obligations to fulfill, without being given the rights of citizens? Will they be excused from paying taxes and from obeying the laws of the State? Will they be obliged to obey the laws and to pay the taxes imposed upon them?

Are they to become the helots of your new Republic? No, citizens, you do not want this; the mothers of your sons cannot be slaves. We address this just demand not merely to the provisional government, which alone cannot decide a question that is of interest to the entire nation. We come to plead our cause—so holy, so legitimate—before the citizens' assembly: our cause is theirs. They will not want to be accused of injustice. When they abolish all privileges, they will not think of conserving the worst one of all and leaving one-half of the nation under the domination of the other half. They will at least give us a role in national representation; some women chosen among the most worthy, the most honorable, the most capable, will be nominated by the men themselves, to come forth in defense of the rights of their sex and the generous principles of our glorious Revolution. Liberty, equality, and fraternity will thus be realized.

Women's Fate in the French Revolution of 1848

SOURCES

71. "Décret sur les clubs," 28 July 1848. *Collection complète des lois, décrets, ordonnances, règlements, et avis du Conseil d'État,* XLVIII (1848), 397, arts. 1-3. Tr. KMO.

72. "Rapport (Projet de décret sur les clubs) par le citoyen Athanase Coquerel—Séance du 22 juillet 1848." *Assemblée constituante, 1848-1849. Impressions,* III, no. 252: 9. Tr. KMO.

72. Anne Knight, *Au Pasteur Coquerel* (Paris, 1848). Tr. KMO.

Jeanne Deroin's dream was short-lived. In July, following the brutal repression of insurgent Parisian workingmen, the government elected by universal manhood suffrage took action to curb freedom of the press and freedom of association. Where women were concerned, however, the measures applied a double standard, closing the women's clubs entirely and forbidding women to participate in political associations of any kind. The text of the July decree on the clubs is the first selection. The provisions were incorporated into law in June 1849, and were reinforced in 1851 by decrees on the press that barred women from publishing newspapers that proposed to discuss political subjects. The rationalization for the 1848 decree is presented in the second selection, by the Assembly's reporter, the liberal protestant pastor and deputy for the Seine, Athanase Coquerel (1795-1868). It ominously recalls the reasons given during the Terror of 1793 for justifying the exclusion of women from French political life.

The decree against the clubs did not, however, go unchallenged by women. The third selection presents the reply of the English Quaker, Anne Knight (1786-1862), who was in Paris during the 1848 revolution. She was one of several women besides Jeanne Deroin who publicly protested the Assembly's action and Coquerel's role in it. Knight was well known to English and American women of her day as an opponent of slavery and a radical thinker on women's issues. In 1847 she had published a pamphlet advocating female suffrage that caused a stir not only in England, but also among the American Quakers like Lucretia Mott, who was to organize the Seneca Falls convention a year later. Anne Knight's reply to Coquerel, written in excellent French, attests her superior education as a linguist; she countered his statements not by appeals to sentiment but by invoking the authority of Christ and Shakespeare. Her tract was reproduced and discussed in the Parisian press.

71. "Décret sur les clubs" (1848)

Art. 1. Citizens have the right to assemble, provided that the following conditions are satisfied.

Art. 2. The opening of any club or citizens' meeting shall be preceded by a declaration made by the founders, in Paris at the Prefecture of Police, and in the departments at the offices of the town mayor and the prefect. This declaration must be made at least forty-eight hours before the beginning of the meeting. It must include the names, addresses, and relevant information about the founders, the locale, and the days and times of meetings. The declaration will be recorded immediately.

No club may have a name other than that of the locale where it meets.

Public or municipal buildings cannot be used, even temporarily, for these meetings.

Art. 3. The clubs will be open to the public and must never restrict, either directly or indirectly, the public nature of their meetings, or meet in secret committee.

To assure such publicity, at least one-fourth of the seats will be reserved for citizens who do not belong to the club.

Women and minor children may not be members of a club nor may they attend the meetings.

Club meetings may not last beyond the closing hour designated by the authorities for the closing of public places.

72. Athanase Coquerel (1848)

Article 3 assures the public nature of meetings, according to the simple and fruitful principle that publicity is the corrective for liberty. . . . A gathering of free citizens should not be allowed to transform itself into a council shrouded in mystery; the matters presented for discussion in the clubs being of interest to all citizens, it follows that everyone should be admitted. This publicity does not extend to minors and women. The minors will have their turn; they can wait and can pursue their studies better elsewhere than in club meetings. The suitable and legitimate place for women is in private life and not in public life. Woman is always the loser when she departs from the former for the latter and, besides, historic memories of the presence of women in political assemblies suffice to exclude them.

73. Anne Knight (1848)

Alas, my brother, is it then true that thy eloquent voice has been heard in the heart of the National Assembly expressing a sentiment so contrary to real republicanism? Can it be that thou hast really protested not only against women's rights to form clubs but also against their right to attend clubs formed by men? Is all this true?

Alas, was this well done, Charmion? (Shakespeare)

Is it possible that thou, a minister of religion, hast spoken a language so contrary to the commandments of thy "Divine Master," for thus I have heard thee call him. This divine Master has said: "Do unto others as thou wouldst have others do unto thee." Well then! Would thee like it if thee were forbidden to hold meetings and to uphold thy opinions there?

Oh! reflect on thy words. What terrible events have taken place since the letter I wrote to thee [in April] soliciting thee to place thy mind and thy voice in the service of women's emancipation. Dost thou remember what M. Legouvé[*] said in one of his lessons on the first revolution? "It failed," he said, "because it was unjust toward women." Then think on this: Could the horrible massacres that took place a few days ago[†] have taken place if the citizens, less preoccupied with their own egotistical interests, had proclaimed liberty *for all men and all women*? Wouldst thou be living under a state of siege? Ah! no. Thou knowest well that if a woman had been seated in the councils at man's side, these horrible events would never have occurred. With the clairvoyance and the sentiment of justice that moves women, they would have opposed such measures, which they foresaw from the beginning would lead to such dreadful consequences. As long as this great injustice toward women remains, misery and insurrection will persist.

Hasten then, I beg thee, in the name of thy beloved fatherland, and also in the name of my country, poor England!

Bound in with shame, with shame, with inky blots and ragged parchment bonds. (Shakespeare)

Demand that the disinherited women of the nation be reintegrated into the rights enjoyed by the women of the Gauls, rights that were not denied to my Anglo-Saxon ancestors in 1515, if history is to be believed. Cast away this awful yoke of prejudice; mount the steps of this tribune, I beg thee, dressed in the armor of the just, like a Christian warrior! Protest in the name of the rights of *humanity*, without distinction of garb.

The righteous have the lion's courage; the cause is just, and it has for its shield the words of our Savior: "Therefore all things whatsoever ye would that men should do to you, do ye even so to them: for this is the law and the prophets." Matt. 7:12.

Yes: "Do unto others as thou wouldst have others do unto thee."

---

[*] The dramatist Ernest Legouvé, who in the spring had lectured on the "moral history of women" at the Collège de France.—EDS.

[†] The infamous June days of 1848 when the government closed the national workshops.—EDS.

Oh! for the love of suffering humanity, *retrace thy steps*. Demand that woman be reintegrated into the rights that have so long been denied her, and let me inform thee that thou wilst not be the only one to labor in our good work. A good American pastor told me in Paris that if two-thirds of the members of Congress were replaced by women, it would be a great blessing for America. An English minister has written that if one-half of our [parliamentary] fox-hunters and steeplechase amateurs were replaced by women, the country would soon attain the height of prosperity. What we lack is a little more of that cautious sensibility and, especially, that sympathy for all, which are the preeminent qualities of woman.

Ally thyself with these two noble brothers and form a glorious trio. Sound the retreat, so that all devoted men can hear thee and, following the example of the noble archbishop of Paris, mount the barricades, proclaim the law of peace, prepare the happiness of thy nation and, thereby, of the earth. Then thou wilst have raised the true tricolor flag destined to circle the world with its slogan: Liberty, equality, fraternity—justice, compassion, and truth.

Fiat justitia!

Thy sister,
Anna Knight

Revolutionary Visions in America

SOURCES

74. "Declaration of Sentiments" and "Resolutions" adopted by the Seneca Falls Convention of July 1848; reprinted from *History of Woman Suffrage*, ed. Elizabeth Cady Stanton, Susan B. Anthony, and Matilda Joslyn Gage, I (New York, 1881), 70-73.

75. Newspaper reports on the Seneca Falls Convention (1848); reprinted from the *History of Woman Suffrage*, I, 802-5.

76. Elizabeth Cady Stanton's reply, from the *National Reformer* (Rochester, N.Y.), 14 September 1848; reprinted from the *History of Woman Suffrage*, I, 806.

News of the European revolutions traveled quickly to America and may have served indirectly to precipitate an extraordinary event during the hot summer months of 1848: the calling in mid-July of a convention on women's rights in the small, upstate New York community of Seneca Falls by a little band of women, mostly Quakers, who had been at the forefront of the abolitionist movement. These women had been concerned with the problem of women's rights ever since their exclusion from the London antislavery convention eight years earlier. Two of them, Quaker activist Lucretia Mott (1793-1880) and Elizabeth Cady Stanton (1815-1902), drew up the "Declaration of Sentiments," paraphrasing the American Declaration of Independence, much in the same way that Olympe de Gouges (Doc. 26) had paraphrased the Declaration of the Rights of Man some sixty years earlier. This declaration and its list of resolutions, drafted by Stanton, marked the beginning of the organized movement for women's rights in the United States. It offers a vivid statement of the injustices that politically aware women perceived in a society generally recognized as the most democratic in the western world.

The Seneca Falls Convention of July 19 attracted considerable attention in the press, as the commentaries in the second selection reveal. Editorial writers ranged from whole-hearted support for the women's cause, through tongue-in-cheek satire, to dire predictions of a world soon to be topsy-turvy. Putting the American events into world context, however, remained the task of James Gordon Bennett's *New York Herald*.

A reply to the press soon came from Elizabeth Cady Stanton. The gifted Stanton had been sensitized to the inferiority of woman's situation through her exposure to her father's law practice, through experiences in her own family as a daughter, wife, and mother of an ever-growing number of children, as well as by her antislavery activities. She wrote this rejoinder concerning women's sphere only a few weeks after the Seneca Falls Convention.

---

74. "Declaration of Sentiments" (1848)

When, in the course of human events, it becomes necessary for one portion of the family of man to assume among the people of the earth a position different from that which they have hitherto occupied, but one to which the laws of nature and of nature's God entitle them, a decent respect to the opinions of mankind requires that they should declare the causes that impel them to such a course.

We hold these truths to be self-evident: that all men and women are created equal; that they are endowed by their Creator with certain inalienable rights; that among these are life, liberty, and the pursuit of happiness; that to secure these rights governments are instituted, deriving their just powers from the consent of the governed. Whenever any form of government becomes destructive of these ends, it is the right of those who suffer from it to refuse allegiance to it, and to insist upon the institution of a new government, laying its foundation on such principles, and organizing its powers in such form, as to them shall seem most likely to effect their safety and happiness. Prudence indeed, will dictate that governments long established should not be changed for light and transient causes; and accordingly all experience hath shown that mankind are more disposed to suffer, while evils are sufferable, than to right themselves by abolishing the forms to which they were accustomed. But when a long train of abuses and usurpations, pursuing invariably the same object evinces a design to reduce them under absolute despotism, it is their duty to throw off such government, and to provide new guards for their future security. Such has been the patient sufferance of the women under this government, and such is now the necessity which constrains them to demand the equal station to which they are entitled.

The history of mankind is a history of repeated injuries and usurpations on the part of man toward woman, having in direct object the establishment of an absolute tyranny over her. To prove this, let facts be submitted to a candid world.

He has never permitted her to exercise her inalienable right to the elective franchise.

He has compelled her to submit to laws, in the formation of which she had no voice.

He has withheld from her rights which are given to the most ignorant and degraded men—both natives and foreigners.

Having deprived her of this first right of a citizen, the elective franchise, thereby leaving her without representation in the halls of legislation, he has oppressed her on all sides.

He has made her, if married, in the eye of the law, civilly dead.

He has taken from her all right in property, even to the wages she earns.

He has made her, morally, an irresponsible being, as she can commit many crimes with impunity, provided they be done in the presence of her husband. In the covenant of marriage, she is compelled to promise obedience to her husband, he becoming, to all intents and purposes, her master—the law giving him power to deprive her of her liberty, and to administer chastisement.

He has so framed the laws of divorce, as to what shall be the proper causes, and in case of separation, to whom the guardianship of the children shall be given, as to be wholly regardless of the happiness of women—the law, in all cases, going upon a false supposition of the supremacy of man, and giving all power into his hands.

After depriving her of all rights as a married woman, if single, and the owner of property, he has taxed her to support a government which recognizes her only when her property can be made profitable to it.

He has monopolized nearly all the profitable employments, and from those she is permitted to follow, she receives but a scanty remuneration. He closes against her all the avenues to wealth and distinction which he considers most honorable to himself. As a teacher of theology, medicine, or law, she is not known.

He has denied her the facilities for obtaining a thorough education, all colleges being closed against her.

He allows her in Church, as well as State, but a subordinate position, claiming Apostolic authority for her exclusion from the ministry, and, with some exceptions, from any public participation in the affairs of the Church.

He has created a false public sentiment by giving to the world a different code of morals for men and women, by which moral delinquencies which exclude women from society, are not only tolerated, but deemed of little account in man.

He has usurped the prerogative of Jehovah himself, claiming it as his right to assign for her a sphere of action, when that belongs to her conscience and to her God.

He has endeavored, in every way that he could, to destroy her confidence in her own powers, to lessen her self-respect, and to make her willing to lead a dependent and abject life.

Now, in view of this entire disfranchisement of one-half the people of this country, their social and religious degradation—in view of the unjust laws above mentioned, and because women do feel themselves aggrieved, oppressed, and fraudulently deprived of their most sacred rights, we insist that they have immediate admission to all the rights and privileges which belong to them as citizens of the United States.

In entering upon the great work before us, we anticipate no small amount of misconception, misrepresentation, and ridicule; but we shall use every instrumentality within our power to effect our object. We shall employ agents, circulate tracts, petition the State and National legislatures, and endeavor to enlist the pulpit and the press in our behalf. We hope this Convention will be followed by a series of Conventions embracing every part of the country.

The following resolutions were discussed by Lucretia Mott, Thomas and Mary Ann McClintock, Amy Post, Catharine A. F. Stebbins, and others, and were adopted:

WHEREAS, The great precept of nature is conceded to be, that "man shall pursue his own true and substantial happiness." Blackstone in his Commentaries remarks, that this law of Nature being coeval with mankind, and dictated by God himself, is of course superior in obligation to any other. It is binding over all the globe, in all countries, and at all times; no human laws are of any validity if contrary to this, and such of them as are valid, derive all their force, and all their validity, and all their authority, mediately and immediately, from this original; therefore;

Resolved, That such laws as conflict, in any way, with the true and substantial happiness of woman, are contrary to the great precept of nature and of no validity, for this is "superior in obligation to any other."

Resolved, That all laws which prevent woman from occupying such a station in society as her conscience shall dictate, or which place her in a position inferior to that of man, are contrary to the great precept of nature, and therefore of no force or authority.

Resolved, That woman is man's equal—was intended to be so by the Creator, and the highest good of the race demands that she should be recognized as such.

Resolved, That the women of this country ought to be enlightened in regard to the laws under which they live, that they may no longer publish their degradation by declaring themselves satisfied with their present position, nor their ignorance by asserting that they have all the rights they want.

Resolved, That inasmuch as man, while claiming for himself intellectual superiority, does accord to woman moral superiority, it is pre-eminently his duty to encourage her to speak and teach, as she has an opportunity, in all religious assemblies.

Resolved, That the same amount of virtue, delicacy, and refinement of behavior that is required of woman in the social state, should also be required of man, and the same transgressions should be visited with equal severity on both man and woman.

Resolved, That the objection of indelicacy and impropriety, which is so often brought against woman when she addresses a public audience, comes with a very ill-grace from those who encourage, by their attendance, her appearance on the stage, in the concert, or in feats of the circus.

Resolved, That woman has too long rested satisfied in the circumscribed limits which corrupt customs and a perverted application of the Scriptures have marked out for her, and that it is time she should move in the enlarged sphere which her great Creator has assigned her.

Resolved, That it is the duty of the women of this country to secure to themselves their sacred right to the elective franchise.

Resolved, That the equality of human rights results necessarily from the fact of the identity of the race in capabilities and responsibilities.

Resolved, therefore, That, being invested by the Creator with the same capabilities, and the same consciousness of responsibility for their exercise, it is demonstrably the right and duty of woman, equally with man, to promote every righteous cause by every righteous means; and especially in regard to the great subjects of morals and religion, it is self-evidently her right to participate with her brother in teaching them, both in private and in public, by writing and by speaking, by any instrumentalities proper to be used, and in any assemblies proper to be held; and this being a self-evident truth growing out of the divinely implanted principles of human nature, any custom or authority adverse to it, whether modern or wearing the hoary sanction of antiquity, is to be regarded as a self-evident falsehood, and at war with mankind.

At the last session Lucretia Mott offered and spoke to the following resolution:

Resolved, That the speedy success of our cause depends upon the zealous and untiring efforts of both men and women, for the overthrow of the monopoly of the pulpit, and for the securing to woman an equal participation with men in the various trades, professions, and commerce.

75. Newspaper Reports on the Seneca Falls Convention (1848)

[From the *Mechanic's Advocate*, Albany, New York]

Women Out of Their Latitude.

We are sorry to see that the women in several parts of this State are holding what they call "Woman's Rights Conventions," and setting forth a formidable list of those Rights in a parody upon the Declaration of American Independence.

The papers of the day contain extended notices of these Conventions. Some of them fall in with their objects and praise the meetings highly; but the majority either deprecate or ridicule both.

The women who attend these meetings, no doubt at the expense of their more appropriate duties, act as committees, write resolutions and addresses, hold much correspondence, make speeches, etc., etc. They affirm, as among their rights, that of unrestricted franchise, and assert that it is wrong to deprive them of the privilege to become legislators, lawyers, doctors, divines, etc., etc.; and they are holding Conventions and making an agitatory movement, with the object in view of revolutionizing public opinion and the laws of the land, and changing their relative position in society in such a way as to divide with the male sex the labors and responsibilities of active life in every branch of art, science, trades, and professions.

Now, it requires no argument to prove that this is all wrong. Every true hearted female will instantly feel that this is unwomanly, and that to be practically carried out, the males must change their position in society to the same extent in an opposite direction, in order to enable them to discharge an equal share of the domestic duties which now appertain to females, and which must be neglected, to a great extent, if women are allowed to exercise all the "rights" that are claimed by these Convention-holders. Society would have to be radically remodelled in order to accommodate itself to so great a change in the most vital part of the compact of the social relations of life; and the order of things established at the creation of mankind, and continued *six thousand years*, would be completely broken up. The organic laws of our country, and of each State, would have to be licked into new shapes, in order to admit of the introduction of the vast change that it contemplated. In a thousand other ways that might be mentioned, if we had room to make, and our readers had patience to hear them, would this sweeping reform be attended by fundamental changes in the public and private, civil and religious, moral and social relations of the sexes, of life, and of the Government.

But this change is impracticable, uncalled for, and unnecessary. If *effected*, it would set the world by the ears, make "confusion worse confounded," demoralize and degrade from their high sphere and noble destiny, women of all respectable and useful classes, and prove a monstrous injury to all mankind. It would be productive of no positive good, that would not be outweighed tenfold by positive evil. It would alter the relations of females without bettering their condition. Besides all, and above all, it presents no remedy for the *real* evils that the millions of industrious, hard-working, and much suffering women of our country groan under and seek to redress.

[From the *Daily Advertiser*, Rochester, New York]

The Reign of Petticoats.

The women in various parts of the State have taken the field in favor of a petticoat empire, with a zeal and energy which show that their hearts are in the cause, and that they are resolved no longer to submit to the tyrannical rule of the *heartless* "lords of creation," but have solemnly determined to demand their "natural and inalienable right" to attend the polls, and assist in electing our Presidents, and Governors, and Members of Congress, and State Representatives, and Sheriffs, and County Clerks, and Supervisors, and Constables, etc., etc., and to unite in the general scramble for office. This is right and proper. It is but just that they should participate in the beautiful and feminine business of politics, and enjoy their proportion of the "spoils of victory." Nature never designed that they should be confined exclusively to the drudgery of raising children, and superintending the kitchens, and to the performance of the various other household duties which the cruelty of men and the customs of society have so long assigned to them. This is emphatically the age of "democratic progression," of *equality* and *fraternization*—the age when all colors and sexes, the bond and free, black and white, male and female, are, as they by right ought to be, all tending downward and upward toward the common level of equality.

The harmony of this great movement in the cause of freedom would not be perfect if women were still to be confined to petticoats, and men to breeches. There must be an "interchange" of these "commodities" to complete the system. Why should it not be so? Can not women fill an office, or cast a vote, or conduct a campaign, as judiciously and vigorously as men? And, on the other hand, can not men "nurse" the babies, or preside at the wash-tub, or boil a pot as safely and as well as women? If they can not, the evil is in that arbitrary organization of society which has excluded them from the practice of these pursuits. It is time these false notions and practices were changed, or, rather, removed, and for the political millennium foreshadowed by this petticoat movement to be ushered in. Let the women keep the ball moving, so bravely started by those who have become tired of the restraints imposed upon them by the antediluvian notions of a Paul or the tyranny of man.

[From the *New York Herald*, New York City]

Woman's Rights Convention.

This is the age of revolutions. To whatever part of the world the attention is directed, the political and social fabric is crumbling to pieces; and changes which far exceed the wildest dreams of the enthusiastic Utopians of the last generation, are now pursued with ardor and perseverance. The principal agent, however, that has hitherto taken part in these movements has been the rougher sex. It was by man the flame of liberty, now burning with such fury on the continent of Europe, was first kindled; and though it is asserted that no inconsiderable assistance was contributed by the gentler sex to the late sanguinary carnage at Paris, we are disposed to believe that such a revolting imputation proceeds from base calumniators, and is a libel upon woman.

By the intelligence, however, which we have lately received, the work of revolution is no longer confined to the Old World, nor to the masculine gender. The flag of independence has been hoisted, for the second time, on this side of the Atlantic; and a solemn league and covenant has just been entered into by a Convention of women at Seneca Falls, to "throw off the despotism under which they are groaning, and provide new guards for their future security." Little did we expect this new element to be thrown into the cauldron of agitation which is now bubbling around us with such fury. We have had one Baltimore Convention, one Philadelphia Convention, one Utica Convention, and we shall also have, in a few days, the Buffalo Convention. But we never dreamed that Lucretia Mott had convened a fifth convention, which, if it be ratified by those whom it proposes to represent, will exercise an influence that will not only control our own Presidential elections, but the whole governmental system throughout the world. . . . The declaration is a most interesting document. We published it in *extenso* the other day. The amusing part is the preamble, where they assert their equality, and that they have certain inalienable rights, to secure which governments, deriving their just powers from the consent of the governed, are instituted; and that after the long train of abuses and usurpations to which they have been subjected, evincing a design to reduce them under absolute despotism, it is their right, it is their duty, to throw off such government.

The declaration is, in some respects, defective. It complains of the want of the elective franchise, and that ladies are not recognized as teachers of theology, medicine, and law. . . . These departments, however, do not comprise the whole of the many avenues to wealth, distinction, and honor. We do not see by what principle of right the angelic creatures should claim to compete with the preacher, and refuse to enter the lists with the merchant. A lawyer's brief would not, we admit, sully the hands so much as the tarry ropes of a man-of-war; and a box of Brandreth's pills are more safely and easily prepared than the sheets of a boiler, or the flukes of an anchor; but if they must have competition in one branch, why not in another? There must be no monopoly or exclusiveness. If they will put on the inexpressibles, it will not do to select those employments only which require the least exertion and are exempt from danger. The laborious employments, however, are not the only ones which the ladies, in right of their admission to all rights and privileges, would have to undertake. It might happen that the citizen would have to doff the apron and buckle on the sword. Now, though we have the most perfect confidence in the courage and daring of Miss Lucretia Mott and several others of our lady acquaintances, we confess it would go to our hearts to see them putting on the panoply of war, and mixing in scenes like those at which, it is said, the fair sex in Paris lately took prominent part.

It is not the business, however, of the despot to decide upon the rights of his victims; nor do we undertake to define the duties of women. Their standard is now unfurled by their own hands. The Convention of Seneca Falls has appealed to the country. Miss Lucretia Mott has propounded the principles of the party. Ratification meetings will no doubt shortly be held, and if it be the general impression that this lady is a more eligible candidate for the presidential chair than McLean or Cass, Van Buren or old "Rough and Ready," then let the Salic laws be abolished forthwith from this great Republic. We are much mistaken if Lucretia would not make a better president than some of those who have lately tenanted the White House.

76. Elizabeth Cady Stanton (1848)

There is no danger of this question dying for want of notice. Every paper you take up has something to say about it, and just in proportion to the refinement and intelligence of the editor, has this movement been favorably noticed. But one might suppose from the articles that you find in some papers, that there were editors so ignorant as to believe that the chief object of these recent Conventions was to seat every lord at the head of a cradle, and to clothe every woman in her lord's attire. Now, neither of these points, however important they be considered by humble minds, were touched upon in the Conventions. . . . For those who do not yet understand the real objects of our recent Conventions at Rochester and Seneca Falls, I would state that we did not meet to discuss fashions, customs, or dress, the rights or duties of man, nor the propriety of the sexes changing positions, but simply our own inalienable rights, our duties, our true sphere. If God has assigned a sphere to man and one to woman, we claim the right to judge ourselves of His design in reference to *us*, and we accord to man the same privilege. We think a man has quite enough in this life to find out his own individual calling, without being taxed to decide where every woman belongs; and the fact that so many men fail in the business they undertake, calls loudly for their concentrating more thought on their own faculties, capabilities, and sphere of action. We have all seen a man making a jackass of himself in the pulpit, at the bar, or in our legislative halls, when he might have shone as a general in our Mexican war, captain of a canal boat, or as a tailor on his bench. Now, is it to be wondered at that woman has some doubts about the present position assigned her being the true one, when her every-day experience shows her that man makes such fatal mistakes in regard to himself?

There is no such thing as a sphere for a sex. Every man has a different sphere, and one in which he may shine, and it is the same with every woman; and the same woman may have a different sphere at different times. The distinguished Angelina Grimké was acknowledged by all the anti-slavery host to be in her sphere, when, years ago, she went through the length and breadth of New England, telling the people of her personal experience of the horrors and abominations of the slave system, and by her eloquence and power as a public speaker, producing an effect unsurpassed by any of the highly gifted men of her day. Who dares to say that in thus using her splendid talents in speaking for the dumb, pleading the cause of the poor friendless slave, that she was out of her sphere? Angelina Grimké is now a wife and the mother of several children. We hear of her no more in public. Her sphere and her duties have changed. She deems it her first and her most sacred duty to devote all her time and talents to her household and to the education of her children. We do not say that she is not *now* in her sphere. The highly gifted Quakeress, Lucretia Mott, married early in life, and brought up a large family of children. All who have seen her at home agree that she was a pattern as a wife, mother, and housekeeper. No one ever fulfilled all the duties of that sphere more perfectly than did she. Her children are now settled in their own homes. Her husband and herself, having a comfortable fortune, pass much of their time in going about and doing good. Lucretia Mott has now no domestic cares. She has a talent for public speaking; her mind is of a high order; her moral perceptions remarkably clear; her religious fervor deep and intense; and who shall tell us that this divinely inspired woman is out of her sphere in her public endeavors to rouse this wicked nation to a sense of its awful guilt, to its great sins of war, slavery, injustice to woman and the laboring poor.

Women's Mission in Revolutionary Europe

SOURCES

77. Jeanne Deroin, "Mission de la femme dans le present et dans l'avenir," *L'Opinion des Femmes* (28 January, 10 March, 10 April 1849). Tr. KMO. The editors are grateful to Professor S. Joan Moon, Sacramento State University, who forwarded copies of these articles.

78. Louise Otto, "Program," *Frauen-Zeitung, Ein Organ für die höheren weiblichen Interessen*, no. 1 (21 April 1849); reprinted in *"Dem Reich der Freiheit werb' ich Bürgerinnen"; Die Frauen-Zeitung von Louise Otto*, ed. Ute Gerhard, Elisabeth Hannover-Drück, and Romania Schmitter (Frankfurt-am-Main, 1980), pp. 37-38. Tr. SGB.

The radical social transformation through class struggle prophesied by Marx and Engels did not find much favor among the other revolutionary activists of 1848. In France, where the revolutions had begun, the euphoria with which many reformers had greeted the fall of the French monarchy and the proclamation of the republic in February soon faded, as working-class demands were repressed by military force later in the summer. Even liberal supporters felt deceived when the nine million newly enfranchised male voters elected the nephew of the legendary emperor Napoleon Bonaparte as president of the new regime. During the height of the revolutionary fervor in Paris, women had once again (as in the 1790's) pressed their own demands. In 1848 Jeanne Deroin (Doc. 70) had organized workshops and self-help associations for women workers. In early 1849 she founded a newspaper, *L'Opinion des Femmes*, to bring their situation to the attention of the public. In the wake of repression, however, the Legislative Assembly took explicit measures to bar women from participating in French political and associational life (Doc. 71). It was in this context that Deroin set forth her own vision of woman's mission. In contrast to the rather bleak vision of Marx and Engels, her argument exhibited the intense humanitarianism, the pacifism, the faith in progress that characterized the mentality of most 1848 revolutionaries, blending Christian social idealism with the secular ideology of liberal individualism that dated from 1789. Deroin viewed society as an organism, with the couple as the fundamental social unit, yet she extended and elaborated traditionally assigned female roles as a platform for demanding women's full participation in the political process. Like the women of Seneca Falls, Deroin based her argument for woman suffrage on an appeal to principles of justice.

Arguments like Jeanne Deroin's were heard in central Europe as well. Louise Otto (Doc. 48) was one of four German women who founded newspapers in this revolutionary period. The other women's papers (Louise Aston's *Der Freischärler*, in Berlin; Louise Dittmar's *Soziale Reform*, in Leipzig; Mathilda Franziska Anneke's *Frauen-Zeitung*, in Cologne) did not survive the revolutionary excitement of 1848. Otto's *Frauen-Zeitung*, published in Meissen (Saxony), had a far-ranging success and survived until 1852. The reasons for its greater success are not far to seek. In contrast to the other German states, in Saxony one-half of the population was to some extent industrialized by the 1840's, with many women in the work-force. Large numbers of women also worked in family textile production in the mountainous districts. Leipzig, one of the state's major cities, was an important trade center, a university town, and the hub of book and newspaper publication. This drew a circle of literary-political figures, among whom the well-known Robert Blum, one of Otto's close friends and supporters, emerged as the chief and eloquent opponent of the government.

Otto's *Frauen-Zeitung* addressed itself to the whole range of political and social problems sparked by the revolution. It became a platform for ideas as diverse as those of socialist Hermann Semmig, and of Johannes Ronge (Doc. 80), who aimed to separate German Catholicism from Rome; it also remains as evidence for the revolutionary activities of women in 1848. In the lead article, reprinted below, Otto presented her own approach to reforming the situation of German women. Though Otto, unlike Deroin, was at that time a single woman, without children, she too emphasized womanliness and sisterhood, arguing from this foundation to build a case for radical reform.

---

77. Jeanne Deroin (1849)

[28 January 1849]

By inscribing the words Liberty, Equality, and Fraternity on its banner, the February Revolution recognized in principle the rights of the people and the rights of woman.

But many women—indeed, the majority—do not understand what changes the power of their influence could bring about in human destinies if they were called on to regain the rank in society that is rightly theirs.

Most of them reject this idea as an outrage to religion and morality, and as a danger to society; they have been persuaded that they were born to obey, love, suffer, and devote themselves to others, and that they must remain shut within the constricted enclosure of the household.

Others, in contrast, have freed themselves from the yoke of these austere principles and openly defy society, which censures them severely; they misunderstand their duties because their rights are misunderstood.

Neither group realizes that they should demand all their rights in the name of religion and morality, and in the interest of society.

They do not understand that the salvation of humanity depends on the triumph of God's law, the rights of the people and of women.

Our most ardent wish is that this truth, on which our future depends, will be engraved on every heart.

It is to make women understand that for them it is not only a right but an obligation to intervene in these distasteful struggles, the sorry result of oppression, suffering, misery, and egotism.

Only they can rise above these party and sectarian hatreds that divide men, and can teach everyone how fraternity should be practiced.

[10 March 1849]

Citoyennes, it is as Christians and mothers that women must demand the rank that belongs to them in the church, the state, and the family.

As Christians—because they too are children of God and because Christ himself called them to be his apostles.

As *citoyennes*, because they belong to the people and have the same right as male citizens to liberty and equality.

But it is especially this sacred function as mother, which some insist is incompatible with the exercise of a citizen's rights, that imposes on woman the duty of watching over the future of her children and confers on her the right to intervene in all the activities not only of civil life but of political life as well.

Up till now politics has been the art not of governing people but rather of oppressing them; for this reason governments can maintain themselves only by the force of bayonets. To govern is to repress more or less cleverly, more or less brutally, according to the time and circumstances. This is why women have been declared incapable—and this is why they must demand the right to intervene in order to aid stout-hearted, intelligent men to transform this politics of violence and repression, which produces only deep hatred and incessant combat and which causes all suffering and social misery.

The immense need to love and be loved that God placed in the heart of woman is the powerful and fertile germ of maternal love that must inspire her and guide her in accomplishing this sacred function as mother of the human race that has been conferred on her. When women understand that they owe obedience to no one but God, that all men are their brothers, that all women are sisters, and that all of them are the mothers not only of their own children but of their sisters' children, and especially of those who hunger and thirst, those who suffer and weep, those who are orphans or abandoned—only when they have comprehended this sublime humanitarian maternity, which should serve them as a powerful bond of solidarity, will humanity really enter the path of progress. . . .

[10 April 1849]

Woman's mission in the present . . . is apostolic; its goal is to realize the kingdom of God on earth, the reign of fraternity and universal harmony. The means is to guide humanity back onto its providential path by reuniting its separated members, divided by their opinions and interests and fighting incessantly with one another—individuals against individuals, families against families, nations against nations. But first we must put a stop to the struggle between the two halves of the grand human family, man and woman. In order to attain this goal we must loudly pro-claim the civil and political equality of the two sexes and demand its ap-plication by all possible means—the press, the spoken word, by constant protests against the negation of the principles of liberty, equality, and fra-ternity that contain the law of God, the rights of woman and the people. We must make it absolutely clear that the abolition of the privileges of race, birth, caste, and fortune cannot be complete and radical unless the privilege of sex is totally abolished. It is the source of all the others, the last head of the hydra. Whatever the nuances of opinion, of the religious or social beliefs of the women who devote themselves to this great mis-sion, they will understand that in this era there is but one single practical means of achieving this goal. By their duty and their devotion, women must constantly demand the right of citizenship.

They must first conquer liberty and equality before concerning them-selves with the constitution of the new marriage and diverse theories re-lating to this great question, which moreover cannot be seriously consid-ered or resolved unless women have the right to discuss it freely and to establish its foundations in perfect equality with men.

78. Louise Otto (1849)

The history of all ages, especially that of the present, teaches us that those who forget to think of themselves will be forgotten! Thus I wrote in May 1848, when I was addressing myself primarily to the men who were concerned with the labor question in Saxony. I drew their attention to the poor women workers, by speaking out on behalf of my sisters so that they should not be forgotten!

The same experiences have inspired me to publish a woman's journal. In the midst of the great revolutions in which we find ourselves, women will find themselves forgotten, if they forget to think of themselves!

Come along then, my sisters, unite with me, so that we do not remain behind while everything around and about us is pressing forward and struggling. We must also demand and earn our part of the great World-Deliverance that must at last come to the whole of humanity, of which we constitute one-half.

We shall demand to have as our share the right to accomplish with all our strength and in unrestricted development that in us which is purely human, and the right to come of age and enjoy independence within the State.

We shall earn our share as follows: we shall offer our forces to advance the work of world salvation, first by promoting the great ideals of the future—Liberty and Humanity (in fact these are synonymous terms)—in all those circles that are accessible to us, in the circles of the world-at-large through the press, and in those of the immediate family through example, instruction, and education.

However, we shall also earn our part by not struggling in isolation—

not everyone for herself, but rather everyone for all the others—and by concerning ourselves primarily with those women who are languishing forgotten and neglected in poverty, misery, and ignorance.

Come, my sisters, help me with this work! Help me first of all to further the ideas here suggested through this journal!

I believe I have said all that needs to be said about the aims of this journal—however, I must agree with those who whisper in my ear (contrary to the usual formula), "to be positive is not enough". I must also present some negative arguments—and I must guard myself and this journal against misunderstandings.

No! I cannot invent words to do this. You shall judge me by my life, by my work as an author since 1843—whoever knows something of this will also know that I do not belong to those so-called "emancipated" women who have discredited the phrase "women's emancipation" by devaluing woman to become a caricature of man. I would like to reassure those who as yet know nothing about me, that it is precisely through this journal that I hope to work against this error, which has often induced those very women who were the most gifted to satisfy their quest for intellectual freedom by succumbing to unbridled passion.

Neither I nor my sisterly co-workers can be included among these "emancipated ones," but we shall be proud to be considered as followers of that noble maiden from Bethany, of whom the illustrious model of all humanity has said: "Mary hath chosen the better part!" *

Therefore I ask all authors, both male and female, who will enter the lists for women's rights, to support me in this undertaking by sending their contributions.

Likewise, I beg those of my sisters who are not authors to send information—first of all those oppressed ones, the poor working women. Even if they do not feel themselves to be skilled authors, I shall gladly edit their simple statements—but I am most eager that their concerns in particular should be published so that they may be the first to be helped.

I invite all of you who think alike to subscribe so that this undertaking may thrive!

The Woman Question and the Catholic Church

SOURCES

79. Pius IX, "Ubi Primum," 2 February 1849, in *Pontificis maximi acta*, I (n.p., n.d.), 162-66. English text in *Papal Documents on Mary*, comps. William J. Doheny and Joseph P. Kelly (Milwaukee, Wisc., 1954), pp. 1-5.

80. Johannes Ronge, *Maria, oder: die Stellung der Frauen der alten und neuen Zeit. Eine Erwiderung auf das Rundschreiben des Papstes wegen dringender Verehrung der Maria* (Hamburg, 1849), pp. 6-15. The editors are grateful to Catherine M. Prelinger, Yale University, for providing them with a copy of this pamphlet, and for her assistance with the translation.

---

* Luke 10:42. The German rendering, "Maria hat das bessere Theil erwählt," gives a different emphasis than that of the King James version.—EDS.

The 1848 debate over women's rights and roles was by no means confined to the revolutionary radicals. The two selections from Pope Pius IX and the founder of German Catholicism, Johannes Ronge, epitomize the controversy over woman within Catholic circles during 1848-1849. Jean-Marie, comte de Mastai-Ferretti (1792-1879), had been elected to the papacy in 1846. This new pope, who was then both a temporal and spiritual ruler, had for a time been viewed as a possible champion of Italian liberalism and a candidate for spearheading the political unification of Italy. But in November 1848 he fled from Rome, relinquishing control of the city and the Papal States to revolutionary forces who proclaimed a republic on February 9, 1849. In the interim Pius IX drafted the encyclical letter *Ubi Primum*, in which he called on bishops to support his intention of honoring the Virgin Mary, elevating her status in the Church by proclaiming her to be free of sin thanks to the exceptional privilege of her Immaculate Conception. The discussion of Mary's purity had occupied theologians since medieval times but had never received formal endorsement by the Church; thus, it seems more than coincidental that Pius IX provoked this move only when the Church was suffering from the tumult of revolution and secular disenchantment, and when the specter of war stalked the Italian peninsula and, indeed, the rest of Europe. What an extraordinary coincidence that the Pope should attempt to rally support by invoking a principle of female purity to buttress the Church in its hour of need! Some six hundred and twenty bishops responded to the encyclical, nearly all in the affirmative, and in December 1854, back in Rome, Pius IX proclaimed the dogma of the Immaculate Conception.

The Pope's initiative met also with some explicit opposition. In German-speaking Europe one of the most vocal dissenters was Johannes Ronge (1813-1887), a one-time Roman Catholic priest who had founded the German Catholic Church following his suspension from the priesthood (for protesting a pilgrimage to a sacred relic at Trier in 1844). Like their earlier Protestant predecessors, the German Catholics rejected papal authority, opposed miracles and superstition, and worshipped in the vernacular. They also adopted an eclectic theology incorporating elements ranging from Christian rationalism to radical Hegelianism. Within a loose conciliar structure, church members organized themselves in quasi-autonomous congregations, electing their own clergy and lay officers; in a radical departure from customary practice, many of the congregations chose to let the women vote. But the spiritual immediacy of German Catholicism, its democratic practices, its support of female educational efforts, and perhaps even the charismatic personality of Ronge, appealed to women like Louise Otto (Docs. 48, 78) who were highly visible in the movement. Ronge published his reply to the Pope on the subject of Mary as a tract, which is here excerpted. Though he can justly be charged with sentimentalizing womanhood, the thrust of his argument systematically supports what was for the time a most progressive view of self-determination for nations, for the working class, and for women as well.

79. Pius IX (1849)

No sooner had We been elevated to the sublime Chair of the Prince of the Apostles and undertook the government of the universal Church (not, indeed, because of Our own worthiness but by the hidden designs of Divine Providence) than We had the great consolation, Venerable Brethren, in recalling that, during the pontificate of Gregory XVI, Our Predecessor of happy memory, there was in the entire Catholic world a most ardent and wondrous revival of the desire that the most holy Mother of God— the beloved Mother of us all, the immaculate Virgin Mary—be finally declared by a solemn definition of the Church to have been conceived without the stain of original sin.

LITURGICAL USE OF THE TERM "IMMACULATE"

Both to Our Predecessor and to Us this most devout desire was clearly and unmistakably made manifest by the petitions of illustrious bishops, esteemed canonical chapters, and religious congregations, among whom was the renowned Order of Preachers. These appeals vied with one another in the insistent request that official permission be granted for the word *Immaculate* to be publicly used and be added to the sacred liturgy, particularly in the Preface of the Mass of the Conception of the Blessed Virgin. With the greatest delight, both Our Predecessor and We acceded to these requests.

REQUESTS FOR DEFINITION

Moreover, Venerable Brethren, many of you have sent letters to Our Predecessor and to Us begging, with repeated insistence and redoubled enthusiasm, that We define as a dogma of the Catholic Church that the most blessed Virgin Mary was conceived immaculate and free in every way of all taint of original sin.

Nor do we lack today eminent theologians—men of intellectual brilliance, of virtue, of holiness and sound doctrine—who have so effectively explained this doctrine and so impressively expounded this proposition that many persons are now wondering why this honor has not already been accorded to the Blessed Virgin by the Church and the Apostolic See—an honor which the widespread piety of the Christian people so fervently desires to have accorded to the Most Holy Virgin by a solemn decree and by the authority of the Church and the Holy See.

THE DEVOTION OF THE HOLY FATHER

Welcome indeed have such requests been to Us. They have filled Us with joy. From our earliest years nothing has ever been closer to Our heart than devotion—filial, profound, and wholehearted—to the most blessed Virgin Mary. Always have We endeavored to do everything that would redound to the greater glory of the Blessed Virgin, promote her honor, and encourage devotion to her. Accordingly, from the very beginning of Our supreme pontificate We have most fervently directed Our energies and Our thoughts to this matter of such great importance. Nor have We failed, through humble and fervent prayers, to beg almighty God to enlighten Our mind with the light of His grace in order that We might know what We should do in this matter.

Great indeed is Our trust in Mary. The resplendent glory of her merits, far exceeding all the choirs of angels, elevates her to the very steps of the throne of God. Her foot has crushed the head of Satan. Set up between

Christ and His Church, Mary, ever lovable and full of grace, always has delivered the Christian people from their greatest calamities and from the snares and assaults of all their enemies, ever rescuing them from ruin.

MARY'S SOLICITUDE FOR HER CHILDREN

And likewise in our own day, Mary, with the ever merciful affection so characteristic of her maternal heart, wishes, through her efficacious intercession with God, to deliver her children from the sad and grief-laden troubles, from the tribulations, the anxiety, the difficulties, and the punishments of God's anger which afflict the world because of the sins of men. Wishing to restrain and to dispel the violent hurricane of evils which, as We lament from the bottom of Our heart, are everywhere afflicting the Church, Mary desires to transform Our sadness into joy. The foundation of all Our confidence, as you know well, Venerable Brethren, is found in the Blessed Virgin Mary. For, God has committed to Mary the treasury of all good things, in order that everyone may know that through her are obtained every hope, every grace, and all salvation. For this is His will, that we obtain everything through Mary. . . .

APPEAL TO THE BISHOPS

Wherefore, Venerable Brethren, We send you this communication that We may effectively encourage your admirable devotion and your pastoral zeal and thus bring it about that each of you, in such manner as you will see fit, will arrange to have public prayers offered in your diocese for this intention: that the most merciful Father of all knowledge will deign to enlighten Us with the heavenly light of His Holy Spirit, so that in a matter of such moment We may proceed to do what will redound to the greater glory of His Holy Name, to the honor of the most Blessed Virgin, and to the profit of the Church Militant.

80. Johannes Ronge (1849)

What then can the image of Mary offer us today? Should the vanished faith in its miracle-producing capacity perhaps be restored once more as the Pope has ordered? All papal bulls calling for damnation and all reprimands issued by bishops following the papal order will be in vain. That faith can no more be revived than the blooming meadow of spring can be revived in the autumn. We no longer need this form of belief in our time. However, we require another faith, which has already matured among the people and which will redeem us. Truly just as our times have generally destroyed the dogmas of the Old Church and made us aware of their underlying ideas, so we seek to know the ideal that underlies the image of Mary and to mold our faith or our conviction according to it. According to *this ideal* we believe in the *majesty and dignity of womanliness* and in the *redeeming power of love*. And this ideal elevates and inspires no less than belief in a supernatural Virgin Mary. . . . As we no longer seek the godly image of the son of man—which we formerly believed resided only in Jesus of Nazareth, exclusively in him and in the self-contained realm of heaven—but rather in all human beings, so should we seek the sanctifying image of Mary only in humanity, and we shall find it in noble woman-liness. While there are still many who do not understand this great re-deeming truth, and many others who do not wish to understand it—you, my German sisters, will believe and recognize it. Oh, I am not deluded in this belief. For I know that many have felt this for a long time, even if they have not recognized it. Therefore, you will hear the call with which the spirit of the times beckons you—particularly through the new young Church, the Bride of recent times—and you will seek to realize within yourselves the image of Mary, not an image of a supernatural Mother of God but the idea of an elevated, sanctifying womanliness that will help to redeem the present just as Mary helped to redeem her own time. If you want to follow this call of history, or the call of the spirit of God, then you must first believe steadfastly in your mission, as Mary believed in hers. You must, hear me German daughters, think highly of yourselves, you must become conscious of your free human dignity and struggle for the right of self-determination for yourselves; formerly you have always been cautioned to think little and modestly of yourselves, thereby limit-ing your right to a free personality. You have been sought more as an ob-ject of property than as the bestowers of a sanctifying love that alone can and should be a free love. . . .

. . . As a general basic principle, attested to by past and present experi-ence, we may say that the higher the women of a nation are regarded, the higher the standing of that nation and the greater its degree of freedom will be. Both the present and the past demonstrate this. Consider the Orient—where women are nothing but slaves; and, on the other hand, consider the United States, where women have the most liberated status, and you will convince yourselves of the above. . . . But since men have lifted themselves to a higher level of independence, women also have rec-ognized the necessity of striving for equal civil rights; they have recog-nized, and indeed feel it as a duty, to participate in the realization of the great ideas of the times. This striving for higher justice exhibited itself more superficially in strange behavior and a desire for emancipation. It was thought that in order to attain this higher justice it was necessary to adopt male actions and attitudes and to ape masculine manners. Such ex-travagances were rare, however—most women recognized the proper faith they must follow in order to fulfill their worldly career. They know that above all they must retain that beautiful sanctifying womanliness—which from now on must be freely developed in its full splendid strength—since up till now it had been shrivelled up and suffocated through narrow-minded pressures and perverse views and customs; they know it is a religious and moral duty to achieve the right of free self-determination because it is only by this means that one may act in the image of God, achieve free human dignity, and become capable of redeeming and ab-solving nations from base ideas and hatred. . . .

. . . It should be easy to see that I am not here voicing so-called theories of emancipation but am rather seeking the inner liberation and elevation of the female sex through a lofty ethical principle. Only malice or crude-ness would cast suspicion on my words and women's striving for higher education and greater independence. Whoever feels and recognizes that here I have touched upon the most sacred living nerve of the future will consider himself in duty bound to offer women not only his protection in their high and noble striving for recognition and true liberation but also his whole-hearted respect.

But what should you do, women and daughters, to realize the calling that has become yours through the spirit of the times? You ought to be the living Mary, the Mary of our time, and seek to represent the concept of lofty womanliness in yourselves. You will not achieve this in isolation, but only in community. . . . Therefore you should strive to achieve the ideal of noble womanhood in community. Inspire yourselves and others to sacred enthusiasm for everything great, noble, and beautiful, and consider yourselves as the sacred living temple of the spirit of God; as such you should help conquer the bondage of falsehood, hypocrisy, pride, selfishness, freedom, and despotism of old. . . . Least of all should you allow yourselves to be brought to the slave market of so-called marriages of convenience. Each marriage without love is unholy, untrue, and ungodly, and brings with it destruction. Only love sanctifies marriage and binds it with God and in heaven. As wives, refresh your spouses through your rich, beautiful world of the spirit, and encourage them to new virtues and sacrifices for the general good. Protect their spirit from cold self-seeking, and ennoble their striving with greatness. You will be able to do this only if you are filled with holy love and unswerving loyalty as the natural accompaniment of this love. Love and loyalty will lead both spouses to ever greater recognition of deep and spiritual permeation and the highest fulfillment, instead of the well-known superficial appearance of morality that conceals the deception of the heart and the spirit. A fundamental condition of such marriages is the equality of rights of both spouses, both in the family and before the law. Therefore you must demand equality of rights, because no one who is a dependent can satisfy a free man or enlarge his being. As mothers, kindle in your children the sacred fire of free human dignity and love, and nurture the holy flame of godliness in them; inspire them to all that is noble, and thus educate a new generation that will suffer neither inferiority nor servitude. As daughters of the German people you must work with joyful enthusiasm for the uplifting, the liberation, and the betterment of this people; you must punish with deep scorn all cowardly and slavish men as well as those shameless self-seekers without conscience who put their personal and class interests above the honor and freedom of the Fatherland. You must attempt especially to heal ancient wounds and to reconcile on a basis of full equality those groups in society that at present confront each other in harsh enmity. You are aware that solving this latter problem is extremely difficult, because the chasm between rich and poor has become tremendously deep; but you are also aware that love is able to fill this chasm—like every other— and you will be less hesitant to begin this great effort of reconciliation of our times because history shows that 600 years ago love was able to overcome slavery and 300 years ago it was able to overcome serfdom, and that social conditions, based at that time upon slavery and serfdom—as they are based now upon class privileges—improved among all classes as a result. However, this reconciliation will be achieved not through empty words but rather through liberating deeds that seek social conditions based upon higher moral principles of justice for workers, and the abolition of indolent, godforsaken, and bleak privilege. Recognize, noble German daughters, that history bound your lot with that of the oppressed classes of the people, that it united redeeming love with misery and toil, and that it has ordained you as priestesses of the new realm of God. Truly, the greatness and holiness of this mission with which you are entrusted will and must fill you with enthusiasm and inflame your hearts with a conquering of self and of sacrifice. Some of you will ask how the solution of this great problem is to be achieved: Begin, German women, by concerning yourselves with the children of those of your brothers and sisters whose lot has been worsened by national circumstances, and try to transform them into human beings. Oh, you surely know that there are many many thousands of parents who cannot earn enough to satisfy the physical needs of their children, not to mention being able to consider the education of their hearts and spirits; and that there are thousands more who may succeed in acquiring the most meager subsistence by working from dawn till deep into the night, but who are still unable to further the mental and moral education of their children. Concern yourselves with these abandoned children and, by educating them, become their living guardian angels. But I must take you further, namely to the sickbeds of those abandoned souls who have been hurled from earliest childhood into a hard, cold struggle for existence, who have never felt the warm hand of a sister, nor known the concerned eye of a mother.

Independent Women and the English Novel

SOURCES
81. Charlotte Brontë, *Jane Eyre* (Oxford, 1969), pp. 398-407. Originally published in London in 1847 as *Jane Eyre: An Autobiography, edited by Currer Bell.*
82. Elizabeth Rigby [Lady Eastlake], "Vanity Fair—and Jane Eyre," *Quarterly Review*, 84, no. 167 (December 1848), 173-76.
83. Charlotte Brontë, *Shirley*, in *The Works of Charlotte Brontë (Currer Bell)*, 4 vols. (Philadelphia, n.d.), III, 196-97, 208-9, 504-5. Originally published in London, 1849, under the pseudonym Currer Bell.

In this revolutionary period, even the personal behavior of literary characters could be interpreted as a political symptom. This became evident in England well before 1848, when Chartist agitation was arousing great anxiety about revolution. In this context appeared the first of a series of major novels by an unknown English writer, whose works propelled the question of women before the English literary public in an unprecedented fashion. This anonymous writer dared to present a female heroine who publicly acknowledged her passionate attraction to a man without having first received his formal offer of marriage. The writer was soon identified as Charlotte Brontë (1816-1855), the gifted daughter of a Yorkshire parson. After completing her education at a school for daughters of impoverished clergymen, Brontë had been called back as an assistant teacher; she subsequently found employment as a governess, an occupation she abhorred. In 1842 she arranged a stay in a Brussels *pensionnat*, to improve her French and German. Only in 1844 did she return home, rarely to leave again, but with a consuming passion for her Belgian schoolmaster, a married man with numerous children.

The selection from Brontë's *Jane Eyre* deals with Jane's refusal of the unhappy Mr. Rochester, who (burdened with an insane wife in a society where divorce was rare and frowned upon) could offer his daughter's governess his love only if she became his mistress. Jane's struggle with her conscience, and her final refusal, vividly depict the complex thoughts of an independent-minded woman. Jane was confronted with a proposal that could never receive social sanction, as well as with society's idealized vision of redeeming womanhood, which she refused to embody for the sake of any man.

The second selection is taken from a widely quoted and virulent review of *Jane Eyre*, which appeared in the *Quarterly Review* and which sent Brontë's friend and first biographer, Elizabeth Gaskell, into a fury. The author of the review, Elizabeth Rigby, Lady Eastlake (1809-1893), the daughter of an eminent physician and one-time mayor of Norwich, was a well-established English writer only a few years older than Brontë herself. Shortly after this review appeared in print, Rigby married for the first time, at the age of forty, the much-admired painter Sir Charles Eastlake, whose position as president of the Royal Academy did nothing to hinder her future as an art critic. Together they collaborated in works of art history.

Rigby's rage against *Jane Eyre* and Jane's passion for Rochester, on the eve of Rigby's own belated marriage, probably betrayed her unrequited passion for her editor John Lockhart. Although Rigby ruthlessly criticized "unchristian" aspects of Brontë's novel, it was a highly moral decision that Brontë's heroine made within a truly Christian social context. Rigby's review unwittingly elucidated Brontë's real life; she sneered, for example, at Jane Eyre's wardrobe, which could not, she said, have belonged to a "lady," but which no doubt reflected all too well Charlotte Brontë's own poverty. Rigby all but accused Brontë of Chartism, because of her concern with the poor and her lack of appreciation of the God-ordained hierarchy of social class. But perhaps the most startling aspect of Rigby's critique is her insistence that Brontë's anonymous novel must have been written by a man, since it was so clearly unwomanly.

The third selection presents excerpts from Brontë's subsequent novel, *Shirley*, which appeared in 1849. Here Brontë offered a series of dialogues that explore the position of middle-class women, and their relationships to the family and freedom, in a far more daring and forthright manner than any previous author had attempted in Victorian fiction.

---

81. Charlotte Brontë (1847)

"You see now how the case stands—do you not?" he continued. "After a youth and manhood, passed half in unutterable misery and half in dreary solitude, I have for the first time found what I can truly love—I have found *you*. You are my sympathy—my better self—my good angel—

I am bound to you with a strong attachment. I think you good, gifted, lovely: a fervent, a solemn passion is conceived in my heart; it leans to you, draws you to my centre and spring of life, wraps my existence about you—and, kindling in pure, powerful flame, fuses you and me in one.

"It was because I felt and knew this, that I resolved to marry you. To tell me that I had already a wife is empty mockery: you know now that I had but a hideous demon. I was wrong to attempt to deceive you; but I feared a stubbornness that exists in your character. I feared early instilled prejudice: I wanted to have you safe before hazarding confidences. This was cowardly: I should have appealed to your nobleness and magnanimity at first, as I do now—opened to you plainly my life of agony— described to you my hunger and thirst after a higher and worthier existence—shown to you, not my *resolution* (that word is weak) but my resistless *bent* to love faithfully and well, where I am faithfully and well loved in return. Then I should have asked you to accept my pledge of fidelity, and to give me yours: Jane—give it me now."

A pause.

"Why are you silent, Jane?"

I was experiencing an ordeal: a hand of fiery iron grasped my vitals. Terrible moment: full of struggle, blackness, burning! Not a human being that ever lived could wish to be loved better than I was loved; and him who thus loved me I absolutely worshipped: and I must renounce love and idol. One drear word comprised my intolerable duty—"Depart!"

"Jane, you understand what I want of you? Just this promise—'I will be yours, Mr. Rochester.'"

"Mr. Rochester, I will *not* be yours."

Another long silence.

"Jane!" recommenced he, with a gentleness that broke me down with grief, and turned me stone-cold with ominous terror—for this still voice was the pant of a lion rising—"Jane, do you mean to go one way in the world, and to let me go another?"

"I do."

"Jane," (bending towards and embracing me) "do you mean it now?"

"I do."

"And now?" softly kissing my forehead and cheek.

"I do—" extricating myself from restraint rapidly and completely.

"Oh, Jane, this is bitter! This—this is wicked. It would not be wicked to love me."

"It would to obey you."

A wild look raised his brows—crossed his features: he rose; but he forbore yet. I laid my hand on the back of a chair for support: I shook, I feared—but I resolved.

"One instant, Jane. Give one glance to my horrible life when you are gone. All happiness will be torn away with you. What then is left? For a wife I have but the maniac up-stairs: as well might you refer me to some corpse in yonder churchyard. What shall I do, Jane? Where turn for a companion, and for some hope?"

"Do as I do: trust in God and yourself. Believe in heaven. Hope to meet again there."

"Then you will not yield?"

"No."

"Then you condemn me to live wretched, and to die accursed?" His voice rose.

"I advise you to live sinless; and I wish you to die tranquil."

"Then you snatch love and innocence from me? You fling me back on lust for a passion—vice for an occupation?"

"Mr. Rochester, I no more assign this fate to you than I grasp at it for myself. We were born to strive and endure—you as well as I: do so. You will forget me before I forget you."

"You make me a liar by such language: you sully my honour. I declared I could not change: you tell me to my face I shall change soon. And what a distortion in your judgment, what a perversity in your ideas, is proved by your conduct! Is it better to drive a fellow-creature to despair than to transgress a mere human law—no man being injured by the breach? for you have neither relatives nor acquaintances whom you need fear to offend by living with me."

This was true: and while he spoke my very Conscience and Reason turned traitors against me, and charged me with crime in resisting him. They spoke almost as loud as Feeling: and that clamoured wildly. "Oh, comply!" it said. "Think of his misery; think of his danger—look at his state when left alone; remember his headlong nature; consider the recklessness following on despair—soothe him; save him; love him: tell him you love him and will be his. Who in the world cares for *you*? or who will be injured by what you do?"

Still indomitable was the reply—"*I* care for myself. The more solitary, the more friendless, the more unsustained I am, the more I will respect myself. I will keep the law given by God; sanctioned by man. I will hold to the principles received by me when I was sane, and not mad—as I am now. Laws and principles are not for the times when there is no temptation: they are for such moments as this, when body and soul rise in mutiny against their rigour: stringent are they; inviolate they shall be. If at my individual convenience I might break them, what would be their worth? They have a worth—so I have always believed; and if I cannot believe it now, it is because I am insane—quite insane: with my veins running fire, and my heart beating faster than I can count its throbs. Preconceived opinions, foregone determinations, are all I have at this hour to stand by: there I plant my foot."

I did. Mr. Rochester, reading my countenance, saw I had done so. His fury was wrought to the highest: he must yield to it for a moment, whatever followed; he crossed the floor and seized my arm, and grasped my waist. He seemed to devour me with his flaming glance: physically, I felt, at the moment, powerless as stubble exposed to the draught and glow of a furnace—mentally, I still possessed my soul, and with it the certainty of ultimate safety. The soul, fortunately, has an interpreter—often an unconscious, but still a truthful interpreter—in the eye. My eye rose to his; and while I looked in his fierce face, I gave an involuntary sigh; his gripe was painful, and my over-tasked strength almost exhausted.

"Never," said he, as he ground his teeth, "never was anything at once so frail and so indomitable. A mere reed she feels in my hand! (and he shook me with the force of his hold.) I could bend her with my finger and thumb: and what good would it do if I bent, if I uptore, if I crushed her? Consider that eye: consider the resolute, wild, free thing looking out of it, defying me, with more than courage—with a stern triumph. Whatever I do with its cage, I cannot get at it—the savage, beautiful creature! If I tear, if I rend the slight prison, my outrage will only let the captive loose. Conqueror I might be of the house; but the inmate would escape to heaven before I could call myself possessor of its clay dwelling-place. And it is you, spirit—with will and energy, and virtue and purity—that I want: not alone your brittle frame. Of yourself, you could come with soft flight and nestle against my heart, if you would: seized against your will, you will elude the grasp like an essence—you will vanish ere I inhale your fragrance. Oh! come, Jane, come!"

As he said this, he released me from his clutch, and only looked at me. The look was far worse to resist than the frantic strain; only an idiot, however, would have succumbed now. I had dared and baffled his fury; I must elude his sorrow: I retired to the door.

"You are going, Jane?"

"I am going, sir."

"You are leaving me?"

"Yes."

"You will not come?—You will not be my comforter, my rescuer?—My deep love, my wild woe, my frantic prayer, are all nothing to you?"

What unutterable pathos was in his voice! How hard it was to reiterate firmly, "I am going."

"Jane!"

"Mr. Rochester."

"Withdraw, then—I consent—but remember, you leave me here in anguish. Go up to your own room; think over all I have said, and, Jane, cast a glance on my sufferings—think of me."

He turned away; he threw himself on his face on the sofa. "Oh, Jane! my hope—my love—my life!" broke in anguish from his lips. Then came a deep, strong sob.

I had already gained the door: but, reader, I walked back—walked back as determinedly as I had retreated. I knelt down by him; I turned his face from the cushion to me; I kissed his cheek; I smoothed his hair with my hand.

"God bless you, my dear master," I said. "God keep you from harm and wrong—direct you, solace you, reward you well for your past kindness to me."

"Little Jane's love would have been my best reward," he answered: "without it, my heart is broken. But Jane will give me her love: yes—nobly, generously."

Up the blood rushed to his face; forth flashed the fire from his eyes; erect he sprang: he held his arms out; but I evaded the embrace, and at once quitted the room.

"Farewell!" was the cry of my heart, as I left him. Despair added,— "Farewell for ever!"

82. Elizabeth Rigby [Eastlake] (1848)

Altogether the auto-biography of Jane Eyre is pre-eminently an anti-Christian composition. There is throughout it a murmuring against the comforts of the rich and against the privations of the poor, which, as far as each individual is concerned, is a murmuring against God's appointment—there is a proud and perpetual assertion of the rights of man, for which we find no authority either in God's word or in God's providence—there is that pervading tone of ungodly discontent which is at once the most prominent and the most subtle evil which the law and the pulpit, which all civilized society in fact has at the present day to contend with. We do not hesitate to say that the tone of mind and thought which has overthrown authority and violated every code human and divine abroad, and fostered Chartism and rebellion at home, is the same which has also written Jane Eyre.

Still we say again this is a very remarkable book. We are painfully alive to the moral, religious, and literary deficiencies of the picture, and such passages of beauty and power as we have quoted cannot redeem it, but it is impossible not to be spellbound with the freedom of the touch. It would be mere hackneyed courtesy to call it 'fine writing.' It bears no impress of being written at all, but is poured out rather in the heat and hurry of an instinct, which flows ungovernably on to its object, indifferent by what means it reaches it, and unconscious too. As regards the author's chief object, however, it is a failure—that, namely, of making a plain, odd woman, destitute of all the conventional features of feminine attraction, interesting in our sight. We deny that he has succeeded in this. Jane Eyre, in spite of some grand things about her, is a being totally uncongenial to our feelings from beginning to end. We acknowledge her firmness—we respect her determination—we feel for her struggles; but, for all that, and setting aside higher considerations, the impression she leaves on our mind is that of a decidedly vulgar-minded woman—one whom we should not care for as an acquaintance, whom we should not seek as a friend, whom we should not desire for a relation, and whom we should scrupulously avoid for a governess.

There seem to have arisen in the novel-reading world some doubts as to who really wrote this book. . . . The question of authorship, therefore, can deserve a moment's curiosity only as far as 'Jane Eyre' is concerned, and though we cannot pronounce that it appertains to a real Mr. Currer Bell and to no other, yet that it appertains to a man, and not, as many assert, to a woman, we are strongly inclined to affirm. Without entering into the question whether the power of the writing be above her, or the vulgarity below her, there are, we believe, minutiæ of circumstantial evidence which at once acquit the feminine hand. No woman—a lady friend, whom we are always happy to consult, assures us—makes mistakes in her own *métier*—no woman *trusses game* and garnishes dessert-dishes with the same hands, or talks of so doing in the same breath. Above all, no woman attires another in such fancy dresses as Jane's ladies assume—Miss Ingram coming down, irresistible, 'in a *morning* robe of sky-blue crape, a gauze azure scarf twisted in her hair!!' No lady, we understand, when suddenly roused in the night, would think of hurrying on '*a frock*.' They have garments more convenient for such occasions, and more becoming too. This evidence seems incontrovertible. Even granting that these incongruities were purposely assumed, for the sake of disguising the female pen, there is nothing gained; for if we ascribe the book to a woman at all, we have no alternative but to ascribe it to one who has, for some sufficient reason, long forfeited the society of her own sex.

83. Charlotte Brontë (1849)

[Shirley Keeldar and Caroline Helstone discuss life]

"I often wonder, Shirley, whether most men resemble my uncle in their domestic relations; whether it is necessary to be new and unfamiliar to them, in order to seem agreeable or estimable in their eyes; and whether it is impossible to their natures to retain a constant interest and affection for those they see every day."

"I don't know: I can't clear up your doubts. I ponder over similar ones myself sometimes. But, to tell you a secret, if I were convinced that they are necessarily and universally different from us—fickle, soon petrifying, unsympathizing—I would never marry. I should not like to find out that what I loved did not love me, that it was weary of me, and whatever effort I might make to please would hereafter be worse than useless, since it was inevitably in its nature to change and become indifferent. That discovery once made, what should I long for? To go away—to remove from a presence where my society gave no pleasure."

"But you could not if you were married."

"No, I could not—there it is. I could never be my own mistress more. A terrible thought!—it suffocates me! Nothing irks me like the idea of being a burden and a bore—an inevitable burden—a ceaseless bore! Now, when I feel my company superfluous, I can comfortably fold my independence round me like a mantle, drop my pride like a veil, and withdraw to solitude. If married, that could not be."

"I wonder we don't all make up our minds to remain single," said Caroline; "we should if we listened to the wisdom of experience. My uncle always speaks of marriage as a burden; and I believe whenever he hears of a man being married, he invariably regards him as a fool, or, at any rate, as doing a foolish thing."

"But, Caroline, men are not all like your uncle; surely not—I hope not."

She paused and mused.

"I suppose we each find an exception in the one we love, till we *are* married," suggested Caroline.

"I suppose so: and this exception we believe to be of sterling materials; we fancy it like ourselves; we imagine a sense of harmony. We think his voice gives the softest, truest promise of a heart that will never harden against us. We read in his eyes that faithful feeling—affection. I don't think we should trust to what they call passion at all, Caroline. I believe it is a mere fire of dry sticks, blazing up and vanishing. But we watch him, and see him kind to animals, to little children, to poor people. He is kind to us, likewise—good—considerate. He does not flatter women, but he is patient with them, and he seems to be easy in their presence, and to find their company genial. He likes them not only for vain and selfish reasons, but as *we* like him—because we like him. Then we observe that he is just—that he always speaks the truth—that he is conscientious. We feel joy and peace when he comes into a room—we feel sadness and trouble when he leaves it. We know that this man has been a kind son—that he is a kind brother. Will any one dare to tell me that he will not be a kind husband?"

"My uncle would affirm it unhesitatingly. 'He will be sick of you in a month,' he would say."

"Mrs. Pryor would seriously intimate the same."

"Mrs. Yorke and Miss Mann would darkly suggest ditto."

[Shirley and Caroline resume their conversation.]

"Caroline," demanded Miss Keeldar, abruptly, "don't you wish you had a profession—a trade?"

"I wish it fifty times a day. As it is, I often wonder what I came into the world for. I long to have something absorbing and compulsory to fill my head and hands, and to occupy my thoughts."

"Can labor alone make a human being happy?"

"No; but it can give varieties of pain, and prevent us from breaking our hearts with a single tyrant master-torture. Besides, successful labor has its recompense; a vacant, weary, lonely, hopeless life has none."

"But hard labor and learned professions, they say, make women masculine, coarse, unwomanly."

"And what does it signify whether married and never-to-be-married women are unattractive and inelegant or not? provided only they are decent, decorous and neat, it is enough. The utmost which ought to be required of old maids, in the way of appearance, is that they should not absolutely offend men's eyes as they pass them in the street; for the rest they should be allowed, without too much scorn, to be as absorbed, grave, plain-looking, and plain-dressed as they please."

"You might be an old maid yourself, Caroline, you speak so earnestly."

"I shall be one; it is my destiny. I will never marry a Malone or a Sykes—and no one else will ever marry me."

[Following a disagreement about marriage, Shirley talks back to her uncle and former guardian.]

"Mr. Sympson. . . . I am sick at heart with all this weak trash; I will bear no more. Your thoughts are not my thoughts, your aims are not my aims, your gods are not my gods. We do not view things in the same light; we do not measure them by the same standard; we hardly speak in the same tongue. Let us part.

"It is not," she resumed, much excited—"It is not that I hate you; you are a good sort of man; perhaps you mean well in your way; but we cannot suit; we are ever at variance. You annoy me with small meddling, with petty tyranny; you exasperate my temper, and make and keep me passionate. As to your small maxims, your narrow rules, your little prejudices, aversions, dogmas, bundle them off. Mr. Sympson, go; offer them a sacrifice to the deity you worship; I'll none of them. I wash my hands of the lot. I walk by another creed, light, faith, and hope than you."

"Another creed! I believe she is an infidel."

"An infidel to *your* religion; an atheist to *your* god."

"*An—atheist!*"

"Your god, sir, is the world. In my eyes, you, too, if not an infidel, are an idolater. I conceive that you ignorantly worship. In all things you appear to me too superstitious. Sir, your god, your great Bel, your fish-tailed Dagon, rises before me as a demon. You, and such as you, have raised him to a throne, put on him a crown, given him a sceptre. Behold how hideously he governs! See him busied at the work he likes best—making marriages. He binds the young to the old, the strong to the imbecile. He stretches out the arm of Mezentius, and fetters the dead to the living. In his realm there is hatred—secret hatred; there is disgust—unspoken disgust; there is treachery—family treachery; there is vice—deep, deadly, domestic vice. In his dominions, children grow unloving between parents who have never loved: infants are nursed on deception from their very birth; they are reared in an atmosphere corrupt with lies. Your god rules at the bridal of kings—look at your royal dynasties! Your deity is the deity of foreign aristocracies—analyze the blue blood of Spain! Your god is the Hymen of France—what is French domestic life? All that surrounds him hastens to decay—all declines and degenerates under his sceptre. *Your* god is a masked Death."

"This language is terrible! My daughters and you must associate no longer, Miss Keeldar: there is danger in such companionship. Had I known you a little earlier—but, extraordinary as I thought you, I could not have believed—"

"Now, sir, do you begin to be aware that it is useless to scheme for me?—that in doing so, you but sow the wind to reap the whirlwind? I sweep your cobweb-projects from my path, that I may pass on unsullied. I am anchored on a resolve you cannot shake. My heart, my conscience, shall dispose of my hand—*they only*. Know this at last."

CHAPTER 9

Women's Political Action in the Face of Repression

A French Woman Seeks Political Office

SOURCES

84. Jeanne Deroin, "Aux Citoyens membres du Comité electoral démocratique et socialiste," *L'Opinion des Femmes*, 10 April 1849; Deroin's election poster, "Aux Electeurs du Département de la Seine," *L'Opinion des Femmes*, 10 April 1849; P.-J. Proudhon, "Protestation du *Peuple* contre la candidature de J. D.," *Le Peuple*, 12 April 1849; Jeanne Deroin, "Réponse à Proudhon," *La Démocratie Pacifique*, 13 April 1849. All reprinted in Adrien Ranvier, "Une Féministe de 1848, Jeanne Deroin," cited in Doc. 70 above, pp. 335-38. Tr. SGB.

85. [Jeanne Deroin], "'À M. Michelet. Droit politique des femmes,' extrait du 7ᵉ numéro de l'*Opinion des Femmes* qui paraîtra prochainement," Paris, 1 May 1850. Tr. KMO. The editors wish to thank Professor S. Joan Moon, Sacramento State University, who forwarded a copy of this brochure.

In the spring of 1849, elections were scheduled for the first Legislative Assembly of the newly established French Second Republic. The proclamation of universal manhood suffrage the previous year meant that every man in France would have a vote. Although one woman, Pauline Roland, had tried to register to vote in the provinces the previous year, this 1849 election marked the first time in the history of Europe that a woman had dared to pose her candidacy for national elective office under a democratic regime. This woman was Jeanne Deroin (1802-1894), who had already made a name for herself as a defender of women's cause (Doc. 70). In January 1849 she founded a newspaper, *L'Opinion des Femmes*, to present a female point of view. In the very first issue she published a rejoinder to the views of Proudhon (1809-1865; Docs. 52, 95), which were tremendously influential in social democratic circles. That April she petitioned to become one of the Paris Democratic Socialist electoral committee's candidates for the Assembly. Her candidacy provoked an important public discussion with Proudhon over the political role of women in the new republic.

The second selection, also by Jeanne Deroin, appeared in May 1850. It was occasioned by historian Jules Michelet's series of public lectures on the family at the Collège de France, in which he elaborated at length his thoughts on woman's place. He offered as his opinion, drawing on his earlier analysis of French women's close relationship to the Catholic Church (Doc. 46), that giving the vote to women was to throw political power to the Church. Especially after the pope's appeal to women through the Marian dogma (Doc. 79), Michelet's invocation of the specter of reactionary clerical interference in secular politics through women had a powerful effect in inhibiting male support for woman suffrage in France well into the twentieth century. Here Deroin (who signed herself "a woman in your audience") refuted Michelet's position, offering an important (though heretofore overlooked) analysis of women's relationship to civic and political life.

---

84. Jeanne Deroin vs. P.-J. Proudhon (1849)

[Jeanne Deroin: "Letter to the Democratic Socialist Electoral Committee"]
Citizens:
    You are democratic socialists; you want to abolish man's exploitation of man, and man's exploitation of woman; you want complete and radical abolition of all privileges of sex, race, birth, caste, and fortune; you sincerely desire all the consequences of our great principles of liberty, equality, and fraternity.
    It is in the name of these principles, which do not admit unjust exclusions, that I present myself as a candidate to the Legislative Assembly and that I come to ask your support—if not to be included on the list of twenty-eight who will be presented to the electorate, at least to obtain assurance, out of your justice, that I should not be excluded from this list in the name of a privilege of sex that violates the principles of equality and fraternity.
    The services rendered to our country and to the social cause, the intellectual superiority, the special capacity and oratorical talents of the large number of candidates who are presenting themselves offer you adequate reasons for excluding me, should you judge this necessary—without your having to invoke a prejudice against which men of the future should protest energetically, if not out of sympathy, then at least out of respect for principle.

[P.-J. Proudhon, *Protest Against the Candidacy of Jeanne Deroin*]
    A very serious incident took place at a recent Socialist banquet that we cannot ignore. A woman seriously proposed her own candidacy for the National Assembly.

[Deroin's election poster, addressed to the Electors of the Department of the Seine.]
Citizens:
    I present myself for your votes, out of devotion to the consecration of a great principle: the civil and political equality of the sexes.
    It is in the name of justice that I appeal to the sovereign people against negating the great principles that are the foundation for the future of our society.
    If, using your right, you call upon woman to take part in the work of the Legislative Assembly, you will consecrate our republican dogmas in all their integrity: Liberty, Equality, Fraternity for all women as well as for all men.
    A Legislative Assembly composed entirely of men is as incompetent to

make the laws that rule a society of men and women, as an assembly composed entirely of privileged people to debate the interests of workers, or an assembly of capitalists to sustain the honor of the country.

Jeanne Deroin, Candidate

[Proudhon continues:]
We cannot allow such pretensions and similar principles to be put forth, without protesting energetically in the name of public morality and of justice itself. It is essential that socialism not accept solidarity with them.

The political equality of both sexes, that is to say the assimilation of women with men in public functions, is one of those sophisms that are contrary not only to logic but also to the human conscience and the nature of things.

Man, to the extent that his reason is developed, sees clearly that woman is his equal, but he will never see her as identical.

[Jeanne Deroin: "Reply to Proudhon"]
Citizen Editor!
I beg you to insert my reply to the peculiar protest on the subject of my candidacy that appeared in the journal *Le Peuple.*

By putting forth my candidacy to the Legislative Assembly I have accomplished a duty: I demanded, in the name of public morality and in the name of justice, that the dogma of equality should not be a lie.

It is precisely because woman is equal to man, and yet not identical to him, that she should take part in the work of social reform and incorporate in it those necessary elements that are lacking in man, so that the work can be complete.

Liberty for woman, as for man, is the right to utilize and to develop one's faculties freely.

Life's unity can be considered to be in three parts: individual life, family life, and social life; this is a complete life. To refuse woman the right to live the social life is to commit a crime against humanity. Thus, it is in the name of socialism, which is henceforth the religion of humanity, that I have appealed to all Democratic Socialists and have urged them to accept solidarity, even with a qualification as to its opportuneness, with the fact that this is a holy and legitimate protest against the errors of the old society and against a clear violation of our sacred principles of liberty, equality, and fraternity.

It is in the name of these principles, which are the basis of socialism, that I ask them, if they do not consider it fitting to protest through their votes, to declare boldly that they are not retreating behind a privilege of sex but rather that grave circumstances require special capacities and eminent qualities to be called to the honor of defending our sacred cause.

As for me, I declare before God and in the name of humanity that it is never too early to stop on a false route, to repair an error, and to proclaim a great truth.

85. Jeanne Deroin (1850)

That's better! The lines are drawn and clear! To the question so often asked of you: "What do you think of women's political rights?" you replied in your last lecture: "Women have the same rights as men, but the means of exercising these rights is not possible under present conditions—we therefore appeal to women themselves. To award women immediately the right to vote would, in effect, drop into the ballot boxes some eighty thousand ballots for the priests." And then, in order to put an end to the question and, doubtless, hoping to console, you added: "moreover, the number of women who claim the right to exercise political rights is very small."

Because you appealed to women's sentiments in this circumstance, Monsieur, I shall try to reply in their name. I ought to do so all the more, perhaps, because of a remarkable fact, which cannot have escaped attentive observers, that proves to me that in contradicting your conclusions on this subject I am in truth the faithful interpreter of woman's sentiments.

Men, to judge by your auditors, agree entirely with your views on votes for women, and the applause that sanctioned your words, when you so easily caused eighty thousand votes for the priests to drop from the hands of women, proved sufficiently that you too, in this regard, expressed exactly the sentiments of your public. But did the women agree with this point of view? Did they also applaud? No, Monsieur, not one did so; and yet usually on every other question, upon hearing your sympathetic voice the applause of both sexes is mingled and blended. Whence came this quite exceptional reserve of the women upon a point that touches them so closely? Did that reserve not carry the weight of a protest? As far as I am concerned, I did not understand it otherwise and, moreover, I have observed that woman's good sense, easily displayed on the spur of the moment, has later been proved correct by reason.

But let us return to your very words, in order to examine various statements.

When you say: "Women have the same rights as men," you offer in its completeness a principle that is increasingly accepted by free thinkers and independent spirits.

But is it the same when you add: "Women under present conditions cannot exercise their political rights without compromising the cause of progress; to let women vote immediately would be to give the priests eighty-thousand ballots"?

On this point we utterly disagree. I believe, on the contrary, that our actual conditions are eminently favorable for the exercise of political rights by women.

Let us consider a case in which women present themselves at the ballot boxes. What would happen in such a case?

Are there large numbers of politically inclined women? That is the first question. This is immaterial; it is not the right question to ask. Are these women of the people or of the bourgeoisie? Are they those who are called

Ladies? None of this is significant. Those women who would like to exercise their right to vote would present themselves in the name of the law; they would claim their privilege, they would base themselves on our republican institutions; that is all. What would happen then? The situation, it will no doubt be said, could become embarrassing, if not downright ridiculous. That is no response. Republicans, Democrats, Socialists all agree unanimously that allowing women to vote under present conditions would be the greatest disaster for the Republic and for the cause of progress and, consequently, women who present themselves must be told that they cannot be allowed to vote. Very well, but if these ladies persist, saying that to let them vote is not at all the same thing as to make them vote; if they protest against the illegality committed against their persons, concerning their RIGHTS as women? If, finally, they require that a formal attestation of denial of justice be drawn up, to document the injustice they claim to have suffered, how will you extricate yourself from that embarrassment, and which side will you take?

Have no doubt, sir; this is the manner in which the question will soon be posed and, indeed, the manner in which it has already been raised by a courageous woman, Madame Pauline Roland. But that was an individual case, which occurred in the provinces and, thus, did not make a great noise.

Do not believe, however, that this example will be lost. On the contrary, you may be sure that it will be repeated and multiplied. Do you not sense this when you see the persistence with which women come back to that very question on every occasion? Is this not a sure indication of the importance they attach to this question?

One woman presented herself in the provinces but in Paris a hundred will present themselves.

That number is not at all impressive, you say? So much the better! You will be better able to choose sides before the number increases to infinity.

Do you wish to make a fiction of the law? Do you wish to repulse women in spite of the law and in the most flagrantly illegal manner? Do the democratic journals, in the manner of *Le Charivari*, wish to settle the question with a few bad jokes? That would be a disastrous course.

This protest of a few women, this example of civic courage and, above all else, your moral persecution will perhaps produce the spark that will leap all the way to the domestic hearth to kindle the fire of independence and liberty!

One should not play either with justice or with fire. Justice is the sacred fire of the conscience; cursed be they who do not tend it!

If Republicans and Socialists join together in refusing women the exercise of their political rights in the present circumstances, it is because they have not considered the matter carefully.

To recognize women's rights *in principle* is to pledge oneself to consecrate them in fact; no one has the right to appoint himself judge of the opportunity for exercising a right. For the simple reason that women are not excluded from political rights by law, the law consecrates these rights; these rights no more await sanction than do the women themselves; these sanctions can no more be opposed or postponed than women can be placed outside the law. Those who dare to attempt this are guilty of attacking justice and progress; they would threaten the very foundations of the Republic.

Nor is this all. From a question of principle, which has nothing to fear from the facts, you would arbitrarily create a political question. The forces of reaction would not hesitate to employ the tool you have scorned to use. Not only would they recognize women's right, which you have acknowledged to no purpose, but also, in order to profit from your mistakes, they would replace the current conditions for voting with new ones; gallantry would triumph over strict equality, and they would easily find the means of reconciling women's exercise of political rights with the modesty of the sex and the etiquette of the world. For women the ballot box at the church would replace the men's ballot box at the mayor's office; then, and then alone, would eighty thousand ballots fall to the priests from the hands of women.

For heaven's sake, gentlemen, do not presume to teach women delicacy!

Do not place yourselves above justice or appoint yourselves the judges of a question of opportuneness that does not concern you. Opportuneness can be sensed and determined only by those who are called to exercise their rights.

A truth recognized, admitted, and proclaimed henceforth carries its own charge, which impels it toward complete realization. It would be very strange, then, if the moment when the truth appeared were not also, within the limits of possibility, the moment of its very realization! It would be very strange if the intelligence that expresses a truth were, at the same time, to issue a respectful summons to that truth, asking it to reappear at a more suitable time! No, no! this is impossible! Every truth, by the very fact that it is recognized, begins to be usable.

To return to the question that concerns us—and to preserve the future from the evils we fear just as much as you do—I have but one thing to say, and I address it to all who cherish the realization of orderly progress.

Do you wish to be *just* as well as prudent? Do you wish to remain within the bounds of legality? Then let women vote freely, and take care only that nothing is changed for them in the present conditions of the vote. These conditions are the very guarantees of progress; every honest opinion submits to them easily.

Does the number of women anxious to exercise their rights still seem too large to you, despite these quite natural restrictions? Would you wish, while still remaining within the confines of legality, to embark on a system that incorporates a more stringent weeding-out? So be it! I shall offer you a last morsel, which I submit to your wise consideration.

Supposing a hundred women present themselves to vote in Paris at the next election, all at different mayors' offices. Among these hundred women will be five widows, fifteen spinsters, and eighty married women.

Bravely make this magnificent purge! Send away the eighty married women, and allow only the other twenty to vote. Why so? What law permits you to act thus, everyone cries? I am much embarrassed to say so, but it is simply by virtue of the Civil Code! Through the very act of marriage, every adult woman is thrown back into legal childhood and may not exercise her civic rights without her husband's authorization. . . . While the twenty spinsters and widows vote freely, the eighty married women return to their conjugal hearths.—Various points of view.— Piquant topics of conversation between the spouses at the dinner table. . . .

Repression and Reaction

SOURCES

86. "Verordnung über die Verhütung eines die gesetzliche Freiheit und Ordnung gefährdenden Missbrauchs des Versammlungs- und Vereinigungsrechtes," 11 March 1850, no. 3261, in *Gesetzsammlung für die Königlichen preussischen Staaten, 1850* (Berlin). Tr. SGB.

87. Jeanne Deroin and Pauline Roland, "Letter to the Convention of the Women of America," 15 June 1851. Published in *History of Woman Suffrage*, I, 234-37.

88. [Harriet Taylor Mill], Review essay on *The New York Tribune for Europe* (issue of 29 October 1850), *Westminster Review* no. 109 (July 1851), pp. 149-55, 160-61.

89. Louise Otto, "Das Ewig Weibliche," *Frauen-Zeitung, Ein Organ für die höheren weiblichen Interessen, begründet und fortgesetzt von Louise Otto*, III, no. 45 (23 Nov. 1851), as reprinted in *Die deutsche Frauenbewegung*, II, *Quellen: 1843-1889*, ed. Margrit Twellmann (Meisenheim am Glan, 1972), 36-38. Tr. SGB.

Organized efforts to advance the cause of women in Europe, like those devoted to the cause of the working class, were effectively disrupted by the measures taken by European governments to douse the fires of revolution. As in France in 1848, other governments soon deployed their power by drastically curbing freedom of political association and of the press, which had been blamed for much of the turbulence that rocked the monarchies in 1848 and 1849. The ways in which these restrictions affected women have been suggested by the French decree against the clubs (Doc. 71). A similar measure was the Prussian king's 1850 "Decree protecting lawful freedom and order from the abuse of the rights of assembly and association," our first selection. Measures of this type were also enacted in Bavaria, Saxony, and Brunswick, and in 1854 were incorporated into the protocols of the German Confederation. Only a few principalities and free cities escaped their rigor.

In France universal manhood suffrage itself was rescinded in May 1850. Later that year French women like Jeanne Deroin, who had continued to be vocal and visible in efforts to organize associations of male and female workers, were arrested and jailed for breaching the sanctions against political association. In the second selection Deroin and her colleague Pauline Roland (1805-1852) appealed to the women of America from their Paris prison, following the successful effort by the American Lucretia Mott (Doc. 74) to establish contact with them. Their appeal was read aloud at the Women's Rights Convention held in Worcester, Massachusetts, in 1851. Their rhetorical plea summarizes many of the themes they had raised earlier during their involvement with the Saint-Simonians and throughout the events of 1848. Following Louis-Napoleon's coup d'état Deroin fled to England, where she remained to the end of her life. Roland, who had remained in France, was deported by military authorities to a prison camp in Algeria; she died shortly after her release in 1852.

The third selection, published in England within weeks of the appeal of Deroin and Roland, was written by Harriet (Hardy) Taylor Mill (1807-1856), long associated with—and, after April 1851, the wife of—the distinguished political philosopher, John Stuart Mill (Docs. 105, 135). She had recently been widowed, after being married for many years to a man she did not love but could not divorce, and had several grown children. Through her long friendship with Mill, whom she had met in the early 1830's, she exerted a deep influence on his thinking on the woman question. Harriet Taylor Mill evidently wrote this long and tightly argued essay in the late 1840's. For several years Mill had encouraged her to publish it, and it finally appeared, anonymously, in the guise of a review article in the liberal *Westminster Review*, of which Mill was an editor. J. S. Mill proudly distributed copies of the essay, stressing his wife's primary authorship, to sympathetic reformers such as Pierre Leroux in France; meanwhile Taylor Mill's son delivered copies to Lucretia Mott in Pennsylvania. Later this article became more widely known under the title, "Enfranchisement of Women." These selections from Harriet Mill's essay reveal, in a different manner than Rigby-Eastlake's review of *Jane Eyre* (Doc. 82), the extent to which the English intelligentsia, though untouched directly by the revolutionary proceedings on the Continent, were acutely aware of those events. They also illustrate the contrast between the harsh repression of women's political action by authorities on the European continent and its continued liberty in England and the United States, a liberty that fostered the uninterrupted growth of an organized Anglo-Saxon women's movement from that time forth.

Despite the repression of women's participation in political associations, assertive statements by women were still forthcoming in the German press, as the final selection, by Louise Otto (1819-1895; Docs. 48, 78, 129), shows. In 1850 a Saxon law prohibiting women from publishing newspapers had forced Otto to move herself and her journal for women across the border. She continued to publish in Gera (Thuringia) until the following year. In these articles from her *Frauen-Zeitung* Otto invoked Goethe's image of the "eternal-womanly" (from *Faust*) to argue for women's right to full participation in political and social life within a framework that would respect and honor sexual differences.

---

86. Decree on Associations (1850)

[Paragraph 8]

Those organizations aiming to discuss political matters in public meetings are bound by the following restrictions [in addition to other, previously stated provisions concerning the times of meetings, restrictions on the bearing of arms, notification of police, etc.—EDS.]:

(a) such organizations may not accept as members women, students, or apprentices;

(b) they may not join with other similar organizations to work for common goals; specifically, they may not thus combine through committees, centralized publications, or any similar arrangements, or through any exchange of written correspondence.

If these restrictions are violated, the local police has the authority, as a provision leading to legal proceedings against the offending organization, to dissolve the organization until a judicial hearing and verdict have been procured.

Women, students, and apprentices may not attend meetings of such political organizations. If such persons are not removed by an attendant representing authority, this is a cause for the official termination of the meeting.

[Paragraph 16]

If a political organization violates the prescriptions drawn up in paragraph 8, the chairmen, organizers, and leaders who contravened these decisions will be liable to fines of from five to fifty thalers, or imprisonment from eight days to three months. Depending upon the seriousness of the circumstances, the judge is also entitled to demand the dissolution of the organization. Such a dissolution must take place if chairmen, organizers, or leaders have repeatedly contravened the law.

Whoever continues to participate as a member, even temporarily, in a dissolved organization is liable to a fine of from five to fifty thalers, or of eight days to three months' imprisonment.

Those who permit themselves to be accepted as members contrary to the proscriptions in paragraph 8, are liable to a fine of from five to fifty thalers.

87. Jeanne Deroin and Pauline Roland (1851)

To the Convention of the Women of America:

Dear Sisters:—Your courageous declaration of Woman's Rights has resounded even to our prison, and has filled our souls with inexpressible joy.

In France the reaction has suppressed the cry of liberty of the women of the future. Deprived, like their brothers, of the Democracy, of the right to civil and political equality, and the fiscal laws which trammel the liberty of the press, hinder the propagation of those eternal truths which must regenerate humanity.

They wish the women of France to found a hospitable tribunal, which shall receive the cry of the oppressed and suffering, and vindicate in the name of humanity, solidarity, the social right for both sexes equally; and where woman, the mother of humanity, may claim in the name of her children, mutilated by tyranny, her right to true liberty, to the complete development and free exercise of all her faculties, and reveal that half of truth which is in her, and without which no social work can be complete.

The darkness of reaction has obscured the sun of 1848, which seemed to rise so radiantly. Why? Because the revolutionary tempest, in overturn-

ing at the same time the throne and the scaffold, in breaking the chain of
the black slave, forgot to break the chain of the most oppressed of all of
the pariahs of humanity.

"There shall be no more slaves," said our brethren. "We proclaim universal suffrage. All shall have the right to elect the agents who shall carry
out the Constitution which should be based on the principles of liberty,
equality, and fraternity. Let each one come and deposit his vote; the barrier of privilege is overturned; before the electoral urn there are no more
oppressed, no more masters and slaves."

Woman, in listening to this appeal, rises and approaches the liberating
urn to exercise her right of suffrage as a member of society. But the barrier of privilege rises also before her. "You must wait," they say. But by
this claim alone woman affirms the right, not yet recognized, of the half
of humanity—the right of woman to liberty, equality, and fraternity. She
obliges man to verify the fatal attack which he makes on the integrity of
his principles.

Soon, in fact during the wonderful days of June, 1848, liberty glides
from her pedestal in the flood of the victims of the reaction; based on the
"right of the strongest," she falls, overturned in the name of "the right of
the strongest."

The Assembly kept silence in regard to the right of one-half of humanity, for which only one of its members raised his voice, but in vain. No
mention was made of the right of woman in a Constitution framed in the
name of Liberty, Equality, and Fraternity.

It is in the name of these principles that woman comes to claim her
right to take part in the Legislative Assembly, and to help to form the
laws which must govern society, of which she is a member.

She comes to demand of the electors the consecration of the principle
of equality by the election of a woman, and by this act she obliges man to
prove that the fundamental law which he has formed in the sole name of
liberty, equality, and fraternity, is still based upon privilege, and soon
privilege triumphs over this phantom of universal suffrage, which, being
but half of itself, sinks on the 31st of May, 1850.

But while those selected by the half of the people—by men alone—
evoke force to stifle liberty, and forge restrictive laws to establish order
by compression, woman, guided by fraternity, foreseeing incessant struggles, and in the hope of putting an end to them, makes an appeal to the
laborer to found liberty and equality on fraternal solidarity. The participation of woman gave to this work of enfranchisement an eminently
pacific character, and the laborer recognizes the right of woman, his companion in labor.

The delegates of a hundred and four associations, united, without distinction of sex, elected two women, with several of their brethren, to participate equally with them in the administration of the interests of labor,
and in the organization of the work of solidarity.

Fraternal associations were formed with the object of enfranchising the laborer from the yoke of spoliage and patronage, but, isolated in the midst of the Old World, their efforts could only produce a feeble amelioration for themselves.

The union of associations based on fraternal solidarity had for its end the organization of labor; that is to say, an equal division of labor, of instruments, and of the products of labor.

The means were, the union of labor, and of credit among the workers of all professions, in order to acquire the instruments of labor and the necessary materials, and to form a mutual guarantee for the education of their children, and to provide for the needs of the old, the sick, and the infirm.

In this organization all the workers, without distinction of sex or profession, having an equal right to election, and being eligible for all functions, and all having equally the initiative and the sovereign decision in the acts of common interests, they laid the foundation of a new society based on liberty, equality, and fraternity.

It is in the name of law framed by man only—by those elected by privilege—that the Old World, wishing to stifle in the germ the holy work of pacific enfranchisement, has shut up within the walls of a prison those who had founded it—those elected by the laborers.

But the impulse has been given, a grand act has been accomplished. The right of woman has been recognized by the laborers, and they have consecrated that right by the election of those who had claimed it in vain for both sexes, before the electoral urn and before the electoral committees. They have received the true civil baptism, were elected by the laborers to accomplish the mission of enfranchisement, and after having shared their rights and their duties, they share to-day their captivity.

It is from the depths of their prison that they address to you the relation of these facts, which contain in themselves high instruction. It is by labor, it is by entering resolutely into the ranks of the working people, that women will conquer the civil and political equality on which depends the happiness of the world. As to moral equality, has she not conquered it by the power of sentiment? It is, therefore, by the sentiment of the love of humanity that the mother of humanity will find power to accomplish her high mission. It is when she shall have well comprehended the holy law of solidarity—which is not an obscure and mysterious dogma, but a living providential fact—that the kingdom of God promised by Jesus, and which is no other than the kingdom of equality and justice, shall be realized on earth.

Sisters of America! your socialist sisters of France are united with you in the vindication of the right of woman to civil and political equality. We have, moreover, the profound conviction that only by the power of association based on solidarity—by the union of the working-classes of both sexes to organize labor—can be acquired, completely and pacifically, the civil and political equality of woman, and the social right for all.

It is in this confidence that, from the depths of the jail which still imprisons our bodies without reaching our hearts, we cry to you, Faith, Love, Hope, and send to you our sisterly salutations.

Jeanne Deroin,
Pauline Roland.

Paris, Prison of St. Lazare, *June* 15, 1851.

88. Harriet Taylor Mill (1851)

Most of our readers will probably learn from these pages for the first time, that there has arisen in the United States, and in the most civilized and enlightened portion of them, an organized agitation on a new question—new, not to thinkers, nor to any one by whom the principles of free and popular government are felt as well as acknowledged, but new, and even unheard-of, as a subject for public meetings and practical political action. This question is, the enfranchisement of women; their admission, in law and in fact, to equality in all rights, political, civil, and social, with the male citizens of the community.

It will add to the surprise with which many will receive this intelligence, that the agitation which has commenced is not a pleading by male writers and orators for women, those who are professedly to be benefited remaining either indifferent or ostensibly hostile. It is a political movement, practical in its objects, carried on in a form which denotes an intention to persevere. And it is a movement not merely *for* women, but *by* them. Its first public manifestation appears to have been a Convention of Women, held in the state of Ohio, in the spring of 1850. Of this meeting we have seen no report. On the 23rd and 24th of October last, a succession of public meetings was held at Worcester in Massachusetts, under the name of a "Women's Rights Convention," of which the president was a woman, and nearly all the chief speakers women: numerously reinforced, however, by men, among whom were some of the most distinguished leaders in the kindred cause of negro emancipation. A general and four special committees were nominated, for the purpose of carrying on the undertaking until the next annual meeting.

According to the report in the *New York Tribune*, above a thousand persons were present throughout, and "if a larger place could have been had, many thousands more would have attended." The place was described as "crowded from the beginning with attentive and interested listeners." In regard to the quality of the speaking, the proceedings bear an advantageous comparison with those of any popular movement with which we are acquainted, either in this country or in America. Very rarely in the oratory of public meetings is the part of verbiage and declamation so small, that of calm good sense and reason so considerable. The result of the Convention was in every respect encouraging to those by whom it was summoned: and it is probably destined to inaugurate one of the most important of the movements towards political and social reform, which are the best characteristics of the present age. . . .

The following is a brief summary of the principal demands.

1. *Education* in primary and high schools, universities, medical, legal, and theological institutions.

2. *Partnership* in the labours and gains, risks and remunerations, of productive industry.

3. *A coequal share* in the formation and administration of laws—municipal, state, and national—through legislative assemblies, courts, and executive offices.

It would be difficult to put so much true, just, and reasonable meaning into a style so little calculated to recommend it as that of some of the resolutions. But whatever objection may be made to some of the expressions, none, in our opinion, can be made to the demands themselves. As a question of justice, the case seems to us too clear for dispute. As one of expediency, the more thoroughly it is examined the stronger it will appear.

That women have as good a claim as men have, in point of personal right, to the suffrage, or to a place in the jury-box, it would be difficult for any one to deny. It cannot certainly be denied by the United States of America, as a people or as a community. Their democratic institutions rest avowedly on the inherent right of every one to a voice in the government. . . .

We do not imagine that any American democrat will evade the force of these expressions by the dishonest or ignorant subterfuge, that "men," in this memorable document, does not stand for human beings, but for one sex only; that "life, liberty, and the pursuit of happiness" are "inalienable rights" of only one moiety of the human species; and that "the governed," whose consent is affirmed to be the only source of just power, are meant for that half of mankind only, who, in relation to the other, have hitherto assumed the character of governors. The contradiction between principle and practice cannot be explained away. A like dereliction of the fundamental maxims of their political creed has been committed by the Americans in the flagrant instance of the negroes; of this they are learning to recognise the turpitude. After a struggle which, by many of its incidents, deserves the name of heroic, the abolitionists are now so strong in numbers and in influence that they hold the balance of parties in the United States. It was fitting that the men whose names will remain associated with the extirpation, from the democratic soil of America, of the aristocracy of colour, should be among the originators, for America and for the rest of the world, of the first collective protest against the aristocracy of sex; a distinction as accidental as that of colour, and fully as irrelevant to all questions of government.

Not only to the democracy of America, the claim of women to civil and political equality makes an irresistible appeal, but also to those Radicals and Chartists in the British islands, and democrats on the Continent, who claim what is called universal suffrage as an inherent right, unjustly and oppressively withheld from them. For with what truth or rationality could the suffrage be termed universal, while half the human species remained excluded from it? To declare that a voice in the government is the right of all, and demand it only for a part—the part, namely, to which the claimant himself belongs—is to renounce even the appearance of principle. The Chartist who denies the suffrage to women, is a Chartist only because he is not a lord: he is one of those levellers who would level only down to themselves.

Even those who do not look upon a voice in the government as a matter of personal right, nor profess principles which require that it should be extended to all, have usually traditional maxims of political justice with which it is impossible to reconcile the exclusion of all women from the common rights of citizenship. It is an axiom of English freedom that taxation and representation should be co-extensive. Even under the laws which give the wife's property to the husband, there are many unmarried women who pay taxes. It is one of the fundamental doctrines of the British Constitution, that all persons should be tried by their peers: yet women, whenever tried, are tried by male judges and a male jury. To foreigners the law accords the privilege of claiming that half the jury should be composed of themselves; not so to women. Apart from maxims of detail, which represent local and national rather than universal ideas, it is an acknowledged dictate of justice to make no degrading distinctions without necessity. In all things the presumption ought to be on the side of equality. A reason must be given why anything should be permitted to one person and interdicted to another. But when that which is interdicted includes nearly everything which those to whom it is permitted most prize, and to be deprived of which they feel to be most insulting; when not only political liberty but personal freedom of action is the prerogative of a caste; when even in the exercise of industry, almost all employments which task the higher faculties in an important field, which lead to distinction, riches, or even pecuniary independence, are fenced round as the exclusive domain of the predominant section, scarcely any doors being left open to the dependent class, except such as all who can enter elsewhere disdainfully pass by; the miserable expediencies which are advanced as excuses for so grossly partial a dispensation, would not be sufficient, even if they were real, to render it other than a flagrant injustice. While, far from being expedient, we are firmly convinced that the division of mankind into two castes, one born to rule over the other, is in this case, as in all cases, an unqualified mischief; a source of perversion and demoralization, both to the favoured class and to those at whose expense they are favoured; producing none of the good which it is the custom to ascribe to it, and forming a bar, almost insuperable while it lasts, to any really vital improvement, either in the character or in the social condition of the human race. . . .

We deny the right of any portion of the species to decide for another portion, or any individual for another individual, what is and what is not their "proper sphere." The proper sphere for all human beings is the largest and highest which they are able to attain to. What this is, cannot be ascertained, without complete liberty of choice. The speakers at the Convention in America have therefore done wisely and right, in refusing to entertain the question of the peculiar aptitudes either of women or of men, or the limits within [which] this or that occupation may be supposed to be more adapted to the one or to the other. They justly maintain, that these questions can only be satisfactorily answered by perfect freedom. Let every occupation be open to all, without favour or discouragement to any, and employments will fall into the hands of those men or women who are found by experience to be most capable of worthily exercising them. There need be no fear that women will take out of the hands of men any occupation which men perform better than they. Each individual will prove his or her capacities, in the only way in which capacities can be proved—by trial; and the world will have the benefit of the best faculties of all its inhabitants. But to interfere beforehand by an arbitrary limit, and declare that whatever be the genius, talent, energy, or force of mind of an individual of a certain sex or class, those faculties shall not be exerted, or shall be exerted only in some few of the many modes in which others are permitted to use theirs, is not only an injustice to the individual, and a detriment to society, which loses what it can ill spare, but is also the most effectual mode of providing that, in the sex or class so fettered, the qualities which are not permitted to be exercised shall not exist. . . .

Concerning the fitness, then, of women for politics, there can be no question: but the dispute is more likely to turn upon the fitness of politics for women. When the reasons alleged for excluding women from active life in all its higher departments are stripped of their garb of declamatory phrases, and reduced to the simple expression of a meaning, they seem to be mainly three: first, the incompatibility of active life with maternity, and with the cares of a household; secondly, its alleged hardening effect on the character; and thirdly, the inexpediency of making an addition to the already excessive pressure of competition in every kind of professional or lucrative employment.

The first, the maternity argument, is usually laid most stress upon: although (it needs hardly be said) this reason, if it be one, can apply only to mothers. It is neither necessary nor just to make imperative on women that they shall be either mothers or nothing; or that if they have been mothers once, they shall be nothing else during the whole remainder of their lives. Neither women nor men need any law to exclude them from an occupation, if they have undertaken another which is incompatible with it. No one proposes to exclude the male sex from Parliament because a man may be a soldier or sailor in active service, or a merchant whose business requires all his time and energies. Nine-tenths of the occupations of men exclude them *de facto* from public life, as effectually as if they were excluded by law; but that is no reason for making laws to exclude even the nine-tenths, much less the remaining tenth. The reason of the case is the same for women as for men. There is no need to make provision by law that a woman shall not carry on the active details of a household, or of the education of children, and at the same time practise a profession, or be elected to parliament. Where incompatibility is real, it will take care of itself: but there is gross injustice in making the incompatibility a pretence for the exclusion of those in whose case it does not exist. And these, if they were free to choose, would be a very large proportion. The maternity argument deserts its supporters in the case of single women, a large and increasing class of the population; a fact which, it is not irrelevant to remark, by tending to diminish the excessive competition of numbers, is calculated to assist greatly the prosperity of all. There is no inherent reason or necessity that all women should voluntarily choose to devote their lives to one animal function and its consequences. Numbers of women are wives and mothers only because there is no other career open to them, no other occupation for their feelings or their activities. Every improvement in their education, and enlargement of their faculties, everything which renders them more qualified for any other mode of life, increases the number of those to whom it is an injury and an oppression to be denied the choice. To say that women must be excluded from active life because maternity disqualifies them for it, is in fact to say, that every other career should be forbidden them in order that maternity may be their only resource.

But secondly, it is urged, that to give the same freedom of occupation to women as to men, would be an injurious addition to the crowd of competitors, by whom the avenues to almost all kinds of employment are choked up, and its remuneration depressed. This argument, it is to be observed, does not reach the political question. It gives no excuse for withholding from women the rights of citizenship. The suffrage, the jury-box, admission to the legislature and to office, it does not touch. It bears only on the industrial branch of the subject. . . .

The third objection to the admission of women to political or professional life, its alleged hardening tendency, belongs to an age now past, and is scarcely to be comprehended by people of the present time. There are still, however, persons who say that the world and its avocations render men selfish and unfeeling; that the struggles, rivalries, and collisions of business and of politics make them harsh and unamiable; that if half the species must unavoidably be given up to these things, it is the more necessary that the other half should be kept free from them; that to preserve women from the bad influences of the world, is the only chance of preventing men from being wholly given up to them.

There would have been plausibility in this argument when the world was still in the age of violence; when life was full of physical conflict, and every man had to redress his injuries or those of others, by the sword or by the strength of his arm. Women, like priests, by being exempted from such responsibilities, and from some part of the accompanying dangers, may have been enabled to exercise a beneficial influence. But in the present condition of human life, we do not know where those hardening influences are to be found, to which men are subject and from which women are at present exempt. Individuals now-a-days are seldom called upon to fight hand to hand, even with peaceful weapons; personal enmities and rivalities count for little in worldly transactions; the general pressure of circumstances, not the adverse will of individuals, is the obstacle men now have to make head against. That pressure, when excessive, breaks the spirit, and cramps and sours the feelings, but not less of women than of men, since they suffer certainly not less from its evils. There are still quarrels and dislikes, but the sources of them are changed. The feudal chief once found his bitterest enemy in his powerful neighbour, the minister or courtier in his rival for place: but opposition of interest in active life, as a cause of personal animosity, is out of date; the enmities of the present day arise not from great things but small, from what people say of one another, more than from what they do; and if there are hatred, malice, and all uncharitableness, they are to be found among women fully as much as among men. In the present state of civilization, the notion of guarding women from the hardening influences of the world, could only be realized by secluding them from society altogether. The common duties of common life, as at present constituted, are incompatible with any other softness in women than weakness. Surely weak minds in weak bodies must ere long cease to be even supposed to be either attractive or amiable.

But, in truth, none of these arguments and considerations touch the foundations of the subject. The real question is, whether it is right and expedient that one-half of the human race should pass through life in a state of forced subordination to the other half. If the best state of human society is that of being divided into two parts, one consisting of persons with a will and a substantive existence, the other of humble companions to these persons, attached, each of them to one, for the purpose of bringing up *his* children, and making *his* home pleasant to him; if this is the place assigned to women, it is but kindness to educate them for this; to make them believe that the greatest good fortune which can befal them, is to be chosen by some man for this purpose; and that every other career which the world deems happy or honourable, is closed to them by the law, not of social institutions, but of nature and destiny.

When, however, we ask why the existence of one-half the species should be merely ancillary to that of the other—why each woman should be a mere appendage to a man, allowed to have no interests of her own, that there may be nothing to compete in her mind with his interests and his pleasure; the only reason which can be given is, that men like it. It is agreeable to them that men should live for their own sake, women for the sake of men: and the qualities and conduct in subjects which are agreeable to rulers, they succeed for a long time in making the subjects themselves consider as their appropriate virtues. Helvetius has met with much obloquy for asserting, that persons usually mean by virtues the qualities which are useful or convenient to themselves. How truly this is said of mankind in general, and how wonderfully the ideas of virtue set afloat by the powerful, are caught and imbibed by those under their dominion, is exemplified by the manner in which the world were once persuaded that

the supreme virtue of subjects was loyalty to kings, and are still persuaded that the paramount virtue of womanhood is loyalty to men. Under a nominal recognition of a moral code common to both, in practice
self-will and self-assertion form the type of what are designated as manly
virtues, while abnegation of self, patience, resignation, and submission to
power, unless when resistance is commanded by other interests than their
own, have been stamped by general consent as pre-eminently the duties
and graces required of women. The meaning being merely, that power
makes itself the centre of moral obligation, and that a man likes to have
his own will, but does not like that his domestic companion should have
a will different from his. . . .

. . . The fact which affords the occasion for this notice, makes it impossible any longer to assert the universal acquiescence of women (saving
individual exceptions) in their dependent condition. In the United States,
at least, there are women, seemingly numerous, and now organized for
action on the public mind, who demand equality in the fullest acceptation
of the word, and demand it by a straightforward appeal to men's sense of
justice, not plead for it with a timid deprecation of their displeasure.

Like other popular movements, however, this may be seriously retarded by the blunders of its adherents. Tried by the ordinary standard of
public meetings, the speeches at the Convention are remarkable for the
preponderance of the rational over the declamatory element; but there
are some exceptions; and things to which it is impossible to attach any
rational meaning, have found their way into the resolutions. Thus, the
resolution which sets forth the claims made in behalf of women, after
claiming equality in education, in industrial pursuits, and in political
rights, enumerates as a fourth head of demand something under the
name of "social and spiritual union," and "a medium of expressing the
highest moral and spiritual views of justice," with other similar verbiage,
serving only to mar the simplicity and rationality of the other demands;
resembling those who would weakly attempt to combine nominal equality between men and women, with enforced distinctions in their privileges and functions. What is wanted for women is equal rights, equal
admission to all social privileges; not a position apart, a sort of sentimental priesthood. To this, the only just and rational principle, both the resolutions and the speeches, for the most part, adhere. They contain so little
which is akin to the nonsensical paragraph in question, that we suspect it
not to be the work of the same hands as most of the other resolutions.
The strength of the cause lies in the support of those who are influenced
by reason and principle; and to attempt to recommend it by sentimen-
talities, absurd in reason, and inconsistent with the principle on which
the movement is founded, is to place a good cause on a level with a
bad one.

There are indications that the example of America will be followed on
this side of the Atlantic; and the first step has been taken in that part of
England where every serious movement in the direction of political progress has its commencement—the manufacturing districts of the North.

On the 13th of February 1851, a petition of women, agreed to by a public meeting at Sheffield, and claiming the elective franchise, was presented to the House of Lords by the Earl of Carlisle.

89. Louise Otto (1851)

> The Indefinable
> Made manifest here—
> The Eternal-Womanly
> Forever uplifts us.
> —Goethe

We have often met philistines and reactionaries who, in their limited lack of understanding—not to say in their malevolence—suggested that all of us who are trying to help women achieve a worthy position, are attempting to educate woman according to a manly model and to imitate man.

On the contrary, we insist on equality of women with men. . . . Man and woman appeared through the hand of God or creation . . . as two complete creatures of equal rank; but the differences in their physical characteristics are also maintained in the life of the spirit. The union of both produces a balance of these differences. The man in himself and the woman in herself are equally significant individuals; only when they are united do they form a whole. This was implicit in the wisdom of the creation.

Woman is equal to man in all higher concerns of life. It is a sin, not only against woman but against mankind and against the principle of creation, to force woman into and to keep her in slavery, to limit her to the narrow circle of domesticity and thus to exclude her from those other aims of humanity that are not related to the family.

Women ought to be able to act in common for the common good, as well as for their own development, with the same freedom as men. In the struggle for woman's freedom it is particularly important to rescue what is truly womanly; to liberate it from that one-sided despotism of judgment that has been developed by men by degrees and from which not only the female sex, but the entire better part of mankind suffers.

Woman should bring the divine inheritance given her to universal acceptance in its entire might and sanctity against the super-power of a cold and brutal force—that is the true, lofty, and beautiful goal, which is the aim of all our exertions. I have not asked for more in the past, nor do I ask now for more, or for less.

[In 1846 a critic, writing about Louise Otto and her work, complained: "She is no Liberal, her politics are those of sentiment, her world is the world of the heart. No, she is no Liberal, she is a woman." To this criticism Louise Otto replied as follows:]

My speaking "more from the heart than from the head" is neither reproach nor praise—it is the essence of woman. I have never desired anything else, never striven to change this. I have offered myself with my heart for the fatherland, for humanity—and the more I participate in and work for public affairs, the more I recognize how much better it would be if in all matters of state or of society the heart played a greater part than it now does.

I am happy to agree to being a woman rather than a liberal. Indeed it is not as a liberal but as a woman that I step beyond the narrow circle to which women have mostly been banished. In the name of women I am demanding the right to take part in the activities and struggles of political parties; I acknowledge this myself and want it acknowledged as my duty as a woman.

Other women have come forth to work for women's emancipation, but many of them have lost the proper path. I will not speak of those caricatures who have adopted the cruder customs and practices of men as their right, and who have even preferred to see themselves in male attire. There have also been innumerable women who consider the development of the female heart and spirit as sentimental and every innate gentle and noble female characteristic as an inferior impetus that must be overcome. These women worked toward a one-sided development of women's faculties; they have tried to replace deeper sensibilities with broader cleverness; to replace warmth with coldness, enthusiasm with abstraction, sacrifice with calculation, yielding with arrogance—this was the sort of exchange they offered women; in fact they demanded it from them. Indeed, we cannot be surprised if women's emancipation has been discredited through such efforts. . . .

The truth of the matter is this: The origin of eternal womanly has almost been lost in slavery, in lack of consciousness, and in the eternal immaturity in which women have been kept for so long. In most women, womanliness has been turned into an ugly caricature, into effeminacy; whatever is woman's highest ornament has been turned into a false adornment; the diamond has been deeply buried and replaced with fake jewels, ostentatiously and vainly surrounded by tinsel. Womanliness has not been cultivated; it has been perverted to effeminacy. . . .

We are laboring to engender the eternal womanly in the consciousness of women and to make humanity accept its value.

Development cannot flourish without freedom. Therefore the same freedom given to man to further the free unfolding of his characteristics must be given to woman to develop hers. The spirit, the humanity that is independent of sex, must find equal rights among women and men.

The eternal womanly is now valued only in the love of single individuals, in the true love of a man for a woman and thus uplifts the loving man to a higher refinement; this concept must be brought to valued acceptance by humanity at large so that not only single individuals, but all of humanity is uplifted to a higher position, to the goal of perfection.

CHAPTER 10

Women Demand Civil Law Reform

A Marriage Reform Initiative in England

SOURCES

90. Barbara Leigh-Smith [Bodichon], *A Brief Summary in Plain Language of the Most Important Laws Concerning Women, Together with a Few Observations Thereon* (London, 1854), pp. 3-11.

91. Margaret Oliphant, "The Laws Concerning Women," *Blackwood's Edinburgh Magazine*, 79, no. 486 (April 1856), 379-81, 381-82, 385-86.

92. Caroline Frances Cornwallis, "Capabilities and Disabilities of Women," review article in the *Westminster Review*, 67, no. 131 (January 1857), 45, 46-47, 49-52.

In the 1850's a small group of Englishwomen dedicated themselves to obtaining reforms in the legal status of women and to opening up educational, professional, and political opportunities for them as well. This group, centered around the *Englishwoman's Journal*, published at Langham Place, London, became known as the "Langham Place Circle"; it included Jessie Boucherett, Bessie Rayner Parkes, Emily Davies, Isa Craig, Emily Faithfull, and Barbara Leigh-Smith, who was later better known by her married name of Bodichon.

Barbara Leigh-Smith (1827-1891) was financially independent even as an unmarried young woman, thanks to the far-sighted generosity of her unconventional father. Leigh-Smith had been a member of the original audiences attending lectures for women at Bedford College (London) in 1849, and eventually expressed her gratitude for this opportunity through large bequests to Bedford College and to Girton College, Cambridge, which she helped to found. In 1854 Leigh-Smith published a pamphlet entitled *A Brief Summary in Plain Language of the Most Important Laws Concerning Women*. This became a key document in the subsequent political agitation that gradually changed the legal position of married Englishwomen, which had remained unaltered since William Blackstone had so approvingly described it (Doc. 5) a hundred years earlier. Leigh-Smith's simplified explanation of the laws concerning women immediately sparked debate in the press and among political figures who subsequently carried the debate into Parliament and successfully sponsored the Divorce Act of 1857, the Married Women's Property Act of 1870, and its successor act of 1882. These three acts transformed the legal position of married women in England.

Leigh-Smith's *Brief Summary*, which was frequently reissued throughout the next decade, prompted many responses, two of which we reprint here. The first is by Margaret Oliphant (1827-1897), one of the most popular and prolific writers of her day. She published over 120 novels and historical works, many in two or three volumes, in addition to some 300 articles in contemporary magazines and journals. Many of her stories and articles were published in *Blackwood's Edinburgh Magazine*, as is her review of Leigh-Smith. Oliphant wrote her article criticizing Leigh-Smith's pamphlet while she was a young married woman. After her husband's lingering illness and death in 1859, however, and the death of her daughter, she took on the care of her widowed brother's children in addition to her own two remaining sons. During the 1860's she became much more responsive to the necessity of reforming laws concerning women's property. She later confided, in her autobiography, that her vast literary output was motivated by financial need and that she might have written "more valuable" books had she been free from such demanding family responsibilities. In this selection, Oliphant objects to Leigh-Smith's pamphlet on the grounds that the law should not trespass on the domain of marital authority.

The second response included here is by Caroline Frances Cornwallis (1786-1858). Cornwallis was the younger daughter of the rector of Wittersham, Kent, who was descended from Thomas Cornwallis, the first governor of Maryland in the 1630's. Caroline Cornwallis remained unmarried, and devoted her life to books, philosophy, and her garden. She published anonymously a series of philosophical works, *Small Books on Great Subjects*, which were admiringly reviewed in respectable journals and by well-known contemporary philosophers. Her work dealt with the relationship between spirituality, psychology, and physiology; one well-known article treated the "Connexion Between Physiology and Mental Philosophy." She was clearly concerned with independence of mind and the biological underpinnings of women's status. Unlike Margaret Oliphant, however, Caroline Cornwallis was annoyed by the criticisms leveled against women. In 1841, having read appreciative reviews of her own anonymously published books, she wrote to a friend: "I long to knock all the big-wigs together by-and-bye, and say 'it was a *Woman* that did all this. . . . A *Woman* that laughed at you all, and despised your praise. . . . It is as a woman and not as the individual CFC that I enjoy my triumph." Cornwallis's last publications, at the age of seventy, were her articles on women, the law, and employment, which appeared in the *Westminster Review* in 1856 and 1857. In "Capabilities and Disabilities of Women," from which the last selection is excerpted, she exhibited a comprehensive understanding of the problem of women's dependence (whether single, married, or widowed), exacerbated as it was by the nineteenth-century concept of marriage and married women's legal annihilation as economic entities.

---

90. Barbara Leigh-Smith [Bodichon] (1854)

LEGAL CONDITIONS OF UNMARRIED WOMEN OR SPINSTERS

A single woman has the same rights to property, to protection from the law, and has to pay the same taxes to the State, as a man.

Yet a woman of the age of twenty-one, having the requisite property qualifications, cannot vote in elections for members of Parliament.

A woman duly qualified can vote upon parish questions, and for parish officers, overseers, surveyors, vestry clerks, etc.

If her father or mother dies *intestate* (i.e., without a will) she takes an equal share with her brothers and sisters of the personal property (i.e., goods, chattels, moveables), but her eldest brother, if she have one, and his children, even daughters, will take the real property (i.e., not personal property, but all other, as land, etc.), as the heir-at-law; males and their issue being preferred to females; if, however, she have sisters only, then all the sisters take the real property equally. If she be an only child, she is entitled to all the intestate real and personal property.

The church and nearly all offices under government are closed to women. The Post-office affords some little employment to them; but there is no important office which they can hold, with the single exception of that of Sovereign.

The professions of law and medicine,* whether or not closed by law, are closed in fact. They may engage in trade, and may occupy inferior situations, such as matron of a charity, sextoness of a church, and a few parochial offices are open to them. Women are occasionally governors of prisons for women, overseers of the poor, and parish clerks. A woman may be ranger of a park; a woman can take part in the government of a great empire by buying East India Stock.

A servant and a master or mistress are bound by a verbal or written agreement. If no special agreement is made, a servant is held by the common custom of the realm to be hired from year to year, and the engagement cannot be put an end to without a month's notice on either side.

If a woman is seduced, she has no remedy against the seducer; nor has her father, excepting as he is considered in law as being her master and she his servant, and the seducer as having deprived him of her services. Very slight service is deemed sufficient in law, but evidence of some service is absolutely necessary, whether the daughter be of full age or under age.

These are the only special laws concerning single women: the law speaks of men only, but women are affected by all the laws and incur the same responsibilities in all their contracts and doings as men.

LAWS CONCERNING MARRIED WOMEN

Matrimony is a civil and indissoluble contract between a consenting man and woman of competent capacity. . . .

A man and wife are one person in law; the wife loses all her rights as a single woman, and her existence is entirely absorbed in that of her husband. He is civilly responsible for her acts; she lives under his protection or cover, and her condition is called coverture.

A woman's body belongs to her husband; she is in his custody, and he can enforce his right by a writ of *habeas corpus.*

What was her personal property before marriage, such as money in hand, money at the bank, jewels, household goods, clothes, etc., becomes absolutely her husband's, and he may assign or dispose of them at his pleasure whether he and his wife live together or not.

* Elizabeth Blackwell, M.D., received her diploma in America before she walked St. Bartholomew's Hospital in London.

A wife's *chattels real* (i.e., estates held during a term of years, or the next presentation to a church living, etc.) become her husband's by his doing some act to appropriate them; but, if the wife survives, she resumes her property.

Equity is defined to be a correction or qualification of the law, generally made in the part wherein it faileth, or is too severe. In other words, the correction of that wherein the law, by reason of its universality, is deficient. While the Common Law gives the whole of a wife's personal property to her husband, the Courts of Equity, when he proceeds therein to recover property in right of his wife, oblige him to make a settlement of some portion of it upon her, if she be unprovided for and virtuous.

If her property be under £200, or £10 a year, a Court of Equity will not interpose.

Neither the Courts of Common Law nor Equity have any direct power to oblige a man to support his wife,—the Ecclesiastical Courts (i.e., Courts held by the Queen's authority as governor of the Church, for matters which chiefly concern religion) and a Magistrate's court at the instance of her parish alone can do this.

A husband has a freehold estate in his wife's lands during the joint existence of himself and his wife, that is to say, he has absolute possession of them as long as they both live. If the wife dies without children, the property goes to her heir, but if she has borne a child, her husband holds possession until his death.

Money earned by a married woman belongs absolutely to her husband; that and all sources of income, excepting those mentioned above, are included in the term personal property.

By the particular permission of her husband she can make a will of her personal property, for by such a permission he gives up his right. But he may revoke his permission at any time before *probate* (i.e., the exhibiting and proving a will before the Ecclesiastical Judge having jurisdiction over the place where the party died).

The legal custody of children belongs to the father. During the life-time of a sane father, the mother has no rights over her children, except a limited power over infants, and the father may take them from her and dispose of them as he thinks fit.

If there be a legal separation of the parents, and there be neither agreement nor order of Court, giving the custody of the children to either parent, then the *right to the custody of the children* (except for the nutriment of infants) belongs legally to the father.

A married woman cannot sue or be sued for contracts—nor can she enter into contracts except as the agent of her husband; that is to say, her word alone is not binding in law, and persons giving a wife credit have no remedy against her. There are some exceptions, as where she contracts debts upon estates settled to her separate use, or where a wife carries on trade separately, according to the custom of London, etc.

A husband is liable for his wife's debts contracted before marriage, and also for her breaches of trust committed before marriage.

Neither a husband nor a wife can be witnesses against one another in criminal cases, not even after the death or divorce of either.

A wife cannot bring actions unless the husband's name is joined.

As the wife acts under the command and control of her husband, she is excused from punishment for certain offences, such as theft, burglary, house-breaking, etc., if committed in his presence and under his influence. A wife cannot be found guilty of concealing her felon husband or of concealing a felon jointly with her husband. She cannot be found guilty of stealing from her husband or of setting his house on fire, as they are one person in law. A husband and wife cannot be found guilty of conspiracy, as that offence cannot be committed unless there are two persons.

USUAL PRECAUTIONS AGAINST THE LAWS CONCERNING THE PROPERTY OF MARRIED WOMEN

When a woman has consented to a proposal of marriage, she cannot dispose or give away her property without the knowledge of her betrothed; if she make any such disposition without his knowledge, even if he be ignorant of the existence of her property, the disposition will not be legal.

It is usual, before marriage, in order to secure a wife and her children against the power of the husband, to make with his consent a settlement of some property on the wife, or to make an agreement before marriage that a settlement shall be made after marriage. It is in the power of the Court of Chancery to enforce the performance of such agreements.

Although the Common Law does not allow a married woman to possess any property, yet in respect of property settled for her separate use, Equity endeavours to treat her as a single woman.

She can acquire such property by contract before marriage with her husband, or by gift from his or other persons.

There are great difficulties and complexities in making settlements, and they should always be made by a competent lawyer.

When a wife's property is stolen, the property (legally belonging to the husband) must be laid as his in the indictment.

SEPARATION AND DIVORCE

A husband and wife can separate upon a deed containing terms for their immediate separation, but they cannot legally agree to separate at a *future* time. The trustees of the wife must be parties to the deed, and agree with the husband as to what property the wife is to take, for a husband and wife cannot covenant together.

Divorce is of two kinds—

1st. Divorce *à mensa et thoro*, being only a separation from bed and board.

2nd. Divorce *à vinculo matrimonii*, being an entire dissolution of the bonds of matrimony.

The grounds for the first kind of divorce are, 1st. Adultery, 2nd. Intolerable Cruelty, and 3rd. Unnatural Practices. The Ecclesiastical Courts can do no more than pronounce for this first kind of divorce, or rather separation, as the matrimonial tie is not severed, and there is always a possibility of reconciliation.

The law cannot dissolve a lawful marriage; it is only in the Legislature that this power is vested. It requires an act of Parliament to constitute a divorce *à vinculo matrimonii*, but the investigation rests by usage with the Lords alone, the House of Commons acting upon the faith that the House of Lords came to a just conclusion.

This divorce is pronounced on account of adultery in the wife, and in some cases of aggravated adultery on the part of the husband.

The expenses of only a common divorce bill are between six hundred and seven hundred pounds, which makes the possibility of release from the matrimonial bond a privilege of the rich.

A wife cannot be plaintiff, defendant, or witness in an important part of the proceeding for a divorce, which evidently must lead to much injustice.

LAWS CONCERNING A WIDOW

A widow recovers her real property, but if there be a settlement she is restricted by its provisions. She recovers her chattels real if her husband has not disposed of them by will or otherwise.

A wife's paraphernalia (i.e., her clothes and ornaments) which her husband owns during his lifetime, and which his creditors can seize for his debts, becomes her property on his death.

A widow is liable for any debts which she contracted before marriage, and which have been left unpaid during her marriage.

A widow is not bound to bury her dead husband it being the duty of his legal representative.

If a man die intestate, the widow, if there are children, is entitled to one-third of the personalty; if there are no children, to one-half: the other is distributed among the next of kin, among whom the widow is not counted. If there is no next of kin the moiety goes to the crown.

A husband can, of course, by will deprive a wife of all right in the personalty.

A right is granted in Magna Charta to a widow to remain forty days in her husband's house after his death, provided she do not marry during that time.

A widow has a right to a third of her husband's lands and tenements for her life. Right of dower is generally superseded by settlements giving the wife a jointure. If she accept a jointure she has no claim to dower.

LAWS CONCERNING WOMEN IN OTHER RELATIONSHIPS

A woman can act as agent for another, and, as an attorney, legally execute her authority. A wife can so act if her husband do not dissent.

An unmarried woman can be vested with a trust, but if she marry, the complexities and difficulties are great, from her inability to enter alone into deeds and assurances.

A single woman can act as executrix under a will, but a wife cannot accept an executorship without her husband's consent.

A woman is capable of holding the office of administratrix to an intestate personalty, and administration will be granted to her if she be next of kin to the intestate. But a wife cannot act without the consent of her husband.

If a man place a woman in his house, and treat her as his wife, he is responsible for her debts.

91. Margaret Oliphant (1856)

The injuries of women have long been a standing subject of complaint and animadversion. Woman's rights will never grow into a popular agitation, yet woman's wrongs are always picturesque and attractive. They are indeed so good to make novels and poems about, so telling as illustrations of patience and gentleness, that we fear any real redress of grievances would do more harm to the literary world than it would do good to the feminine. We speak with a very serious and well-meaning pamphlet * on the subject before us—no impassioned statement of personal wrongs, but a quiet summary of real laws and positive (apparent) injustices. We have no desire, for our own part, to throw ridicule upon any temperate and well-considered movement of real social amelioration; but words and terms are unchancy things to deal with, and half the quarrels in the world come from different interpretations put by different people on the same phraseology. These laws which concern women do not seem at the first glance either just or complimentary. At the first glance, it is reasonable to suppose that the masculine law-maker has made use of his advantages for the enslavement of his feebler companion. Mrs. Browning's

> "Women sobbing out of sight,
> Because men made the laws"

appears, in fact, a real condition, when we glance at the surface and outside of the question; and we are disposed, in immediate indignation, to break a lance upon the grand abstract tyrant, Man, who keeps this princess in a perpetual dungeon. Yet let us pause a moment. The law may be unnecessarily particular; but are its opponents upon just ground?

We have small faith, for our own part, in what is called class legislation, and smallest faith of all in that species of class legislation which could make the man an intentional and voluntary oppressor of the woman. This idea, that the two portions of humankind are natural antagonists to each other, is, to our thinking, at the very outset, a monstrous and unnatural idea. The very man who made the laws which send "women sobbing out of sight," had not only a wife, whom we may charitably suppose he was glad of a legal argument for tyrannising over, but doubtless such things as sisters and daughters, whom he could have no desire to subject to the tyranny of other men. There is no man in exis-

---

* *A Brief Summary, in Plain Language, of the Most Important Laws Concerning Women, Together With a Few Observations Thereon* (Chapman, London) [Doc. 90].

tence so utterly separated from one-half of his fellow-creatures as to be able to legislate against them in the interests of his own sex. No official character whatever can make so absurd and artificial a distinction. Let us vindicate, in the first instance, the law and the law-maker. It is possible that the poor may legislate against the rich, or the rich against the poor, but to make such an antagonism between men and women is against all reason and all nature.

This is the first grand mistake of a movement which certainly has the appearance of justice on its side. The laws which govern human intercourse are for the most part only fixed and arbitrary demonstrations of natural rights and necessities; and it is taking altogether false ground to interpret them by motives of petty jealousy, such as a particular man might entertain towards his wife, but which men in general never have entertained, nor can entertain, towards the abstract Woman. This is the very vanity of reasoning—fallacious and untrustworthy in its first beginning.

If this antagonism is not true of man and woman in the abstract, how much less true is it of the particular relationship of man and wife. It is no fallacy of the law to say that these two are one person; it is a mere truism of nature. Let us grant that in most cases they have their differences; that they do a little private fighting quietly under their own roof on various domestic occasions; that Elysian harmony and content is by no means a prevailing atmosphere even in the happiest households—yet our proposition remains unaltered. Marrying is like dying—as distinct, as irrevocable, as complete. In moments of excitement, in the flush of injury, real or supposed, or under the intolerable sting of injustice, we may chafe and strain at the chain that binds us; but sober thought and cooler temper say what the law says, with a deep and silent emphasis stronger than the law. The "marriage of true minds" may be as rare as it is lofty and fortunate. The marriage of interests, hopes, and purposes is universal. The more independent husband and wife are of each other, the less sure is the basis of society. We desire no injustice to women; we are reluctant even to shut out from hope of redress those desperate exceptional cases which occur now and then to prove barbarism and injustice in every law; but no considerate and unbiassed mind can omit to perceive that legislation for the exceptional cases, if it were possible, would be at once foolish and wrong. It is true that most of us have outgrown the utilitarian principle which held "the greatest happiness of the greatest number" for the chief article of its system; but it is impossible to outgrow those general principles of nature of which the law is but a distinct and authoritative exposition. Nor can we accept individual hardship in a dozen or in a hundred cases as sufficient motive for the alteration of a rule which regulates the fate of millions, which is no invented tyranny, but which, to a plain and visible arrangement of nature, pronounces its emphatic Amen!

For all the laws complained of as affecting women concern themselves with women *married*; women unmarried are under no humiliations of legal bondage. It is the *wife*, and not the *woman*, whose separate existence the law denies. This is a fiction in one sense, but not in another; in one point of view, a visible piece of nonsense; in another, an infallible truth. It is hard to enter upon this subject without falling into the authoritative hardness of legal phraseology, or the sweet jargon of poetic nonsense, on one side or the other. "The wife loses her rights as a single woman, and her existence is entirely absorbed in that of her husband," says this *Brief Summary in Plain Language* of the formal law. "His house she enters," says the poet,

> "A guardian angel o'er his life presiding,
> Doubling his pleasures, and his cares dividing."

The one utterance is somewhat humiliating, the other unquestionably pretty; and both fail of the truth. Lawyer and Poet alike survey the surface and external aspect of the question—common experience pronounces a fuller verdict. This question, of all others, is a question which cannot be decided by individual cases—and we are all perfectly aware that, as a general principle, the wife *is* the husband quite as much as the husband *is* the wife. In truth and in nature—with the reality of sober fact and without romancing—these two people set their hands to it, that they are no longer two people, but one person. And let us not suppose that, in considering any social question, we have to consider principally a succession of sensitive and high-spirited individual temperaments or states of exalted feeling. No law can suffice to baulk of their natural portion of misery those susceptible personages who are alive to every touch of possible offence. The broad general principle crushes over them, regardless of their outcries. Common law and rule take no cognisance of feelings excited and heroical. We grant it is sometimes unjust to judge the chance Edwin and Angelina, as it is right to judge the Johns and the Marys of ordinary existence; but how much more unjust to fit our regulations to the chance case instead of to the ordinary! We can come to no true and safe conclusion upon a matter so delicate and personal as this, without carefully discriminating between the common and the uncommon. No law of human origin can reach every possible development of human temper and organisation; injured wives and unhappy husbands are accidents uncurable by law; and it would be almost as wise to legislate for the race, on the supposition that every member of it had a broken leg, as on the more injurious hypothesis that tyranny, oppression, and injustice, rankled within the heart of every home. . . .

But every man and every woman knows, with the most absolute certainty, that a household divided against itself cannot stand. It is the very first principle of domestic existence. In all this great world, with all its myriads of creatures, it is vain to think of forming a single home unless it is built upon this foundation. One interest and one fortune is an indispensable necessity. The constitution of the household is more entirely representative than even that glorious constitution of which we all have heard so much, and which keeps our ship of state afloat. The man is the natural representative of his wife in one set of duties—the wife is the natural representative of the husband in another; and if any one will tell us that the nursery is less important than the Exchange, or that it is a more dignified business to vote for a county member than to regulate a Christian household, we will grant that the woman has an inferior range of duty. Otherwise, there is a perfect balance between the two members of this one person. In this view—and we defy the most visionary champion of abstract female rights to disprove that this is the ordinary rule of common society—it is a mere trick of words to say that the woman loses her existence, and is absorbed in her husband. Were it so in reality—and were it indeed true "that the poor rivulet loseth her name, is carried and recarried with her new associate, beareth no sway, possesseth nothing"— then would the question of female inferiority be fairly proved and settled once for all. Mighty indeed must be the Titanic current of that soul which could receive one whole human being, full of thoughts, affections, and emotions, into its tide and yet remain uncoloured and unchanged. There is no such monster of a man, and no such nonentity of a woman, in ordinary life. Which of us does not carry our wife's thoughts in our brain, and our wife's likings in our heart, with the most innocent unconsciousness that they are not our own original property? And how vain is the reasoning which goes upon any other premises. In fact, this agitation is only defensible when it deals with matters of practice; it has no principle to carry in its front—for the only true rule of Marriage remains unimpugnable; and if it is either a legal or a poetic fiction to call man and wife one person, then all sacredness, purity, and noble sentiment, departs from the bond between them.

It may be said that this sacred and entire union is not to be made by law: True; yet undoubtedly these very restrictions, harsh and arbitrary, which "absorb the existence" of the wife in that of the husband, help towards this consummation. Let us not mistake. The law has nothing to do with that union of souls and sympathies of which lovers dream; but it has to do with the common security, the peace of families, the safe foundation of the social world. Rash enough at all times are the young entrants into this irrevocable bond; painful enough often is the breaking-in of two impetuous and impatient spirits to the common yoke of life; and love itself is irritable and headstrong—the greatest mischief-maker in the world. Before the threshold of this uncertain house stands the law, barring all exit. For the interests of society, and for the comfort of the commonwealth, this authoritative voice says it is impossible. The nomadic principle has already too much sway over our social arrangements; here it cannot enter. The business of a righteous and rational law is not to provide facilities for escaping, but to rivet and enforce the claims of that relationship upon which all society is founded. It is not possible to permit those who have once been man and wife to go forth to the world separate units, uninjured by the failure of so vital an experiment. All purity, all certainty, all the sober and steadfast continuance which is the heart and strength of a nation, are perilled by such a possibility. The law compels no one, either man or woman, to enter into this perilous estate of marriage; but, being once within it, it is the law's first duty to hedge this important territory round with its strongest and highest barriers. The justice which means an equal division of rights has no place between those two persons whom natural policy as well as Divine institution teach us to consider as one. It seems a harsh saying, but it is a true one—Justice cannot be done between them; their rights are not to be divided; they are beyond the reach of all ordinary principles of equity. In the event of a disjunction between the father and the mother, the wife and the husband, you must choose which of them you shall be just to; for it is impossible to do justice to both.

For it is not the question of the wife's earnings or the wife's property which lies nearest the heart of this controversy: there are the children— living witnesses of the undividableness of the parents. You give their custody to the husband. It is a grievous and sore injustice to the mother who bore them. But let us alter the case. Let the wife have the little ones, and how does the question stand? The ground is changed, but the principle is the same. Still injustice, hard, unnatural, and pitiless; still wrong, grievous, and inexcusable. . . .

This one great thing the law cannot do—it cannot defend married people from each other. It may make certain arbitrary regulations to secure a possible disjunction for them in case they will not bear with each other. It cannot interpose a shield between the two, nor determine boundaries of right and separate possession. It could, indeed, in defiance of all the rules of nature, elect the woman as the representative of the family instead of the man; but it has no standing-ground for both. In every scheme of social polity, great or small, a house counts for one. This is the true original of all government. We give a married man a more important standing than an unmarried, simply because he is a representative, and holds in his hands more interests and influences than those which belong exclusively to himself. Nature confers this official character upon the head of a household, the law has no choice but to confirm it, and all honest expediency and suitableness justifies this ordination of God and of man. We *might* certainly, in one of our perverse human vagaries, change the person while we keep the office, and make the wife the legal family representative; but really, under present circumstances, and while women retain so much untransferable business for their share of the world's labours, we do not see how this would mend the question; and one head, voice, and representative in the public eye the household must have. But the law cannot come into the heart of the house. Like an evil spirit, it must be dragged across the threshold, to make injuries bitterer and feuds less appeasable. It can smite with fiercer swords into the hearts of the combatants. It cannot end their quarrels, or defend them from each other. So long as it makes its boundaries outside, and far away, it is in its legitimate position; but if any one attempts to bring it in to hedge off half the rights, half the possessions, half the comforts of a house, it is a mockery and a delusion. Let no one be deceived. By the help of the law we can command (sometimes) the restoration of stolen goods and borrowed money—but we cannot command the return of happiness, love, or a pure heart. Marrying, however the young ladies and the young gentlemen may look upon it—and we can hear the laugh of that saucy happy confidence, to which heaven send no doubting!—is a solemn and perilous experiment. Bridegroom and bride alike enter defenceless into their life; no one can come between them to help the weakest. The law will not let them kill each other, and public opinion will not permit any very serious mutual wrong; but beyond this it is a fair field and no favour.

92. Caroline Cornwallis (1857)

The effect of a law can rarely be measured by its active interference in the affairs of life; its influence is spread over a much wider area; for custom assimilates itself to the law when it has existed unchanged for any long time. The law of Gavelkind takes upon itself the distribution of property only where the owner dies intestate—a rare circumstance; yet, in districts where it prevails, it has led to testamentary arrangements in conformity to the legal distribution, and consequently in such districts the subdivision of property into equal or nearly equal parts among all the children, prevails as a custom—a custom very much at variance with that of other parts of England. It has had the effect of substituting a race of yeomen, using their own land, for the usual country gentlemen and tenantry; and this merely by a kind of legal *induction*, as is said of electricity when it is conveyed to another body by juxta-position without contact. It is a good instance of the wide-spread influence of an old law, intended only for particular and rather exceptional cases. It is thus that the law with respect to the property of *married* women has influenced the position of *all* females; for fathers and guardians, in determining on the kind of education to be given to a child, are guided by what is likely to be its future career in life; and thus, though a girl may never marry, she bears the burthen of a married woman's disabilities; for, marriage being the assumed end of female existence, parents think it needless to teach what will be useless when learned. The showy accomplishments likely to entrap a husband are taught; while the solid acquirements which would enable her to manage property, or find lucrative employment, are not thought of. "What is the use of teaching a girl more of arithmetic than will enable her to cast up a bill?" is the argument of many a father, when thinking of the education of his daughters; and this bad reason descends through all classes, for over all has been extended the iron grasp of the Common Law. . . .

The consequence of this utter want of education in regard to the common business of life is in many cases disastrous. Very few women have enough information on such subjects to render them capable of taking care of their property when they are left alone, which, in the course of human events, must frequently happen: and even if they are fortunate enough to retain relations and friends around them to the last, they, at any rate, lose the respect of both husband and sons, from their ignorance of things which men know because they have been taught, and which women do not know because they have not been taught. How often do we hear a grown-up son expressing the utmost affection for his mother, but at the same time despising her judgment on all matters of business, or politics, or theology, because he knows that she has never had enough information communicated to her on any of these subjects to enable her to form a sound opinion; adding, probably, "Poor dear woman! I love her with all my heart, but she knows nothing about these things." Of course her advice is not sought, though, were she qualified by her education and knowledge of the common affairs of life to have an opinion, she would be the friend whose counsel would be the most readily listened to. But further than this—persons whom the law has doomed to perpetual dependence, unless they embrace a life of celibacy—who, if they enter into the state which is most natural to all human beings, can have no legal control over their person, their actions, or their property, are not likely to take much trouble in order to learn what might, indeed, be profitable in a pecuniary point of view, or useful to their fellow-creatures, but which will afford them no personal advantage: for, however sorry we may be to allow it, there is no doubt that when we ourselves are to derive no benefit from our exertions, none but the very highest minds will be brought to exert themselves at all; and this height of disinterestedness and self-devotion is not very likely to be attained by persons whose education in general is but a series of smatterings. Parents who are anxious "to marry off" their daughters, know that a woman of independent spirit might hesitate to enter into a state in which "her being and legal existence are suspended"; and therefore they educate them to be dependent. They are told that it is "unfeminine" and "blue" to know much or to have strong opinions on any point beyond the set of a dress or the fashion of a bonnet; they are not to read newspapers, lest their delicacy should be rubbed off; and "women have no business with politics"—they are to mix in none of the affairs of life which engage the attention of the men of their family, lest they should become "masculine";—till they end by becoming mere drawing-room ornaments, scarcely so useful as a French clock or a fire-screen, when young, and when old, sink down into reading novels with a gold eyeglass, lest they should show their advancing age by the use of spectacles—and entrapping young men of fortune into marrying their daughters, as they themselves were married before them. The sons, meantime, are left to themselves at the period when a mother's counsels are most needed, and probably run a wild career of vice and folly, which a prudent female adviser might have prevented, till precious years are wasted in idleness, health injured, and talent thrown away; and then, when the nation looks for men to administer its affairs, it finds—what?— the experience of the last three years has told the tale to all Europe. . . .

But these direct evils which flow from the law in question, are not all:—having crushed all independence of spirit in woman, and left her so incapable of business as to make her an easy prey to designing persons, it acts as a direct tempter to man. Every one knows that the law gives the

husband more or less of the property of the woman he marries; and one
who has either set out in life with slender means, or who has squandered
imprudently, may naturally think—or if he does not, kind friends will
suggest the thought—that a rich wife would be an easy and safe way of
attaining fortune without toil. Then comes counterfeited affection, dishonorable contrivances—sins of every grade and colour, which would
probably never have entered his head but for the temptation of the law.
This, of course, happens in every rank of life, and it would be easy to
multiply examples. . . .

The first result of the tendency of the sexes to this union is the check it
puts upon selfishness. . . .

. . . What, then, is the business of the law in regard to this part of the
constitution of our nature? Love cannot be created by statute; motives of
action cannot be coerced by pains and penalties. Social law, then, is
powerless before the higher law of the Creator; and all that it can do is to
avoid clashing with it. To meddle when it cannot aid effectually, is to introduce yet farther confusion where the instincts and passions of ill-
regulated minds have already produced a large crop of evil. Does our
common law, or even the remedy for its injustice provided in equity, pursue this prudent course? What is its operation? The moment a woman
entertains a proposal of marriage, the man to whom she has given the
highest proof of affection becomes, to a certain degree, master of her
property—that is to say, she can no longer alienate any part of it without
his consent; and if she attempted it, such contracts would be void. Lawyers tell her that this is because, if she were now allowed to give away any
portion of her property, it would be a fraud practised on her intended
husband, who might thus not get the fortune he expected. Here is a first
check to the *abandon* of a disinterested affection. Then friends step in,
and caution her to secure her interests by a settlement. If she does not
distrust, at least she must act as if she did, and the first flow of generous
affection is dammed up by legal instruments. The man, on his part, feels
that he has no other mode of proving that he is disinterested, than by
renouncing all control over his wife's affairs. Trustees are appointed, who
have far less interest in the matter, and in whose hands the property frequently suffers; and thus, in the very best-assorted union, the law contrives to dash a certain portion of bitter ingredients into the cup, and selfishness and distrust too often peep out from the marriage-settlement. All
this evil would be avoided were the common rules of the laws with regard
to property generally observed in regard to married women; for her interests would then be guarded by the law without making any provisions
which imply distrust; and if any settlement were thought needful, it
would be an unselfish renunciation, on the part of both, of some rights,
for the benefit of their future offspring. What follows next? Let one of the
most eager advocates of the common law explain its operation:—

The law compels no one, either man or woman, to enter into this perilous estate of marriage; but being once within it, it is the law's first duty to hedge this

important territory round with its strongest and highest barriers. The justice which means an equal division of rights, has no place between these two persons, whom natural policy, as well as Divine institution, teach us to consider as one. It seems a harsh saying, but it is a true one. Justice cannot be done between them; their rights are not to be divided: they are beyond the reach of all ordinary principles of equity.

Were this so—did the law insist that in no case the parties should sever, and that under all circumstances they should be obliged to have all things in common—something might be said in its favour; and we might deem it the gentle dream of some Utopian legislator, who, in his primitive innocence, had never heard of extravagant wives or brutal husbands. But our law is by no means so ignorant of evil: it contemplates the contingencies of the wife's infidelity, of her absconding, of her rebellion; and it provides in the first case—divorce—*for a rich man*; in the second, a power of imprisoning in his own house, *also for a rich man*; and in the third, according to Mr. Justice Coleridge, the correction of a small crabstick for the poor one; and for all, rich and poor, the power of laying hands on all that the wife possesses; and therefore, in this country of costly law, the practical denial of all justice, where the husband exercises his privileges, beyond the point which even the English code allows. To balance all this, the wife is allowed to mulct her husband by incurring debts which he is obliged to pay, unless he have been beforehand with her by notifying publicly that he does not hold himself responsible for them; and it exempts her from the penalty of all crime but murder, which she may commit under his tutelage; thus insuring to a worthless fellow an accomplice in his depredations, who can assist him with impunity! Is there anything in all this calculated to promote the moral ends of the institution of marriage? We wound, and thus do harm, by interfering with the natural course of true affection and honourable feeling, where such is the basis of the union. We do yet farther mischief, by "hedging this important territory with the law's strongest and highest barriers"; for the man of wealth contrives to overleap them all, while the poor and the defenceless alone are subjected to their restraint. The fact is, that the whole system is a fiction, and the more it is attempted to justify it, the more glaring does its injustice become. Why the woman's infidelity should be sufficient to procure a divorce for those who can pay for it, but not for the poor—why the man's infidelity, which is surely as great a wrong as that of the wife, is not to be punished with divorce, unless he have added two or three other crimes to it—why the woman who leaves her husband may be imprisoned by him, when he can catch her, without any form of trial, while the man who misuses her so far as to drive her from him can do it with impunity—all this may be very clear to conservative legislators, but it passes the comprehension of liberal reviewers.

Legal Reform and the Scandinavian Novel

SOURCES

93. Camilla Collett, *Amtmadens dötre* (Christiania, 1854-55). The editors are grateful to Kirsten A. Seaver, Stanford, California, for allowing them to publish this excerpt from her forthcoming translation of Collett's work.

94. Fredrika Bremer, *Hertha*. Tr. Mary Howitt (New York and London, 1856). Originally published in Swedish, Stockholm, 1855, as *Hertha; eller. En själs historia*.

During the 1850's the debate over women re-emerged in two countries that were at some remove from the scenes of the revolutionary troubles of 1848—Norway and Sweden. In both cases the debate was reopened by women writers familiar with the literature of continental thought on women, Camilla Wergeland Collett (1813-1895) in Norway, and Fredrika Bremer (1801-1865) in Sweden.

In 1815 Norway had been forcibly joined in political union with Sweden, under a common sovereign, though culturally it remained a distinct entity with closer ties to Denmark (to which Norway had formerly been joined). During the 1830's and 1840's members of the Norwegian intelligentsia mounted an intense nationalist movement, in which a rediscovery of Norwegian traditional culture, language, and institutions intersected with a critique of the status quo that was informed by liberal and idealist notions then current in Germany and France. It was in this context that Camilla Wergeland Collett composed her important social novel, *Amtmadens dötre* (The District Governor's Daughter).

Camilla Collett was the daughter of the pastor Nicolai Wergeland, a signer of the Norwegian constitution and, with his son Henrik, one of the leaders of the Norwegian nationalist movement. She was educated by tutors and in schools in Christiania (Oslo) and Copenhagen. Beautiful and talented, she fell passionately in love with a poet who was not only poor but was also a political adversary of her brother; under such circumstances, marriage was an impossible dream—though their mutual attraction sustained them both for some seven years. In 1834 Collett's father took her to Paris in an effort to make her forget the poet, and she later spent several years with a family in Hamburg, cultivating her taste for German, as well as French, literature. In 1841 she married Peter Jonas Collett, who was a more acceptable suitor and loved her deeply; she returned his love and bore him four sons before his untimely death from overwork in 1851. In the meantime, with her husband's encouragement, Collett had begun to write. After his death she turned her attention to the plight of women in Norwegian society, a theme that obsessed her throughout the remainder of her career as a writer. In *Amtmadens dötre* Collett presented women's plight as lying not in the law but in custom and prejudice; the story tells of a promising romance between two mutually suited young people, Sophie Raum and Georg Kold, which is shattered by their own fears of social pressure, of other people's opinions about proprieties and the etiquette of courtship. Here Collett built on her own unhappy experience with such proprieties; she allowed her heroine to violate bourgeois taboo by declaring to Georg her love for him before he had formally declared his own intentions. In this selection, excerpted from an older woman friend's commentary addressed to Georg Kold, Collett sketches the dilemma of the young Norwegian woman within a framework shaped by what she knew or had heard about other lands.

The second selection comes from an equally important Swedish novel, *Hertha*, by Fredrika Bremer, a single and well-read woman. Bremer was much better known in English-speaking lands than Collett, both because of her extensive travels and through English translations of her many published works by the well-known English Quaker author Mary Howitt. In this novel, Bremer attacked the law itself—in this case, the system of patriarchal guardianship over daughters, embodied in Sweden's "Paternal Statutes" of 1734. In composing *Hertha*, Bremer drew heavily on her observations of the relative freedom allowed to American women, which had so impressed her during her travels in the United States in 1849-51. Significantly, the public outcry aroused in Sweden by Bremer's novel led to the modification in 1858 of the paternal statutes concerning daughters, and in 1872 to the full legal emancipation of unmarried Swedish women at the age of twenty-five. In this instance, a fictional work with a social purpose did help to achieve legislative action on behalf of women. In this excerpt, Bremer's heroine Hertha discusses with her sister Alma the helplessness of Swedish daughters under the old law.

---

93. Camilla Collett (1854)

I certainly thought there was another reason behind it. There is something profoundly deplorable and demeaning in these facts, as I have finally heard them from yourself. Deplorable for you, demeaning for us. The real puzzle is that none of the ladies with whom you fell in love, has truly loved you. Yet there was absolutely no reason why you could not have become married to any one of them. Thank God that did not happen.

Some sort of sentiment they have surely entertained, and they would have been offended indeed, had it not been referred to as love; it had all the proper whims and demands. They did have a sort of sentiment, or they would not have been able to encounter you thus. But it was not a *genuine* feeling. It was not that spontaneous, uninvited and irresistible force which, like a plant born in the shade, nourishes itself, unseen and uncared for, by its own sap, and which one cannot pull up without at the same time pulling up its taproot.

It was that artificial hothouse sensation, the unripe fruit of coincidence; it was the feeble reflection of male desire, which is produced by an interplay of flattered vanity, commonsensical calculation, and an inherited habit of submission.

This is what a man is satisfied with; he demands nothing better, and if, into the bargain, he has to struggle a little to conquer it, he is as proud as a deity.

Whenever possible, the men ought not to do the selecting. They mostly choose according to sensual whims; they put possession above all else.

Women ought not to choose, either. They are so undeveloped that they cannot even make a sensible choice based on common sense. One would be horrified to see the motives that often move them to accept an offer.

The so-called arranged marriages may therefore often carry with them a greater assurance of mutual happiness than one tends to believe. One ought not to scorn them.

The choice should truly be left to only one thing, and that is to *woman's love*.

Among all the imagined and actual qualities that attract a man to the woman of his choice, he forgets about just one small, insignificant one; that is *her love*.

Should he notice, nevertheless, that this little matter is wanting, he thinks: it will surely come.

All men believe themselves to be Pygmalions, who can give life to the statue when the time comes when she of necessity must descend from her pedestal.

But marriage is not apt to kindle love; on the contrary, a good measure of that article should be brought into marriage in order to enable the woman to stand it.

Even if a man is not a tender husband, he may well be a *good* husband. He may tend to his calling just as eagerly, just as conscientiously. His duties have very definite limits.

A wife, on the other hand, must be *tender* if she is to be *good*. A wife's calling has no such limits. It consists of a horde of undefined, various, nameless particulars, invisible as the falling dew, which only derive their significance from the spirit in which they are done. In this, in love, lies its boundlessness. Without this, it shrivels to become a burden, a trivial execution of duty, by which it immediately becomes limited.

A man may sit all day at his desk without once thinking of her for whom he nevertheless works. On the other hand, he devotes a lot of thought to how the article on which he is working is going to look in the newspaper, and what effect it may have on his next promotion.

The wife who loves, thinks only of him in everything she does. To *him*, for *him*, by *him*, everything. He is her ambition, her public, her ministerial department.

It is strange the way one can sense, the minute one steps into a house, whether or not this life-giving spark is present. One notices it particularly in the atmosphere of the living rooms. Where it is in command, everything will show the mark of gentleness and inspired beauty; where it is lacking, everything is dead, cold, and prosaic, even in the richest surroundings. In that case, she either tears herself loose from the burden and lets the machinery carry on without her, while she tries to submerge her life outside the home, or she becomes completely absorbed in it, she herself becoming a growling machine that one would prefer to avoid.

The novels of *Madame Dudevant* are causing a stir these days. It is true, they are dreadful, as dreadful as the occasions that may have given rise to them. Here it will not do to assume the usual attitude of bourgeois criticism or to bring out the ordinary yardstick for what constitutes transgression. We must be able to read these novels calmly, with the dreadful interest with which, from a safe vantage point, one observes one of those violent eruptions of nature that spread terror and destruction in its vicinity. It is not suitable for our conditions. We and French society may just about be considered two extremes; the incipient, undeveloped, tightly furled in its bud that is threatened only by cold and lack of care, and the sophisticatedly overcultivated that is close to its own dissolution; and it is from the morasses of the latter that she sends out her cries for help over the entire civilized world. She allows no conditions; she wants total liberation, complete equality with men in all matters of everyday and social life, right up to the point of participating in their customs, their habits, right up to their manner of dress. Now, all this goes way beyond our own humble wishes and serves only to repel us. No—we do not understand it. Until time everlasting, men must be our natural support and protectors. Mme Dudevant wants the dissolution of marriage, which for our women constitutes the only harbor and sole salvation, although they, just like the French ones, harbor a feeling that they could and ought to be happier.*

In France, marriages are usually contracted out of monetary considerations; *there* with money and without love, *here* without money and . . . without love; but with the great difference that here the men are less corrupt, by which the disparity is made much less noticeable; indeed, one ought not to deny that our men, by means of a peculiar and tender protectiveness toward their wives, seek as if unconsciously to even out some of the disparities in their circumstances. No, with all admiration for that brilliant authoress, and in full acknowledgment of what may have been made necessary by social motives—Georges Sand does not suit our conditions. She has no tongue for our mute complaints; her writings only serve to cause agony and irritation, like all false comfort. We need only those forces that work unseen, silently, within their domain, and that unnoticed gnaw off the ropes that tie us to the old ballast. It was the poor, unknown Madame *Le Gros* who by her quiet fortitude in the *la Tude* case caused the fall of the Bastille. Our attempts at liberation are still confined to their own invisible domains, and we do not in the least understand the sort of conquests that are to be made outside them. God preserve us from competing with the men in their daily business or wresting from them the pleasure of wearing a uniform and a tall hat. What we want is a greater freedom of *thought* and *feeling*, the nullification of all the innumerable, ridiculous considerations and prejudices that inhibit such thoughts and feelings; more accurate, less high-flown concepts of virtue, a healthier sense of morals, which by itself would repel all assaults

---

* In her understanding of Georges Sand, Margrethe here seems to be somewhat misled by the misunderstanding attending her debut as an author, a very commonly held opinion of her works, which was considerably modified by her later productions. [Author's note in 1879 edition.—EDS.]

by an immoral, public judgment, against which nobody now is safe; a greater mental independence of men, which would enable us to get closer to them and to be more to them in a deeper sense than is now possible.

An author, who, incidentally, is vigorously opposed to the cry for emancipation that has arisen in France, says: Women have only one source for their experiences: their *love* is their understanding, their faith, their genius, their *emancipation*. Very well, we demand nothing better. But then this love must first be emancipated, that is: saved from barbarism and thraldom. Protect then, oh humanity, this first flower of our lives, because from it all blessing is later to mature! Take heed of its growth and its fruits. Do not frivolously disturb its fragile central leaf in the stupid belief that the coarse leaves succeeding it are good enough. No, they are not good enough. There is just as big a difference as there is between the tea with which we ordinary mortals content ourselves and refer to as tea, and that which only the Emperor of the Celestial Kingdom drinks and which is the *real* tea; it is harvested first and is so delicate that it must be picked with gloved hands, after the pickers have washed themselves twenty-four times, I think it is.

Yes, there are many such harsh conditions in our lives that make us unable to fulfill our task as we should. Yes, yes, let it be shouted to those thousand deaf ears, there is something askew, something wrong, in our position. Ought there not to be a reason for those bitter complaints from both sides? We do not hear any, you will say. But yet they come, these laments, like those inexplicable wails that seem to rise from the shining seas or to vibrate in the air; but few ears are capable of hearing them.

Yes, we deserve to be better situated; we are better, much better, than our upbringing, our institutions, and common judgment make us out to be. There are splendid natures who well know how to obtain their rights in their relationship with another individual. A particular person many a time surmounts the faults of his family as a whole. Is it because the men, the married ones, have more respect for our sex and are more pleasant in their social intercourse with us than are the young? At least they honor their wives and daughters. It is to no woman's advantage to be the topic of conversation in a circle of bachelors, and it is well known that the only way in which one may excel and be honored there, is by not being *mentioned*.

Much is being said about the elevated position that American women have in their country. It may well be that this is due to something we do not quite want to acknowledge. This does not prevent it, however, from being just as weighty in its results. I would imagine that the practical way in which they are reared, the laws that accord them every advantage, the men who with intelligently calculated, exquisite egotism protect their position, make them right from the cradle into those proud, independent creatures whose influence extends from the drawing room to all aspects of public life.

By way of contrast I shall try to give a sketch, just a rough sketch, of the conditions under which our young girls live. Even before they are born into the world, the laws have plundered them.* At that point it is already believed necessary that they must be provided for by a man who will marry them. The husband thus becomes a sort of vocational study for them, like the law or officer's training for the sons. Their upbringing is planned accordingly, that is, with much more emphasis upon being admitted to their vocation than mastering it. In this manner they grow up, without any real skills or knowledge, without deeper interests, in an idle life full of empty pleasures. It is as if their parents, out of a sort of pitying weakness, cannot obtain for them enough of these empty pleasures, as if they cannot sufficiently anesthetize them against the grave fate that awaits them; they are at least to have fun and be well cared for as long as they are living with their parents. To this situation is often added a hidden heartache, which ravages their inner being like those stealthy forest fires that one cannot see in the clear summer light. Then they find themselves by the dividing line: Helplessness on the one side, a wretched marriage based on chance on the other. The choice is not the worst thing that can happen. As we know, the silk cord is always more honorable than the hangman's rope. At least they get married. And now it is expected that at least the best among them will obtain for themselves an importance greater than that which a few miserable ballroom triumphs have given them. No, it only means that at this point they enter into the hopeless night of obscurity and insignificance. A noticeable fading characterizes this transition. Nothing is known any longer of these beings, who were once referred to as the pretty so-and-sos; one scarcely recognizes them any longer when they show their faded selves in public. They are no longer individuals; they are Norwegian housewives. Do you know what a Norwegian housewife is? I am not really sure, either, but I do know that I am not acquainted with a single woman who has a quickening effect upon a wider circle, either by her charm or by her spirit, and yet I know many who both could and should have this effect.

Oh, you sad city, where one is doomed forever to drink up the dregs of memory! Have you no potion for hope and oblivion! Whoever has become heartsick at your bosom, can never more be happy. Everywhere one goes, there are crosses showing where a joy, an illusion, lies buried. They walk again everywhere, these restless ghosts. They float past you on the stairs; they meet you at street corners; they wave to you from the windows of now this house, now that, which itself stands like a monument, desolate and petrified.

94. Fredrika Bremer (1856)

"I have held my peace so long, I have left unspoken so much that stirs my whole being, Alma! With you alone can I give vent to my feelings. You only can read my heart. I feel as if your glance had a healing power.

---

* In the interest of truth we must remind the reader that time, with regard to this point of law to which Margrethe alludes, has brought a change which is more in keeping with what is right and acceptable. [Author's note in 1879 edition.—EDS.]

Lay your hand there; let it rest there for a moment; perhaps it may allay this bitterness, which I now feel towards them who gave us life, against them whom we call our father in Heaven, and our father on earth. Bitterness against one's father is a frightful feeling! Oh, Alma! when I think that it is our father's fault that you are lying here heart-broken; that you might have been the happy wife of the man who loved you if our father's obstinacy and covetousness had not separated you!"

"Do not speak of it, Hertha!" interrupted Alma, whilst a death-like paleness overspread her countenance; "do not touch upon that subject."

"Forgive me, beloved! But I know that it is *that* which is killing you. Ever since then have I seen you fade and waste away, as by some secret malady; your eyes become larger; your cheeks emaciated, and you—oh, Alma, sweet Alma! I feel I shall hate him!"

"Do not hate him. Pity him rather. Believe me, he is not happy. He has not always been as he is now. Ever since our mother's death, Anna says that his temper has become gloomy and morbid; and our aunt made him more morose than he otherwise would have been."

"But he is also unjust and severe! Had he given us our right, then you would not have been as you now are. Why does he withhold from us our mother's property? Why does he render us no account of what we possess, or of what we ought to have?"

"We have, in fact, no right to desire it. We are, according to the laws of our country, still minors, and he is our lawful guardian."

"And we shall always continue to be minors, if we do not go to law with our father, because it is his will that we should ever be dependent upon him, and the laws of our country forbid us to act as if we were rational, independent beings! Look, Alma, it is this injustice towards us, as women, which provokes me, not merely with my father, but with the men who make these my country's unjust laws, and with all who contrary to reason and justice maintain them, and in so doing contribute to keep us in our fettered condition. We have property which we inherit from our mother; yet can we not dispose of one single farthing of it. We are old enough to know what we desire, and to be able to take care of ourselves and others, yet at the same time we are kept as children under our father and guardian, because he chooses to consider us as such, and treat us as such. We are prohibited every action, every thought which would tend to independent activity or the opening of a future for ourselves, because our father and guardian says that we are minors, that we are children, and the law says, 'it is his right; you have nothing to say!'"

"Yes," said Alma, "it is unjust, and harder than people think. But, nevertheless, our father means well by us, and manages our property justly and prudently with regard to our best interests."

"And who will be the better for it? We? When we are old and stupid, and no more good for anything? See, I shall soon be twenty-seven, you are twenty-nine already, and for what have we lived?"

Alma made no reply, and Hertha continued:

"If we had even been able to learn anything thoroughly, and had had

the liberty to put forth our powers, as young men have, I would not complain. Is it not extraordinary, Alma, that people always ask boys what
they would like to be, what they have a fancy or taste for, and then give
them the opportunity to learn, and to develop themselves according to
the best of their minds, but they never do so with girls! They cannot even
think or choose for themselves a profession or way of life. Ah, I would so
gladly have lived upon bread and water, and have been superlatively
happy, if I might but have studied as young men study at universities, and
by my own efforts have made my own way. The arts, the sciences—oh,
how happy are men who are able to study them; to penetrate the mysteries of the beautiful and the sublime, and then go forth into the world and
communicate to others the wisdom they have learned, the good they have
found. How glorious to live and labor day by day, for that which makes
the world better, more beautiful, lighter. How happy should one feel,
how good, how mild; how different that life must be to what it is, where
there seems to be no other question in the world but, 'What shall we eat
and drink, and what shall we put on?' and where all life's solicitude
seems to resolve itself into this. Oh, Alma, are we not born into this
world for something else? How wretched!" and as if overwhelmed by the
thought, Hertha buried her face in her hands. Presently she became
calmer, and continued, looking steadily upwards:

"How dissimilar are objects in the world, as well as in nature as among
mankind. The Creator has given to each and all their different impulse
and destination, which they cannot violate without becoming unnatural,
or perishing. This is allowed to be an unquestioned law as regards the
children of nature. People do not require from the oak that it shall be like
a birch, nor from the lily that it shall resemble the creeping cistus. With
men it is the same; they are allowed each one to grow according to his
bent and his nature, and to become that which the Creator has called
them to be; but women, precisely they who should improve every power
to the utmost, they must become unnatural, thoughtless, submissive tools
of that lot to which men have destined them. They must all be cast in one
mould and follow one line, which is chalked out for them as if they had
no souls of their own to show them the way, and to give them an individual bent. And yet how different are the gifts and the dispositions of
women; what a difference there is, for instance, among us sisters, all children of the same parents. What a clever and active practical woman will
our Martha become, and Maria, on the contrary, how unusually thoughtful and pleased with study is she! You, my Alma, are made to be the angel
of domestic life, and I—ah, I do not know, I cannot tell what I was created to become. I yet seek for myself; but if I had been able to develop
myself in freedom, if the hunger and thirst which I felt within me had
been satisfied, then I might perhaps have become something more than
ordinarily good and beneficial to my fellow-creatures. Because, though it
may be bold to say or think it, I know that I might have been able to
acquire the good gifts of life in order to impart them to the many; I
would liberate the captive and make the oppressed soul happy; I would

work, and live and die for humanity. Other objects are for me too trivial. There was a time when I believed what people and books said about home and domestic life, as woman's only object and world; when I thought that it was a duty to crush all desires after a larger horizon, or any other sphere of action; weak, stupid thoughts those, which I have long since cast behind me! My inward eye has become clearer, my own feelings and thoughts have become too powerful for me, and I can no longer, as formerly, judge myself by others. There was a time when, above all things, I thirsted after an artist's life and freedom; but that, even that, is a selfish, circumscribed aim, if it be not sanctified by something higher. Marriage is to me a secondary thing, nay, a wretched thing, if it do not tend to a higher human development in the service of light and freedom. That which I seek for and which I desire is, a life, a sphere of labor, which makes me feel that I live fully, not merely for myself, but for the whole community, for my country, my people, for humanity, for God, yes, for God! if he be the God of justice and goodness—the father of all. Perhaps I may never attain to that which I wish for; perhaps I may sink down, buried in the inner life, which is mine and so many other women's portion in this world; but never, never will I say that it is woman's proper inheritance and lot, never will I submit, never will I cease to maintain that she has been created for something better, something more; yes, if she were able fairly and fully to develop all the noble powers which the Creator has given her, then she would make the world happier. Oh! that I could live and labor for the emancipation of these captive, struggling souls, these souls which are yearning after life and light; with what joy should I live, with what gladness should I then die, yes, even if to die were to cease for ever! I should then, nevertheless, have lived immortally!"

"How handsome you are, after all, Hertha!" exclaimed Alma, as she looked up with rapture to her sister, who looked radiant in her longings after freedom and love.

"Handsome," repeated Hertha, blushing and smiling sorrowfully. "Ah, there was a time when I know I might have become, might have been good-looking, if—but that time is gone by. Now I grow plainer every day, because my soul and mind are embittered more and more against both God and man. I have sometimes had the most extravagant thoughts of how I might deliver us from this misery. I have thought of going to Stockholm and speaking to the King!"

"To the King! Ah, Hertha!"

"Yes, to the King. They say that King Oscar is noble and just; that he does not refuse their rights to any of his subjects. I should speak to him in this manner (now you are the King and I am your subject): 'Your Majesty, I come on behalf of myself and many of my sisters. We have been kept as children, in ignorance of our human rights and duties, and held as minors, in order that we may not become mature human beings. Both our souls and our hands are in bonds, although God has bade us to be free, and although we demand nothing but that which is good and right.

In other Christian countries, and even in our own sister-land, your Majesty's kingdom of Norway, her rights have been determined by law to woman at a certain age, and this the age of her best powers; but in our country, in Sweden, the law ordains, that the daughters of the country shall for all time be under bondage, and declared to be under age, unless they happen to be widows, whatever their age may be; or they must appeal to the seat of justice to demand that freedom, which still their guardians can prevent their obtaining.'"

"But now, if the King should say, 'My dear child, you and your many sisters need support and guidance. You could not manage or keep things in order for yourselves.'"

"Then would I reply, 'Your Majesty, let us be tried, and your Majesty will then see that it is quite the reverse. Many noble-minded and liberal-minded women have shown it to be so, and these might become more, might become many, if the laws of our country allowed it. Children could not learn to walk alone, if they were not released from the leading strings; they could not use their eyes unless light were allowed to enter their rooms.

"'Let us only know that we may be, that we are permitted to be our own supporters, and we shall learn to support ourselves and others. Your Majesty! grant us freedom, grant us the right over our own souls, our lives, our property, our future, and we will serve you, and our country, and all that is good, with all our heart and all our soul, and with all our powers, as only they who are free can do!'"

"Well said, my beautiful, noble Hertha!" exclaimed Alma. "I wish that the King and the estates of the realm could both see and hear you, they would then repent of having done an injustice to the Swedish woman—having been willing to depreciate her worth and limit her future."

"And that of the community at the same time," added Hertha, warmly, "because a great deal of that which is so wretched in morals and in disposition, proceeds from the want of esteem which women have for themselves, the want of fully comprehending their high vocation as human beings. . . ."

CHAPTER 11

Syntheses and New Horizons in Post-revolutionary Europe

The Debate Deepens in France

SOURCES

95. P.-J. Proudhon, *De la Justice dans la Révolution et dans l'Église* (1858), in *Oeuvres complètes de P.-J. Proudhon*, new ed., ed. C. Bouglé and H. Moysset, XII (Paris, 1935), 179-83, 185-87, 190, 196-97, 199, 201, 203-4, 211, 213. Tr. KMO.

96. Juliette Lambert [Adam], *Idées anti-proudhoniennes sur l'amour, la femme et le mariage*, 2d ed. (Paris, 1861), pp. 41-44, 59-60, 75-82. Originally published in 1858. Tr. KMO. The editors wish to thank Professor Claire Goldberg Moses, University of Maryland, for a copy of this work.

In the wake of the revolutionary repression of 1849-50 and the bitter disillusionment experienced by idealists and reformers, the worker-philosopher and polemicist Pierre-Joseph Proudhon (Docs. 52, 84) refined his own definitive views concerning the nature and organization of human society in a purely secular world. In the spring of 1858 he published *De la Justice dans la Révolution et dans l'Église*, a major theoretical treatise predicated on the forty-nine-year-old Proudhon's atheism, materialism, and devotion to logic. On behalf of the "true revolution" he invoked nature and justice as his chosen allies in combating the spiritualism of the church and its teachings.

Proudhon devoted two chapters of his book to a discussion of love and marriage, elaborating his authoritarian and patriarchal views concerning women and the family in their most uncompromising form to date. He likewise unleashed his fury at emancipated women such as George Sand and Daniel Stern [Marie d'Agoult], and challenged defenders of female emancipation to grapple with his theories. No doubt his judgments were stimulated as much by his reflections about his own personal experiences as by more abstract considerations. Following the events of 1849-50 he had married "a working girl who was young and poor," not because he loved her, as he wrote to a friend, but because he "cherished the idea of a *household* and PATERNITY." He was not disappointed; by 1854 he had fathered three daughters.

The following excerpts from *De la Justice* encapsulate Proudhon's views on women. Like many nineteenth-century men, Proudhon subscribed to an ancient Aristotelian male-centered physiological view of the sexes, which has since been labeled the "spermatic economy." In this view, the male principle incarnated by the semen was defined as active and the female as passive; scientific knowledge of the actual physiology of reproduction was not then widely known. This belief provides the underpinnings for his mathematical "proof" of female inferiority that required women's subordination in the family and the state. Although these features of Proudhon's work were even then disturbing to women like Juliette Adam, his atheism and materialism alarmed government censors even more; the imperial government confiscated his treatise and threatened Proudhon with prosecution. To avoid going to prison, he fled to Belgium where a second edition of *De la Justice* was published in 1860.

Proudhon's brutal judgments were soon contested by a spirited young woman of twenty-two, Juliette Lambert La Messine (1836-1936), who later became famous as Madame Edmond Adam (the surname by which we will henceforth refer to her). Raised in Picardy, amid a running argument between her free-thinking, republican father and her royalist, Catholic grandmother, Juliette Adam became a wife at eighteen and a mother by the age of twenty. She subsequently moved to Paris with her first husband, a government official, and established connections with members of a Saint-Simonian-inspired literary circle. Later she became incensed at Proudhon's harsh judgments on women in general, and offended by his denigration of her literary idols Sand and Stern as well. Encouraged by her coterie, she drafted a lively counter-offensive, which she published at her own expense in August 1858 under the name Lamber, an altered version of her maiden name, a maneuver designed to prevent her first, estranged husband from confiscating her royalties. *Idées anti-proudhoniennes* was an immediate critical success and launched Adam on a distinguished literary career.

In the face of Proudhon's misogyny, Adam's words read as brave expressions of advanced opinion. In these excerpts she raises a host of questions concerning the role of women, especially that of the mature woman, that even now have not been resolved. Her vocabulary, too, is strangely modern. She posed the question of "woman as other" in the existential terminology of immanence and transcendence that we will encounter again nearly one hundred years later in the works of Simone de Beauvoir.

---

95. P.-J. Proudhon (1858)

Are man and woman each other's equals or equivalents? Or are they merely complementary to one another, in such a manner that there can be neither equality nor equivalence between them? In any case, what is the social function of woman? Following from this, what is her dignity? What is her right? How should she be considered in the Republic? . . .

I hesitated a long time before deciding to treat this question. Certain brusque statements that fell from my pen—less against woman—who would think of attacking woman?—than against her so-called emancipators—have brought down on me so many quarrels, that I promised myself never to return to the subject and to let matters be. I wanted to abolish these troublesome words *equality* and *inequality* with reference to our other halves, an untarnished source for divisiveness, internal quarrels, treason, and shame. In the interest of the common dignity and domestic peace, I would gladly have accepted a pact of silence, more in conformity with the old-style reserve and chivalrous habits of our forefathers.

Apparently my fears were exaggerated. Others before me, absurdly brave, have resurrected this debate that now menaces the tranquility of our households. Feminine indiscretion has caught fire; a half-dozen inky-fingered insurgents obstinately try to make woman into something we do not want, reclaim their *rights* with insults, and defy us to bring the question out into the light of day. After I have established on the basis of facts and evidence the PHYSICAL, INTELLECTUAL, AND MORAL inferiority of woman; after I have demonstrated by glaring examples that what they call her emancipation is the same thing as her prostitution, it remains only to determine by other measures the nature of her prerogatives and to take up her defense against the digressions of a certain number of impure women who have been rendered insane by sin.

PHYSICAL INFERIORITY OF WOMEN

It is a fact of life, common to all mammals, that until puberty the make-up of the young man and the girl are scarcely different, but from the moment masculine development begins, man takes the lead in several respects: the squareness of his shoulders, the thickness of his neck, the hardness of his muscles, the girth of his biceps, the strength of his loins, the agility of his entire body, the power of his voice. It is a fact that this development can be arrested and retained, so to speak, in the neutral state by mutilating the young male; and that the adult male himself, undergoing castration, redescends insensibly and loses his virile qualities, as if by the generative faculties with which he is endowed the man, before engendering his kind, engenders himself and brings himself to a degree of strength such as woman never attains.

It is also a fact of life that the abuse of amorous encounters and seminal losses, like castration itself, deprives man of his strength and its accompanying qualities—agility, ardor, courage—and that the age at which he begins to grow old is that at which his organs produce less of this semen, of which the greatest part is used, it appears, for the production of strength.

Finally, it is a fact of life that between individual males the differences in strength and physical agility are not generally proportional to the height, mass, and weight, but to virile energy and to the relative efficiency with which this energy serves and maintains the system. This accounts for those softer temperaments, the less angular forms, the less well endowed bodies that the peasants of Franche-Comté refer to as *femmelins*, all the more inclined toward love as their constitutions seem weaker, or in other words, that their bodies reabsorb the semen less completely.

According to these observations, therefore, the physical inferiority of woman is the product of her *non-masculinity*.

The complete human being, adequate to his destiny (I am speaking here of physique), is the male, who by means of his virility attains the highest degree of muscular and nervous tension that his nature and his destiny require, and thereby the maximum of activity in work and in combat.

The woman is a diminutive of man, and lacks an organ necessary to become anything other than a potential adult.

Why has nature given only to man this seminal virtue, whereas it has made woman a passive being, a receptacle for the seed that man alone produces, a place of incubation—like the earth for the grain of wheat—by itself an inert organ, lacking its own goal, which can be activated only by the fertilizing action of the father, but for another goal than that of the mother? This contrasts with the case of man, for whom the generative power has its positive utility independent of generation itself.

Such an arrangement can have no reason to exist other than in the couple and the family; it presupposes the subordination of the subject, outside which its self-sufficiency would be impossible, and it could rightly speak of itself as afflicted by nature and as the suffering victim of Providence. . . .

Whatever the inequality of vigor, suppleness, agility, constancy, that one can observe between men and women, it can be said without much risk of error that on the average the ratio of physical force of man to that of woman is 3 to 2.

Thus, from this perspective, the numerical ratio of 3 to 2 indicates the ratio of value between the sexes. . . .

What I have said so far is based on theory: in practice, the condition of woman encounters an even greater subordination through maternity. . . .

Without mentioning her periods, which take up eight days of the month, ninety-six days per year, one must count nine months for pregnancy; for recovery, forty days; for nursing, 12 to 15 months; for child care after weaning, five years: for a total of seven years for a single birth. In the case of four births at two-year intervals, maternity requires twelve years from a woman.

Here we must not engage in quibbling or haggling. No doubt the pregnant woman and the nursing mother, along with some one who cares for bigger children, is capable of some service. In my own estimate, during these twelve years the woman's time is absorbed almost entirely in bearing and raising children; whatever she can do beyond this without deteriorating is strictly fortuitous, and thus she and her children inevitably become dependent on man.

If, therefore, during the better part of her existence, woman is condemned by her nature to subsist only with the help of a man; if he—whether father, brother, husband, or lover—definitively becomes her sole protector and supplier, how (I reason always from pure logic and without regard to any other influence), how, I say, will he be able to submit to the control and the direction of a woman? How is it that she who does not work [for a living], who lives on the work of others, could—in her continual pregnancies and births—govern the worker? However you propose to regulate the relations of the sexes and the education of children—whether in a Platonic community or by an insurance system, as M. de

Girardin proposes—or, if you prefer, by maintaining the monogamous couple and the family—whatever you do, you arrive at this same result—that woman, because of her organic weakness and the *interesting situation* she inevitably falls into (however little the man contributes to it), will be fatally and juridically excluded from all political, administrative, doctrinal, industrial governance, and from all military action.

INTELLECTUAL INFERIORITY OF WOMEN

The doctrine that has, more than all others, contributed toward imagining the utopia of sexual equality is the Platonic-Christian doctrine of the nature of the soul, to which Descartes added the final touches.

According to this doctrine, the soul is a non-material substance, essentially different from the body. This soul constitutes the whole of man; the body is only its envelope, its instrument. Considered in themselves, souls are equal; only the body determines the various inequalities of organic and intellectual power that can be observed between persons. Now, if the destiny of the species is to free itself, by religion, science, Justice, and industry, from the determinants of the flesh as well as from nature, it follows that the equality of souls should appear bit by bit between people, and that every difference in the prerogatives of the two sexes should be eradicated. It is only a question of education, similar to that of the proletariat. . . .

Thus [according to this doctrine] the physical inferiority of woman and the consequences that follow from it are not denied; nor is woman's intellectual inferiority—at least in the present state of things—denied.

It is argued [by George Sand, Daniel Stern, and others] only that the inferiority of organic power ought to be neutralized by industrial progress, and intellectual inferiority neutralized in its turn by the education of the subjects and by the social constitution; in such a manner that the two sexes remain in presence . . . as some sort of pure spirits, from which death and Heaven have extracted all sexuality and matter. . . .

Indeed, progress does move toward equality between subjects of the same order and of equivalent constitution, who have been rendered unequal by ignorance or by fate. This means that progress can be toward equality between man and man, or between woman and woman. But it is not true that progress moves toward equality between man and woman; in order for that to happen, the former would have to stop progressing in the totality of his being, while the latter would progress in the totality of hers—which is impossible.

What, then, remains in conclusion of this elegant reasoning about the souls of women?

What remains is that, in order to allow them to catch up with us, one would have to render strength and intelligence useless; call a halt to the progress of science, industry, work; prevent humanity from developing its virile power; mutilate it in body and soul; lie in the face of destiny; and repress nature, all for the greater glory of this poor little woman's soul, which can neither rival her companion nor follow him. . . .

Like man, woman has five senses; she is constituted like man; like man she sees, she smells, she feeds herself, she walks, she loves. From the standpoint of physical force, she lacks only one thing in order to rival man, which is to produce seed.

Similarly, from the standpoint of intelligence, woman has perceptions, memory, imagination; she is capable of paying attention, of reflecting, of judging. What does she lack? To produce seeds, that is to say, ideas; what the Latins called *genius*, the generative faculty of the mind.

What is genius? . . .

Genius is . . . virility of spirit and its accompanying powers of abstraction, generalization, invention, conceptualization, which are lacking in equal measure in children, eunuchs, and women. And such is the solidarity of the two organs that, just as the athlete must separate himself from woman in order to conserve his vigor, the thinker must also separate himself in order to conserve his genius—as if the reabsorption of the semen were any less necessary to the brain of the latter than to the muscles of the former.

. . . To the generation of ideas as to the generation [of children] woman brings nothing of her own; she is a passive, enervating being, whose conversation exhausts you as much as her embraces. He who wishes to conserve in its entirety the strength of his body and his mind will flee her: she is a murderer. *Inveni amariorem morte mulierem*, said Solomon. . . .

Since, in view of all that I have said, intelligence correlates with strength, we rediscover here the ratio established earlier, that is, that the intellectual power of man is 3, and that of woman, 2.

And insofar as in economic, political, and social action the strength of the body and that of the mind go in tandem and are multiplied by one another, the physical and intellectual value of man will be, with respect to the physical and intellectual value of woman, as 3 x 3 is to 2 x 2, that is as 9 is to 4.

No doubt woman contributes, insofar as she is able, to the social order and to the production of wealth, and it is just that her voice should be heard. But, whereas in general assembly the vote of the man will count as 9, that of woman will count as 4. Thus do arithmetic and Justice agree.

MORAL INFERIORITY OF WOMAN

. . . But is it true that in the moral order of things, from the standpoint of Justice, of liberty, courage, and modesty, woman might be the equal of man? Already we have seen that, in both, intelligence is proportional to strength; how can virtue not also be proportional? . . .

The question becomes one of asking whether woman possesses her own virtue, every bit of it, or whether by chance she does not derive her moral value, in part or in totality, from man, just as we know she derives her intellectual value thus. . . .

Woman is a receptacle. Just as she receives the embryo from man, so too she receives her intellect and her sense of duty from him.

By nature unproductive, inert, lacking industry or understanding, lacking a sense of Justice or modesty, she requires a father, a brother, a lover, a husband, a master, a man of some sort to give her, if I may put it this way, the wherewithal that will render her capable of the virile virtues, and of social and intellectual faculties.

From this one can appreciate her devotion to love; it is not merely the instinct for maturity that encourages her; it is the emptiness of her soul, the need for courage, Justice, and honor that propel her. For her it is insufficient to be chaste, *virgo*; she must also become a heroine, *virago*. Her heart and her brain require fertilization no less than her body. . . .

All these facts about the physical and moral comparableness of man and woman must be stated, not in a vain spirit of denigration and for the stupid pleasure of exalting one sex at the expense of the other, but because they reveal the truth, because truth alone is moral and cannot be mistaken by anyone for either praise or insult. If Nature wanted the two sexes to be unequal and thereby united according to the law of subordination rather than by that of equivalence, she had her reasons—deeper and more conclusive than the utopias of the philosophers, and more advantageous not only to man, but to woman, to the child, to the entire family. It has long been said that the further humanity has risen from its base origins, the more glorious its morality has become. What is true for the conjugal collectivity is equally true for each individual partner; leave to man the heroism, the genius, the jurisdictions that are his prerogative, and you will soon see woman succeed in overcoming the imperfections of her nature to arrive at an incomparable transparence, which by itself is worth the sum of our virtues.

Thus, follow our reasoning to its conclusion.

Inferior to man in conscience as much as in intellectual and muscular power, woman finds herself as member of domestic as well as of civil society definitively relegated to the second rank; from the moral point of view as well as from the physical and intellectual point of view, her comparative value is still 2 to 3.

And since society is constituted according to a combination of these three elements—work, science, and Justice—the total value of man and woman—their relationship and consequently their comparative share of influence will be 3 x 3 x 3 to 2 x 2 x 2, or 27 to 8.

Under these conditions, woman cannot pretend to balance man's virile power; her subordination is inevitable. According both to Nature and before Justice she weighs only a third of man; this means that the emancipation being sought in her name would be the legal consecration of her misery, if not of her servitude. The sole hope remaining to her is to find, without violating Justice, an arrangement that will redeem her: all my readers have identified this arrangement as marriage.

96. Juliette Lambert [Adam] (1858)

M. Proudhon's theories on love are too retrograde, too far outside general opinion, to exert any proselytizing power on our contemporaries.

But his dangerous doctrines concerning women are another matter; they express the general opinion of men who—whatever party they belong to, progressive or reactionary, monarchist or republican, Christian or pagan, atheist or deist—would be delighted to find a means of reconciling their egoism and their conscience in a system that would permit them to conserve the benefits of exploitation based on strength without having anything to fear from protests founded on right.

Power asserts itself because it is necessary, but it cannot maintain itself except by proving its legitimacy.

M. Proudhon has tried to establish that the subordination of woman is based on nature, and he has attempted to construct an *order* that would maintain this subordination and a justice that would sanction it. He wanted to perpetuate the reign of force by legitimizing it: that is his crime.

This crime is unpardonable.

As of this moment, it is unpardonable in the eyes of any woman who is conscious of her own *moral value, her personality, her natural autonomy.* God willing—and woman too—it will soon be equally unpardonable in the eyes of thinking human beings of both sexes.

Without hesitation M. Proudhon affirms the *physical, intellectual, and moral inferiority of woman.* This is saying a lot. Let us examine his case.

First of all, as concerns physical inferiority, he says: "On this point the discussion can be brief; everyone gives a guilty verdict."

Not so fast, Monsieur, if you please; before going further, it would be useful to reach an understanding.

If M. Proudhon, in comparing woman to man from the physical standpoint, intends to speak solely in terms of muscular strength, it is indeed probable that everyone would agree—i.e., that everyone would agree that, in general, man can surpass woman on the dynamometer. But one has to be blind or at least one-eyed and see things only from one side to observe nothing about the human body but [muscular] strength. For if in terms of physical strength man compares to woman in the ratio of 3 to 2, in turn—as M. Proudhon himself agrees further on—woman surpasses man in physical beauty by a ratio of 3 to 2. Thus, in speaking of physique, there is compensation. We ought to add that woman has her brand of strength just as man has his. If, by the size of his muscles and the thickness of his neck, man excels in lifting or bearing heavy burdens, woman by the predominance of fluids, the greater elasticity of her fibers, and the nature of her nervous system, outlasts man in resistive strength. She bends but doesn't break. Who is the Hercules who would endure, without being broken, the efforts of giving birth? . . . Nothing M. Proudhon says about the *masculinity* of strength should be taken seriously; moreover, it proves nothing except for demonstrating his urge to employ a physiological technology that borders on the obscene. . . .

Such are M. Proudhon's ideas about woman. It is apparent that it would be difficult to put her any lower. And then, after all that, M. Proudhon assumes the airs of a cavalier and tries to make himself pass for a defender. After refusing everything to woman in the name of law and justice, he [tries to] offer her the most beautiful sort of world, in the name of the family and of what he calls religion. . . .

On the contrary, Monsieur . . . we want justice, not favors. We will obtain it from you yourself, or at least from your kind. Will you refuse it when we have proved to you not only that equity requires that you accord us our due but that your most pressing interest commands it, and that your salvation and ours, social salvation, makes it mandatory?

By following you step by step I could point out your fallacies and your numerous contradictions. That would have been a petty war.

But I would rather convince you than defeat you; I would rather cure you, for you are ill. This is my most ardent wish. Let me believe it might come true. In any case I will try, so that others who share your views on women will be healed, and so that those who might be disposed to adopt them will be spared contagion. This is my duty. It seemed to me that, in order to fulfill it, the best thing to do would be not to refute your arguments, which are worth very little by themselves, but to show the resolution to the problem you have posed but did not yourself know how to resolve: Justice in society for woman as well as for man. . . .

It must be well understood that, as society organizes itself, it creates organs that correspond to its degree of development and that must be increasingly perfect; these organs are called institutions. Whereas the goal of primitive institutions was to organize strength, those being created nowadays tend instead to organize the love of humanity.

The institutions of the present and the future are institutions of mutual help, of guarantees, and of charity. Their special goal is to extend knowledge, to spread well-being, to guarantee individual existence through the help of the community, to succor the weak, the infirm, and the sick.

Far more than the institutions of previous periods, institutions of this nature call for the assistance of women, and when one looks at society's needs today and the direction of social movement, it is impossible not to recognize the increasing importance of the role women are called upon to fill in society.

Men who, like M. Proudhon, want to return us to patriarchy by imprisoning women in the family are *quintessential abstractors* who do not see what is happening around them and do not recognize the collective life that is developing new needs every day, engendering new forces, and giving way to social foundations that respond to these needs and organize these forces. No doubt they have good intentions; they think they are at least serving the cause of morality, which always turns out to be the cause of progress, if not the cause of progress itself. By obliging women to shut themselves up in the family, by forcing them to be solely wives and mothers, they hope to remedy this fever for luxury and dissipation that possesses women more and more and becomes a cause of social dissolution, an element of moral corruption and disorder.

But they are mistaken. It is not by further restricting the area of women's activity that they will put a stop to her misconduct; on the contrary, it can be done only by giving this activity the means to satisfy itself within legitimate channels.

Women must be given a serious education and, to the extent possible, a vocational education. They must become *productive*. Work alone has emancipated men; work alone can emancipate women. Woman must be able to earn honestly the clothing that adorns and embellishes her and, instead of dragging her silken dresses and lace shawls in the dust of the sidewalk, she can then walk freely and proudly in modest gowns that will allow her beauty to be seen without sullying her virtue and putting a price on her honor. In view of the fact that the education women are given is good for nothing except making dolls out of them, should one be astonished when they pose as dolls before men and end, poor girls, by taking seriously the stupid role they have been taught since childhood.

Do not accuse me of misunderstanding woman's role in the family; as much as M. Proudhon, I think women should apply themselves to being wives and mothers; but I maintain that family life does not suffice for the physical, moral, and intellectual activity of woman. The role of broody hen is, no doubt, most respectable, but it is not suited to everyone; nor is it so absorbing as has been represented. For one thing, there are many women who do not marry; then, too, there are a great number who are obliged to work every day as do their husbands. Two productive workers in a household are worth more than one, and in a family where the father, who has only his own work, is obliged to meet the needs of his wife and three or four children as well, I ask how they can live, if they can live, how they eat, if they eat, how they are clothed, warmed, lodged, and what sort of education the children receive. In any case, work can contribute to good morality when it is not excessive—but when it is, it is brutalizing. I do not see how the virtue of the wife should ever have to suffer from the fact that she works. What are the common recruiting agents of prostitution if not the impossibility of finding honest work, and the inadequacy of salaries, and, finally, idleness, the ever present ancestor of all vice? Opening to women careers in freely chosen and adequately paid work would mean closing the doors of the brothels. Men, are you ready for this?

Beyond the hypocrisy with which men unmercifully blame feminine vice, which is nourished and supported by masculine corruption, the thing that has always shocked me is the profound disdain with which men treat women who have reached middle age. From this moment on, even the most sensitive reformers cease to be concerned with her lot. At thirty-five or forty, men begin to be fit for every kind of job; until then they do not inspire much confidence. Their intellectual development is not really complete until this age. Then public functions become incumbent on them. For men it takes thirty-five or forty years to shape their individual morality and acquire a physiognomy. How can it be, if men only begin to amount to something after having reached middle age, that women, by contrast, from this moment on cease to amount to anything? Is woman then worthless after her flowering? Is man alone allowed to bear fruit?

Until recently woman was considered only from the standpoint of male pleasure or the conservation of the species, and was valued only for her beauty and her maternity. In a society constituted by men for their own profit, woman was appreciated only as a wife and mother; but if woman is a free individual, intellectually and morally active, she will have her own value, she will make her own law. She will no more receive her conscience and dignity from man than he receives his own dignity and conscience from a being outside himself. This is clearly the doctrine of *immanence* (Proudhon's term) applied to woman. When we have forced M. Proudhon to admit that woman is a human being, an independently organized being, we will make him admit all that follows—and perhaps he will go further than we ourselves might, because he is ever excessive and sees only the logic of the matter, regardless of circumstances.

In the meantime, let us restrict ourselves to the affirmation that woman is a free being who develops to intellectual maturity exactly as man does; that if she is a beauty at twenty, she may not be such in all aspects of her being; that her mind and heart ripen and develop for just as long as do those of man himself; that she can arrive at comprehension of general ideas and general interests by applying her faculties and using them; that, finally, like man, she has a conscience and intelligence and that, like him, she can progress indefinitely so long as her organs have not become too tired or worn out.

After seven or eight years of marriage, woman ceases to be absorbed by the cares of maternity.

The preoccupations of love have lessened; she lives less in others—in her husband, in her children, and aspires to live more for herself. Let me tell you, too, that woman is freed earlier and more completely than man from sexual desires. What do you do with this activity that wants to apply itself to external things? Do you shut it in, at the risk of producing those reactions that are so fatal to women of thirty to forty? Will you condemn this woman, who wants to produce things intellectually to an unending sterility, or will you oblige her to turn toward gallantry? Catholicism at least offered frequentation of the church, which, if it did not satisfy her mind, satisfied her heart or at least deceived its hunger. See here, *messieurs les maîtres*, be reasonable; acknowledge that a woman who is no longer interested in pleasing and is no longer absorbed by family cares is good for something—that she can render social services, administer, oversee, sell, buy, *produce*, in fact, in arts, crafts, and industry, and that the time she can spend outside the household represents at least two-thirds of the time she has been accorded to live. This is certainly worth the effort of discussing! Great heavens, messieurs! We are made of flesh and bone like you; we know we have souls, whatever M. Proudhon says; we have heads with something inside them. Is it so silly to want to utilize all these gifts of heaven—after you, but still for you? For in the final analysis it is for your happiness and your comfort that we ask to share with you the burden of social work, just as you share with us that of the propagation of the species.

French Writers Fuel the International Debate

SOURCES

97. Jules Michelet, *Love*. Tr. J. W. Palmer, M.D. (New York, 1860), pp. 1, 43-48, 53-54, 140-41. Originally published in Paris, 1859. Also, Jules Michelet, *Woman (La Femme)*. Tr. J. W. Palmer, M.D. (New York, 1873), pp. 50-52, 79-80, 200-201. Originally published in Paris, 1860.

98. Jenny P. d'Héricourt, *A Woman's Philosophy of Woman, or Woman Affranchised: An Answer to Michelet, Proudhon, Girardin, Legouvé, Comte, and Other Modern Innovators* (New York, 1864), pp. 17-22, 24-25, 28-29, 220-23, 314-17. Originally published in Brussels, 1860.

The 1858 confrontation between Proudhon and Adam attracted much attention. Within only a few years two other French writers published major contributions to the discussion of the woman question that were also widely read, not only in France but abroad. Indeed, both the English translations we have drawn on for these selections were published in the early 1860's by Rudd & Carleton, a New York publishing firm.

We have already encountered the world-famous historian and moralist Jules Michelet (1798-1874; Doc. 46). After 1848 Michelet, who was by then in his fifties, turned his attention increasingly to the woman question. He had become deeply concerned about the declining French marriage and birth rates, and had delivered several series of public lectures on women and the family at the Collège de France. In 1859 and 1860 he published the two volumes, *Love* and *Woman*, which contained the most elaborate statements of his views to date. These two books can be viewed as marriage manuals addressed to men. Like Proudhon, Michelet was profoundly impressed by the discoveries in female reproductive physiology made by French medical men during the 1840's; indeed, during his second marriage to the much younger Athénaïs Mialaret, this fascination developed into a virtual obsession. In these two works Michelet blends an unrelenting physiological reductionism with his inherent romanticism to infuse heterosexual relations within marriage with new poetic meaning. Yet his meaning is cast in purely masculine terms: woman is, physiologically speaking, an invalid, he announced in *Love*. Yet woman, in his eyes, could also be a secular goddess, a cult figure worthy of inspiring man to his highest attainments. But she must necessarily remain under man's authority within his household, her mind as well as her body fertilized by his superior attributes. He wanted to cut woman off from her own family and, thereby, make her totally dependent on her husband. Michelet's double-binding imagery would cast a long shadow throughout Europe and America during the remainder of the nineteenth century, especially among educators, as will be evident in subsequent chapters. Indeed, it would be impossible to overestimate the historical importance of his arguments.

The French writer Jenny P. d'Héricourt (1807-1875) was, like Juliette Adam, a member of the *Revue Philosophique* circle in Paris. It was she, in fact, who had rekindled the flames of Proudhon's anger by several articles she had published in 1856-57. It is difficult to obtain information about Héricourt's life, but it is known that she was a native of Franche-Comté, that she studied medicine privately in Paris after she was forty, and that she subsequently practiced midwifery in Paris and in Chicago. Juliette Adam considered her a "fierce bluestocking," who set herself against George Sand and Daniel Stern by maintaining and priding herself upon a self-righteously upright personal conduct. In her treatise, *A Woman's Philosophy of Woman*, from which the second selection is taken, Héricourt resoundly contradicts Michelet's views and presents her own philosophy of woman. This treatise was read and discussed by women's advocates in northern Italy and in Russia, as well as in the United States.

---

97. Jules Michelet (1859 and 1860)

[*Love* (1859)]

The title which would fully express the design of this book, its signification, and its import, would be: Moral Enfranchisement, Effected by True Love.

This question of Love is lodged, immense and obscure, under the depths of human life. It even supports its bases and its lowermost foundations. The Family rests upon Love, and Society upon the family. Hence Love goes before everything.

As the manners are, so is the community. Liberty would be but a word if we preserved the habits of slaves.

Here we seek the Ideal. The ideal which can be realized to-day, not that which we must postpone for a better state of society. It is the reform of Love and of the Family which must precede all others, for it alone can render them possible. . . .

The object of love, woman, is a being who stands quite alone, and is much more unlike man than would at first appear; even more than differing from, opposed to him, but pleasingly opposed, in a playful and harmonic contest, which constitutes the great charm of this world.

In herself alone, she presents to us another opposition, a struggle of contrary qualities. Elevated by her beauty, her natural poetry, her quick intuition, and divining faculty, she is not the less held down by nature in the bonds of weakness and suffering. Every month she wings her flight upward, our poor dear Sybil, and, every month, nature admonishes her by pain, and by a painful crisis returns her to the hands of love.

She does nothing as we do. She thinks, speaks, and acts differently. Her tastes are different from our tastes. Her blood even does not flow in her veins as ours does, at times it rushes through them like a foaming mountain torrent. She does not respire as we do. Making provision for pregnancy and the future ascension of the lower organs, nature has so constructed her that she breathes, for the most part, by the four upper ribs. From this necessity, results woman's greatest beauty, the gently undulating bosom, which expresses all her sentiments by a mute eloquence.

She does not eat like us—neither as much, nor of the same dishes. Why? Chiefly, because she does not digest as we do. Her digestion is every moment troubled by one thing: she yearns with her very bowels. The deep cup of love (which is called the pelvis) is a sea of varying emotions, hindering the regularity of the nutritive functions.

These internal peculiarities are translated externally by one still more striking. Woman has a language peculiar to herself.

Insects and fish are mute. The bird sings, and would articulate. Man has a distinct tongue, well-defined and explicit words, and a clear tone of voice. But woman, above the man's voice and the bird's song, has a magic language, with which she intermingles this voice or this song: it is the sigh, the impassioned breath.

This is an incalculable power. Though it may but just make itself felt, the heart is at once moved. Her bosom heaves; she cannot speak; and we are won over in advance to everything she wishes. What manly harangue could produce such effect as a woman's silence?

Often, seated pensively by the sea-shore, I have watched the first movement, beginning silently, then palpably increasing until it became fearful, which surged the flood back upon the beach. I have been overwhelmed, absorbed by the potent electricity which danced on the legion of spark-crested waves.

But with how much more of emotion, with what religious and tender respect, have I noted the first signs, light, delicate, and concealed, then violent and painful, of the nervous impressions which periodically announce the flux and reflux of that other ocean, woman!

Besides, these signs are so evident that, even to the eyes of a stranger, they are manifest at the first glance. With some, who seem strong (but who at this time are so much the more weak), a visible agitation, like a tempest, or the approach of a severe illness, commences. In others, who, being more severely attacked, look pale and embarrassed, you can divine something like the destructive agencies of an undermining torrent. In the more common case, the milder influence seems the most salutary; the woman grows younger and renews herself, but always at the cost of suffering, at the cost of that mental uneasiness, which singularly affects her temper, enfeebles her will, and makes quite a new and different person of her, even to him who for a long time has known her best.

The most vulgar woman, at this period, is not without poetry. Long in advance of, and often at the middle of, the lunar month, she gives touching indications of her approaching transformation. Already the wave is coming and the tide rising.

She is agitated or pensive. She has no confidence in herself. By turns, she sheds tears and heaves sighs. Then treat her tenderly, speak to her with extreme consideration, care for her, treat her with attentions, yet abstain from importunity, lest she be made aware of them. Hers is a very defenceless state. She bears within her a power greater than herself, and formidable as a god. She astonishes you with singular speeches, sometimes eloquent, and scarcely to be expected from her. But (except when you have the brutality to irritate her) an increase of tenderness, of love even, overpowers all else. The warmth of the blood quickens the impulses of the heart. . . .

She loves, she suffers, and needs the support of a loving arm. This, more than anything else, has strengthened love in the human race— firmly established matrimonial union.

It has often been said, that it was the helplessness of the child which, prolonging the cares of education, had created the Family. True, the child does retain the mother, but the man is kept at his fireside by the mother herself, by his tenderness for his wife, and the happiness he experiences in protecting her.

Higher, and yet lower, than man; humiliated by nature, the weight of whose hand she feels heavily upon her; but, at the same time, elevated by dreams, presentiments, and superior intuitions, that man could never have, she has fascinated him, innocently bewitched him forever. He remains enchanted. And this is Society.

An imperious power, a charming tyranny, has prevented his stirring from her side. This ever-renewing crisis, this mystery of love and pain, from month to month, has kept him there. She has deprived him of the power of motion by a single sentence: "I love you still the more when I am sick!" . . .

They are called capricious. Nothing could be more untrue. They are, on the contrary, very regular, and submissive to the laws of nature. Knowing the state of the atmosphere, the date of the month, and, finally, the influence of these two things on a third, of which I shall speak hereafter, they are able to predict with more certainty than the ancient augurs. You can tell, almost to a certainty, what the woman's humor will be—sad or gay; what turn her thoughts, her desires, her dreams will take.

Of themselves they are very kind, gentle, and considerate to him upon whom they depend for support. Their sharpness, and little fits of anger, are nearly always the results of suffering. That man is a great fool who takes any notice of these. He should rather, at such times, care for her, attend to her, and sympathize with her the more.

Presently, they are themselves again; then they regret these sad moments, excuse themselves often with tears, throw their arms around your neck, and say: "You know it is not my fault."

Is this a transitory state, then? Not at all. Wherever woman does not blot out her sex by excessive labor (like our hardy peasant women, who, at an early age, make men of themselves), wherever she remains a woman, she is generally ailing at least one week out of four.

But the week that precedes that of the crisis is also a troublesome one. And into the eight or ten days which follow this week of pain, is prolonged a languor and a weakness, which formerly could not be defined, but which is now known to be the cicatrization of an interior wound, the real cause of all this tragedy. So that, in reality, 15 or 20 days out of 28 (we may say nearly always) woman is not only an invalid, but a wounded one. She ceaselessly suffers from love's eternal wound. . . .

It is the paradise of marriage that the man shall work for the woman; that he alone shall support her, take pleasure in enduring fatigue for her sake, and spare her the hardships of labor, and rude contact with the world.

He returns home in the evening, harassed, suffering from toil, mental or bodily, from the weariness of worldly things, from the baseness of men. But in his reception at home there is such an infinite kindness, a calm so intense, that he hardly believes in the cruel realities he has gone through all the day. "No," he says, "that could not have been; it was but an ugly dream. There is but one *real* thing in the world, and that is *you!*"

This is woman's mission (more important than generation even), to re-new the heart of man. Protected and nourished by the man, she in turn nourishes him with love.

In love is her true sphere of labor, the only labor that it is essential she should perform. It was that she should reserve herself entirely for this, that nature made her so incapable of performing the ruder sorts of earthly toil.

Man's business it is to earn money, hers to spend it: that is to say, to regulate the household expenditures, better than man would.

This renders him indifferent to all enjoyment that is bought, and makes it seem to him insipid. Why should he go elsewhere in quest of pleasure? What pleasure is there apart from the woman whom he loves? . . .

What we have just said about the rhythmical life of the woman affects her whole education, and makes it essentially different from that of the man.

Care must be taken to do nothing with her inopportunely, but to fol-low the suggestions of nature. If you do this carefully, she will aid you. What an advantage, for example, to commence every experiment of men-tal initiation in the ascending phase of her sanguine life, when the flood rises, and her sensibility is exalted with a more abundant flow, and a more generous tone! On the contrary, during her crisis, or the languor in which it leaves her, she should not be fatigued with new ideas, but should be left quietly to recover, to dream, to think over those she has already received.

This should be attended to by the prudent mother, by the wise in-structress, who commences the education of the young girl; and by the lover, the husband, who continues that of the young wife. The impregna-tion of the mind, as well as that of the body, demands that nothing be done but in season, at the most favorable time. For this there is needed a constant and unrelaxing watch over, a tender respect for, the beloved. No violence, no impatience; select her time, her day, her hour.

[*Woman* (1860)]

My dear sirs, the reason for which you will marry, the strongest motive for your hearts, is, as I told you, that:

Woman cannot live without man.

No more than the child without woman. All foundlings die; and does man live without woman? You yourselves have just said: Your life is

sombre and bitter. In the midst of amusements and vain feminine shadows, you possess neither wife, nor happiness, nor repose. You have
not the sure foundation, the harmonious equilibrium, so favorable to
productiveness.

Nature has bound up life within a triple and absolute tie: man, woman,
and child. Separately, they are sure to perish, and are only saved together.

All the disputes about the two sexes, and their opposing peculiarities,
go for nothing; we should put an end to them; we must not imitate Italy,
Poland, Ireland, and Spain, where the weakening of family ties, and solitary egotisms, have contributed so much to destroy the State. In the only
book of the age that contains a great poetic conception (the poem of the
Last Man), the author supposes the earth exhausted and the world about
to come to an end. But there is one sublime obstacle:

The world cannot come to an end while one man still loves. . . .

The true woman for a wife is she whose portrait I have painted in my
Book of *Love*—she who, simple and loving, having as yet received no
definite impress, shall least repel the modern thought, shall not beforehand be an enemy to science and to truth. I prefer that she should be
poor, and isolated, with few family connexions—her position and education are secondary matters. Every French woman is born a queen or is on
the point of becoming so.

As a wife, the simple woman, who can be somewhat instructed, and as
a daughter, the confiding woman, who can at once be taught by her father: these will break that vicious circle in which we revolve, in which
woman prevents us from creating women.

With so excellent a wife, sharing, in heart at least, the faith of her husband, the latter, following the very easy path of nature, will maintain over
the child an incredible ascendency of authority and tenderness. The
daughter does so trust in her father! He may make of her what he will.
The strength of this second love, so lofty and so pure, will create in her
the woman, the adorable ideal of grace and wisdom, by which alone family and society are to be restored in the future.

I am not now writing a book on education, and should not stop to
discuss general views, but proceed to my special subject, *the education of
the daughter*. Let us have done then with what is common between the
girl and boy, and dwell on the difference.

It is profound, and this it is:

The education of the boy, in the modern sense, aims to *organize a
force*, an effective and productive force, to create a creator; which is the
modern man.

The education of the girl is to produce harmony, to *harmonize a
religion*.

Woman is a religion.

Her destiny is such, that the higher she stands as religious poetry, the
more effective will she be in common and practical life.

The utility of man, being in creative, productive power, may exist apart
from the ideal; an art which yields noble products may sometimes have

the effect of vulgarizing the artist, who may himself retain very little of the beauty he infuses into his works.

There is never anything like this in woman.

The woman of prosaic heart, she who is not a living power, a harmony to exalt a husband, to educate a child, to constantly sanctify and ennoble a family, has failed in her mission, and will exert no influence even in what is vulgar.

A mother, seated by the cradle of her daughter, should say to herself: "I have here the war or the peace of the world, what will trouble the hearts of men or give them the tranquillity and high harmony of God.

"She it is who, if I die, will at twelve years of age, on my tomb, raise her father on her little wings, and carry him back to heaven. (See the Life of Manin.)

"She it is who, at sixteen, may with a word of proud enthusiasm, exalt a man far above himself, and make him cry, 'I *will* be great!'

"She it is who, at twenty, and at thirty, and all her life long, will renew her husband, every night, as he returns deadened by his labor, and make his wilderness of interests and cares blossom like the rose.

"She again, who, in the wretched days, when the heavens are dark, and everything is disenchanted, will bring God back to him, making him find and feel Him on her bosom."

To educate a daughter is to educate society itself. Society proceeds from the family, of which the wife is the living bond. To educate a daughter is a sublime and disinterested task; for you create her, O mother, only that she may leave you, and make your heart bleed. She is destined for another. She will live for others, not for you, not for herself; it is this relative character which places her higher than man, and makes her a religion. She is the flame of love, and the flame of the hearth; she is the cradle of the future, and she is the school, another cradle—in a word: *She is the altar.* . . .

The true happiness of the teacher is in finding himself surpassed by his pupil. Woman, constantly cultivated by man and enriched by his thought, soon believes; and some morning she finds herself superior to him.

She becomes superior to him, as well by these new elements as by her personal gifts, which without the inspirations she derives from man would scarcely have come to light. Melodious aspirations, and sensibility to nature, these were in her, but they have flourished by love. Add one gift (so high, that it is the all in all, that which chiefly distinguishes our race from others): a true and charming womanly heart, opulent with compassion, with knowledge to console all, the divinations of pity.

She is docile, she is modest, she is unconscious of her splendor; but at every moment it blazes forth. . . .

You are strong; she is divine—a daughter and a sister of nature. She leans upon your arm, and yet she has wings. She is feeble, she is in pain; and it is just when her beautiful languishing eyes bear witness that she suffers, that the dear sibyl soars to lofty heights and inaccessible summits. Who knows how she mounts thither?

Your tenderness has done much towards that. If she has this power, if as woman and mother, united with man, she possesses in the midst of marriage the sibylline virginity, it is because your anxious love, surrounding the dear treasure, has divided and distributed your life—for you, hard labor and the rude contacts of the world—for her, peace and love, maternity, art, and all the tender cares of domesticity.

How well you have done! and how grateful am I for it! Oh! woman, fragile globe of incomparable alabaster, wherein burns the lamp of God, one must care for thee well, bear thee with a pious hand, and guard thee closely in the warmth of his bosom.

It is by sharing with her the miseries of the special labor with which your days are occupied, dear workman, that you will preserve her in the nobleness which only children and women have—that amiable aristocracy of the human race. She is your nobleness, your own, to raise you above yourself. When you return from the forge, panting, fatigued with labor, she, young and fresh, pours over you her youth, brings the sacred wave of life to you, and makes you a god again, with a kiss. With so divine an object near you, you will not blindly follow the temptations which allure you from your rugged and narrow path. You will each moment feel the happy necessity of elevating and extending your conceptions, in order to follow your dear pupil whither you have elevated her. Your young friend, your scholar, as she modestly calls herself, will not permit you, O master, to shut yourself up in your avocation. She beseeches you every moment to come out from it, and aid her to remain in harmony with all that is noble and beautiful. To suffice for the humble needs of your little comrade, you will be forced to be great.

98. Jenny P. d'Héricourt (1860)

Several women have sharply criticised Michelet's "Love."

Why are intelligent women thus dissatisfied with so upright a man as Michelet?

Because to him woman is a perpetual invalid, who should be shut up in a gynœceum in company with a dairy maid, as fit company only for chickens and turkeys.

Now we, women of the west, have the audacity to contend that we are not invalids, and that we have a holy horror of the harem and the gynœceum.

Woman, *according to Michelet*, is a being of a nature opposite to that of man; a creature weak, *always wounded, exceedingly barometrical*, and, consequently, unfit for labor.

She is incapable of abstracting, of generalizing, of comprehending conscientious labors. She does not like to occupy herself with business, and she is destitute, in part, of judicial sense. But, in return, she is revealed all gentleness, all love, all grace, all devotion.

Created for man, she is the altar of his heart, his refreshment, his consolation. In her presence he gains new vigor, becomes inspirited, draws the strength necessary to the accomplishment of his high mission as worker, creator, organizer.

He should love her, watch over her, maintain her; be at once her father, her lover, her instructor, her priest, her physician, her nurse, and her waiting-maid.

When, at eighteen, a virgin in reason, heart and body, she is given to this husband, who should be twenty-eight, neither more nor less, he confines her in the country in a charming cottage, at a distance from her parents and friends, with the rustic maid that we just mentioned.

Why this sequestration in the midst of the nineteenth century, do you ask?

Because the husband can have no power over his wife in society, and can have full power over her in solitude. Now, it is necessary that he should have this full power over her, since it belongs to him to form her heart, to give her ideas, to sketch within her the incarnation of himself. For know, readers, that woman is destined to reflect her husband, more and more, until the last shade of difference, namely, that which is maintained by the separation of the sexes, shall be at last effaced by death, and unity in love be thus effected.

At the end of half a score years of housekeeping, the wife is permitted to cross the threshold of the gynœceum, and to enter the world, or *the great Battle of Life*. Here she will meet more than one danger; but she will escape them all if she keeps the oath she has taken *to make her husband her confessor*. . . . It is evident that Michelet respects the rights of the soul. . . .

You see, my readers, that in Michelet's book, woman is created for man; without him she would be nothing; he it is who pronounces the *fiat lux* in her intellect; he it is who makes her in his image, as God made man in his own.

Accepting the Biblical Genesis, we women can appeal from Adam to God; for it was not Adam, but God, who created Eve. Admitting the Genesis of Michelet, there is no pretext, no excuse for disobedience; woman must be subordinate to man and must yield to him, for she belongs to him as the work to the workman, as the vessel to the potter.

The book of Michelet and the two studies of Proudhon on woman, are but two forms of the same thought. The sole difference that exists between these gentlemen is, that the first is as sweet as honey, and the second as bitter as wormwood.

Nevertheless, I prefer the rude assailant to the poet; for insults and blows rouse us to rebel and to clamor for liberty, while compliments lull us to sleep and make us weakly endure our chains.

It would be somewhat cruel to be harsh to Michelet, who piques himself on love and poetry, and, consequently, is thin skinned; we will therefore castigate him only over the shoulders of M. Proudhon, who may be cannonaded with red-hot shot; and we will content ourselves with criticising in his book what is not found in that of Proudhon.

The two chief pillars of the book on Love are,

First, that woman is a wounded, weak, barometrical, constantly diseased being;

Second, that the woman belongs to the man who has fructified and incarnated himself in her; a proposition proved by the resemblance of the children of the wife to the husband, whoever may be the father.

Michelet and his admirers and disciples do not dispute that the only good method of proving the truth of a principle, or the legitimateness of a generalization, is *verification by facts*; neither do they dispute that to make general rules of exceptions, to create imaginary laws, and to take these pretended laws for the basis of argument, belongs only to the aberrations of the Middle Age, profoundly disdained by men of earnest thought and severe reason. Let us apply these data unsparingly to the two principal affirmations of M. Michelet.

It is a principle in biology that *no physiological condition is a morbid condition*; consequently, the monthly crisis peculiar to woman is not a disease, but a normal phenomenon, the derangement of which causes disturbance in the general health. Woman, therefore, is not an invalid because her sex is subject to a peculiar law. Can it be said that woman is wounded because she is subjected to a periodical fracture, the cicatrice of which is almost imperceptible? By no means. It would be absurd to call a man perpetually wounded who should take a fancy to scratch the end of his finger every month.

Michelet is too well informed to render it necessary for me to tell him that the normal hemorrhage does not proceed from this wound of the ovary, about which he makes so much ado, but from a congestion of the gestative organ.

Are women ill on the recurrence of the law peculiar to their sex?

Very exceptionally, yes; but in the indolent classes, in which transgressions in diet, the lack of an intelligent physical education, and a thousand causes which I need not point out here, render women valetudinarians.

Generally, no. All our vigorous peasant women, our robust laundresses, who stand the whole time with their feet in water, our workwomen, our tradeswomen, our teachers, our servant-maids, who attend with alacrity to their business and pleasures, experience no uncomfortableness, or at most, very little.

Michelet, therefore, has not only erred in erecting a physiological law into a morbid condition, but he has also sinned against rational method by making general rules of a few exceptions, and by proceeding from this generalization, contradicted by the great majority of facts, to construct a system of subjection.

If it is of the faculty of abstracting and generalizing that Michelet, as he employs it, robs woman, we can only congratulate her on the deprivation.

Not only is woman diseased, says Michelet, in consequence of a bio-

logical law, but she is always diseased; she has uterine affections, hereditary tendencies, which may assume a terrible form in her sex, etc.

We would ask Michelet whether he considers his own sex as always
diseased because it is corroded by cancer, disfigured by eruptions, tortured as much as ours by hereditary tendencies; for hereditary tendencies
torture it as much as ours, and it is decimated and enfeebled far more
fearfully by shameful diseases, the fruits of its excesses.

Of what, then, is Michelet thinking, in laying such stress on the diseases of women in the face of the quite as numerous diseases of men? . . .

Michelet will pardon me this short lesson in method. I should not presume to give it to him, were not men repeating, like well-trained parrots,
after him and Proudhon, that woman is destitute of high intellectual faculties, that she is unsuited to science, that she has no comprehension of
method, and other absurdities of like weight.

Allegations such as these place women in a wholly exceptional position, with respect to courtesy and reserve: they owe no consideration to
those who deny them these; their most important business at the present
time is to prove to men that they deceive themselves, and that they are
deceived; that a woman is fully capable of teaching the chief among them
how a law is discovered, how its reality is verified, how, and on what conditions we have a right to believe, and to style ourselves, rational, and
rationalists. . . .

Can you prove to me, a woman, that I desire to possess knowledge differently from you?

Take care! disciple of liberty, you have not the right to think and to
wish in my place. I have, like you, an intellect and a free will, to which
you are bound, by your principles, to pay sovereign respect. Now I forbid
you to speak for any woman; I forbid you in the name of what you call
the rights of the soul. . . .

The women who ask to be free, great, mistaken poet, are those who are
conscious of their dignity, of the true rôle of their sex in humanity; those
who desire that the women who follow them in the career of labor should
no longer be obliged *to live by man*, because to live by him is at least to
prostitute their dignity, and almost always, their whole person. They
wish that woman should be the equal of man, in order to love him holily,
to devote herself without calculation, to cease to deceive him or to rule
him by artifice, and to become to him a useful auxiliary, instead of a servant or a toy. They know our influence over you; slaves, we can only
debase you; at present, we render you cowardly, selfish, and dishonest;
we sent you out every morning, like vultures, upon society, to provide for
our foolish expenses or to endow our children; we, women of emancipation, are unwilling that our sex should longer play this odious rôle, and
be, through its slavery, an instrument of demoralization and of social
degradation—and this you impute to us as a crime!

Ah! I do not believe it; you yourself will say that I ought not to believe it.

Looking from a deplorably narrow stand point, you fancied that you saw all woman-kind in a few valetudinarians, your kind heart was moved for them, and you sought to protect them. Had you looked far and high, you would have seen the workers of thought and muscle; you would have comprehended that inequality is to them a source of corruption and suffering.

Then, in your lofty and glowing style, you would have written, not this book of Love which repels all intelligent and reflective women, but a great and beautiful work to demand the right of half the human race.

The misfortune, the irreparable misfortune, is that instead of climbing to the mountain top to look at every moving thing under the vast horizon, you have shut yourself up in a narrow valley, where, seeing nothing but pale violets, you have concluded that every flower must be also a pale violet; whilst Nature has created a thousand other species, on the contrary, strong and vigorous, with a right, like you, to earth, air, water and sunshine.

Whatever may be your love, your kindness and your good intentions towards woman, your book would be immensely dangerous to the cause of her liberty, if men were in a mood to relish your ethics: but they will remain as they are; and the dignity of woman, kept waking by their brutality, their despotism, their desertion, their foul morals, will not be lulled to sleep under the fresh, verdant, alluring and treacherously perfumed foliage of this manchineel tree, called the book of *Love.* . . .

We demand our place at your side, gentlemen, because identity of species gives us the right to occupy it.

We demand our right, because the inferiority in which we are kept is one of the most active causes of the decay of morals.

We demand our right, because we are persuaded that woman has to set her stamp on Science, Philosophy, Justice and Politics.

We demand our right, lastly, because we are convinced that the general questions, the lack of solution of which threatens our modern civilization with ruin, can only be resolved by the co-operation of woman delivered from her fetters and left free in her genius.

Is it not a great proof of our insanity, our *impurity*, gentlemen, that we feel this ardent desire to check the corruption of morals, and to labor for the triumph of Justice, the coming of the reign of Duty and Reason, the establishment of an order of things in which humanity, worthier and happier, shall pursue its glorious destinies without the accompaniment of cannon or the shedding of blood?

Is it not because the advocates of emancipation are *impure women whom sin has rendered mad, beings incapable of comprehending Justice and conscientious works?*

Gentlemen, we will conclude.

Though that were true which I deny; that woman is inferior to you; though that were true which *facts* prove false; that she can perform none of the functions which you perform, that she is fit only for maternity and the household, she would be none the less your equal in right, because right is based neither on superiority of faculties nor on that of the functions which proceed from them, but on identity of species.

A human being, like you, having, like you, intellect, will, free will and various aptitudes, woman has the right, like you, to be free and autonomous, to develop her faculties freely, to exercise her activity freely; to mark out her path, to reduce her to subjection, as you do, is therefore a violation of Human Right in the person of woman—an odious abuse of force.

From the stand point of facts, this violation of right takes the form of grievous inconsistency; for we find many women far superior to the majority of men; whence it follows that right is granted to those who ought not to have it, according to your doctrine, and refused to those who ought to possess it, according to the same doctrine, since they make good their claim to the qualities requisite.

We find that you accord right to qualities and functions, *because the individual is a man*, and that you cease to recognize it in the same case, *because the individual is a woman*.

Yet you boast of your lofty reason—yet you boast of possessing the sense of justice!

Take care, gentlemen! Our rights have the same foundation as yours: in denying the former, you deny the latter in principle.

A word more to you, pretended disciples of the doctrines of '89, and we have done. Do you know why so many women took part with our Revolution, armed the men, and rocked their children to the song of the *Marseillaise*! It was because they thought they saw under the Declaration of the rights of men and citizens, the declaration of the rights of women and female citizens.

When the Assembly took it upon itself to undeceive them, by lacking logic with respect to them, and closing their meetings, they abandoned the Revolution, and you know what ensued.

Do you know why, in 1848, so many women, especially among the people, declared themselves for the Revolution? It was because they hoped that this Revolution would be more consistent with respect to them than the former had been.

When, in their senseless arrogance and lack of intelligence, the representatives not only forbid them to assemble, but *drove* them from the assemblies of men, the women abandoned the Revolution by detaching their husbands and sons from it, and you know what ensued.

Do you comprehend at last?

I tell you truly; all your struggles are in vain, if woman does not go with you.

An order of things may be established by a *coup de main*, but it is only maintained by the adhesion of majorities; and these majorities, gentlemen, are formed by us women, through the influence that we possess over men, through the education that we give them with our milk.

We have it in our power to inspire them from their cradles with love, hatred or indifference for certain principles; in this is our strength; and you are blind not to comprehend that if man is on one side and woman on the other, humanity is condemned to weave Penelope's web.

Gentlemen, woman is ripe for civil liberty, and we declare to you that we shall henceforth regard whoever shall rise against our lawful claim as an enemy of progress and of the Revolution; while we shall rank among the friends of progress and of the Revolution, those who declare themselves in favor of our civil emancipation, SHOULD THEY BE YOUR ADVERSARIES?

If you refuse to listen to our lawful demands, we shall accuse you before posterity of the crime with which you reproach the holders of slaves.

We shall accuse you before posterity of having denied the faculties of woman, because you feared her competition.

We shall accuse you before posterity of having refused her justice, because you wished to make her your servant and plaything. We shall accuse you before posterity of being enemies of right and progress.

And our accusation will remain standing and living before future generations who, more enlightened, more just, more moral than you, will turn away their eyes with disdain and contempt from the tomb of their fathers. . . .

Progressive women, to you, I address my last words, Listen in the name of the general good, in the name of your sons and your daughters.

You say: the manners of our time are corrupt; the laws concerning our sex need reform.

It is true; but do you think that to verify the evil suffices to cure it?

You say: so long as woman shall be a minor in the city, the state and marriage, she will be so in social labor; she will be forced to be supported by man; that is to debase him while humbling herself.

It is true; but do you believe that to verify these things suffices to remedy our abasement?

You say: the education that both sexes receive is deplorable in view of the destiny of humanity.

It is true; but do you believe that to affirm this suffices to improve, to transform the method of education?

Will words, complaints and protestations have power to change any of these things?

It is not to lament over them that is needed; it is to act.

It is not merely to demand justice and reform that is needed; it is to labor ourselves for reform; it is to prove *by our works* that we are worthy to obtain justice; it is to take possession resolutely of the contested place; it is, in a word, to have intellect, courage and activity.

Upon whom then will you have a right to count, if you abandon yourselves?

Upon men? Your carelessness and silence have in part discouraged those who maintained your right; it is much if they defend you against those who, to oppress you, call to their aid every species of ignorance, every species of despotism, every selfish passion, all the paradoxes which they despise when their own sex is in question.

You are insulted, you are outraged, you are denied, or you are blamed in order that you may be reduced to subjection, and it is much if your indignation is roused thereby!

When will you be ashamed of the part to which you are condemned?

When will you respond to the appeal that generous and intelligent men have made to you?

When will you cease to be masculine photographs, and resolve to complete the revolution of humanity by finally making the word of woman heard in Religion, in Justice, in Politics and in Science?

What are we to do, you say?

What are you to do, ladies? Well! what is done by women believing. Look at those who have given their soul to a dogma; they form organizations, teach, write, act on their surroundings and on the rising generation in order to secure the triumph of the faith that has the support of their conscience. Why do not you do as much as they?

Your rivals write books stamped with supernaturalism and individualistic morality; why do you not write those that bear the stamp of rationalism, of solidary morality and of a holy faith in Progress?

Your rivals found educational institutions and train up professors in order to gain over the new generation to their dogmas and their practices; why do not you do as much for the benefit of the new ideas?

Your rivals organize industrial associations; why do not you imitate them?

Would not what is lawful to them be so to you.

Could a government which professes to revive the principles of '89, and which is the offspring of Revolutionary right, entertain the thought of fettering the direct heirs of the principles laid down by '89, while leaving those free to act who are more or less their enemies? Can any one of you admit such a possibility?

What are we to do?

You are to establish a journal to maintain your claims.

You are to appoint an encyclopedic committee to draw up a series of treatises on the principal branches of human knowledge for the enlightenment of women and the people.

You are to found a Polytechnic Institute for women.

You are to aid your sisters of the laboring classes to organize themselves in trades associations on economical principles more equitable than those of the present time.

You are to facilitate the return to virtue of the lost women who ask you for aid and counsel.

You are to labor with all your might for the reform of educational methods.

Yet, in the face of a task so complicated, you ask: what are we to do?

Ah, ye women who have attained majority, arise, if ye have heart and courage!

Arise, and let those among you who are the most intelligent, the most instructed, and who have the most time and liberty constitute an *Apostleship of women.*

Around this Apostleship, let all the women of Progress be ranged, that each one may serve the common cause according to her means.

And remember, remember above all things, that *Union is strength.*

The Debate Reaches Russia

SOURCES

99. M. L. Mikhailov, "Women: Their Education and Significance in the Family and in Society," *Sochineniia* [Memoirs], ed. B. P. Koz'min et al., III (Moscow, 1958), 426-30. Originally published in *Sovremennik*, 1860. The editors are indebted to Professor Richard Stites, Georgetown University, for his translation of this article from the Russian and for background information.

100. N. G. Chernyshevsky, *What Is to Be Done? Tales About New People* [*Chto Delat'?*]. Tr. Benjamin Tucker, revised and abridged by Ludmilla B. Turkevich (New York, 1961), pp. 292-93, 293-94, 294-95, 296-99. Originally published in *Sovremennik*, 1863.

Mikhail Larionovich Mikhailov (1829-1865) was a minor Russian poet and publicist who gained notoriety in the 1860's as a revolutionary. In 1853 he had fallen in love with his best friend's wife, Ludmilla Shelgunova, who had been raised by her mother to be an independent woman. Mikhailov became seriously interested in the woman question in the late 1850's, when he went abroad with the Shelgunovs. While in Paris he became closely associated with the *Revue Philosophique* and was particularly influenced by the arguments of Jenny d'Héricourt (Doc. 98), a friend of Shelgunova. Mikhailov was prompted to undertake a synthesis of the French debate for Russian readers after encountering the works of Michelet and Proudhon printed earlier in this chapter. After refuting their arguments with counter-arguments similar to those of Héricourt and Harriet Taylor Mill (he subsequently published a translation of the latter's 1851 article, Doc. 88), Mikhailov laid out his own program for emancipating Russian women of the educated classes. A half-dozen of his articles, dealing wholly or in part with this issue, appeared in influential Russian journals, especially *Sovremennik* [The Contemporary] during the early 1860's. The most important of these is excerpted here. Mikhailov's optimistic prescriptions—for educational reform, vocational opportunities, and marriage reform—though moderate by Western European standards, broke new ground in Russia where, as historian Richard Stites has shown, his synthesis "established [the woman question] as a major theme in the ideological constellation of the Russian intelligentsia." But in Russia, such ideas were still viewed with great suspicion. Indeed, not long after these articles were published, Mikhailov was arrested and imprisoned for writing a revolutionary proclamation; in 1865 he died in Siberia, a martyr to the cause of social change.

In contrast to his contemporary Mikhailov, the radical social critic Nikolai Gavrilovich Chernyshevsky (1828-1889) did not join the debate about women until after his arrest in 1863 for other political activities. The son of a provincial priest, he had studied at a Russian university and had become intensely interested in the revolutions of 1848 further to the west. He was familiar with French discussion of the woman question (notably with the works of George Sand and Charles Fourier) and had tried to implement certain innovations in his personal life; in his opposition to the double standard he had made a pact with his wife to allow her full personal—including sexual—freedom. In prison Chernyshevsky began to draft his realistic novel, *Chto Delat'?* (What Is to Be Done?), which is excerpted here. In the novel, which can be said to take up the question where Almqvist (Doc. 38) left off, the young heroine Vera Pavlovna struggles to obtain personal freedom and economic independence for herself and other women (though in the conspicuous absence of children) through a series of confrontations with the orthodoxy, autocracy, and repressive morality that characterized Russian society under Alexander II. Chernyshevsky was, like Proudhon, an ardent materialist; unlike Proudhon, he turned this attitude to women's account. Consequently, he underscored the subject of eroticism in human affairs—an emphasis that was considered scandalous not only in his time but ever since. *Chto Delat'?* became a revolutionary classic, inspiring generations of educated and disaffected young Russians, and providing a model of a counter-cultural lifestyle that many of them copied.

---

99. M. L. Mikhailov (1860)

Early upbringing and primary education, as well as education in the broadest sense, general and specialized, should be the same in all essential respects for both sexes. The same concern must be shown for the mental growth of both boys and girls. The deliberate elimination from female education of the established areas of knowledge would mean in effect limiting the intellectual capabilities of a gifted mind. All knowledge recognized as useful for a man must also be seen as useful for a woman. The individual capabilities of each will determine the stage for his or her participation in scientific achievements and in the affairs of social life. But in order for a person to take up an occupation suited to his or her abilities, and to find meaning and happiness in life in it, requires full freedom of development. This is true for both sexes. To designate a woman from childhood on for a specific and limited role is as absurd as planning a career in engineering or medicine from childhood on for a boy who, if allowed to develop freely according to his ability, might be more talented in agronomy or history. By eliminating the uncivilized division of knowledge into masculine and feminine, we must also eliminate external divisions—that is, segregation. Let boys study together with girls; let education itself prepare them for common endeavors in life. There can be no moral turpitude here; only a diseased imagination could suspect the purity of relations between children and fear some kind of danger in them. According to this line of thought, even the interaction between brothers and sisters would have to be considered harmful, and they would have to be separated by a high wall as soon as they had begun to stand up and chatter.

Higher education, however it might be organized, must be made available to women and men on an equal basis. Let the university, the academy, and every specialized institution of learning accept both sexes as pupils and students, according to the aspirations and special demands of each. Let there be an arena open to all talents, whoever may possess those talents—persons in skirts or persons in trousers. Here threats to public morality would be completely out of place. The continuous segregation of the sexes from childhood on encourages most of all an abnormal development of the imagination, and with it sensuality and immorality. The best examples of this are the closed boarding schools [institutes] for girls. The stupidest and most barbarous notions about human relations are formed behind their walls—notions that bring discord, unpleasantness, and even misery into life for a long time. The continuous segregation of the sexes during the best years of youth inhibits both masculine and feminine feelings from strengthening into genuine affection and from concentrating on a single goal that is most satisfactory to our needs. The impermanence of our affections, the light-heartedness of our relations is nothing more than a serious search for enduring satisfaction by hearts that are unacquainted with an environment in which such satisfaction might readily be found.

In university classrooms lifetime friendships are made, based on identity of aspirations, equality of intellectual and moral growth, and similarity of natures. Add to this the natural attraction between the sexes— and you have a durable foundation for a rational and freely-contracted union for mutually interesting activity and mutual joy. Fear not for young boys and girls bound by such ties; they know how to guard themselves against those distractions that, for some people, are so harmful to the soul. Pure love is inseparable from mutual respect. Remember, too, that they are bound by something more solid than mere sexual attraction, an attraction that plays such an important role among men and women who have been isolated from the opposite sex. Among the kind of people we are talking about, the sexual dimension is appreciably moderated by other mutual sympathies. Precocious physical development, which so distresses some people, will gradually be brought within reasonable limits through the system of upbringing I am suggesting; children and youth with depraved imaginations and abnormal demands on life will become rare and pitiable exceptions.

Another malady of our society—marriages based on financial need or on calculation (often very uncalculated)—would also be impossible when both partners have a better and deeper understanding of their obligations and advantages as well as of their relationship to society. People fear that such an understanding, issuing from a free and rational education, would be a cause of vice and moral corruption; yet their moral sensibilities are not offended by the prevailing state of affairs, which allows marriages between worn-out old men and sixteen-year-old girls, or "good matches" between young people who hardly know each other.

Thus, expanding education for women is not enough. It is necessary to grant women free access to all sorts of occupations that are now the exclusive preserve of men. Otherwise, education itself will not achieve its purpose and will remain dead capital for society and, often, a burdensome advantage for a woman who finds no chance of putting her gifts and her knowledge to use. There is no need to fear that, given a free choice, woman will take it into her head to seize upon something unsuitable to her nature and to her maternal obligations, which at a certain time do require her particular—indeed exclusive—attention. It can probably be assumed, for example, that there will be very few women of a military bent, thirsting for bayonets and blood. But even if there were many, no harm would be done: no doubt, experience would eventually limit their numbers. Every adult member of society must be admitted to labor in industry, in science, and in art. If this is not yet the case, we are nevertheless headed toward such an order of things. This is evident from the entire movement of present-day society. Moreover, recognizing woman as a member of society—as we do in words—means to grant her all its rights. How and to what extent she will use these rights is not really our concern. She demands these rights as a conscious human being, and we are obliged to grant them to her, just as we will grant them sooner or later to the proletarian and to the negro slave. One thing is certain: her activities will be directed, to the same extent as man's, toward the maintenance and development of personal, family, and social interests.

By solving the problem of woman's participation in all these civil rights and obligations which until now only man has enjoyed, her sexual role—that of motherhood—will in no way be harmed. With a proper system of family relations, marriages will not take place so early, to the detriment of the physical and moral powers of both mother and child. With better moral development, childbirth will occur in the life of a woman only when she is at full physical maturity, not in her later years of declining strength. The average number of children per woman should not exceed four or five, and thus the period of pregnancy, childbirth, and nursing would occupy no more than eight or ten years in her life. Even if we admit that these years are absolutely unsuitable for activity in anything other than household concerns, even if we recognize them as years of suffering and every sort of weakness—mental, moral, physical—even then our demands are not fundamentally unreasonable. Can we sacrifice the freedom and happiness of a woman's entire life for the sake of the eight-to-ten years in which she will not be able to exercise them? How, by whom, and to what extent the woman must be supported in these years—even if they are emphatically judged to be unproductive ones—this is a question of practical application, unsuited for discussion in these general remarks. But there can be no doubt that its solution would appear as a matter of course after the family is reorganized along lines that flow from a healthy-minded view of things.

According to the conditions we have outlined above, marriage would become a union founded on exalted moral lines, the interest of wives and husbands would coincide, their activity would be directed toward a common goal, and the prevailing instability of marital relations would become almost impossible. The primary result of a new order must be the upbringing of the next generation, one which is pure in morals and in harmony with the general good. From its earliest years, the child will observe in the relations between his parents the harmony of rights, obligations, and actions, which—like a bright ideal of the future happiness of society—is beginning to prevail in the minds of the best people of our time, though often only after an arduous struggle with the prevailing evil and falsity.

100. N. G. Chernyshevsky (1863)

. . . Women have always been told that they are weak, and so they feel weak and to all intents and purposes are weak. You know instances where men really in good health have been seen to waste away and die from the single thought that they were going to weaken and die. But there are also instances of this in the conduct of great masses of people, entire humanity. . . .

"True, Sásha. We are weak because we consider ourselves so. But it seems to me that there is still another cause. I have us two in mind. Does it not seem to you that I changed a great deal during the two weeks when you did not see me?"

"Yes, you grew very thin and pale."

"It is precisely that which is revolting to my pride when I remember that no one noticed you grow thin or pale, though you suffered and struggled as much as I. How did you do it?"

"This is the reason, then, why these lines about Kátya, who escapes sorrow through labor, have made such an impression on you! I endured struggle and suffering with reasonable ease, because I had not much time to think about them. During the time that I devoted to them I suffered horribly, but my urgent daily duties forced me to forget them the greater part of the time. I had to prepare my lessons and attend to my patients. In spite of myself I rested during that time from my bitter thoughts. On the rare days when I had leisure, I felt my strength leaving me. It seems to me that, if I had abandoned myself for a week to my thoughts, I should have gone mad."

"That's it, exactly. Of late I have seen that the origin of the difference between us was there. One must have work that cannot be neglected or postponed, and then one is incomparably securer against sorrow."

"But you had a great deal of work too."

"My household duties, to be sure, but I was not obliged to attend to them, and often, when my sadness was too strong, I neglected them to abandon myself to my thoughts; one always abandons that which is least important. As soon as one's feelings get firm possession of them, these drive all petty cares out of the mind. I have lessons; these are more important. My main support then came from Dmítry's work as it now comes from yours. The lessons allow me to flatter myself that I am independent, and are by no means useless. But then I could get along without them.

"Then I tried, in order to drive away tormenting thoughts, to busy myself in the shop more than usual. But I did it only by an effort of will. I understood well enough that my presence in the shop was necessary only for an hour or an hour and a half, and that, if I stayed longer, I was tying myself down to a fatigue that, though certainly useful, was not at all indispensable. . . . What we need in such cases is a personal, urgent occupation, upon which our life depends; such an occupation, considering my feelings and condition, would weigh more with me than all the impulses of passion; it alone could serve to support me in a struggle against an omnipotent passion; it alone gives strength and rest. I want such an occupation."

"You are right, my friend," said Kirsánov, warmly, kissing his wife, whose eyes sparkled with animation. "To think that it hadn't occurred to me before, when it would have been so simple; I didn't even notice it! Yes, Vérochka, no one can think for another. If you wish to be comfortable, think for yourself of yourself; no one can take your place. To love as I love, and not to have understood all this before you explained it to me! But," he continued, laughing, and still kissing his wife, "why do you think this occupation necessary now? Are you becoming amorously inclined towards any one?"

Véra Pávlovna began to laugh heartily, and for some minutes mad laughter prevented them from speaking.

"Yes, we can laugh at that now," she said, at last: "both of us can now be sure that nothing of the kind will ever happen to either of us. But seriously, do you know what I am thinking about now? Though my love for Dmítry was not the love of a completely developed woman, neither did he love me in the way in which we understand love. His feeling for me was a mixture of strong friendship with the fire of amorous passion. He had a great friendship for me, but his amorous transports needed but a woman for their satisfaction, not me personally. No, that was not love. Did he care much about my thoughts? No, no more than I did about his. There was no real love between us."

"You are unjust to him, Vérochka."

"No, Sásha, it is really so. Between us it is useless to praise him. We both know very well in what high esteem we hold him; it is vain for him to say that it would have been easy to separate me from him; it is not so; you said in the same way that it was easy for you to struggle against your passion. Yet, however sincere his words and yours, they must not be understood or construed literally.

"Oh! my friend, I understand how much you suffered. And this is how I understand it."

"Vérochka, you stifle me. Confess that, besides the force of sentiment, you also wanted to show me your muscular force. How strong you are, indeed! But how could you be otherwise with such a chest?"

"My dear Sásha . . .

"But you did not let me talk business, Sásha," began Véra Pávlovna, when, two hours later, they sat down to tea.

"I did not let you talk? Was it my fault?"

"Certainly."

"Who began the indulgence?"

"Are you not ashamed to say that?"

"What?"

"That I began the *indulgence*. Fie! the idea of thus compromising a modest woman on the plea of coldness!"

"Indeed! Do you not preach equality? Why not equality of initiative as well?"

"Ha, ha, ha! a fine argument! But would you dare to accuse me of being illogical? Do I not try to maintain equality in initiative also? I take now the initiative of continuing our serious conversation, which we have too thoroughly forgotten."

"Take it, if you will, but I refuse to follow you, and I take the initiative of continuing to forget it. Give me your hand."

"But we must finish our talk, Sásha."

"We shall have time enough tomorrow. Now, you see, I am absorbed in an analysis of this hand."

"Sásha, let's finish our conversation of yesterday. We must do so, because I am getting ready to go with you, and you must know why," said Véra Pávlovna the next morning.

"You are coming with me?"

"Certainly. You asked me, Sásha, why I wanted a job upon which my life should depend, which I should look upon as seriously as you on yours, which should be as interesting as yours, and which should require as much attention as yours requires. I want this job, dearest, because I am very proud. When I think that during my days of trial my feelings became so visible in my person that others could analyze them, I am thoroughly ashamed. I do not speak of my sufferings. You had to struggle and suffer no less than I, and you triumphed where I was conquered. I want to be as strong as you, your equal in everything. And I have found the way; I have thought a great deal since we left each other yesterday, and I have found it all alone; you were unwilling to aid me with your advice; so much the worse for you. It is too late now. Yes, Sásha, you may be very anxious about me, my dear friend, but how happy we shall be if I am successful!"

Véra Pávlovna had just thought of an occupation which, under Kirsánov's guidance and her hand in his, she could engage in successfully. . . . Kirsánov does not wait for his wife to ask him to participate in all that she does. He is as interested in everything that is dear to her as she is in everything that relates to him.

From this new life Véra Pávlovna derives new strength, and what formerly seemed to her as if it would never leave the realms of the ideal now appears entirely within reach.

As for her thoughts, this is the order in which they came to her:

"Almost all the paths of civil life are formally closed to us, and those which are not closed by formal obstacles are closed by practical difficulties. Only the family is left us. What occupation can we engage in, outside of the family? That of a governess is almost the only one; perhaps we have one other resource—that of giving lessons (such lessons as are left after the men have chosen). But we all rush into this single path and stifle there. We are too numerous to find independence in it. There are so many to choose from that no one needs us. Who could care to be a governess? When any one wants one, he is besieged by ten, a hundred, or even more applicants, each trying to get the place to the detriment of the others.

"No, until women launch out into a greater number of careers, they will not enjoy independence. It is difficult, to be sure, to open a new road. But I occupy an especially favorable position for doing it. I should be ashamed not to profit by it. We are not prepared for serious duties. For my part, I do not know how far a guide is indispensable to me in order to confront them. But I do know that every time I need him I shall find him, and that he will always take great pleasure in helping me.

"Public prejudice has closed to us such paths of independent activity as the law has not forbidden us to enter. But I can enter whichever of these paths I choose, provided I am willing to brave the usual gossip. Which shall I choose? My husband is a doctor; he devotes all his leisure time to me. With such a man it would be easy for me to attempt to follow the medical profession.

"Indeed, it is very important that there should be women-physicians. They would be very useful to persons of their own sex. It is much easier for a woman to talk to another woman than to a man. How much distress, suffering, and death would thus be averted! The experiment must be tried."

Véra Pávlovna finished the conversation with her husband by putting on her hat to follow him to the hospital, where she wished to try her nerves and see if she could stand the sight of blood and whether she would be capable of pursuing the study of anatomy. In view of Kirsánov's position in the hospital, there certainly would be no obstacles in the way of this attempt.

I have already compromised Véra Pávlovna several times from the poetical standpoint; I have not concealed the fact, for instance, that she dined every day, and generally with a good appetite, and that further she took tea twice a day. But I have now reached a point where, in spite of the depravity of my tastes, I am seized with scruples, and timidly I ask myself: Would it not be better to conceal this circumstance? What will be thought of a woman capable of studying medicine?

What coarse nerves, what a hard heart, she must have! She is not a woman, she is a butcher. Nevertheless, remembering that I do not set up my characters as ideal types, I calm myself: let them judge as they will of the coarseness of Véra Pávlovna's nature; how can that concern me? She is coarse? Well! so be it.

Consequently I calmly state that she found a vast difference between idle contemplation of matters and active work on them for the good of one's own self and of others. Indeed, whoever is at work has no time to be frightened and feel repugnance or disgust. So Véra Pávlovna studies medicine, and I number among my acquaintances one of those who introduced this novelty among us. She felt transformed by the study, and she said to herself: In a few years I shall get a foothold.

That is a great thought. There is no complete happiness without complete independence. Poor women that you are, how few of you enjoy this happiness!

PART IV

Evolution, Education, and Economics, 1860-1880

B Y 1860 WOMEN'S CHALLENGE to patriarchy was fully mounted on the basis of their "equality in difference." Meanwhile the defenders of patriarchal social order had begun to formulate a new set of counter-arguments, which turned the arguments for equality-in-difference to their own advantage. As we have seen in the writings of Michelet, a main theme in the counter-argument was to acknowledge women's moral superiority and then to insist on its being subjected to male control. This approach would be further bolstered by evolutionary theorists building on the work of Darwin.

In the 1860's the counter-argument began to appear in the developing world of secular scholarship. The reformulators of opposition to women's emancipation no longer resorted to Scripture and the authority of the church, but spoke a new authoritative language. As scholars in the newly professionalized (yet overlapping) specialties of history, anthropology, and sociology, as well as biology and physiology, investigated the laws and customs of earlier and contemporary societies, they found the family and, therefore, the position of women, to be a central concern. Some of them found too that women's subjection could seemingly be justified by their discoveries. Men with university training and the leisure to pursue research lectured to audiences that were awed by their learning and respectful of their conclusions—surely an unfair advantage in an age where women were not even admitted to university studies, as some of them were quick to point out. The historians Henry Sumner Maine and J.-J. Bachofen (Docs. 101, 102), the biologist Charles Darwin, and the sociologist Herbert Spencer (Docs. 110, 112), who unhesitatingly applied Darwin's theories of natural selection to explain the course of European development and to emphasize the divergence of sexual spheres in the nineteenth century, represented a new current of thinking that permeated intellectual discourse during this period; it also included the contributions of such full-time "amateurs" as the engineer-turned-sociologist

Frédéric Le Play in France and the lawyer-anthropologist Lewis Henry Morgan in the United States.[1]

Not all male scholars—even those who accepted the evolutionists' argument that men and women were becoming increasingly different from one another—devoted themselves to proving the necessity of subjugating women. One such scholar was the French physiologist Paul Broca (Doc. 111), who had studied the respective brain size of women and men among prehistoric peoples. The main thrust of the discussion by most of the scientists was, however, to counter demands of women and their male supporters for women's rights wherever such demands challenged the prerogatives of men. This is apparent in the transatlantic controversy over sex in education, set in motion by Professor Edward H. Clarke at Harvard (Doc. 115), and in the related controversy that arose in Britain over women's demands for medical education and access to the profession itself (Docs. 133, 134).[2] It was during the period 1860-1880 that men such as Spencer, Jules Simon, and the followers of Michelet, who considered themselves Liberals, hoping to minimize state intrusion on individual liberty of men and advocating free market economics, began to question the meaning of "progress" for women. They opposed women's incursions into what they considered to be the male sphere, especially in the professions, in older skilled trades such as printing, which were threatened with mechanization, and also in the new forms of industrial labor. Instead, they insisted more firmly than ever that the sexual division of labor itself (as discussed in Spencer and, before Spencer, in Auguste Comte [Docs. 62, 63]) was indeed progressive. They incorporated into their theory of social evolution their belief that such extra-domestic activities were incompatible with women's "irreplaceable" social function as reproducers (not merely educators) of the race. This was, as we have noted before, the trump argument of the defenders of patriarchal society, and they deployed it repeatedly as the ultimate response to women's demands for comparable freedom. The biological determinism of Rousseau, argued on the authority of nature, was here recast in terms of evolution and cultural history—old wine in new bottles. Evolutionary determinism decreed, said the sociologists, that in an industrial society increasing specialization of functions by sex was the wave of the future. In this configuration, women's function was reproduction, not production. In this view, then, woman was not—and could never be—an autonomous individual in the same way as man; her fate was necessarily linked with children and, therefore, in these mens' view, with dependence on male breadwinners. However much recent social evolution might have

[1] Various sources discuss the emergence of the woman question in the developing social sciences. For anthropology, see Burrow 1966 and Fee 1974. For psychology, see S. Shields 1975; Fee 1976; and Alaya 1977. For bio-sociology, see Mosedale 1978. See also Schiller 1979 and Harvey 1981.

[2] See Todd 1918; B. Stephen 1927; E. Bell 1953; Burstyn 1973, 1980; Wein 1974a, 1974b; Donnison 1976; and Walsh 1977.

eroded patriarchy, it could never be eliminated; indeed, the male-headed family was increasingly presented as a requirement of social progress.[3]

To this, women's advocates in England and the United States replied with a new, more radical line of argument—that opportunities for women must not be developed on the grounds of equality-in-difference, which was being turned against women, or on the grounds of cultivating women's special qualities, or with the hope that new models incorporating such qualities could be generated. Opportunities for women could be based only on undifferentiated equality of opportunity within existing institutions. This new perception was clearly articulated by Emily Davies, founder of Girton College (Doc. 113), in the conflict over the organization of women's higher education at Cambridge University. Davies insisted on hard-line, male university standards, however flawed, against the advocates of the woman-oriented, revisionist Newnham College approach. In the United States the separate single-sex colleges established for women in the 1860's and 1870's (Vassar, Smith, Wellesley), dedicated to educating women as women, did not provoke an outcry as did women students' attempt to infiltrate the male bastion of Harvard University and their success in infiltrating Cornell in the early 1870's. At that point a heated debate developed in the United States (see Docs. 115, 116) reminiscent of the debate sparked in England with women's challenge to the male establishment at Cambridge University. By contrast, in France, education for women remained conceptualized within a framework riddled by acknowledgment of sexual difference and a continuing emphasis on the mother-educator ideal (on both the secular and the religious side), as the documents on the establishment of national secondary education for girls (Docs. 118-121) attest. The same emphasis was apparent in Germany and elsewhere.[4]

This new, hard line of argument of women's rights advocates was greatly aided in the later 1860's by the contribution of a single man—the internationally recognized economist and political philosopher John Stuart Mill (Docs. 105, 135). The publication, in 1869, of his *Subjection of Women* was an event of truly international significance for the cause of women's rights. The crux of Mill's eloquent argument was that woman's "nature" could never be properly determined until all the legal and cultural constraints on women's full development as human beings were removed. This argument allowed women's rights advocates to take the offensive in demanding reforms in women's legal status and education without having to justify such demands on the basis of women's special nature, as even Elizabeth Cady Stanton (Doc. 137) was still doing in

---

[3] Elaborated by Spencer and others. The distinction between production and reproduction became a commonplace in European social science well before 1879, when Engels appropriated it for Marxism.

[4] For England, see Clough 1903; B. Stephen 1927; and McWilliams-Tullberg 1975, 1977. On the United States, see Newcomer 1959; Bishop 1962; Conable 1974; Wein 1974; and Simmons 1976. For a comparative survey, see Stock 1978.

1869. The London edition of Mill's work was quickly reprinted in New York; translations appeared shortly thereafter in nearly every European language, including Danish and Polish. Significantly, many of his translators were women, among them the Italian Anna Maria Mozzoni (see Doc. 123) and the German Jenny Hirsch (see Doc. 140). Mill's contribution was constantly cited in other countries, as in France, where Jules Ferry (Doc. 119) called it "the beginning of wisdom."[5]

Aided by this new ideological formulation, the proponents of women's rights found it easier to organize for action. From this period dates the emergence of organized national movements for specific women's rights—legal, educational, economic, and political—in virtually every country where such group activity was legal. In countries where it remained illegal, as in Prussia and other German states, organizers insisted that their groups were pressing for purely economic or educational reforms, the political nature of which they attempted to mute as much as possible. Accompanying this was a growing insistence by the organizers that no substantive reforms could be achieved without the mass support of women themselves.[6]

Political developments during the 1860's and 1870's directly affected the direction of arguments for and against women's rights and the organization of pressure groups. In Italy the pursuit by women of changes in their own legal status was closely connected to the success of the movement for national unification. French ideas, along with a Mazzinian concept of revolutionary motherhood (Doc. 103), informed debate over the recasting of Italian civil law, as can be seen in the arguments of Italian women's rights advocate Anna Maria Mozzoni (Doc. 123) for women's full civil and political equality in the new nation. But resistance to such change was strong, as is apparent from the better-known study of women's legal status by Italian jurist Carlo Francesco Gabba (Doc. 122).

Similarly, in France, advocacy of legal reforms for women became closely associated with nationalist anticlerical republicanism. In 1870 the Second Empire fell, as a consequence of the Prussian defeat of France. The imperial position on women's rights, however, had been mixed: support for secular education of girls and even, thanks to Empress Eugénie, for a medical school for women, but continued stiff opposition to their participation in political life. The latter had been underscored not only by the continued exclusion of women from attendance at political clubs and from newspaper editorships, but also by a provision in the constitutional changes ratified in early 1870 that formally barred women from

[5] On Mill and women's subjection, see in particular Hayek 1951; Robson 1968; Rossi 1970; Okin 1973, 1979; and Pugh 1978, 1980, 1982.
[6] For an international appreciation of organized national movements, see R. Evans 1977. For English educational developments before 1880, see Kamm 1965. For English political developments before 1880, see Strachey 1928; Fulford 1956; and Rover 1967. For the early phases of the French women's rights movement, see Bidelman 1977, 1982. For Italy, see Pieroni-Bortolotti 1963; and Howard 1977, 1978. For the United States, see Flexner 1959; Riegel 1963; DuBois 1978, 1981. For Russia, see Engel & Rosenthal 1975; Broido 1977; and Stites 1978.

the succession to the imperial throne—a telling action that did not escape criticism by women hostile to the Empire.[7] Henceforth, most advocates of women's rights would be found in the republican camp, whose partisans came to power in the 1870's. Even the friends of women's rights in France, however, felt it necessary to tread cautiously in order not to identify themselves too closely with the exiled partisans of the Paris Commune, whose supporters included a number of women militants.[8]

Despite the eloquence brought to women's cause by Maria Deraismes, Victor Hugo, and Hubertine Auclert (Docs. 142, 143), the French campaign for women's rights during this time was muted. The anticlerical supporters of the women's cause insisted that friends of the new republican regime must insist on reforms in women's status lest this regime fail, like its predecessors in 1792 and 1848, because women would abandon it. This attributed to women a considerable degree of negative political influence over men but fell short of being a positive argument for their active participation. High on the list were specific legal reforms in the civil and penal codes, the goal of Léon Richer (Doc. 141), the enactment of legislation that would allow civil divorce, and—by now an old theme—the secularization of women's education.[9] In Russia, the agitation for women's rights arose directly out of discussion of emancipating the serfs and, in the German states, was coupled with the cause of the working class.[10] In the United States, as was mentioned in Parts II and III, it was closely connected to the struggle to abolish slavery.

As a result of disappointments experienced by women's rights advocates in these parallel reform movements, however, women acquired a mounting awareness of the fact that they must take their liberation into their own hands, instead of relying on men with somewhat different (and often conflicting) priorities to do it for them. This had become especially evident in the United States, where Elizabeth Cady Stanton and the militant suffragists confronted abolitionist men and the Republican party over the Fifteenth Amendment (Docs. 137, 138).[11] Without the support of a mass movement of women, organizers recognized that they could achieve no substantive reforms. In Great Britain, the petition for woman suffrage signed by 1,499 well-known women, and presented to the House of Commons by John Stuart Mill and Henry Fawcett in 1866, was an attempt to demonstrate that women's support could be mobilized. In France Léon Richer and Hubertine Auclert both urged women to become active supporters of their own cause. Raising women's political consciousness on a mass basis was, even in the 1870's, far more difficult than formulating arguments for their rights—the situation was not unlike that

[7] See Angélique Arnaud, "La Loi salique," *Le Droit des Femmes*, 2, no. 58 (5 June 1870).

[8] Women's issues were not central issues in the Paris Commune, although they were certainly present. See Schulkind 1950; E. Thomas 1966, 1971; and Hunt 1971.

[9] See Bidelman 1977, 1982.

[10] On Russia the best account is that of Stites 1978. On the German movement before 1880, see Puckett 1930; Thönnessen 1973; Hackett 1976; Sanford 1976; Niggemann 1981; and Prelinger (in progress).

[11] On this confrontation, see McPherson 1965 and DuBois 1978.

faced by Marx and his supporters in the First International Workingmen's Association, when they attempted to raise the political consciousness of the working class.[12]

One of the most revealing conflicts with respect to women's rights took
place over the question of women's right to work. Concern over women's
work, as we have seen, had gravely preoccupied social critics from the
1830's on, but women's "right to work" for pay had been asserted only
by those few hardy souls inspired by the Saint-Simonian and Fourierist
women. In the early 1860's women's labor force participation once again
became the subject of public discussion; not only liberal reformers like
Jules Simon (Doc. 126), but also the organizers of workingmen's movements in England, France, Germany, and Belgium all addressed the issue.
Few of them supported women's "right" to work. In Leipzig Louise Otto
found herself at odds with the followers of the German socialist Ferdinand Lasalle, who opposed the presence of women in the industrial labor
force. In 1866 she founded a General Association of German Women,
devoted to furthering women's right to education and to "the liberation
of women's work from all those hindrances that stand in the way of its
development" (Doc. 129). Such claims were poorly received by the
Lasalleans, whose efforts to better the condition of German workers were
predicated, like those of the French reformer Simon, on assistance to
male workers and on the assumption that domesticity, not paid labor,
was best for women. This same disagreement surfaced soon thereafter in
the annual congresses of the First International, where women's work in
manufacturing was debated by all-male delegations in both 1866 and
1867. As is clear from these debates—and from the impassioned rejoinder of Paule Mink in Paris (Docs. 130-132)—resistance to women's
labor force participation was no less strong among leaders of the labor
movement than it was among the bourgeoisie.[13]

When the focus of discussion on women's right to work moved from
industrial labor to the professions, resistance to women's participation
was just as firm and equally international in its dimensions. This is exemplified by the controversy over the entry of women into the British medical profession. The campaign of Sophia Jex-Blake in Great Britain, which
began in 1869 (almost simultaneously with the founding of Girton and
Newnham colleges), was inspired by the success of American women in
founding their own medical institutions—and undoubtedly also by the
example of the Russian women who were studying medicine in Zurich in
the 1860's. But Jex-Blake decided that the time had come to deliver an
organized challenge in her homeland. Once women students had entered
the medical school at the University of Edinburgh, however, their success
did nothing but generate resistance from male students and teachers
(Docs. 133, 134).[14] Beyond this, moreover, the appearance of women in

[12] See the records of the First International in Freymond 1962. On Marx's role, see Berlin
1963 and McLellan 1974. See also Drachkovich 1966 and Braunthal 1967.
[13] See Boxer 1975, 1978; and Niggemann 1981.
[14] In England and on the Continent, there was great concern about an overproduction of
educated men and, especially, overcrowding in the liberal professions. See O'Boyle 1970.

the medical profession challenged male control of scientific knowledge about women's anatomy and thereby produced a body of revisionist research literature that countered the obstetrical and gynaecological profession's prescriptive approach to female health.[15]

The question of political rights for women arose once again in the late 1860's, this time with a specific focus on the vote and with more persistence and support than had been forthcoming in the 1840's. It was, as before, an issue tightly linked to better-known agitation for national electoral reform to benefit men, which was based on the slow erosion of property ownership as the sole criterion for political participation. It was, therefore, an unabashedly political demand. In England, John Stuart Mill introduced a measure in Parliament to give votes to unmarried women on exactly the same basis as to men; his arguments for the "expediency" of woman suffrage garnered a substantial amount of parliamentary support (Docs. 135, 136). Unmarried English women did receive the vote in municipal affairs in 1869. In the post-Civil War United States, women abolitionists broke with their former associates when it appeared, after emancipation of the slaves, that their victorious colleagues were effectively abandoning their promises to work for the women's vote in order to assure suffrage for negro males by constitutional amendment (Docs. 137, 138). Yet they were heartened when Wyoming became the first state in the union to enact woman suffrage at all levels. In unified Germany, as in France in 1848, the establishment of universal manhood suffrage for the election of Reichstag delegates (who could debate issues but not make decisions) provoked discussion of a similar extension of suffrage to German women, though little support for such a reform was forthcoming (Docs. 139, 140). In republican France, as we have mentioned, advocacy of woman suffrage was felt by the leading supporters of women's rights to be too dangerous to the new republican regime because of the assistance "reactionary" women might bring to the republic's enemies (Docs. 141-143).

Significantly, by the end of the 1860's successive demands for woman suffrage had forced the defenders of the established patriarchal order in most Western countries to clarify at law their belief that maleness was a prerequisite for national citizenship: this had happened in Britain with the first Reform Act of 1832, in France in 1848, and in the United States in 1869 (Docs. 31, 84, 85, 137, 138). Thus, masculine prerogative was formally asserted. That assertion was promptly condemned by women's rights advocates (just as by Guyomar in 1793) for establishing an "aristocracy of sex." The fact that sex was explicitly mentioned in the law, however, also meant that it might be removed through due process—the tactic used henceforth in the United States, in France, and in Great Brit-

---

[15] On the male medical preoccupation with the societal implications of sexuality in the United States, see Haller & Haller 1974; R. Walters 1974; Barker-Benfield 1976; and Degler 1974, 1980. For England, see S. Marcus 1964. For the use of bio-medical arguments to justify women's subjection, see Bullough & Voght 1973; Burstyn 1973, 1980; Smith-Rosenberg & Rosenberg 1973; Smith-Rosenberg 1974; Hellerstein 1976, 1980; Knibiehler 1976a, 1976b; Ehrenreich & English 1978; and Hellerstein, Hume & Offen 1981.

ain. The suffrage issue had thus been effectively clarified by repeated challenges, in the face of the new social scientific endorsement of separate and diverging social roles for men and women, and women's fight for equity in education and employment. These events underscored, at last, the truly radical character of the demand for woman suffrage in the history of Western political thought.

CHAPTER 12

Woman's Sphere Reconsidered: From Romantic Idealism to Historical Materialism

Scholars Investigate Woman's Position in the Ancient Family

SOURCES

101. Sir Henry Sumner Maine, *Ancient Law; Its Connection with the Early History of Society, and Its Relation to Modern Ideas*, 6th ed. (London, 1876), pp. 122-26, 133-35, 146-50, 152-55, 157-59, 168-70. Originally published in London, 1861.

102. Johann-Jakob Bachofen, *Myth, Religion, and Mother Right*, tr. Ralph Manheim (Princeton, N.J., 1967), pp. 69-74, 79, 86-89, 91-92, 109-11. Originally published as *Das Mutterrecht: Eine Untersuchung über die Gynakokratie der alten Welt nach ihrer religiösen und rechtlichen Natur* (Stuttgart, 1861).

The rise of historical scholarship in the nineteenth century focused attention on the origins and development of human societies. Writing before the era of great archaeological excavations and on-site anthropological expeditions, these scholars had to rely on evidence drawn from early written records preserved in law and literature. They prided themselves on observing a scientific, scholarly approach to the past, though they wrote with an unapologetic eye on the present.

Two major works published in 1861 reveal the centrality of the woman question to theories about the history of societal development. *Ancient Law* by Sir Henry Sumner Maine (1822-1888) has long been considered, together with Blackstone's *Commentaries* (Doc. 5), one of the great works of the legal literature in the English language. Maine made his reputation as a classical scholar and jurist at Cambridge, where he pioneered the study of comparative law as practiced by the school of Friedrich Karl von Savigny in Berlin. Following publication of *Ancient Law*, Maine spent six years working on codification of the laws of India; during this time he extended his perceptions concerning the evolution of law from status to contract and confirmed his predisposition for governance by an enlightened male oligarchy. In *Ancient Law* Maine argued that since time immemorial Indo-European societies have been organized around patriarchal families, though the absolute authority of the father has been subject to increasing erosion in more recent times as the personal and proprietary freedom of individuals, especially female individuals, increased.

The first to challenge the patriarchal theory of social evolution was the Swiss Johann-Jakob Bachofen (1815-1887). Like his slightly younger counterpart Maine, Bachofen was a scholar of classical philology and jurisprudence and held an academic chair in Roman law at the University of Basel. But unlike Maine, who relied on the legal record, Bachofen was deeply impressed with the significance of religion and the importance of myth as an interpretative tool. Bachofen, the son of a long-established Basel family, had traveled widely in Europe, studying in Berlin with von Savigny, and in Paris and London; he was in Rome during the revolutionary upheaval of 1848. In 1861 he published his landmark study *Das Mutterrecht*, in which he attempted to reconstruct the rise and fall of matriarchy, drawing his evidence from a detailed analysis of ancient Greek mythology and religion, and comparing his findings with studies of other primitive societies. His enduring contribution was to demonstrate authoritatively the existence of matrilineal kinship patterns in early Mediterranean culture, though not to prove—as he thought he had—actual female governance. Though many progressive nineteenth-century men and women believed that Bachofen's assertions that women had once ruled had more positive implications for female emancipation than those of Maine, the contrary may indeed be true. Bachofen was, in fact, a thorough-going Romantic as concerned women; moreover, he clearly considered patriarchy to be a superior state in social organization, representing a step toward the triumph of spirit over matter.

Maine and Bachofen did not know of each other's work in 1861. But Maine soon learned about mother-right through the work of another scholar, the Scot John Fergusson McLennan, who incorporated Bachofen's matrilineal theories into his own analysis of primitive marriage. Maine the jurist nevertheless remained skeptical about Bachofen's conclusions, given the Swiss scholar's extreme reliance on religion and myth as evidence. Yet Bachofen's findings, together with those of McLennan and the American Lewis Henry Morgan, did deeply influence other writers, in particular Friedrich Engels, who subsequently asserted that "the overthrow of mother right was the *world-historical defeat of the female sex*" (Vol. II, Doc. 13). Bachofen's analysis likewise provided food for thought to the brilliant young philosopher Friedrich Nietzsche (Vol. II, Doc. 6), who was a regular visitor to the Bachofen household during his years as a professor in Basel.

---

101. Henry Sumner Maine (1861)

The effect of the evidence derived from comparative jurisprudence is to establish that view of the primæval condition of the human race which is known as the Patriarchal Theory. There is no doubt, of course, that this theory was originally based on the Scriptural history of the Hebrew patriarchs in Lower Asia. . . .

The points which lie on the surface of the history are these:—The eldest male parent—the eldest ascendant—is absolutely supreme in his household. His dominion extends to life and death, and is as unqualified over his children and their houses as over his slaves; indeed, the relations of sonship and serfdom appear to differ in little beyond the higher capacity which the child in blood possesses of becoming one day the head of a family himself. The flocks and herds of the children are the flocks and herds of the father. . . . A less obvious inference from the Scriptural accounts is that they seem to plant us on the traces of the breach which is first effected in the empire of the parent. The families of Jacob and Esau separate and form two nations; but the families of Jacob's children hold together and become a people. This looks like the immature germ of a state or commonwealth, and of an order of rights superior to the claims of family relation.

If I were attempting, for the more special purposes of the jurist, to express compendiously the characteristics of the situation in which mankind disclose themselves at the dawn of their history, I should be satisfied to quote a few verses from the *Odyssey* of Homer: "They have neither assemblies for consultation nor *themistes*, but every one exercises jurisdiction over his wives and his children, and they pay no regard to one another.". . . The verses condense in themselves the sum of the hints which are given us by legal antiquities. Men are first seen distributed in perfectly insulated groups, held together by obedience to the parent. Law is the parent's word, but it is not yet in the condition of those *themistes* which were analysed in the first chapter of this work. When we go forward to the state of society in which these early legal conceptions show themselves as formed, we find that they still partake of the mystery and spontaneity which must have seemed to characterise a despotic father's commands, but that at the same time, inasmuch as they proceed from a sovereign, they presuppose a union of family groups in some wider organization. The next question is, what is the nature of this union and the degree of intimacy which it involves? It is just here that archaic law renders us one of the greatest of its services, and fills up a gap which otherwise could only have been bridged by conjecture. It is full, in all its provinces, of the clearest indications that society in primitive times was not what it is assumed to be at present, a collection of *individuals*. In fact, and in the view of the men who composed it, it was *an aggregation of families*. The contrast may be most forcibly expressed by saying that the *unit* of an ancient society was the Family, of a modern society the individual. We must be prepared to find in ancient law all the consequences of this difference. It is so framed as to be adjusted to a system of small independent corporations. It is therefore scanty, because it is supplemented by the despotic commands of the heads of households. It is ceremonious, because the transactions to which it pays regard resemble international concerns much more than the quick play of intercourse between individuals. Above all, it has a peculiarity of which the full importance cannot be shown at present. It takes a view of *life* wholly unlike any which appears in developed jurisprudence. Corporations *never die*, and accordingly primitive law considers the entities with which it deals, *i.e.*, the patriarchal or family groups, as perpetual and inextinguishable. . . .

The family, then, is the type of an archaic society in all the modifications which it was capable of assuming; but the family here spoken of is not exactly the family as understood by a modern. In order to reach the ancient conception we must give to our modern ideas an important extension and an important limitation. We must look on the family as constantly enlarged by the absorption of strangers within its circle, and we must try to regard the ficton of adoption as so closely simulating the reality of kinship that neither law nor opinion makes the slightest difference between a real and an adoptive connexion. On the other hand, the persons theoretically amalgamated into a family by their common descent are practically held together by common obedience to their highest living ascendant, the father, grandfather, or great-grandfather. The patriarchal authority of a chieftain is as necessary an ingredient in the notion of the family group as the fact (or assumed fact) of its having sprung from his loins; and hence we must understand that if there be any persons who, however truly included in the brotherhood by virtue of their blood-relationship, have nevertheless *de facto* withdrawn themselves from the empire of its ruler, they are always, in the beginnings of law, considered as lost to the family. It is this patriarchal aggregate—the modern family thus cut down on one side and extended on the other—which meets us on the threshold of primitive jurisprudence. Older, probably, than the State, the Tribe, and the House, it left traces of itself on private law long after the House and the Tribe had been forgotten, and long after consanguinity had ceased to be associated with the composition of States. It will be found to have stamped itself on all the great departments of jurisprudence, and may be detected, I think, as the true source of many of their most important and most durable characteristics. At the outset, the peculiarities of law in its most ancient state lead us irresistibly to the conclusion that it took precisely the same view of the family group which is taken of individual men by the systems of rights and duties now prevalent throughout Europe. There are societies open to our observation at this very moment whose laws and usages can scarcely be explained unless they are supposed never to have emerged from this primitive condition; but in communities more fortunately circumstanced the fabric of jurisprudence fell gradually to pieces, and if we carefully observe the disintegration we shall perceive that it took place principally in those portions of each system which were most deeply affected by the primitive conception of the family. In one all-important instance, that of the Roman law, the change was effected so slowly, that from epoch to epoch we can observe the line and direction which it followed, and can even give some idea of the ultimate result to which it was tending. And in pursuing this last inquiry we need not suffer ourselves to be stopped by the imaginary barrier which separates the modern from the ancient world. For one effect of that mixture of refined Roman law with primitive barbaric usage, which is known to us by the deceptive name of feudalism, was to revive many features of archaic jurisprudence which had died out of the Roman world, so that the decomposition which had seemed to be over commenced again, and to some extent is still proceeding.

On a few systems of law the family organisation of the earliest society has left a plain and broad mark in the life-long authority of the Father or other ancestor over the person and property of his descendants, an authority which we may conveniently call by its later Roman name of Patria Potestas. No feature of the rudimentary associations of mankind is deposed to by a greater amount of evidence than this, and yet none seems to have disappeared so generally and so rapidly from the usages of advancing communities. . . .

The Patria Potestas, in its normal shape, has not been, and, as it seems to me, could not have been, a generally durable institution. The proof of its former universality is therefore incomplete so long as we consider it by itself; but the demonstration may be carried much further by examining other departments of ancient law which depend on it ultimately, but not by a thread of connexion visible in all its parts or to all eyes. Let us turn for example to Kinship, or in other words, to the scale on which the proximity of relatives to each other is calculated in archaic jurisprudence. Here again it will be convenient to employ the Roman terms, Agnatic and Cognatic relationship. . . .

Cognates then are all those persons who can trace their blood to a single ancestor and ancestress; or if we take the strict technical meaning of the word in Roman law, they are all who trace their blood to the legitimate marriage of a common pair. "Cognation" is therefore a relative term, and the degree of connexion in blood which it indicates depends on the particular marriage which is selected as the commencement of the calculation. If we begin with the marriage of father and mother, Cognation will only express the relationship of brothers and sisters; if we take that of the grandfather and grandmother, then uncles, aunts, and their descendants will also be included in the notion of Cognation, and following the same process a larger number of Cognates may be continually obtained by choosing the starting point higher and higher up in the line of ascent. All this is easily understood by a modern; but who are the Agnates? In the first place, they are all the Cognates who trace their connexion exclusively through males. A table of Cognates is, of course, formed by taking each lineal ancestor in turn and including all his descendants of both sexes in the tabular view; if then, in tracing the various branches of such a genealogical table or tree, we stop whenever we come to the name of a female and pursue that particular branch or ramification no further, all who remain after the descendants of women have been excluded are Agnates, and their connection together is Agnatic Relationship. I dwell a little on the process which is practically followed in separating them from the Cognates, because it explains a memorable legal maxim, "Mulier est finis familiæ"—a woman is the terminus of the family. A female name closes the branch or twig of the genealogy in which it occurs. None of the descendants of a female are included in the primitive notion of family relationship. . . .

. . . The foundation of Agnation is not the marriage of Father and Mother, but the authority of the Father. All persons are Agnatically connected together who are under the same Paternal Power, or who have been under it, or who might have been under it if their lineal ancestor had lived long enough to exercise his empire. In truth, in the primitive view,

Relationship is exactly limited by Patria Potestas. Where the Potestas begins, Kinship begins; and therefore adoptive relatives are among the kindred. Where the Potestas ends, Kinship ends; so that a son emancipated by his father loses all rights of Agnation. And here we have the reason why the descendants of females are outside the limits of archaic kinship. If a woman died unmarried, she could have no legitimate descendants. If she married, her children fell under the Patria Potestas, not of her Father, but of her Husband, and thus were lost to her own family. It is obvious that the organization of primitive societies would have been confounded, if men had called themselves relatives of their mother's relatives. The inference would have been that a person might be subject to two distinct Patriæ Potestates; but distinct Patriæ Potestates implied distinct jurisdictions, so that anybody amenable to two of them at the same time would have lived under two different dispensations. As long as the Family was an imperium in imperio, a community within the commonwealth governed by its own institutions of which the parent was the source, the limitation of relationship to the Agnates was a necessary security against a conflict of laws in the domestic forum. . . .

It may be shown, I think, that the Family, as held together by the Patria Potestas, is the nidus out of which the entire Law of Persons has germinated. Of all the chapters of that Law the most important is that which is concerned with the status of Females. It has just been stated that Primitive Jurisprudence, though it does not allow a Woman to communicate any rights of Agnation to her descendants, includes herself nevertheless in the Agnatic bond. Indeed, the relation of a female to the family in which she was born is much stricter, closer, and more durable than that which unites her male kinsmen. We have several times laid down that early law takes notice of Families only; this is the same thing as saying that it only takes notice of persons exercising Patria Potestas, and accordingly the only principle on which it enfranchises a son or grandson at the death of his Parent, is a consideration of the capacity inherent in such son or grandson to become himself the head of a new family and the root of a new set of Parental Powers. But a woman, of course, has no capacity of the kind, and no title accordingly to the liberation which it confers. There is therefore a peculiar contrivance of archaic jurisprudence for retaining her in the bondage of the Family for life. This is the institution known to the oldest Roman law as the Perpetual Tutelage of Women, under which a Female, though relieved from her Parent's authority by his decease, continues subject through life to her nearest male relations, or to her father's nominees, as her Guardians. Perpetual Guardianship is obviously neither more nor less than an artificial prolongation of the Patria Potestas, when for other purposes it has been dissolved. In India, the system survives in absolute completeness, and its operation is so strict that a Hindoo Mother frequently becomes the ward of her own sons. Even in Europe, the laws of the Scandinavian nations respecting women preserved it until quite recently. . . .

Ancient law subordinates the woman to her blood-relations, while a prime phenomenon of modern jurisprudence has been her subordination to her husband. The history of the change is remarkable. It begins far back in the annals of Rome. Anciently, there were three modes in which marriage might be contracted according to Roman usage, one involving a religious solemnity, the other two the observance of certain secular formalities. By the religious marriage or *Confarreation*; by the higher form of civil marriage, which was called *Coemption*; and by the lower form, which was termed *Usus*, the Husband acquired a number of rights over the person and property of his wife, which were on the whole in excess of such as are conferred on him in any system of modern jurisprudence. But in what capacity did he acquire them? Not as *Husband*, but as *Father*. By the Confarreation, Coemption, and Usus, the woman passed *in manum viri*, that is, in law she became the *Daughter* of her husband. She was included in his Patria Potestas. She incurred all the liabilities springing out of it while it subsisted, and surviving it when it had expired. All her property became absolutely his, and she was retained in tutelage after his death to the guardian whom he had appointed by will. These three ancient forms of marriage fell, however, gradually into disuse, so that at the most splendid period of Roman greatness, they had almost entirely given place to a fashion of wedlock—old apparently, but not hitherto considered reputable—which was founded on a modification of the lower form of civil marriage. Without explaining the technical mechanism of the institution now generally popular, I may describe it as amounting in law to a little more than a temporary deposit of the woman by her family. . . .

. . . When we move onwards, and the code of the middle ages has been formed by the amalgamation of the two systems, the law relating to women carries the stamp of its double origin. The principle of the Roman jurisprudence is so far triumphant that unmarried females are generally (though there are local exceptions to the rule) relieved from the bondage of the family; but the archaic principle of the barbarians has fixed the position of married women, and the husband has drawn to himself in his marital character the powers which had once belonged to his wife's male kindred, the only difference being that he no longer purchases his privileges. At this point therefore the modern law of Southern and Western Europe begins to be distinguished by one of its chief characteristics, the comparative freedom it allows to unmarried women and widows, the heavy disabilities it imposes on wives. It was very long before the subordination entailed on the other sex by marriage was sensibly diminished. The principal and most powerful solvent of the revived barbarism of Europe was always the codified jurisprudence of Justinian, wherever it was studied with that passionate enthusiasm which it seldom failed to awaken. It covertly but most efficaciously undermined the customs which it pretended merely to interpret. But the Chapter of law relating to married women was for the most part read by the light, not of Roman, but of Canon Law, which in no one particular departs so widely from the spirit of the secular jurisprudence as in the view it takes of the relations created by marriage. . . .

. . . The systems however which are least indulgent to married women are invariably those which have followed the Canon Law exclusively, or those which, from the lateness of their contact with European civilisation, have never had their archaisms weeded out. The Danish and Swedish laws, harsh for many centuries to all females, are still much less favourable to wives than the generality of Continental codes. And yet more stringent in the proprietary incapacities it imposes is the English Common Law, which borrows far the greatest number of its fundamental principles from the jurisprudence of the Canonists. Indeed, the part of the Common Law which prescribes the legal situation of married women may serve to give an Englishman clear notions of the great institution which has been the principal subject of this chapter. I do not know how the operation and nature of the ancient Patria Potestas can be brought so vividly before the mind as by reflecting on the prerogatives attached to the husband by the pure English Common Law, and by recalling the rigorous consistency with which the view of a complete legal subjection on the part of the wife is carried by it, where it is untouched by equity or statutes, through every department of rights, duties, and remedies. . . .

The movement of the progressive societies has been uniform in one respect. Through all its course it has been distinguished by the gradual dissolution of family dependency, and the growth of individual obligation in its place. The Individual is steadily substituted for the Family, as the unit of which civil laws take account. . . . Nor is it difficult to see what is the tie between man and man which replaces by degrees those forms of reciprocity in rights and duties which have their origin in the Family. It is Contract. Starting, as from one terminus of history, from a condition of society in which all the relations of Persons are summed up in the relations of Family, we seem to have steadily moved towards a phase of social order in which all these relations arise from the free agreement of Individuals. In Western Europe the progress achieved in this direction has been considerable. Thus the status of the Slave has disappeared—it has been superseded by the contractual relation of the servant to his master. The status of the Female under Tutelage, if the tutelage be understood of persons other than her husband, has also ceased to exist; from her coming of age to her marriage all the relations she may form are relations of contract. So too the status of the Son under Power has no true place in the law of modern European societies. If any civil obligation binds together the Parent and the child of full age, it is one to which only contract gives its legal validity.

. . . The word Status may be usefully employed to construct a formula expressing the law of progress thus indicated, which, whatever be its value, seems to me to be sufficiently ascertained. All the forms of Status taken notice of in the Law of Persons were derived from, and to some extent are still coloured by, the powers and privileges anciently residing in the Family. If then we employ Status, agreeably with the usage of the best writers, to signify these personal conditions only, and avoid applying the term to such conditions as are the immediate or remote result of agreement, we may say that the movement of the progressive societies has hitherto been a movement *from Status to Contract.*

102. J.-J. Bachofen (1861)

The present work deals with a historical phenomenon which few have observed and no one has investigated in its full scope. Up until now archaeologists have had nothing to say of mother right. The term is new and the family situation it designates unknown. The subject is extremely attractive, but it also raises great difficulties. The most elementary spadework remains to be done, for the culture period to which mother right pertains has never been seriously studied. Thus we are entering upon virgin territory.

We find ourselves carried back to times antedating classical antiquity, to an older world of ideas totally different from those with which we are familiar. Leaving the nations we commonly associate with the glory of the ancient world, we find ourselves among peoples who never achieved the level of classical culture. An unknown world opens before our eyes, and the more we learn of it, the stranger it seems. Everything contrasts with the idea of a highly developed culture; everywhere we find older conceptions, an independent way of life that can only be judged according to its own fundamental law. The matriarchal organization of the family seems strange in the light not only of modern but also of classical ideas. And the more primitive way of life to which it pertains, from which it arose, and through which alone it can be explained, seems very strange beside the Hellenic. The main purpose of the following pages is to set forth the moving principle of the matriarchal age, and to give its proper place in relationship both to the lower stages of development and to the higher levels of culture. Thus the scope of this work is far broader than its title indicates. I propose to investigate all aspects of matriarchal culture, to disclose its diverse traits and the fundamental idea which unites them. In this way I hope to restore the picture of a cultural stage which was overlaid or totally destroyed by the later development of the ancient world. This is an ambitious undertaking. But it is only by broadening our horizon that we can achieve true understanding and carry scientific thinking to that clarity and completeness which are the very essence of knowledge.

And now I shall attempt a general survey of my ideas, which, I believe, will facilitate the study of the work itself.

Of all records relating and pertaining to mother right, those concerning the Lycian people are the clearest and most valuable. The Lycians, Herodotus reports, did not name their children after their fathers like the Hellenes, but exclusively after their mothers; in their genealogical records they dealt entirely with the maternal line, and the status of children was defined solely in accordance with that of the mother. Nicolaus of Damascus completes this testimony by telling us that only the daughters possessed the right of inheritance, and traces this institution back to the

Lycian common law, the unwritten law which, as defined by Socrates, was handed down by the godhead itself. All these customs are manifestations of one and the same basic conception. Although Herodotus regards them merely as an odd deviation from Hellenic customs, closer observation must lead to a deeper view. We find not disorder but system, not fancy but necessity. And since it is expressly denied that these customs were influenced by any positive body of legislation, the hypothesis of a meaningless anomaly loses its last shred of justification. We find, then, side by side with the Hellenic-Roman father principle, a family organization which differs diametrically both in its foundation and in its development, as a comparison of the two clearly shows. This opinion is confirmed by the discovery of related conceptions among other peoples. The limitation of the right of inheritance to the daughters among the Lycians finds a parallel in the obligation (recorded by Diodorus for Egypt) of the daughters alone to provide for aged parents. And in line with the same basic conception Strabo reports that among the Cantabri the sisters provided their brothers with dowries.

All these traits join to form a single picture and lead to the conclusion that mother right is not confined to any particular people but marks a cultural stage. In view of the universal qualities of human nature, this cultural stage cannot be restricted to any particular ethnic family. And consequently what must concern us is not so much the similarities between isolated phenomena as the unity of the basic conception. Polybius' passage about the matriarchal genealogy of the hundred noble families among the Epizephyrian Locrians suggests two further observations which have been confirmed in the course of our investigation: (1) mother right belongs to a cultural period preceding that of the patriarchal system; (2) it began to decline only with the victorious development of the paternal system. The patriarchal forms are observed chiefly among the pre-Hellenic peoples and are an essential component of this archaic culture, upon which they set their imprint as much as do patriarchal forms upon Greek culture.

The principles which we have here deduced from a few observations are confirmed in the course of our investigation by an abundance of data. The Locrians lead us to the Leleges, Carians, Aetolians, Pelasgians, Caucones, Arcadians, Epeians, Minyae, and Teleboeans, who furnish a diversified picture of mother right and the culture based on it. The prestige of womanhood among these peoples was a source of astonishment to the ancients, and gives them all, regardless of individual coloration, a character of archaic sublimity that stands in striking contrast to Hellenic culture. Here we discern the basic idea from which sprang the genealogical system set forth in the Hesiodic *Eoiai* and "Catalogues," the unions of immortal mothers wedded to mortal fathers, the emphasis on maternal property and the name of the maternal line, the closeness of maternal kinship, which gave rise to the term "mother country," the appellation "motherland," the greater sanctity of female sacrifices, and the inexpiability of matricide.

In these prefatory remarks, concerned not with individual data but with general perspectives, we must stress the importance of the mythical tradition for our investigation. In view of the central position of mother right among the earliest Greek peoples, we may expect this system to be reflected in myth. And accordingly this oldest form of tradition becomes an important source for our knowledge of matriarchal institutions. The question therefore arises: What importance may we impute to this primordial form of human tradition, and what use are we justified in making of its testimony? The answer to this question is provided by a single example drawn from Lycian mythology.

The maternal transmission of inheritance is attested for this sphere not only by the purely historical account of Herodotus but also by the mythical history of the Lycian kings. Not the sons of Sarpedon, but Laodamia, his daughter, is entitled to his heritage, and she passes the kingdom on to her son, to the exclusion of his uncles. A story recorded by Eustathius gives this system of inheritance a symbolic expression, disclosing the basic idea of mother right in all its sensuous sexuality. If the reports of Herodotus and of Nicolaus had been lost, those who hold the prevailing view would have attempted to discredit Eustathius' story on the ground that its authenticity could not be supported by any older, not to mention contemporaneous sources; they would have argued that its cryptic character indicated invention by some foolish mythographer. They would have said, not that the myth had formed around the fact like a shell, but on the contrary, that the fact had been abstracted from the myth. They would have set it down as worthless rubbish and relegated it to the discard pile whose steady growth marks the destructive progress of the so-called "critical" approach to mythology. But comparison of the myth and the historical account shows the fallacy of this entire method. Tested by historically established truths, the mythical tradition is seen to be an authentic, independent record of the primordial age, a record in which invention plays no part. The preference of Laodamia over her brothers must then be taken as adequate proof that mother right prevailed in Lycia.

There is scarcely a feature of the matriarchal system that cannot be documented in this way, although the parallels cannot always be taken from one and the same people. In fact, we have such parallels even for the general picture of matriarchal culture; and the reason is that mother right was preserved at least partially down to relatively recent times. Both the mythical and the strictly historical traditions present very similar pictures of the system. Products of archaic and of much later periods show such an astonishing accord that we almost forget the long interval between the times when they originated. This parallelism proves the value of the mythical tradition and shows that the attitude of present-day scholarship toward it is untenable. Precisely in regard to the most important aspect of history, namely, the knowledge of ancient ideas and institutions, the already shaky distinction between historic and prehistoric times loses its last shred of justification.

Our question has been answered: the mythical tradition may be taken as a faithful reflection of the life of those times in which historical antiquity is rooted. It is a manifestation of primordial thinking, an immediate historical revelation, and consequently a highly reliable historical source.

Eustathius declares that the favoring of Laodamia over her brothers is entirely contrary to Hellenic attitudes. His remark is all the more noteworthy in view of its recent date. Unlike modern critics, the learned Byzantine does not question, much less modify the tradition because of the anomaly he seems to find in it. Such uncritical, candid acceptance of tradition, often attacked as thoughtless copying, provides the best pledge of the reliability of our sources even when they are relatively late. Among all the ancients who wrote about the earliest times we find the same meticulous fidelity in preserving and handing down tradition, the same reluctance to tamper with the vestiges of the primordial world. It is to this attitude that we owe the possibility of discerning with any degree of certainty the essential character of the most ancient periods and of tracing the history of human ideas back to their beginnings. The less inclined he is toward critique and subjective combination, the more reliable an author will be, and the less prone to falsification.

There is still another reason why myth demonstrates the authenticity of mother right. The contrast between mythical conceptions and those of subsequent days is so marked that where more recent ideas prevailed, it would not have been possible to invent the phenomena of matriarchy. The older system represented an utter puzzle to the patriarchal mind, which consequently could not have conceived any part of it. Hellenic thought could not possibly have fabricated Laodamia's priority, for it is in diametric opposition to such a conception. The same is true of the innumerable vestiges of matriarchal form woven into the prehistory of all ancient peoples—not excluding Athens and Rome, two most resolute advocates of paternity. The thinking and literature of any period unconsciously follow the laws of its life form. So great is the power of such laws that the natural tendency is always to set the new imprint on the divergent features of former times.

The matriarchal traditions did not escape this fate. We shall encounter some very surprising phenomena produced by the impact of late conceptions on the vestiges of older views and by the weakness which led some writers to replace the incomprehensible by what was comprehensible from the standpoint of their own culture. Old features are overlaid by new ones, the venerable figures of the matriarchal past are introduced to contemporaries in forms consonant with the spirit of the new period, harsh features are presented in a softened light; institutions, attitudes, motives, passions are reappraised from a contemporary point of view. Not infrequently new and old occur together; or the same fact, the same person, may appear in two versions, one prescribed by the earlier, one by the later world; one innocent, one criminal; one full of nobility and dignity, one an object of horror and the subject of a palinode. In other cases the mother gives way to the father, the sister to the brother, who now takes her place in the legend or alternates with her, while the feminine name is replaced by a masculine one. In a word, maternal conceptions cede to the requirements of patriarchal theory. . . .

. . . At the lowest, darkest stages of human existence the love between the mother and her offspring is the bright spot in life, the only light in the moral darkness, the only joy amid profound misery. By recalling this fact to our attention, the observation of still living peoples of other continents has clarified the mythical tradition which represents the appearance of the φιλοπάτορες (father lovers) as an important turning point in the development of human culture. The close relation between child and father, the son's self-sacrifice for his begetter, require a far higher degree of moral development than mother love, that mysterious power which equally permeates all earthly creatures. Paternal love appears later. The relationship which stands at the origin of all culture, of every virtue, of every nobler aspect of existence, is that between mother and child; it operates in a world of violence as the divine principle of love, of union, of peace. Raising her young, the woman learns earlier than the man to extend her loving care beyond the limits of the ego to another creature, and to direct whatever gift of invention she possesses to the preservation and improvement of this other's existence. Woman at this stage is the repository of all culture, of all benevolence, of all devotion, of all concern for the living and grief for the dead.

Myth and history express this idea in any number of ways. The Cretan expressed his love for the land of his birth by the term "mother country"; origin in a common womb is regarded as the closest bond, as the true and originally the only relation of kinship; to help, to protect, and to avenge the mother is seen as the highest duty, while to threaten her life is looked upon as a crime beyond all expiation, even if it is done in the service of offended fatherhood. . . .

We have numerous indications of the intimate connection between matriarchy and woman's religious character. Among the Locrians only a maiden could enact the rite of the φιαληφορία (bearing of the sacrificial bowl). In citing this custom as the proof that mother right prevailed among the Epizephyrians, Polybius recognized its connection with the basic matriarchal idea. Moreover, the Locrians sacrificed a maiden in expiation of Ajax's sacrilege. This confirms the same relation and indicates the basis of the widespread belief that female sacrifices are more pleasing to the godhead. And this line of thought carries us to the deepest foundation and meaning of the matriarchal idea. Traced back to the prototype of Demeter, the earthly mother becomes the mortal representative of the primordial tellurian mother, her priestess and hierophant, entrusted with the administration of her mystery. All these phenomena are of a piece, manifestations of one and the same cultural stage. This religious primacy of motherhood leads to a primacy of the mortal woman; Demeter's exclusive bond with Kore leads to the no less exclusive relation of succession between mother and daughter; and finally, the inner link between the mystery and the chthonian-feminine cults leads to the priesthood of the mother, who here achieves the highest degree of religious consecration.

These considerations bring new insight into the cultural stage characterized by matriarchy. We are faced with the essential greatness of the pre-Hellenic culture: in the Demetrian mystery and the religious and civil primacy of womanhood it possessed the seed of noble achievement which was suppressed and often destroyed by later developments. The barbarity of the Pelasgian world, the incompatibility of matriarchy with a noble way of life, the late origin of the mysterious element in religion—such traditional opinions are dethroned once and for all. It has long been a hobby with students of antiquity to impute the noblest historical manifestations to the basest motives. Could they be expected to spare religion, to acknowledge that what was noblest in it—its concern with the supernatural, the transcendent, the mystical—was rooted in the profoundest needs of the human soul? In the opinion of these scholars only self-seeking false prophets could have darkened the limpid sky of the Hellenic world with such ugly clouds, only an era of decadence could have gone so far astray. But mystery is the true essence of every religion, and wherever woman dominates religion or life, she will cultivate the mysterious. Mystery is rooted in her very nature, with its close alliance between the material and the supersensory; mystery springs from her kinship with material nature, whose eternal death creates a need for comforting thoughts and awakens hope through pain; and mystery is inherent in the law of Demetrian motherhood, manifested to woman in the transformations of the seed grain and in the reciprocal relation between perishing and coming into being, disclosing death as the indispensable forerunner of higher rebirth, as prerequisite to the ἐπίκτησις τῆς τελετῆς (higher good of consecration).*

All these implications of the maternal are fully confirmed by history. Wherever we encounter matriarchy, it is bound up with the mystery of the chthonian religion, whether it invokes Demeter or is embodied by an equivalent goddess. The relation between the two phenomena is clearly exemplified in the lives of the Lycians and Epizephyrians, whose high development of the mystery—revealed by a number of remarkable phenomena that have hitherto been misunderstood—accounts for the unusual survival of mother right among them. This historical fact leads us to an inescapable conclusion. If we acknowledge the primordial character of mother right and its connection with an older cultural stage, we must say the same of the mystery, for the two phenomena are merely different aspects of the same cultural form; they are inseparable twins. And this is all the more certain when we consider that the religious aspect of matriarchy is at the root of its social manifestations. The cultic conceptions are the source, the social forms are their consequence and expression. Kore's bond with Demeter was the source of the primacy of mother

* Bachofen says in *Gräbersymbolik* (*Gesammelte Werke*, vol. 4, p. 44): "The two blessings bestowed on mortal men by the Demetrian initiation are material well-being on earth and a higher hope in death. This latter is predominant in τελετή. Εὐθηνία, the blessing of abundance and well-being, is the gain for the duration of this life; ἐπίκτησις is the higher gain, the *adventicium lucrum* (gratuitous gain) which grants a happy outlook for the time after death."

over father, of daughter over son, and was not abstracted from the social relationship. Or, in ancient terms: the cultic-religious meaning of the maternal κτείς (weaver's shuttle, comb, weaving woman) is primary and dominant; while the social, juridical sense *pudenda* (shame) is derivative. The feminine *sporium* (womb) is seen primarily as a representation of the Demetrian mystery, both in its lower physical sense and in its higher transcendent implication, and only by derivation becomes an expression of the social matriarchy, as in the Lycian myth of Sarpedon. This refutes the assertion of modern historians that mystery is appropriate only to times of decadence and is a late degeneration of Hellenism. History reveals exactly the opposite relationship: the maternal mystery is the old element, and the classic age represents a late stage of religious development; the later age, and not the mystery, may be regarded as a degeneration, as a religious leveling that sacrificed transcendence to immanence and the mysterious obscurity of higher hope to clarity of form.

Hellenism is hostile to such a world. . . .

I shall pursue the religious basis of matriarchy no further: it is most deeply rooted in woman's vocation for the religious life. Who will continue to ask why devotion, justice, and all the qualities that embellish man's life are known by feminine names, why τελετή (initiation) is personified by a woman? This choice is no free invention or accident, but is an expression of historical truth. We find the matriarchal peoples distinguished by εὐνομία, εὐσέβεια, παιδεία (rectitude, piety, and culture); we see women serving as conscientious guardians of the mystery, of justice and peace, and the accord between the historical facts and the linguistic phenomenon is evident. Seen in this light, matriarchy becomes a sign of cultural progress, a source and guarantee of its benefits, a necessary period in the education of mankind, and hence the fulfillment of a natural law which governs peoples as well as individuals.

Here we are carried back to our starting point. We began by showing matriarchy to be a universal phenomenon, independent of any special dogma or legislation. Now we can go further in our characterization and establish its quality of natural truth. Like childbearing motherhood, which is its physical image, matriarchy is entirely subservient to matter and to the phenomena of natural life, from which it derives the laws of its inner and outward existence; more strongly than later generations, the matriarchal peoples feel the unity of all life, the harmony of the universe, which they have not yet outgrown; they are more keenly aware of the pain of death and the fragility of tellurian existence, lamented by woman and particularly the mother. They yearn more fervently for higher consolation, which they find in the phenomena of natural life, and they relate this consolation to the generative womb, to conceiving, sheltering, nurturing mother love. Obedient in all things to the laws of physical existence, they fasten their eyes upon the earth, setting the chthonian powers over the powers of uranian light. They identify the male principle chiefly with the tellurian waters and subordinate the generative moisture to the *gremium matris* (maternal womb), the ocean to the earth. In a wholly material sense they devote themselves to the embellishment of material existence, to the πρακτική ἀρετή (practical virtues). Both in agriculture, which was first fostered by women, and in the erection of walls, which the ancients identified with the chthonian cult, they achieved a perfection which astonished later generations. No era has attached so much importance to outward form, to the sanctity of the body, and so little to the inner spiritual factor; in juridical life no other era has so consistently advocated maternal dualism and the principle of actual possession; and none has been so given to lyrical enthusiasm, this eminently feminine sentiment, rooted in the feeling of nature. In a word, matriarchal existence is regulated naturalism, its thinking is material, its development predominantly physical. Mother right is just as essential to this cultural stage as it is alien and unintelligible to the era of patriarchy. . . .

The progress from the maternal to the paternal conception of man forms the most important turning point in the history of the relations between the sexes. The Demetrian and the Aphroditean-hetaeric stages both hold to the primacy of generative motherhood, and it is only the greater or lesser purity of its interpretation that distinguishes the two forms of existence. But with the transition to the paternal system occurs a change in fundamental principle; the older conception is wholly surpassed. An entirely new attitude makes itself felt. The mother's connection with the child is based on a material relationship, it is accessible to sense perception and remains always a natural truth. But the father as begetter presents an entirely different aspect. Standing in no visible relation to the child, he can never, even in the marital relation, cast off a certain fictive character. Belonging to the offspring only through the mediation of the mother, he always appears as the remoter potency. As promoting cause, he discloses an immateriality over against which the sheltering and nourishing mother appears as ὕλη (matter), as χώρα καὶ δεξαμενὴ γενέσεως (place and house of generation), as τιθήνη (nurse).

All these attributes of fatherhood lead to one conclusion: the triumph of paternity brings with it the liberation of the spirit from the manifestations of nature, a sublimation of human existence over the laws of material life. While the principle of motherhood is common to all spheres of tellurian life, man, by the preponderant position he accords to the begetting potency, emerges from this relationship and becomes conscious of his higher calling. Spiritual life rises over corporeal existence, and the relation with the lower spheres of existence is restricted to the physical aspect. Maternity pertains to the physical side of man, the only thing he shares with the animals: the paternal-spiritual principle belongs to him alone. Here he breaks through the bonds of tellurism and lifts his eyes to the higher regions of the cosmos. Triumphant paternity partakes of the heavenly light, while childbearing motherhood is bound up with the earth that bears all things; the establishment of paternal right is universally represented as an act of the uranian solar hero, while the defense of mother right is the first duty of the chthonian mother goddesses.

Myth takes this view of the conflict between the old and the new principle in the matricide of Orestes and Alcmaeon, and links the great turning point of existence to the sublimation of religion. These traditions undoubtedly embody a memory of real experiences of the human race. If the historical character of matriarchy cannot be doubted, the events accompanying its downfall must also be more than a poetic fiction. In the adventures of Orestes we find a reflection of the upheavals and struggles leading to the triumph of paternity over the chthonian-maternal principle. Whatever influence we may impute to poetic fancy, there is historical truth in the struggle between the two principles as set forth by Aeschylus and Euripides. The old law is that of the Erinyes, according to which Orestes is guilty and his mother's blood inexpiable; but Apollo and Athene usher in the victory as a new law; that of the higher paternity and of the heavenly light. This is no dialectical opposition but a historical struggle, and the gods themselves decide its outcome. The old era dies, and another, the Apollonian age, rises on its ruins. A new ethos is in preparation, diametrically opposed to the old one. The divinity of the mother gives way to that of the father, the night cedes its primacy to the day, the left side to the right, and it is only in their contrast that the character of the two stages stands out sharply. The Pelasgian culture derives its stamp from its emphasis on maternity, Hellenism is inseparable from the patriarchal view. The Pelasgians present a picture of material confinement, the Hellenes of spiritual development; the life of the Pelasgians is marked by the operation of unconscious law, that of the Hellenes by individualism; on the one hand we find acceptance of nature, on the other, a transcending of nature; the old limits of existence are burst, the striving and suffering of Promethean life takes the place of perpetual rest, peaceful enjoyment, and eternal childhood in an aging body. The higher hope of the Demetrian mystery lies in the mother's free gift, which is seen in the sprouting of the seed corn; the Hellene wishes to achieve everything, even the supreme goal, by his own efforts. In struggle he becomes aware of his paternal nature, in battle he raises himself above the maternity to which he had wholly belonged, in battle he strives upward to his own divinity. For him the source of immortality is no longer the childbearing woman but the male-creative principle, which he endows with the divinity that the earlier world imputed only to the mother.

It is assuredly the Attic race that carried the Zeus character of paternity to its highest development. Though Athens itself has its roots in the Pelasgian culture, it wholly subordinated the Demetrian to the Apollonian principle in the course of its development. The Athenians revered Theseus as a second woman-hating Heracles; in the person of Athene they set motherless paternity in the place of fatherless maternity; and even in their legislation they endowed the universal principle of paternity with a character of inviolability which the old law of the Erinyes imputed only to motherhood. The virgin goddess is well disposed to the masculine, helpful to the heroes of the paternal solar law; in her, the warlike Amazonism of the old day reappears in spiritual form. Her city is hostile to the women who moor their ships on the coasts of Attica in search of help in defending the rights of their sex. Here the opposition between the Apollonian and the Demetrian principle stands out sharply. This city, whose earliest history discloses traces of matriarchal conditions, carried paternity to its highest development; and in one-sided exaggeration it condemned woman to a status of inferiority particularly surprising in its contrast to the foundations of the Eleusinian mysteries.

The Twilight of the Romantics

SOURCES

103. Giuseppe Mazzini, *An Essay on the Duties of Man Addressed to Workingmen* (New York, 1892), pp. 64-69. Originally published as *Doveri dell'uomo* in Naples, 1860. Tr. Emilie Ashurst Venturi in 1862.

104. John Ruskin, "Of Queen's Gardens," in *Sesame and Lilies* (London, 1907), pp. 49-50, 58-60, 71-74. Originally published in London, 1865.

The surge of scholarly interest in investigating the history of woman's position in society, as illustrated in this volume by Maine and Bachofen, should not obscure the continuing importance of the philosophical vision of womanhood celebrated by Romantic writers in this era. In these selections, we present two additional, influential statements of the Romantic idealist perspective, published at about the same time.

The first selection is by Giuseppe Mazzini (1805-1872), the longtime revolutionary and champion of Italian unification. Raised and educated in Genoa, Mazzini lived in exile for many years in France, Switzerland, and England, where he augmented his background in the classics of European literature with the teachings of the Saint-Simonians and other "utopian" socialists, and of republicanism. Never married, though close to many women, his vision of woman's sphere, as revealed in this excerpt, was one of "radical maternity" and of the family as an irreducible institution and a vital agent of social change. Here Mazzini exhorts working-class men to honor their families and to recognize their wives as angels in the house.

The second selection is John Ruskin's vision, first presented to the public as a lecture in the Manchester Town Hall in 1864. Ruskin (1819-1900) was perhaps one of the most original and best known of the English Victorians. The son of a wealthy wine merchant and his overprotective wife, young Ruskin had been encouraged to develop his artistic talents and aesthetic sensibilities; in the course of an otherwise confining youth, he developed a lasting enthusiasm for Gothic art and things medieval, for the Alps, and for the controversial paintings of J. M. W. Turner, whose champion Ruskin became. Indeed, in "Of Queen's Gardens" Ruskin draws heavily on the imagery of medieval chivalry. His message of social regeneration through woman's agency should be compared with those of Aimé-Martin and Michelet (Docs. 43, 97), with whose writings Ruskin was clearly familiar. Though seductively poetic and in certain respects egalitarian, his vision of sexual complementarity must ultimately be judged a male projection; in it woman is "other," an ideal type whose very mythic qualities Ruskin believed might be invoked to uplift ordinary men. One is led to seek the sources of this idealization. As it turns out, Ruskin's personal relationships with real women were never satisfactory: his wife had their marriage annulled, claiming that Ruskin was impotent. In Ruskin's defense, however, it must be acknowledged that he did advocate a substantive education for women, and his vision of female superiority, despite its fancifulness, does propose a serious mission for women of the leisure class at a time when they were once again being roundly criticized for their frivolity.

---

103. Giuseppe Mazzini (1860)

The Family is the Heart's Fatherland. There is in the Family an Angel, possessed of a mysterious influence of grace, sweetness, love; an Angel who renders our duties less arid and our sorrows less bitter. The only pure and unalloyed happiness, the only joys untainted by grief granted to man on this earth are—thanks be given to this Angel!—the happiness and joys of the family. He who, from some fatality of position, has been unable to live the calm life of the Family, sheltered beneath this Angel's wing, has a shadow of sadness cast over his soul, and a void in his heart which naught can fill, as I, who write these pages for you, know.

Bless the God who created this Angel, O you who share the joys and consolations of the Family! Hold them not in light esteem, because you fancy you might find more ardent pleasures and more facile consolations elsewhere. There is in the family an element rarely found elsewhere—the element of durability. Family affections wind themselves round your heart slowly and all unobserved; but tenacious and enduring as the ivy round the tree, they cling to you hour by hour, mingling with and becoming a portion of your very existence. Very often you are unconscious of them, because they are a part of yourselves; but when once you lose them, you feel as if an intimate and necessary portion of your life were gone. You wander restless and unhappy; it may be that you again succeed in finding some brief delights and consolations, but never the supreme consolation of calm; the calm of the waters of the lake, the calm of trusting sleep, a repose like that of the child on its mother's breast.

This Angel of the family is woman. Whether as mother, wife, or sister, woman is the caress of existence, the soft sweetness of affection diffused over its fatigues, a reflection in the individual of that loving Providence which watches over Humanity. She has in her a treasure of gentle consolation sufficient to soothe every sorrow. Moreover, she is for each of us the Initiatrix of the future. The child learns its first lesson of love from its mother's kiss. In the first sacred kiss of the beloved one, man learns the lesson of hope and faith in life, and hope and faith create that yearning after progress, and that power to achieve it step by step—that *future*, in short—whose living symbol is the infant, our link with the generations to come. It is through woman that the family—with its Divine mystery of reproduction—points to Eternity.

Hold, then, the family sacred, my brothers! Look upon it as one of the indestructible conditions of life, and reject every attempt made to undermine it, either by men imbued with a false and brutish philosophy, or by shallow thinkers, who, irritated at seeing it too often made the nursery of selfishness and the spirit of caste, imagine, like the savage, that the sole remedy for this evil growth, is the destruction of the tree itself.

The conception of the family is not human, but Divine, and no human power can extinguish it. Like the Fatherland—even more than the Fatherland—the family is an element of existence.

I have said, even more than the Fatherland. Distinctions of country—sacred now—may possibly disappear whenever man shall bear the moral law of Humanity inscribed upon his own heart, but the family will endure while man himself endures. It is the cradle of Humanity. Like every other element of human life, it is, of course, susceptible of progress, and from epoch to epoch its tendencies and aspirations are improved, but it can never be cancelled. Your mission is evermore to sanctify the family, and to link it ever more closely with the country. That which the country is to Humanity, the family must be to the country. Even as the scope and object of our love of country is, as I have told you, to educate you as *men*, so the scope and object of the family is to educate you as *citizens*. The family and the country are the two extreme points of one and the same line. And wheresoever this is not the case the family degenerates into selfishness, a selfishness the more odious and brutal, inasmuch as it prostitutes and perverts from their true aim the most sacred things that be—our affections.

Love and respect woman. See in her not merely a comfort, but a force, an inspiration, the redoubling of your intellectual and moral faculties.

Cancel from your minds every idea of superiority over woman. You have none whatsoever.

Long prejudice, an inferior education, and a perennial legal inequality and injustice, have created that *apparent* intellectual inferiority which has been converted into an argument for continued oppression.

But does not the history of every oppression teach us how the oppressor ever seeks his justification and support by appealing to a fact of his own creation? The feudal castes that withheld education from the sons of the people, excluded them, on the grounds of that very want of education, from the rights of the citizen, from the sanctuary wherein laws are framed, and from that right to vote which is the initiation of their social mission. The slaveholders of America declare the black race radically inferior and incapable of education, and yet persecute those who seek to instruct them. For half a century the supporters of the reigning families in Italy have declared the Italians unfit for freedom, and meanwhile, by their laws, and by the brute force of hireling armies, they close every path through which we might overcome the obstacles to our improvement, where such really exist, as if tyranny could ever be a means of educating men for liberty.

Now, we men have ever been, and still are, guilty of a similar crime towards woman. Avoid even the shadow or semblance of this crime; there is none heavier in the sight of God, for it divides the human family into two classes, and imposes or accepts the subjugation of one class to the other.

In the sight of God the Father there is neither *man* or *woman*. There is only the *human being*, that being in whom, whether the form be of male or female, those characteristics which distinguish Humanity from the brute creation are united, namely: the social tendency, and the capacity of education and progress.

Wheresoever these characteristics exist, the human nature is revealed, and thence perfect equality both of rights and of duties.

Like two distinct branches springing from the same trunk, man and woman are varieties springing from the common basis—Humanity. There is no inequality between them, but, even as is often the case among men, diversity of tendency and of special vocation. Are two notes of the same musical chord unequal or of different nature? Man and woman are the two notes without which the Human chord is impossible.

Suppose two peoples, one of which is called by circumstances and by special tendencies to the mission of diffusing the idea of human association by means of colonization, and the other to teach that idea by the production of universally admired literature and art; are their general rights and duties therefore different? Both of these people are, consciously or unconsciously, Apostles of the same Divine Idea, equals and brothers in that idea.

Man and Woman, even as these two peoples, fulfill different functions in Humanity, but these functions are equally sacred, equally manifestations of that Thought of God which He has made the soul of the universe.

Consider woman, therefore, as the partner and companion, not merely of your joys and sorrows, but of your thoughts, your aspirations, your studies and your endeavours after social amelioration. Consider her your equal in your civil and political life. Be ye the two human wings that lift the soul towards the Ideal we are destined to attain. The Mosaic Bible has declared: *God created man, and woman from man*; but your Bible, the Bible of the Future, will proclaim that *God created Humanity, made manifest in the woman and the man.*

104. John Ruskin (1865)

Believing that all literature and all education are only useful so far as they tend to confirm this calm, beneficent, and *therefore* kingly, power—first, over ourselves, and, through ourselves, over all around us, I am now going to ask you to consider with me farther, what special portion or kind of this royal authority, arising out of noble education, may rightly be possessed by women; and how far they also are called to a true queenly power. Not in their households merely, but over all within their sphere. And in what sense, if they rightly understood and exercised this royal or gracious influence, the order and beauty induced by such benignant power would justify us in speaking of the territories over which each of them reigned, as "Queens' Gardens."

And here, in the very outset, we are met by a far deeper question, which—strange though this may seem—remains among many of us yet quite undecided, in spite of its infinite importance.

We cannot determine what the queenly power of women should be, until we are agreed what their ordinary power should be. We cannot consider how education may fit them for any widely extending duty, until we are agreed what is their true constant duty. And there never was a time when wilder words were spoken, or more vain imagination permitted, respecting this question—quite vital to all social happiness. The relations of the womanly to the manly nature, their different capacities of intellect or of virtue, seem never to have been yet measured with entire consent. We hear of the mission and of the rights of Woman, as if these could ever be separate from the mission and the rights of Man—as if she and her lord were creatures of independent kind and of irreconcileable claim. This, at least, is wrong. And not less wrong—perhaps even more foolishly wrong (for I will anticipate thus far what I hope to prove)—is the idea that woman is only the shadow and attendant image of her lord, owing him a thoughtless and servile obedience, and supported altogether in her weakness by the pre-eminence of his fortitude.

This, I say, is the most foolish of all errors respecting her who was made to be the helpmate of man. As if he could be helped effectively by a shadow, or worthily by a slave!

Let us try, then, whether we cannot get at some clear and harmonious idea (it must be harmonious if it is true) of what womanly mind and virtue are in power and office, with respect to man's; and how their relations, rightly accepted, aid, and increase, the vigour, and honour, and authority of both. . . .

. . . But what we too often doubt is the fitness of the continuance of such a relation throughout the whole of human life. We think it right in the lover and mistress, not in the husband and wife. That is to say, we think that a reverent and tender duty is due to one whose affection we still doubt, and whose character we as yet do but partially and distantly discern; and that this reverence and duty are to be withdrawn, when the affection has become wholly and limitlessly our own, and the character has been so sifted and tried that we fear not to entrust it with the happiness of our lives. Do you not see how ignoble this is, as well as how unreasonable? Do you not feel that marriage—when it is marriage at all—is only the seal which marks the vowed transition of temporary into untiring service, and of fitful into eternal love?

But how, you will ask, is the idea of this guiding function of the woman reconcileable with a true wifely subjection? Simply in that it is a *guiding*, not a determining, function. Let me try to show you briefly how these powers seem to be rightly distinguishable.

We are foolish, and without excuse foolish, in speaking of the "superiority" of one sex to the other, as if they could be compared in similar things. Each has what the other has not: each completes the other, and is completed by the other: they are in nothing alike, and the happiness and perfection of both depends on each asking and receiving from the other what the other only can give.

Now their separate characters are briefly these. The man's power is active, progressive, defensive. He is eminently the doer, the creator, the discoverer, the defender. His intellect is for speculation and invention; his energy for adventure, for war, and for conquest, wherever war is just, wherever conquest necessary. But the woman's power is for rule, not for battle—and her intellect is not for invention or creation, but for sweet ordering, arrangement, and decision. She sees the qualities of things, their claims, and their places. Her great function is Praise: she enters into no contest, but infallibly adjudges the crown of contest. By her office, and place, she is protected from all danger and temptation. The man, in his rough work in open world, must encounter all peril and trial:—to him, therefore, the failure, the offence, the inevitable error: often he must be wounded, or subdued, often misled, and *always* hardened. But he guards the woman from all this; within his house, as ruled by her, unless she herself has sought it, need enter no danger, no temptation, no cause of error or offence. This is the true nature of home—it is the place of Peace; the shelter, not only from all injury, but from all terror, doubt, and division. In so far as it is not this, it is not home; so far as the anxieties of the outer life penetrate into it, and the inconsistently-minded, unknown, unloved, or hostile society of the outer world is allowed by either husband or wife to cross the threshold, it ceases to be home; it is then only a part of that outer world which you have roofed over, and lighted fire in. But so far as it is a sacred place, a vestal temple, a temple of the hearth watched over by Household Gods, before whose faces none may come but those whom they can receive with love—so far as it is this, and roof and fire are types only of a nobler shade and light—shade as of the rock in a weary land, and light as of the Pharos in the stormy sea—so far it vindicates the name, and fulfils the praise, of Home.

And wherever a true wife comes, this home is always round her. The stars only may be over her head; the glowworm in the night-cold grass may be the only fire at her foot: but home is yet wherever she is; and for a noble woman it stretches far round her, better than ceiled with cedar, or painted with vermilion, shedding its quiet light far, for those who else were homeless.

This, then, I believe to be—will you not admit it to be—the woman's true place and power? But do not you see that, to fulfil this, she must—as far as one can use such terms of a human creature—be incapable of error? So far as she rules, all must be right, or nothing is. She must be enduringly, incorruptibly good; instinctively, infallibly wise—wise, not for self-development, but for self-renunciation: wise, not that she may set herself above her husband, but that she may never fail from his side: wise, not with the narrowness of insolent and loveless pride, but with the passionate gentleness of an infinitely variable, because infinitely applicable, modesty of service—the true changefulness of woman. In that great sense—"La donna e mobile," not "Qual piùm' al vento"; no, nor yet "Variable as the shade, by the light quivering aspen made"; but variable as the *light*, manifold in fair and serene division, that it may take the colour of all that it falls upon, and exalt it. . . .

. . . Thus far, then, of the nature, thus far of the teaching, of woman, and thus of her household office, and queenliness. We come now to our last, our widest question—What is her queenly office with respect to the state?

Generally, we are under an impression that a man's duties are public, and a woman's private. But this is not altogether so. A man has a personal work or duty, relating to his own home, and a public work or duty, which is the expansion of the other, relating to the state. So a woman has a personal work or duty, relating to her own home, and a public work and duty, which is also the expansion of that.

Now the man's work for his own home is, as has been said, to secure its maintenance, progress, and defence; the woman's to secure its order, comfort, and loveliness.

Expand both these functions. The man's duty, as a member of a commonwealth, is to assist in the maintenance, in the advance, in the defence of the state. The woman's duty, as a member of the commonwealth, is to assist in the ordering, in the comforting, and in the beautiful adornment of the state.

What the man is at his own gate, defending it, if need be, against insult and spoil, that also, not in a less, but in a more devoted measure, he is to be at the gate of his country, leaving his home, if need be, even to the spoiler, to do his more incumbent work there.

And, in like manner, what the woman is to be within her gates, as the centre of order, the balm of distress, and the mirror of beauty; that she is also to be without her gates, where order is more difficult, distress more imminent, loveliness more rare.

And as within the human heart there is always set an instinct for all its real duties—an instinct which you cannot quench, but only warp and corrupt if you withdraw it from its true purpose—as there is the intense instinct of love, which, rightly disciplined, maintains all the sanctities of life, and, misdirected, undermines them; and *must* do either the one or the other;—so there is in the human heart an inextinguishable instinct, the love of power, which, rightly directed, maintains all the majesty of law and life, and misdirected, wrecks them.

Deep rooted in the innermost life of the heart of man, and of the heart of woman, God set it there, and God keeps it there. Vainly, as falsely, you blame or rebuke the desire of power!—For Heaven's sake, and for Man's sake, desire it all you can. But *what* power? That is all the question. Power to destroy? the lion's limb, and the dragon's breath? No so. Power to heal, to redeem, to guide, and to guard. Power of the sceptre and shield; the power of the royal hand that heals in touching—that binds the fiend, and looses the captive; the throne that is founded on the rock of

Justice, and descended from only by steps of mercy. Will you not covet such power as this, and seek such throne as this, and be no more house-wives, but queens?

. . . That highest dignity is open to you, if you will also accept that highest duty. Rex et Regina—Roi et Reine—"*Right*-doers"; they differ but from the Lady and Lord, in that their power is supreme over the mind as over the person—that they not only feed and clothe, but direct and teach. And whether consciously or not, you must be, in many a heart, enthroned: there is no putting by that crown; queens you must always be; queens to your lovers; queens to your husbands and your sons; queens of higher mystery to the world beyond, which bows itself, and will for ever bow, before the myrtle crown, and the stainless sceptre, of womanhood.

Ending the Subjection of Women

SOURCES

105. John Stuart Mill, *The Subjection of Women* (New York, 1869), pp. 48-52, 71-82, 177.

106. Margaret Oliphant, "Mill's *Subjection of Women*," *Edinburgh Review*, 130 (October 1869), 572-73, 577-80, 581-82, 583, 586-87.

107. Review of Mill's *Subjection of Women*, in *The Lancet*, 2, no. 2406 (9 October 1869), 510, 511-12.

108. Edouard de Pompéry, "L'Assujéttissement des femmes, par Stuart Mill," *La Philosophie Positive*, 6, no. 5 (March-April 1870), 314-15. Tr. KMO.

109. *A Reply to John Stuart Mill on the Subjection of Women* (Philadelphia, 1870), pp. 10-14.

In the heat of arguments over ancient history, women's place in the scheme of evolution, and resurgent romanticization of their role, John Stuart Mill (1806-1873) composed his most eloquent argument for women's legal emancipation from patriarchal institutions.

Mill, celebrated as an economist and political philosopher throughout Europe and in America, needs little introduction. One has only to recall his intellectual heritage of philosophic radicalism and his slow retreat from its principles, his precocious education at the hands of his strong-minded father, James Mill (Doc. 31), his early participation in the birth-control campaigns of Richard Carlile, the associate of Eliza Sharples (Doc. 33), his intense interest in Saint-Simonian and Fourierist social criticism (Docs. 34-36), and his long-standing debate with Auguste Comte (Docs. 62, 63), with whom Mill ultimately fell out over the issue of biological determinism, to recognize his importance in Western thought.

The woman question was central to his thinking from the 1830's, during his many years of collaboration with Harriet Taylor (Doc. 88). He remained convinced that there was no reason to admit the "necessary subordination of one sex to the other." Extending the principle he had developed in the great tract *On Liberty* (1859), Mill suggested that all artificial or socially constructed barriers to the flourishing of the female personality should be eliminated, thereby allowing the issue of women's nature to be decided once and for all. Women, he argued, should be allowed the same opportunity for personal liberty, the same freedom to acquire individual dignity, as was allowed to men. No romantic idealist like Ruskin (Doc. 104), Mill's eyes were open to the perversities of human nature— particularly male human nature. But he sustained his focus on the possible benefits that the development of female capacities might have for society as a whole. In the many countries where Mill's work was published or circulated, readers of both sexes found his view of marriage between equals breathtaking.

The four reviews of Mill's *Subjection of Women* excerpted here reveal the diverse ways in which the woman question debate forced thinkers to grapple with fundamental issues of political and social theory.

The second and third selections are excerpted from contemporary British publications. The long review by Margaret Oliphant (Doc. 91) in the *Edinburgh Review* was written when she had been ten years a struggling widow, supporting herself, her own children, and those of her brother, by her writing. Oliphant here revealed a fundamental difference in perception from that of Mill, charging that his arguments for lifting social constraints on the flowering of women's individuality simply ignored certain fundamental bio-social realities. For Oliphant, as for other subsequent critics of Mill, in marriage the couple, not the individual, was paramount, and maternity determined the basic division of social labor between the sexes. The reviewer in the *Lancet*, the weekly publication of the British medical profession, invoked—in a different fashion—the fact of significant physiological differences between the sexes to assure his readers that women were, on the whole, simply disadvantaged in competition with men and that, although there were many areas in which their social contributions could be useful, neither the political arena nor that of the liberal professions such as medicine were suitable places for them.

The selection by Edouard de Pompéry (1812-1895) offers a very different sort of critique of Mill's *Subjection*. Pompéry, a fervent French republican and humanist from Brittany, was a partisan of Fourier (Docs. 9, 35) and in 1864 had published a treatise, *La Femme dans l'humanité, sa nature, son rôle, et sa valeur sociale*. Though his review of Mill was published in the Comtist-positivist *Revue Philosophique*, Pompéry criticized Mill not (as might have been expected) for ignoring Comte's biological determinism but—startlingly—for departing from an argument based solely on principles of intrinsic moral equality.

The final selection, from a book published in Philadelphia by an anonymous author, sometimes identified as Donald MacCaig, was dedicated "to all who believe, or are open to the conviction, that their fathers were not all tyrants, nor their mothers all slaves." In contrast to Pompéry this author, after contesting Mill's championing of equality arguments themselves, in subsequent chapters attempted to refute Mill's arguments on a chapter-by-chapter basis.

---

105. John Stuart Mill (1869)

One thing we may be certain of—that what is contrary to women's nature to do, they never will be made to do by simply giving their nature free play. The anxiety of mankind to interfere in behalf of nature, for fear lest nature should not succeed in effecting its purpose, is an altogether unnecessary solicitude. What women by nature cannot do, it is quite superfluous to forbid them from doing. What they can do, but not so well as the men who are their competitors, competition suffices to exclude them from; since nobody asks for protective duties and bounties in favour of women; it is only asked that the present bounties and protective duties in favour of men should be recalled. If women have a greater natural inclination for some things than for others, there is no need of laws or social inculcation to make the majority of them do the former in preference to the latter. Whatever women's services are most wanted for, the free play of competition will hold out the strongest inducements to them to undertake. And, as the words imply, they are most wanted for the things for which they are most fit; by the apportionment of which to them, the collective faculties of the two sexes can be applied on the whole with the greatest sum of valuable result.

The general opinion of men is supposed to be, that the natural vocation of a woman is that of a wife and mother. I say, is supposed to be, because, judging from acts—from the whole of the present constitution of society—one might infer that their opinion was the direct contrary. They might be supposed to think that the alleged natural vocation of women was of all things the most repugnant to their nature; insomuch that if they are free to do anything else—if any other means of living, or occupation of their time and faculties, is open, which has any chance of appearing desirable to them—there will not be enough of them who will be willing to accept the condition said to be natural to them. If this is the real opinion of men in general, it would be well that it should be spoken out. I should like to hear somebody openly enunciating the doctrine (it is already implied in much that is written on the subject)—"It is necessary to society that women should marry and produce children. They will not do so unless they are compelled. Therefore it is necessary to compel them." The merits of the case would then be clearly defined. It would be exactly that of the slaveholders of South Carolina and Louisiana. "It is necessary that cotton and sugar should be grown. White men cannot produce them. Negroes will not, for any wages which we choose to give. *Ergo* they must be compelled." An illustration still closer to the point is that of impressment. Sailors must absolutely be had to defend the country. It often happens that they will not voluntarily enlist. Therefore there must be the power of forcing them. How often has this logic been used! and, but for one flaw in it, without doubt it would have been successful up to this day. But it is open to the retort—First pay the sailors the honest value of their labour. When you have made it as well worth their while to serve you, as to work for other employers, you will have no more difficulty than others have in obtaining their services. To this there is no logical answer except "I will not": and as people are now not only ashamed, but are not desirous, to rob the labourer of his hire, impressment is no longer advocated. Those who attempt to force women into marriage by closing all other doors against them, lay themselves open to a similar retort. If they mean what they say, their opinion must evidently be, that men do not render the married condition so desirable to women, as to induce them to accept it for its own recommendations. It is not a sign of one's thinking the boon one offers very attractive, when one allows only Hobson's choice, "that or none." And here, I believe, is the clue to the feelings of those men, who have a real antipathy to the equal freedom of women. I believe they are afraid, not lest women should be unwilling to marry, for I do not think that any one in reality has that apprehension; but lest they should insist that marriage should be on equal conditions; lest all women of spirit and capacity should prefer doing almost anything else, not in their own eyes degrading, rather than marry, when marrying is giving themselves a master, and a master too of all their earthly possessions. And truly, if this consequence were necessarily incident to marriage, I think that the apprehension would be very well founded. I agree in thinking it probable that few women, capable of anything else, would, unless under an irresistible *entrainement*, rendering them for the time insensible to anything but itself, choose such a lot, when any other means were open to them of filling a conventionally honourable place in life: and if men are determined that the law of marriage shall be a law of despotism, they are quite right, in point of mere policy, in leaving to women only Hobson's choice. But, in that case, all that has been done in the modern world to relax the chain on the minds of women, has been a mistake. They never should have been allowed to receive a literary education. Women who read, much more women who write, are, in the existing constitution of things, a contradiction and a disturbing element: and it was wrong to bring women up with any acquirements but those of an odalisque, or of a domestic servant. . . .

But how, it will be asked, can any society exist without government? In a family, as in a state, some one person must be the ultimate ruler. Who shall decide when married people differ in opinion? Both cannot have their way, yet a decision one way or the other must be come to.

It is not true that in all voluntary association between two people, one of them must be absolute master: still less that the law must determine which of them it shall be. The most frequent case of voluntary association, next to marriage, is partnership in business: and it is not found or thought necessary to enact that in every partnership, one partner shall have entire control over the concern, and the others shall be bound to obey his orders. No one would enter into partnership on terms which would subject him to the responsibilities of a principal, with only the powers and privileges of a clerk or agent. If the law dealt with other contracts as it does with marriage, it would ordain that one partner should administer the common business as if it was his private concern; that the others should have only delegated powers; and that this one should be designated by some general presumption of law, for example as being the eldest. The law never does this: nor does experience show it to be necessary that any theoretical inequality of power should exist between the partners, or that the partnership should have any other conditions than what they may themselves appoint by their articles of agreement. Yet it might seem that the exclusive power might be conceded with less danger to the rights and interests of the inferior, in the case of partnership than in that of marriage, since he is free to cancel the power by withdrawing from the connexion. The wife has no such power, and even if she had, it is almost always desirable that she should try all measures before resorting to it.

It is quite true that things which have to be decided every day, and cannot adjust themselves gradually, or wait for a compromise, ought to depend on one will: one person must have their sole control. But it does not follow that this should always be the same person. The natural arrangement is a division of powers between the two; each being absolute in the executive branch of their own department, and any change of system and principle requiring the consent of both. The division neither can nor should be pre-established by the law, since it must depend on individual capacities and suitabilities. If the two persons chose, they might pre-appoint it by the marriage contract, as pecuniary arrangements are now often pre-appointed. There would seldom be any difficulty in deciding such things by mutual consent, unless the marriage was one of those unhappy ones in which all other things as well as this, become subjects of bickering and dispute. The division of rights would naturally follow the division of duties and functions; and that is already made by consent, or at all events not by law, but by general custom, modified and modifiable at the pleasure of the persons concerned.

The real practical decision of affairs, to whichever may be given the legal authority, will greatly depend, as it even now does, upon comparative qualifications. The mere fact that he is usually the eldest, will in most cases give the preponderance to the man; at least until they both attain a time of life at which the difference in their years is of no importance. There will naturally also be a more potential voice on the side, whichever it is, that brings the means of support. Inequality from this source does not depend on the law of marriage, but on the general conditions of human society, as now constituted. The influence of mental superiority, either general or special, and of superior decision of character, will necessarily tell for much. It always does so at present. And this fact shows how little foundation there is for the apprehension that the powers and responsibilities of partners in life (as of partners in business), cannot be satisfactorily apportioned by agreement between themselves. They always are so apportioned, except in cases in which the marriage institution is a failure. Things never come to an issue of downright power on one side, and obedience on the other, except where the connexion altogether has been a mistake, and it would be a blessing to both parties to be relieved from it. . . . The despotic power which the law gives to the husband may be a reason to make the wife assent to any compromise by which power is practically shared between the two, but it cannot be the reason why the husband does. That there is always among decently conducted people a practical compromise, though one of them at least is under no physical or moral necessity of making it, shows that the natural motives which lead to a voluntary adjustment of the united life of two persons in a manner acceptable to both, do on the whole, except in unfavourable cases, prevail. The matter is certainly not improved by laying down as an ordinance of law, that the superstructure of free government shall be raised upon a legal basis of despotism on one side and subjection on the other, and that every concession which the despot makes may, at his mere pleasure, and without any warning, be recalled. Besides that no freedom is worth much when held on so precarious a tenure, its conditions are not likely to be the most equitable when the law throws so prodigious a weight into one scale; when the adjustment rests between two persons one of whom is declared to be entitled to everything, the other not only entitled to nothing except during the good pleasure of the first, but under the strongest moral and religious obligation not to rebel under any excess of oppression.

A pertinacious adversary, pushed to extremities, may say, that husbands indeed are willing to be reasonable, and to make fair concessions to their partners without being compelled to it, but that wives are not: that if allowed any rights of their own, they will acknowledge no rights at all in any one else, and never will yield in anything, unless they can be compelled, by the man's mere authority, to yield in everything. This would have been said by many persons some generations ago, when satires on women were in vogue, and men thought it a clever thing to insult women for being what men made them. But it will be said by no one now who is worth replying to. It is not the doctrine of the present day that women are less susceptible of good feeling, and consideration for those with whom they are united by the strongest ties, than men are. On the contrary, we are perpetually told that women are better than men, by those who are totally opposed to treating them as if they were as good; so that the saying has passed into a piece of tiresome cant, intended to put a complimentary face upon an injury, and resembling those celebrations of royal clemency which, according to Gulliver, the king of Lilliput always prefixed to his most sanguinary decrees. If women are better than men in anything, it surely is in individual self-sacrifice for those of their own family. But I lay little stress on this, so long as they are universally taught that they are born and created for self-sacrifice. I believe that equality of rights would abate the exaggerated self-abnegation which is the present artificial ideal of feminine character, and that a good woman would not be more self-sacrificing than the best man: but on the other hand, men would be much more unselfish and self-sacrificing than at present, because they would no longer be taught to worship their own will as such a grand thing that it is actually the law for another rational being. There is nothing which men so easily learn as this self-worship: all privileged persons, and all privileged classes, have had it. The more we descend in the scale of humanity, the intenser it is; and most of all in those who are not, and can never expect to be, raised above any one except an unfortunate wife and children. The honourable exceptions are proportionally fewer than in the case of almost any other human infirmity. Philosophy and religion, instead of keeping it in check, are generally suborned to defend it; and nothing controls it but that practical feeling of the equality of human beings, which is the theory of Christianity, but which Christianity will never practically teach, while it sanctions institutions grounded on an arbitrary preference of one human being over another. . . .

The equality of married persons before the law, is not only the sole mode in which that particular relation can be made consistent with justice to both sides, and conducive to the happiness of both, but it is the only means of rendering the daily life of mankind, in any high sense, a school of moral cultivation. Though the truth may not be felt or generally acknowledged for generations to come, the only school of genuine moral sentiment is society between equals. The moral education of mankind has hitherto emanated chiefly from the law of force, and is adapted almost solely to the relations which force creates. In the less advanced states of society, people hardly recognise any relation with their equals. To be an equal is to be an enemy. Society, from its highest place to its lowest, is one long chain, or rather ladder, where every individual is either above or below his nearest neighbour, and wherever he does not command he must obey. Existing moralities accordingly, are mainly fitted to a relation of command and obedience. Yet command and obedience are but unfortunate necessities of human life: society in equality is its normal state. Already in modern life, and more and more as it progressively improves, command and obedience become exceptional facts in life, equal association its general rule. The morality of the first ages rested on the obligation to submit to power; that of the ages next following, on the right of the weak to the forbearance and protection of the strong. How much longer is one form of society and life to content itself with the morality made for another? We have had the morality of submission, and the morality of chivalry and generosity; the time is now come for the morality of justice. Whenever, in former ages, any approach has been made to society in equality, Justice has asserted its claims as the foundation of virtue. It was thus in the free republics of antiquity. But even in the best of these, the equals were limited to the free male citizens; slaves, women, and the unenfranchised residents were under the law of force. The joint influence of Roman civilization and of Christianity obliterated these distinctions, and in theory (if only partially in practice) declared the claims of the human being, as such, to be paramount to those of sex, class, or social position. The barriers which had begun to be levelled were raised again by the northern conquests; and the whole of modern history consists of the slow process by which they have since been wearing away. We are entering into an order of things in which justice will again be the primary virtue; grounded as before on equal, but now also on sympathetic association; having its root no longer in the instinct of equals for self-protection, but in a cultivated sympathy between them; and no one being now left out, but an equal measure being extended to all. It is no novelty that mankind do not distinctly foresee their own changes, and that their sentiments are adapted to past, not to coming ages. To see the futurity of the species has always been the privilege of the intellectual élite, or of those who have learnt from them; to have the feelings of that futurity has been the distinction, and usually the martyrdom, of a still rarer élite. Institutions, books, education, society, all go on training human beings for the old, long after the new has come; much more when it is only coming. But the true virtue of human beings is fitness to live together as equals; claiming nothing for themselves but what they as freely concede to every one else; regarding command of any kind as an exceptional necessity, and in all cases a temporary one; and preferring, whenever possible, the society of those with whom leading and following can be alternate and reciprocal. To these virtues, nothing in life as at present constituted gives cultivation by exercise. The family is a school of despotism, in which the virtues of despotism, but also its vices, are largely nourished. Citizenship, in free countries, is partly a school of society in equality; but citizenship fills only a small place in modern life, and does not come near the daily habits or inmost sentiments. The family, justly constituted, would be the real school of the virtues of freedom. It is sure to be a sufficient one of everything else. It will always be a school of obedience for the children, of command for the parents. What is needed is, that it should be a school of sympathy in equality, of living together in love, without power on one side or obedience on the other. This it ought to be between the parents. It would then be an exercise of those virtues which each requires to fit them for all other association, and a model to the children of the feelings and conduct which their temporary training by means of obedience is designed to render habitual, and therefore natural, to them. The moral training of mankind will never be adapted to the conditions of the life for which all other human progress is a preparation, until they practise in the family the same moral rule which is adapted to the normal constitution of human society. . . .

What marriage may be in the case of two persons of cultivated faculties, identical in opinions and purposes, between whom there exists that best kind of equality, similarity of powers and capacities with reciprocal superiority in them—so that each can enjoy the luxury of looking up to the other, and can have alternately the pleasure of leading and of being led in the path of development—I will not attempt to describe. To those who can conceive it, there is no need; to those who cannot, it would appear the dream of an enthusiast. But I maintain, with the profoundest conviction, that this, and this only, is the ideal of marriage; and that all opinions, customs, and institutions which favour any other notion of it, or turn the conceptions and aspirations connected with it into any other direction, by whatever pretences they may be coloured, are relics of primitive barbarism. The moral regeneration of mankind will only really commence, when the most fundamental of the social relations is placed under the rule of equal justice, and when human beings learn to cultivate their strongest sympathy with an equal in rights and in cultivation.

106. Margaret Oliphant (1869)

Of all writers on the claims of women, Mr. Mill alone has treated the question on its fundamental principles. The apologists of woman have eluded the first dilemma in many ingenious ways. They have not ventured to go to the fountainhead and begin with the beginning. We have heard much talk about moral superiority and mental equality, but more in the shape of guesses than of argument; and we have had an amount of wild statement on both sides which it is amazing should have been tolerated in any reasonable discussion. Men have gravely informed us that women were incapable of self-government, or of any share in the serious work of the world, notwithstanding the patent facts which we have only to open our eyes and see; and women, with equal gravity and more heat, have endeavoured to impress upon us the belief that they were competent to undertake the work of men, not instead of, but in addition to, their own. We have been told that the one sex is better and that it is worse than the other; that it is full of intuitive wisdom and intuitive folly; that it is stronger, that it is weaker, that it is purer, that it is wickeder. We have been told that most of the harm done in the world has originated with women; and we have been told that all the good comes from their influence and soft example. In the face of such assertions what is the puzzled spectator to do? . . .

. . . When Mr. Mill asserts that slavery is the basis of the law of marriage, he forgets that it is a contract by which the master is bound to labour for the slave, not the slave for the master.

And even after this preface which has somewhat shaken our confidence in him, it is disappointing to find that such an authority as Mr. Mill takes us to no higher ground in his attempt to clear up the old question between men and women than that limited area of equality upon which so many futile duels have been fought. Of all doubtful questions, this is one which must be the most doubtful to any thoughtful mind. Is there such a thing as equality, not only between men and women, but between any two creatures in the whole round of existence? Mr. Mill's very argument settles the question between the sexes without a moment's difficulty; for the fundamental and undeniable difference of bodily strength, which alone would make the subjection he describes possible, throws the balance so overwhelmingly in favour of one of the claimants, that the superiority of the other in point of intellect and character would need to be immense in order to neutralise that first advantage. Intellect is a great power; and no doubt in the long run it is that which solves all the difficulties, and finally settles the movements of humanity; but it does not reign at first hand, nor is it the undisputed monarch of the universe; and even did woman possess a monopoly of it, which is so far from being the case, it is doubtful whether that would have sufficed in the rude conflicts of the ages to enable her to hold her ground as an antagonist and athlete against the greater strength, the bolder temper, and the uninterrupted robustness of man. But, strangely enough, it is in this aspect alone that Mr. Mill apparently cares to consider it. It is to him no complicated matter which a hundred subtleties of nature combine to render difficult, but a simple question to be settled by that sleight of hand which is called legislation. It is strange to find so profound a mind taking so superficial a view. Even were his theory of equality a perfectly right and just one, did men and women stand upon precisely the same ground, adapted for the same work, framed on the same model, qualified to perform the same functions in the world, yet the very fact that for so many centuries they have not realised this, and in the meantime have been weaving themselves up in confused and intricate webs of prejudice and tradition, should move the philosopher to a keener sense of the infinite difficulties of the subject. These difficulties, which to us seem well nigh insurmountable, are in his opinion overcome by a simple change of conditions. He mixes up the fundamental question—which we may call that of the official superiority of man in the economy of the world—with local laws of marriage and individual hardships resulting from the same; strangely conceiving the greater to be produced by the less, and not the less by the greater. And looking on the matter in this light, the remedy becomes easy enough. It is but to repeal the laws which subject women to the legal authority of their husbands, and to place the sexes on a footing of external equality. These words no doubt describe an outward revolution which would change, though not so much as appears on the face, many circumstances of our lives. It would not, however, change in one iota the laws or conditions of nature. The alteration would be simply external. The disabilities of woman removed, the superstition of her different standing in the world abolished, her equality recognised, her rights guaranteed, a perfect legal level of position established between men and women—this is Mr. Mill's remedy for all her evils. He does not flatter us, indeed, that the immediate result will be perfect blessedness, for she is, he thinks, too profoundly debased by her subjection to recover all in a moment. But the acknowledgment of her equality is all that is wanted in the long run; and as soon as she has become accustomed to her enfranchisement her griefs will disappear by degrees, and Woman for the first time will be happy, being free.

This is a summary way of settling the difficulty, and, if it were possible, would be a very easy one; but Mr. Mill does not seem to perceive that any law on such a subject must be but an expression of some deep primitive sentiment, and that while the former can be dealt with, the latter is beyond the reach of legislation. For our own part, we agree with Mr. Mill to a great extent as to the injustice of some existing laws which press very hardly upon women; and are perfectly disposed to accept the alterations he suggests, believing that they would furnish a real remedy for a distinct grievance. We believe that a great and universal injury—the injury of an insult—is done to all women by the present state of the marriage law in England. Were it universally—as it is in the vast majority of cases—a dead letter, it would still outrage the sensibilities of one half of the race; and no end that is worth serving can be served by that. To say that a woman loses all rights, all property, all identity, as soon as she is married —although it is the merest legal fiction and idle breath—is in its actual words an insult to every woman. Nobody believes that the bride, when her husband leads her from the church door over the scattered flowers, herself the very flower and blossom of humanity, the perfection and the origin of life, is the chattel of the man by her side—a thing transformed, lost to the world and the race, absorbed in him, and with no further claim to personal existence. But yet the law says as much in the plainest language, and Mr. Mill builds upon this his dismal survey of the condition of women. It is not true, and all the enactments in the world could not make it so; and—not to speak of marriage settlements and the precautions of anxious parents—that mutual dependence which is the law of nature, and love which is the origin of wedlock, and the most ordinary good sense and good feeling suffice, except in individual instances, to nullify the law. The grievance chiefly complained of is, let us say, a sentimental grievance, and practically makes very little difference to the happiness of married women generally; but there are not perhaps a hundred married women in England to whom at one time or other the phraseology of the law has not conveyed a stinging sense of humiliation and insult. This has little to do with the abstract question of equality—it does not affect the subordination of the wife to the husband or the virtual authority of the bread-winner. It is a gratuitous offence and an actual falsehood. And at the same time it sets a door of opportunity open to the exceptional monsters of the race. "Absolute fiends are as rare as angels, perhaps rarer," says Mr. Mill; but when the fiend appears, as happens at intervals, the law hands his victim over to him with cheerful readiness. It provides the knife and the cord, and places every instrument of torture within the reach of the operator. It will not let him kill her, unless he is exceptionally gifted; but it lets him rob her, starve her, ruin her, beat away her hands from every help she clings to, neutralise all her efforts, take the bread out of her mouth and the children out of her arms, and make her life a continued torture. All this can be done in the name of the law which insults the happiest wife, while it thus crushes the unfortunate. This is a question altogether apart from the general question between the sexes. It is a special practical matter, susceptible of amendment. The Married Woman's Property Bill, without offering any facilities for separation, or interfering in any way with the husband's position as a husband, offers a remedy which will cancel the sentimental grievance, and do as much for the real evil as can be done in this life. . . . But it would not affect, except nominally and in the most limited way, those arrangements which to him seem its artificial produce and to us appear the laws of nature. The bond of marriage is too intimate, and the parties are left too completely at each other's mercy, to make any external code absolutely supreme between them. We must search farther and go deeper before we can see where the foundation of the matter actually lies.

And strangely enough in this unjust and cruel and insulting law of marriage there is a germ of natural truth, which recognises something deeper in the question than Mr. Mill is disposed to recognise. "The two," he says with indignation, "are called one person in the law, for the purpose of inferring that whatever is hers is his; but the parallel inference is never drawn, that whatever is his is hers; the maxim is not applied against the man, except to make him responsible to third parties for her acts, as a master is for the acts of his servants or his cattle." Here then is the hypothesis which Mr. Mill will not take into consideration, but which we are compelled to take into consideration, and which in reality affects the whole question. They are "one person in law." This Mr. Mill asserts to be a cruel fiction. It is utterly contrary to the idea of two equally endowed, similarly able persons entering into a contract of mutual profit and assistance. It is here that we completely join issue with the so-called champion of women. It is here also that the real principle comes in, which he has treated, externally, as a matter of legislation alone—and far though we should be from placing ourselves on any other question on the same level with Mr. Mill, we have a conviction that in this point we speak with a fuller knowledge of the feeling of women, who are the parties most concerned. And we assert that this faulty law has yet amid all its offensive and tyrannical enactments caught sight of the principle in which lies all the difficulties of the question, and which Mr. Mill ignores. It is, that the man and the woman united in the first of all primitive bonds, the union upon which the world and the race depend, *are* one person. We say it not sentimentally or poetically, but with the profoundest sense of reality and seriousness. If they were two the matter would be easy. It would but be to establish the balance by law as Mr. Mill suggests and to keep it even; a business requiring the watchfulness of Argus, yet probably manageable by dint of pains and trouble. The secret of all that is hard and dangerous and bewildering in the matter, is simply the fact that in very truth the two *are* one. . . .

. . . A woman is a woman, and not a lesser edition of man. The competition in which we are for ever labouring to involve them, has no existence in nature. They are not rivals, nor antagonists. They are two halves of a complete being. The offices they hold in the world are essentially different. There is scarcely any natural standing ground which we can realise on which these two creatures appear as rivals. The very thought is preposterous. Shall the woman challenge the man to a trial of strength? Shall the man pit himself against the woman for delicacy of eye and taste? Shall she plough the heavy fields with him, wading through the new-turned mould, or shall he watch the children with her, patient through the weary vigil? An exchange of place and toil, the man taking the indoor work and the woman the outdoor, in order to prove the futility of their mutual discontent, was a favourite subject with the old ballad-makers; and the witty minstrel is generally very great on the domestic confusion that follows, and gives the wife the best of it. But the fact is that such a rivalry can be nothing but a jest. The two are not rivals, they are not alike. They are different creatures. They are one. . . .

. . . Far be it from us to dwell with prurient sentiment upon the details of that grand function which is the distinguishing work of woman in the world. But any theory of her being which ignores it, or gives it a secondary place, or in any way whatever leaves it out of the calculation, is inevitably a futile theory. Let us imagine even that at other times she may be capable of maintaining her own independence and securing her livelihood apart from the help of man—yet at these times she is not so capable. It is then that his strength which is liable to no interruption asserts its superiority. He has nothing to do which calls him off his day's work, prompts him to seek the covert, puts him aside from ordinary employments. Such a fact makes rivalry utterly impossible. It would be as reasonable to expect that a soldier engaged in a dangerous campaign, and with the necessity upon him of periodically confronting death, and running all the risks of a battle, should at the same time compete with a civilian in some art or handicraft. The comparison is weak, for there is no reason why the soldier should not be in robust health up to the moment of marching, and it is his own life only which is concerned. But the women who are men's wives are bound in most cases to undergo periodically a risk which is as great as that which any individual soldier encounters in a battle. And they have not only to brace their nerves to encounter this danger for themselves, but it is their grand moment of responsibility, when they must vindicate the trust reposed in them by God and the world. Can there be any doubt that this essential element of her life at once and for ever disables a woman from all trial of strength and rude equality with man? Nobody but a fool, we believe, will assert that the burden of this great trust stamps her as inferior. It would be just as reasonable to say that it gave her a superior place in the economy of nature as the possessor of a faculty more utterly essential to the continuance of the race. But there can be no doubt about the fact that it separates her and her work and her office from the office and work of man. The two are not made to contend and compete and run races for the same prize. There is no natural opposition, but on the contrary harmony unbounded in their differences of nature—harmony which can never be attained by two creatures framed on the self-same plan.

And thus, we repeat, the old harsh contemptuous law which Mr. Mill condemns, and which we no less condemn, melts into a certain sense of the necessities of nature which he refuses to acknowledge. With an economic provision for this most important of woman's disabilities, it qualifies her husband to act for her at all times, and binds him to provide for her. Marriage has its conditions which are hard upon him as well as upon her. He cannot be free any more than she is. By the laws of equality, might not he too demand to leave off his work by times, and let her shift for herself? The hardships are not all on her side. He must go on whether he likes it or no, while she may pause and rest; there can be no break in his labours, for everything depends upon him; not only the moral but a legal obligation binds him hand and foot. He is as subject as his wife is. The claims made upon him by her needs and the needs of her children impede his natural liberty as completely as the yoke of conjugal submission does hers.

107. *The Lancet* (1869)

So many pressing matters of professional interest have of late occupied our attention, that we have had neither leisure nor space for considering Mr. JOHN STUART MILL's work on the "Subjection of Women." In deference to the wish of several of our correspondents, we will, however, without attempting any elaborate discussion, express some of the objections to his views and those of the same school which appear to us to lie, as it were, upon the surface. Like every production of its author, "The Subjection of Women" is clearly and thoughtfully written; but it fails to carry conviction to our minds. The construction of an essay in the retirement of a study, where obstacles can be easily disposed of, is one thing; but it is quite another thing to encounter and overcome, in detail, the difficulties which practically meet us in real life: and this question of the subjection of women is environed with difficulties of a practical character. . . . We have no desire to curtail woman's sphere of usefulness, or prevent her from engaging in an active competition with man; on the contrary, we hold that, viewing the enormous amount of energy now wasted, it would be cruel to bar the door to anything likely to lead to some amelioration of the condition of thousands of women doomed to inactivity and poverty from the small number of occupations open to them. There are several of these for which they are specially fitted, but from which they are now either wholly or partially excluded by the presence of men who might well be engaged in more manly or arduous duties. By all means let these occupations be made available for women. But there are spheres where they already exercise great if not exclusive influence, and where the presence of well-trained and intelligent women was never more required than now. The enormous number of governesses is truly lamentable; but how many of them have no aptitude for their work, or are unfitted by nature or education for it? When the question of public education has been settled on some fixed basis, and the State recognizes the duties which it owes to all individuals alike, instead of only taking care to impose duties upon them for the well-being of society, there will be ample scope for the employment of women in our national schools, in instructing children not only in matters of a general or technical education, but in those which more especially belong to them as human beings in their domestic and social relations, and of which they are now so lamentably ignorant. How few girls really know anything of the management of a household, or about the proper dieting, clothing, and care of infants and children; and yet the lack of this knowledge brings poverty on themselves and is a source of disease and sorrow to others. How many a puny creature owes a feeble frame and delicate health to the ignorance of those who tended it in infancy or childhood. . . .

While we fully agree that it is a mark of the lowest and most depraved form of civilisation for women to be reduced to the position of being little more than slaves to man's passions or child-bearers, we do not think that anyone acquainted with the physiology of the female organism could deny that they would, in this respect, labour under grave disadvantages in the race with men. Philosophers and men of abstraction may, but practical every-day people cannot, ignore these distinctions. As long as it is the fashion of this world to "marry and be given in marriage," just so long will natural instincts propel the majority of young people in that direction, [in] spite of philosophers. . . . It will be said that we must still provide for the case of the large number of unmarried women. Be it so. In the human struggle for existence the victory will remain with the possessor of the most powerful and best-trained intellect; but where the mental qualities are equal, the possession of superior physical powers, such as men undoubtedly enjoy, will make all the difference nevertheless.

108. Edouard de Pompéry (1870)

This little book is a remarkable and powerful speech for the defense. . . . The work by the English philosopher is wholly worthy of him and of the noble cause he defends. It is also worthy enough to solicit public attention to a question of the greatest importance.

However, I do not share all of Mr. Mill's ideas and I think that, like most defenders of women's rights, he has fallen into an error that prejudices his cause. . . . The error for which I reproach Mr. Stuart Mill is to have rested his thesis concerning equality of rights for women and men on the thesis of the equality of their faculties. This leads to confusion, and Mr. Mill himself avows that the question of equality of faculties should be put to one side since at present it cannot be verified from experience.

I would argue that there is no need to demonstrate any equality of faculties between women and men in order to establish the equality of their rights. This equality is founded on an incontestable and superior principle.

In fact, in human society all those who are part of humanity enjoy in essence an equal right to development of their being. If it were not so, there would no longer be any society, no unity of the species, and no basis for a common justice. Whether you are black or white, yellow or red, man or woman, whether you are a genius or whether you are not, whether you are a child or an adult, your right is the same. For everyone the legitimacy of rights is equal, and each possesses it by the same entitlement, as a member of the species.

But equality of rights in no way implies equality of faculties or even their equivalence. Questions of superiority or inferiority of the beings who compose the species lie entirely outside the subject of equality and the legitimacy of their rights to individual expansion, and the development of their faculties. There can be no doubt that faculties are unequal and different among individuals of the same sex as among those of different sexes. This has little significance so long as the principle of equal right to individual development remains intact. If the principle is respected, it is evident that no member of society in his right mind can pretend that the social law assures him of faculties equal or equivalent to those of one or another of his kind. . . .

It is not in the name of equality of faculties between man and woman that the rights of woman should be demanded, but in the name of human justice, which should assure to each member of society the fullest and most complete expansion of his being. For it is self-evident that society has the greatest interest in seeing that each of its members is neither handicapped nor mutilated but, on the contrary, can contribute his best efforts in conformity with his natural faculties. Slavery, serfdom, the subjection of women have been passing necessities, along with war, theocracies, despotism, and that paternal power which extends to the right of life and death over every member of the family; but none of these institutions can find justification in rights or stand firm in the face of reason.

109. "A Reply to John Stuart Mill" (1870)

. . . It may be observed, for the benefit of those who have not had the opportunity of perusing Mr. Mill's essay, that the main features of this agitation consist in the advocacy of certain radical changes in the social condition of women; especially as regards marriage laws, and all other legal restrictions and disabilities not in accordance with certain hypothetical doctrines of equality to be more fully considered during the progress of this discussion.

The first fifty-two pages, or more than one-quarter of his essay, is devoted by Mr. Mill to securing a footing, or preparing his readers for the reform, the essential features of which are more fully explained throughout the second and third chapters of his book. These preparatory labors consist chiefly in an unqualified condemnation of old laws, old customs, and old institutions generally, but more especially such as relate to marriage, and the hitherto almost universally recognized distinctions in the occupations and legal position of the sexes. The existence to so late a date of the errors or injustice by which these distinctions are still maintained, and the authority of the laws which regulate them, is ascribed by the essayist to the idolatry of instinct, which, in the present century, is said to be greatly in the ascendant.

In order to bring those relics of barbarism into disrepute, and exhibit the enormities and wrongs which have been, and are still perpetrated against one-half of the human race under their sanction, the assumed equality of the sexes, if not the most philosophical, is perhaps the most effective instrument which could be adopted to catch the popular ear. Mr. Mill, however, cannot be accredited with making any original discovery in seizing upon this oft-exploded doctrine of equality, though his application of it is certainly original, but withal, the most absurdly unfortunate in which it has been made to serve the interests of any cause. Equality as a practical theory, except in the incipient stages of a reform or revolution, never can have any weight; for the very first shade of order or government is fatal to its pretensions. The equality by which man may secure power or place to-day, is the very means by which it may be wrested from him to-morrow. The failures and follies of all systems established on this basis are a sufficient comment on this aspect of the doctrine.

But if, practically, equality is a myth, naturally it is much more so. No kind of mental, moral, or physical equality exists among men themselves as the basis of any legislative privileges, much less between men and women. The very near approaches which men and women make to a similar mentality must, after all, be a very coarse-grained kind of equality, when it is always measured by bulk; for this is the only criterion employed in making the estimate. Woman manifests a certain amount of physical endurance, mental power, or moral acumen: she is, therefore, the equal or superior of man upon some one, or all of these considerations, and must, as a necessary consequence, be launched upon the sphere of masculine struggles and ambition, to measure herself against him. The doctrine, even with all this coarseness, and the other absurdities and inconsistencies which cling to it, might have some force if men were elevated to any enviable positions on the ground of equality. Practically instituted and carried out, such a system would be fatal to all government. Equality recognized, is the god of the mob, and mob-law. The most republican government on the face of the earth dare not practically adopt this theory. Indeed, it is on the recognized inequality of men that position, preferment, and authority are at all admissible in the state, and that there can be any justice in placing one man over another, even with delegated powers.

Mr. Mill does not find it convenient to analyze the doctrines on which the claims for his reform are based; for nothing more nor less than a loud-mouthed, coarse-grained equality, which means nothing, could serve his purpose. If intended to catch the popular but uncultivated ear and intellect, his choice has been most fortunate for success, but fatal to his reputation as a philosopher; for he has been preparing a companion piece to the doggerel, "When Adam delved and Eve span," and he will have his corresponding type of followers.

Every age and nation has its reforms, and reformers who propose to renovate the world, and establish all human institutions on the basis of equality and justice, and these find hosts ready to respond to their war-cry. If John Mill flatters himself that the system which he would introduce has a nobler foundation than others, and rests solely on justice and reason, he can scarcely congratulate himself on the majority of his followers and admirers; for these will certainly be made up, to a very great extent, of those who hold the most radical opinions with regard to all law and government; since, whatever be the intention of the author in his essay, his doctrines are the legitimate food of those who honor no higher god than their own crude imaginings.

Evolution, Science, and the Subjection of Women

SOURCES

110. Charles Darwin, *The Descent of Man and Selection in Relation to Sex* (New York, 1879), pp. 563-65. Originally published in London, 1871.

111. Paul Broca, "Sur les Cranes de la caverne de l'Homme-Mort," *Revue d'Anthropologie*, 2, no. 1 (Paris, 1873), 45-46. Tr. KMO.

112. Herbert Spencer, *The Principles of Sociology*, I (New York, 1893), 755-58. Originally published in London, 1876.

Victorian scholars did not limit their interest in the position of women to explorations of classical antiquity, especially in the wake of the controversy over evolution precipitated in 1859 by Darwin's *Origin of Species*. By 1870 a number of scientists in other fields had begun to address the woman question within the evolutionary framework offered by Darwin, drawing on more recent findings in biology and anthropology.

In 1871 Charles Darwin (1809-1882) published a second important book, *The Descent of Man*. In it he proposed the evolutionary importance of sexual selection, or choice of mate, for increasing the differentiation between men and women—as concerns not only their physiology but their mental and emotional make-up as well. Darwin was no misogynist of the temperament of a Proudhon (Docs. 52, 95) or a Comte (Docs. 62, 63), but—given his own theories and evidence from related empirical studies by others—he found it difficult to accept the arguments for women's emancipation of such liberal thinkers as John Stuart Mill. In Darwin's eyes, the very history of man's ancestors—in particular the fact that women, however much preyed upon by men, had become increasingly protected by them as societies grew more complex—suggested that women had lost the necessity of having to sharpen their faculties in the unremitting struggle for survival, thereby assuring their relatively inferior development. Though Darwin, ever cautious, refused to draw wholly deterministic conclusions from this pessimistic analysis, he was clearly convinced that the results of evolutionary sexual differentiation could never be undone, whatever nineteenth-century women's rights advocates might desire.

Darwin's arguments were of particular interest to pioneer anthropologists such as the French physician Paul Broca (1824-1880). A professor of clinical pathology in Paris and a member of the French Academy of Medicine, Broca was also one of the founders of physical anthropology in France and, as a senator, a proponent of state secondary education for women. In this selection Broca considers the evidence for sexual differentiation found in a recent discovery of Stone Age human remains in a burial cave named Homme-Mort, located in the mountains of southeastern France.

In contrast to Darwin and Broca, the widely read British social philosopher Herbert Spencer (1820-1903) developed a far more comprehensive interpretation. Considering the woman question from the standpoint of evolutionary progress in human social organization, focusing on the domestic institution of the family, and drawing on a wide range of examples from other cultures, Spencer argued that, with the advent of civilization, industry and monogamy tend to facilitate improvements in the status of women. Like a number of the French social scientists, Spencer's first career had been that of a civil engineer. But he soon turned to social analysis and began writing for progressive London periodicals. Never married, he devoted himself exclusively to the development of a "synthetic philosophy" that ultimately appeared in consecutive volumes on the principles of biology, psychology, morality, and sociology. Unlike Comte (Doc. 62), his predecessor in system-building, or even Darwin, Spencer was by no means hostile to effecting certain legal and educational improvements on behalf of women; he measured all such improvements within an analytical framework predicated on biological difference and on the premise that evolution brought increasing complexity in the organization of human affairs. Such complexity, Spencer believed, manifested itself in an ever-finer division of labor and in increased tension between the growing state and the now-disintegrating, once-autonomous family. Informed by Darwin's theories on natural and sexual selection, Spencer preached the gospel of laissez-faire individualism—for men—and coined the term "survival of the fittest." But for women, he insisted, any growth in individualism must be tempered by the prior requirements of the species for its continued reproduction.

---

110. Charles Darwin (1871)

Difference in the Mental Powers of the two Sexes.—With respect to differences of this nature between man and woman, it is probable that sexual selection has played a highly important part. I am aware that some writers doubt whether there is any such inherent difference; but this is at least probable from the analogy of the lower animals which present other secondary sexual characters. No one disputes that the bull differs in disposition from the cow, the wild-boar from the sow, the stallion from the mare, and, as is well known to the keepers of menageries, the males of the larger apes from the females. Woman seems to differ from man in mental disposition, chiefly in her greater tenderness and less selfishness; and this holds good even with savages, as shewn by a well-known passage in Mungo Park's Travels, and by statements made by many other travellers. Woman, owing to her maternal instincts, displays these qualities towards her infants in an eminent degree; therefore it is likely that she would often extend them towards her fellow-creatures. Man is the rival of other men; he delights in competition, and this leads to ambition which passes too easily into selfishness. These latter qualities seem to be his natural and unfortunate birthright. It is generally admitted that with woman the powers of intuition, of rapid perception, and perhaps of imitation, are more strongly marked than in man; but some, at least, of these faculties are characteristic of the lower races, and therefore of a past and lower state of civilisation.

The chief distinction in the intellectual powers of the two sexes is shewn by man's attaining to a higher eminence, in whatever he takes up, than can woman—whether requiring deep thought, reason, or imagination, or merely the use of the senses and hands. If two lists were made of the most eminent men and women in poetry, painting, sculpture, music (inclusive both of composition and performance), history, science, and philosophy, with half-a-dozen names under each subject, the two lists would not bear comparison. We may also infer, from the law of the deviation from averages, so well illustrated by Mr. Galton, in his work on 'Hereditary Genius,' that if men are capable of a decided pre-eminence over women in many subjects, the average of mental power in man must be above that of woman.

Amongst the half-human progenitors of man, and amongst savages, there have been struggles between the males during many generations for the possession of the females. But mere bodily strength and size would do little for victory, unless associated with courage, perseverance, and determined energy. With social animals, the young males have to pass through many a contest before they win a female, and the older males have to retain their females by renewed battles. They have, also, in the case of mankind, to defend their females, as well as their young, from enemies of all kinds, and to hunt for their joint subsistence. But to avoid enemies or to attack them with success, to capture wild animals, and to fashion weapons, requires the aid of the higher mental faculties, namely, observation, reason, invention, or imagination. These various faculties will thus have been continually put to the test and selected during manhood; they will, moreover, have been strengthened by use during this same period of life. Consequently, in accordance with the principle often alluded to, we might expect that they would at least tend to be transmitted chiefly to the male offspring at the corresponding period of manhood.

Now, when two men are put into competition, or a man with a woman, both possessed of every mental quality in equal perfection, save that one has higher energy, perseverance, and courage, the latter will generally become more eminent in every pursuit, and will gain the ascendancy.* He may be said to possess genius—for genius has been declared by a great authority to be patience; and patience, in this sense, means unflinching, undaunted perseverance. But this view of genius is perhaps deficient; for without the higher powers of the imagination and reason, no eminent success can be gained in many subjects. These latter faculties, as well as the former, will have been developed in man, partly through sexual selection—that is, through the contest of rival males, and partly through natural selection—that is, from success in the general struggle for life; and as in both cases the struggle will have been during maturity, the characters gained will have been transmitted more fully to the male than to the female offspring. It accords in a striking manner with this view of the modification and re-inforcement of many of our mental fac-

---

* J. Stuart Mill remarks ("The Subjection of Women," 1869, p. 122), "The things in which man most excels woman are those which require most plodding, and long hammering at single thoughts." What is this but energy and perseverance?

ulties by sexual selection, that, firstly, they notoriously undergo a considerable change at puberty,* and, secondly, that eunuchs remain throughout life inferior in these same qualities. Thus man has ultimately become superior to woman. It is, indeed, fortunate that the law of the equal transmission of characters to both sexes prevails with mammals; otherwise it is probable that man would have become as superior in mental endowment to woman, as the peacock is in ornamental plumage to the peahen.

It must be borne in mind that the tendency in characters acquired by either sex late in life, to be transmitted to the same sex at the same age, and of early acquired characters to be transmitted to both sexes, are rules which, though general, do not always hold. If they always held good, we might conclude (but I here exceed my proper bounds) that the inherited effects of the early education of boys and girls would be transmitted equally to both sexes; so that the present inequality in mental power between the sexes would not be effaced by a similar course of early training; nor can it have been caused by their dissimilar early training. In order that woman should reach the same standard as man, she ought, when nearly adult, to be trained to energy and perseverance, and to have her reason and imagination exercised to the highest point; and then she would probably transmit these qualities chiefly to her adult daughters. All women, however, could not be thus raised, unless during many generations those who excelled in the above robust virtues were married, and produced offspring in larger numbers than other women. As before remarked of bodily strength, although men do not now fight for their wives, and this form of selection has passed away, yet during manhood, they generally undergo a severe struggle in order to maintain themselves and their families; and this will tend to keep up or even increase their mental powers, and, as a consequence, the present inequality between the sexes.[†]

III. Paul Broca (1873)

I will now return to a curious detail that I mentioned previously, though I postponed the discussion until now. One of the most remarkable features of the Homme-Mort skull series is the relatively large capacity of the female skulls. It is only 99.5 cc. [cubic centimeters] less than that of the male skulls. None of the other races . . . offer such a small

---

*Darwin's reference is to Henry Maudsley, *Body and Mind: An Inquiry into their Connection and Mutual Influence, Specially in Reference to Mental Disorders; Being the Gulstonian Lectures for 1870, Delivered before the Royal College of Physicians* (New York, 1871), p. 31. On Maudsley, see below, headnote to Document 117.—EDS.

[†]An observation by Vogt bears on this subject: he says, "It is a remarkable circumstance that the difference between the sexes, as regards the cranial cavity, increases with the development of the race, so that the male European excels much more the female, than the negro the negress. Welcker confirms this statement of Iluschko from his measurements of negro and German skulls." But Vogt admits ("Lectures on Man," Eng. translat. 1864, p. 81) that more observations are requisite on this point.

sexual difference. In the Parisian series, in particular, the relative difference is twice as great. But the contrast between the two series becomes even more striking when we compare the proportional figures instead of the absolute figures. The female skulls from Homme-Mort measure less than the male skulls by only 6.6% of the total capacity. However, the difference between the skulls of the Parisian women . . . and the male skulls in the same series represents . . . 16.5% of their capacity. Thus the superiority of the men among the troglodytes amounts to only 6.5%, but for the Parisians it rises to 16.5%.

Earlier considerations allow us to note this fact without astonishment. Nothing varies more than the position and role of women in the various civilized and barbarian societies; but it is generally clear that the progress of civilization tends increasingly to assure woman of male protection. As a respected member of a family, she concentrates her efforts there, while man struggles outside it for [their mutual] existence; social organization, which already markedly attenuates for man the harshness of the laws of natural selection, eases them even more in the woman's case; thus with respect to man, she finds herself in conditions somewhat analogous to those in which the civilized person, sustained and protected by society, finds himself in comparison to the savage, who sustains himself solely by his own efforts. And just as we have seen civilization introduce into a race conditions of such a nature as to decrease the average volume of the skull, likewise we find in the social situation of civilized woman conditions that exaggerate the naturally existing difference between the volume of her brain and that of man's brain.

These conditions do not generally exist among savages. Their women share in the labor, the struggles, and the dangers of the tribe. Almost equally with man, they submit to the laws of natural selection. They go hunting, fishing, even into combat. The Cro-Magnon woman died from an axe blow that split her skull, and it must be remembered that one of the women in the Homme-Mort cavern carried the traces of an old and severe skull wound. Moreover, it is a well-known fact that among many savage or merely barbarian peoples, the constitution of the woman differs far less from that of the man than is the case among our own people. This remark cannot be elevated to the level of a general principle, because even among savages the position of woman varies a great deal, from the most abject slavery that reduces her to the rank of a domestic animal, to a more or less complete emancipation that associates her to the public life of her tribe.

112. Herbert Spencer (1876)

If, still guiding ourselves by observing the course of past evolution, we ask what changes in the *status* of women may be anticipated, the answer must be that a further approach towards equality of position between the sexes will take place. With decline of militancy and rise of industrialism— with decrease of compulsory co-operation and increase of voluntary co-operation—with strengthening sense of personal rights and accompanying sympathetic regard for the personal rights of others; must go a diminution of the political and domestic disabilities of women, until there remain only such as differences of constitution entail.

To draw inferences more specific is hazardous: probabilities and possibilities only can be indicated. While in some directions the emancipation of women has to be carried further, we may suspect that in other directions their claims have already been pushed beyond the normal limits. If from that stage of primitive degradation in which they were habitually stolen, bought and sold, made beasts of burden, inherited as property, and killed at will, we pass to the stage America shows us, in which a lady wanting a seat stares at a gentleman occupying one until he surrenders it, and then takes it without thanking him, we may infer that the rhythm traceable throughout all changes has carried this to an extreme from which there will be a recoil. The like may be said of some other cases: what were originally concessions have come to be claimed as rights, and in gaining the character of assumed rights, have lost much of the grace they had as concessions. Doubtless, however, there will remain in the social relations of men and women, not only observances of a kind called forth by sympathy of the strong for the weak irrespective of sex, and still more called forth by sympathy of the stronger sex for the weaker sex; but also observances which originate in the wish, not consciously formulated but felt, to compensate women for certain disadvantages entailed by their constitutions, and so to equalize the lives of the sexes as far as possible.

In domestic life, the relative position of women will doubtless rise; but it seems improbable that absolute equality with men will be reached. Legal decisions from time to time demanded by marital differences, involving the question which shall yield, are not likely to reverse all past decisions. Evenly though law may balance claims, it will, as the least evil, continue to give, in case of need, supremacy to the husband, as being the more judicially-minded. And, similarly, in the moral relations of married life, the preponderance of power, resulting from greater massiveness of nature, must, however unobtrusive it may become, continue with the man.

When we remember that up from the lowest savagery, civilization has, among other results, caused an increasing exemption of women from bread-winning labour, and that in the highest societies they have become most restricted to domestic duties and the rearing of children; we may be struck by the anomaly that in our days restriction to indoor occupations has come to be regarded as a grievance, and a claim is made to free competition with men in all outdoor occupations. This anomaly is traceable in part to the abnormal excess of women; and obviously a state of things which excludes many women from those natural careers in which they are dependent on men for subsistence, justifies the demand for freedom to pursue independent careers. That hindrances standing in their way should be, and will be, abolished must be admitted. At the same time it must be concluded that no considerable alteration in the careers of women in general, can be, or should be, so produced; and further, that any extensive change in the education of women, made with the view of fitting them for businesses and professions, would be mischievous. If women comprehended all that is contained in the domestic sphere, they would ask no other. If they could see everything which is implied in the right education of children, to a full conception of which no man has yet risen, much less any woman, they would seek no higher function.

That in time to come the political *status* of women may be raised to something like equality with that of men, seems a deduction naturally accompanying the preceding ones. But such an approximate equalization, normally accompanying a social structure of the completely industrial type, is not a normal accompaniment of social types still partially militant. Just noting that giving to men and women equal amounts of political power, while the political responsibilities entailed by war fell on men only, would involve a serious inequality, and that the desired equality is therefore impracticable while wars continue; it may be contended that though the possession of political power by women might improve a society in which State-regulation had been brought within the limits proper to pure industrialism, it would injure a society in which State-regulation has the wider range characterizing a more or less militant type. Several influences would conduce to retrogression. The greater respect for authority and weaker sentiment of individual freedom characterizing the feminine nature, would tend towards the maintenance and multiplication of restraints. Eagerness for special and immediate results, joined with inability to appreciate general and remote results, characterizing the majority of men and still more characterizing women, would, if women had power, entail increase of coercive measures for achieving present good, at the cost of future evil caused by excess of control. But there is a more direct reason for anticipating mischief from the exercise of political power by women, while the industrial form of political regulation is incomplete. We have seen that the welfare of a society requires that the ethics of the Family and the ethics of the State shall be kept distinct. Under the one the greatest benefits must be given where the merits are the smallest; under the other the benefits must be proportioned to the merits. For the infant unqualified generosity; for the adult citizen absolute justice. Now the ethics of the family are upheld by the parental instincts and sentiments, which, in the female, are qualified in a smaller degree by other feelings than in the male. Already these emotions proper to parenthood as they exist in men, lead them to carry the ethics of the Family into the policy of the State; and the mischief resulting would be increased were these emotions as existing in women, directly to influence that policy. The progress towards justice in social arrangements would be retarded; and demerit would be fostered at the expense of merit still more than now.

But in proportion as the conceptions of pure equity become clearer— as fast as the *régime* of voluntary co-operation develops to the full the sentiment of personal freedom, with a correlative regard for the like freedom of others—as fast as there is approached a state under which no restrictions on individual liberty will be tolerated, save those which the equal liberties of fellow-citizens entail—as fast as industrialism evolves its appropriate political agency, which, while commissioned to maintain equitable relations among citizens, is shorn of all those powers of further regulation characterizing the militant type; so fast may the extension of political power to women go on without evil. The moral evolution which leads to concession of it, will be the same moral evolution which renders it harmless and probably beneficial.

CHAPTER 13

New Controversies over Women's Education

University Education for Englishwomen

SOURCES

113. Emily Davies, "Special Systems of Education for Women," in *Thoughts on Some Questions Relating to Women, 1860-1908* (Cambridge, England, 1910), pp. 118-28 *passim*, 130-34. Originally published in *The London Student*, June 1868.

114. Anne Jemima Clough, "Merton Hall and the Cambridge Lectures for Women," prospectus dated 22 October 1873, Newnham College Archives.

In the 1860's higher education for women became a focal point in the discussion of the woman question at Oxford and Cambridge, where a number of academic radicals were engaged in efforts to change both the status of university teachers and the curriculum itself. Members of both these ancient English universities contributed to the early higher education of women, but it was at Cambridge that the first two colleges for women—Girton and Newnham—were founded.

These two colleges and their principals exemplify the split in ideology not only over women's higher education during this particular period, but over the broader issue of how to achieve women's goals within the confines of an established male society. Emily Davies (1830-1921), the founder of Girton College, strove in every particular for continuing the male educational tradition, even to the point of choosing the title "Mistress" of Girton College (Master being the title for heads of the men's colleges). Davies and her supporters argued that only by proving their capacity for equal study by achieving good marks on the competitive examinations for men, would women prove their right to emancipation. In their eyes any deviation from the classical curriculum—or emphasis on cultural female traits or requirements—would detract from reaching this goal, by allowing opponents to label women's intellectual capacity "inferior" or "second rate."

Anne Jemima Clough (1820-1892) became the first "principal" of Newnham, the competing Cambridge college for women, which began its existence in Merton Hall. Clough's contrasting approach grew out of her experience as the proprietor of a country school and as the organizer of the original North of England Council of University Extension Lectures, which attracted thousands of women in Manchester, Liverpool, Sheffield, and Newcastle during the late 1860's. She and her principal ally, the Cambridge philosopher Henry Sidgwick, argued for an independent, less organized, less rigorous type of study, suited to the individual according to age, temperament, and need. They recognized a vital difference between early Cambridge women students and their male counterparts that had less to do with femaleness *per se* than with cultural concerns: the female students were often older, and their previous education very different from that of the schoolboys who entered Cambridge; their immediate task was to acquire training as secondary teachers for a still largely ill-educated female population. Thus, the Clough-Sidgwick team at Newnham (after Clough's death, Sidgwick's wife Eleanor succeeded her as principal) believed from the outset in integrating women through the development of new, more flexible educational institutions, while Davies at Girton believed in integration by assimilation to male educational patterns, with the hope for change postponed to a later date.

In the article of 1868 reprinted below, Davies insisted that it was vital for women to submit to the same university entrance examinations as men. In contrast, Anne Jemima Clough's prospectus for "Merton Hall and the Cambridge Lectures for Women," which solicited funds for the construction of what would become Newnham College in 1874, stressed in the most non-threatening language the usefulness of the special lectures for women begun in 1871 as a necessary and valuable interim step for women's higher education at Cambridge.

---

113. Emily Davies (1868)

Among the controversies to which the movement for improving the education of women has given rise, there is one which presses for settlement. The question has arisen and must be answered—Is the improved education which, it is hoped, is about to be brought within reach of women, to be identical with that of men, or is it to be as good as possible, but in some way or other specifically feminine? The form in which the question practically first presents itself is—What shall be the standards of examination? . . . [The controversy may] be assumed to be between two parties, each equally accepting examinations as "valuable and indispensable things" alike for women and for men—each equally admitting that "their use is limited," and that they may be abused.

Of these two parties, one regards it as essential that the standards of examination for both sexes should be the same; the other holds that they may without harm—perhaps with advantage—be different.

. . . It may do something towards clearing away the haze to endeavour to give some answer to the question—Why do you ask for a common standard? Do you want to prove the intellectual equality of the sexes? or their identity? If you desire to improve female education, why not strive after what is ideally best, instead of trying to get things for women which have produced results far short of perfection in men?

The abstract questions as to equality and identity may be quickly dismissed. The advocates of the "common" principle—those who hold what may be called the *humane* theory—altogether disclaim any ambition to assert either. . . .

We come down, therefore, to the narrower and more hopeful inquiry—

Which is best, to extend methods of education admitted to be imperfect, or to invent new ones presumably better?

The latter course is urged on the ground that there are differences between men and women which educational systems ought to recognise; or supposing this to be disputed, that at any rate the conditions of women's lives are special, and ought to be specially prepared for; or there is a latent feeling of repugnance to what may appear like an ungraceful, perhaps childish, attempt to grasp at masculine privileges—an idea which jars upon a refined taste. Considerations of this sort, resting mainly upon sentiment or prejudice, can scarcely be met by argument. It is usually admitted that we are as yet in the dark as to the specific differences between men and women—that we do not know how far they are native, and to what extent those which strike the eye may have been produced by artificial influences—that even if we knew much more than we do about the nature of the material to be dealt with, we should still have much to learn as to the kind of intellectual discipline which might be most suitable. Nor have we as yet any trustworthy evidence—scarcely so much as a plausible suggestion—as to the manner in which the differences of the work in life to which men and women respectively are said to be called, could be met by corresponding differences in mental training. The arbitrary differences established by fashion seem to have been directed by the rule of contraries rather than by any intelligent judgment. Practically, what we come to is something like this—People who want to impose a special system have some theories as to the comparative merits of certain studies, which they feel a friendly impulse to press upon others at every convenient opportunity; or they have a vague impression that as certain subjects and methods have been in a manner set apart for women ever since they can remember, there is most likely something in them which distinguishes them either as suitable to the female mind, or as specially useful to women in practical life. To discover how much of truth there may be behind this opinion would be a tedious and difficult task. It may be enough to remark that experience seems to be against it. It is precisely because the special system, as hitherto tried, has proved a signal failure, that reform is called for.

There are other advocates, however, of independent schemes, who take up a totally different ground. They only half believe, or perhaps altogether repudiate, the female mind theory; and they are prepared to go great lengths in assimilating the education of the sexes. But they say— 1. Male education is in a very bad state—therefore it is not worth while to spread it. 2. Rightly or wrongly, it *is* different from that of women. It would be useless to examine people in things they have not learnt; and women do not as a rule learn Latin and Greek and Mathematics. We must recognise facts.

By all means let us recognise facts. But let us remember also that facts are created things, and mortal. There are old facts, of a bad sort, which want to be put an end to, and there are new and better facts, which may by wise measures be called into being. And speaking of facts, let this be considered—that however bad the education of men may be, that of women is undoubtedly worse. On this point the Report of the Schools Inquiry Commission speaks very distinctly. After adverting to the general deficiency in girls' education, which "is stated with the utmost confidence and with entire agreement, with whatever difference of words, by many witnesses of authority," the Commissioners observe that "the same complaints apply to a great extent to boys' education. But on the whole, the evidence is clear that, not as they might be but as they are, the girls' schools are inferior in this view to the boys' schools." And if this is the evidence as regards the school period, during which girls are receiving more or less regular and systematic instruction, it is likely to be still more unanimous and emphatic as to the later stage, during which men are, in however antiquated and foolish a manner, as the reformers tell us, at any rate in some sort taken in hand by the universities, while women are for the most part left altogether to their own resources. It will probably be admitted, without further argument, that to make the education of average women only as good as that of men, would be a step in advance of what it is now.

But is this intermediate step an indispensable one? Are we obliged to go through a course of wandering along paths which have been found to lead away from the desired end? Cannot we use the light of experience, and, avoiding exploded errors, march straight on to perfection by the nearest road? To a great extent, Yes. There is no reason, for example, to imitate boys' schools in their excessive devotion to physical sports; or in the exclusion of music from the ordinary school routine; or to take up methods of teaching of which the defects have been discovered. Again, looking to the higher stage, no one would wish to reproduce among women either the luxurious idleness of the lower average of university men, or the excessive strain of the competition for honours which is said to act so injuriously on the studious class. But these are evils from which women are pretty securely guarded by existing social conditions. . . .

The immediate controversy turns, as has been said, upon examinations—examinations regarded as a controlling force, directing the course of instruction into certain channels; pronouncing upon the comparative value of subjects, fixing the amount of time and attention bestowed upon each, and to some extent guiding the method of teaching; wholesomely stimulating; and aptly fulfilling its great function of plucking. What are the conditions required to produce the right kind of controlling force? We want authority—that no one disputes. We want the best subjects encouraged. What they are, the most competent judges have not yet settled; but most people, perhaps not all, will agree that when they have made up their minds their verdict ought to be acted upon. We want an examination which can be worked beneficially. . . . an examination for which candidates will be forthcoming. Finally, we want an examination which will sift. We do not want to have certificates of proficiency given to half-educated women. There are examinations which will do this already within reach.

Authority; wise choice of subjects; so much skill in the construction of questions that at any rate they do not invite shallow and unthorough preparation; practicability; and due severity—these are requisites which most people will agree in regarding as essential. But the agreement does not go much farther. As to authority, what constitutes it? Is it the personal reputation of the examiners, or is it their official position? Or is it the prestige acquired by prescription? Or has the quality of the candidates anything to do with it? It is as to the two last points that opinions differ. We can agree so far as this, that an examination by men of high repute will carry more weight than one by men unknown, and that an examination by an official body such as a university, will be more readily believed in than one by any self-constituted board, however respectable. But supposing these two points secured, is a new examination conducted by competent examiners appointed by a university all that is to be desired? Will an unknown standard, having expressly in view candidates drawn from a limited and notoriously illiterate class, be worth much as regards authority? . . .

The most highly cultivated women would not care to submit themselves to an ordeal in which to fail might be disgrace, but to pass would be no distinction. The mere fact of its special character would in itself repel them. That the greatest of female novelists should have taken the precaution to assume a masculine *nom de plume* for the express purpose of securing their work against being measured by a class standard, is significant of the feeling entertained by women. Right or wrong, wise or foolish, here is at any rate a fact to be recognised, and a fact having a manifest bearing on the question in hand. An examination limited to a class, and with which the *élite* of that class will have nothing to do, is not likely to command very high respect. . . .

The questions of practicability and severity may be taken together. A medium is required between a test so far out of reach that no one will go in for it, and one so loose that it fails to discriminate. And here we must not forget that, though without any fault of their own, the great majority of women *are* very imperfectly educated, and it is therefore impossible, in the nature of things, to devise any test which can at once embrace the great mass and yet be sufficiently exclusive. There are a few educated women. We want to find them. We may be very sorry that other women, perhaps equally intelligent and willing, have not had the chance of being educated too. We are bound to do all we can to bring education within their reach. But we are not bound to perpetuate the evils with which we are struggling, by certifying competent knowledge where it does not exist.

And it is not, except perhaps to some small extent, that the education of women has taken a different line, and that they do know some things thoroughly well, if only they had the opportunity of showing it. The defectiveness of female education tells all the way through. The schools are indeed improving, but then it is to be observed that the best girls' schools are precisely those in which the "masculine" subjects have been introduced, and by which therefore the imposition of a feminine test is least likely to be desired. The real question of practicability therefore seems to be, not what would exactly fit female education as it is, but what it may be made to fit itself to, within a reasonable time and without great inconvenience and difficulty. . . .

The tendency of examinations to adjust themselves to studies is a consideration of great importance. At present the weak points in the education of men are the comparatively strong points in that of women, and therefore less need attention. It is where men are strong that women want stimulus and encouragement—and it may be added, they need this only in order to produce satisfactory results. The Cambridge Local Examinations furnish a case in point. In the first examination to which girls were admitted, 90 per cent of the senior candidates failed in the preliminary arithmetic. Fortunately, the standard was fixed by reference to an immense preponderance of boy candidates, and it was understood that the girls must be brought up to it. Extra time, and probably better teaching, aided by greater willingness on the part of the pupils, who had been made aware of their deficiency, were devoted to the unpopular and "useless" subject. In the next examination, out of the whole number of girls only three failed in it.

Other reasons for desiring a common standard, of a more subtle character, can scarcely be apprehended perhaps in their full force without personal experience. Probably only women who have laboured under it can understand the weight of discouragement produced by being perpetually told that, as women, nothing much is ever to be expected of them, and it is not worth their while to exert themselves—that they can write lively letters, full of graphic description and homely touches, but that anything like original research or profound learning is not for them to think of—that whatever they do they must not interest themselves, except in a second-hand and shallow way, in the pursuits of men, for in such pursuits they must always expect to fail. Women who have lived in the atmosphere produced by such teaching know how it stifles and chills; how hard it is to work courageously through it. Every effort to improve the education of women which assumes that they may, without reprehensible ambition, study the same subjects as their brothers and be measured by the same standards, does something towards lifting them out of the state of listless despair of themselves into which so many fall. Supposing that the percentage of success attained by women should be considerably less than that of men, the sense of discouragement thus engendered would be as nothing compared with the general self-distrust produced by having it taken for granted that they are by nature disqualified to stand the ordinary tests. To make the discovery of individual incompetence may be wholesomely humbling or stimulating, as the case may be, but no one is the better for being told, on mere arbitrary authority, that he belongs to a weak and incapable class. And this, whatever may be the intention, is said in effect by the offer of any test of an exclusively female character. No doubt there are university men whose opinion of their own education is so low that they can honestly propose a special standard for women with the intention and expectation of its being better than anything that has been known before, and an example to be imitated in male examinations. But this idea is so new and so bewildering to the outside world that it is simply incomprehensible. The statement of it is regarded as irony.

If it were otherwise—supposing that in the future the relative positions of men and women as regards learning should be reversed—the arguments in favour of common standards would be changed in their application, but would remain substantially the same. There would still be the same reasons for desiring that in all departments of study boys and girls, men and women, should walk together in the same paths. Why should they be separated? And the whole specializing system has a tendency, so far as its influence goes, to separate—to divide where union is most to be desired. The easy way in which it is often taken for granted that, as a matter of course, men care for men and women for women—that a certain *esprit de corps* is natural, if not positively commendable—must surely arise from a most inhuman way of looking at things. Conceive a family in which the brothers and sisters form rival *corps*, headed by the father and mother respectively! If on the small scale the spectacle is revolting, surely it ought to be no less so in the great human family. In the rebellion of the best instincts of human nature against such a theory, we have a security that it will never prevail. But sympathy may be checked even where it cannot be destroyed; and to put barriers in the way of companionship in the highest kinds of work and pleasure, is to carry out in the most effectual way the devices of the dividing spirit.

But when all has been said that can be, or that need be, said in favour of common standards, it may still be urged—All this is very well, but can you get them? What university is likely to open its degree-examinations to women? Would it not be well to try some judicious compromise?

To those who are aware that women have at this moment free access to the degrees of several foreign universities, to say nothing of historic precedent, the idea of extending those of our own country is not so very startling. We see in the papers from time to time notices of ladies who have taken the degree of Bachelière-ès-Sciences, or Bachelière-ès-Lettres, at Paris, Lyons, or elsewhere; and three English ladies are now studying for the medical degree at the University of Zurich, without hindrance or restriction of any sort. In England the only university which could at present be reasonably asked to open its examinations to women is that of London. The condition of residence imposed by the old universities must exclude women until they are able, by means of a college of their own, to offer guarantees as to instruction and discipline similar to those which are required at Oxford and Cambridge. It is probable that within no very distant period the opportunity of complying with this essential condition will be within reach of women, and there is reason to hope that the examinations of the University of Cambridge may then be substantially, if not in name—and this last is a secondary consideration—as accessible to women as they are to men.

114. Anne Jemima Clough (1873)

Among the many plans devised for improving the Education of Women, an important place may fairly be claimed for the Scheme of Lectures established in Cambridge. These Lectures give to Women an opportunity of gaining a more exact knowledge of the subjects taught in schools; and also of pursuing their studies further, in any department which they may select.

It is well before saying any more, to draw attention to the remarkable fact, that these Lectures were a free-will offering of Higher Culture made to Women by Members of the University—to enable them to fit themselves to pass with credit the Examination for Women over 18, which had been granted by the University in the year 1868, on the receipt of a Memorial praying for such an Examination.

The Lectures were begun in January, 1870, and have been continued ever since, with increasing success. In October, 1871, at the request of one of the Promoters of the scheme, I took the management of a house for Students, and five Ladies came into residence. In October, 1872, this small community was removed to Merton Hall, that house being considered more suitable for the purpose, as being retired and close to the country.

In October, 1873, it became needful to supplement this undertaking by hiring another house for the accommodation of the increasing number of Students; and with the help of kind friends twenty-four are now provided with homes where they can pursue their studies under the guidance of teachers who are at the same time giving instruction in similar subjects to Undergraduates. There is still a growing demand for admission to Merton Hall, and at Christmas it will be very difficult to provide for all who wish to come. Another difficulty has arisen, namely, that in October, 1874, Merton Hall must be given up, and the promoters of the Lectures, and of the Hall, are most anxious to provide for the future.

The most reasonable plan seems to be that a suitable building should be erected, giving to each Student a Bedroom, which could also be used as a Study, and a general Study for every six Students, and providing a large Dining-room, together with sufficient accommodation for the Principal, and perhaps one other Lady. This plan has been partly acted on; a subscription has been set on foot, £1320. has been promised in five donations of different amounts, £1500. taken in shares of £50. each, on which it is proposed to endeavour to pay a yearly dividend at the rate of 4 per cent. But this sum will not be sufficient to cover the expenses of building and furnishing a house capable of holding twenty-six Students, and laying out a garden of two acres. It is thought that many would be willing to contribute towards these expenses, if they were made acquainted with the objects, both of the Lectures and of the Hall, and the work that has been already done.

The Lectures were begun with a view to instructing Women who wished to pass the Higher Examination, and opening out to them the study of a large range of Subjects.

The Examination includes the following Subjects:—Divinity, English Language, Literature and History, and Arithmetic: Languages, Ancient and Modern: Mathematics: certain branches of Natural Science: Logic and Political Economy: Harmony and Drawing.

The Lecture scheme has made provisions for almost all these Subjects, together with one or two more, and is capable of being further extended.

This wide range of Studies is well suited to the requirements and present attainments of Women. They are encouraged to begin with familiar subjects, such as Arithmetic, History, English Language and Literature, and then to take up whatever special department may interest them most. Having thus obtained the University Certificate, they are encouraged to proceed further in the line of study that they have chosen: which (having felt the value of thorough and systematic teaching) the Cambridge Students are usually anxious to do, if they are able to prolong their residence. Several who have left early have expressed their intention to return and continue their Studies, as soon as they can afford the expense.

The Lectures were originally instituted for the benefit of persons living in Cambridge: but it was soon thought desirable that their advantages should be more widely extended: and accordingly one of the promoters of the scheme provided funds for furnishing and opening a house to receive students. In this way a number of women of different occupations and different stations in life, and different religious persuasions, have been brought together to receive at least some share of academic education. So far the result has been very satisfactory; there has been much kindly feeling and good fellowship among the students: and their close proximity to the town, while opening to them a much greater variety and extent of teaching than they could otherwise have obtained, has also enabled them to attend their own places of worship.

The expenses of the house—though they have been kept as low as was compatible with health and necessary comfort—have from the first been somewhat greater than the receipts: but so long as the scheme was regarded as an experiment, they have been willingly borne by one or two persons. Now, however, that the Lectures have taken their place as a permanent institution; and, at the same time, the increasing numbers of our students render it desirable to provide increased accommodation; we venture to appeal to the public for support. It may perhaps be thought that the growing popularity of the scheme ought to bring with it financial success. But it is an essential part of our plan to offer academic education on the lowest possible terms to those who are preparing to be teachers: accordingly we receive such students for three-fourths of the ordinary payment (£15. instead of £20. for the term of 8 weeks). This sum merely pays for board, service, &c., leaving nothing for rent or management: *

---

* The item of management has not hitherto been included in our expenditure: and the present Principal, as long as she is able to do what is required, will gladly give her services without trespassing on the very limited resources of the Hall. But in forecasting the future, we must take into account the contingency of our finding it desirable to offer a small salary to another Principal.

but even this payment is somewhat heavy for the scanty resources of this class of students: and we are anxious to be able to reduce it still further. And thus the increase in our numbers must be expected to be, financially speaking, a burden rather than a gain. It is on this ground that we ask for donations towards building: in order that the annual expenditure of the house may not be too much swelled by interest to be paid on the original outlay. If we are right in thinking our object one of national importance, surely the burden which it entails ought not to be thrown entirely upon residents in Cambridge: much less should the members of the University, who are already giving their time ungrudgingly, be called upon to give money also.

These Lecturers are not rich: their time is much occupied with other duties, and yet they take on themselves voluntarily much additional work, and for a most trifling remuneration, that of One Guinea per Student for each course of Lectures, during a term of eight weeks. They teach in most cases two hours weekly, set questions and look over papers besides. All persons preparing to be teachers are admitted to these advantages for half-price. Thus the cost of education alone is reduced to a comparatively trifling amount.

As the Principal of Merton Hall I have had constant opportunities of watching this work, and seeing the results, and I can bear witness to the great pains bestowed on the Students, with very good success. I do feel strongly that the efforts made by University-men in their own University, to give to Women the best educational advantages, deserve to be recognised by the public, and I cannot but hope that when all they have done is known, support will be given to the scheme they have devised and so generously carried out.

Anne J. Clough
Merton Hall.

October 22, 1873.

Sex and Education

SOURCES
115. Edward H. Clarke, *Sex in Education; or A Fair Chance for Girls* (Boston and New York, 1873), pp. 11-15, 16-19, 124-29.
116. Caroline Dall's rejoinder in *Sex and Education: A Reply to Dr. E. H. Clarke's "Sex in Education"*, ed. Julia Ward Howe (Boston, 1874), pp. 87-88, 91-93, 94-95, 107-8.
117. Elizabeth Garrett Anderson, "Sex in Mind and in Education: A Reply," *Fortnightly Review*, o.s. 21 (May 1874), 588-94.

As pressure mounted in Boston during the early 1870's to admit women to Harvard College, the authority of medical science was invoked to combat women's claims to equal opportunity in American higher education on grounds of biological difference. In 1873 Edward H. Clarke (1820-1877), a Philadelphia-trained physician who had retired as professor of *Materia medica* at Harvard the previous year, addressed the New England Women's Club on the topic of his new book, *Sex in Education; or A Fair Chance for Girls*. He argued against coeducation and in favor of a completely separate educational regime for young women. Clarke had a large general practice in the Boston area and, according to one biographer, "believed that the woman's rights movement was responsible for many nervous troubles" among women. He was especially concerned about the adverse effects of intensive study on the reproductive development of pubescent girls. Clarke's concern for the economy of sexual energy and mental powers bears traces of the same French physiological arguments that had earlier influenced Proudhon and Michelet; nor should this be surprising, given the vogue enjoyed in Philadelphia (where Clarke had trained in the 1840's) by French medicine and social thought. The good doctor later took his case, which had turned into something of a crusade, before the National Education Association; its importance for the subsequent development of women's higher education in the United States was immense, as developments throughout the next century were to demonstrate.

Clarke's challenge aroused the anger of women reformers who in fact shared his basic premises concerning the importance of sexual differences. One of his best known adversaries was his contemporary Julia Ward Howe (1819-1910), then president of both the New England Women's Club and the American Woman Suffrage Association, and editor of the *Woman's Journal*. Mrs. Howe, who had four grown daughters of her own, quite agreed that the differences between the sexes were important. Nevertheless, she stoutly defended coeducation as a means of reinforcing sexual complementarity. She insisted, however, that the present educational system was too harsh for boys as well; changes were required in the learning environment for both sexes.

To counter Clarke Howe assembled a volume of rebuttals, from which the selection by Caroline Dall (1822-1912) is taken. Caroline Wells Healey Dall came to the New England women's movement by way of religion and philanthropy. Her husband, a Unitarian minister, had gone to India in 1855 as a missionary, leaving his wife and their two small children behind to fend for themselves. During the 1860's Dall became well known in the Boston area as a speaker and writer on the woman question. Like Howe, Dall fully accepted the premises of sexual difference and defended prevailing standards of gentility by objecting to Clarke's use of clinical language in discussing female reproductive problems; such women preferred to drop the curtain of womanly privacy before men on such matters. In these excerpts Caroline Dall makes telling points against medical men like Clarke, who presume to tell women what is best for them.

Edward Clarke's arguments were soon picked up by opponents of women's higher education in England, where an article published in the April 1874 *Fortnightly Review* by a fellow physician, Henry Maudsley, set off a debate comparable to that already underway in New England. Quick to reply to Maudsley and Clarke in the May issue was Elizabeth Garrett Anderson (1836-1917), Britain's first licensed woman physician and a close associate of Emily Davies (Doc. 113). Like Howe and Dall, Garrett Anderson (who married and continued her medical practice) did not contest the argument that young women should not overstrain their minds at puberty. She was less concerned about coeducation than her American counterparts but asserted that the efforts of her colleagues to open up higher education to English women did in fact take women's special needs into account. More tellingly, she insisted (based on her own experiences) that serious mental work is far less hazardous to the health of young upper-class girls than the state of enforced idleness that had hitherto been their fate, and turned her rejoinder into a call for support.

---

115. Edward H. Clarke (1873)

It is idle to say that what is right for man is wrong for woman. Pure reason, abstract right and wrong, have nothing to do with sex: they neither recognize nor know it. They teach that what is right or wrong for man is equally right and wrong for woman. Both sexes are bound by the same code of morals; both are amenable to the same divine law. Both have a right to do the best they can; or, to speak more justly, both should feel the duty, and have the opportunity, to do their best. Each must justify its existence by becoming a complete development of manhood and womanhood; and each should refuse whatever limits or dwarfs that development.

The problem of woman's sphere, to use the modern phrase, is not to be solved by applying to it abstract principles of right and wrong. Its solution must be obtained from physiology, not from ethics or metaphysics. The question must be submitted to Agassiz and Huxley, not to Kant or Calvin, to Church or Pope. Without denying the self-evident proposition, that whatever a woman can do, she has a right to do, the question at once arises, What can she do? And this includes the further question, What can she best do? A girl can hold a plough, and ply a needle, after a fashion. If she can do both better than a man, she ought to be both farmer and seamstress; but if, on the whole, her husband can hold best the plough, and she ply best the needle, they should divide the labor. He should be master of the plough, and she mistress of the loom. The *quœstio vexata* of woman's sphere will be decided by her organization. This limits her power, and reveals her divinely-appointed tasks, just as man's organization limits his power, and reveals his work. In the development of the organization is to be found the way of strength and power for both sexes. Limitation or abortion of development leads both to weakness and failure.

Neither is there any such thing as inferiority or superiority in this matter. Man is not superior to woman, nor woman to man. The relation of the sexes is one of equality, not of better and worse, or of higher and lower. By this it is not intended to say that the sexes are the same. They are different, widely different from each other, and so different that each can do, in certain directions, what the other cannot; and in other directions, where both can do the same things, one sex, as a rule, can do them better than the other; and in still other matters they seem to be so nearly alike, that they can interchange labor without perceptible difference. All this is so well known, that it would be useless to refer to it, were it not that much of the discussion of the irrepressible woman-question, and many of the efforts for bettering her education and widening her sphere, seem to ignore any difference of the sexes; seem to treat her as if she were identical with man, and to be trained in precisely the same way; as if her organization, and consequently her function, were masculine, not feminine. There are those who write and act as if their object were to assimilate woman as much as possible to man, by dropping all that is distinctively feminine out of her, and putting into her as large an amount of masculineness as possible. These persons tacitly admit the error just alluded to, that woman is inferior to man, and strive to get rid of the inferiority by making her a man. There may be some subtle physiological basis for such views—some strange quality of brain; for some who hold and advocate them are of those, who, having missed the symmetry and organic balance that harmonious development yields, have drifted into an hermaphroditic condition. One of this class, who was glad to have escaped the chains of matrimony, but knew the value and lamented the loss of maternity, wished she had been born a widow with two children. These misconceptions arise from mistaking difference of organization and function for difference of position in the scale of being, which is equivalent to saying that man is rated higher in the divine order because he has more muscle, and woman lower because she has more fat. The loftiest ideal of humanity, rejecting all comparisons of inferiority and superiority between the sexes, demands that each shall be perfect in its kind, and not be hindered in its best work. The lily is not inferior to the rose, nor the oak superior to the clover: yet the glory of the lily is one, and the glory of the oak is another; and the use of the oak is not the use of the clover. That is poor horticulture which would train them all alike. . . .

The fact that women have often equalled and sometimes excelled men in physical labor, intellectual effort, and lofty heroism, is sufficient proof that women have muscle, mind, and soul, as well as men; but it is no proof that they have had, or should have, the same kind of training; nor is it any proof that they are destined for the same career as men. The presumption is, that if woman, subjected to a masculine training, arranged for the development of a masculine organization, can equal man, she ought to excel him if educated by a feminine training, arranged to develop a feminine organization. Indeed, I have somewhere encountered an author who boldly affirms the superiority of women to all existences on this planet, because of the complexity of their organization. Without undertaking to indorse such an opinion, it may be affirmed, that an appropriate method of education for girls—one that should not ignore the mechanism of their bodies or blight any of their vital organs—would yield a better result than the world has yet seen.

Gail Hamilton's statement is true, that, "a girl can go to school, pursue all the studies which Dr. Todd enumerates, except *ad infinitum*; know them, not as well as a chemist knows chemistry or a botanist botany, but as well as they are known by boys of her age and training, as well, indeed, as they are known by many college-taught men, enough, at least, to be a solace and a resource to her; then graduate before she is eighteen, and come out of school as healthy, as fresh, as eager, as she went in." But it is not true that she can do all this, and retain uninjured health and a future secure from neuralgia, uterine disease, hysteria, and other derangements of the nervous system, if she follows the same method that boys are trained in. Boys must study and work in a boy's way, and girls in a girl's way. They may study the same books, and attain an equal result, but should not follow the same method. Mary can master Virgil and Euclid as well as George; but both will be dwarfed—defrauded of their rightful attainment—if both are confined to the same methods. It is said that Elena Cornaro, the accomplished professor of six languages, whose statue adorns and honors Padua, was educated like a boy. This means that she was initiated into, and mastered, the studies that were considered to be the peculiar dower of men. It does not mean that her life was a man's life, her way of study a man's way of study, or that, in acquiring six languages, she ignored her own organization. Women who choose to do so can master the humanities and the mathematics, encounter the labor of the law and the pulpit, endure the hardness of physic and the conflicts of politics; but they must do it all in woman's way, not in man's way. In all their work they must respect their own organization, and remain women, not strive to be men, or they will ignominiously fail. For both sexes, there is no exception to the law, that their greatest power and largest attainment lie in the perfect development of their organization. "Woman," says a late writer, "must be regarded as woman, not as a nondescript animal, with greater or less capacity for assimilation to man." If we would give our girls a fair chance, and see them become and do their best by reaching after and attaining an ideal beauty and power, which shall be a crown of glory and a tower of strength to the republic, we must look after their complete development as women. Wherein they are men, they should be educated as men; wherein they are women, they should be educated as women. The physiological motto is, Educate a man for manhood, a woman for womanhood, both for humanity. In this lies the hope of the race. . . .

Obedient to the American educational maxim, that boys' schools and girls' schools are one, and that the one is the boys' school, the female schools have copied the methods which have grown out of the requirements of the male organization. Schools for girls have been modelled after schools for boys. Were it not for differences of dress and figure, it would be impossible, even for an expert, after visiting a high school for boys and one for girls, to tell which was arranged for the male and which for the female organization. Our girls' schools, whether public or private, have imposed upon their pupils a boy's regimen; and it is now proposed, in some quarters, to carry this principle still farther, by burdening girls, after they leave school, with a quadrennium of masculine college regimen. And so girls are to learn the alphabet in college, as they have learned it in the grammar-school, just as boys do. This is grounded upon the supposition that sustained regularity of action and attendance may be as safely required of a girl as of a boy; that there is no physical necessity for periodically relieving her from walking, standing, reciting, or studying; that the chapel-bell may call her, as well as him, to a daily morning walk, with a standing prayer at the end of it, regardless of the danger that such exercises, by deranging the tides of her organization, may add to her piety at the expense of her blood; that she may work her brain over mathematics, botany, chemistry, German, and the like, with equal and sustained force on every day of the month, and so safely divert blood from the reproductive apparatus to the head; in short, that she, like her brother, develops health and strength, blood and nerve, intellect and life, by a regular, uninterrupted, and sustained course of work. All this is not justified, either by experience or physiology. The gardener may plant, if he choose, the lily and the rose, the oak and the vine, within the same enclosure; let the same soil nourish them, the same air visit them, and the same sunshine warm and cheer them; still, he trains each of them with a separate art, warding from each its peculiar dangers, developing within each its peculiar powers, and teaching each to put forth to the utmost its divine and peculiar gifts of strength and beauty. Girls lose health, strength, blood, and nerve, by a regimen that ignores the periodical tides and reproductive apparatus of their organization. The mothers and instructors, the homes and schools, of our country's daughters, would profit by occasionally reading the old Levitical law. The race has not yet quite outgrown the physiology of Moses.

Co-education, then, signifies in common acceptation identical co-education. This identity of training is what many at the present day seem to be praying for and working for. Appropriate education of the two sexes, carried as far as possible, is a consummation most devoutly to be desired; identical education of the two sexes is a crime before God and humanity, that physiology protests against, and that experience weeps over. Because the education of boys has met with tolerable success, hitherto—but only tolerable it must be confessed—in developing them into men, there are those who would make girls grow into women by the same process. Because a gardener has nursed an acorn till it grew into an oak, they would have him cradle a grape in the same soil and way, and make it a vine. Identical education, or identical co-education, of the sexes defrauds one sex or the other, or perhaps both. It defies the Roman maxim, which physiology has fully justified, *mens sana in corpore sano*. The sustained regimen, regular recitation, erect posture, daily walk, persistent exercise, and unintermitted labor that toughens a boy, and makes a man of him, can only be partially applied to a girl. The regimen of intermittance, periodicity of exercise and rest, work three-fourths of each month, and remission, if not abstinence, the other fourth, physiological interchange of the erect and reclining posture, care of the reproductive system that is the cradle of the race, all this, that toughens a girl and makes a woman of her, will emasculate a lad. A combination of the two methods of education, a compromise between them, would probably yield an average result, excluding the best of both. It would give a fair chance neither to a boy nor a girl. Of all compromises, such a physiological one is the worst. It cultivates mediocrity, and cheats the future of its rightful legacy of lofty manhood and womanhood. It emasculates boys, stunts girls; makes semi-eunuchs of one sex, and agenes of the other.

The error which has led to the identical education of the two sexes, and which prophecies their identical co-education in colleges and universities, is not confined to technical education. It permeates society. It is found in the home, the workshop, the factory, and in all the ramifications of social life. The identity of boys and girls, of men and women, is practically asserted out of the school as much as in it, and it is theoretically proclaimed from the pulpit and the rostrum. Woman seems to be looking up to man and his development, as the goal and ideal of womanhood. The new gospel of female development glorifies what she possesses in common with him, and tramples under her feet, as a source of weakness and badge of inferiority, the mechanism and functions peculiar to herself.

116. Caroline Healey Dall (1874)

"The hand of iron in the glove of silk!" How utter one word in the face of testimony like this—honest, conscientious, earnest; adding to the highest professional reputation all the force of a pure and noble individual character? How do it, still further, in the face of personal obligations accumulating for more than twenty years, and of that loving respect with which the physician who is also priest is held in every household? I have anticipated this book with pain. I lay it down with pain, far sharper and far different from any that I foresaw. I start from the same premises with Dr. Clarke; for I believe the spiritual and intellectual functions of men and women to tend differently to their one end; and their development to this end, through the physical, to be best achieved by different methods. But I do not believe that any greater difference of capacity, whether physical or psychical, *will be* found between man and woman than *is* found between man and man; and my faith in the co-education of the sexes has been greatly stimulated by the present inelastic method, from which many boys *do* shrink as much as any girl *could*.

Under a proper system boys and girls help each other forward, not merely towards excellent scholarship, but towards a perfect humanity— that is, a perfect self-possession—the attainment for each of a sound mind in a sound body. To understand this, however, not even the President of Harvard will find possible unless he does more than *look* at a mixed college. . . .

When I laid down this book I felt the emphasis of my pain in a direction wholly unexpected. Every woman who takes up her pen to reject its conclusions knows very well that it will penetrate hundreds of households where her protest cannot follow; and Dr. Clarke must be patient with the number and weight of our remonstrances, since he knows very well that upon the major part of the community our words will fall with no authority, our experiences invite no confidence. We must gain the public ear by constant iteration, and by our "importunity" prevail. This book will fall into the hands of the young, and that I deplore. They should be taught the proper care of their growing bodies; but any such cases of disease as are here recorded are fruitful of evil stimulus to any girl inclined to hysterics. If this subject ought to be discussed publicly at all, a matter open to doubt, teachers and mothers should discuss it. No amount of professional skill can avail in place of that sympathetic intuition of causes which should spring from identical physical constitution. In no pages that I ever read is the need of educated women physicians so painfully apparent as in these. I expected to find premises from which I should dissent, but, with the exception of that upon which the book is based, I did not find any; and, so far as it is an argument against co-education, the book utterly fails. . . .

The most painful thing in the book is its *tone.* Mr. Higginson has said that it is not *coarse!* Surely never was a sentence written that more eloquently betrayed the need women have to speak for themselves! Women read this essay with personal humiliation and dismay. A certain materialistic taint is felt throughout the whole, such as saddens most of our intercourse with our young physicians, but which we had hoped never to associate with this man, so long and so justly revered. The natural outgrowth of this tone are the sneers which disfigure its pages, the motto from Plautus, and a few most unhappy illustrations.

These things might be easily forgiven to the immature student, as we pardon the rude manners of growing boys; but should not our friend have denied himself the small relief of their utterance? We cannot excuse the trait merely because the work has been undertaken in the midst of more pressing cares. We feel that it indicates something in the author which is no accident. We do not accept it as suitable in the "beloved physician" for whose delicate and thoughtful care so many have been grateful. He, at least, should have given us pages that a woman might read without a blush.

We are sorry that he thought it worth while to invent a word to give point to his sneer. If there are any "agenes" in the world, surely we do not find them in the women who, seeking to do some good work in the world, have sought the development of their best powers in ways unwise or absurd, and have in consequence failed to satisfy the yearnings that they feel. "Other tasks in other worlds" await them, and the yearning may still prove the germ of a completed development. The true "agenes" are the men who have lost manhood through vicious courses, and whose innocent wives will never hear the voices of their children in consequence. We look from the possible mother to the father, and I mean all that my words imply. It is the testimony of one even more familiar with the nursery and the sick-room than with the theories of the platform. The vices of *men* imperil the populations of the earth far more than the unwise studies of women. . . .

In all books that concern the education of women, one very important fact is continually overlooked.

Women, and even young girls at school, take their studies *in addition* to their home-cares. If boys are preparing for college, they do not have to take care of the baby, make the beds, or help to serve the meals. A great many girls at the High Schools do all this. Then, if a man who is a student marries, he is carefully protected from all annoyance. His study is sacred, his wife does the marketing. If his baby cries, he sleeps in the spare room.

So far women have written in the nursery or the dining-room, often with one foot on the cradle. They must provide for their households, and nurse their sick, before they can follow any artistic or intellectual bent.

When it is once fairly acknowledged that women properly have a vocation, they may be protected in it as a man is. At present there is no propriety in making comparisons of results in regard to the two sexes. . . .

Nothing is so absurd as to press upon a young woman's thought the idea that she is to become a mother. What if she is? Let her make herself a healthy, happy human being, and what will may befall. What would be thought of a community which definitely undertook to train young men to the functions and duties of fathers? A shout of derision would be raised at once. "Let us have citizens!" the world would cry. I echo the demand. Mothers are no more important to the race than fathers. We must gain both by seeking first the "kingdom of God." People should live out their young and happy days, unconscious of this issue, as the flowers take no thought of seed. This is best done when their minds are occupied with other subjects than "periodicity" or "development."

117. Elizabeth Garrett Anderson (1874)

It must not be overlooked, that the difficulties which attend the period of rapid functional development are not confined to women, though they are expressed differently in the two sexes. Analogous changes take place in the constitution and organization of young men, and the period of immature manhood is frequently one of weakness, and one during which any severe strain upon the mental and nervous powers is productive of more mischief than it is in later life. It is possible that the physiological demand thus made is lighter than that made upon young women at the corresponding age, but on the other hand it is certain that, in many other ways unknown to women, young men still further tax their strength, *e.g.* by drinking, smoking, unduly severe physical exercise, and frequently by late hours and dissipation generally. Whether, regard being had to all these varying influences, young men are much less hindered than young women in intellectual work by the demands made upon their physical and nervous strength during the period of development, it is probably impossible to determine. All that we wish to show is that the difficulties which attend development are not entirely confined to women, and that in point of fact great allowance ought to be made, and has already been made, for them in deciding what may reasonably be expected in the way of intellectual attainment from young men. It is not much to the point to prove that men could work harder than women, if the work demanded from either is very far from overtaxing the powers of even the weaker of the two. If we had no opportunity of measuring the attainments of ordinary young men, or if they really were the intellectual athletes Dr. Maudsley's warnings would lead us to suppose them to be, the question, "Is it well for women to contend on equal terms with men for the goal of man's ambition?" might be as full of solemnity to us as it is to Dr. Maudsley. As it is, it sounds almost ironical. Hitherto most of the women who have "contended with men for the goal of man's ambition" have had no chance of being any the worse for being allowed to do so on equal terms. They have had all the benefit of being heavily handicapped. Over and above their assumed physical and mental inferiority, they have had to start in the race without a great part of the training men have enjoyed, or they have gained what training they have been able to obtain in an atmosphere of hostility, to remain in which has taxed their strength and endurance far more than any amount of mental work could tax it. Would, for instance, the ladies who for five years have been trying to get a medical education at Edinburgh find their task increased, or immeasurably lightened, by being allowed to contend "on equal terms with men" for that goal? The intellectual work required from other medical students is nothing compared with what it has been made to them by obliging them to spend time and energy in contesting every step of their course, and yet in spite of this heavy additional burden they have not at present shown any signs of enfeebled health or of inadequate mental power. To all who know what it is to pursue intellectual work under such conditions as these, Dr. Maudsley's pity for the more fortunate women who may pursue it in peace and on equal terms with men sounds superfluous. But Dr. Maudsley would probably say that, in speaking of the pace at which young men at the Universities work as being dangerously rapid for average women, he was not referring to anything less ambitious than the competition for honours. No one denies that in some cases this is severe; many men knock up under it, and it would doubtless tax the strength of women. But it must be borne in mind that that element in the competition which incites men to the greatest effort, and increases the strain to its utmost, is one which, for the present at least, would not operate upon women. Pecuniary rewards, large enough to affect a man's whole after-life, are given for distinction in these examinations; and it is the eager desire for a Fellowship which raises the pressure of competition to so high and, as many think, to so unwholesome a point. As there are at present no Fellowships for women, this incentive does not operate upon them.

It must always be remembered, too, that University work does not come at the age when Dr. Maudsley and Dr. Clarke think it is likely to be too exciting. No one is proposing that girls of seventeen or eighteen should be allowed to try for a place in the Cambridge Honours' Lists. What is proposed is that after a girlhood of healthful work and healthful play, when her development is complete and her constitution settled, the student, at the age of eighteen or nineteen, should begin the college course, and should be prepared to end it at twenty-two or twenty-three.

As we shall see later on, this is a very different plan from that pursued in America, and censured by Dr. Clarke.

In estimating the possible consequences of extending the time spent in education, and even those of increasing somewhat the pressure put upon girls under eighteen, it should be borne in mind that even if the risk of overwork, pure and simple, work unmixed with worry, is more serious than we are disposed to think it, it is not the only, nor even the most pressing, danger during the period of active physiological development. The newly developed functions of womanhood awaken instincts which are more apt at this age to make themselves unduly prominent than to be hidden or forgotten. Even were the dangers of continuous mental work as great as Dr. Maudsley thinks they are, the dangers of a life adapted to develop only the specially and consciously feminine side of the girl's nature would be much greater. From the purely physiological point of view, it is difficult to believe that study much more serious than that usually pursued by young men would do a girl's health as much harm as a life directly calculated to over-stimulate the emotional and sexual instincts, and to weaken the guiding and controlling forces which these instincts so imperatively need. The stimulus found in novel-reading, in the theatre and ball-room, the excitement whch attends a premature entry into society, the competition of vanity and frivolity, these involve far more real dangers to the health of young women than the competition for knowledge, or for scientific or literary honors, ever has done, or is ever likely to do. And even if, in the absence of real culture, dissipation be avoided, there is another danger still more difficult to escape, of which the evil physical results are scarcely less grave, and this is dulness. It is not easy for those whose lives are full to overflowing of the interests which accumulate as life matures, to realise how insupportably dull the life of a young woman just out of the schoolroom is apt to be, nor the powerful influence for evil this dulness has upon her health and morals. There is no tonic in the pharmacopœia to be compared with happiness, and happiness worth calling such is not known where the days drag along filled with make-believe occupations and dreary sham amusements.

The cases that Dr. Clarke brings forward in support of his opinion against continuous mental work during the period of development could be outnumbered many times over even in our own limited experience, by those in which the break-down of nervous and physical health seems at any rate to be distinctly traceable to want of adequate mental interest and occupation in the years immediately succeeding school life. Thousands of young women, strong and blooming at eighteen, become gradually languid and feeble under the depressing influence of dulness, not only in the special functions of womanhood, but in the entire cycle of the processes of nutrition and innervation, till in a few years they are morbid and self-absorbed, or even hysterical. If they had had upon leaving school some solid intellectual work which demanded real thought and excited genuine interest, and if this interest had been helped by the stimulus of an examination, in which distinction would have been a legitimate source of pride, the number of such cases would probably be indefinitely smaller than it is now. It may doubtless be objected that even if this plan were pursued, and young women were allowed and expected to continue at tolerably hard mental work till they were twenty-one or twenty-two, it would only be postponing the evil day, and that when they left college they would dislike idleness as much, and be as much injured by it as when they left school. This is true; but by this time they would have more internal resources against idleness and dulness, and they would have reached an age in which some share in practical work and responsibility—the lasting refuge from dulness—is more easily obtained than it is in girlhood. Moreover, by entering society at a somewhat less immature age, a young woman is more able to take an intelligent part in it; is prepared to get more real pleasure from the companionship it affords, and, suffering less from *ennui*, she is less apt to make a hasty and foolish marriage. From the physiological point of view this last advantage is no small or doubtful one. Any change in the arrangements of young women's lives which tends to discourage very early marriages will probably do more for their health and for the health of their children than any other change could do. But it is hopeless to expect girls, who are at heart very very dull, to wait till they are physiologically fit for the wear and tear consequent upon marriage if they see their way to it at eighteen or nineteen. There is always a hope that the unknown may be less dull than the known, and in the mean time the mere mention of a change gives life a fillip. It is also hopeless to expect them to be even reasonably critical in their choice. Coleridge says, "If Ferdinand hadn't come, Miranda *must* have married Caliban"; and many a Miranda finds her fate by not being free to wait a little longer for her Ferdinand.

But Dr. Maudsley supports his argument by references to American experience. He says in effect, "That which the English educational reformers advocate has been tried in America and has failed; the women there go through the same educational course as the men, and the result is that they are nervous, specially prone to the various ailments peculiar to their sex, not good at bearing children, and unable to nurse them." These are grave charges, and we can scarcely wonder at Dr. Maudsley's thinking "it is right to call attention to them." But it is also right to see if they are true. One fact certainly seems to be plain, and that is, that American women are frequently nervous, and do too often break down in the particular ways described in the quotation, though, if we may judge at all from those whom we have an opportunity of seeing in Europe, it may be hoped that the race is not quite in such a bad plight as Dr. Maudsley's quotations would lead us to fear. But granting that the facts are stated correctly, the doubtful point is, what causes this condition of things? Dr. Clarke says that, among other causes, it is due to an education which is at once too continuous, too exciting, too much pressed, and which is taken at too early an age. But against this we have to notice the testimony of many independent witnesses to the effect that the evils complained of are seen to a much greater extent among the fashionable and idle American women—those guiltless of ever having passed an examination—than they are among those who have gone through the course of study complained of. Then, again, it is notorious that the American type in both sexes is "nervous." The men show it as distinctly, if not even more distinctly than the women; and not those men only who have any claim to be considered above the average in intellect or culture. If Dr. Clarke's explanation of the existence of this type in women is correct, what is its explanation in men?

Dr. Clarke himself gives us some valuable hints as to possible causes, other than study. He says: "We live in a zone of perpetual pie and doughnut"; "our girls revel in these unassimilable abominations." He also justly blames the dress of American women, "its stiff corsets and its heavy skirts"; but somewhat inconsequently, as it seems to us, he says, "these cannot be supposed to affect directly the woman's special functions." If one thing more than another is likely to do a woman harm in these directions, we should say it is heavy skirts; and it certainly shakes our faith in Dr. Clarke's acumen to find him attributing less direct influence to them than to mental occupation. Our own notion would be that till American girls wear light dresses and thick boots, and spend as much time out of doors as their brothers, no one knows how many examinations they could pass not only without injury but with positive benefit to their health and spirits. We find, however, no mention made by Dr. Clarke of the influence of the stove-heated rooms in which American women live, nor of the indoor lives they lead. These two things only would, we believe, suffice to explain the general and special delicacy of which he complains, and the inferiority in point of health of American to English women.

But the truth is, that the system against which Dr. Clarke protests, and to which his arguments are directed, is, in some of the very points upon which he most insists, essentially different from that which is now being gradually introduced in England. Dr. Maudsley has, with what we must call some unfairness, applied what was written against one plan, to another which is unlike it in almost every important point. Whether the system in America deserves all that Dr. Clarke says against it, Americans must determine. We are not in a position at this distance to weigh conflicting evidence, or to determine which out of many causes is the most potent in producing the ill-health he deplores. But we can speak of the conditions under which English girls work, and we are able to say distinctly that on many vital points they are just those which Dr. Clarke and the other American doctors urge as desirable.

For instance, the stress of educational effort comes in America before eighteen. Graduation takes place at that age. At our own college for women at Girton, girls under eighteen are not admitted, and the final examinations take place three years or more later. Dr. Weir Mitchell's evidence on this point, as quoted by Dr. Clarke, is very emphatic. He says: "Worst of all is the American view of female education. The time taken for the more serious instruction of girls extends to the age of eighteen, and rarely over this." There is nothing that the English advocates of a change of system have striven more heartily to effect, than an extension of the time given to education; and what they have urged is in complete agreement with the opinions of Dr. Clarke and Dr. Mitchell. Then, again, Dr. Clarke distinguishes very clearly between girls learning the same subjects as boys, and sharing the same final examinations (which he does not disapprove), and identical coeducation, where they are subjected to exactly the same rules and daily system, and where emulation between the two is constantly at work. He says (p. 135): "It is one thing to put up a goal a long way off—five or six months, or three or four years distant— and to tell girls and boys, each in their own way, to strive for it; and quite a different thing to put up the same goal, at the same distance, and oblige each sex to run their race for it side by side on the same road, in daily competition with each other, and with equal expenditure of force at all times. Identical co-education is racing in the latter way." Now, there is no organized movement in England for identical co-education in this sense. What is advocated is just what Dr. Clarke approves, viz. setting up the same goal, and allowing young men and young women to reach it each in their own way, and without the stimulus of daily rivalry. The public recitations, and the long hours of standing they involve, so much blamed by Dr. Clarke, are unknown in England, except in schools of the most old-fashioned and unenlightened type. The number of hours per day spent in mental work seems also to be much greater than that which is usual or even allowed in the best English schools. Eight or ten hours is said to be the usual time given to study in the American schools. In England, six hours is the time suggested by the Schoolmistresses' Association, and this is to include time given to music and needlework. Naturally, there is no time in America for physical exercise or outdoor games.

. . . We will venture to draw another conclusion from the discussion, and it is this; that those who wish to give a fair hearing to all that is urged in support of a higher education for women must examine the evidence for themselves, not saying to themselves loosely that medical men seem to be afraid of this higher education, or that it seems to have been tried in America, and to have failed. Let them inform themselves thoroughly of what is proposed, and of the difference between the new system and the old; and if the result be, that, by improvement in the training and education of women, as much may be hoped for their physical as for their mental development, let them, in the interests not of women only, but of the children who claim from their mothers so much more than mere existence and nurture, give to those who are labouring at this difficult work, not languid approval, but sustained and energetic support.

State Secondary Education for Frenchwomen

SOURCES

118. Félix Dupanloup, "Femmes savantes et femmes studieuses," *Le Correspondant*, 70, no. 4 (25 April 1867), 749. Tr. KMO.

119. Jules Ferry, "Discours sur l'égalité d'éducation" (10 Avril 1870, Salle Molière), *Discours et opinions de Jules Ferry*, I (Paris, 1893), 301-5. Tr. KMO.

120. Émile Keller, speech before the Chamber of Deputies, 19 January 1880, in *Annales, Sénat et Chambre des Députés*, I, pt. 1, *1880, Chambre des Députés*, pp. 80, 86. Tr. KMO.
121. Camille Sée, speech, 19 January 1880. *Annales, Sénat et Chambre des Députés*, I, pt. 1, *1880, Chambre des Députés*, pp. 89-90. Tr. KMO.

Throughout the nineteenth century French educators upheld and reinforced a view of the power of women that manifested itself in a conflict for control of their minds through a separate and sexually specific type of schooling. This was as true of secularizing republican educators of the 1860's and 1880's as it had been of countless generations of Catholic educators before them, as the following selections reveal.

The first selection comes from an influential article by the Bishop of Orléans, Félix-Antoine-Philbert Dupanloup (1802-1878). It was occasioned by his entry into a major controversy over girls' secondary education that broke out during the late Second Empire. In 1866 Napoleon III's reforming minister of public instruction, Victor Duruy, inaugurated a series of secondary courses for young upper-class women in Paris and other French cities. These courses were to be taught in public buildings by state-employed educators, and were intended to introduce women to "scientific" subjects such as physiology as well as the more acceptable humanistic subjects. In a bitter polemic in the press, Monseigneur Dupanloup led the Catholic counter-charge against Duruy's project; he even threatened excommunication for members of his own diocese who dared to allow their daughters to attend these "godless" courses. Yet Dupanloup was by no means an opponent of female education; indeed, he argued that both Jewish and Christian tradition supported thorough literacy and mental development for females, though with constant reference to their roles as wives and mothers. In this excerpt from his article (later published in book form in French and in English) "Studious Women," Dupanloup sets forth his own definition of a well-educated Christian woman within the tradition of Proverbs 31.

The second selection is excerpted from a landmark speech on the future of French education delivered in Paris by Jules Ferry (1832-1893) in the spring of 1870. Here Ferry, an attorney from a textile-manufacturing family in eastern France (who was considered one of the most promising political figures in the republican opposition to the Empire), sets out a program for mass education to be undertaken by the French state. Ferry was himself to implement this program in the 1880's, when he served as minister of public instruction and prime minister. Already in the 1860's, however, he had taken an active interest in the woman question, from the standpoint of both educational and legal reform. In this speech he demonstrated the importance of his exposure to women's rights advocates, as well as his reading of Mill's *Subjection of Women*, for the future organization of education for French girls. Although a few Frenchwomen were by 1870 already engaged in university study in France, the French ideal remained that of the "mother-educator." Consequently, neither Ferry nor his peers were as obsessed as their English and American counterparts with the "sex in education" issue (Docs. 115-117)—despite the influence of biological deterministic thinking, through Comte's positivism and Michelet's anticlericalism, on the republican tradition.

The third and fourth selections are excerpted from the 1880 debates in the Chamber of Deputies on the bill that established state secondary schools for

French upper-class girls. Several issues, each of which concerned male authority over women, stood out during these debates: (1) specifically, whether the new republicanized state could wrest control of female education away from the church and thereby (it was assumed) manipulate the formation of female intelligence; (2) whether the state had the right to intrude upon the rights of the *père de famille*; and (3) outright fear of female "emancipation." The first speech in opposition to the bill was given by Émile Keller (1828-1909), a leading Alsatian Catholic deputy then representing the territory of Belfort, near the Swiss border. Keller ardently opposed coeducation, and objected to the "dechristianization" of French women; elsewhere in his speech he invoked the all too notorious example of the Russian nihilist women to illustrate his point. The second speech, in support of the bill, was given by its principal champion, the young deputy Camille Sée (1847-1919). Here Sée, whose vision of the scope of girls' education was extremely broad, paralleling in many respects the views of Condorcet a century earlier (Doc. 19), attempts to allay the fears of more apprehensive members of the Chamber whose votes were essential to passage of the bill. Even with Jules Ferry's support, Camille Sée's law won by only a narrow majority in both houses; it became law in December 1880.

---

118. Monseigneur Dupanloup (1867)

But let me make myself perfectly understood. What I should like to see above all else is not a race of learned women, but—what is necessary to their husbands, their children, and their households—intelligent, judicious, attentive women, well instructed in everything that is necessary and useful for them to know as mothers, mistresses of households, and women of the world; never despising any manual labor, but knowing how to keep not only their fingers busy but their minds as well, and how to cultivate their souls and their entire being. And I will add that what must be dreaded as much as the very worst of scourges are the frivolous, fickle, flabby, idle, ignorant, dissipated women who are devoted to pleasure and amusement and who are, consequently, opposed to every exertion and to nearly every duty, incapable of any studious pursuit, of any sustained attention, and therefore in no condition to take any real share in the education of their children, or in the affairs of their husbands and their households.

119. Jules Ferry (1870)

. . . To call for equal education for all classes is only half the job, half of what is necessary, half of what is due. I demand such equality for both sexes and I want to spend a few moments considering this aspect of the question. Here the [major] difficulty, the obstacle, is not merely expense but one of custom; it consists, more than anything else, of an adverse masculine attitude. There are two sorts of pride in the world: pride of class and pride of sex. The latter is far more evil, far more persistent, and far more ferocious than the former. This male pride, this feeling of male superiority exists in a great number of minds, and among many who would not admit to it; it insinuates itself into the best souls and, indeed, it might be said that it digs into the deepest recesses of our hearts. Yes, gentlemen, we must confess: in the hearts of even the best of us there resides a sultan (Much laughter); this is especially true of Frenchmen. I would not dare admit this except for the fact that moralists who have observed us for decades, who have analyzed our [national] character, have written that in France, under the façade of the most exquisite gallantry, there exists a secret contempt of man for woman. Truly, this is a trait of the French character, a sort of conceit that even the most civilized among us carries within himself: we must speak plainly, it is male pride (Laughter). This is the first obstacle to equalizing the conditions of instruction for both sexes.

There is a second obstacle, no less serious, and this one originates with you, ladies. For this opinion that men have of their intellectual superiority is one you constantly encourage; it is you who ratify it; on this point you conduct a perpetual plebiscite. (Applause and laughter).

You accept what I will call, not your servitude, but to borrow a word that describes it exactly, that of Stuart Mill, you accept this *subjection* of women that establishes itself as a consequence of women's intellectual inferiority, and you have heard this repeated so many times that you have ended up believing it. Well, ladies, you are mistaken, believe me, and if we had enough time I would prove it to you. At least read the book of Mr. Stuart Mill on the *subjection of women*; you should all read it, for it is the beginning of wisdom. It will teach you that you have the same faculties as men. Men say the opposite, but really, how do they know? I haven't the slightest idea. . . .

Women, you say, are this and that. But, my dear sir, what do you know? To judge all women thus, can you say that you are acquainted with all women? Perhaps you know one—or even more! (Laughter).

You must learn that it is impossible to say of women, who are complex, many-sided, delicate, changeable, and unpredictable, that they are this or that. In the present state of their education, it is impossible to say that they could not be something else if they were raised differently. In consequence, given our ignorance of the true aptitudes of women, we do not have the right to handicap her. (Applause).

Moreover, experience proves the contrary of this French prejudice, and it is America that furnishes us with the proof. Mr. Hippeau* visited Boston, Philadelphia, and New York. He visited institutions for girls that are intended to prepare them for higher education; he visited co-educational institutions where—extraordinary phenomenon—girls and boys sit together under the eye of the teacher without any disturbance to morals—as we must point out, to the honor of the American race, which we sometimes treat so archly and consider just a bit savage. In France it

* Celestin Hippeau visited the United States to inspect its educational institutions as an official delegate of the French ministry of public instruction. His report was subsequently published in serial form in the *Revue de Deux Mondes* during the late 1860's.—EDS.

was considered a great step forward to eliminate coeducational schools. In America woman is so respected that she can travel alone from St. Louis to New York without running the risk of insult, whereas here a mother could not let her daughter go from the Bastille to the Madeleine with the same confidence. (Laughter).

In these schools I have just mentioned, twelve to fifteen hundred young people of both sexes study the same subjects; a happy subject for comparison. Mr. Hippeau did so with care. He wanted to see everything and to learn about everything. After interrogating the teachers and the students, he declared that it is impossible to discover any difference whatsoever between the aptitudes of the girls and those of the boys; that they are equal in intelligence; that there are excellent students and weak students to be found in both sexes and in equal proportions. I conclude from this that the test has been made and that equality of education is a right not only for both classes but for both sexes as well.

In my opinion the current problem of the equality of woman with man should be considered within these limits. Let us proceed in orderly fashion: let us begin the reform at the beginning. We are told that we must give women the same rights, the same functions—I don't know about this, and I don't want to know. I am content to seek for them the thing they have a right to, what we can offer them today, and let free competition do the rest.

120. Émile Keller (1880)

Gentlemen, I ask your permission to present, with reference to the first article, a few observations concerning the law that has been submitted to us.

On different occasions, I have pointed out to you an overall plan in the education laws, having for its goal the separation of the Church from the schools, of religion from education; its goal is to re-establish and aggrandize the University monopoly and to make of the University—controlling primary as well as secondary instruction, the instruction of girls as well as of boys—the lay clergy of a new state religion, the lay clergy of freethought. . . .

The proposed law concerning secondary schools (*collèges*) for girls marks a new step in this dangerous and profoundly anti-liberal path.

Indeed, what is being proposed to replace the girls' boarding schools (*pensionnats*), which will be closed by the notorious Article 7 [of Jules Ferry's proposed law on associations] and which contain no less than 40,000 pupils? What is proposed is to establish in every department and in every important town, girls' preparatory schools [*lycées*], paid for by the State, that is, by the taxpayers. These lycées would be directed entirely by the minister of public instruction.

Here we see realized for the first time the dearest wish of the honorable Paul Bert [professor of physiology at the Sorbonne and an anticlerical republican deputy]—that is to say, the total suppression of religious instruction.

And to populate these establishments, in which it is feared there would not be many pupils, an entire system of scholarships has been organized, to be paid for by the taxpayers and awarded by the ministry of public instruction. Here, gentlemen, is the essence of the project that has been submitted to you.

Basically, they are not happy with French women who are, in great majority, Christians, and whom they consider to be bad citizens for a radical republic that makes war on the Church; and in order to demonstrate this, they express their thoughts concerning [these women] in the most severe—I should say, in the most outrageous—fashion. . . .

. . . This project will realize the vow of M. Jules Ferry that I have already brought to your attention from this tribune and that you would do well to remember—it was in 1870, and M. Jules Ferry declared that democracy, under penalty of death, must deliver woman from the Church. "Yes," he said, "woman must no longer belong to the Church, but to Science."

Today the proposal is to deliver women from the Church and to give them over to Science—and to accomplish this you are being asked to create, at the taxpayers' expense, in every department and every city in France, secondary schools for girls directed by the minister, and having for their goal to mould not only the young men but also the girls in the likeness of M. Jules Ferry. (Loud laughter on the right.)

And to fill these *collèges* of which families are so fearful . . . you are asked to vote for enough scholarships to populate these establishments, again at the taxpayers' expense. This is the sum total of the law!

121. Camille Sée (1880)

I am not saying that, like the United States, we must organize higher education for women. Higher education is intended for young men who, generally speaking, wish to take up a career: this one will enter the school of law to become a lawyer or a functionary; that one, the school of medicine to become a doctor. I know there are young women who have their diplomas of doctor of medicine, but they are rare exceptions, and if I must speak my mind completely, I believe that we will always have too few midwives and quite enough female doctors.

Young men enroll in the courses at the faculties* at an age at which a young woman, simply because she is a woman, has other duties to fulfill. A young woman at seventeen or eighteen gets married; sometimes she is already a mother. . . .

Moreover, I am not taking up the question of whether women should be introduced to careers in the liberal professions or in the administration.

It is not prejudice, but nature herself that confines women to the family circle. It is in their interest, in our interest, in the interest of the entire society that they remain at home. The goal of the schools we want to

---

* At this time there was one university in France, with faculties of law, medicine, letters, etc., located in various cities. The idea of *university* in France also encompassed secondary education.—EDS.

found is not to tear them away from their natural vocation but to render them more capable of fulfilling their obligations as wives, mothers, and mistresses of households. It is within these limits that we confine our hopes and desires; but there we can invoke both justice and the social interest. . . .

Not only does a sense of justice encourage us to do for young women what we do for young men, but we have also an interest here of the first order, a social interest, a political interest. It is vital that between husband and wife there be a community of ideas, in order for a community of feelings to exist. It is vital that they not be deeply separated by their beliefs and their hopes; that the mother does not pass on to her children opinions, customs, and traditions contrary to those believed in and desired by the father; that contradiction and chaos do not reign at the domestic hearth; that each sex does not hold to its own language, its own ideas, its prejudices if you will, and soon its own separate life. But, on the contrary, concord and unity in the family ought to be the model and the source of concord and unity in the State.

CHAPTER 14

Women and the Civil Law

A New Code for a Unified Italy

SOURCES

122. Carlo Francesco Gabba, *Della condizione giuridica delle donne nelle legislazioni francese, austriaca e sarda: Studio di legislazione comparata* (Milan, 1861), pp. 4-5. The editors are indebted to Dr. Judith Jeffrey Howard, Arlington, Virginia, for her translations and annotations of the Gabba and Mozzoni selections.

123. Anna Maria Mozzoni, *La donna e i suoi rapporti sociali in occasione della revisione del codice civile italiano* (Milan, 1864), pp. 219-22.

A vital aspect of building a unified Italian nation after 1861 was to consolidate the laws governing the five major pre-existing political regions, which had been under the respective jurisdictions of Austria, the kingdom of Naples and the Two Sicilies, the kingdom of Piedmont, the duchy of Tuscany, and the Papal States. Each of these jurisdictions treated the legal position of women somewhat differently, allowing single and married women varying degrees of legal authority over their own persons and property. In the following selections, two writers present conflicting approaches to the determination of women's civil status in the new Italian kingdom. The first is from a treatise on comparative law by Carlo Francesco Gabba (1838-1920), a professor of law at the University of Pisa. Gabba, though a Catholic, quoted from Michelet's *Woman* (Doc. 97) to preface his distinction between women's legal competence as single adult individuals and their loss of civil rights as married women. He drew the line in such a way as to preserve the full authority of husbands and fathers in the family unit. Gabba's work was very influential and was constantly cited during the Italian Parliament's debates on the civil code. In contrast, Anna Maria Mozzoni (1837-1920?) advocated full civil and political emancipation of Italian women. Mozzoni was the daughter of an upper-class family from Milan that had long espoused Mazzinian republican ideas. She herself acknowledged the influence of the Saint-Simonians, Fourier, Sand, Deroin, and d'Héricourt on her own thinking, and was quick to translate John Stuart Mill's essay on the subjection of women into Italian when it was first published. In this selection Mozzoni argues that a married woman's functions as wife and mother should no more exclude her from full civil and political rights than a man's functions as husband and father should exclude a man. Mozzoni, who remained single until she was nearly forty, went on to become a leader of the Italian women's rights movement.

In its treatment of women the Italian Civil Code enacted by the constitutional monarchy in 1865 followed the pattern set by the Piedmontese [Albertine] Code of 1837, which itself drew heavily on the French Code, with the major difference that its provisions for separation of property in marriage imposed less of a handicap on married women.

---

122. Carlo Francesco Gabba (1861)

One of the major questions concerns the legal status of woman. . . . The importance of this subject needs no explanation in a century such as ours, where protests have so often been made against the remnants of women's ancient legal inferiority, a century inspired by general ideas of liberty and equality and also, a little, by the stimulation of more cordial relations between the sexes. We confess that some such remnants still exist in the legislation of many parts of Italy; they are compatible neither with the civility of the century, nor with the dignity of the human race, nor with the well-being of families, so that it is not possible or permissible in our day to discuss these holdovers in good faith without condemning them. We do not hesitate, however, to confess likewise that, besides this justifiable condemnation, exaggerated and absurd aspirations going under the very vague names of [women's] emancipation and equality have often been and continue to be espoused by jurists and non-jurists alike. These people would not want to admit of any difference between man and woman other than sex, [admitting] no differences in civil and political competencies. They do not consider that, in order to double the size of the population that exercises civil rights in this way, it would be necessary not only to carry out an intellectual revolution and to turn absolutely upside down the ideas and traditions of all times and places; it would also be necessary to eradicate the influences that these same sex differences, including divergencies of strength and inclinations, naturally exercise on men's and women's moral and civic aptitudes. And in this lies the error of those aspirations. If, then, it is our duty to champion those principles governing the legal status of women, which seem proper to us, no less do we have to gird ourselves to combat those that strike us as absurd and impossible; such is precisely the two-fold intent of the present work.

The comprehensive and general formula for the ideas we advocate concerning the legal status of women is this: woman is equal to man in legal competency, but in the exercise of rights during marriage she must endure her characteristic limitations. It seems to us that this formula satisfies the various requirements of modern civility with reference to the [natural] rights (*diritto*) of women, and at the same time avoids the exaggerations referred to above. Inasmuch as legal competency refers precisely to the most humiliating aspects of the so-called *legal inferiority* of woman, which was very grave in former times and has not yet been totally eliminated in every part of Italy, it is precisely in marriage that the particular tendencies and natural aptitudes of woman contrast with those of men. Thus it also becomes evident that the former have less legal competence and strength than the latter in the management of affairs, and that fact cannot help but influence the exercise of rights. In the course of this work, the reader will see the reasons for this distinction between legal competence and the exercise of rights, as well as the precise limits we have assigned to women in this latter respect and the reasons for assigning such limits.

123. Anna Maria Mozzoni (1864)

Since [natural] rights (*il diritto*) are based on attributes common to the human race and not on individual attributes, and since [natural] rights are perceived as the legitimate claim of every person to the development of characteristic human faculties, and to the fulfillment of all the functions that allow him to attain his goals [in life], I will not hesitate to demonstrate that woman, as a human being, has no fewer rights than man, so long as privilege does not usurp the sacred name of rights.

I will say only that all jurists, even though they do not formulate their opinions according to any philosophical basis of [natural] rights, perceive the will to justice and reason as lying in the notion that rights should be extended to every human being. Yet, since they find themselves unable to deny that woman belongs to the human race, they all begin to contradict themselves whenever they introduce inequality between man and woman. And thus does justice cut with a two-edged sword; while it denies a right to one, it grants a privilege to the other.

So it is that, of all the charges brought against woman with the intention of justifying the iniquitous way she is treated by the laws—charges sanctioned neither by nature nor by reason, but only by the passions— none can be upheld in the face of a very few observations and in view of the true basis of [natural] rights.

[The jurists] say: woman is unfit to exercise rights.

But it is impossible to deny the intelligence of many women, any more than one can refuse to recognize the imbecility of many men. But [natural] rights are not based on individual intelligence.

They say: woman is weak.

But it is impossible to deny the power and strength of many women, just as it is impossible to deny the puniness and chronic illness of many men. But [natural] rights are not based on strength and good health.

You object to the nature of her social roles?

It is impossible to demonstrate and to prove that maternity, running a household, often teaching, trade, industrial production, are less necessary and less noble occupations than those of the ragpicker, street cleaner, or the liveried servant. But [natural] rights are not based on social roles.

Perhaps woman's special physical make-up, which subjects her to crises and ups and downs, makes her inadaptable to the exercise of rights?

The exercise of any civil rights (*diritto civile*) whatever, not being a mere trifle, will always be performed much better by a healthy woman than by a sick man, whose rights are, nonetheless, not taken away from him. All of which demonstrates that rights are not based on physical make-up.

But her ignorance renders her unfit!

It is impossible to deny the erudition of many women, any more than it is possible to refuse to recognize the ignorance of many men. Who is more cultured, a woman who directs an educational institution or the servant who leads the pigs to pasture? But rights are not based on learning.

Nor could one argue with greater success on the basis of the protection that the man exercises over the woman; we have just seen that this protection is illusory and denied by the law itself whenever it assumes responsibility for checking the husband and defending the woman against him. Nor could one argue on grounds of support, because nowadays the woman contributes to meeting family expenses, either with her dowry, or with her wealth, or with her personal labor, so that the house in which she lives is no longer the husband's house but a conjugal house. Moreover, with regard to a woman who is of legal age, the question of support has no reason to be raised. . . .

Furthermore, one cannot argue [against women's rights] by invoking the manifold cares of the family, because these are no more taxing than those of a smithy who hammers on an anvil twelve hours a day, or those of a government minister who handles the affairs of an entire kingdom, or those of a soldier who is under the burden of stern and precise discipline night and day. . . .

If rights were based on social roles, on productivity, or on personal merit, again one would not be able, without inconsistency and injustice, to exclude women who work, women who produce, or women who have social value as mothers, as manufacturers, or as proprietors. But rights are not and have never been based on any of the above.

Rights are based on the acknowledged, characteristic capacity of a given nature; as such every being of every species has its characteristic rights.

Attacks on the Civil Code in France

SOURCES

124. Léon Richer, *La Femme libre* (Paris, 1877), pp. 46-55. Tr. KMO. The editors are grateful to Professor Claire Goldberg Moses, University of Maryland, for allowing us to consult her microfilms of Richer's book and newspaper.

125. Congrès international du Droit des Femmes, "Voeux: Section de Législation," in *L'Avenir des Femmes*, no. 166 (1 September 1878), pp. 133-34. Tr. KMO.

Despite continued criticism of women's inferior situation in the Civil Code of 1804, no reforms were achieved before 1880. But with Napoleon III's liberalization of the Second Empire during the 1860's, agitation for abolition of married women's legal disabilities was renewed and, in spite of the dislocations of 1870-71, continued with mounting vigor during the early years of the Third Republic. What is striking is the extent to which advocacy of such changes was taken up by liberal men within the legal and notarial professions, many of whom were also closely associated with French freemasonry. Most of these men drew inspiration from the revolutionary rhetoric of 1848, which emphasized women's companionate mission as wife and mother. They strove to ameliorate women's legal situation within this framework.

The first selection is by Léon Richer (1824-1911), a pivotal figure in this phase of the French women's movement. Richer had been sensitized to the woman question during the fifteen years he spent as clerk for a notary in Choisy-le-Roi, just outside Paris. In 1865 he moved to Paris, became active in freemasonry and republican politics, and began writing for the anticlerical *L'Opinion Nationale*. In 1869 he founded a group dedicated to changing the position of women in French law, the "Ligue Française pour le Droit des Femmes" (which still exists), and began publishing a weekly newspaper, *Le Droit des Femmes* (also known during the 1870's as *L'Avenir des Femmes*), which appeared regularly until 1891. In 1877 Richer published *La Femme libre*, the 340-page work from which this selection is excerpted; Richer viewed this book as a preface to his subsequent book, *Le Code des femmes* (1883), which consisted of a careful exposé, section by section, of women's status in the Code, accompanied by detailed proposals for legislation to amend the law so as to remove women's disabilities.

Richer's arguments for legal reform were carefully keyed to appeal to the sensibilities of his republican contemporaries. The establishment of the Third Republic enabled him to invoke on women's behalf republican traditions of liberty and justice for all, and the elimination of servitude, while at the same time underscoring (as this selection suggests) how substantive reforms in the Code were required to give wives more freedom of action and more legitimate power within the framework of separate spheres for the sexes. To convince his fellow republicans that such reforms were essential, Richer argued first that France's recovery following defeat by the Germans in 1870 necessitated women's emancipation, and secondly, that the republicans must carry out a whole program of reforms in order to attach women to the new regime. The republic, he insisted, would never be truly consolidated in France if women remained hostile to it.

The second selection consists of a series of resolutions adopted by the first international congress on women's rights, held in Paris during the summer of 1878. This congress, organized by Léon Richer and Maria Deraismes, was scheduled to coincide with the World Exposition and attracted a sizable number of French republican leaders as well as representatives from abroad. Most of the measures demanded in 1878 did become law by 1914.

---

124. Léon Richer (1877)

The present situation of women seems to me to be most precarious. It is no way in accord, I will say, not only with the law in the strict sense—this is incontestable—but with the services that women are called upon to render, the influence they exercise on the general current of ideas, and the real level of their intelligence. I might also say that it is not in accord with our own interests; this we will see later.

I think I can characterize this abnormal situation in very few words, and I will try to prescribe the remedy even as I define the evil:

The present status of woman is *servitude.*

The true state, the moral state of woman is—just as for you—LIBERTY.

Show me one situation in life where the woman is not a serf, one circumstance—even an exceptional one—where the right of woman is not subordinated to our own, and I will agree that I am guilty of exaggerating.

But our morals, our law, innumerable facts show that I am a thousand times right. In all life situations, whether public or private, woman is a *serf.*

Everyone knows—and I need not speak at length about this—how she is treated in marriage.

I am not accusing husbands exclusively; there are good husbands—indeed, most of them are good. Unfortunately, however, the law renders the best intentions null and void. If, generally speaking, the husband is benevolent, the law is always brutal.

Thus, according to the Code, this masterpiece . . . the mother has no sort of authority over her children. Do not think that I exaggerate. I speak the exact truth.

One might, I agree, triumphantly cite against me two articles thus conceived: . . .

Art. 371. The child, at any age, owes honor and respect to his *father* and his *mother.*

Art. 372. [The child] remains under *their* authority until the age of majority or until his emancipation.

Under *their* authority; isn't this very clear? It could not be more formal, more clear, more affirmative. It could not be more explicitly stated that the husband and wife share the authority, that they are both invested with it to the same degree.

By no means! This is quite simply a lie.

Article 373, which follows immediately afterward, DECREES:

"The father ALONE exercises this authority during the marriage."

And the Code is full of these contradictions, these traps, these hypocrisies.

Is it a question of marrying off the children?

Common practice—and the appearance of respect that is affected for whatever concerns the family—insists that the consent of the father and that of the mother be requested.

When I say common practice *insists*, it is evidently a manner of speaking, for common practice insists on nothing—common practice conforms to the law.

Let us then have a look at the law.

It says (art. 148):

"A son who has not reached the age of twenty-five or a daughter who has not reached the age of twenty-one cannot contract marriage *without the consent of their father and* MOTHER.

Let us stop there.

Does this mean that the *mother* has a recognized, proclaimed, written right?

No.

For, after the period and comma, marking a pause, the same article 148 continues thus:

"*In case of disagreement, the consent of the father will suffice.*"

What does this signify, if not that the consent of the mother has no effect—no effect, just as her refusal has no effect?

In the case of marriage, the mother's wishes do not count.

If the husband says *yes*, it is enough. Even though the mother lives closer to her children than the father and knows them better, knows their tastes, their needs, takes account of their preferences, especially in the case of a daughter!—Even though this confidante of the child's intimate thoughts might say *no*, her refusal would prevent nothing. If she does not give her consent, it can be dispensed with.

If, on the other hand, the husband is opposed, the true interests of the child may be sacrificed, but the marriage will not take place.

Thus, the mother's consent is demanded only for form's sake. It has no value except under one condition—that it is in agreement with that of the father.

Is this not ridiculous?

Now let us speak of the role accorded to wives in the conduct of domestic affairs.

One thing has always struck me—that along with the inconsistency of the law goes the inconsistency of certain minds, whose obstinacy in not breaking away from prejudice generates the most striking contradictions.

Everyone is aware that there are women who demand the exercise of political rights—a revindication that I would certainly agree is premature in France.

Now, the major argument of men against any woman who exhibits any trace of political freedom consists of sending her back to her household, where family obligations await her.

It is there, they say, that she should perform her activity, there that her faculties will find employment, there that she will reign as sovereign.

And indeed, the domestic functions, which consist especially of keeping order and of economizing—the high functions of *minister of the interior*, to use a frequently employed expression—are woman's particular domain; she understands them marvelously. Many households are held together only by the good administration of the mother of the family. The husband, swept up by multiple preoccupations, does not always budget; often he spends blindly. The wife, more prudent, wiser, more reserved, reestablishes equilibrium in the house.

Well, I hear you saying, this doctrine is perfect!

Undoubtedly. Only I will point out that between theory and practice there is a flagrant contradiction. If the wife has the great qualities that one deigns to recognize in her; if she is an excellent housekeeper; if she understands so well how to administer, why do our laws—the laws we have made—contest precisely the most indispensable of [women's] liberties, which is at the same time the most useful—that of putting to account the economic talents that they are supposed to possess in such high degree?

What does it gain us to pretend that woman is especially gifted in administration if, by formal disposition of the code, she is classed among minors and those who have lost their civil rights? She is recognized as possessing an especial talent, and it is precisely this talent that the law prohibits her from exercising freely.

We must agree that nothing could be more illogical.

Article 1421 of the Civil Code is thus formulated:

"The husband *alone administers* the community property. He can sell it, transfer it, mortgage it, without the agreement of his wife." . . .

Article 1422 in turn says:

"The husband can dispose of chattels gratis and privately, as he pleases."

This allows him a host of dishonorable dealings; this (oh, depth of ignominy!) gives him the means of keeping a concubine, of *favoring* a mistress to the detriment of his own wife and children!

Article 1428 is even more precise. It reads:

"The husband administers all personal property of his wife."

"Personal" property means the very patrimony of the wife.

"The husband," Jules Favre has written, "is a dictator who can dispose of the fortune of his wife at his pleasure and ruin her, without leaving her any other recourse than to file for separation of property, which always comes too late."

But all of that, you might say, is applicable only to the community property system.

This is true, but the other systems—the dowry system and the separate property system—give husbands the same rights, except for several slight modifications that at bottom change absolutely nothing.

Thus, we send woman back to the household, and when she is there, we take away from her all initiative and all authority. With the Code in hand, we contest her very right to get involved—I was going to say, in our affairs, but I will say, in her *own interests.* We proclaim her an excellent administrator, with the understanding that she will administer nothing.

She is our very humble vassal. She does not manage our domestic affairs (for I do not call "management" the washing of children in the morning, brushing the suits, washing the dishes, and mending the linen); she will not *manage* our domestic affairs unless we allow her to do so.

In the fullness of the law, the incapable husband is the administrator; the capable wife becomes the administrator only with Monsieur's permission. If in such conditions, and when the husband is a spendthrift—which one sometimes sees—the wife manages to make order and economies, we must agree that she has a great deal of merit!

However, it is necessary that these things be put in harmony. Insofar as domestic administration is woman's lot, let the law at least permit wives to *administer.* How can they set about making order if their husbands retain the right to dissipate, without their consent, all the profits of their employment? How can they realize savings, if it is in men's power to sell the furniture and to withdraw investments?

When one realizes that the husband's right extends down to the *personal* property of the wife, of her very own, to what she inherits from her own family, one is astounded!

Without doubt, distinctions must be made, in order to avoid charges of exaggeration:

If the personal property of the married woman consists of real property, its alienation by the man alone presents some difficulties; but it can be arrived at by means of relatively inexpensive legal formalities. If it is a matter of transferable securities [*valeurs mobilières*], however, all obstacles disappear: husbands are absolute masters. They cannot sell a cheap little shanty, but they are free to spend a personal fortune worth a million francs. They can even take this million and give it to a concubine without the dispossessed spouse having any legal means of protest.

In a time when many fortunes are purely monetary [*mobilière*], this facility in the hands of husbands seems to me excessive, to say the least.

125. The First International Congress on Women's Rights (1878)

I.

Considering that woman is a civil personality;

Whereas, according to natural law, the adult woman is the equal of the adult man,

The Congress resolves that, in every country where woman is made inferior, the entire body of civil legislation be revised in the direction of the most absolute and complete equality between the two sexes.

II.

Convinced as we are that the legislation presently in force is inadequate; that the system of legal separation is immoral and should be eradi-

454   *Evolution, Education, and Economics, 1860-80*

cated; that the indissolubility of marriage is contrary both to the principle of individual liberty and to morality and has the most unfortunate and terrible consequences; that divorce is necessary from the perspective of humanity, of morals, and, in a word, of the future of society;

The Section concerned with legislation—illuminated by the debates and drawing inspiration from the hopes common to all nations as expressed by the members that represent them; leaving to the legislators the task of formulating the text of the law and determining a mode of special jurisdiction—puts forth the following propositions, which it believes respond to the wishes of the majority and which it submits to the consideration of the Congress:

The Congress demands:

1. The suppression of the regime of bodily separation [*régime de la séparation de corps*].

2. The establishment or reestablishment of divorce, according to the principle of equality between the spouses.

III.

The Congress considers the absolute freedom to divorce as the best remedy against the inequality of the man and the woman with regard to the laws on adultery.

IV.

Whereas there is only one morality;

Whereas the degree of guilt for the same crime or misdemeanor cannot vary according to sex.

With regard to the misdemeanor of adultery:

Considering that adultery by the man is as sinful as that of the woman, since the man, like the woman, can introduce into someone else's family bastards of his authorship.

Considering that, even apart from this circumstance, the adultery of man, no less than that of woman, carries in its wake social disorders whose seriousness, whether from the perspective of family bonds or of public morality, is not contested by anyone.

Considering that if the reestablishment of divorce on the foundation of the greatest liberty should result in the decrease of instances of adultery, it will not be able to prevent them all:

The Congress resolves that the penal laws should not acknowledge any difference between the adultery of the wife and the adultery of the husband, wherever the act is committed.

V.

The Congress expresses its ardent desire to see enacted as soon as possible, in those nations currently deprived of it, a law establishing as a misdemeanor the act of seduction of an underage girl, accomplished with the help of lies and a false promise of marriage.

Such a law should empower the appropriate tribunals to sentence, when appropriate, the guilty party to pay damages to the plaintiff.

VI.

The Congress,

Considering that both morality and social order require equally that the parentage of every human being should be a matter of record:

Resolves that the search for paternity [*recherche de paternité*] by judicial process be allowed and pursued, without charge, on behalf of any child who has not been legally recognized, and also at the request of an underage girl whose seduction by lies and promises of marriage has been verified.

The Congress adds that it would be useful to have the laws on the right of inheritance of the father's estate be equalized for all his children, with no distinctions being made between them.

VII.

Considering that the first and most sacred right of the human being is his right to absolute sovereignty over his own person:

Considering that citizens (*citoyens*) and citizenesses (*citoyennes*) are equal in common law;

Considering that the arbitrary powers accorded to the morals police are in flagrant violation of the juridical guarantees assured by the law to each individual, even to the worst criminal;

The Congress demands the suppression of the morals police.

CHAPTER 15

Women, Work, and the Professions

A New Look at Working Women in France

SOURCES

126. Jules Simon, *L'Ouvrière*, 4th ed. (Paris, 1862), pp. iii-vii, 80-81. Originally published in 1861. Tr. KMO.

127. Julie-Victoire Daubié, *La Femme pauvre au XIXᵉ siècle* (Paris, 1866), pp. 1-6, 8, 40-41. Tr. KMO.

The 1860's witnessed a rash of renewed concern in France over the plight of working men and women and the state of working-class family life. These selections are taken from two of the most influential books published on the subject of working women during the Second Empire, Jules Simon's *L'Ouvrière* (1861) and Julie-Victoire Daubié's *La Femme pauvre au XIXᵉ siècle* (1866).

Jules Simon (1814-1896) addressed the working-woman issue in his capacity as a liberal republican educator and moralist. Simon, who would later become a senator and prime minister, was an ardent proponent of the work ethic for both sexes and criticized the uselessness of idle and frivolous bourgeois women. But he ardently opposed any sort of work for women—particularly factory work—that would remove them from the home. Simon was keenly aware of all the social problems that had developed among working-class families in English textile manufacturing towns and examined their counterparts in France with those problems in mind. Though historians have shown that a surprisingly high proportion of the women employed in textiles were young and single, Simon discusses their work in terms of married women, the implicit assumption (a common one at the time) being that every single woman was a prospective wife and mother of a large family whose work-force participation not only actively prevented the acquiring and practice of her domestic skills but threatened her virtue as well. Simon argued in fact that women should be barred altogether from taking employment in the manufacturing sector; that their wages in other "minor industries," in which they could still produce items in their homes, should be increased; and that the imperial government should initiate legal steps to facilitate formal marriage and family formation among working-class persons, to improve their educational opportunities, to encourage them to save money and acquire property of their own.

Julie-Victoire Daubié (1824-1874) was the grand-daughter of an ironmaster from the Vosges. The youngest of eight children, she learned Latin and German, studying with an older brother who was a priest, and later supported herself as a governess. In Lyons she attracted the attention of the Saint-Simonian industrialist François Arlès-Dufour, who encouraged her to put forth her candidacy for the baccalaureate, the first university degree; at the age of thirty-seven she successfully passed it, to the consternation of the minister of public instruction. Arlès-Dufour also encouraged Daubié to write, and in 1866 her book, *La Femme pauvre*, won first prize in a competition sponsored by the Academy of Lyons. Daubié's analysis of the working-woman's problems was both more systematic and far more critical than that of Simon. Rather than attempting, like Simon, to return working women to a dependent familial role by raising men's wages, Daubié urged reforms that would permit women to become economically independent. She pointed an accusing finger at society's tendency toward concentration, or centralization as she called it, of the rural population in the cities, of commercial and industrial facilities in massive, highly capitalized stores and factories; at the accompanying pseudo-professionalization of many occupations that placed women at a disadvantage; and, most importantly, at the absence of laws that would curb sexual harassment and thereby allow women more freedom of movement in French society. For Daubié, anti-capitalist though she was, as for the less radical Simon, moral reform through law and better education remained a prerequisite to economic reform. Julie Daubié dedicated the remainder of her life to the pursuit of this goal.

---

126. Jules Simon (1861)

. . . There is a horrible vice in our economic organization that generates misery and must be vanquished at all cost if we do not want to perish: the suppression of family life.

In former times the worker was himself an intelligent force; today he is nothing more than an intelligence who directs a force. The immediate consequence of this transformation has been to replace men with women almost everywhere, by virtue of the law of industry, which impels it to produce a great deal with little money, and of the law of wages, which lowers them incessantly to the level of need of the unskilled worker. One recalls the eloquent invectives of M. Michelet: "The working woman! impious, sordid word, which before this age of iron no other tongue, no other time would have comprehended, and which by itself counteracts all our pretended progress!" If one bemoans the introduction of women into manufacturing, it is not because their material condition there is very bad. There are very few deleterious workshops, and very few tiring functions in these workshops—at least not for women. A carder has no other task but to watch over the movement of the card and, from time to time, to reconnect a broken thread. Compared to her living quarters, the room where she works is an agreeable place to be, thanks to its good ventilation, its cleanliness, its gaiety. She receives a good salary, or at least one much higher than she would have earned in former times as a seamstress or embroiderer. What then is the problem? It is this: that the woman, having become a worker, is no longer a woman. Instead of leading this retired, sheltered, modest life, surrounded by those dear to her, which is so necessary to her own happiness and to ours, by an indirect yet inevitable consequence she lives under the domination of a foreman, amid companions of doubtful morality, in perpetual contact with [other] men, separated from her husband and her children. In a worker's household, the father and mother are absent, each in turn, fourteen hours per day. Thus, there is no longer any family. The mother, who can no longer nurse her infant, abandons it to a badly-paid wetnurse, sometimes even to a caretaker, who feeds it soups. The result is a frightfully high mortality rate, morbid habits among the children who survive, a growing degeneration of the race, and the complete absence of moral education. Children three and four years old roam through the fetid streets, pursued by hunger and cold. At seven in the evening, when father, mother, and children find themselves once again in the single room that offers them asylum—the father and mother worn out from their work, and the children from their vagabonding—what is there ready to receive them? The room has been empty all day: no one has seen to the most elementary requirements of cleanliness; the fire is out; the exhausted mother hasn't the strength to prepare anything to eat; all their clothing is falling to pieces; this is the family that manufacturing has to offer us. One should not be too astonished if the father, upon leaving the workshop that has exhausted him, returns in disgust to this confining, unclean, stagnant room, where a poorly prepared meal awaits him, half-wild children, a wife who has become nearly a stranger to him because she no longer inhabits the house and returns only to grab a hasty rest between two working days. If he gives in to the seduction of the cabaret, his profits will be swallowed up and his health destroyed; and the result is this—pauperism in the midst of a prosperous industry—a result one could scarcely believe possible.

What, then, can be done? Without a doubt the augmentation of [men's] wages would be the surest and most immediate means of returning women to their natural destiny; for it is need that drives them from the household; it is to supplement the insufficiency of earnings of the *père de famille* that women are condemned to workshop life. We ardently hope that it will be possible to render their work more productive; we will not despair. But we cannot forget the existence of a law stronger than all the laws inscribed in the law codes, stronger than the most dedicated charity—this is the economic law that governs all industrial development, that forces the manufacturer to measure his expenses against his chances for profit and to struggle against competition by means of lower prices. Even an increase in wages would not bring an end to pauperism unless it were accompanied by profound moral reform. . . .

. . . If there is one thing nature clearly teaches us, it is that woman is made to be protected, to live as a girl with her mother, as a wife under the protection and authority of her husband. To tear her away, from childhood on, from this necessary refuge, to impose on her a sort of public life in a workshop, is to wound her in all her instincts, alarm her modesty, deprive her of the sole milieu in which she can truly be happy.

127. Julie-Victoire Daubié (1866)

In former times French society assured women's subsistence in the cloister, in industry, and in the family; numerous institutions came to their aid. The corporations of arts and crafts and the municipalities furnished funds to dower young women, and until 1790 the state budget set aside 24,000 *livres* to dower them in the provinces. Besides this, individual initiative created the institutions called *rosières* in a large number of localities.

The system of freedom and common law, replacing the numerous regulations that established the respective rights of each sex, is undoubtedly preferable to the former state of affairs, and I am far from seeking my ideal in the past. But the present state of our society demonstrates that under the misleading names of liberty and equality woman is held back in deplorable inferiority and excluded from employments that were formerly guaranteed her by both legislation and custom.

Thus woman, dispossessed, once again seeks asylum in the convent, in order to enjoy instruction, sanitary assistance, etc., privileges that she cannot enjoy as a laywoman. Even in industry the vices of our social organization are so extensive, and the conditions for free apprenticeship so disadvantageous for young women, that our industrial cloisters are growing rich by concluding contracts with apprentices that engage them to offer the use of their time in exchange for nourishment.

These industrial convents alone attest to the difficult, if not impossible position in which the woman of the people finds herself; they offer miserly nourishment in exchange for hard work; meanwhile, they attract girls at such a rate that, in the last fifteen years, the State has authorized 80 to 100 [religious] communities of women annually [to administer them]. . . .

The poor woman excluded from the types of employment that were formerly hers vegetates in indigence or falls into vice, for lack of a means of subsistence. If this encroachment of men is the result of liberty, the natural inferiority of women would demand special protection, but it is easy to convince oneself that the oppression that weighs her down is, on the contrary, the effect of the denial of liberty. When we investigate carefully the causes of the poor woman's precarious state, we see that they can be attributed to an administrative centralization that arbitrarily excludes her from schools and employments, and to an irresponsible immorality that, after banishing her from the family, has loaded her down with the triple oppression of laws, institutions, and customs.

Everywhere the State, the departments, and the municipalities are opening and organizing vocational schools. They take in a certain number of scholarship pupils, but not one of them welcomes women. Even when a woman gifted with a special or exceptional aptitude achieves some rank in industry, the State almost always refuses to give her the patents for invention or improvements that she applies for; the ordinary excuse given in these instances is that women do not have access to credit, which deprives them of Parisian correspondants and leading houses to represent them. In the same manner they are barred from nominating experts to the commercial tribunals; they can neither intervene in the election of *prud'hommes* nor take part in their deliberations.

In the arts, in letters, and in science, even more than in industry, a severe interdict hangs over woman. Not only are the artistic, literary, and scientific schools closed to her, when she prepares for practicing a profession, but the woman who acquires by herself the required knowledge for trades taught in the special schools would not thereby acquire the right to practice them. Thus, it can be said that for a woman instruction is more of an ornament than a means of earning a living, for the University will not offer her the least assignment; the medical profession excludes her from the application of this science, even though the good sense of the people, morals, and social interest all call for her to do so. Centralization distributes in the most arbitrary manner a host of subordinate employments that require no special aptitudes. Thus, we would search in vain for women to tend our museums or our public libraries, and even in our hospitals we see men applying leeches to women and waiting on them as nurses. The regulations of the municipality or of the Parisian police also ordinarily obstruct women's exercising the profession of street sweeper.

Could one believe that the *baccalauréat* and the medal of the Legion of Honor have become requisites for being hired as shopgirls?

One such novelty shop requires that a bachelor of letters staff one of its departments. At this point so few [women] are in possession of the *baccalauréat* that we humbly admit our total inferiority when confronted by the right to measure ribbons and laces by university authorization. . . .

This centralization, so prejudicial to woman, finds its *raison d'être* in society's immorality, which prohibits coeducation, an enormous benefit for every society possessed of good morals. In France a young woman cannot even do her apprenticeship under the same conditions as young men because she always has to be safeguarded against society by the family or the convent; this is a severe blow to individual liberty and to the right to earn a living through one's own labor. In other countries, shopgirls can circulate in town as freely as salesmen and, like them, can transact with merchants those types of business called commissions. In France, the absence of laws to repress immorality expose these women too much to allow them to enjoy complete freedom; all sorts of traps are laid for them; their isolation is exploited by every means; and our laws cannot prevent even one of the abuses that other peoples repress in the severest manner.

Even in the so-called free schools, women remain in an inferior position. To cite but one example: it is recognized that the knowledge of modern languages, especially English, which in Paris is often required of store employees, is often much appreciated and allows them to earn more money.

The salesmen gather in evening courses, which cost relatively little, given the large numbers of students; but the shopgirls cannot take advantage of these lessons because they have less freedom than the young men and because our customs give them every opportunity to be corrupted by the men, which prohibits them from acquiring this instruction. . . . Not only that, but the parents will voluntarily make the necessary sacrifices of time and money to assure the future of the salesman, whether by instruction or, sometimes, by putting up bond money, but will not offer any security of subsistence to a woman in the same situation.

When these causes do not constitute a motive for excluding the young woman, they necessarily contribute to the reduction of her salary.

I will frequently speak of the associations that seek to preserve young women from the dangers of their situation; this troublesome intervention is necessitated by our social system; thus in Paris a religious association protects the shopgirls and attempts to remove them from all the exploitation that menaces them.

Woman also finds herself dispossessed of her former employments in the towns because men are deserting the countryside, the consequence of bad morals. Unfortunately, when legislators no longer understand how to prevent debauchery and accord to it all the facilities they take away from marriage and the family, the rights of pleasure-seeking men can become established and varied only in the cities; there wealthy corrupters abound on every side; thus the cities alone absorb nearly all the public fortune, and the population of every class finds itself forced to desert its quarters to seek the income that can no longer be found in the impoverished countryside.

Thus woman, whose needs and expenses are augmented by the embellishments of the towns and their opulence, finds herself almost always with insufficient resources; man competes with her, takes away the easy and lucrative jobs; he takes everything away from her precisely because he owes her nothing; he leaves her to collapse from the excesses of unproductive and killing labor, when he does not make her a victim of his passions.

This *déclassement*, which calls man into the cities, this usurpation that precipitates him into feminine employments, is characteristic of all corrupt societies. . . .

With centralization and immorality thus accumulating all capital in the hands of men, the woman without fortune also finds herself excluded from every industry that requires an investment of funds, which the poor man normally obtains from his wife's dowry. In this manner, the woman, being reduced to a subordinate kind of work, often cannot even direct the fashion houses for ladies.

Capital, the basis of the humblest merchants, serves to stock these houses, which rely on large investments. Thus it is that the great industrialists, the opulent capitalists, have invaded dressmaking and have already succeeded in corrupting the traditional good taste of Frenchwomen that had imposed the yoke of our fashions everywhere.

Even the women who do business with these men, these bearded *couturières*, complain of the bad direction they give to fashion; of the heaviness of the short jackets cut and sewn by their great masculine hands; of the disgraceful and inelegant decorations they applique onto the light fabrics; of the monumental dresses of which they are the architects, etc. . . .

In summary, I have affirmed that, as concerns her subsistence, centralization smothers woman and immorality crushes her; thus I will call upon the principles of liberty and justice to emancipate her from paying this heavy tribute to these two minotaurs.

Women and the Work Force in Germany

SOURCES

128. Joseph Heinrichs, "Vorwort" to Louise Otto, *Das Recht der Frauen auf Erwerb: Blicke auf das Frauenleben der Gegenwart* (Hamburg, 1866), pp. v-viii. Tr. SGB.

129. Louise Otto, *Das Recht der Frauen auf Erwerb: Blicke auf das Frauenleben der Gegenwart* (Hamburg, 1866), pp. 60-62, 67. Tr. SGB.

The question of women's participation in the labor force became a truly international issue in the 1860's as these two selections, drawn from the German debate, reveal. Joseph Heinrichs (dates not known), a philanthropist from Lisse (Posen), had published a pamphlet on women's emancipation in 1863. Little is known about Heinrichs beyond this, except that he did attend the founding congress of *Der allgemeine deutsche Frauenverein* in 1865. Here, in his preface to Louise Otto's book, *Das Recht der Frauen auf Erwerb*, Heinrichs emphasized the pragmatic necessity of developing suitable employment for women that would accommodate itself to the special nature of women in which he clearly believed. Though familiar with the French debate as depicted in the writings of Jules Michelet (whose ideas are reflected in the *Breslauer Zeitung* articles he opposed), Jules Simon, and others, Heinrichs insisted that the Germans, unlike the French, need not save society from decadence through women and the family, but must contend with the fact that women were performing unsuitable kinds of wage labor.

The second selection is from Louise Otto (1819-1865; Docs. 48, 78). By 1865 she had expanded her interest in the problems of middle- and working-class women (which had begun in the 1840's) to a general social critique, which led her to found a general association of German women in 1865. This excerpt from her book reveals the extent to which she had come to adopt a male-centered perspective of the narrowness of the domestic sphere relative to the importance of the "public sphere." By this time she had become obsessed with the need for women to develop their independence—both economic and mental—from men. She viewed women's participation in economic life as an essential means for fostering their self-development and broadening their perspective on the world.

---

128. Joseph Heinrichs (1866)

The current agitation about women's right to work has no connection with those vague emancipation ideals of the forties. The present agitation concentrates exclusively on economic matters; it is concerned with actual tangible wrongs that it aims to improve or to abolish; it rests firmly on a practical base and will triumph in the end. Thus, much as we admire English models, our actions are neither as stirring nor as decisive as those on the other side of the Channel; we ponder and search with much ingenuity for the most suitable means to attack a problem: some day, however, we shall guide it into the right groove and, with German perseverance and German thoroughness, achieve our goal. The reform we want to carry through is an end in itself, not as in France (Simon, Pelletan) a means to other ends. Thank God, German family life is as yet untouched by immorality, and it is not necessary for our reformers to educate women in order to save the family and society. We stand so far on firm ground—the ancient Teutonic virtues, the depth of German sensitivity, German loyalty, German morality and sobriety are no myths. *The only emancipation we seek for our women is the emancipation of their labor.* . . .

. . . It is said: "Woman is intended for family life—she shall rule the home. All attempts to organize her activity in the public sphere are a threat to her womanly nature, and sooner or later they must fail. Such pronouncements are based upon laws of physiology, laws of statistics and of history." The anonymous author of a series of essays on "the woman question" in the *Breslauer Zeitung* that we review here, in order to show what kind of objections we have to combat, insists that the entire reform movement is based on a mistaken view of woman's being—that the central figures of the reform movement are the so-called privy councillors' daughters who, when they have suffered a disaster as a result of their excessive demands on life, having scorned the possibility of founding their own homes, abandon themselves to some obscure longing for independence that they want to achieve through a "right to work." The similarity that this author discovers between the woman question and socialism, his insistence that we are confronting a struggle against the law of nature, and the view that only "privy councillors' daughters" are at the root of the entire agitation—such assumptions are erroneous and all demands based upon them meaningless.

We agree with him in viewing the family sphere as woman's most noble career; his defense of marriage is based upon great truth. When, however, he wants to solve the [woman] question through the magic word "marry," he misunderstands the real conditions that, with bitter seriousness, make it necessary for a large number of women to support themselves, even when they are lucky enough to make a happy marriage. These essays have considered the misery of certain classes of society—the "noble proletariat" of the civil service, and the unjustified demands of "privy councillors' daughters." However justified such criticism may be, it is clear that the reforms we seek would benefit quite different and much larger circles, which the author ignores. In his polemic against the Leipzig *Frauen-Verein* (Women's Union), against Lette and Virchow, against Stuart Mill, Pelletan, and Jules Simon, he attempts to persuade us that we need no reforms similar to those sought by them—that, in fact, total salvation lies in a simple education and in marriage. Even an improvement in education is unnecessary: "The husband shall be the teacher of woman." He attempts to prove that the demand for women's work exceeds the supply; he scorns women scholars; he is skeptical of women's ability to deal with most of the new careers suggested for them, especially their aptitude for medicine, even though as he regrets earnestly, "there is a need that is greater than can be described." Brougham's* invocations to the workers to "become capitalists" cannot solve the problem of the social question; neither can the woman question be settled by a well-meaning command to "marry." One might just as well urge a drowning man to swim! . . .

We do not seek to create new careers for women. We only want to choose those for which they are distinctly suitable and in which they have a prospect of using their talents in a suitable manner. We wish to advance this goal, the possibility for which has been much diminished through custom and prejudice, by improving women's education, by making them more aware of their strengths, and by clarifying for them those economic laws upon which our society is founded. Beyond this, we demand only freedom for individual development, which will allow every woman, in whatever circumstances, to take up any career for which she has inclination or talent. Even romantics like Michelet who consider it a loss of dignity for woman's nature when she is forced to work, is aware of the necessity for woman's labor. In this respect we do the same; we begin with existing conditions. Our sole aims are as follows: to guide woman's work into areas that do not conflict with the singularity of her nature, that are compatible with her destiny in family life. The nightmare of imagining a female Samson is as nothing compared to the existing misery of women working in factories, or their participation in men's work that crushes their physical strength and injures their natural sense of delicacy.

129. Louise Otto (1866)

. . . We have already mentioned in passing how industrial workers fear the competition of women, how as early as 1848, in several places, the workers chased women out of the factories. Recently similar thoughts are to be found here and there; indeed, the Lassallean principle states that

* Lord Brougham (Henry Peter Brougham, 1st baron Brougham and Vaux, 1778-1868), internationally known British social reformer.—EDS.

women's position can be improved only through the position of men. *Such* a principle, which mocks all morality and humanitarianism, is contrary to our philosophy of life and to the ideas in this book. The very party that promises itself so much from the "help of the State," that insists upon *universal* suffrage, excludes women from all its efforts—and thereby proves that its empire of freedom, which is "the rule of the fourth estate," is to be founded upon the slavery of women, because those who may not be *freely and gainfully employed for themselves are slaves.* But, thank God, this is only a minority of the workers. The majority supported women's work at a workers' congress in Stuttgart and later agreed to a women's conference. Its journals, such as the *Arbeitgeber* and *Arbeiter-Zeitung* among others, support women's work.

It is impossible to comprehend how anyone with open eyes could not favor women's work. Even if one were to accept as the outcome of competition—that some men would have less work and profit than at present because of the supply of female labor—it is surely all the same whether it is the men or the women who experience feast or famine: undeniably they share the need for bread! And when it is no longer necessary for men to provide bread for their wives, daughters, and mothers, it is they who will benefit most from the introduction of women's work since it is no longer possible for one pair of hands to work and earn enough to nourish an entire family for a lifetime. These considerations are at the root of all our womanly efforts—not, as some of our opponents insist, a hostility and declaration of war against men. We want to free men from pressure, the most severe pressure nowadays being the worry over sustenance, and from conditions in which it is a crime to devote time and energy to a project that might benefit society as a whole—but not the family. We also want to free ourselves from the pressure of dependence by demanding a natural sharing of labor for men and women.

A man wishing to work can always, everywhere find an opportunity for *profitable employment*; only those who are lazy, irresponsible, proud, and wicked, who lose their work and thus sink into shame and misery, are debased by the "struggle for existence." Moreover, no one says to them, "you need not work; you will be better off and earn more if you do not work, and devote your life to sacrifice and self-denial." No one says this to a man, but a girl is so instructed a thousand times, both subtly and crudely. She hears it from men who are enslaved by their sensuality, from old women long since hardened and plunged into the depth of vice, from young women still cheerfully wallowing in their sins—perhaps even from her own parents.

And thus thousands upon thousands listen to these voices and grasp the means so easily available. Some give themselves to men who seduce them with gifts and promises, and convert their desolate position into one of friendship; some throw themselves into the arms of the most gruesome trade because it was the only one available to them. Then there is great consternation about the corruption of the female sex, which is held responsible for criminal life, supposedly abusing the most sacred laws of nature and destroying the sanctity of the family. The situation becomes a problem for lawmakers, and no satisfactory solution is to be found!

And whose fault are these crimes? The immorality of men and women, is the quickest and, presumably, a just answer, because men are not excluded from the judgment.

But who is to blame for this immorality? It is not only the fault of those individuals who are affected by it; the blame must lie with the conscience of all men and women, even the most moral, who believe the principle that women exist only for the sake of men. The blame must lie with all those men and women who do not educate their daughters to be able to provide for themselves; it must lie with all those men who object *to women's right to gainful employment*, with all those who condemn women to idleness and do not allow them the means to education, labor, and an independent position in life. The burden of guilt rests also upon the State when it permits encroachment upon women's right to gainful employment. In order to eradicate at least a tiny portion of this enormous burden of our times, I have written this book.

The First International and Working Women

SOURCES

130. The First International Workingmen's Association, Geneva Congress 1866, "Compte rendu des débats," in *La Première Internationale: Recueil des documents*, ed. Jacques Freymond, I (Geneva, 1962), 49-51. Tr. KMO.

131. The First International Workingmen's Association, Lausanne Congress 1867, "Rapports lu au Congrès ouvrier réuni du 2 au 8 septembre 1867 à Lausanne," in *La Première Internationale*, I, 211-13. Tr. KMO.

132. Paule Mink, "Le Travail des femmes, Discours prononcé par Mme Paul [*sic*] Mink à la réunion publique du Vauxhall, le 13 juillet 1868," Bibliothèque Nationale, Paris, microfiche Rp 12236. Tr. KMO. The editors are grateful to Professor Marilyn J. Boxer, San Diego State University, for kindly transmitting a copy of this speech.

As the previous selections suggest, discussion of women's right to work was profound, heated, and detailed. Nor were bourgeois social critics alone in their concern and disagreements. The selections that follow offer a glimpse into the working-class discussion of women's right to work in manufacturing within the context of the First International Workingmen's Association, founded in the mid-1860's. Here the theories of Proudhon confronted those not only of Michelet but also of Marx, as the delegates attempted to reach agreement on the issue. At the Geneva Congress of 1866, two distinct points of view are in evidence among the French-speaking delegates: a Proudhonian view represented by the worker Chemalé and his supporters, and a more libertarian view espoused by Varlin and Bourdon, as the first selection shows.

When the International convened in Lausanne in 1867, a commission delegated to report on the question of women and work presented its conclusions. The excerpts from this report, offered here as the second selection, rebuke the

Proudhonian workers for their theories of female inferiority, at the same time stoutly defending the patriarchal family and the strict division of labor along sexual lines and condemning the very principle of female labor outside the home. In an accompanying report (not included here), a Belgian delegation condemned the principle of industrial labor for women on similar, but more comprehensive grounds. Women's work outside the home, the Belgians argued: (1) competes with men's work and undercuts their salaries; (2) leads women to neglect their households; (3) tends to perpetuate working-class ignorance, by allowing women no time to acquire education for themselves or to teach their children; (4) contributes to physical degeneration of the working class by undermining women's health and preventing them from nursing their own infants; and (5) is philosophically and practically incompatible with women's destiny as spouses, housewives, and mothers.

Such arguments as these by working men provoked the ire of a young woman of Polish descent, Paule Mink (1839-1901) who, recently arrived in Paris, had become active in the women's rights and working-class movements. In July 1868 Mink addressed the public on behalf of women's right to work, at the great Vauxhall assembly hall in Paris. Contesting the position of the First International (which had been presented at the Vauxhall the previous week), Mink argued that women's work did not overlap with that of men; indeed, she was a strong advocate of "equality in difference" and, like Louise Otto, a critic of the so-called emancipated woman. As a woman, however, she found it impossible to tolerate either the Proudhonian or the relatively milder patriarchal arguments then being advanced by the workers' movement. Her eloquent speech was subsequently posted in Paris, where it received much attention. Mink later worked on behalf of the first French workers' political party, the *Parti Ouvrier Français*, founded by Jules Guesde. The POF was one of the few groups on the French Left that consistently supported the principle of women's right to work.

---

130. The First International Workingmen's Association, Geneva Congress (1866)

Citizen COULLERY (La Chaux-de-Fonds). I am happy to see the congress take up the question of woman. We must declare in a categorical manner that we are working just as much for woman's emancipation as for that of man. We must tear her away not only from the prostitution of the streets but also from that of the workshop. Her instruction, like that of man, must be complete, so that she does not become the prey of ministers of any religion. In short, she must be enabled to achieve complete development, both cerebral and corporeal, for she is the hope of the human race.

Citizens CHEMALÉ, FRIBOURG, PERRACHON, CAMÉLINAT put forth the following proposition:

"From the physical, moral, and social standpoint, the work of women and children in manufacturing should be energetically condemned in principle as one of the most active causes of the degeneration of the human race and as one of the most powerful means of demoralization set in motion by the capitalist caste."

"Woman," they add, "is not created to work. Her place is in the family *foyer*, she is the natural educator of the child; only she can prepare the child for civic existence, manly and free. This question should be placed on the agenda for the next congress. Statistics will furnish documentation persuasive enough that we will be able to condemn the work of women in manufacturing."

Citizen VARLIN (Paris). Like all of you, I recognize that women's work in manufacturing, as it is currently practiced, ruins the body and engenders corruption. But, proceeding from this fact, we cannot condemn women's work altogether; how will you who want to rescue women from prostitution be able to do so if you don't give them another means of making a living? What will become of the widows and orphans? They will be obliged either to beg or to enter into prostitution. To condemn women's work is to ratify charity and to authorize prostitution as well.

Citizen FRIBOURG (Paris). Widows and orphans will always remain an exception and can in no way weaken the proposition we are putting forth. For, he said, while believing it necessary for all men to work, we know perfectly well that many will be prevented from doing so by natural accidents; nevertheless, we support the general principle. Widows and orphans are in the same class as the infirm.

Citizen TOLAIN (Paris). As long as woman is engaged in manufacturing, she will never be a free being; she will never be able to develop her natural faculties. The workshop bastardizes her.

Citizen LAWRENCE (London). There is something more powerful than all the reasoning being put forward here, more true than all the philanthropic sentiments being voiced—the movement of society. We should not be theorizing; we are workers, practical men and not utopians. Well then, if we want to assist usefully in the emancipation of our class, we should limit our role to observing what is going on around us, to understanding the course of social movement instead of trying to impose on it our feelings and particular views. As the Central Committee's report said so well, the tendency of modern industry is to engage women and children in social production. And this is so true that, in certain parts of England, the woman no longer remains at home, and it is the man who is reduced to doing the cooking. We are far from admiring the manner in which women are made to work, but the fact exists and it would be madness to condemn woman's work across the board. But what we can do is to protest energetically against such exploitation of woman as is practiced by the capitalist caste.

The extract of the Central Committee's report dealing with women's work is put to a vote and passed by a large majority.

The following amendment, presented by citizens VARLIN (Paris) and BOURDON (Paris), intended to strengthen the English report, is put to a vote and rejected:

Lack of education, excessive work, inadequate pay, and bad hygienic conditions in manufacturing are, at present, causes of physical and moral degradation for the women who work there. These causes can be eliminated by a better organization of labor and by cooperation. Since women need to work in order to live an honorable life, one should seek to ameliorate their work rather than to suppress it. As for children, one should seek to retard their entry into manufacturing and restrict the hours they are allowed to work as much as possible.

The proposition put forth by citizens CHEMALÉ, FRIBOURG, PERRACHON, CAMÉLINAT is put to a vote and adopted.

131. The First International Workingmen's Association, Lausanne Congress (1867)

Inasmuch as societal renewal is based on the principle of *mutuality* and on *equivalence of functions*, it must—in order to be possible and practical—have fraternity as its basis, which is encountered only in honest and generous hearts. Egoists exclude themselves from the benefits of fraternity. If all men were animated by such fraternity, societal renewal would be easy and promptly accomplished—or rather, it would not be necessary. Thus, one must locate the source from which this fraternity emanates.

In vain will the most eloquent predications be heard if they do not penetrate into the bosom of the family, the principal base of the social edifice.

The family will exist in vain if woman, who is its guiding spirit, is not treated with respect, benevolence, and justice. Errors and prejudices concerning woman and her moral and intellectual faculties can be encountered in every country and in every social class. These errors and prejudices have entered into the laws, formulated by whom? by man, superb protector of his life's companion, without whom existence would not only lose its charm but would be impossible. Questions pertaining to the social condition of women have preoccupied legislators and philosophers, but alas! without serious results, because of the fact that the legislators and philosophers have based their reasoning on a capital error, namely on the *inferiority of woman*. . . .

Woman makes us think naturally of the family. Indeed, among so many institutions that are perishing, among so many authorities that are succumbing, there remains one imperishable thing, one authority higher than all the others! The greatest name on earth is the name of the father; the greatest thing is paternal authority: these are the creative and conserving elements of the family. The name of king has suffered greatly, and peoples have sworn hatred to royalty, but the name of father has suffered far less: happily it is still a name that commands authority and respect.

Fatigued by the unfortunate and scandalous scenes of present-day life, people prefer to cast their eyes on the sweet and touching spectacle of the inner family, where the father and mother together raise their children in virtue. What in human society could be greater and more beautiful! The family is the cornerstone of the entire social edifice. . . . It is in the bosom of the family that all the virtues must be created that will develop later on in practical and social life.

Without the family there is no complete and harmonious development for man. It is also the consoling refuge for saddened hearts, for anguished and desperate souls. It is humanity in miniature, in sum, and its modest theater should suffice to fulfill the greatest ambition: in its bosom one finds activity and work, suffering and consolation, peace and happiness. It is the very source of brotherhood.

Woman, by her physical and moral nature, is naturally called to the peaceable minutiae of the domestic hearth; this is her department. We do not believe it is useful for society to give her any other charge. If the wife of the proletarian is able to become a deputy to the Chamber, the worker's soup may well be inadequately seasoned. As a mother, woman is the child's first educator, but on the express condition that the father acts as the directing agent. First impressions exercise a powerful effect, whether physically or morally, and prepare the future of the man. This is why education must begin at the cradle and must, by a rational system, well understood, accompany man throughout the course of his practical life. Education must concern itself with the complete and harmonious development of the moral, physical, and intellectual faculties of man. A good education should produce a virile, energetic, and free will, an enlightened mind, free of prejudice, a heart inclined toward feelings of benevolence, justice, and fraternity. Domestic education should be the object of the most tender care on the part of the parents.

No material reform is possible without moral reforms through the medium of family, education, and instruction.

132. Paule Mink (1868)

If I were a man, I would probably not have taken part in this debate, for after all the fine, eloquent words that have been spoken here, to reopen the discussion is to risk repetition and perhaps even to verge on plagiarism.

What impels me to address you is my status as a woman. I believe it is my obligation to protest energetically against the tendencies of certain persons who are, no doubt, very well intentioned but who, in their ardor for progress . . . rush to the outer limits of what they believe to be the best solution, without paying any attention to the intermediate positions. . . .

Many of you, gentlemen, recognize no duty for woman other than that of being a wife, no right other than that of being a mother.

This is the feminine ideal, so you say. Ah! Let's have less of the ideal, thank you! Let's stay a bit more on practical ground, for these appeals to the ideal tend to destroy the best, most fruitful questions.

The ideal changes with the times. Our current ideal is that of perpetual and incessant progress; no theory these days can offer an ideal if it does not offer some progress.

Now, let's see whether your ideal constitutes progress. . . .

You want to suppress all work for women except for reproduction?

Women's work! This is one of the most vital questions of our time.

This question carries with it the moral and even the physical regeneration of the future race.

But I am speaking here about a suitable kind of work, not this abusive exploitation that turns the worker in general, and the poor woman in particular, into a slave, the serf of modern society, the subject of speculation at pleasure. . . .

It has been suggested that work exhausts and kills, and the dissimilarities of appearance between women in Bordeaux and Marseille and those in the manufacturing towns of Rouen, Lille, etc. has been remarked. One could perhaps point out the differences in hygiene of these places; for the first, the proximity to the sea; for the second, the deadly necessity of living in airless cellars with no space and no sunlight. But meanwhile let us admit that the difference in work has a good deal to do with the development of the first group of women and the withering of the second. In the latter case, certainly, the suffering is immense and the results are terrible! But where and when have excesses not been an evil? Can we then say, nonetheless, that the good cannot be found at a certain distance from one extreme without having to go all the way to the opposite extreme? Must one then conclude that woman works too much, therefore she should not work at all, and let her avoid the wreckage produced by excessive work by plunging her into an enervation caused by idleness?

Let us ensure rather that women's salaries are raised, that they are commensurate with the end-product, that they are raised in proportion to the cost of the necessities of life. Then there will be no excess, no extreme sapping of strength leading inevitably to corruption, degeneration, and even to death.

It has been suggested that the excessive work of women causes a bastardization of the race. Certainly, excessive work—whether by woman or by man—is an atrocious anomaly that ought to disappear. But we ourselves believe that the bastardization of the race can be attributed far more to the excessive vice and depravity produced by flaws in the distribution of wages to women that lead so fatally to debauchery and all the evils it engenders.

Woman should not work, they say, because it will destroy her beauty and grace. Certainly this is a noble concern on the part of those whom we have too long spoken of as our lords and masters; but we must admit that it doesn't seem to us that work necessarily destroys this beauty.

Normal work develops the body rather than wearing it out; it maintains one's skills in a happy state of activity; it maintains equilibrium among one's various physical faculties and expands them, endowing them with a new fullness of life that is rarely encountered among those depressed, enervated, suffering, nearly invalid creatures who are condemned to idleness.

It is certainly appropriate to be concerned with physical beauty, but moral beauty should by no means be entirely overlooked. Now—and I will say it loudly—work is the only means to progress and perfection that has been given to us. Through work, the mind is developed, the heart is fortified, the level of intelligence is raised. Through work, suffering can be forgotten; through work, one can acquire additional energy for struggling and winning; through work, one can better withstand adversity, combat evil, and master life.

And you want to deprive woman of this supreme happiness, of this immense consolation! You want to deprive the woman who, alone, often isolated, wounded in her deepest feelings, has found peace and consolation in her work; you want to deprive the woman who fell through weakness, and who, solely through her work, has lifted herself up again and has ennobled herself. Ah! Gentlemen, do not cast such reprobation on her, for then, more than ever, we will have to despair for the future of humanity!

You claim that women are too weak, too delicate for work; you claim that you love them too much to deliver them over to such exhausting and absorbing fatigue. Well, we know all that, gentlemen, and we have understood it for a long time; it is by such lovely thoughts that, from one age to another, you have gilded our moral subjection, our social dependence, our intellectual inferiority. But we have had enough of these sonorous and banal phrases, whose inanity we have come to recognize. We want to live and blossom in the light of liberty, and not continue to vegetate and to sigh voicelessly, without strength and almost without thinking.

Certain among you want to make woman a queen, an idol, or I don't know what else! A queen laden with chains that are not, alas, always made of flowers. An idol that had better not move, nor leave the niche where it is kept under glass. . . .

No, gentlemen, no! Woman is neither a slave nor a queen nor an idol. She is a human being like yourselves; like you, she has a right to autonomy. She is the friend and companion of her husband, not his saint, his overseer, or his servant. She does not pretend to submit with bowed head or to be adored; above all else, she wants to be loved and esteemed!

By denying woman the right to work, you degrade her; you put her under man's yoke and deliver her over to man's good pleasure. By ceasing to make her a worker, you deprive her of her liberty and, thereby, of her responsibility (and this is why I insist so much on this issue), so that she will no longer be a free and intelligent creature, but merely a reflection, a small part of her husband.

Certainly there will come a time—and I hope it is not too far off—when our honor will come primarily from our work, where no one will be worth more than he produces. Then what will woman's role be if, inert and passive, she is entirely at the disposal of whatever husband she may have? If she is forbidden to think of work? If she has no future apart from marriage? And if she is deprived forever of liberty and a life of her own?

Pardon me for dwelling at such length on this subject, but I believe it is the keystone. It is work alone that makes independence possible and without which there is no dignity. . . .

I understand very well the feelings that made you want to prohibit women from working. In theory, they are very noble and very praiseworthy. Your wives and daughters have been taken from you for so long that you want to keep them with you in spite of everything. But let us not exaggerate. . . .

You say that wives and mothers should not work. This is all very well, but what of the others? All women are not wives and mothers; some could not or did not want to be, some are not yet, others are no longer.

We must not sacrifice a large number of women to a form of social life that is, I admit, widespread but not completely universal.

What of the daughters, the widows, the women who have bad husbands or who have been abandoned—and that sometimes happens—what about them? Who will take care of them if woman is fatally condemned to inaction? . . .

Certainly it is essential that woman produce goods and earn money, but it does not follow that her work must necessarily lower the salaries of men: equal pay for equal work, this is the only true justice. . . .

Why should we fear that women will invade men's work and exclude them from certain positions? If those jobs that require skilled hands have come to women, is this not just and entirely natural? There are many other kinds of work for men: those of great thought and those of the earth. We still have immense researches, numerous discoveries to make, and the land is far from being exhausted, but too often it lacks farmhands. Science, inventions, the land, all offer vast horizons for masculine activity. Have no fear that women will usurp your prerogatives in these things; this is not in their nature!

But at present everything is abnormal. . . . If the men were in their proper place, the women would be in theirs.

Wouldn't you all agree with me that many of the jobs in the stores, in industry, or even in the administration would be better given to women? If that were the case, how many young men who come to wither away in Paris and the other large towns, would remain in the countryside and make the earth bear more and better quality products? . . .

We are not asking for unnatural types of work for women that physically deform her and sometimes even deprave her morally by making her a hybrid being, without charm, without sex, and without attraction. . . .

In calling for the independence of woman, we must not pretend to want to make a man of her. By no means. Too often, I know well, this has been the goal of the emancipators of women, and I believe that this has been their downfall, the reason for their repeated failures.

Why can't woman be man's equal without wanting to become like him? Copying is inevitably a form of weakness; above all, one must affirm and remain oneself. Women have virtues that are their own, and men have qualities peculiar to themselves. Why meld them into a formless mass whose parts are unrecognizable?

We affirm our individuality, but we want to remain women. It is not with arrogance, neither by weeping nor by supplicating, that we demand our independence, but with calm, with head held high, and firm hearts; for we believe ourselves to be playing a noble role by claiming the rights of an entire half of the human person,* and we are conscious of rendering, by this emancipation, an immense service to humanity in giving it a double force, double activity, double facility to move ahead, by the impulse that we will bring to it. And for affirming this right, for putting this obligation into practice, future generations will later thank us!

The British Controversy over Women in Medicine

SOURCES

133. Sophia Jex-Blake, "Medicine as a Profession for Women," in her *Medical Women*, 2d ed. (Edinburgh, 1886), pp. 38-39, 39-45, 49, 50-51. This essay was originally published in somewhat different form in 1869.

134. George Hoggan's account of the problems at Edinburgh, in Frances Elizabeth Hoggan, "Women in Medicine," in *The Woman Question in Europe*, ed. Theodore Stanton (New York, 1884), pp. 72-77.

Among the charges made against nineteenth-century men by the American women at Seneca Falls (Doc. 74) was that of monopolizing "nearly all the profitable employments" and closing "all the avenues to wealth and distinction which he considers most honorable to himself." They were no doubt alluding to the experience of Elizabeth Blackwell, an Englishwoman who had settled in the United States and succeeded in face of great opposition to earn a medical degree. After practicing medicine for a decade in New York, Blackwell returned to England, where she secured registration as a physician; shortly thereafter Parliament passed the Medical Act of 1858, which restricted entry into the field henceforth to holders of British university degrees.

Disturbed by this development, a few dedicated Englishwomen launched a campaign to storm the bastions of the British medical profession. Sophia Jex-Blake (1840-1912), the strong-minded daughter of an attorney, led the movement. A graduate of Queen's College (London) and herself an educator, she was much influenced by the example of an American follower of Blackwell, the physician Lucy Sewall, with whom she had stayed in Boston. Called back to England by a death in her family, Jex-Blake determined to become a doctor in Britain. By 1869 the twenty-nine-year-old Jex-Blake and a small group of younger women obtained permission to study medicine in separate "ladies' classes" at the University of Edinburgh. Three conflict-ridden years later, the University Senatus refused them permission to register for the graduation examinations that led to the degrees; the women took the University Senatus to court and won their case. But the university officials stalled by appealing the court decision and the delays and continued expense finally forced the women to leave. Most of them completed their studies abroad. In 1876, however, Parliament amended the Medical Act so as to remove all restrictions grounded in sexual difference, and in 1877 London University became the first English university to grant medical degrees to women. "I believe," wrote Jex-Blake in the preface to *Medical Women*, "that it was the

---

* Mink refers to the Saint-Simonian notion of the "human person" as a male-female couple (see Doc. 34).—EDS.

seed sown in tears in Edinburgh that was reaped in joy elsewhere." The first selection below is excerpted from Jex-Blake's widely read essay, "Medicine as a Profession for Women," first published in 1869.

The second selection, an account of the problems Jex-Blake and her associates encountered at Edinburgh, is from an article by Frances Elizabeth Morgan Hoggan (1843-1927). Hoggan had begun her medical education at London but completed it at Zurich in 1870. She subsequently established a private practice for the treatment of women in London and joined Elizabeth Blackwell, who had returned to England, in founding the National Health Society in 1871. The text excerpted here was written by Frances Hoggan's husband and collaborator, George Hoggan, who was an enthusiastic supporter of medical education for women at Edinburgh yet was highly critical of Jex-Blake's tactics. Frances Hoggan's footnotes provide a revealing counterpoint to her husband's comments. It is significant that George Hoggan emphasized the desire of male medical students to retain financial benefits for themselves as the basis of their hostility toward women as students and as physicians.

---

133. Sophia Jex-Blake (1869)

If, then, nature does not instinctively forbid the practice of the healing art by women, and if it cannot be denied that some at least of its branches have long been in their hands, we must go further to seek on what grounds their admission to the medical profession should be opposed.

Probably the next argument will be that women do not require, and are not fitted to receive, the scientific education needful for a first-rate physician, and that "for their own sakes" it is not desirable that they should pursue some of the studies indispensably necessary. To this the answer must be, that the wisest thinkers teach us to believe that each human being must be "a law unto himself," and must decide what is, and what is not, suitable for his needs; what will, and what will not, contribute to his own development, and fit him best to fulfil the life-work most congenial to his tastes. If women claim that they do need and can appreciate instruction in any or all sciences, I do not know who has the right to deny the assertion. . . .

If it be argued that the study of natural science may injure a woman's character, I would answer, in the words of one of the purest-minded women I know, that "if a woman's womanliness is not deep enough in her nature to bear the brunt of any needful education, it is not worth guarding." It is, I think, inconceivable that any one who considers the study of natural science to be but another word for earnest and reverent inquiry into the works of God, and who believes that, in David's words, these are to be "sought out of all them that have pleasure therein," can imagine that any such study can be otherwise than elevating and helpful to the moral, as well as to the mental, nature of every student who pursues it in a right spirit. In the words of Scripture, "To the pure, all things are pure," and in the phrase of chivalry, "Honi soit qui mal y pense."

It has always struck me as a curious inconsistency, that while almost everybody applauds and respects Miss Nightingale and her followers for

their brave disregard of conventionalities on behalf of suffering humanity, and while hardly any one would pretend that there was any want of
feminine delicacy in their going among the foulest sights and most painful scenes to succour, not their own sex, but the other, many people yet
profess to be shocked when other women desire to fit themselves to take
the medical care of those of their sisters who would gladly welcome their
aid. Where is the real difference? If a woman is to be applauded for facing
the horrors of an army hospital, when she believes that she can there do
good work, why is she to be condemned as indelicate when she professes
her willingness to go through an ordeal certainly no greater, to obtain the
education necessary for a medical practitioner? Surely work is in no way
degraded by being made scientific; it cannot be commendable to obey in-
structions as a nurse, when it would be unseemly to learn the reasons for
them as a student, or to give them as a doctor; more especially as the
nurse's duties may lead her, as they did in the Crimea, to attend on men
with injuries and diseases of all kinds, whereas the woman who practises
as a physician would probably confine her practice to women only. It is
indeed hard to see any reason of delicacy, at least, which can be adduced
in favour of women as nurses, and against them as physicians.

Their natural capacity for the one sphere or the other is, of course, a
wholly different matter, and is, indeed, a thing not to be argued about,
but to be tested. If women fail to pass the required examinations for the
ordinary medical degree, or if, after their entrance into practice, they fail
to succeed in it, the whole question is naturally and finally disposed of.
But that is not the point now at issue.

That the most thorough and scientific medical education need do no
injury to any woman, might safely be prophesied, even if the experiment
had never been tried; but we have, moreover, the absolute confirmation
of experience on the point, as I, for one, will gladly testify from personal
acquaintance in America with many women who have made Medicine
their profession; having had myself the advantage of studying under one
who was characterized, by a medical gentleman known throughout the
professional world, as "one of the best physicians in Boston," and who,
certainly, was more remarkable for thorough refinement of mind than
most women I know—Dr. Lucy Sewall. . . .

The next argument usually advanced against the practice of Medicine
by women is, that there is no demand for it; that women, as a rule, have
little confidence in their own sex, and had rather be attended by a man.
That everybody had rather be attended by a competent physician is no
doubt true; that women have hitherto had little experience of competent
physicians of their own sex is equally true; nor can it be denied that the
education bestowed on most women is not one likely to inspire much
confidence. It is probably a fact, that until lately there has been "no demand" for women doctors, because it does not occur to most people to
demand what does not exist; but that very many women have wished that
they could be medically attended by those of their own sex, I am very
sure, and I know of more than one case where ladies have habitually gone

through one confinement after another without proper attendance, because the idea of employing a man was so repugnant to them. I have, indeed, repeatedly found that even doctors, not altogether favourable to the present movement, allow that they consider men rather out of place in midwifery practice; and an eminent American practitioner once remarked to me that he never entered a lady's room to attend her in confinement, without wishing to apologize for what he felt to be an intrusion, though a necessary and beneficent intrusion, in one of his sex.

I suppose that the real test of "demand" is not in the opinions expressed by those women who have never even seen a thoroughly educated female physician, but in the practice which flows in to any such physician when her qualifications are clearly satisfactory. On this point I shall have something to say in a future page.

Of the Boston Hospital for Women and Children I can speak from lengthened experience in it as a student. When standing in its dispensary I have over and over again heard rough women of a very poor class say, when questioned why they had not had earlier treatment for certain diseases, "Oh, I *could not* go to a man with such a trouble, and I did not know till just now that ladies did this work;" and from others have repeatedly heard different expressions of the feeling that, "It's so nice, isn't it, to be able at last to ask ladies about such things?"

As I am alluding to my own experience in this matter, I may perhaps be allowed to say how often in the same place I have been struck with the *contingent* advantages attendant on the medical care by women of women; how often I have seen cases connected with stories of shame or sorrow to which a woman's hand could far most fittingly minister, and where sisterly help and counsel could give far more appropriate succour than could be expected from the average young medical man, however good his intentions. Perhaps we shall find the solution of some of our saddest social problems when educated and pure-minded women are brought more constantly in contact with their sinning and suffering sisters, in other relations as well as those of missionary effort.

So far from there being no demand for women as physicians, I believe that there is at this moment a large amount of work actually awaiting them; that a large amount of suffering exists among women which never comes under the notice of medical men at all, and which will remain unmitigated till women are ready in sufficient numbers to attend medically to those of their own sex who need them, and this in all parts of the world. . . .

And indeed, if no such special suffering were often involved in the idea of consulting a man on all points, it seems self-evident that a woman's most natural adviser would be one of her own sex, who must surely be most able to understand and sympathize with her in times of sickness as well as of health, and who can often far more fully appreciate her state, both of mind and body, than any medical man would be likely to do.

Nor can I leave the subject without expressing a hope that, when women are once practising medicine in large numbers, great gain may accrue to medical science from the observations and discoveries which their sex will give them double facilities of making among other women. . . .

Moreover, there is reason to hope that women doctors may do even more for the health of their own sex in the way of prevention than of cure, and surely this is the very noblest province of the true physician. Already it is being proved with what eagerness women will attend lectures on physiology and hygiene when delivered to them by a woman, though perhaps not one in ten would go to the same course of lectures if given by a medical man. I look forward to the day when a competent knowledge of these subjects shall be as general among women as it now is rare; and when that day arrives, I trust that the "poor health" which is now so sadly common in our sex, and which so frequently comes from sheer ignorance of sanitary laws, will become rather the exception than, as now, too often, the rule. I hope that then we shall find far fewer instances of life-long illness entailed on herself by a girl's thoughtless ignorance; I believe we shall see a generation of women far fitter in mind and body to take their share in the work of the world, and that the registrar will have to record a much lower rate of infantile mortality, when mothers themselves have learned to know something at least of the elementary laws of health. It has been well said, that the noblest end of education is to make the educator no longer necessary; and I, at least, shall think it the highest proof of success if women doctors can in time succeed in so raising the standard of health among their sister women, that but half the present percentage of medical practitioners are required in comparison to the female population.

134. Frances and George Hoggan (1884)

As one of the most devoted servants and supporters of the cause of medical women at that time in Edinburgh, I may describe what I, from personal knowledge, know to be the turning point at which the cause, which seemed to have a fair chance of success, was destroyed by the injudicious conduct of its leader. That point was the agitation connected with the Hope Scholarship. In order to understand the question, a few preliminary words are necessary. In the first place, it was clearly understood that the ladies were admitted into the University of Edinburgh only on the basis of an experiment. There was no equality of rights granted to them with the regular students, but only certain privileges, which allowed them to receive instruction from some friendly professors, who had previously announced their willingness to teach them, provided that those professors who were opposed to the whole question should not be called upon to teach them against their will. . . . It was on these terms only that the ladies were allowed to matriculate, and to receive instruction in special classes, apart from the regular classes of the University. At that time, Professor Crum Brown was the lecturer on chemistry, and a warm friend of the women's cause. He agreed to give the ladies the same course of lectures that he gave to his regular class, receiving, however, for the former a fee amounting only to about a thirtieth part of that which he received from his regular class, and giving, moreover, to the ladies certain privileges which his male students did not enjoy. He granted the women special class examinations, at which the same printed paper of questions was used as that for the men students at the competitions for the class medals, and for the scholarship bequeathed by a former professor, and named after him the Hope Scholarship.* In doing so, he little imagined that he was forging a weapon that would be used against himself.

An authority of the most absolute nature was exercised over the women students by the leader of the party, as she naturally imagined that for the ladies to show extraordinary capacity would at once enlist public sympathy, and force the University to admit them, as of right, to all the privileges of students. Miss Pechey, a student of great ability, was, therefore, provided with a good chemical laboratory and private tuition, in order that she might be enabled to pass the best chemistry examination.

Professor Crum Brown not only used the same examination papers for both classes, but he also used the same valuation terms, and found that Miss Pechey's paper was the best of any male or female student's of her year, and that, had she been a member of the regular class, instead of *the private class* only, she would have become entitled to hold the Hope Scholarship, which had a nominal money value, but was actually given in the shape of three months' tuition in the University laboratory for analytical chemistry.

A demand was made that the Hope Scholarship should be awarded to Miss Pechey. But even had her private examination entitled her to this, it was impossible to grant it to her, for, in order to enjoy it, either she would have had to study with the male students, who worked all day in the chemical laboratory, or the laboratory would have had to be reserved for her alone, by turning out all the men; one of the most stringent regulations under which the female student experiment was conducted being that there should be no mixed classes permitted. She had, however, no legal right to the Hope Scholarship, which was a prize for the students of the regular class, and not for members of any irregular, exceptional, or experimental class which the professor might be allowed to form.† A long series of violent attacks was made by the press upon the University authorities in general, and upon Professor Crum Brown in particular, who, however, did all he could to pacify and satisfy the ladies. He gave the University (bronze) class medal to Miss Pechey, and even offered to add to this the actual money value of the scholarship out of his own pocket, as the rule against mixed classes prevented him from giving the educational equivalent in his laboratory, but this was refused, the

* These scholarships were founded with the proceeds of some very successful lectures given to ladies, and it is hardly to be wondered at that the ladies should feel they had some special claim to compete for them.—F. E. H.

† In Great Britain alone could such an anomaly exist as students allowed to matriculate and yet not legally admitted to the rights and privileges of University students.—F. E. H.

entrance to a mixed class, and not the actual prize, being the point aimed at.

It is difficult for any one not then present in Edinburgh to realize the excitement which prevailed in the local press and in the University. That excitement produced its natural and inevitable result. Those professors who had remained benevolently neutral, when they might have been actively antagonistic, and who had expressed themselves at the beginning as willing to give the experiment a fair chance, now thought that they had made a mistake, and determined to get rid of the rebellious element, which, in the guise of a few young ladies had determined to hold them up to public obloquy. The consequences were foreseen and foretold by many, including myself, to those most interested. Friendly professors became first neutral, next hostile. The ladies were driven out of the University and out of the medical school, and the question which, judiciously conducted, might have had a favorable solution within five years, was thrown back fifty years further in Edinburgh than in any other medical school of the three kingdoms.

The same kind of injudicious action which initiated the exclusion of women from the University, had the same effect subsequently in excluding them from the independent school of medicine at the College of Surgeons, only that in the latter case it was the antipathy of the students which was roused, and it was the influence of the students which excluded them. The board of lecturers at the College of Surgeons was favorable to trying the experiment of teaching the ladies in mixed classes, and the experiment was first tried in the classes of anatomy and surgery. In the latter department, I had the honor of giving the ladies their first lesson in practical anatomy, besides delivering the winter course of lectures on regional anatomy to a mixed class of male and female students.

The episode of the Hope Scholarship had just taken place, and the bitterness which it had aroused made it impossible that mixed classes, with competition for prizes, could be then and for some time afterward a success. One of the professors permitted this rivalry, however, and even showed a certain leaning toward the ladies while adjudicating the daily marks which ultimately determined the question of prizes. The anger of the students, thus called forth, knew no bounds. They organized an opposition, and on the next occasion of an examination in anatomy the first of that series of dastardly riots occurred which disgraced so deeply the Edinburgh Medical School.

The history of these riots is a painful one, and exceedingly discreditable to medical students.* On the other hand it has been sought to show, as a set-off to their misconduct, that, stung by the disgrace of the riots, a body of the more respectable students formed a guard, who in turn defied and maltreated the rioters, and escorted the ladies home every night while the riots lasted. As the organizer and leader of that escort, I regret

---

* Professor Blackie, an eminent professor of the Faculty of Arts, exclaimed on hearing of it: "Ye can say now that ye've fought with wild beasts at Ephesus!"—F. E. H.

to say that its constitution did not bear out the alleged facts. Of the whole guard, only four were medical students, not one of whom belonged properly to the extra-mural school. In fact, the main body of the escort was composed of Irish students, studying at the Royal Veterinary College, who were marshalled up each evening by their leader, brave and simple Micky O'Halloran, an Irish Bachelor of Arts, and an ex-trooper in the Confederate States' Army. These men, each armed with the national shillelah (anticipating by some years the act of justice to medical women which the Irish College of Physicians was the first to accomplish, by admitting women to examinations for the diploma of the college), soon showed the medical students that rioting was a hazardous game. When the riots proved a failure, the students almost unanimously signed and presented a memorial, asking that ladies should be ejected from the mixed classes; the effect of this being that the lecturers actually rescinded the permission given by them at the beginning of the session, and excluded the female students altogether from the school. That rivalry and jealousy were the great factors at the extra-mural school, was made evident by the fact that personal antipathy was shown by the male students to one lecturer only, the one in whose class the men and women contended for the same prizes. In Dr. Patrick Heron Watson's mixed class of surgery not the slightest sign of disturbance was ever shown; but then, while the ladies had no better, more determined, and unselfish supporter than Dr. Watson, in Edinburgh, he refused to accede to their wish that the men and women of his class should be allowed to compete for the same class-prizes, choosing rather to give a second set of prizes to the women out of his own pocket.

CHAPTER 16

Women and the Vote

The Second British Reform Bill—Should Women Be Included?

SOURCES

135. John Stuart Mill, Speech before the House of Commons, 20 May 1867, in Hansard, *British Parliamentary Debates*, 187: 817-23, 825-29.

136. Debate in the House of Commons following Mill's speech, 20 May 1867. Remarks by Mr. Edward Kent Karslake, Mr. Henry Fawcett, Sir George Boyer, Viscount Galway, in Hansard, *British Parliamentary Debates*, 187: 829-33, 835-37, 840-43.

Extending the franchise once again became a political issue in England in the later 1860's. In March 1866 the Conservative government introduced a measure in the House of Commons to extend the suffrage to the prosperous members of the working class by broadening the property-holding qualifications. Into the midst of the parliamentary conflict over this issue, John Stuart Mill (Doc. 105), who had been elected to the Commons in 1865, interjected a new theme by proposing that the franchise be extended to women on the same basis as to men. In May 1867 he addressed the House on this question, proposing to change the word "man" to "person" wherever it occurred in the bill.

Mill's speech drew attention to the magnitude of the "woman question" and provoked lively debate, as excerpts from several speakers' remarks attest. When the proposed word change was put to a vote, 73 members voted in favor; it was opposed by 196 others. Although his amendment failed, Mill had nevertheless succeeded in putting the question before the country and the world, an act he considered to be "by far the most important public service" he performed while serving in Parliament. In August 1867 the Second Reform Act became law, virtually doubling the size of the British electorate—which was now specifically confirmed by law as a male electorate. The organized movement for woman suffrage in England effectively dates from this time.

---

135. John Stuart Mill (1867)

Mr. J. STUART MILL: I rise, Sir, to propose an extension of the suffrage which can excite no party or class feeling in this House; which can give no umbrage to the keenest asserter of the claims either of property or of numbers; an extension which has not the smallest tendency to disturb what we have heard so much about lately, the balance of political power, which cannot afflict the most timid alarmist with revolutionary terrors, or offend the most jealous democrat as an infringement of popular rights, or a privilege granted to one class of society at the expense of another. There is nothing to distract our attention from the simple question, whether there is any adequate justification for continuing to exclude an entire half of the community, not only from admission, but from the capability of being ever admitted within the pale of the Constitution, though they may fulfil all the conditions legally and constitutionally sufficient in every case but theirs. Sir, within the limits of our Constitution this is a solitary case. There is no other example of an exclusion which is absolute. If the law denied a vote to all but the possessors of £5,000 a year, the poorest man in the nation might—and now and then would—acquire the suffrage; but neither birth, nor fortune, nor merit, nor exertion, nor intellect, nor even that great disposer of human affairs, accident, can ever enable any woman to have her voice counted in those national affairs which touch her and hers as nearly as any other person in the nation.

Nor, Sir, before going any further, allow me to say that a *prima facie* case is already made out. It is not just to make distinctions, in rights and privileges, without a positive reason. I do not mean that the electoral franchise, or any other public function, is an abstract right, and that to withhold it from any one, on sufficient grounds of expediency, is a personal wrong; it is a complete misunderstanding of the principle I maintain, to counfound this with it; my argument is entirely one of expediency. But there are different orders of expediency; all expediencies are not exactly on the same level; there is an important branch of expediency called justice; and justice, though it does not necessarily require that we should confer political functions on every one, does require that we should not, capriciously and without cause, withhold from one what we give to another. As was most truly said by my right hon. Friend the Member for South Lancashire, in the most misunderstood and misrepresented speech I ever remember; to lay a ground for refusing the suffrage to any one, it is necessary to allege either personal unfitness or public danger. Now, can either of these be alleged in the present case? Can it be pretended that women who manage an estate or conduct a business—who pay rates and taxes, often to a large amount, and frequently from their own earnings—many of whom are responsible heads of families, and some of whom, in the capacity of schoolmistresses, teach much more than a great number of the male electors have ever learnt—are not capable of a function of which every male householder is capable? Or is it feared that if they were admitted to the suffrage they would revolutionize the State—would deprive us of any of our valued institutions, or that we should have worse laws, or be in any way whatever worse governed through the effect of their suffrages? No one, Sir, believes anything of the kind. And it is not only the general principles of justice that are infringed, or at least set aside, by the exclusion of women, merely as women, from any share in the representation; that exclusion is also repugnant to the particular principles of the British Constitution. It violates one of the oldest of our constitutional maxims—a doctrine dear to Reformers, and theoretically acknowledged by most Conservatives—that taxation and representation should be co-extensive. Do not women pay taxes? Does not every woman who is *sui juris* contribute exactly as much to the revenue as a man who has the same electoral qualification? If a stake in the country means anything, the owner of freehold or leasehold property has the same stake, whether it is owned by a man or a woman. . . .

. . . Politics, it is said, are not a woman's business. Well, Sir, I rather think that politics are not a man's business either; unless he is one of the few who are selected and paid to devote their time to the public service, or is a Member of this or of the other House. The vast majority of male electors have each his own business which absorbs nearly the whole of his time; but I have not heard that the few hours occupied, once in a few years, in attending at a polling-booth, even if we throw in the time spent in reading newspapers and political treatises, ever causes them to neglect their shops or their counting-houses. I have never understood that those who have votes are worse merchants, or worse lawyers, or worse physicians, or even worse clergymen than other people. One would almost suppose that the British Constitution denied a vote to every one who could not give the greater part of his time to politics; if this were the case we should have a very limited constituency. But allow me to ask, what is the meaning of political freedom? Is it anything but the control of those who do make their business of politics, by those who do not? Is it not the very essence of constitutional liberty, that men come from their looms and their forges to decide, and decide well, whether they are properly governed, and whom they will be governed by? And the nations which prize this privilege the most, and exercise it most fully, are invariably those who excel the most in the common concerns of life. The ordinary occupations of most women are, and are likely to remain, principally domestic; but the notion that these occupations are incompatible with the keenest interest in national affairs, and in all the great interests of humanity, is as utterly futile as the apprehension, once sincerely entertained, that artizans would desert their workshops and their factories if they were taught to read. I know there is an obscure feeling—a feeling which is ashamed to express itself openly—as if women had no right to care about anything, except how they may be the most useful and devoted servants of some man. But as I am convinced that there is not a single Member of this House, whose conscience accuses him of so mean a feeling, I may say without offence, that this claim to confiscate the whole existence of one half of the species for the supposed convenience of the other, appears to me, independently of its injustice, particularly silly. For who that has had ordinary experience of human affairs, and ordinary capacity of profiting by that experience, fancies that those do their own work best who understand nothing else? A man has lived to little purpose who has not learnt that without general mental cultivation, no particular work that requires understanding is ever done in the best manner. It requires brains to use practical experience; and brains, even without practical experience, go further than any amount of practical experience without brains. But perhaps it is thought that the ordinary occupations of women are more antagonistic than those of men are to the comprehension of public affairs. It is thought, perhaps, that those who are principally charged with the moral education of the future generations of men, cannot be fit to form an opinion about the moral and educational interests of a people; and that those whose chief daily business is the judicious laying-out of money, so as to produce the greatest results with the smallest means, cannot possibly give any lessons to right hon. Gentlemen on the other side of the House or on this, who contrive to produce such singularly small results with such vast means. I feel a degree of confidence, Sir, on this subject, which I could not feel, if the political change, in itself not great or formidable, which I advocate, were not grounded, as beneficent and salutary political changes almost always are, upon a previous social change. The notion of a hard and fast line of separation between women's occupations and men's—of forbidding women to take interest in the things which interest men—belongs to a gone-by state of society which is receding further and further into the past. We talk of political revolutions, but we do not sufficiently attend to the fact that there has taken place around us a silent domestic revolution; women and men are, for the first time in history, really each other's companions. . . .

. . . Sir, the time is now come when, unless women are raised to the level of men, men will be pulled down to theirs. The women of a man's family are either a stimulus and a support to his highest aspirations, or a drag upon them. You may keep them ignorant of politics, but you cannot prevent them from concerning themselves with the least respectable part of politics—its personalities; if they do not understand and cannot enter into the man's feelings of public duty, they do care about his personal interest, and that is the scale into which their weight will certainly be thrown. They will be an influence always at hand, co-operating with the man's selfish promptings, lying in wait for his moments of moral irresolution, and doubling the strength of every temptation. Even if they maintain a modest forbearance, the mere absence of their sympathy will hang a dead-weight on his moral energies, making him unwilling to make sacrifices which they will feel, and to forego social advantages and successes in which they would share, for objects which they cannot appreciate. Supposing him fortunate enough to escape any actual sacrifice of conscience, the indirect effect on the higher parts of his own character is still deplorable. Under an idle notion that the beauties of character of the two sexes are mutually incompatible, men are afraid of manly women; but those who have considered the nature and power of social influences well know, that unless there are manly women, there will not much longer be manly men. When men and women are really companions, if women are frivolous, men will be frivolous; if women care for nothing but personal interest and idle vanities, men in general will care for little else; the two sexes must now rise or sink together. It may be said that women may take interest in great public questions without having votes; they may, certainly; but how many of them will? Education and society have exhausted their power in inculcating on women that their proper rule of conduct is what society expects from them; and the denial of the vote is a proclamation intelligible to every one, that whatever else society may expect, it does not expect that they should concern themselves with public interests. . . .

. . . Sir, it is true that women have great power. It is part of my case that they have great power; but they have it under the worst possible conditions because it is indirect, and therefore irresponsible. I want to make this great power a responsible power. I want to make the woman feel her conscience interested in its honest exercise. I want her to feel that it is not given to her as a mere means of personal ascendency. I want to make her influence work by a manly interchange of opinion, and not by cajolery. I want to awaken in her the political point of honour. Many a woman already influences greatly the political conduct of the men connected with her, and sometimes, by force of will, actually governs it; but she is never supposed to have anything to do with it; the man whom she influences, and perhaps misleads, is alone responsible; her power is like the backstairs influence of a favourite. Sir, I demand that all who exercise power should have the burden laid on them of knowing something about the things they have power over. With the acknowledged right to a voice, would come a sense of the corresponding duty. Women are not usually inferior in tenderness of conscience to men. Make the woman a moral agent in these matters; show that you expect from her a political conscience; and when she has learnt to understand the transcendent importance of these things, she will know why it is wrong to sacrifice political convictions to personal interest or vanity; she will understand that political integrity is not a foolish personal crotchet, which a man is bound, for the sake of his family, to give up, but a solemn duty; and the men whom she can influence will be better men in all public matters, and not, as they often are now, worse men by the whole amount of her influence. But at least, it will be said, women do not suffer any practical inconvenience, as women, by not having a vote. The interests of all women are safe in the hands of their fathers, husbands, and brothers, who have the same interest with them, and not only know, far better than they do, what is good for them, but care much more for them than they care for themselves. Sir, this is exactly what is said of all unrepresented classes. The operatives, for instance; are they not virtually represented by the representation of their employers? Are not the interest of the employers and that of the employed, when properly understood, the same? To insinuate the contrary, is it not the horrible crime of setting class against class? Is not the farmer equally interested with the labourer in the prosperity of agriculture—the cotton manufacturer equally with his workmen in the high price of calicoes? Are they not both interested alike in taking off taxes? And, generally, have not employers and employed a common interest against all outsiders, just as husband and wife have against all outside the family? And what is more, are not all employers good, kind, benevolent men, who love their workpeople, and always desire to do what is most for their good? All these assertions are as true, and as much to the purpose, as the corresponding assertions respecting men and women. Sir, we do not live in Arcadia, but, as we were lately reminded, *in fœce Romuli*: and in that region workmen need other protection than that of their employers, and women other protection than that of their men. I should like to have a Return laid before this House of the number of women who are annually beaten to death, kicked to death, or trampled to death by their male protectors; and, in an opposite column, the amount of the sentences passed in those cases in which the dastardly criminals did not get off altogether. I should also like to have, in a third column, the amount of property, the unlawful taking of which was, at the same sessions or assizes, by the same judge, thought worthy of the same amount of punishment. We should then have an arithmetical estimate of the value set by a male legislature and male tribunals on the murder of a woman, often by torture continued through years, which, if there is any shame in us, would make us hang our heads. Sir, before it is affirmed that women do not suffer in their interests, as women, by the denial of a vote, it should be considered whether women have no grievances; whether the laws, and those practices which laws can reach, are in every way as favourable to women as to men. Now, how stands the fact? . . .

. . . How does it fare with that great and increasing portion of the sex, who, sprung from the educated classes, have not inherited a provision, and not having obtained one by marriage, or disdaining to marry merely for a provision, depend on their exertions for subsistence? Hardly any decent educated occupation, save one, is open to them. They are either governesses or nothing. A fact has recently occurred, well worthy of commemoration in connection with this subject. A young lady, Miss Garrett, from no pressure of necessity, but from an honourable desire to employ her activity in alleviating human suffering, studied the medical profession. Having duly qualified herself, she, with an energy and perseverance which cannot be too highly praised, knocked successively at all the doors through which, by law, access is obtained into the medical profession. Having found all other doors fast shut, she fortunately discovered one which had accidentally been left ajar. The Society of Apothecaries, it seems, had forgotten to shut out those who they never thought would attempt to come in, and through this narrow entrance this young lady found her way into this profession. But so objectionable did it appear to this learned body that women should be the medical attendants even of women, that the narrow wicket through which Miss Garrett entered has been closed after her, and no second Miss Garrett will be allowed to pass through it. And this is *instar omnium*. No sooner do women show themselves capable of competing with men in any career, than that career, if it be lucrative or honourable, is closed to them. A short time ago women

might be associates of the Royal Academy; but they were so distinguishing themselves, they were assuming so honourable a place in their art,
that this privilege also has been withdrawn. This is the sort of care taken
of women's interests by the men who so faithfully represent them. This is
the way we treat unmarried women. And how is it with the married?
They, it may be said, are not interested in this Motion; and they are not
directly interested; but it interests, even directly, many who have been
married, as well as others who will be. . . .

. . . Sir, grievances of less magnitude than the law of the property of
married women, when suffered by parties less inured to passive submission, have provoked revolutions. We ought not to take advantage of the
security we feel against any such consequence in the present case, to
withhold from a limited number of women that moderate amount of participation in the enactment and improvement of our laws, which this
Motion solicits for them, and which would enable the general feelings of
women to be heard in this House through a few male representatives. We
ought not to deny to them, what we are conceding to everybody else—a
right to be consulted; the ordinary chance of placing in the great Council
of the nation a few organs of their sentiments—of having, what every
petty trade or profession has, a few members who feel specially called on
to attend to their interests, and to point out how those interests are affected by the law, or by any proposed changes in it. No more is asked by
this Motion; and when the time comes, as it certainly will come, when
this will be granted, I feel the firmest conviction that you will never repent of the concession.

Amendment proposed, in page 2, line 16, to leave out the word "man,"
in order to insert the word "person"—(*Mr. Mill*)—instead thereof.

136. The Debate in the House of Commons (1867)

MR. KARSLAKE said, he had listened, as the rest of the House had done,
with great attention to the argument of the hon. Member for Westminster, for there was this peculiarity in the subject—that there was not a
man in England, whatever his rank in life, who was not interested in it:—
for though the observations of the hon. Member pointed only to the admission of spinsters and widows to the suffrage, the hon. Member's argument, as well as the arguments in his published writings, which he (Mr.
Karslake) had studied with great care, all pointed to the admission of
married women. Now it was somewhat remarkable that during the short
period he had been in that House he had not received a single petition or
letter in favour of such a proposition. He was obliged, however, to take
into consideration that question, because of the spinsters and widows it
might be said with all delicacy that they were in a transition state—the
spinsters might marry, and the widows might marry again. Now, if the
ladies of England were once to obtain this boon—this inestimable boon
of the franchise (as the hon. Member for Westminster seemed to consider

it), and if they attached that importance to it which the hon. Member supposed them to do, could the House expect that they would part with it again by marrying? He was obliged to consider the question of married women possessing the franchise not only by this consideration, but also by the writings of the hon. Member, for all who were familiar with his writings knew that the suffrage of married women was a favourite hobby of his, though it must be admitted he had ridden his hobby very temperately that evening. But the Committee must consider what the result would be, and that if the hon. Member got in the thin end of the wedge by the admission of unmarried women to the electoral roll he would afterwards claim that married women should also be admitted to the franchise. But take the present proposal of the hon. Member that spinsters and widows alone should have a right to the franchise: then every poor lady who went to the altar would lose the franchise; and was it to be supposed that after having exercised this right for a few years—after having enjoyed the sweets of the franchise—they would be content to forego it by entering into the married state. . . . Until the disability of coverture was removed a married lady was to be held a debased and degraded creature, something in the position of the poor compound-householder of whose exclusion they lately heard so much. He must therefore remind the Committee that the question of the unmarried woman and the widow was but a small part of the subject, and that they must face the more important question whether or no married women ought to have the suffrage. . . .

. . . In the course of his canvass, which was still vividly in his recollection, he often canvassed the wives of voters. And he generally found that the female persons were "blue." It was their usual reply—"Oh, I am blue; but my husband votes yellow." Sometimes, he admitted, it was the other way. How did the hon. Gentleman propose to deal with these differences of opinion between the head of the family and her whom the poet called "the lesser man"? He pointed out this as showing the difficulties that would exist in the way of women exercising their right of voting in opposition to their husbands. He did not wish to pursue this subject farther; but he believed that the farther they did refer to it the more would they be met with the difficulties of the subject. . . .

. . . [Mr. Karslake] certainly expected from the hon. Member for Westminster reasoning of a much more logical kind than any he had as yet used in respect to this question. He thought that the Committee would come to the opinion that the hon. Gentleman was wrong in his first principles. In one of his very able works the hon. Member had laid it down that there was no greater difference between a woman and a man than there was between two human beings, one with red hair and one with black, or one with a fair skin and the other with a dark one. He (Mr. Karslake) humbly begged to differ from him, for while he believed that a man qualified to possess the franchise would be ennobled by its possession, woman, in his humble opinion, would be almost debased or degraded by it. She would be in danger of losing those admirable attributes of her sex—namely, her gentleness, her affection, and her domesticity. . . .

. . . As not a lady in Essex had asked him to support the proposition in favor of a female franchise, and believing that the women in other parts of England were equally indifferent on the subject, he came to the conclusion that the women of this country would prefer to remain as they were, being content with the happy homes and advantages they now possessed, even with the disabilities referred to by Chief Justice Blackstone. ["Oh!"] He inferred from that exclamation that the hon. and learned Member for Tiverton was in favour of giving the franchise to "female" persons; but he wished to observe that he concurred in the observation of Blackstone, who had said that the very disabilities to which women were subject, taken on the whole, showed how great a favourite was the female sex to the laws of England. . . .

MR. FAWCETT said, he was extremely sorry to detain the Committee; but this was a question which he had thought upon for years, and there was no subject connected with the representation of the people with regard to which he had a more decided or more earnest opinion. Possibly he might have come to that opinion because he had always looked up to the hon. Member for Westminster as his teacher, and from him he had learnt all his lessons of political life. Certainly, he thought that of all the arguments the hon. Member had ever brought forward, there was no case to which he had supplied more conclusive reasoning than that to which the Committee had listened that evening. What was the reasoning of the hon. and learned Member for Colchester (Mr. Karslake)? The hon. and learned Gentleman said that the ladies of Essex had not intrusted him with a single petition nor written a single letter to him in favour of women suffrage. Now, if the hon. and learned Gentleman had said in his canvass as much as he had said to-night upon the subject of women, he (Mr. Fawcett) must say he thought that the ladies of Essex had exercised a sound judgment in not intrusting him with their letters. . . . The hon. and learned Member for Colchester said, that if they conferred the franchise on a single woman they conferred on her a precious privilege. That was conclusive on their side; but ought they to constitute themselves judges, and say they should not enjoy what they so much valued? The hon. and learned Member also went on to state that after women had enjoyed the privilege for two or three years they would value it so highly that they would not relinquish it for marriage. But was he to decide whether it was a good thing or not for women to marry? Surely he might leave that question for women to decide. The whole of the hon. and learned Member's speech was based on the fallacy that man possessed a superior kind of wisdom, which enabled him to decide what was best for the other half of the human race. There had not been an argument advanced in any speech made by Mr. Beales, or had been put forth in the most extreme programme of the Reform League, in favour of a wide extension of the franchise, but what equally applied to conferring it on women. They urged that taxation and representation should go together. Now, women paid taxes as well as men, and the argument that the franchise should be given to working men, in order that their particular interests might be represented, applied with equal force to women. The hon. Member for Westminster had exhausted that part of the subject, and had shown that there were no laws on the statute book which so much demanded immediate attention as those which referred to the condition of women, and surely it was as fair, right, just, and politic that before Parliament undertook legislation for women they should give them representatives in that House, as that they should give them to working men. It had been contended that if women took an interest in political matters it would very much deteriorate from their character; but he challenged hon. Members to prove that those women of their acquaintance who interested themselves in politics lost any of those qualities which entitled them to the admiration of the world any more than those who cared nothing about politics. It did not prevent them from performing all those social and domestic duties which it was their peculiar right and duty to perform. The most illustrious Lady of the land had as many political duties to perform as a Cabinet Minister; and was it not proverbial the admirable manner in which she discharged her social duties herself? Experience justified him in saying that if they gave women the same opportunity as they did men it would by no means tend to destroy their character, but to make them in intellectual power equal to men, and to strengthen all those qualities which were most valuable in them. . . .

SIR GEORGE BOWYER expressed a hope that the right hon. Member for South Lancashire, who some time ago laid it down as a principle that everybody was entitled, in the absence of some special disqualification, to exercise the franchise [Mr. GLADSTONE: No, no!], would inform the Committee how far he would apply that principle to the case under discussion. He (Sir George Bowyer) also believed that provided a person possessed the requisite qualification laid down by the law, *primá facie* that person had a right to the vote, unless it could be shown that some disqualification attached to him. Was there any reason for excluding women from the franchise? He thought that no such reason existed, and that the claim of women to the suffrage could not be answered logically. This country was governed by our Sovereign Lady the Queen; and in other countries there were or had been female Monarchs, among whom, indeed, on the page of history, was to be found a larger proportion of great and distinguished Sovereigns than among male rulers. Women, moreover, were qualified for churchwardens and for other parochial offices. He was no advocate for strong-minded women; but he believed they might exercise the suffrage without abrogating those qualities which specially adorned their sex. He presumed, however, that the hon. Member for Westminster would propose that they should use voting papers, for it would be manifestly indecorous for them to attend the hustings or the polling-booth; but voting papers, duly guarded, would enable the sex to vote in a manner free from objection. He approved the proposal in a constitutional point of view, for it was a principle of our Constitution that taxation should be as nearly as possible co-extensive with representation. Subject to the limitation that no one should have a vote who could not exercise it for the benefit of the community everybody ought to share in the representation. Now, women held a considerable amount of property which was subject to taxation, and of this there was a remarkable instance in a lady distinguished not so much for her wealth as for the noble use she made of it. Yet that property, being held by a woman, was not represented. This he thought unjust, and though, generally speaking, women do not occupy themselves with politics—nor was it desirable that they should do so—he maintained that, being taxed, they ought to be represented.

VISCOUNT GALWAY, believing that the Committee were anxious to proceed to more important business, would appeal to the hon. Member for Westminster to withdraw his Motion, which, if pressed to a division, would place many Gentlemen who were great admirers of the fair sex in an embarrassing point. The hon. Member for Brighton (Mr. Fawcett) had said that the female sex had no representatives in the House. Now he thought they had a very able one in the hon. Gentleman himself, though his experience with regard to the sex was not very prolonged, as the hon. Gentleman, he believed, had not been married above a fortnight. Moreover, every one acquainted with elections was aware of the influence which was exercised by women. In making his appeal to the hon. Member for Westminster he would remind him of the remark which was made last year by the hon. Member for Bristol—that if the hon. Gentleman's father could give him an excellent piece of advice it would be, "John, stick to the Ballot, and leave the women alone.". . .

MR. J. STUART MILL: I will merely say, in answer to the noble Lord who requested me to withdraw the Motion, that I am a great deal too well pleased with the speeches that have been made against it—his own included—to think of withdrawing it. There is nothing that has pleased me more in those speeches than to find that every one who has attempted to argue at all, has argued against something which is not before the House: they have argued against the admission of married women, which is not in the Motion; or they have argued against the admission of women as Members of this House; or again, as the hon. Member for the Wick boroughs (Mr. Laing) has done, they have argued against allowing women to be generals and officers in the army; a question which I need scarcely say is not before the House. I certainly do think that when we come to universal suffrage, as some time or other we probably shall come—if we extend the vote to all men, we should extend it to all women also. So long, however, as you maintain a property qualification, I do not propose to extend the suffrage to any women but those who have the qualification. If, as is surmised by one of the speakers, young ladies should attach so much value to the suffrage that they should be unwilling to divest themselves of it in order to marry, I can only say that if they will not marry without it, they will probably be allowed to retain it. As to any question that may arise in reference to the removal of any other disabilities of women, it is not before the House. There are evidently many arguments and many considerations that cannot be overlooked in dealing with these larger questions, but which do not arise on the present Motion, and on which, therefore, it is not necessry that I should comment. I will only say that if we should in the progress of experience—especially after experience of the effect of granting the suffrage—come to the decision that married women ought to have the suffrage, or that women should be admitted to any employment or occupation which they are not now admitted to—if it should become the general opinion that they ought to have it, they will have it.

Question put, "That the word 'man' stand part of the Clause."
The Committee *divided*:—Ayes 196; Noes 73: Majority 123.

The Fifteenth Amendment—Votes for Black Men Only?

SOURCES
137. Elizabeth Cady Stanton, Speech before the Woman Suffrage Convention in Washington, D.C., 18 January 1869. In *History of Woman Suffrage*, II, 348-55.
138. Wendell Phillips, "The Fifteenth Amendment," *The Woman's Advocate* (New York), 2, no. 1 (July 1869), 34-39.

At the same time as the English were debating the enfranchisement of working-class men and women, the Americans were confronting the logical consequences for citizenship of emancipating the slaves. Women had been active participants in the abolition movement and had believed that their male allies clearly understood that the lot of the negro slave and that of women were inextricably linked and must be improved together. When the Civil War ended, however, the more radical women abolitionists found that many of their earlier allies, led by Wendell Phillips (1811-1884), were casting their lot with the Reconstructionist politics of the Republican party, which meant putting negro male suffrage first on their list of priorities. It was, Phillips proclaimed in 1865, "the Negro's hour." In the wake of a woman suffrage referendum defeat in Kansas in 1867, therefore, the militant suffragists headed by Elizabeth Cady Stanton (Doc. 76) and Susan B. Anthony, split from the abolitionists, the Republican party, and many other female suffrage advocates over the proposed Fifteenth Amendment. They sought instead an alliance with the Democratic party to urge passage of an additional amendment that would specifically give the vote to all American women.

The speech given by Stanton at the national woman suffrage convention in January 1869, reprinted below, spells out a new "expedient" and elitist line of argument, one that was to engender controversy through the suffrage movement in the United States for the next fifty years. More immediately, Stanton's speech set the seal on an organizational schism that did not heal for over twenty years after the ratification of the Fifteenth Amendment.

The tactics of Stanton and Anthony scandalized the more moderate New England abolitionists and suffragists, and their formation of the American Woman Suffrage Association provoked formation of a rival National Association. The selection by Wendell Phillips, Boston born and bred, and long a major spokesman for the abolition movement, makes clear the nature and extent of the differences between the two factions.

---

137. Elizabeth Cady Stanton (1869)

MRS. STANTON said:—A great idea of progress is near its consummation, when statesmen in the councils of the nation propose to frame it into statutes and constitutions; when Reverend Fathers recognize it by a new interpretation of their creeds and canons; when the Bar and Bench at its command set aside the legislation of centuries, and girls of twenty put their heels on the Cokes and Blackstones of the past.

Those who represent what is called "the Woman's Rights Movement," have argued their right to political equality from every standpoint of justice, religion, and logic, for the last twenty years. They have quoted the Constitution, the Declaration of Independence, the Bible, the opinions of great men and women in all ages; they have plead the theory of our government; suffrage a natural, inalienable right; shown from the lessons of history, that one class can not legislate for another; that disfranchised classes must ever be neglected and degraded; and that all privileges are but mockery to the citizen, until he has a voice in the making and administering of law. Such arguments have been made over and over in conventions and before the legislatures of the several States. Judges, lawyers, priests, and politicians have said again and again, that our logic was unanswerable, and although much nonsense has emanated from the male tongue and pen on this subject, no man has yet made a fair argument on the other side. Knowing that we hold the Gibraltar rock of reason on this question, they resort to ridicule and petty objections. . . . There are no new arguments to be made on human rights, our work to-day is to apply to ourselves those so familiar to all; to teach man that woman is not an anomalous being, outside all laws and constitutions, but one whose rights are to be established by the same process of reason as that by which he demands his own.

When our Fathers made out their famous bill of impeachment against England, they specified eighteen grievances. When the women of this country surveyed the situation in their first convention, they found they had precisely that number, and quite similar in character; and reading over the old revolutionary arguments of Jefferson, Patrick Henry, Otis, and Adams, they found they applied remarkably well to their case. The same arguments made in this country for extending suffrage from time to time, to white men, native born citizens, without property and education, and to foreigners; the same used by John Bright in England, to extend it to a million new voters, and the same used by the great Republican party to enfranchise a million black men in the South, all these arguments we have to-day to offer for woman, and one, in addition, stronger than all besides, the difference in man and woman. Because man and woman are the complement of one another, we need woman's thought in national affairs to make a safe and stable government.

The Republican party to-day congratulates itself on having carried the Fifteenth Amendment of the Constitution, thus securing "manhood suffrage" and establishing an aristocracy of sex on this continent. As several bills to secure Woman's Suffrage in the District and the Territories have been already presented in both houses of Congress, and as by Mr. Julian's bill, the question of so amending the Constitution as to extend suffrage to all the women of the country has been presented to the nation for consideration, it is not only the right but the duty of every thoughtful woman to express her opinion on a Sixteenth Amendment. While I hail the late discussions in Congress and the various bills presented as so many signs of progress, I am especially gratified with those of Messrs. Julian and Pomeroy, which forbid any State to deny the right of suffrage to any of its citizens on account of sex or color.

This fundamental principle of our government—the equality of all the citizens of the republic—should be incorporated in the Federal Constitution, there to remain forever. To leave this question to the States and partial acts of Congress, is to defer indefinitely its settlement, for what is done by this Congress may be repealed by the next; and politics in the several States differ so widely, that no harmonious action on any question. can ever be secured, except as a strict party measure. Hence, we appeal to the party now in power, everywhere, to end this protracted debate on suffrage, and declare it the inalienable right of every citizen who is amenable to the laws of the land, who pays taxes and the penalty of crime. We have a splendid theory of a genuine republic, why not realize it and make our government homogeneous, from Maine to California. The Republican party has the power to do this, and now is its only opportunity. Woman's Suffrage, in 1872, may be as good a card for the Republicans as Gen. Grant was in the last election. It is said that the Republican party made him President, not because they thought him the most desirable man in the nation for that office, but they were afraid the Democrats would take him if they did not. We would suggest, there may be the same danger of Democrats taking up Woman Suffrage if they do not. God, in his providence, may have purified that party in the furnace of affliction. They have had the opportunity, safe from the turmoil of political life and the temptations of office, to study and apply the divine principles of justice and equality to life; for minorities are always in a position to carry principles to their logical results, while majorities are governed only by votes. You see my faith in Democrats is based on sound philosophy. In the next Congress, the Democratic party will gain thirty-four new members, hence the Republicans have had their last chance to do justice to woman. It will be no enviable record for the Fortieth Congress that in the darkest days of the republic it placed our free institutions in the care and keeping of every type of manhood, ignoring womanhood, all the elevating and purifying influences of the most virtuous and humane half of the American people. . . .

I urge a speedy adoption of a Sixteenth Amendment for the following reasons:

1. A government, based on the principle of caste and class, can not stand. The aristocratic idea, in any form, is opposed to the genius of our free institutions, to our own declaration of rights, and to the civilization of the age. All artificial distinctions, whether of family, blood, wealth, color, or sex, are equally oppressive to the subject classes, and equally destructive to national life and prosperity. Governments based on every form of aristocracy, on every degree and variety of inequality, have been tried in despotisms, monarchies, and republics, and all alike have perished. . . . On all sides the cry is echoed, "Republicanism is a failure," though that great principle of a government "by the people, of the people, for the people," has never been tried. Thus far, all nations have been built on caste and failed. Why, in this hour of reconstruction, with the experience of generations before us, make another experiment in the same direction? If serfdom, peasantry, and slavery have shattered kingdoms, deluged continents with blood, scattered republics like dust before the wind, and rent our own Union asunder, what kind of a government, think you, American statesmen, you can build, with the mothers of the race crouching at your feet, while iron-heeled peasants, serfs, and slaves, exalted by your hands, tread our inalienable rights into the dust? While all men, everywhere, are rejoicing in new-found liberties, shall woman alone be denied the rights, privileges, and immunities of citizenship? While in England men are coming up from the coal mines of Cornwall, from the factories of Birmingham and Manchester, demanding the suffrage; while in frigid Russia the 22,000,000 newly-emancipated serfs are already claiming a voice in the government; while here, in our own land, slaves, but just rejoicing in the proclamation of emancipation, ignorant alike of its power and significance, have the ballot unasked, unsought, already laid at their feet—think you the daughters of Adams, Jefferson, and Patrick Henry, in whose veins flows the blood of two Revolutions, will forever linger round the campfires of an old barbarism, with no longings to join this grand army of freedom in its onward march to roll back the golden gates of a higher and better civilization? Of all kinds of aristocracy, that of sex is the most odious and unnatural; invading, as it does, our homes, desecrating our family altars, dividing those whom God has joined together, exalting the son above the mother who bore him, and subjugating, everywhere, moral power to brute force. Such a government would not be worth the blood and treasure so freely poured out in its long struggles for freedom. . . .

2. I urge a Sixteenth Amendment, because "manhood suffrage" or a man's government, is civil, religious, and social disorganization. The male element is a destructive force, stern, selfish, aggrandizing, loving war, violence, conquest, acquisition, breeding in the material and moral world alike discord, disorder, disease, and death. See what a record of blood and cruelty the pages of history reveal! Through what slavery, slaughter, and sacrifice, through what inquisitions and imprisonments,

pains and persecutions, black codes and gloomy creeds, the soul of humanity has struggled for the centuries, while mercy has veiled her face and all hearts have been dead alike to love and hope! The male element has held high carnival thus far, it has fairly run riot from the beginning, overpowering the feminine element everywhere, crushing out all the diviner qualities in human nature, until we know but little of true manhood and womanhood, of the latter comparatively nothing, for it has scarce been recognized as a power until within the last century. Society is but the reflection of man himself, untempered by woman's thought, the hard iron rule we feel alike in the church, the state, and the home. No one need wonder at the disorganization, at the fragmentary condition of everything, when we remember that man, who represents but half a complete being, with but half an idea on every subject, has undertaken the absolute control of all sublunary matters.

People object to the demands of those whom they choose to call the strong-minded, because they say, "the right of suffrage will make the women masculine." That is just the difficulty in which we are involved today. Though disfranchised we have few women in the best sense; we have simply so many reflections, varieties, and dilutions of the masculine gender. The strong, natural characteristics of womanhood are repressed and ignored in dependence, for so long as man feeds woman she will try to please the giver and adapt herself to his condition. To keep a foothold in society woman must be as near like man as possible, reflect his ideas, opinions, virtues, motives, prejudices, and vices. She must respect his statutes, though they strip her of every inalienable right, and conflict with that higher law written by the finger of God on her own soul. She must believe his theology, though it pave the highways of hell with the skulls of new-born infants, and make God a monster of vengeance and hypocrisy. She must look at everything from its dollar and cent point of view, or she is a mere romancer. She must accept things as they are and make the best of them. To mourn over the miseries of others, the poverty of the poor, their hardships in jails, prisons, asylums, the horrors of war, cruelty, and brutality in every form, all this would be mere sentimentalizing. To protest against the intrigue, bribery, and corruption of public life, to desire that her sons might follow some business that did not involve lying, cheating, and a hard, grinding selfishness, would be arrant nonsense. In this way man has been moulding woman to his ideas by direct and positive influences, while she, if not a negation, has used indirect means to control him, and in most cases developed the very characteristics both in him and herself that needed repression. And now man himself stands appalled at the results of his own excesses, and mourns in bitterness that falsehood, selfishness, and violence are the law of life. The need of this hour is not territory, gold mines, railroads, or specie payments, but a new evangel of womanhood, to exalt purity, virtue, morality, true religion, to lift man up into the higher realms of thought and action.

We ask woman's enfranchisement, as the first step toward the recognition of that essential element in government that can only secure the health, strength, and prosperity of the nation. Whatever is done to lift woman to her true position will help to usher in a new day of peace and perfection for the race. In speaking of the masculine element, I do not wish to be understood to say that all men are hard, selfish, and brutal, for many of the most beautiful spirits the world has known have been clothed with manhood; but I refer to those characteristics, though often marked in woman, that distinguish what is called the stronger sex. For example, the love of acquisition and conquest, the very pioneers of civilization, when expended on the earth, the sea, the elements, the riches and forces of Nature, are powers of destruction when used to subjugate one man to another or to sacrifice nations to ambition. Here that great conservator of woman's love, if permitted to assert itself, as it naturally would in freedom against oppression, violence, and war, would hold all these destructive forces in check, for woman knows the cost of life better than man does, and not with her consent would one drop of blood ever be shed, one life sacrificed in vain. With violence and disturbance in the natural world, we see a constant effort to maintain an equilibrium of forces. Nature, like a loving mother, is ever trying to keep land and sea, mountain and valley each in its place, to hush the angry winds and waves, balance the extremes of heat and cold, of rain and drought, that peace, harmony, and beauty may reign supreme. There is a striking analogy between matter and mind, and the present disorganization of society warns us, that in the dethronement of woman we have let loose the elements of violence and ruin that she only has the power to curb. If the civilization of the age calls for an extension of the suffrage, surely a government of the most virtuous, educated men and women would better represent the whole, and protect the interests of all, than could the representation of either sex alone. But government gains no new element of strength in admitting all men to the ballot-box, for we have too much of the man-power there already. We see this in every department of legislation, and it is a common remark, that unless some new virtue is infused into our public life the nation is doomed to destruction. Will the foreign element, the dregs of China, Germany, England, Ireland, and Africa supply this needed force, or the nobler types of American womanhood who have taught our presidents, senators, and congressmen the rudiments of all they know?

3. I urge a Sixteenth Amendment because, when "manhood suffrage" is established from Maine to California, woman has reached the lowest depths of political degradation. So long as there is a disfranchised class in this country, and that class its women, a man's government is worse than a white man's government with suffrage limited by property and educational qualifications, because in proportion as you multiply the rulers, the condition of the politically ostracised is more hopeless and degraded. John Stuart Mill, in his work on "Liberty," shows that the condition of one disfranchised man in a nation is worse than when the whole nation is under one man, because in the latter case, if the one man is despotic, the nation can easily throw him off, but what can one man do with a nation

of tyrants over him? If American women find it hard to bear the oppressions of their own Saxon fathers, the best orders of manhood, what may they not be called to endure when all the lower orders of foreigners now crowding our shores legislate for them and their daughters. Think of Patrick and Sambo and Hans and Yung Tung, who do not know the difference between a monarchy and a republic, who can not read the Declaration of Independence or Webster's spelling-book, making laws for Lucretia Mott, Ernestine L. Rose, and Anna E. Dickinson. Think of jurors and jailors drawn from these ranks to watch and try young girls for the crime of infanticide, to decide the moral code by which the mothers of this Republic shall be governed? This manhood suffrage is an appalling question, and it would be well for thinking women, who seem to consider it so magnanimous to hold their own claims in abeyance until all men are crowned with citizenship, to remember that the most ignorant men are ever the most hostile to the equality of women, as they have known them only in slavery and degradation.

Go to our courts of justice, our jails and prisons; go into the world of work; into the trades and professions; into the temples of science and learning, and see what is meted out everywhere to women—to those who have no advocates in our courts, no representatives in the councils of the nation. Shall we prolong and perpetuate such injustice, and by increasing this power risk worse oppressions for ourselves and daughters? It is an open, deliberate insult to American womanhood to be cast down under the iron-heeled peasantry of the Old World and the slaves of the New, as we shall be in the practical working of the Fifteenth Amendment, and the only atonement the Republican party can make is now to complete its work, by enfranchising the women of the nation. I have not forgotten their action four years ago, when Article XIV., Sec. 2, was amended* by invidiously introducing the word "male" into the Federal Constitution, where it had never been before, thus counting out of the basis of representation all men not permitted to vote, thereby making it the interest of every State to enfranchise its male citizens, and virtually declaring it no crime to disfranchise its women. As political sagacity moved our rulers thus to guard the interests of the negro for party purposes, common justice might have compelled them to show like respect for their own mothers, by counting woman too out of the basis of representation, that she might no longer swell the numbers to legislate adversely to her interests. And this desecration of the last will and testament of the fathers, this retrogressive legislation for woman, was in the face of the earnest protests of thousands of the best educated, most refined and cultivated women of the North.

Now, when the attention of the whole world is turned to this question of suffrage, and women themselves are throwing off the lethargy of ages,

---

* The amendment as proposed by the Hon. Thaddeus Stevens, of Pennsylvania, extended the right of suffrage to "all citizens," which included both white and black women. At the bare thought of such an impending calamity, the more timid Republicans were filled with alarm, and the word "male" promptly inserted.

and in England, France, Germany, Switzerland, and Russia are holding their conventions, and their rulers are everywhere giving them a respectful hearing, shall American statesmen, claiming to be liberal, so amend their constitutions as to make their wives and mothers the political inferiors of unlettered and unwashed ditch-diggers, boot-blacks, butchers, and barbers, fresh from the slave plantations of the South, and the effete civilizations of the Old World? While poets and philosophers, statesmen and men of science are all alike pointing to woman as the new hope for the redemption of the race, shall the freest Government on the earth be the first to establish an aristocracy based on sex alone? to exalt ignorance above education, vice above virtue, brutality and barbarism above refinement and religion? Not since God first called light out of darkness and order out of chaos, was there ever made so base a proposition as "manhood suffrage" in this American Republic, after all the discussions we have had on human rights in the last century. On all the blackest pages of history there is no record of an act like this, in any nation, where native born citizens, having the same religion, speaking the same language, equal to their rulers in wealth, family, and education, have been politically ostracised by their own countrymen, outlawed with savages, and subjected to the government of outside barbarians. Remember the Fifteenth Amendment takes in a larger population than the 2,000,000 black men on the Southern plantation. It takes in all the foreigners daily landing in our eastern cities, the Chinese crowding our western shores, the inhabitants of Alaska, and all those western isles that will soon be ours. American statesmen may flatter themselves that by superior intelligence and political sagacity the higher orders of men will always govern, but when the ignorant foreign vote already holds the balance of power in all the large cities by sheer force of numbers, it is simply a question of impulse or passion, bribery or fraud, how our elections will be carried. When the highest offices in the gift of the people are bought and sold in Wall Street, it is a mere chance who will be our rulers. Whither is a nation tending when brains count for less than bullion, and clowns make laws for queens?

138. Wendell Phillips (1869)

A friend in Rhode Island writes to us that there is a wide opposition to the Fifteenth Amendment among the advocates of Women's Rights; especially among those who have not been trained in the Anti-Slavery cause. The fact does not much surprise us. Education in reform is such a slow process, simple faith in absolute right is so very rare an element, that it is natural beginners should be confused by the crafty demagogues about them and shrink from what seems such a perilous step. A little experience and a more profound consideration will, we believe, lift them to the level of a full faith in principles.

What is the Fifteenth Amendment? It runs thus:

ARTICLE 15.—The right of the citizens of the United States to vote shall not be denied or abridged by the United States or by any State, on account of race, color, or previous condition of servitude.

SEC. 2. The Congress shall have power to enforce this article by appropriate legislation.

The form is unexceptionable. If the thing sought is good, the language used could not be better. There is no word *"male"* (odious to us all, in laws and constitutions) to be found here. Wherever and whenever women vote it will protect their rights as fully as those of men, and be as valuable to them as to men. The object sought is to oblige the States to allow black *persons* to vote on the same conditions that white *persons* do. As men only are now allowed to vote, of course the immediate effect will be to oblige the States to allow black *men* to vote just as white *men* do.

This is *all its effect.* The talk about its giving the vote to Chinamen, Irish, Germans and other "ignorant foreigners," is wholly out of place. It does not admit one such to the ballot-box; does not affect them in any way. Such men are excluded from the ballot-box, until they are naturalized, on account of their *birthplace*, not on account of their *race*. These are totally distinct elements. It is *foreigners* not *races* (excepting in the Negro's case) that we exclude from voting.

Race means *blood*. Nationality means *birthplace*. Englishmen are men of a dozen *races*, all *born* in England. *Americans* are made up of a score of *races*, all *born* here. All *races* here are equal, all Americans vote—except the black. The object of this Amendment is to abolish that inequality. A Jew born in New York does not change his race: he is still a Jew. This Amendment provides that he shall not, *on account of his race*, be denied his vote. A Jew born in Paris is still a Jew in race. He cannot vote, however, till naturalized, because he is a *foreigner*. This Amendment does not hasten his right to vote at all, does not in the least change his present rights as to voting. So of all other foreigners—Irish, Chinese, and the rest.

Let us omit therefore all this idle talk, which only confuses the question at issue. The whole object of this Amendment is to prevent a person's being shut out from voting because he is a Jew, or a Celt, or a Negro. Its immediate effect will be to prevent negro men from being forbidden to vote.

What then is the objection to it? We are told that if these negro men vote they will tyrannize over their wives just as white men do; and that so large an ignorant class voting, will make it still more difficult to get woman's right to the ballot recognized. Suppose all this were true—what then? Does it authorize us to resist the recognition, by Government, of the negro man's right to vote?

A man has the same "inherent, unalienable" right to vote that a woman has. We humbly presume that the marvellous progress of these last few months has not upset that principle, or produced any woman so terribly in earnest as to deny it.

If that be so, is there any intelligent reformer prepared to maintain that we have a right to deny to any human being his, or her, *natural rights* because we fear he, or she, will misuse them? I should like to see the Abolitionist, of thirty years standing, who will look his own record in the face and maintain such a proposition. All history laughs at it. The Pope said, "I cannot allow men to read the Bible, each in his own language and pick out his own faith—the 'right will certainly be misused.'" Tories say, "we cannot let poor and unlearned men vote, 'they will misuse the right.'" What said the Declaration of Independence to that? The Episcopalian said, "I cannot let the Catholic vote, 'he will misuse it and harm me.'" What said O'Connell to that?

Slaveholders said, "the black has a right to liberty, but we cannot recognize it, 'he will misuse the right.'" Ask the last thirty years and the war how God answered that. Capital says to the eight hour men—"Yes, an immortal being has a right to some leisure to prepare for this life and the next, but I cannot recognize it, 'he will misuse it.'" What do we reply?— "Recognize your fellow man's natural rights—those God gave him—aid him, as you can, to use them wisely—but leave him, at last, responsible to God alone for their use—'art thou thy brother's keeper?'"

If the negro man should therefore, in his ignorance, misuse *his right* and delay woman's recognition many a year, we are not authorized *on that account*, to forbid Government to recognize his natural and inalienable right to vote; that is, to oppose the Fifteenth Amendment.

It was one of the great promises of MAGNA CHARTA, extorted from the King by his Barons, that he would "neither *delay* nor refuse Justice." God lays the same duty on all of us.

We were not sent into the world responsible that negroes, or any other race, should behave themselves. But God will hold us responsible if we presume to deny to our fellow man any of his natural rights.

Fashion—woman's realm—was one of the strongest bulwarks of slavery; sometimes equal to Church and State combined. It is to-day the special bulwark of negro hate. *Woman* could extinguish that scourge in half-a-dozen years. Suppose twenty years ago when fashion laughed at us, it had been proposed to give women the vote and that Abolitionists had cried out "no—we've enough to convert now, selfish merchants and bigoted church-members; do not throw contemptuous and silly women into the scale. It is an 'infamous' proposition." Should we have been justified?

But leaving this argument with those who recognize and fully trust all God-given rights, let us come down to those who settle this question by reasons of expediency.

Those friends say it is not wise to recognize these rights piece-meal. The Amendment is faulty because it does not cover the whole ground, man and woman's vote too, all that relates to voting. Well then, here is Mr. A——, he believes the vote is a snare and a strengthening of the Aristocracy unless every voter is secured a homestead, his natural right. Here is Mr. B——, he believes voting only plays into the hands of Capital, unless our whole system of finance is changed and Government allowed to issue paper money at discretion, without interest. Here is Mr. C.——, who believes no drunkard should be allowed to vote and no convicted criminal, as is sometimes the law abroad. Here is Mr. D.——, who believes the whole method of choosing the Senate is a violation of natural right.

Shall we wait till the whole country gets educated up to all these ideas and make no change till we can settle the subject in its whole breadth? Absurd. Man gets forward step by step—the recognition of half a truth helping him to see the other half. First we had individual liberty, then separate property, then right of inheritance, then freedom of opinion, then freedom of speech, then voting: thus, one by one, ray by ray, men got able to bear the full light of day. In what order these steps shall be taken—which first, which second—is God's ordaining, not of our plan. Every change large and distinct enough to serve as a point upon which to rally the nation, should have a separate discussion and be decided by itself. This is the most economical and speediest method of reform. Every other method, mixing up separate issues, is like good Davie Deans' attachment to the Scottish Covenant. From his sick pillow he asked if the Doctor had subscribed the Covenant. "That's no matter now, father," said his child. "Indeed it is," cried the old Covenanter, "for if he has not, never a drop of his medicine shall go down the stomach of my father's son."

In the present instance this great rule holds. We have drawn the weight so far up; fasten it there; and thus get a purchase to lift it still higher. There have been several different tests excluding men from voting in this country. Church membership, property, book-learning, race, sex. The first we have got rid of everywhere. The second is almost gone, except in obsolete corners like Rhode Island. Book learning is fast vanishing as a test. The abolition of each one has helped to get rid of his comrade. Race and sex alone are left. Abolish the first and you will clear the ground and simplify the question. It will leave the naked, bare, intolerable, and illogical test of sex so monstrous as it stands isolated, that it will almost topple over of its own weight.

No doubt the ignorant prejudice of the working class is one of the great obstacles to the recognition of Woman's Rights. Some over-sanguine advocates seem to forget this, and imagine that when a Legislature is carried the work is mainly done. Not so by any means. When the first line of the enemy's works—the Legislature—is carried, there remain two behind—the Church and the laboring class. Whether the Church line will contest the fight remains to be seen. It looks sometimes and in some places as if it would not. But there's no trustworthy evidence on that point. The working men will, without doubt. And with that whole class the same thorough and weary work is to be done as fell to the lot of the Abolitionists between 1830 and 1850, with the mass of the Nation; patient lecturing, line upon line, precept upon precept, "without haste, without rest." But the enfranchisement of the negro need not give us the alarm which Democrats, masquerading in Woman's Rights uniform, try to create.

This reform—woman's voting—will never probably be carried by national action. It will be granted State by State. Slavery would have been abolished so but for the war. It was the "war power" which brought and enabled the Nation to kill slavery. Abolitionists looked forward to the peaceful action of successive States. This will probably be the course relative to woman's voting.

The addition therefore of seventy thousand black votes in South Carolina will not retard the action of Iowa or Massachusetts on this question. It will rather hasten their action. Desirous to guard as fully as possible against any conceivable ill consequence from such sudden increase of voters, the Northern States will be spurred to call, all the sooner into the field, whatever there is of good and conservative and well intentioned in woman. Just as the lager beer infatuation of the German Republicans out West moves the Republican Temperance men there to accept woman's rights in order to correct that bias in the party, so the negro vote will operate in this case. Once carry this reform in half-a-dozen Northern States, and the negro looks so much to us for his example that his vote will be sure to follow ours. If the North once accepts our principles, the time will come when Woman will find her best friend in the negro, as the Union did. You may be sure he will keep step to the music of any improvement his trusted North initiates.

Let ignorance then believe that the only way to improve the world is to do everything at once—"I shall never get to the top of the hill by single steps; the only way is to wait till I can leap the whole way at one bound." Let selfishness cry—"He shall not have his rights till I get mine." The true reformer will say, "Let every class have its rights the very moment the world is ready to recognize them. Thus and thus only will every other class get one step nearer to the recognition of its own. 'First the blade, then the ear, after that the full corn in the ear.'"

German Unification and Political Rights for Women

SOURCES

139. Hedwig Dohm, *Der Jesuitismus im Hausstande, ein Beitrag zur Frauenfrage* (Berlin, 1873). As reprinted in *Die deutsche Frauenbewegung*, II, *Quellen: 1843-1889*, ed. Margrit Twellmann (Meisenheim am Glan, 1972), 227-37. Tr. SGB.

140. Jenny Hirsch, "Hedwig Dohm: Der Jesuitismus im Hausstande," *Frauen-Anwalt*, 4, nos. 8/9 (1873-74), 165-66. Tr. SGB.

Disagreement over the pursuit of political rights for women divided German supporters of female emancipation following the unification of Germany in 1871 under Wilhelm I and Bismarck. Unification raised a flurry of controversy over the state of civic and political liberty then prevailing among the emperor's subjects, both male and female. The constitution of 1871 established universal manhood suffrage for the election of Reichstag delegates and thus precipitated, for the first time since Hippel (Doc. 29), a demand for political rights for women—this time the Reichstag vote—by a woman, Hedwig Schleh Dohm (1833-1919).

The eleventh of eighteen children born to a lower-middle-class family, Hedwig Dohm (to use the name under which she later became known) looked back on a frustrated girlhood. She spent her youth reading novels, detesting the fine needle-work with which she was expected to occupy her time, and daydreaming of a prince charming who, by marrying her, would free her from a situation she con-sidered intolerable. In 1848, when she was fifteen, she caught a glimpse of the corpse of a young revolutionary, slain in the street; it was this experience that turned Dohm into an ardent social democrat. Her dissatisfaction with petit bour-geois life, and the ennui of a short stay in a lackluster teachers' seminary, provoked her to marry the writer and journalist Ernst Dohm. Though the marriage was not altogether satisfactory, she bore five children and profited from the stimulating intellectual conversations with the many writers and social reformers whom she and her husband had befriended. When Dohm began to publish, her outspoken and acerbic prose startled friends and acquaintances by its contrast to the mod-esty and shyness she exhibited in her personal life. Dohm's book *Der Jesuitismus im Hausstande*, which she published at the age of forty, was the second of four works she devoted to the woman question. The passages reprinted here highlight Dohm's astute appreciation of the danger inherent in state power, and of the im-portance of democratic participation and political liberties in combating arbi-trary uses of that power. Her description of the debate on the Second British Re-form Bill (Docs. 135, 136) also reveals her awareness of the liberal tradition of Western Europe and America and of Mill's contribution to the cause of woman suffrage. Her rationale for woman suffrage in the militaristic, authoritar-ian German Empire should be compared with that of Elizabeth Cady Stanton (Doc. 137).

A dissenting view of Dohm's contribution came from Jenny Hirsch (pseudonym for F. Arnefeldt; 1829-1902). Hirsch edited the *Frauen-Anwalt* (Women's Advo-cate), which was published by the paternalistic "Lette-Verein." This organization had been created in 1865 by Dr. Adolf Lette under the patronage of the Prussian crown princess in order to help women to become self-supporting through pro-fessional training for service jobs.

A poet and a schoolteacher in her native Anhalt-Zerbst (an enclave in Saxony), Hirsch had come to Berlin in the 1860's. Before she became secretary and editor of the Lette-Verein, she had worked with Louise Otto (now Otto-Peters) on the journal of the newly established General German Women's Association (Der All-gemeine Deutsche Frauen-Verein), which had muted its activities to conform to the Prussian Law on Associations of 1851 (Doc. 86). She had translated Mill's *Subjection of Woman* as *Die Hörigkeit der Frau* in 1869, the year it was origi-nally published. In this selection Hirsch insists that Dohm's pro-suffrage argu-ments were harmful to the Lette-Verein's efforts to advance women's education and vocational training. Yet, like Dohm, she could not entirely suppress her rage against the prejudice and injustice that characterized women's situation.

---

139. Hedwig Dohm (1873)

. . . Recently, in conversation with a liberal statesman, when I briefly raised the question of women's professional capabilities and their right to vote, he firmly rejected such views. He responded more or less as follows: "The state does not exist in order to promote experimentation. The state is responsible for existing conditions, not for seedlings of what might be.

It is for human society to create and develop such seedlings. Only the developed and mature seedling becomes the concern of the state."

A strange principle. According to this principle the state appears to be an elderly grandmother, sitting quietly in her chair, watching the battle and plucking one laurel leaf after another from the hands of the victor, able at last to crown her own head with the completed wreath.

What indeed is "mature" and what is not? Which seedlings are portentous for the future and which will die in embryo? By what right would the state suppress this or that movement if this principle of "wait and see" politics were to be carried out; by what right is the state presently opposed to the social-republican movement?

Never since the dawn of history have we seen the state follow such a "wait and see" principle. It has always taken sides and used the might of its power to realize its ideals. Who does not know that from inner necessity truth must break free, either with the help of the state or in opposition to it—perhaps, however, the state suppresses only those seedlings that might sprout a bloody grain?

The Social Democrats, like the advocates of the liberation of women, seek a new world order. The latter are ridiculed, the former not. Why?— Laughter is silenced by pallid fear. Blood streaming from wounds is shunned and avoided; no one feels safe at the sight of such wounds—a common attitude.

For me the beginning of all true progress in the woman question lies in women's right to the vote. Of those laws that are of interest to women, most operate against them, because women have no part in creating them.

A government amassing unlimited authority over its people against their will and desires is considered despotic. Almost all lawgivers of the last few centuries stress the concept that no one should be bound by laws that he did not help to formulate. Among innumerable such statements, that of Benjamin Franklin comes to mind. . . .

The objection can be raised that women's votes would by and large hardly result in any laws except those enacted by the one-sided male franchise. This point of view is totally false. Are not men always the first to insist that women have other interests, that they have other intellectual, spiritual, and physical needs than men?

The stronger the emphasis on the difference between the sexes, the clearer the need for the specific representation of women. And since, according to Franklin, the poor man has a greater need to be represented than the rich man, likewise a woman, belonging to the weaker sex, has greater need to be represented than a man. This question requires no specially deep argument. The facts speak loudly for themselves, and if men would not plug their ears and hearts with a two-fold egoism they would understand this point.

I ask every honest man to imagine a country in which women were empowered to vote on laws on women's property, on custody rights over children, on marriage, divorce, etc. If they had the power, they would change these laws completely. Like men, women pay taxes; they are accountable to laws they had no part in making; thus they are forced to abide by laws made by others. In all languages of the world, this is called tyranny. However mildly executed, it is still tyranny. . . .

Few of my readers will have followed the British parliamentary debate on women's enfranchisement. Perhaps they will be grateful if I acquaint them briefly with the main points of the opposition.

Two theories, based upon contrasting points of view, are immediately evident. We may call the first a "stilts theory" and the second a "Cinderella theory." The first is based on woman's exalted state; the second bases its negative position on woman's intellectual inferiority.

We shall quickly be convinced that the comfortable "honorable gentlemen" satisfied themselves with a few dips into the great phrase grab-bag of the century, without fishing out anything of particular brilliance.

The "stilts theoreticians" discuss the matter as follows: First gentleman: "The position of women is far too elevated for them to be exposed to the dirt and mire of political activity." Second gentleman: "shudders at the idea that a woman should take part in the dissolute activity, in the disagreeable and hostile world of political agitation." Third gentleman exclaims firmly and briefly: "Active participation at an election would taint and pollute the entire sex."

Similar to these "stilts theorists" is another honorable gentleman who objects, "The vote would alter the character of the sex." The honorable sir actually fears, as his further discussion demonstrates, not so much a change in woman's character, as a blurring, an obliteration of sexual differences. He fears that the entire female sex might disappear along the unfamiliar path of voting rights.

This is the terror, the shuddering fear that grips all opponents of the women's movement and drives them into dusky woods . . . where as manly Cassandras they cry, "Woe to us!" because they imagine that the small amusements of their lives are threatened. The terror drives them to poetry, and they cite Schiller: "What is life without intrigues of love, adventure, romance, and so forth". . . .

A companion of the knight of purity fears that voting rights will cause women to lose their timidity and their blushes—and timidity and blushes surely serve as chastity belts. . . .

Let us now hear from the chief proponents of the Cinderella theory: One of them suggests that the sexes are distinctly different, that man is more suitable for government, and woman for private influence. Reason rules in man, feelings and sympathy in woman. She finds her satisfaction in sensibility, he in reason. The danger of giving woman the vote is that the tendency to emotionalism thus created might paralyze, and perhaps even overwhelm, reason, whereas the opposite condition is of course the only proper one. . . .

Until now man has ruled supreme. With what results? Let us open any page of history at random: [We find] battles, and blood, superstition, moral depravity, and social chaos.

If there be truth in what men are so pleased to insist upon—that they are a sex that is wild, gruesome, hungry for battles, thirsty for activity, with a tendency to vulgarity and vice, while women lean toward virtue, gentleness, and idealism—I see no reason to exclude virtue, gentleness, and ideals from the promulgation of laws. . . .

The most fluent speaker claims that women's votes would produce a political reaction because they are strongly influenced by the church. And who would be responsible if women were to cast their votes under priestly guidance? Who created religious conditions? Who invented confession? To this day women have not invented a religion. Men have driven women into the churches by excluding them from all other areas of spiritual life. This clerical influence will diminish in proportion to women's being permitted to participate in higher duties. . . .

Everyone agrees that the municipal vote for Englishwomen is nothing but a precursor of general national voting rights. The principle is thereby accepted; we are concerned now with a broadening of the practice.

Other precursors of general enfranchisement are the women who in some American states already exercise the right to vote. . . .

It may be true that at present only a minority of German women are concerned with the liberation of women and demand radical reform. Many women are deterred from participating in the agitation for the reforms by a simple reasoning. They say to themselves: I eat well and drink well, I have elegant clothes, I frequent theaters, balls, etc., What do these crazy women want? I have what I need—why concern myself about others? The ten thousand women who are happy ridicule the millions who are unhappy.

Whoever is happy rarely senses the unhappiness of others, as rarely as anyone who craves freedom craves it also for others.

It is not modesty nor the recognition of an unchangeable decision of nature that restrains thousands upon thousands of women from the great revolutionary movement; it is common selfishness. . . .

"Are you perchance demanding that women should eventually sit in the chambers of parliaments?," suggests a sarcastic voice. Why not? Even though the liberal statesman to whom we mentioned this possibility felt that it could never come to pass—since, as he argued, many capable men would find their voting and political resolve confused by feelings of love. . . .

As a matter of fact, gentlemen, one must ask: Are women in this world only in order to eliminate all possible obstacles to male virtue? Could not men themselves occasionally do something for their own virtue? In my opinion the interests of half of humanity are of greater importance than the danger that some weak-minded representatives might lose their political acumen along with their hearts.

140. Jenny Hirsch (1873-74)

The author who has already demonstrated her energy as a champion of female social equality in her previous work, *Was die Pastoren von den*

Frauen denken, does so in this new book with even greater spirit, wit, and reckless determination. We wish to offer appreciation of her courage and of the recklessness with which she loudly proclaims to the world what she believes to be true, without caring about the hostility and vilification that she will reap. We offer our appreciation—gratitude we cannot offer. While reading this book by Frau Hedwig Dohm, we were strongly reminded of the old saw: "May God protect me from my friends—From my enemies I can protect myself.". . . As editors concerned with improving women's education and business opportunities we must primarily consider two matters that affect the woman question in the appearance of new literary works: First, can we recommend this work to our readers? Second, will this work further or hinder our efforts?

We do recommend this book to our readers because it is spirited, bright, racy, and contains much material for thought and much that can be used as a basis for further activity. Moreover, readers of our journal *Frauen-Anwalt* have identified themselves with our viewpoint; they are enthusiastic and won over to our efforts to such a degree that they will not permit this book to confuse them. For those who reject and are hostile to the "woman question" we should—and we confess it quite openly—prefer to put *Jesuitismus im Hausstande* on a list of forbidden books. Risking Frau Dohm's accusation of hypocritical jesuitry, we admit that we cannot find much that is positive in furtherance of the woman question in this book (which she calls "a contribution"); on the contrary, we suspect that it will do much harm.

Will this book educate? No. Does this book expose social crimes and offer means to solve them? No. Does it offer means by which the woman question can be solved? Yes, one: voting rights and enfranchisement for women, which the author expects to be achieved in Germany within fifty years at the earliest. Meanwhile, she throws down the gauntlet to existing institutions, ridiculing the errors and prejudices that we also recognize, which have often enough hampered us and filled us with rage, but which cannot be abolished in this way; rather it causes them to become ever more entrenched and obdurate. Meanwhile, she looks down pityingly at those virtuous German women "who are struggling to recommend a few improvements in girls' schools; to build small, neat educational institutions, and who crave a small position in the postal or telegraph offices." Indeed, honored Madam, these are truly small and modest beginnings, and the women who "struggle" with them know it only too well. Does it not also require some courage, some self-denial, and some endurance, to work doggedly and quietly, fully recognizing that it is very little, that more might be asked, to conquer the terrain step by step, to let oneself be enveloped in hostility, criticism, and derision from the masses, and to say to oneself: You will never see the fruits of your labor, but your cause will enrich future generations. Does this not also require some courage—though perhaps not quite as much as to air one's rage and anger through the pages of a book, the errors in which one does not acknowledge, but blames instead upon men?

Does it not also require some courage to survive the battle with one-self? This is the battle that German women, whose activity is so con-temptible to you, must survive daily, even hourly. They must be silent, when they want to speak; they must beg, when they want to demand; they must wait, when with flaming enthusiasm they want to advance; they must listen to clichés and cannot rip off their hypocritical masks. They must prove to the world, to men, and to authority that their point of view is correct. For all this, words help very little—only deeds. The latter have been accomplished and have contributed a great deal to re-verse public opinion. As an issue of educating women for higher aca-demic, artistic, and business activity the woman question has achieved a civic right. Only rarely will its justice be doubted, though foolish jokes are made at its expense—but who is proof against that? Given our Ger-man character and social arrangements, it is only in this fashion that we can proceed. Progress it is nevertheless, sure and certain. And when it comes to pass that women vote and take their seats as members of parlia-ment (always supposing that by then we have not adopted another form of government, which is not impossible), this goal will have been achieved through the efforts and patience of "good and modest German women."

. . . We agree with much that has been said; with some of it we do not agree. We are, however, more concerned with the "how" than with the "what," which to us seemed very dubious. We are more concerned to know whether it will be possible [for women to have the vote] than with the fact that it has been talked about. This is our point of view; our criti-cism must be considered only from this angle.

The Suffrage Issue in Republican France

SOURCES

141. Léon Richer, *La Femme libre* (Paris, 1877), pp. 238-41. Tr. KMO. The editors wish to thank Professor Claire Goldberg Moses, University of Maryland, for allowing us to consult her microfilms of both the Richer book and Auclert's *Droit politique*, which are otherwise unavailable in the United States.

142. Hubertine Auclert, *Le Droit politique des femmes, question qui n'est pas traitée au Congrès international des femmes* (Paris, 1878), pp. 3-6, 8-11, 13-14. Tr. KMO.

143. Hubertine Auclert, *Egalité sociale et politique de la femme et de l'homme, discours prononcé au Congrès ouvrier socialiste de Marseille* (Marseille, 1879), as reproduced in *Romantisme*, nos. 13-14 (1976), pp. 123-24, 125, 126, 127. Tr. KMO.

In France the campaign for woman suffrage was muted throughout the 1870's by the struggle for political supremacy between republicans and monarchists that followed the overthrow of the Second Empire. This struggle came to a climax in 1877, following which the republicans consolidated their control of the legisla-ture and forced the president to submit to parliamentary rule. Even in the wake of this republican victory, however, the two leaders of the anticlerical republican women's movement, Léon Richer (Doc. 124) and Maria Deraismes, did not feel secure in pushing for the vote, arguing as had Jeanne Deroin's opponents in 1850 (Docs. 84, 85) that giving women the vote would throw the balance of power back to the priests and the monarchists. Richer preferred to place his emphasis on achieving specific legal reforms: reestablishment of divorce, enactment of strict paternity laws, improvement of educational opportunities, and abolition of regulated prostitution. By giving preference to these reforms Richer provoked the wrath of a former colleague, Hubertine Auclert (1848-1914), a young woman of independent means, who had come to Paris expressly to work with Richer and Deraismes on behalf of women's rights.

Richer and Auclert came into open conflict in 1877-78, when Richer and Deraismes organized the first International Congress on Women's Rights, held in Paris during the International Exposition. Woman suffrage was explicitly excluded from the agenda, which did, however, take up history, education, economics, morals, and legislation. This omission infuriated Auclert, who, like Elizabeth Cady Stanton (Doc. 137) a decade earlier, marshalled arguments of principle against erstwhile allies whom she considered to be sacrificing justice to expediency—an argument that was hurled with increasing frequency by many other radical republicans against the "opportunism" of their more moderate counterparts who had recently come to power.

The first selection is excerpted from Richer's book, *La Femme libre*, published in 1877. The second selection is drawn from Auclert's 1878 pamphlet, *Le Droit politique des femmes*, in which she protested against the purposeful exclusion of the suffrage issue from the international congress, invoking the arguments of Condorcet and Olympe de Gouges (Docs. 24, 26) to support her case. The third selection comes from a speech Auclert gave a year later when, totally disenchanted by the timidity of her republican colleagues, she sought support for woman suffrage among the once-Proudhonian militants of the newly blossoming French socialist workers' movement. In this speech, Auclert makes explicit the connection between class oppression and sex oppression, echoing in new language the long-forgotten arguments of her Saint-Simonian precursors. The workers' congress voted to support her resolution. The honeymoon lasted only a few years, however, for the pursuit of any women's rights whatever fell victim to the intranecine strife in the workers' party, as bourgeois reformists parted company with the Marxist group that advocated collectivism and revolution. Auclert, who lived off interest from family investments, found the collectivist program unacceptable and established her own organization and propaganda center for the pursuit of woman suffrage in republican France.

---

141. Léon Richer (1877)

I have said before, and insist on repeating again in the name of clarity, that at the present time women, generally speaking, are not demanding political rights. They know all too well—I speak of those who are capable of understanding—who would profit from this hasty reform. Out of nine million adult women, some few thousand would vote freely; the rest would receive their orders from the confessional.

The intelligent, educated, republican women are quite well aware of this situation.

Thus they have preferred not to raise the political question at this time.

Although it is put aside for the moment, the right to vote is nonetheless affirmed in theory.

For my part, I have no hesitation in so declaring.

Now I pose a question.

Is it not true that, in acting with the prudence I have just indicated, the women who, thanks to their education, would be able to make good use of their right to vote today, are not exhibiting incontestable proof of their political wisdom?

Their disinterested attitude seems all the more remarkable to me when, in other countries—notably in England and the United States—the question of female emancipation is framed almost exclusively in terms of political rights. Already, even in certain parts of America, it has been resolved in the direction of absolute equality for both sexes.

I have sometimes heard it proposed that French women be admitted by categories to the exercise of suffrage. Only those would be registered who could justify it on the basis of sufficient schooling. This idea has not been very successful, and I am glad of it. I daresay that every time it has come up in my presence, I have fought against it. Most of the women themselves also reject this procedure.

Why should women be subjected to an examination that men are exempt from? Why should women be subjected to the humiliation of interrogation when a mere farmhand who cannot either read or write is a full-fledged voter? Moreover, such an examination would prove absolutely nothing from the standpoint of political intelligence. It is not because of her knowledge of religious history, grammar, geography, drawing, piano, and other useful things that a rich woman who has spent ten years in a convent or in a well-known *pensionnat* would vote any better than a stout-hearted working woman, enlightened by her own suffering as to the real needs of the country. Not only would such a system be absurd, unjust, and insulting, but it would go against the very goal we want to reach. Either we must call on all women or call on none. If it is still too early, let us wait; but let us not create exceptions, let us not establish classes. I repeat that most women agree with this.

Thus, for the time being, the question of political rights for women is not on the agenda. Nevertheless, we are obligated to examine it. In the event that, in light of other developments, this matter comes up again, we must not be taken by surprise. If a movement in its favor emerges, at least we must know what we are about; we will be familiar with all the elements of the problem, and we will be ready for discussion.

142. Hubertine Auclert (1878)

I am astonished that under a republic it is still necessary to cry out for such and such a right for one segment of humankind. The complete human being is man and woman: to restrict right with regard to woman is to restrict the right of humanity: it is to lessen the right of man.

Being equal before nature, and equally indispensable for the perpetuation of society, man and woman should together govern this society that they form part of, and share in exercising the same rights, as much in public life as in private life.

I demand woman's right, her absolute right.

One can no more oppose her political emancipation than one can oppose her civil emancipation. Right is Right, and in spite of all the many ways in which women's right has been usurped, it remains inviolable.

I am aware that many partisans of women's emancipation find the demand for political rights premature. I have no response to them other than to declare that woman is a ravaged creature who demands justice instead of remaining in the situation in which she has been placed, that of a beggarwoman who implores man's charity. Liberty is no longer being accorded parsimoniously to slaves. Can it continue to be accorded parsimoniously to women?

In our call for women's rights, it is essential to avoid derogation of the principle, to proceed straight to the goal. Would we be fit to help women emancipate themselves if those of us who have taken up their cause preoccupied ourselves primarily with not antagonizing their oppressors and with meekly demanding for them only a little bit more schooling, a little bit more bread, a few less humiliations in marriage or difficulties in life?

When nearly all of France lay in servitude, what would the great emancipators of '89 have obtained if they had been content to expose humbly the needs of our fathers and reclaim from the powerful of yesteryear—the nobility, the clergy, royalty—some relief from their troubles? [Instead] they marched against the existing order of things that made them serfs, just as the present order of things makes us serfs. They declared, they proclaimed the right of man, an audacious act that freed man. But yesterday's oppressed remained the next day's oppressor.

Our mothers, who cooperated in making the revolution, did not harvest its fruits. Nevertheless, we saw women active everywhere during this great drama, in the assemblies, in the clubs, in the public squares, on the battlefields. They agitated, they spoke, they fought, they wrote the men's speeches, they knew how to die for liberty. . . . Alas, man, once emancipated, forgot to remember that woman's liberty would serve as the guarantee of his own. . . .

Long before the men, women have been won over to the republic; during these great eras [1789; 1848—EDS.] they were in a greater hurry than the men to swear the civic oath. Today, without realizing it, they have the republican feeling as much as men. But then—strange phenomenon— this Republic so loved by women—this Republic pushes them away. . . . At present the opportunist republic closes all its doors to us and then finds it strange that the women, rebuffed and disdained, go over to reinforce the enemy's ranks, to march in assault upon this public enterprise that is by no means the enterprise of all.

The [monarchist Catholic] reaction conducts itself differently.

The reaction cultivates the aid of the women; without this would it not, in its iniquity, be crushed by a truly just Republic? . . .

The women are rebuffed by those who preach equality and who nevertheless leave women beyond the limits of this equality, by continuing to recognize the supremacy of one sex over the other. With only a few rare exceptions, the republicans disdain and jeer at woman; meanwhile, the monarchists and bonapartists arm her for combat. . . .

The reaction understands marvelously well how to prepare women for the struggle: through the confessional, the sermon, the watchword comes. In the salons and boudoirs the beautiful great ladies will stoke enthusiasm for the candidates. They will intrigue stealthily, influencing husbands, fathers, brothers, friends, visitors. By a word, by an act of friendship, they operate by flattering [men's] self-esteem. The business women and wage-earning women do likewise. Outwardly they don't vote, but they do exercise influence—they slip the ballot into the hand that places it in the ballot box. Strong indeed is the man who can resist their power.

In order to counterbalance the adverse influence of reactionary women, we need the beneficent influence of republican women. We must be interested in public affairs. By leaving us on the periphery of civic life, you retard the arrival of liberty; but it is impossible to prevent or to retard for long the movement that leads every being to realize its own complete development, its complete autonomy. If this is the case, why then deprive the nation of the fullness of its reason, of its force, by depriving it of half its intelligence? Our chambers, which could work usefully if they represented the whole of humanity (men and women), find themselves paralyzed because they lack a vital element in order to resolve a number of questions. I am convinced that our senators and deputies have the will to make equitable laws; most of the time, however, they make incomplete laws, laws that lack the cachet of justice and that notion of humanity that ought to induce the legislator to concern himself especially with the poor and the weak.

In the social reforms required by progress, woman's assistance would be of inestimable value; aided by man, she would be able to incorporate enough goodness, enough humanity in the details of social arrangements to prevent the revolts and revolutions that are brought on by an excess of suffering.

All men and all women have the same social and political interests. Why has man been able to arrogate to himself the privilege of making laws? Does he believe himself to be an infallible king? You laugh loudly, you free-thinking gentlemen, about the infallibility of the pope; but in the present circumstances, you are all infallible popes. You oblige us—we who constitute one-half of humanity—and oblige us under threat of condemnation, to submit without examination or discussion to the laws you make for us. It is evident that you are not susceptible of being mistaken; it is evident that you are infallible because, good sense and reason notwithstanding, you take it upon yourselves to govern humanity, and for this purpose you have instituted a suffrage to which you have given a misleading name: a suffrage that allows you to exclude from the electoral lists nine million women is far too restrictive to bear the name universal. . . .

Ladies, we must remind ourselves that the weapon of the vote will be for us, just as it is for man, the only means of obtaining the reforms we desire. As long as we remain excluded from civic life, men will attend to their own interests rather than to ours. The proletariat understood as much when, in 1848, it demanded the vote as the sole means of achieving other liberties.

Would we love liberty less than men love it? Do we not blush over the situation in which we now find ourselves? We are nine million adult women who constitute a nation of slaves amid a nation of free men. We are subject to the same repressive laws, to the same taxes as men. We must be able to delegate to our representatives the making of laws and budgets to support our interests. Without this we will continue to be left out on all counts. The laws will be made against us, and the least possible amount of money will be spent on our behalf. . . .

By virtue of the fact that one pays taxes, one has the right to participate in establishing the tax rate. A taxpayer ought to be a voter. The rights and the well-paid government positions belong to men alone. Woman is still taxed to death unjustly* because, although she participates in the community's expenses, she is not consulted about the community's arrangements. You refuse women the vote on the grounds that they would vote for the priests and the Jesuits—which is hardly a proven fact—and yet you do not hesitate to allow the Jesuits and priests to vote. Do you suppose that the priests and the Jesuits do not vote for their own kind?

Republicans, you who believe yourselves to be radicals, socialists, and who deny woman's political right, you are nothing but autocrats. You deny liberty, you deny equality. Do you think you can thus seriously establish a republican government by retaining slaves who will make of France a country that remains in a continual state of ferment?

Reflect well, gentlemen, and in the name of justice, in the name of liberty, abdicate your masculine kingship. It is time to proclaim equality. It is time that there are no longer inferiors and superiors in the world except for those judged on intelligence and thought.

Until you have recognized the complete right of women—civil rights and political rights—your struggle to attain a greater liberty can appear to impartial witnesses and to us, the neglected half of humanity, only as a quarrel between despotisms.

143. Hubertine Auclert (1879)

. . . Like you [workers], we [women] have been the victims of abusive force. In our modern society we, like you, still endure the tyrannical force of those who are in power, to which one must add, in our case, the tyrannical force of those who now enjoy their rights.

And all this takes place under the protection of the Republic! Of the Republic whose very name designates an era in which everything that be-

---

* Auclert is speaking here of propertied single women like herself.—EDS.

longed to those who wielded might and had usurped the wealth, should have ceased belonging to them, to become the property of one and all.

Ah! we live in a type of Republic that proves that the most sublime words can become empty slogans, shocking to the eye, when the principles they represent for a society are not integrally applied. A Republic that keeps women in an inferior situation cannot make men equal. Before you men can earn the right to raise yourselves to the level of your masters, you are obliged to raise your slaves, the women, up to your own level.

Many of you have never thought about this before. For that matter, if in this imposing gathering I asked this question: Are you partisans of human equality? everyone would reply: Yes. For the great majority understand by human equality the equality of men among one other. But if I were to change the theme, if, emphasizing these two terms—man and woman—in which humanity manifests itself, I were to say to you: Are you partisans of the equality of man and woman? many would reply: No. Then, how can you speak of equality, you who—being yourselves under the yoke—wish to keep other beings under your control? What complaints can you make about the ruling classes, when you, the ruled, treat women the same way the ruling classes treat you? . . .

Either women are the equals of workers and bourgeois, or else the bourgeois, as they claim, are the superiors of workers and of women.

Believe me, citizens, it is only upon the equality of all beings that you can base your claims to freedom. If you do not ground your demands in justice and natural law; if you, the proletariat, also wish to conserve privileges, privileges of sex, I ask you on what authority you can contest class privileges? On what grounds can you reproach those in power who dominate you and exploit you, if you favor retaining any categories at all of superior and inferior within the human race?

Beware of being accused by your masters of challenging their prerogatives that you covet. Proclaim equality between the human beings that the accident of birth has made male and female; or, if you dare, deny this equality and, as good logicians, recognize your innate inferiority and the right of the ruling classes to think, act, and enjoy life in your stead.

Let us have done with these questions of pride and egotism. The rights of woman do not take away your rights. Then freely replace authority by natural right: for if, by virtue of authority, man oppresses woman, then by virtue of this same authority, man oppresses man.

I have spoken so far to the majority. Now I will speak to those who declare themselves the partisans of equality between man and woman, but for whom the password is: "Shhh! . . . Let's not waste our time worrying about that detail." A detail! The exploitation of half of humanity by the other half! In the society of the future, these would-be socialists continue, women will have their rights. In this manner they imitate the priests who promise the pleasures of heaven to the wretched of the earth. Neither those disinherited in fortune nor those disinherited in the law, neither the poor nor the women, will be able to content themselves forever with holy promises. . . .

. . .Women should beware of those who preach equality in the future and who, in the present, reject the contribution of their intelligence, their ideas, and their tastes to the planning of this future society.

Women of France, I tell you from the loftiness of this podium: Those who deny our equality in the present, will deny it also in the future. Thus we must count on ourselves to achieve our own freedom; we must not abandon our claims. For centuries we have been too much the victims of bad faith to forget ourselves any longer and to believe that by working for the general good we will obtain our share of the general good. (Applause.)

Ah! If at the beginning women had been able to draw up a contract with men that would guarantee the equality of their rights in the face of conquests made in common, I would say: Let us forget our particular fate as slaves. Let us confound our claims with those of men! Alas! Without a guarantee, I am truly afraid that human equality, as preached by every socialist school, will still mean the equality of men, and that the women will be duped by the proletarian men just as the latter have been duped by the bourgeois.

The heads of the various socialist groups are far from recognizing our equality unanimously. We cannot count on the authoritarians, who say, in order to deter us from what we regard as the source and principle of every right, the vote: "Why should we argue over civil rights; there will be no need for them in the society of the future." In the society of the future even more than in that of the present, an idea will have to be approved by the majority in order to triumph. Moreover, we have not yet arrived at this society of the future, and in order to build it in such a manner that women are not left out, they need the right to participate in its construction; they need the tool that can already be found in the hands of men—the ballot. . . .

We, the women, will not busy ourselves with aiding despotism to change hands. What we want is to kill privilege, not merely to reallocate it.

REFERENCE MATTER

SUGGESTED FURTHER READING

ADAM, JULIETTE LAMBERT LAMESSINE (Doc. 96)
  Adam 1904; Whale 1917; Morcos 1962; E. Thomas 1966; Moses 1978.
AIMÉ-MARTIN, LOUIS (Doc. 43)
  Aimé-Martin 1843.
ALLGEMEINES LANDRECHT (Doc. 7)
  Koch 1862.
ALMQVIST, CARL (Doc. 38)
  Qvist 1960; Berg 1962; Romberg 1977.
ANDERSON, ELIZABETH GARRETT (Doc. 117)
  Strachey 1928; E. Bell 1953; Wymer 1959; Manton 1965; Burstyn 1973,
  1980; L'Esperance 1977; Atkinson 1978.
ATELIER, L' (Docs. 57, 66)
  Cuvillier 1954; S. J. Moon 1978a.
AUCLERT, HUBERTINE (Docs. 142, 143)
  Dzeh-Djen 1934; Bidelman 1976, 1977, 1982; Sowerwine 1977a, 1982; Taïeb
  1982.
BACHOFEN, JOHANN-JAKOB (Doc. 102)
  Briffault 1927; J. Campbell 1967; Bamberger 1974.
BALZAC, HONORÉ DE (Doc. 39)
  Faillie 1960; Pradalié 1960; Bolster 1970.
BAUDEAU, NICOLAS (Doc. 17)
  J. Bloch 1979. See also Black 1979; Nash 1981.
BEAUMER, MADAME DE (Doc. 2)
  Gelbart 1980.
BEECHER, CATHARINE (Doc. 49)
  Cross 1965; Sklar 1973; A. Douglas 1977; Rose 1982.
BLACKSTONE, WILLIAM (and Anglo-Saxon civil law) (Doc. 5)
  R. Morris 1930; Beard 1946; Rabkin 1974, 1980; N. Basch 1979; Salmon
  1979, 1980.
BODICHON, BARBARA LEIGH-SMITH (Doc. 90)
  Rice 1934; Burton 1949; Graveson & Crane 1957; Bradbrook 1976; Hol-
  combe 1977, 1982.
BONALD, LOUIS VICOMTE DE (Doc. 21)
  Moulinie 1916; Deniel 1965.
BREMER, FREDRIKA (Doc. 94)
  Qvist 1969; Wieselgren 1978.
BROCA, PAUL (Doc. 111)
  S. Shields 1975; Schiller 1979; Gould 1981; J. Harvey 1982.

BRONTË, CHARLOTTE (Docs. 81, 83)
Wise & Symington 1932; Gérin 1967; F. Basch 1974; Gilbert & Gubar 1980.
CABET, ETIENNE (Doc. 51)
C. Johnson 1974.
CHERNYSHEVSKY, N. G. (Doc. 100)
Woehrlin 1971; Stites 1978.
CLARKE, EDWARD H. (Doc. 115)
Bullough & Voght 1973; Haller & Haller 1974; Atkinson 1978; Burstyn 1980.
CLOUGH, ANNE JEMIMA (Doc. 114)
Clough 1903; Strachey 1928; Hamilton 1936; McWilliams-Tullberg 1975, 1977; Phillips 1979; Burstyn 1980; S. Bell 1981.
COLLETT, CAMILLA (Doc. 93)
Gravier 1965; Seaver (unpub. ms).
COMTE, AUGUSTE (and Clotilde de Vaux) (Docs. 62, 63)
Teixiera-Mendes 1915-18; Rouvre 1917; Willey 1949; Hayek 1952; Charlton 1963; Simon 1963; Lenzer 1975; Kent 1978; Haines 1978.
CONDORCET, MARIE-JEAN-NICOLAS CARITAT, MARQUIS DE (Docs. 19, 24)
Shapiro 1934; Manuel 1962; Gay 1966, 1969; Williams 1971; Baker 1975; Fisher 1975; Kleinbaum 1977; Hoffmann 1978; Gardner 1979.
COQUEREL, ATHANASE (Doc. 72)
Prévost 1961.
CORNWALLIS, CAROLINE (Doc. 92)
Cornwallis 1864.
DALL, CAROLINE HEALEY (Doc. 116)
Riegel 1963; Conrad 1976; Welter 1976; Leach 1980.
DARWIN, CHARLES (Doc. 110)
Burrow 1966; Himmelfarb 1968; Fee 1974, 1976; Alaya 1977; Kanner 1977; Duffin 1978; Mosedale 1978.
DAUBIÉ, JULIE-VICTOIRE (Doc. 127)
Magellon 1898; Bascou-Bance 1972.
DAVIES, EMILY (Doc. 113)
B. Stephen 1927; Strachey 1928; McWilliams-Tullberg 1975, 1977; Burstyn 1980; S. Bell 1981.
"DECLARATION OF SENTIMENTS" (Seneca Falls) (Docs. 74, 75)
E. Stanton 1898; Cromwell 1958; Flexner 1959; C. Taylor 1974; DuBois 1978; Bacon 1980; Banner 1980; D. Greene 1980.
DECREE ON ASSOCIATIONS (Prussia) (Doc. 86)
Quataert 1979.
DEROIN, JEANNE (Docs. 70, 77, 84, 85, 87)
Ranvier 1908; Tixerant 1908; Abensour 1913; Le Van Kim 1926; Zévaès 1931; E. Thomas 1948; Sullerot 1966a; Fraisse 1975; S. J. Moon 1976b, 1978b; Dufrancatel 1977; Moses 1978, 1982.
DOHM, HEDWIG (Doc. 139)
Schreiber 1914; Janssen-Jurreit 1981.
DUBUISSON, JANE (and *Le Conseiller des Femmes*) (Doc. 55)
Struminger 1976, 1978.
DUPANLOUP, FELIX (Doc. 118)
Horvath 1975; Mayeur & Gadille 1980.
ELLIS, SARAH STICKNEY (Doc. 53)
F. Basch 1974; Showalter 1977.

ENCYCLOPÉDIE, L' (Louis, chevalier de Jaucourt) (Doc. 6)
Gay 1966, 1969; Roger 1971; Darnton 1977; Hoffmann 1978. On Diderot, see Venturi 1939; Wilson 1957, 1976; Jacobs 1979; Niklaus 1979. On Jaucourt, see Schwab 1957; Lough 1960; M. Morris 1979; Perla 1980.

ENFANTIN, PROSPER (and the Saint-Simonians) (Doc. 34)
Butler 1926; Thibert 1926; Charléty 1931; Pankhurst [1957]; Killham 1958; Charlton 1963; Altman 1977; Moses 1982.

ENGELS, FRIEDRICH (Docs. 61, 69)
Henderson & Challoner 1968; Leacock 1972; Marcus 1974; Sacks 1974; Delmar 1976; Lane 1976.

FEMALE POLITICAL UNION OF NEWCASTLE UPON TYNE (Doc. 64)
D. Thompson 1971, 1976.

FEMME LIBRE, LA (and the Saint-Simonian women) (Doc. 36)
Abensour 1913; Thibert 1926; Jehan d'Ivray 1930; Killham 1958; Sullerot 1966b; S. J. Moon 1976a, 1977, 1978b; Dufrancatel 1977; Elhadad 1977; Adler 1979; Mallet 1980; Moses 1982.

FERRY, JULES (Doc. 119)
Acomb 1941; Legrand 1961.

FOURIER, CHARLES (Docs. 9, 35)
Thibert 1926; Sourine 1936; Pankhurst 1956; Manuel 1962; Riasanovsky 1969; Beecher & Bienvenue 1971; Altman 1977; Hayden 1981.

FOX, CHARLES JAMES (Doc. 30)
Hammond 1903; Hobhouse 1935; Goodwin 1979.

FREDERICIAN CODE (Samuel von Cocceji) (Doc. 4)
Weill 1961; Petschauer 1972; H. Johnson 1975; Hausen 1981.

GABBA, CARLO FRANCESCO (Doc. 122)
Howard 1977, 1978.

GASKELL, ELIZABETH CLEGHORN (Doc. 58)
Rubenius 1950; Cazamian 1973; Gérin 1976; Showalter 1977.

GOETHE, JOHANN WOLFGANG VON (Doc. 28)
Koepke 1979; Hausen 1981; Mommsen 1983a, 1983b.

GOUGES, OLYMPE DE (Doc. 26)
Lacour 1900; Duhet 1971; Abray 1975; Chaudhuri 1975; Devance 1977; Levy, Applewhite & Johnson 1979.

GRIMKÉ, ANGELINA (Doc. 50)
Lerner 1967; Lumpkin 1974; Melder 1977; Rose 1982.

HEINRICHS, JOSEPH (Doc. 128)
Sanford 1976.

HÉRICOURT, JENNY P. D' (Doc. 98)
E. Thomas 1966; Stites 1969; C. Johnson 1974.

HIPPEL, THEODOR GOTTLIEB VON (Doc. 29)
Sanford 1976; R. Evans 1977; Sellner 1979.

HIRSCH, JENNY (Doc. 140)
Hauff 1928.

HOGGAN, FRANCES MORGAN, AND GEORGE HOGGAN (Doc. 134)
E. Bell 1953; Donnison 1976.

HUMBOLDT, WILHELM VON (Doc. 15)
Hertz 1978; Sweet 1978; Hausen 1981; Mommsen 1983b.

INTERNATIONAL CONGRESS ON WOMEN'S RIGHTS, FIRST (Doc. 125)
Bidelman 1977, 1982.

INTERNATIONAL WORKINGMEN'S ASSOCIATION (Docs. 130, 131)
Freymond 1962; Drachkovich 1966; Braunthal 1967; Perrot 1976.

JEX-BLAKE, SOPHIA (and women in medicine) (Doc. 133)
  Todd 1918; E. Bell 1953; Donnison 1976. See also Meijer 1955; Walsh 1977.
JÜDISCH DEUTSCHE MONATSSCHRIFT (Doc. 22)
  Kestenberg-Gladstein 1969; Hertz 1978.
KANT, IMMANUEL (Doc. 27)
  Vorländer 1924; Broad 1978.
KELLER, ÉMILE (Doc. 120)
  Gautherot 1922.
KNIGHT, ANNE (Doc. 73)
  C. Taylor 1974; Malmgreen 1982.
MACAULAY-GRAHAM, CATHARINE (Doc. 11)
  Stenton 1957; Boos 1976; Schnorrenberg 1979a; Boos & Boos 1980; Davis
  1980; Rogers 1983.
MAINE, HENRY SUMNER (Doc. 101)
  Feaver 1969; Kanner 1977.
MAISTRE, JOSEPH DE (Docs. 42, 45)
  Bayle 1945; Deniel 1965; Lebrun 1965; Lively 1965; Lombard 1976.
MARX, KARL (Doc. 69)
  Berlin 1963; McLellan 1974.
MAURICE, MARY ATKINSON (Doc. 47)
  Maurice 1884; Grylls 1948; Kaye 1972.
MAZZINI, GIUSEPPE (Doc. 103)
  Griffith 1932; Salvemini 1957.
MICHELET, JULES (Docs. 46, 97)
  Pisano 1974; Calo 1975.
MIKHAILOV, M. L. (Doc. 99)
  Stites 1969, 1978.
MILL, HARRIET TAYLOR (Doc. 88)
  Hayek 1951; Pappe 1960; Robson 1968; Rossi 1970; Held 1971; Pugh 1978;
  Okin 1979.
MILL, JAMES (and the *Encyclopedia Britannica*) (Doc. 31)
  Mazlish 1975; Okin 1979.
MILL, JOHN STUART (Docs. 105, 135, 136)
  Hayek 1951; Packe 1954; C. Shields 1956; Pankhurst [1957]; Pappe 1960;
  Robson 1968; Rossi 1970; Himmelfarb 1970, 1974; Okin 1973, 1979; Maz-
  lish 1975; Annas 1977; Pugh 1978, 1980, 1982; Bostick 1980.
MINK, PAULE (Doc. 132)
  Sowerwine 1978; Hellerstein, Hume & Offen 1981.
MORE, HANNAH (Doc. 20)
  Jones 1952; Myers 1982.
MOZZONI, ANNA MARIA (Doc. 123)
  Pieroni-Bortolotti 1963; Mozzoni 1975; Howard 1977, 1978, 1980.
MURRAY, JUDITH SARGENT (Doc. 3)
  Field 1931; Kerber 1974, 1980; Fisher 1975; J. Wilson 1976; Cott 1977; Nor-
  ton 1980.
NAPOLEON (the Civil Code and girls' education) (Docs. 8, 23)
  Brasier 1901; Gautier 1903; Balde 1921; Abensour 1923; Bonnecase 1928;
  Reval 1931; Rheinstein 1956; Portemer 1959; Knibiehler 1976b.
NATIONAL TRADES' UNION COMMITTEE ON FEMALE LABOR (Docs. 56, 59)
  Commons & Sumner 1910-11; Foner 1979.
NORTON, CAROLINE SHERIDAN (Doc. 41)
  Strachey 1928; Rice 1934; Marreco 1948.

OLIPHANT, MARGARET OLIPHANT (Docs. 91, 106)
Oliphant 1899; Showalter 1977.

OTTO, LOUISE (Docs. 48, 78, 89, 129)
Otto-Peters 1876; Schmidt & Rösch 1898; Magnus-Hausen 1922; Semmig 1957; Twellmann 1972; Sanford 1976; Gerhard, Hannover-Drück & Schmitter 1979.

PALM D'AELDERS, ETTA (Doc. 25)
Duhet 1971; Abray 1975; Devance 1977; Levy, Applewhite & Johnson 1979.

PHILLIPS, WENDELL (Doc. 138)
J. McPherson 1965.

PIUS IX (and the Immaculate Conception of Mary) (Doc. 79)
Digby 1845-47; Doheny & Kelly 1954; O'Connor 1958; Gruber 1967; Coppa 1979.

POMPÉRY, EDOUARD DE (Doc. 108)
Vapereau, *Dictionnaire des Contemporains*, 1880.

POUTRET DE MAUCHAMPS, MARIE-MADELEINE (Doc. 40)
M.-L. Puech 1935; Sullerot 1966.

PROUDHON, PIERRE-JOSEPH (Docs. 52, 84, 95)
Domergue 1902; Thibert 1926; Maitron 1954; D. Halévy 1955; Edwards 1969; Ritter 1969; Hall 1971; Hoffman 1972; Boxer 1974, 1977; Moses 1978.

REID, MARION KIRKLAND (Docs. 44, 54, 68)
Only available information in *DNB*; s.v. "Reid, Hugo."

RICHARDSON, R. J. (Doc. 65)
D. Thompson 1971.

RICHER, LÉON (Docs. 124, 141)
Dzeh-Djen 1934; Bidelman 1976, 1977, 1982.

RIGBY (EASTLAKE), ELIZABETH (Doc. 82)
Lochhead 1961.

ROLAND, PAULINE (Doc. 87)
E. Thomas 1956; Moses 1982.

RONGE, JOHANNES (Doc. 80)
Droz 1966; Prelinger 1976a, 1976b.

ROUSSEAU, JEAN-JACQUES (Doc. 10)
Alstad 1971; Graham 1976; LeGates 1976; Sanford 1976; Wexler 1976; Kleinbaum 1977; Jimack 1979; Okin 1979; Bloch & Bloch 1980; Keohane 1980a.

RUSH, BENJAMIN (Doc. 18)
Binger 1966; Cott 1977; R. Bloch 1978a; A. Gordon 1979; Kerber 1974, 1976, 1980.

RUSKIN, JOHN (Doc. 104)
Millett 1969, 1972; Sonstroem 1977; Abse 1981.

SAND, GEORGE (Doc. 37)
Monin 1899/1900; D.-O. Evans 1930; Pradalié 1960; Malia 1961; Lubin 1973; Cate 1975; P. Thompson 1977.

SCHLEGEL, FRIEDRICH VON (Doc. 16)
Eichner 1970; Schlegel 1971; Hertz 1978; Hausen 1981. *See also* Pange 1938.

SÉE, CAMILLE (Doc. 121)
Offen 1973b; Mayeur 1977.

SHARPLES [CARLILE], ELIZA (Doc. 33)
T. Campbell 1899; Fryer 1965; Royle 1974; B. Taylor 1977.

SIMON, JULES (Doc. 126)
  Bertocci 1978.
SOPHIA, A PERSON OF QUALITY (Doc. 1)
  Schnorrenberg 1980; Kelly 1982; Rogers 1983; Ferguson (forthcoming); Bell & Offen (forthcoming).
SPENCER, HERBERT (Doc. 112)
  J. Greene 1959; Burrow 1966; Fee 1974, 1976; Kanner 1977; Duffin 1978; Mosedale 1978.
STAËL, GERMAINE DE (Docs. 13, 14)
  Gautier 1903; Pange 1938; Gennari 1947; Gutwirth 1971, 1978; Balayé 1979.
STANTON, ELIZABETH CADY (Docs. 74, 76, 137)
  E. Stanton 1898; Lutz 1940; Riegel 1962; J. McPherson 1965; Rabkin 1974, 1980; DuBois 1978, 1981; Banner 1980.
THOMPSON, WILLIAM, AND ANNA DOYLE WHEELER (Doc. 32)
  Pankhurst 1954a, 1954b; Stenton 1957; Galgano 1979; B. Taylor 1979.
TRISTAN, FLORA (Doc. 60)
  J. Puech 1925; Baelen 1972; S. J. Moon 1978a.
WOLLSTONECRAFT, MARY (Doc. 12)
  Rauschenbusch-Clough 1898; Bouten 1922; Wardle 1951; George 1970; Flexner 1972; Tomalin 1974; Fisher 1975; Korsmeyer 1976; Walters 1976; Kleinbaum 1977; Myers 1977, 1982; Janes 1978; Rogers 1983.

BIBLIOGRAPHY

Abensour, Léon. 1913. *Le Féminisme sous le règne de Louis-Philippe et en 1848.* Paris.

———. 1923. *La Femme et le féminisme avant la Révolution.* Paris.

Abray, Jane. 1975. "Feminism in the French Revolution," *American Historical Review*, 80, no. 1 (Feb.), 43-62.

Abse, Joan. 1981. *John Ruskin: The Passionate Moralist.* London and New York.

Acomb, Evelyn M. 1941. *The French Laic Laws (1879-1889), The First Anti-Clerical Campaign of the Third Republic.* New York.

Adam, Juliette. 1904. *My Literary Life.* London and New York.

Adler, Laure. 1979. *A l'Aube du féminisme: Les premières journalistes (1830-1850).* Paris.

Agonito, Rosemary, ed. 1977. *History of Ideas on Woman: A Sourcebook.* New York.

Aimé-Martin, Louis. 1843. Introduction to Aimé-Martin, *The Education of Mothers; or, the Civilization of Mankind by Women.* Tr. Edwin Lee. Philadelphia. Originally published in Paris, 1834.

Alaya, Flavia. 1977. "Victorian Science and the 'Genius' of Women," *Journal of the History of Ideas*, vol. 38, no. 2 (Apr.-June), 261-80.

Albistur, Maïté, and Daniel Armogathe. 1978a. *Histoire du féminisme français.* 2 vols. Paris.

———. 1978b. *Le Grief des femmes.* 2 vols. Paris.

Alexander, Sally. 1976. "Women's Work in Nineteenth-Century London; A Study of the Years 1820-50," in *The Rights and Wrongs of Women*, ed. Juliet Mitchell and Ann Oakley. London.

Alstad, Dianne Lynn. 1971. "The Ideology of the Family in 18th-Century France," Ph.D. dissertation, Yale University.

Altman, Elizabeth C. 1977. "The Philosophical Foundations of Feminism: The Feminist Doctrines of the Saint-Simonians and Charles Fourier," *Philosophical Forum*, 8, nos. 3-4: 277-93.

Annas, Julia. 1977. "Mill and the Subjection of Women," *Philosophy*, 52 (April), 179-94.

Ariès, Philippe. 1962. *Centuries of Childhood: A Social History of Family Life.* Tr. Robert Baldick. New York. Originally published in French, 1960.

Atkinson, Paul. 1978. "Fitness, Feminism, and Schooling," in *The Nineteenth-Century Woman: Her Cultural and Physical World*, ed. Sara Delamont and Lorna Duffin. London and New York.

Bacon, Margaret Hope. 1980. *Valiant Friend: The Life of Lucretia Mott.* New York.

Baelen, Jean. 1972. *La Vie de Flora Tristan: Socialisme et féminisme au XIXe siècle.* Paris.

Baker, Keith Michael. 1975. *Condorcet, from Natural Philosophy to Social Mathematics.* Chicago.

Balayé, Simone. 1979. *Madame de Staël, lumières et liberté.* Paris.

Balde, Jean [Jeanne Allemane]. 1921. "Napoléon et l'éducation des filles (Souvenirs sur Madame Campan)," *Revue Hebdomadaire,* 30, no. 34 (20 Aug.), 333-51.

Bamberger, Joan. 1974. "The Myth of Matriarchy: Why Men Rule in Primitive Society," in *Women, Culture, and Society,* ed. Michelle Rosaldo and Louise Lamphere. Stanford, Calif.

Banks, J. A., and Olive Banks. 1964. *Feminism and Family Planning in Victorian England.* New York.

Banner, Lois W. 1980. *Elizabeth Cady Stanton: A Radical for Woman's Rights.* Boston.

Barker-Benfield, G. J. 1976. *The Horrors of the Half-Known Life: Male Attitudes Toward Women and Sexuality in Nineteenth-Century America.* New York.

Barrow, Margaret. 1981. *Women 1870-1928, A Select Guide to Printed and Archival Sources in the United Kingdom.* London and New York.

Basch, Françoise. 1974. *Relative Creatures: Victorian Women in Society and the Novel.* New York.

Basch, Norma. 1979. "Invisible Women: The Legal Fiction of Marital Unity in Nineteenth-Century America," *Feminist Studies,* 5, no. 2 (Summer), 346-66.

Bascou-Bance, P. 1972. "La Première femme bachelière: Julie Daubié," *Bulletin de l'Association Guillaume Budé,* 4th ser., no. 1 (Mar. 1972), 107-13.

Bauer, Carol, and Lawrence Ritt. 1979. *Free and Ennobled: Source Readings in the Development of Victorian Feminism.* Oxford and New York.

Bayle, Francis. 1945. *Les Idées politiques de Joseph de Maistre.* Paris.

Beard, Mary R. 1946. *Woman as Force in History.* New York. Reprint, 1971.

Beecher, Jonathan, and Richard Bienvenu, eds. 1971. *The Utopian Vision of Charles Fourier.* Boston.

Bell, Enid Hester Chataway Moberly. 1953. *Storming the Citadel: The Rise of the Woman Doctor.* London.

Bell, Susan Groag. 1980. *Women from the Greeks to the French Revolution: An Historical Anthology.* Stanford, Calif. Originally published in 1973.

———. 1981. "The Green Lawns of Newnham," *University Publishing,* 2 (Spring), 15-24.

———, and Karen M. Offen. Forthcoming. "Woman Not Inferior to Man: The French-English Connection."

Berg, Karin Westman. 1962. *C. J. L. Almqvists kvinnouppfattning.* Göteborg.

Berkin, Carol R., and Clara M. Lovett, eds., 1980. *Women, War, and Revolution.* New York.

Berlin, Isaiah. 1963. *Karl Marx: His Life and Environment.* 3rd ed. Oxford and New York.

Bertocci, Philip A. 1978. *Jules Simon: Republican Anticlericalism and Cultural Politics in France, 1848-1886.* Columbia, Mo.

Bettelheim, Bruno. 1962. "The Problem of Generations," *Daedalus* (Winter), 68-96.

Bidelman, Patrick Kay. 1976. "The Politics of French Feminism: Léon Richer and the Ligue Française pour le Droit des Femmes, 1882-1891," *Historical Reflections,* 3, no. 1 (Summer), 93-120.

———. 1977. "Maria Deraismes, Léon Richer, and the Founding of the French

Feminist Movement, 1866-1878," *Third Republic/Troisième République*, nos. 3-4 (Spring/Fall), 20-73.

———. 1982. *Pariahs Stand Up! The Founding of the Liberal Feminist Movement in France, 1858-1889.* Westport, Conn.

Binger, Carl. 1966. *Revolutionary Doctor, Benjamin Rush, 1746-1813.* New York.

Binion, Rudolph. 1968. *Frau Lou: Nietzsche's Wayward Disciple.* Princeton, N.J.

Bishop, Morris. 1962. *Early Cornell, 1865-1900.* Ithaca, N.Y.

Black, Joseph Lawrence. 1979. "Educating Women in Eighteenth-Century Russia," in *Citizens for the Fatherland: Education, Educators, and Pedagogical Ideals in Eighteenth-Century Russia*, ed. J. L. Black. Boulder, Colo.

Blackburn, Helen. 1902. *Woman Suffrage.* London.

Bloch, Jean H. 1979. "Women and the Reform of the Nation," in *Women and Society in 18th Century France: Essays in Honor of J. S. Spink*, ed. Eva Jacobs et al. London and New York.

Bloch, Maurice, and Jean H. Bloch. 1980. "Women and the Dialectics of Nature in Eighteenth-Century French Thought," in *Nature, Culture, and Gender*, ed. Carol MacCormack and Marilyn Strathern. Cambridge, Eng., and New York.

Bloch, Ruth H. 1978a. "American Feminine Ideals in Transition: The Rise of the Moral Mother, 1785-1815," *Feminist Studies*, 4, no. 2 (June), 101-26.

———. 1978b. "Untangling the Roots of Modern Sex Roles: A Survey of Four Centuries of Change," *SIGNS: Journal of Women in Culture and Society*, 4, no. 2 (Winter), 236-52.

Bolster, Richard. 1970. *Stendhal, Balzac et le féminisme romantique.* Paris.

Bonnecase, Julien. 1928. *La Philosophie du Code Napoléon appliquée au droit de famille: Ses destinées dans le droit civil contemporain.* 2d ed. Paris.

Boos, Florence S. 1976. "Catharine Macaulay's *Letters on Education* (1790), An Early Feminist Polemic," University of Michigan *Papers in Women's Studies*, 2, no. 2, 64-78.

———, and William Boos. 1980. "Catharine Macaulay: Historian and Political Reformer," *International Journal of Women's Studies*, 3, no. 1 (Jan.-Feb.), 49-65.

Bostick, Theodora. 1980. "Women's Suffrage, the Press, and the Reform Bill of 1867," *International Journal of Women's Studies*, 3, no. 4: 373-90.

Bouten, Jacob. 1922. *Mary Wollstonecraft and the Beginnings of Female Emancipation in France and England.* Amsterdam.

Boxer, Marilyn Jacoby. 1974. "Foyer or Factory: Working Class Women in Nineteenth-Century France," *Proceedings of the Western Society for French History*, 21 (1975), 192-203.

———. 1975. "Socialism Faces Feminism in France: 1879-1913." Ph.D. dissertation, University of California at Riverside.

———. 1977. "French Socialism, Feminism, and the Family," *Third Republic/ Troisième République*, 3-4 (Spring/Fall), 128-67.

———. 1978. "Socialism Faces Feminism: The Failure of Synthesis in France, 1879-1914," in *Socialist Women*, ed. Marilyn Boxer and Jean H. Quataert. New York.

———, and Jean H. Quataert. 1978. *Socialist Women.* New York.

Bradbrook, M. C. 1976. *Barbara Bodichon, George Eliot, and the Limits of Feminism.* Oxford.

Branca, Patricia. 1975. *Silent Sisterhood: Middle-Class Women in the Victorian Home.* Pittsburgh, Penn.

Brasier, Léon. [1901.] *Histoire des Maisons d'éducation de la légion d'honneur.* Paris.

Braunthal, Julius. 1967. *History of the International.* Vol. I: *1864-1914.* Tr. Henry Collins and Kenneth Mitchell. New York. Originally published in German, 1961.

Bremner, Robert H. 1971. "Josephine Clara Goldmark," in *Notable American Women,* ed. Edward T. James, Janet Wilson James, and Paul S. Boyer. 3 vols., Cambridge, Mass.

Brennan, Teresa, and Carole Pateman. 1979. "'Mere Auxiliaries to the Commonwealth': Women and the Origins of Liberalism," *Political Studies,* 27, no. 2 (June), 183-200.

Briffault, Robert. 1927. *The Mothers; A Study of the Origins of Sentiments and Institutions.* 3 vols. New York. Abridged ed., New York, 1963.

Broad, Charlie Dunbar. 1978. *Kant: An Introduction.* Cambridge, Eng.

Broido, Vera. 1977. *Apostles into Terrorists: Women and the Revolutionary Movement in the Russia of Alexander II.* London and New York.

Brooks, Carol Flora. 1966. "The Early History of the Anti-Contraceptive Laws in Massachusetts and Connecticut," *American Quarterly,* 18, no. 1 (Spring), 3-23.

Bullough, Vern. 1974. *The Subordinate Sex: A History of Attitudes Toward Women.* Baltimore, Md.

———, and Martha Voght. 1973. "Women, Menstruation, and Nineteenth-Century Medicine," *Bulletin of the History of Medicine,* 47, no. 1 (Jan.-Feb.), 66-82.

Burrow, John Wyon. 1966. *Evolution and Society: A Study in Victorian Social Theory.* Cambridge, Eng.

Burstyn, Joan N. 1973. "Education and Sex: The Medical Case Against Higher Education for Women in England, 1870-1900," *Proceedings of the American Philosophical Society,* 117:79-89.

———. 1980. *Victorian Education and the Ideal of Womanhood.* Totowa, N.J.

Burton, Hester. 1949. *Barbara Bodichon, 1827-1891.* London.

Butler, Eliza M. 1926. *The Saint-Simonian Religion in Germany: A Study of the Young German Movement.* Cambridge, Eng.

Calder, Jenni. 1976. *Women and Marriage in Victorian Fiction.* New York.

Calo, Jeanne. 1975. *La Création de la femme chez Michelet.* Paris.

Campbell, Joseph. 1967. Introduction to J. J. Bachofen, *Myth, Religion, and Mother Right.* Princeton, N.J.

Campbell, Theophilia Carlile. 1899. *The Battle of the Press, as Told in the Story of the Life of Richard Carlile.* London.

Cate, Curtis. 1975. *George Sand.* Boston.

Cazamian, Louis. 1973. *The Social Novel in England, 1830-1850: Dickens, Disraeli, Mrs. Gaskell, Kingsley.* Tr. Marin Fido. London and Boston.

Charléty, Sebastian-Camille-Gustave. 1931. *Histoire du Saint-Simonisme.* Paris. Reprint, 1964.

Charlton, D. G. 1963. *Secular Religion in France, 1815-1870.* Oxford.

Chaudhuri, Nupur. 1975. "Feminism of Olympe de Gouges." Paper presented at the 1975 Conference of Women Historians of the Midwest.

Chodorow, Nancy. 1978. *The Reproduction of Mothering.* Berkeley and Los Angeles, Calif., and London.

Clements, Frances M. 1973. "The Rights of Women in the Eighteenth-Century Novel," *Enlightenment Essays,* 4, nos. 3-4 (Fall/Winter), 63-70.

Clinton, Katherine B. 1975. "Femme et Philosophe: Enlightenment Origins of Feminism," *Eighteenth-Century Studies*, 8, no. 3 (Spring), 283-99.

Clough, Blanche Athena. 1903. *A Memoir of Anne Jemima Clough, First Principal of Newnham College, Cambridge, by her Niece*. 2d ed. London.

Commons, John R., and Helen L. Sumner, eds. 1910-11. *Documentary History of American Industrial Society*. VI: *Labor Movement, 1820-1840*, pt. 2. Cleveland.

Conable, Charlotte Williams. 1977. *Women at Cornell: The Myth of Equal Education*. Ithaca, N.Y., and London.

Conrad, Susan Phinney. 1976. *Perish the Thought: Intellectual Women in Romantic America, 1830-1860*. New York.

Coppa, Frank J. 1979. *Pope Pius IX: Crusader in a Secular Age*. Boston.

Cornwallis, Caroline Frances. 1864. *Selections from the Letters of Caroline Frances Cornwallis*, ed. M. C. Power. London.

Cott, Nancy L. 1977. *The Bonds of Sisterhood: Women's Sphere in New England, 1780-1835*. New Haven, Conn.

Cromwell, Otelia. 1958. *Lucretia Mott*. Cambridge, Mass. Reprint, 1971.

Cross, Barbara M., ed. 1965. *The Educated Woman in America: Selected Writings of Catharine Beecher, Margaret Fuller, and M. Carey Thomas*. New York.

Cuvillier, Armand. 1954. *Un Journal d'ouvriers: "L'Atelier," 1840-1850*. Paris.

Dahl, Kathleen. 1975. "The Feminist-Literary Movement in 19th-Century Scandinavia." Unpublished manuscript.

Darnton, Robert. 1977. *The Business of Enlightenment: A Publishing History of the 'Encyclopédie,' 1775-1880*. Cambridge, Mass.

Darrow, Margaret. 1979. "French Noblewomen and the New Domesticity, 1750-1850," *Feminist Studies*, 5, no. 1 (Spring), 41-65.

Davidoff, Lenore. 1973. *The Best Circles: Society, Etiquette, and the Season*. London.

————, Jean L'Esperance, and Howard Newby. 1976. "Landscape with Figures: Home and Community in English Society," in *The Rights and Wrongs of Women*, ed. Juliet Mitchell and Ann Oakley. London.

Davis Natalie Z. 1975. *Society and Culture in Early Modern France*. Stanford, Calif. Esp. ch. 3, "City Women and Religious Change," and ch. 5, "Women on Top."

————. 1980. "Gender and Genre: Women As Historical Writers 1400-1820," in *Beyond Their Sex: Learned Women of the European Past*, ed. Patricia H. Labalme. New York.

Degler, Carl N. 1974. "What Ought To Be and What Was: Women's Sexuality in the Nineteenth Century," *American Historical Review*, 79, no. 5 (Dec.), 1467-90.

————. 1980. *At Odds: Women and the Family in America from the Revolution to the Present*. Oxford and New York.

Delmar, Rosalind. 1976. "Looking Again at Engels's *Origin of the Family, Private Property, and the State*," in *The Rights and Wrongs of Women*, ed. Juliet Mitchell and Ann Oakley. London.

Deniel, Raymond. 1965. *Une Image de la famille et de la société sous la Restauration (1815-1830): Étude de la presse catholique*. Paris.

Desforges, Jacques. 1954. "La Loi Naquet," in *Renouveau des idées sur la famille*, ed. Robert Prigent. Paris.

Devance, Louis. 1977. "Le Féminisme pendant la Révolution française," *Annales Historiques de la Révolution Française*, no. 229 (Jul.-Sept.), 341-76.

Digby, Kenelm Henry. 1845-47. *Mores Catholici: or Ages of Faith.* 3 vols. London. Originally published in 1831-42.

Ditzion, Sidney. 1955. *Marriage, Morals, and Sex in America: A History of Ideas.* New York. Expanded ed., 1978.

Doheny, William J., and Joseph P. Kelly. 1954. *Papal Documents on Mary.* Milwaukee, Wisc.

Domergue, Gabriel. 1902. "Proudhon et le féminisme," *La Quinzaine,* 16 Jan. 1902, pp. 222-35.

Donnison, Jean. 1976. "Medical Women and Lady Midwives, A Case Study in Medical and Feminist Politics," *Women's Studies,* 3, no. 3: 229-50.

Dornemann, Luise. 1973. *Clara Zetkin: Leben und Wirken.* Rev. ed. Berlin.

Douglas, Ann. 1977. *The Feminization of American Culture.* New York.

Douglas, Jane Dempsey. 1974. "Women and the Continental Reformation," in *Religion and Sexism; Images of Woman in the Jewish and Christian Tradition,* ed. Rosemary Radford Ruether. New York.

Drachkovich, Milorad, ed. 1966. *The Revolutionary Internationals, 1864-1943.* Stanford, Calif.

Draper, Hal, and Anne G. Kipow. 1976. "Marxist Women versus Bourgeois Feminism," in *The Socialist Register 1976,* ed. John Saville and Ralph Miliband. London.

Droz, Jacques. 1966. "Religious Aspects of the Revolutions of 1848 in Europe," in *French Society and Culture Since the Old Regime,* ed. Evelyn M. Acomb and Marvin L. Brown, Jr. New York.

DuBois, Ellen Carol. 1975. "The Radicalism of the Woman Suffrage Movement: Notes Toward the Reconstruction of Nineteenth-Century Feminism," *Feminist Studies,* 3, no. 1-2 (Fall), 63-71.

———. 1978. *Feminism and Suffrage: The Emergence of an Independent Women's Movement in America, 1848-1869.* Ithaca, N.Y.

———, ed. 1981. *Elizabeth Cady Stanton and Susan B. Anthony: Correspondence, Writings, Speeches.* New York.

Duffin, Lorna. 1978. "Prisoners of Progress: Women and Evolution," in *The Nineteenth-Century Woman, Her Cultural and Physical World,* ed. Sara Delamont and Lorna Duffin. London.

Dufrancatel, Christiane. 1977. "Les Amants de la liberté? Strategies de femme, luttes républicaines, luttes ouvrières," *Les Révoltes Logiques,* no. 5 (Spring/Summer), 61-93.

Duhet, Paule Marie. 1971. *Les Femmes et la Révolution, 1789-1794.* Paris.

Duncan, Carol. 1982. "Happy Mothers and Other New Ideas in Eighteenth-Century French Art," in *Feminism and Art History; Questioning the Litany,* ed. Norma Broude and Mary D. Garrard. New York. Originally published in *The Art Bulletin,* 55 (Dec. 1973), 570-83.

Duveau, Georges. 1969. *1848: The Making of a Revolution.* New York.

Dzeh-Djen, Li. 1934. *La Presse féministe en France de 1869 à 1914.* Paris.

Edwards, Stewart, ed. 1969. *Selected Writings of Pierre-Joseph Proudhon.* Princeton, N.J.

Ehrenreich, Barbara, and Deirdre English. 1978. *For Her Own Good: 150 Years of the Experts' Advice to Women.* Garden City, N.Y.

Eichner, Hans. 1970. *Friedrich Schlegel.* New York.

Eisenstein, Zillah R. 1980. *The Radical Future of Liberal Feminism.* New York.

Elhadad, Lydia. 1977. "Femmes prénommées: Les proletaires Saint-Simoniennes rédactrices de 'La Femme Libre' 1832-1834," *Les Révoltes Logiques,* no. 4 (Winter), 62-88, and no. 5 (Spring/Summer), 29-60.

Engel, Barbara Alpern, and Clifford N. Rosenthal. 1975. *Five Sisters: Women Against the Tsar*. New York.

Evans, David-Owen. 1923. *Le Drame moderne à l'époque romantique (1827-1850)*. Paris.

———. 1930. *Le Roman social sous la Monarchie de Juillet*. Paris.

———. 1948. *Le Socialisme romantique: Pierre Leroux et ses contemporains*. Paris.

———. 1951. *Social Romanticism in France, 1830-1848*. Oxford.

Evans, Richard J. 1977. *The Feminists: Women's Emancipation Movements in Europe, America, and Australasia, 1840-1920*. London and New York.

Faillie, Marie-Henriette. 1960. *La Femme et le Code civil dans "La Comédie Humaine" d'Honoré de Balzac*. Paris.

Fauchery, Pierre. 1972. *La Destinée féminine dans le roman européen du XVIIIe siècle, 1713-1807*. Paris.

Feaver, George. 1969. *From Status to Contract: A Biography of Sir Henry Maine, 1822-1888*. London.

Fee, Elizabeth. 1974. "The Sexual Politics of Victorian Social Anthropology," in *Clio's Consciousness Raised*, ed. Mary Hartman and Lois W. Banner. New York.

———. 1976. "Science and the Woman Problem: Historical Perspectives," in *Sex Differences: Social and Biological Perspectives*, ed. Michael S. Teitelbaum. Garden City, N.Y.

———, and Michael Wallace. 1979. "The History and Politics of Birth Control: A Review Essay," *Feminist Studies*, 5, no. 1 (Spring), 201-15.

Ferguson, Moira, ed. Forthcoming. *First Feminists*. Old Westbury, N.Y.

Field, Vena. 1931. *Constantia; A Study of the Life and Works of Judith Sargent Murray, 1751-1820*. Orono, Me.

Figes, Eva. 1970. *Patriarchal Attitudes*. London and Greenwich, Conn.

Fisher, Marguerite. 1975. "Eighteenth-Century Theorists of Women's Liberation," in *"Remember the Ladies:" New Perspectives on Women in American History. Essays in Honor of Nelson Manfred Blake*, ed. Carol C. R. George. Syracuse, N.Y.

Flandrin, Jean-Louis. 1979. *Families in Former Times: Kinship, Household, and Sexuality*. Cambridge, Eng. Originally published in Paris, 1975.

Fletcher, Sheila. 1980. *Feminists and Bureaucrats: A Study in the Development of Girls' Education in the 19th Century*. Cambridge, Eng., and New York.

Flexner, Eleanor. 1959. *Century of Struggle: The Woman's Rights Movement in the United States*. Cambridge, Mass. New ed., 1972.

———. 1972. *Mary Wollstonecraft*. New York.

Foner, Philip S. 1979-80. *Women and the American Labor Movement: From Colonial Times to the Eve of World War I*. 2 vols. New York.

Forbes, Thomas R. 1966. *The Midwife and the Witch*. New Haven and London.

Fraisse, Geneviève. 1975. "Les Femmes libres de 48, moralisme et féminisme," *Les Révoltes Logiques*, no. 1 (Winter): 23-50.

Fredeman, William E. 1974. "Emily Faithful and the Victoria Press: An Experiment in Sociological Bibliography," *The Library*, 29, no. 2 (June), 139-64.

Freymond, Jacques, ed. 1962. *La Première Internationale: recueil de documents*. 2 vols. Geneva.

Fritz, Paul, and Richard Morton, eds. 1976. *Woman in the 18th Century and Other Essays*. Toronto and Sarasota.

Fryer, Peter. 1965. *The Birth Controllers*. London.

Fulford, Roger. 1956. *Votes for Women: The Story of a Struggle*. London.

Galgano, Michael. 1979. "Anna Doyle Wheeler," in *Biographical Dictionary of Modern British Radicals*, I, ed. Joseph O. Baylen and Norbert J. Gossman. Brighton, Eng., and Atlantic Highlands, N.J.

Gardner, Elizabeth J. 1979. "The *Philosophes* and Women: Sensationalism and Sentiment," in *Women and Society in 18th-Century France*, ed. Eva Jacobs et al. London and New York.

Gautherot, Gustave. 1922. *Un Demi-siècle de défense nationale et religieuse: Émile Keller, 1828-1909*. Paris.

Gautier, Paul. 1903. *Madame de Staël et Napoléon*. Paris.

Gay, Peter. 1966. *The Enlightenment: An Interpretation*. Vol. I: *The Rise of Modern Paganism*. New York.

———. 1969. *The Enlightenment: An Interpretation*. Vol. II: *The Science of Freedom*. New York.

———. 1973. *The Enlightenment: A Comprehensive Anthology*. New York.

Geffriand-Rosso, Jeannette. 1977. *Montesquieu et la fémininité*. Pisa.

Gelbart, Nina. 1980. "The *Journal des Dames* and Its Women Editors." Paper presented at the eleventh annual meeting of the American Society for Eighteenth-Century Studies, San Francisco.

Gennari, Geneviève. 1947. *Le Premier Voyage de Mme de Staël en Italie, et la génèse de Corinne*. Paris.

———. 1967. *Simone de Beauvoir*. Rev. ed. Paris.

George, Margaret. 1970. *One Woman's "Situation": A Study of Mary Wollstonecraft*. Urbana, Ill.

Gerhard, Ute, Elisabeth Hannover-Drück, and Romina Schmitter. 1980. "*Dem Reich der Freiheit werb' ich Bürgerinnen": Die Frauen-Zeitung von Louise Otto*. Frankfurt-am-Main.

Gérin, Winifred. 1967. *Charlotte Brontë: The Evolution of Genius*. Oxford and New York.

———. 1976. *Elizabeth Gaskell: A Biography*. Oxford and New York.

Gilbert, Sandra M., and Susan Gubar. 1980. *The Madwoman in the Attic*. New Haven and London.

Goodwin, Albert. 1979. *The Friends of Liberty: The English Democratic Movement in the Age of the French Revolution*. London and Cambridge, Mass.

Gordon, Ann D. 1979. "The Young Ladies' Academy of Philadelphia," in *Women of America*, ed. Carol R. Berkin and Mary Beth Norton. Boston.

Gordon, Linda. 1976. *Woman's Body, Woman's Right: A Social History of Birth Control in America*. New York.

Gould, Stephen Jay. 1981. *The Mismeasure of Man*. New York.

Graham, Ruth. 1976. "Rousseau's Sexism Revolutionized," in *Woman in the 18th Century and Other Essays*, ed. Paul Fritz and Richard Morton. Toronto and Sarasota.

———. 1977. "Loaves and Liberty: Women in the French Revolution," in *Becoming Visible: Women in European History*, ed. Renate Bridenthal and Claudia Koonz. Boston.

Graveson, R. H., and F. R. Crane. 1957. *A Century of Family Law, 1857-1957*. London.

Gravier, Maurice. 1965. "Camilla Collett et la France," *Scandinavica*, 4:38-51.

Green, Elizabeth Alden. 1979. *Mary Lyon and Mount Holyoke: Opening the Gates*. Hanover, N.H.

Greene, Dana, ed. 1980. *Lucretia Mott: Her Complete Speeches and Sermons*. Lewiston, N.Y.

Greene, John C. 1959. "Biology and Social Theory in the Nineteenth Century:

Auguste Comte and Herbert Spencer," in *Critical Problems in the History of Science*, ed. Marshall Clagett. Madison, Wisc.

Griffith, Gwilym O. 1932. *Mazzini: Prophet of Modern Europe*. London.

Gruber, S. 1967. *Das Vorspiel zur Dogmatisierung des unbefleckten Empfängnis Mariens in Deutschland (1849-1854)*. Dissertation, University of Erlangen.

Grylls, Rosalie Glynn. 1948. *Queen's College, 1848-1948*. London.

Gutwirth, Madelyn. 1971. "Madame de Staël, Rousseau, and the Woman Question," *Proceedings of the Modern Language Association*, 86 (Jan.), 100-109.

————. 1978. *Madame de Staël, Novelist: The Emergence of the Artist as Woman*. Urbana, Ill.

Hackett, Amy Kathleen. 1976. "The Politics of Feminism in Wilhelmine Germany 1890-1918." 2 vols. Ph.D. dissertation, Columbia University.

Haines, Barbara. 1978. "The Interrelations Between Social, Biological, and Medical Thought, 1750-1850: Saint-Simon and Comte," *British Journal for the History of Science*, 11, pt. 1, no. 37 (Mar.), 19-35.

Halévy, Daniel. 1955. *Le Mariage de Proudhon*. Paris.

Halévy, Elie. 1928. *The Growth of Philosophic Radicalism*. Tr. M. Morris. New York. New ed., London, 1972.

Hall, Constance M. 1971. *The Sociology of P.-J. Proudhon*. New York.

Haller, John S. Jr., and Robin M. Haller. 1974. *The Physician and Sexuality in Victorian America*. Urbana, Ill.

Hamilton, Mary Agnes. 1936. *Newnham: An Informal Biography*. London.

Hammond, J. L. Le Breton. 1903. *Charles James Fox, A Political Study*. London.

Harrison, Brian. 1978. *Separate Spheres: The Opposition to Women's Suffrage in Britain*. London and New York.

Hartmann, Heidi I. 1981. "The Family as Locus of Gender, Class, and Political Struggle: The Example of Housework," *SIGNS: Journal of Women in Culture and Society*, 6, no. 3 (Spring), 366-95.

Harvey, Joy. 1982. "Les Sélections: A Study of Race, Social Evolution, and Social Consequences in 19th-Century French Anthropology." Paper presented at the Society for French Historical Studies, New York.

Hauff, Lilly. 1928. *Der Lette-Verein in der Geschichte der Frauenbewegung*. Berlin.

Hausen, Karin. 1981. "Family and Role Division: The Polarization of Sexual Stereotypes in the 19th-Century—An Aspect of the Dissociation of Work and Family Life," in *The German Family: Essays on the Social History of the Family in 19th- and 20th-Century Germany*, ed. Richard J. Evans and W. R. Lee. London and New York.

Hayden, Dolores. 1981. *The Grand Domestic Revolution: A History of Feminist Designs for American Homes, Neighborhoods, and Cities*. Cambridge, Mass., and London.

Hayek, F. A., ed. 1951. *John Stuart Mill and Harriet Taylor: Their Correspondence and Subsequent Marriage*. Chicago.

————. 1952. *The Counter-Revolution of Science: Studies on the Abuse of Reason*. Glencoe, Ill. Reprint, 1979.

Hays, H. R. 1964. *The Dangerous Sex: The Myth of Feminine Evil*. New York.

Hazard, Paul. 1963a. *The European Mind, 1680-1715*. Cleveland, Ohio. Originally published in French, 1935.

————. 1963b. *European Thought in the Eighteenth Century: From Montesquieu to Lessing*. Cleveland, Ohio.

Hedman, Edwin R. 1954. "Early French Feminism from the Eighteenth Century to 1848." Ph.D. dissertation, New York University.

Heilbrun, Carolyn. 1974. *Toward a Recognition of Androgyny*. New York.

Held, Virginia. 1971. "Justice and Harriet Taylor," *The Nation*, 25 October, pp. 405-6.

Hellerstein, Erna Olafson. 1976. "Secular Rules and Secular Sanctions: The Regulation of Female Sexuality in Nineteenth-Century France." Paper presented at the Third Berkshire Conference on the History of Women, Bryn Mawr College.

———. 1980. "Women, Social Order, and the City: Rules for French Ladies, 1830-1870." Ph.D. dissertation, University of California, Berkeley.

———, Leslie Parker Hume, and Karen M. Offen. 1981. *Victorian Women: A Documentary Account of Women's Lives in Nineteenth-Century England, France, and the United States*. Stanford, Calif.

Henderson, W. O., and W. H. Chaloner, eds. 1968. Introduction to Friedrich Engels, *The Condition of the Working Class in England*. Stanford, Calif.

Hertz, Deborah. 1978. "Salonières and Literary Women in Late Eighteenth-Century Berlin," *New German Critique*, 14:97-108.

Heymann, Lida Gustava. 1972. *Erlebtes—Erschautes, Deutsche Frauen kämpfen für Freiheit, Recht, und Frieden, 1850-1940*, ed. Margrit Twellmann. Meisenheim-am-Glan.

Himmelfarb, Gertrude. 1968. *Darwin and the Darwinian Revolution*. New York.

———. 1970. "The Other John Stuart Mill," in Himmelfarb, *Victorian Minds*. New York.

———. 1974. *On Liberty and Liberalism: The Case of John Stuart Mill*. New York.

Hine, Ellen McNiven. 1973. "The Woman Question in Early 18th Century French Literature: The Influence of François Poulain de la Barre," *Studies on Voltaire and the 18th Century*, 116:65-79.

Hobhouse, Christopher. 1935. *Charles James Fox*. London.

Hobsbawm, Eric J. 1962. *The Age of Revolution, 1789-1848*. London.

Hoffman, Robert L. 1972. *Revolutionary Justice: The Social and Political Theory of P.-J. Proudhon*. Urbana, Ill.

Hoffmann, Paul. 1978. *La Femme dans la pensée des lumières*. Strasbourg.

Holcombe, Lee. 1973. *Victorian Ladies at Work*. Hamden, Conn.

———. 1977. "Victorian Wives and Property: Reform of the Married Women's Property Law, 1857-1882," in *A Widening Sphere*, ed. Martha Vicinus. Bloomington, Ind.

———. 1982. *Wives and Property: Reform of the Married Women's Property Law in Nineteenth-Century England*. Toronto.

Hollis, Patricia. 1979. *Women in Public, 1850-1900; Documents of the Victorian Women's Movement*. London.

Horowitz, Maryanne Kline. 1976. "Aristotle and Woman," *Journal of the History of Biology*, 9, no. 2 (Fall), 183-213.

Horvath, Sandra Ann. 1975. "Victor Duruy and the Controversy over Secondary Education for Girls," *French Historical Studies*, 9, no. 1 (Spring), 83-104.

Houghton, Walter E. 1957. *The Victorian Frame of Mind, 1830-1870*. New Haven, Conn.

Howard, Judith Jeffrey. 1977. "The Woman Question in Italy, 1861-1880." Ph.D. dissertation, University of Connecticut.

———. 1978. "The Civil Code of 1865 and the Origins of the Feminist Movement in Italy," in *The Italian Immigrant Woman in North America: Proceedings of the 10th Annual Conference of the American Italian Historical Asso-*

ciation and the Canadian Italian Historical Association, ed. Betty Boyd Caroli, Robert F. Harney, and Ledio F. Thomasi. Toronto.

———. 1980. "Patriot Mothers in the Post-Risorgimento: Women After the Italian Revolution," in *Women, War, and Revolution*, ed. Carol R. Berkin and Clara M. Lovett. New York and London.

Hunt, Persis Charles. 1971. "Feminism and Anti-Clericalism Under the Commune," *Massachusetts Review*, 12, no. 3 (Summer), 418-20, 429-31.

Ivray, Jehan d' [Jeanne Fahmy Bey]. 1930. *L'Aventure Saint-Simonienne et les femmes*. Paris.

Jacobs, Eva. 1979. "Diderot and the Education of Girls," in *Woman and Society in 18th-Century France*, ed. Eva Jacobs et al. London and New York.

——— et al. 1979. *Woman and Society in 18th Century France: Essays in Honour of John Stephenson Spink*. London and New York.

Janes, R. M. 1978. "On the Reception of Mary Wollstonecraft's *A Vindication of the Rights of Woman*," *Journal of the History of Ideas*, 39, no. 2 (Apr.-June), 293-302.

Janssen-Jurreit, Marielouise. 1981. *Sexism: The Male Monopoly on History and Thought*. New York.

Jimack, P. D. 1979. "The Paradox of Sophie and Julie: Contemporary Response to Rousseau's Ideal Wife and Ideal Mother," in *Women and Society in 18th Century France*, ed. Eva Jacobs et al. London and New York.

Johansson, Sheila Ryan. 1979. "Demographic Contributions to the History of Victorian Women," in S. Barbara Kanner, ed., *The Women of England from Anglo-Saxon Times to the Present: Interpretative Bibliographical Essays*. Hamden, Conn.

John, Angela V. 1980. *By the Sweat of Their Brow: Women Workers at Victorian Coal Mines*. London.

Johnson, Christopher H. 1974. *Utopian Communism in France: Cabet and the Icarians, 1839-1851*. Ithaca, N.Y.

Johnson, Hubert C. 1975. *Frederick the Great and His Officials*. New Haven, Conn.

Jones, Mary Gwladys. 1952. *Hannah More*. New York. Reprint, 1968.

Jordanova, Ludmilla J. 1980. "Natural Facts: A Historical Perspective on Science and Sexuality," in *Nature, Culture, and Gender*, ed. Carol MacCormack and Marilyn Strathern. Cambridge, Eng.

Kamm, Josephine. 1965. *Hope Deferred, Girls' Education in English History*. London.

Kanner, S. Barbara. 1973. "The Women of England in a Century of Social Change, 1815-1914: A Select Bibliography, Part I," in *Suffer and Be Still: Women in the Victorian Age*, ed. Martha Vicinus, Bloomington, Ind., and London.

———. 1977. "The Women of England in a Century of Social Change, 1815-1914: A Select Bibliography, Part II," in *A Widening Sphere: Changing Roles of Victorian Women*, ed. Martha Vicinus. Bloomington, Ind., and London.

———, ed. 1979. *The Women of England from Anglo-Saxon Times to the Present: Interpretive Bibliographical Essays*. Hamden, Conn., and London.

Kaye, Elaine. 1972. *A History of Queen's College, London*. London.

Kelley, Mary. ed. 1979. *Woman's Being, Woman's Place: Female Identity and Vocation in American History*. Boston.

Kelly-Gadol, Joan. 1977. "Did Women Have A Renaissance?," in *Becoming Visible: Women in European History*, ed. Renate Bridenthal and Claudia Koonz. Boston.

———. 1982. "Early Feminists: Theory and the *Querelle des Femmes*, 1400-

1789," *SIGNS: Journal of Women in Culture and Society*, 8, no. 1 (Autumn), 4-28.

Kent, Christopher. 1978. *Brains and Numbers: Elitism, Comtism, and Democracy in Mid-Victorian England*. Toronto, Can.

Keohane, Nannerl O. 1980a. "'But for Her Sex . . .': The Domestication of Sophie," *Revue de l'Université d'Ottawa*, 49, nos. 3-4: 390-400.

———. 1980b. *Philosophy and the State in France: The Renaissance to the Enlightenment*. Princeton, N.J.

Kerber, Linda K. 1974. "Daughters of Columbia: Educating Women for the Republic, 1789-1805," in *The Hofstadter Aegis: A Memorial*, ed. Stanley Elkins and Eric McKitrick. New York.

———. 1976. "The Republican Mother; Women and the Enlightenment—An American Perspective," *American Quarterly*, 28, no. 2 (Summer), 187-205.

———. 1980. *Women of the Republic: Intellect and Ideology in Revolutionary America*. Chapel Hill, N.C.

Kestenberg-Gladstein, Ruth. 1969. *Neuere Geschichte der Juden in den Böhmischen Ländern, I: Das Zeitalter der Aufklärung, 1780-1830*. Tübingen.

Killham, John. 1958. *Tennyson and the Princess: Reflections of an Age*. London.

Klaus, Patricia Otto. 1979. "Women in the Mirror: Using Novels to Study Victorian Women," in *The Women of England: From Anglo-Saxon Times to the Present: Interpretative Bibliographical Essays*, ed. Barbara Kanner. Hamden, Conn., and London.

Kleinbaum, Abby R. 1977. "Women in the Age of Light," in *Becoming Visible: Women in European History*, ed. Renate Bridenthal and Claudia Koonz. Boston.

Knibiehler, Yvonne. 1976a. "Le Discours médical sur la femme," *Romantisme: Revue du Dix-Neuvième Siècle*, nos. 13-14:41-55.

———. 1976b. "Les Médecins et la 'nature féminine' au temps du Code Civil," *Annales: Economies, Sociétés, Civilisations*, 31, no. 4 (July-Aug.), 824-45.

———, and Catherine Fouquet, 1980. *L'Histoire des mères du Moyen Age à nos jours*. Paris.

Koch, C. F. 1862. "Kommentar" to C. F. Koch, ed., *Allegemeines Landrecht für die Preussischen Staaten*. Berlin.

Koepke, Wulf. 1979. "Die emanzipierte Frau in der Goethezeit und ihre Darstellung in der Literatur," in *Die Frau als Heldin und Autorin. Neue kritische Aufsätze zur deutschen Literatur*, ed. Wolfgang Paulsen. Bern.

Kornberg, Jacques. 1974. "Feminism and the Liberal Dialectic: John Stuart Mill on Women's Rights," *Historical Papers, 1974* (Canadian Historical Association), pp. 37-63.

Korsmeyer, Carolyn W. 1976. "Reason and Morals in the Early Feminist Movement: Mary Wollstonecraft," in *Women and Philosophy: Toward a Theory of Liberation*, ed. Carol C. Gould and Marx W. Wartofsky. New York.

Lacour, Léopold. 1900. *Trois Femmes de la Révolution: Olympe de Gouges, Théroigne de Méricourt, Rose Lacombe*. Paris.

Landes, David S. 1969. *The Unbound Prometheus: Technological Change and Industrial Development in Western Europe from 1750 to the Present*. Cambridge, Eng.

Lane, Ann J. 1976. "Women in Society: A Critique of Frederick Engels," in *Liberating Women's History*, ed. Berenice Carroll. Urbana, Ill.

Langer, William L. 1969. *Political and Social Upheaval, 1832-1852*. New York.

Lasch, Christopher. 1977. *Haven in a Heartless World: The Family Besieged*. New York.

Leach, William R. 1980. *True Love and Perfect Union: The Feminist Reform of Sex and Society.* New York.

Leacock, Eleanor Burke. 1972. Introduction to F. Engels, *The Origin of the Family, Private Property, and the State.* New York.

———. 1977. "Women in Egalitarian Societies," in *Becoming Visible,* ed. Renate Bridenthal and Claudia Koonz. Boston.

Lebrun, Richard. 1965. *Throne and Altar: The Political and Religious Thought of Joseph de Maistre.* Ottawa.

Lederer, Wolfgang. 1968. *The Fear of Women.* New York.

LeGates, Marlene. 1976. "The Cult of Womanhood in Eighteenth-Century Thought," *Eighteenth-Century Studies,* 10, no. 1 (Fall), 21-39.

Legrand, Louis. 1961. *L'Influence du positivisme dans l'oeuvre scholaire de Jules Ferry.* Paris.

Lehmann, Andrée. 1924. *De la Réglementation légale du travail féminin (Etude de législation comparée).* Paris.

Lenzer, Gertrud, ed. 1975. *Auguste Comte and Positivism: The Essential Writings.* New York.

Lerner, Gerda. 1967. *The Grimké Sisters from South Carolina: Pioneers for Women's Rights and Abolition.* New York.

———. 1979. *The Majority Finds Its Past.* Oxford.

L'Esperance, Jean. 1977. "Doctors and Women in Nineteenth Century Society: Sexuality and Role," in *Health Care and Popular Medicine in Nineteenth Century England,* ed. John Woodward and David Richards. New York.

Le Van Kim. 1926. *Féminisme et travail féminin dans les doctrines et dans les faits.* Paris.

Levy, Darlene, Harriet Applewhite, and Mary Durham Johnson. 1979. *Women in Revolutionary Paris.* Urbana, Ill.

Lively, Jack, ed. 1971. *The Works of Joseph de Maistre.* New York.

Lochhead, Marion. 1961. *Elizabeth Rigby, Lady Eastlake.* London.

Lombard, Charles M. 1976. *Joseph de Maistre.* Boston.

Lougee, Carolyn C. 1976. *Le Paradis des Femmes: Women, Salons, and Social Stratification in Seventeenth-Century France.* Princeton, N.J.

Lougee, Robert W. 1972. *Midcentury Revolution, 1848: Society and Revolution in France and Germany.* Lexington, Mass.

Lough, John. 1960. "Louis, Chevalier de Jaucourt (1704-1780), A Biographical Sketch," in *Essays Presented to C. M. Girdlestone,* ed. E. T. Dubois et al. Durham, Eng.

Lubin, Georges. 1973. "George Sand et la révolte des femmes contre les institutions," *Roman et Societé* (Colloque, Société d'histoire littéraire de la France, 1971), pp. 42-50. Paris.

Lumpkin, Katharine DuPré. 1974. *The Emancipation of Angelina Grimké.* Chapel Hill, N.C.

Lutz, Alma. 1940. *Created Equal: A Biography of Elizabeth Cady Stanton.* New York. Reprint, 1974.

McDougall, Mary Lynn. 1977. "Working Class Women During the Industrial Revolution, 1780-1914," in *Becoming Visible,* ed. Renate Bridenthal and Claudia Koonz. Boston.

MacKinnon, Catharine A. 1982. "Feminism, Marxism, Method, and the State: An Agenda for Theory," *SIGNS: Journal of Women in Culture and Society,* 7, no. 3 (Spring), 515-44.

McLaren, Angus. 1978a. "Abortion in France: Women and the Regulation of

Family Size, 1800-1914," *French Historical Studies*, 10, no. 3 (Spring), 461-85.

———. 1978b. *Birth Control in Nineteenth-Century England*. London.

McLellan, David. 1974. *Karl Marx, His Life and Thought*. New York.

MacPherson, C. B. 1962. *The Political Theory of Possessive Individualism*. Oxford.

McPherson, James M. 1965. "Abolitionists, Woman Suffrage, and the Negro, 1865-1869," *Mid-America*, 47, no. 1 (Jan.), 40-47.

McWilliams-Tullberg, Rita. 1975. *Women at Cambridge—A Men's University, Though of a Mixed Type*. London.

———. 1977. "Women and Degrees at Cambridge University, 1862-1897," in *A Widening Sphere: Changing Roles of Victorian Women*, ed. Martha Vicinus. Bloomington, Ind., and London.

Magellon, Comtesse de. 1898. "Le Féminisme. Victoire Daubié," *Nouvelle Revue*, 15 Aug. 1898, pp. 677-95.

Magnus-Hausen, Frances. 1922. "Ziel und Weg in der deutschen Frauenbewegung des XIX. Jahrhunderts," in *Deutscher Staat und deutsche Parteien: Beiträge zur deutschen Partei- und Ideensgeschichte, Friedrich Meinecke zum 60. Geburtstag dargebracht*, etc., ed. Paul Wentzcke, Munich. Reprint, Aalen, 1973.

Maitron, Jean. 1954. "Les Penseurs sociaux et la famille dans la première moitié du XIXe siècle," in *Renouveau des idées sur la famille*, ed. Robert Prigent. Paris.

Malia, Martin. 1961. "Realism in Love: George Sand," in Malia, *Alexander Herzen and the Birth of Russian Socialism 1812-1855*, ch. 11. Cambridge, Mass.

Mallet, Sylvie. 1980. "Tribune des femmes: Une éducation pour l'indépendance économique (1830)," *Romantisme: Revue du dix-neuvième siècle*, no. 28-29, pp. 203-12.

Malmgreen, Gail. 1982. "Anne Knight and the Radical Sub-culture," *Quaker History*, 71, no. 2 (Fall), 100-113.

Manton, Jo. 1965. *Elizabeth Garrett Anderson*. London.

Manuel, Frank E. 1962. *The Prophets of Paris: Turgot, Condorcet, Saint-Simon, Fourier, Comte*. Cambridge, Mass.

Marandon, Sylvaine. 1967. *L'Image de la France dans l'Angleterre victorienne, 1848-1900*. Paris.

Marcus, Steven. 1964. *The Other Victorians: A Study of Sexuality and Pornography in Mid-Nineteenth Century England*. New York. New ed., 1975.

———. 1974. *Engels, Manchester, and the Working Class*. New York.

Marreco, Anne. 1948. *Caroline Norton*. London.

Masters, R. E. L., and Eduard Lea. 1964. *The Anti-Sex: The Belief in the Natural Inferiority of Women. Studies in Male Frustration and Sexual Conflict*. New York.

Maurice, J. F. 1884. *Life of F. D. Maurice*. 2 vols. London.

May, Georges Claude. 1963. "Féminisme et roman," in *Le Dilemme du roman au XVIIIe siècle; étude sur les rapports du roman et de la critique, 1715-1761*. New York and Paris.

May, Henry F. 1976. *The Enlightenment in America*. New York.

Mayeur, Françoise. 1977. *L'Enseignement secondaire des jeunes filles sous la Troisième République*. Paris.

———, and Jacques Gadille, eds. 1980. *Education et images de la femme chrétienne en France au début du XXème siècle*. Lyons.

Mazlish, Bruce. 1975. *James and John Stuart Mill: Father and Son in the Nineteenth Century*. New York.

Meijer, Jan Marinus. 1955. *Knowledge and Evolution: The Russian Colony in Zurich (1870-1873)—A Contribution to the Study of Russian Populism.* Assen, The Netherlands.

Melder, Keith E. 1977. *Beginnings of Sisterhood: The American Woman's Rights Movement, 1800-1850.* New York.

Merchant, Carolyn. 1980. *The Death of Nature: A Feminist Reappraisal of the Scientific Revolution.* New York.

Midelfort, H. C. Erik. 1972. *Witch-Hunting in Southwestern Germany, 1562-1684: The Social and Intellectual Foundations.* Stanford, Calif.

Millett, Kate. 1969. *Sexual Politics.* New York.

———. 1972. "The Debate over Women: Ruskin vs. Mill," in *Suffer and Be Still: Women in the Victorian Age,* ed. Martha Vicinus. Bloomington, Ind., and London.

Mitchell, Juliet. 1966. "Women: The Longest Revolution," *New Left Review,* 40 (Dec.), 11-37.

———. 1971. *Woman's Estate.* New York.

———. 1976. "Women and Equality," in *The Rights and Wrongs of Women,* ed. Juliet Mitchell and Ann Oakley. London.

Mohr, James C. 1978. *Abortion in America.* Oxford and New York.

Mommsen, Katharina. 1983a. "Goethe as a Precursor of Women's Emancipation," *Goethe Sesquicentennial, 1832-1982.* Davis, Calif.

———. 1983b. "Goethe's View of Women—A Modern Perspective," in *Goethe in the Twentieth Century: An Intercultural and Interdisciplinary Inquiry into His Works, His World and the Impact of His Views.* Hempstead, N.Y.

Monin, Hippolyte. 1899-1900. "George Sand et la République de Février 1848," *La Révolution Française,* 38 (Nov.-Dec. 1899), 428-48, 543-61, and 39 (Jan.-Feb. 1900), 53-64, 167-85.

Monter, E. William. 1976. *Witchcraft in France and Switzerland.* Ithaca, N.Y.

———. 1977. "The Pedestal and the Stake: Courtly Love and Witchcraft," in *Becoming Visible,* ed. Renate Bridenthal and Claudia Koonz. Boston.

Moon, Parker T. 1921. *The Labor Problem and the Social Catholic Movement in France: A Study in the History of Social Politics.* New York.

Moon, S. Joan. 1976a. "Social Relationship and Sexual Liberation Among the Utopian Socialists." Paper delivered at the Third Berkshire Conference on the History of Women, Bryn Mawr College.

———. 1976b. "The Utopian Socialist Sources of French Feminism: The Movement for Women's Rights During the Second Republic." Paper presented at the American Historical Association, Washington, D.C.

———. 1977. "The Saint-Simonian Association of Working-Class Women," *Proceedings of the Western Society for French History,* 5:274-80.

———. 1978a. "Feminism and Socialism: The Utopian Synthesis of Flora Tristan," in *Socialist Women: European Socialist Feminism in the Nineteenth and Early Twentieth Centuries,* ed. Marilyn J. Boxer and Jean H. Quataert. New York.

———. 1978b. "The Saint-Simoniennes and the Moral Revolution," *Proceedings of the Consortium on Revolutionary Europe, 1976.* Athens, Ga.

Morcos, Saad. 1962. *Juliette Adam.* Cairo, Egypt.

Morris, Madeleine F. 1979. *Le Chevalier de Jaucourt, un ami de la terre (1704-1780).* Geneva, Switzerland.

Morris, Richard B. 1930. "Women's Rights in Early American Law," in Morris, *Studies in the History of American Law.* New York.

Mosedale, Susan Sleeth. 1978. "Science Corrupted: Victorian Biologists Consider 'The Woman Question,'" *Journal of the History of Biology*, 11, no. 1 (Spring), 1-55.

Moses, Claire Goldberg. 1978. "The Evolution of Feminist Thought in France, 1829-1889." Ph.D. dissertation, George Washington University.

————. 1982. "Saint-Simonian Men/Saint-Simonian Women: The Transformation of Feminist Thought in 1830s France," *Journal of Modern History*, 54, no. 2 (June), 240-67.

Moss, Bernard H. 1976. *The Origins of the French Labor Movement*. Berkeley and Los Angeles, Calif.

Moulinié, Henri. 1916. *De Bonald: La Vie, la carrière politique, la doctrine*. Paris.

Mozzoni, Anna Maria. 1975. *La liberazione delle donna*, ed. Franca Pieroni-Bortolotti. Milan.

Myers, Mitzi. 1977. "Politics from the Outside: Mary Wollstonecraft's First *Vindication*," in *Studies in Eighteenth-Century Culture*, VI, ed. Ronald C. Rosbottom. Madison, Wisc.

————. 1982. "Reform or Ruin: A Revolution in Female Manners," *Studies in Eighteenth-Century Culture*, XI, ed. Henry C. Payne. Madison, Wisc.

Nash, Carol S. 1981. "Educating New Mothers: Women and the Enlightenment in Russia," *History of Education Quarterly*, 21, no. 3 (Fall), 301-16.

Neff, Wanda Fraiken. 1929. *Victorian Working Women*. New York.

Newcomer, Mabel. 1959. *A Century of Higher Education for American Women*. New York.

Niggeman, Heinz. 1981. *Emanzipation zwischen Sozialismus und Feminismus: Die sozialdemokratische Frauenbewegung im Kaiserreich*. Wuppertal, Germany.

Niklaus, Robert. 1979. "Diderot and Women," in *Women and Society in 18th-Century France*, ed. Eva Jacobs et al. London and New York.

Noonan, John T., Jr. 1966. *Contraception: A History of Its Treatment by the Catholic Theologians and Canonists*. Cambridge, Mass.

Norton, Mary Beth. 1980. *Liberty's Daughters: The Revolutionary Experience of American Woman, 1750-1800*. Boston.

O'Boyle, Lenore. 1970. "The Problem of an Excess of Educated Men in Western Europe, 1800-1850," *Journal of Modern History*, 42, no. 4 (Dec.), 471-95.

O'Connor, Edward D., ed. 1958. *The Dogma of the Immaculate Conception: History and Significance*. South Bend, Ind.

Offen, Karen M. 1973a. "The 'Woman Question' as a Social Issue in Republican France Before 1914." Unpublished manuscript.

————. 1973b. "A Feminist Challenge to the Third Republic's Public Education for Girls: The Campaign for Equal Access to the *Baccalauréat*, 1880-1924." Paper presented at the American Historical Association, San Francisco.

————. 1977. "The 'Woman Question' as a Social Issue in Nineteenth-Century France: A Bibliographical Essay," *Third Republic/Troisième République*, no. 3-4 (Spring/Fall), 238-99.

————. 1982. "First Wave Feminism in France: New Work and Resources," in *Women's Studies International Quarterly* (London), 5, no. 6:685-89.

Okin, Susan Moller. 1973. "John Stuart Mill's Feminism: The *Subjection of Women* and the Improvement of Mankind," *New Zealand Journal of History*, 7, no. 2 (Oct.), 105-27.

————. 1979. *Women in Western Political Thought*. Princeton, N.J.

Oliphant, Margaret. 1899. *The Autobiography and Letters of Mrs. M. O. Oliphant*, arranged and ed. Mrs. Harry Coghill. Edinburgh and New York.

O'Neill, William L. 1969a. *Everyone Was Brave: The Rise and Fall of Feminism in America*. Chicago, Ill.

————. 1969b. *The Woman Movement; Feminism in the United States and England*. London. Reprint, Chicago, 1971.

O'Reilly, Robert F. 1973. "Montesquieu: Anti-Feminist," *Studies on Voltaire and the 18th Century*, 102:143-56.

Osborne, Martha Lee. 1979. *Woman in Western Thought*. New York.

Otto-Peters, Louise. 1876. *Frauenleben im deutschen Reich: Erinnerungen aus der Vergangenheit*. Leipzig.

Packe, Michael St. John. 1954. *The Life of John Stuart Mill*. London.

Palmer, R. R. 1959. *The Age of the Democratic Revolution*. I, *The Challenge*. Princeton, N.J.

Pange, Comtesse Jean de. 1938. *Auguste-Guillaume Schlegel et Madame de Staël, d'après des documents inédits*. Paris.

Pankhurst, Richard K. P. 1954a. "Anna Wheeler—A Pioneer Socialist, Feminist, and Co-operator," *Political Quarterly*, 25, no. 2:132-43.

————. 1954b. *William Thompson (1775-1833); Britain's Pioneer Socialist, Feminist, and Co-operator*. London.

————. 1956. "Fourierism in Britain," *International Review of Social History*, 1, pt. 3:398-432.

————. [1957]. *The Saint-Simonians, Mill and Carlyle: A Preface to Modern Thought*. London.

Pappe, H. O. 1960. *John Stuart Mill and the Harriet Taylor Myth*. Melbourne, Australia.

Pateman, Carole. 1980. "'The Disorder of Women': Women, Love, and the Sense of Justice," *Ethics*, 91, no. 1 (Oct.), 20-34.

Pellison, Maurice. 1910. "Une Femme moraliste au XVIIIe siècle. Mme de Puisieux," *Revue Pédagogique*, 57, no. 9 (15 Sept.), 201-18.

Perla, George A. 1980. "La Philosophie de Jaucourt dans *l'Encyclopédie*," *Revue de l'histoire des religions*, 197, no. 1 (Jan.-Mar.), 59-78.

Perrot, Michelle. 1976. "L'Éloge de la ménagère dans le discours des ouvriers français au XIXe siècle," *Romantisme: Revue du dix-neuvième siècle*, no. 13-14: 105-21.

Peterson, M. Jeanne. 1972. "The Victorian Governess: Status Incongruence in Family and Society," in *Suffer and Be Still: Women in the Victorian Age*, ed. Martha Vicinus. Bloomington, Ind., and London.

Petschauer, Peter. 1972. "Tradition and Enlightenment: Women's Legal Position in Southwest Germany," *Enlightenment Essays*, no. 3 (Fall/Winter), 160-68.

————. Forthcoming. "The Education of Women in Southwest Germany in the Eighteenth Century." *Societas*.

Phillips, Ann. 1979. *A Newnham Anthology*. Cambridge, London, and New York.

Pichanick, Valerie Kossew. 1980. *Harriet Martineau: The Woman and Her Work*. Ann Arbor, Mich.

Pieroni-Bortolotti, Franca. 1963. *Alle origini del movimento femminile in Italia 1848-1892*. Turin. Reprint, 1975.

Pinchbeck, Ivy. 1930. *Women Workers and the Industrial Revolution, 1750-1850*. London. Reprint, 1975.

Pisano, Anthony P. 1974. "La Nouvelle Beatrice: The Role of Woman in the Life and Writings of Jules Michelet, 1848-1860." Ph.d. dissertation, University of Notre Dame (Ind.).

Pivar, David J. 1973. *Purity Crusade: Sexual Morality and Social Control, 1868-1900*. Westport, Conn.

Pope, Barbara Corrado. 1977. "Angels in the Devil's Workshop: Leisured and Charitable Women in Nineteenth-Century England and France," in *Becoming Visible*, ed. Renate Bridenthal and Claudia Koonz. Boston.

———. 1980. "Revolution and Retreat: Upper-Class French Women after 1789," in *Women, War, and Revolution*, ed. Carol R. Berkin and Clara M. Lovett. New York.

Portemer, Jean. 1959. "Le Statut de la femme en France, depuis la réformation des coutumes jusqu'à la rédaction du Code civil," *Recueils de la Société Jean Bodin pour l'Histoire Comparative des Institutions*, 12 : 447-97.

Power, Eileen. 1975. *Medieval Women*, ed. M. M. Postan. Cambridge, London, and New York.

Pradalié, Georges. 1960. "Dialogue entre Balzac et George Sand sur le problème du mariage," *La Table Ronde*, no. 153 (Sept.), 88-101.

Prelinger, Catherine M. 1976a. "The Religious Context of Mid-Nineteenth Century German Feminism." Paper presented to the American Historical Association, Washington, D.C.

———. 1976b. "Religious Dissent, Women's Rights, and the *Hamburger Hochschule für das weibliche Geschlecht* in Mid-Nineteenth Century Germany," *Church History*, 45, no. 1 (Mar.), 42-55.

———. In progress. "In a Charitable Context: The Mid-Nineteenth Century German Women's Movement."

Prévost, Marcel. 1961. "Coquerel (Athenase-Laurent-Charles)," *Dictionnaire de biographie française*, IX (Paris, 1961), 674-75.

Price, Roger D. 1972. *The French Second Republic: A Social History*. London.

Prochaska, F. K. 1980. *Women and Philanthropy in 19th Century England*. Oxford and New York.

Puckett, Hugh Wiley. 1930. *Germany's Women Go Forward*. New York.

Puech, Jules L. 1925. *La Vie et l'oeuvre de Flora Tristan, 1803-1844*. Paris.

Puech, Marie-Louise. 1935. "Le Mystère de la Gazette des Femmes," *La Grande Revue*, 147, no. 3 (Mar.), 39-76.

Pugh, Evelyn L. 1978. "John Stuart Mill and Harriet Taylor, and Women's Rights in America, 1850-1873," *Canadian Journal of History*, 13, no. 3 (Dec.), 423-42.

———. 1980. "John Stuart Mill and the Women's Question in Parliament, 1865-1868," *The Historian*, 42 (May), 399-418.

———. 1982. "Florence Nightingale and J. S. Mill Debate Women's Rights," *Journal of British Studies*, 21, no. 2 (Spring), 118-38.

Quataert, Jean H. 1979. *Reluctant Feminists in German Social Democracy, 1885-1917*. Princeton, N.J.

Qvist, Gunnar. 1960. *Kvinnofragan i Sverige 1809-46; Studier rörande kvinnans näringsfrihet inom de borgerliga yrkena*. Göteborg.

———. 1969. *Fredrika Bremer och kvinnans emancipation*. Göteborg.

Rabkin, Peggy A. 1974. "The Origins of Law Reform: The Social Significance of the Nineteenth-Century Codification Movement and Its Contribution to the Passage of the Early Married Women's Property Acts." *Buffalo* [N.Y.] *Law Review*, 24 : 683-760.

————. 1980. *Fathers to Daughters: The Legal Foundations of Female Emancipation.* Westport, Conn.

Ranvier, Adrien. 1908. "Une Féministe de 1848, Jeanne Deroin," *La Révolution de 1848*, 4, no. 24 (Jan.-Feb.), 317-55; 5, no. 25 (Mar.-Apr.), 421-30; 5, no. 26 (May-June), 480-98; 5, no. 30 (Jan.-Feb.), 816-25.

Rauschenbusch-Clough, Emma. 1898. *A Study of Mary Wollstonecraft and the Rights of Woman.* London and New York.

Reed, James. 1978. *From Private Vice to Public Virtue: The Birth Control Movement and American Society Since 1830.* New York.

Reiss, Erna. 1934. *The Rights and Duties of Englishwomen: A Study in Law and Public Opinion.* Manchester, Eng.

Reval, Gabrielle [pseud.]. 1931. *Madame Campan, assistante de Napoléon.* Paris.

Rheinstein, Max. 1956. "The Code and the Family," in *The Code Napoleon and the Common-Law World*, ed. Bernard Schartz. New York.

Riasanovsky, Nicholas V. 1969. *The Teaching of Charles Fourier.* Berkeley, Calif.

Rich, Adrienne. 1979. *On Lies, Secrets, and Silence: Selected Prose, 1966-1978.* New York.

Riegel, Robert E. 1962. "The Split of the Feminist Movement in 1869," *Mississippi Valley Historical Review*, 49, no. 3 (Dec.), 485-96.

————. 1963. *American Feminists.* Lawrence, Kans.

Ritter, Alan. 1969. *The Political Thought of Pierre-Joseph Proudhon.* Garden City, N.J.

Robertson, Priscilla. 1952. *Revolutions of 1848: A Social History.* Princeton, N.J. Reprint, New York, 1960.

Robson, John M. 1968. *The Improvement of Mankind: The Social and Political Thought of John Stuart Mill.* Toronto.

Roger, Jacques. 1971. *Les Sciences de la vie dans la pensée française du 18e siècle; la génération des animaux de Descartes à l'Encyclopédie.* Paris.

Rogers, Katharine M. 1983. *Eighteenth-Century English Feminism.* Urbana, Ill.

Romberg, Bertil. 1977. *Carl Jonas Love Almqvist.* Boston.

Rose, Willie Lee. 1982. "Reforming Women," *New York Review of Books*, 29, no. 15 (7 Oct.), 45-49.

Rossi, Alice S. 1970. "Sentiment and Intellect: The Story of John Stuart Mill and Harriet Taylor Mill," in *Essays on Sex Equality*, ed. Alice S. Rossi. Chicago.

————. 1973a. "Feminist History in Perspective: Sociological Contributions to Biographic Analysis," in *A Sampler of Women's Studies*, ed. Dorothy Gies McGuignan. Ann Arbor, Mich.

————, ed. 1973b. *The Feminist Papers, from Adams to De Beauvoir.* New York.

Rouvre, Charles de. 1917. *L'Amoureuse histoire d'Auguste Comte et de Clotilde de Vaux.* Paris.

Rover, Constance. 1967. *Women's Suffrage and Party Politics in Britain, 1866-1914.* London.

————. 1970. *Love, Morals, and the Feminists.* London.

Rowbotham, Sheila. 1973. *Hidden from History: Rediscovering Women in History from the 17th Century to the Present.* London and New York.

Royle, Edward. 1974. *Victorian Infidels: The Origins of the British Secularist Movement, 1791-1866.* Manchester, Eng.

Rubenius, Aina. 1950. *The Woman Question in Mrs. Gaskell's Life and Works.* Uppsala, Sweden, and Cambridge, Mass.

Ryan, Mary P. 1975. *Womanhood in America.* New York.

Sacks, Karen. 1974. "Engels Revisited: Woman, the Organization of Production, and Private Property," in *Woman, Culture, and Society*, ed. Michelle Rosaldo and Louise Lamphere. Stanford, Calif.

Salleron, Claude. 1954. "La Littérature au XIXe siècle et la famille," in *Renouveau des idées sur la famille*, ed. Robert Prigent. Paris.

Salmon, Marylynn. 1979. "Equality or Submersion? *Feme Covert* Status in Early Pennsylvania," in *Women of America: A History*, ed. Carol R. Berkin and Mary Beth Norton. Boston.

———. 1980. "Life, Liberty and Dower: The Legal Status of Women after the American Revolution," in *Women, War, and Revolution*, ed. Carol R. Berkin and Clara M. Lovett. New York.

Salvemini, Gaetano. 1957. *Mazzini*. London and Stanford, Calif.

Sanford, Jutta Schroers. 1976. "The Origins of German Feminism: German Women, 1789-1870." Ph.D. dissertation, Ohio State University.

Sargent, Lydia, ed. 1981. *Women and Revolution: A Discussion of the Unhappy Marriage of Marxism and Feminism*. Boston.

Schiller, Francis. 1979. *Paul Broca, Founder of French Anthropology, Explorer of the Brain*. Berkeley, Calif.

Schlegel, Friedrich von. 1971. *Friedrich Schlegel's "Lucinde" and the Fragments*. Tr. and introd., Peter Firchow. Minneapolis, Minn.

Schmidt, Auguste, and Hugo Rösch. 1898. *Louise Otto-Peters, die Dichterin und Vorkämpferin für Frauenrecht: Ein Lebensbild*. Leipzig.

Schneir, Miriam, ed. 1972. *Feminism: The Essential Historical Writings*. New York.

Schnorrenberg, Barbara Brandon. 1979a. "The Brood Hen of Faction: Mrs. Macaulay and Radical Politics, 1765-1775," *Albion*, 11, no. 1 (Spring), 33-46.

———, with Jean E. Hunter. 1979b. "The Eighteenth-Century Englishwoman," in *The Women of England from Anglo-Saxon Times to the Present: Interpretive Bibliographical Essays*, ed. Barbara Kanner. Hamden, Conn.

———. 1980. "Sophia: English Feminism at Mid-Century." Paper presented at the Eleventh Annual Meeting of the American Society for Eighteenth-Century Studies, San Francisco.

Schochet, Gordon J. 1975. *Patriarchalism and Political Thought: The Authoritarian Family and Political Speculation and Attitudes, Especially in Seventeenth-Century England*. Oxford.

Schreiber, Adele. 1914. *Hedwig Dohm als Vorkämpferin und Vordenkerin neuer Frauenideale*. Berlin.

Schroeder, Hannelore. 1981. *Die Frau ist frei geboren: Texte zur Frauenemanzipation*, II, *1870-1918*. Munich.

Schulkind, Eugene W. 1950. "Le Rôle des femmes dans la Commune de 1871," *1848: Revue des Révolutions Contemporaines*, 42 (Feb.), 15-29.

Schwab, Richard N. 1957. "The Chevalier de Jaucourt and Diderot's 'Encyclopédie,'" *Modern Language Forum*, 42, no. 1 (June), 44-51.

Scott, Anne Firor. 1978. "What, Then, Is the American: This New Woman?," *Journal of American History*, 65, no. 3 (Dec.), 679-703.

———. 1979. "The Ever Widening Circle: The Diffusion of Feminist Values from the Troy Female Seminary, 1822-1872," *History of Education Quarterly*, 19, no. 1 (Spring), 3-25.

Scrimgeour, R. M., ed. 1950. *The North London Collegiate School, 1850-1950: A Hundred Years of Girls' Education: Essays in Honour of the Frances Mary Buss Foundation*. London.

Seaver, Kirsten A. Introduction to her translation of Camilla Collett, *Amtmadens dötre*. Unpublished manuscript.

Sellner, Timothy F., tr. and ed. 1979. *Theodor Gottlieb von Hippel, "On Improving the Status of Women."* Detroit, Mich.

Semming, Jeanne B. 1957. *Louise Otto-Peters: Lebensbild einer deutschen Kämpferin.* Berlin.

Sewell, William H., Jr. 1980. *Work and Revolution in France: The Language of Labor from the Old Regime to 1848.* Cambridge, Eng.

Shanley, Mary Lyndon. 1979. "Marriage Contract and Social Contract in Seventeenth Century Political Thought," *Western Political Quarterly*, 32, no. 1 (Mar.), 79-91.

Shapiro, J. Salwyn. 1934. *Condorcet and the Rise of Liberalism.* New York.

Shields, Currin V., ed. 1956. Introduction to John Stuart Mill, *On Liberty*. Indianapolis, Ind., and New York.

Shields, Stephanie A. 1975. "Functionalism, Darwinism, and the Psychology of Women: A Study in Social Myth," *American Psychologist*, 30, no. 7 (July), 739-54.

Shorter, Edward. 1973. "Female Emancipation, Birth Control, and Fertility in European History," *American Historical Review*, 78, no. 3 (June), 605-40.

―――. 1975. *The Making of the Modern Family.* New York.

Showalter, Elaine. 1975. "Literary Criticism: A Review Essay." *SIGNS: Journal of Women in Culture and Society*, 1, no. 2 (Winter), 435-60.

―――. 1977. *A Literature of Their Own: British Women Novelists from Brontë to Lessing.* Princeton, N.J.

Siegel, Idell E. 1975. "Feminism in the French Popular Playwrights: 1830-1848." Ph.D. dissertation, University of Missouri, Columbia.

Simmons, Adele. 1976. "Education and Ideology in Nineteenth-Century America: The Response of Educational Institutions to the Changing Role of Women," in *Liberating Women's History*, ed. Berenice Carroll. Urbana, Ill.

Simon, Walter Michael. 1963. *European Positivism in the Nineteenth Century: An Essay in Intellectual History.* Ithaca, N.Y.

Sklar, Kathryn Kish. 1973. *Catharine Beecher: A Study in American Domesticity.* New Haven, Conn., and London.

Slaughter, Jane. 1979. "Feminism and Socialism: Theoretical Debates in Historical Perspective," *Marxist Perspectives*, 2, no. 3 (Fall), 32-49.

―――, and Robert Kern, eds. 1981. *European Women on the Left: Socialism, Feminism, and the Problems Faced by Political Women, 1880 to the Present.* Westport, Conn.

Smith, Bonnie G. 1981. *Ladies of the Leisure Class: The Bourgeoises of Northern France in the Nineteenth Century.* Princeton, N.J.

Smith, F. Barry. 1977. "Sexuality in Britain, 1800-1900: Some Suggested Revisions," in *A Widening Sphere*, ed. Martha Vicinus. Bloomington, Ind., and London.

Smith, Hilda. 1981. "Masculinity as a Political Concept in English Thought, 1600-1850." Paper presented at the Fifth Berkshire Conference on the History of Women, Vassar College.

Smith-Rosenberg, Carroll. 1974. "Puberty to Menopause: The Cycle of Femininity in Nineteenth-Century America," in *Clio's Consciousness Raised: New Perspectives on the History of Women*, ed. Mary Hartman and Lois W. Banner. New York.

―――, and Charles Rosenberg. 1973. "The Female Animal: Medical and Biological Views of Women in Nineteenth-Century America," *Journal of American History*, 60, no. 2 (Sept. 1973), 332-56.

Sonstroem, David. 1977. "Millet versus Ruskin: A Defense of Ruskin's 'Of Queens' Gardens,'" *Victorian Studies*, 20, no. 3 (Spring), 183-97.

Sourine, Georges. 1936. *Le Fourierisme en Russie: Contribution à l'histoire du socialisme russe.* Thesis, Faculté de Droit, Paris.

Sowerwine, Charles. 1975. "Le Group féministe socialiste, 1899-1902," *Le Mouvement Social,* 90 (Jan.-Mar.), 87-120.

———. 1976. "The Organization of French Socialist Women, 1880-1914; A European Perspective for Women's Movements," *Historical Reflections,* 3, no. 2 (Winter), 3-24.

———. 1977a. "Women and the Origins of the French Socialist Party: A Neglected Contribution," *Third Republic/Troisième République,* no. 3-4 (Spring/Fall), 104-27.

———. 1977b. "Women, Socialism, and Feminism, 1872-1922: A Bibliography," *Third Republic/Troisième République,* no. 3-4 (Spring/Fall), 300-366.

———. 1978. *Les Femmes et le Socialisme.* Paris.

———. 1979. "Women Against War: A Feminine Basis for Internationalism and Pacifism?," *Proceedings of the Western Society for French History,* 6: 361-70.

———. 1982. *Sisters or Citizens? Women and Socialism in France Since 1876.* Cambridge, Eng., and New York.

Stanton, Elizabeth Cady. 1898. *Eighty Years and More: Reminiscences 1815-1897.* Reprint, 1971, New York.

Stanton, Theodore, ed. 1884. *The Woman Question in Europe.* New York. Reprint, 1970.

Stearns, Peter N. 1974. *1848: The Revolutionary Tide in Europe.* New York.

———. 1979. *Be A Man! Males in Modern Society.* New York.

Steinen, Karl von den. 1979. "The Discovery of Women in Eighteenth-Century English Political Life," in *The Women of England from Anglo-Saxon Times to the Present: Interpretive Bibliographical Essays,* ed. Barbara Kanner. Hamden, Conn.

Stenton, Doris Mary. 1957. *The English Woman in History.* London and New York.

Stephen, Barbara Nightingale. 1927. *Emily Davies and Girton College.* London. Reprint, Westport, Conn., 1976.

Stephen, Leslie. 1876. *History of English Thought in the Eighteenth Century.* 2 vols. London.

———. 1900. *The English Utilitarians.* London and New York.

Stern, Karl. 1965. *The Flight From Woman.* New York.

Stites, Richard. 1969. "M. L. Mikhailov and the Emergence of the Woman Question in Russia," *Canadian-American Slavic Studies,* 3, no. 2 (Summer), 178-99.

———. 1977. "Women and the Russian Intelligentsia: Three Perspectives," in *Women in Russia,* ed. Dorothy Atkinson, Alexander Dallin, and Gail Lapidus. Stanford, Calif.

———. 1978. *The Women's Liberation Movement in Russia: Nihilism, Feminism, and Bolshevism, 1860-1930.* Princeton, N.J.

Stock, Phyllis. 1978. *Better than Rubies: A History of Women's Education.* New York.

Stone, Lawrence. 1977. *The Family, Sex, and Marriage in England, 1500-1800.* London and New York.

Strachey, Ray. 1928. *The Cause: A Short History of the Women's Movement in Great Britain.* London. Reprinted with a new introduction, 1978.

———. 1931. *Millicent Garrett Fawcett.* London.

Strumingher, Laura. 1974. "Les Canutes: Women Workers in the Lyonnais Silk Industry, 1835-48." Ph.D. dissertation, University of Rochester (N.Y.).

————. 1976. "Mythes et réalités de la condition féminine à travers la presse féministe lyonnaise des années 1830," *Cahiers d'Histoire* (Lyons), 21, no. 4: 409-24.

————. 1978. *Women and the Making of the Working Class: Lyon, 1830-1870.* Toronto.

Sugg, Redding S., Jr. 1978. *Motherteacher: The Feminization of American Education.* Charlottesville, Va.

Sullerot, Evelyne. 1966a. "Journaux féminins et luttes ouvrières, 1848-1849," in *La Presse ouvrière 1819-1850*, ed. Jacques Godechot. Paris.

————. 1966b. *Histoire de la presse féminine en France, des origines à 1848.* Paris.

————. 1968. *Histoire et sociologie du travail féminin.* Paris.

Sweet, Paul R. 1978. *Wilhelm von Humboldt: A Biography*, I, *1767-1808.* Columbus, Ohio.

Taïeb, Edith, ed. 1982. *Hubertine Auclert: La Citoyenne, 1848-1914.* Paris.

Taylor, Barbara. 1977. "The Woman Power: Religious Heresy and Feminism in Early English Socialism," in *Tearing the Veil: Essays in Femininity*, ed. Susan Lipshitz. London.

————. 1979. "'The Men Are as Bad as Their Masters. . .': Socialism, Feminism, and Sexual Antagonism in the London Tailoring Trade in the Early 1830s," *Feminist Studies*, 5, no. 1 (Spring), 7-40.

Taylor, Clare, ed. 1974. *British and American Abolitionists: An Episode in Transatlantic Understanding.* Edinburgh and Chicago.

Taylor, Gordon Rattray. 1958. *The Angel-Makers: A Study in the Psychological Origins of Historical Change, 1750-1850.* New York. Reprint, 1974.

Teixiera-Mendes, Raymundo. 1915-18. *Clotilde et Comte, très-saints fondateurs de la religion de l'humanité.* 2 vols. in 3. Rio de Janeiro.

Thibert, Marguerite. 1926. *Le Féminisme dans le socialisme français de 1830 à 1850.* Paris.

Thomas, Edith. 1948. *Les Femmes de 1848.* Paris.

————. 1956. *Pauline Roland: Socialisme et féminisme au XIXe siècle.* Paris.

————. 1966. *The Women Incendiaries.* New York.

————. 1971. *Louise Michel, ou la velléda de l'anarchie.* Paris.

Thomas, Keith. 1958. "Women in the Civil War Sects," *Past and Present*, no. 13 (Apr.), 42-62.

————. 1959. "The Double Standard," *Journal of the History of Ideas*, 20, no. 2 (Apr.), 195-216.

————. 1971. *Religion and the Decline of Magic.* New York.

Thompson, Dorothy, ed. 1971. *The Early Chartists.* Columbia, S.C.

————. 1976. "Women and Nineteenth-Century Radical Politics: A Lost Dimension," in *The Rights and Wrongs of Women*, ed. Juliet Mitchell and Ann Oakley. London.

Thompson, E. P. 1963. *The Making of the English Working Class.* New York.

Thompson, Patricia. 1977. *George Sand and the Victorians.* London.

Thönnessen, Werner. 1973. *The Emancipation of Women: The Rise and Decline of the Women's Movement in German Social Democracy, 1863-1933.* Tr. Joris de Bres. London. Originally published in German, Frankfurt, 1969.

Tilly, Louise A., and Joan W. Scott. 1978. *Women, Work, and Family.* New York.

Tilly, Louise A., Joan W. Scott, and Miriam Cohen. 1976. "Women's Work and European Fertility Patterns," *Journal of Interdisciplinary History*, 6, no. 3 (Winter), 447-76.

Tixerant, Jules. 1908. *Le Féminisme à l'époque de 1848 dans l'ordre politique et dans l'ordre économique.* Thesis, Faculté de Droit, Paris.

Todd, Margaret Georgina. 1918. *The Life of Sophia Jex-Blake.* London.

Tomalin, Clare. 1974. *The Life and Death of Mary Wollstonecraft.* New York.

Touaillon, Christine. 1919. *Der deutsche Frauenroman des 18. Jahrhunderts.* Vienna and Leipzig. Reprint, 1979.

Traer, James F. 1980. *Marriage and Family in Eighteenth-Century France.* Ithaca, N.Y.

Tuke, Margaret. 1939. *A History of Bedford College for Women, 1849-1937.* London.

Twellmann, Margrit. 1972. *Die deutsche Frauenbewegung im Spiegel repräsentativer Frauenzeitschriften, ihre Anfänge und erste Entwicklung.* 2 vols. Meisenheim am Glan.

Van Tieghem, Paul. 1927. "Les Droits de l'amour et l'union libre dans le roman français et allemand (1760-1790)," *Neophilologus,* no. 12:96-103.

Venturi, Franco. 1939. *Jeunesse de Diderot (1713-1753).* Tr. Juliette Bertrand. Paris.

Vorländer, Karl. 1924. *Immanuel Kant, der Mann und das Werk.* 2 vols. Leipzig. Reprint, Hamburg, 1977.

Walsh, Mary Roth. 1977. *"Doctors Wanted: No Women Need Apply": Sexual Barriers in the Medical Profession, 1835-1975.* New Haven, Conn.

Walters, Margaret. 1976. "The Rights and Wrongs of Women: Mary Wollstonecraft, Harriet Martineau, Simone de Beauvoir," in *The Rights and Wrongs of Women,* ed. Juliet Mitchell and Ann Oakley. London.

Walters, Ronald G., ed. 1974. *Primers for Prudery: Sexual Advice to Victorian America.* Englewood Cliffs, N.J.

Wardle, Ralph. 1951. *Mary Wollstonecraft: A Critical Biography.* Reprint, Lincoln, Neb., 1967.

Watt, Ian. 1957. "The New Woman: Samuel Richardson's Pamela," in Watt, *The Rise of the Novel.* Berkeley, Calif.

Webb, Robert Kiefer. 1960. *Harriet Martineau: A Radical Victorian.* New York.

Weill, Herman. 1961. *Frederick the Great and Samuel von Cocceji; A Study in the Reform of the Prussian Judicial Administration, 1740-1755.* Madison, Wisc.

Wein, Roberta. 1974a. "Educated Women and the Limits of Domesticity." Ph.D. Dissertation. New York University.

———. 1974b. "Women's Colleges and Domesticity, 1875-1918," in *Liberating Women's History,* ed. Berenice Carroll. Urbana, Ill.

Weinstein, Fred, and Gerald M. Platt. 1969. *The Wish to Be Free: Society, Psyche, and Value Change.* Berkeley and Los Angeles, Calif.

Welter, Barbara. 1966. "The Cult of True Womanhood, 1820-1860," *American Quarterly,* 18, no. 2 (Summer), 151-74.

———. 1974. "The Feminization of American Religion: 1800-1860," in *Clio's Consciousness Raised,* ed. Mary Hartman and Lois W. Banner. New York.

———. 1976. "The Merchant's Daughter: A Tale from Life," in Welter, *Dimity Convictions: The American Woman in the Nineteenth Century.* Athens, Ohio.

Wemple, Suzanne F., and JoAnn McNamara. 1977. "Sanctity and Power: The Dual Pursuit of Medieval Women," in *Becoming Visible: Women in European History,* ed. Renate Bridenthal and Claudia Koonz. Boston.

Westwater, Martha. 1981. "Emily Faithfull: The Trials of Feminist Publishing."

Paper presented to the Pacific Coast Conference on British Studies, Santa Barbara, Calif.

Wexler, Victor G. 1976. "Made for Man's Delight: Rousseau as Antifeminist," *American Historical Review*, 81, no. 2 (Apr.), 266-91.

Whale, Winifred Stephens. 1917. *Madame Adam (Juliette Lambert), la grande française: From Louis-Philippe Until 1917*. New York.

Wieselgren, Greta. 1978. *Fredrika Bremer och verkligheten romanen Herthas tillblivelse*. Stockholm.

Willey, Basil. 1949. *Nineteenth-Century Studies*. New York and London.

Williams, David. 1971. "The Politics of Feminism in the French Enlightenment," in *The Varied Pattern: Studies in the Eighteenth Century*, ed. Peter Hughes and David Williams. Toronto.

Wilson, Arthur M. 1957. *Diderot: The Testing Years,1713-1759*. New York.

———. 1976. "'Treated Like Imbecile Children' (Diderot), The Enlightenment and the Status of Women," in *Woman in the 18th Century and Other Essays*, ed. Paul Fritz and Richard Morton. Toronto and Sarasota.

Wilson, Joan Hoff. 1976. "The Illusion of Change: Women and the American Revolution," in *The American Revolution*, ed. Alfred F. Young. De Kalb, Ill.

Wise, Thomas James, and John Alexander Symington, eds. 1932. *The Brontës: Their Lives, Friendships, and Correspondence*. 4 vols. Oxford.

Woehrlin, William F. 1971. *Chernyshevskii: The Man and the Journalist*. Cambridge, Mass.

Woody, Thomas. 1929. *A History of Women's Education in the United States*. 2 vols. New York and Lancaster, Pa. Reprint, 1966.

Worzala, Diane. 1980. "The Critics of J. S. Mill's *The Subjection of Women*." Paper read at the Pacific Coast Conference on British Studies, Berkeley, Calif.

Wymer, Norman G. 1959. *Elizabeth Garrett Anderson*. Oxford.

Zévaès, Alexandre. 1931. "Une Candidature féministe en 1849," *La Révolution de 1848*, 28, no. 138 (Sept.-Oct.), 127-34.

ACKNOWLEDGMENTS

C. J. L. Almqvist, *Sara Videbeck/The Chapel*, trans. A. B. Benson. Copyright © 1972 by the American-Scandinavian Foundation. Selections reprinted by permission of the American-Scandinavian Foundation.

J.-J. Bachofen, *Myth, Religion, and Mother Right*, trans. Ralph Manheim, Bollingen Series LXXXIV. Copyright © 1967 by Princeton University Press. Selections reprinted by permission of Princeton University Press.

N. G. Chernyshevsky, *What Is to Be Done? Tales About New People* (*Chto Delat'?*), trans. Benjamin Tucker, revised and abridged by Ludmilla B. Turkevich. Copyright © 1961 by Random House, Inc. Selections reprinted by permission of Random House, Inc.

Friedrich Engels, *The Condition of the Working Class in England*, tr. W. O. Henderson and W. H. Chaloner. Copyright © 1958 by Basil Blackwell. Selections reprinted by permission of Basil Blackwell and Stanford University Press.

Immanuel Kant, *Anthropology from a Pragmatic Point of View*, trans. Victor L. Dowdell, revised and edited by Hans H. Rudnick. Copyright © 1978 by Southern Illinois University Press. Selection reprinted by permission of Southern Illinois University Press.

INDEX